The Collected Writings of Walt Whitman

John McLenan. Caricature of WW in a pencil notebook in the Prints Division, The New York Public Library, Astor, Lenox, and Tilden Foundations. McLenan was a well-known book illustrator whose work included Sarah Josepha Hale's *Northwood,* Joseph Glover Baldwin's *The Flush Times of Alabama and Mississippi* and the appearances of Dickens's *A Tale of Two Cities* and *Great Expectations* and of Wilkie Collins's *The Woman in White* in *Harper's Weekly*. He may have known WW at Pfaff's and his name may appear in "81 Clerman" (p. 431) as a semilegible entry transcribed in this edition as "Mr M Leman." The pencil sketches and caricatures in "81 Clerman" (q.v.) do not appear to be from the same hand as this caricature.

WALT WHITMAN

Notebooks and Unpublished Prose Manuscripts

VOLUME I: FAMILY NOTES AND AUTOBIOGRAPHY
BROOKLYN AND NEW YORK

Edited by Edward F. Gricr

NEW YORK UNIVERSITY PRESS 1984

Library of Congress Cataloging in Publication Data
Whitman, Walt, 1819–1892.
Notebooks and unpublished prose manuscripts.

(The Collected Writings of Walt Whitman)
Bibliography: p.
Includes index.
1. Whitman, Walt, 1819–1892—Diaries. 2. Poets, American—19th century—Biography. I. Grier, Edward F. II. Title. III. Series: Whitman, Walt, 1819–1892. Works. 1961.
PS3231.A36 1984 818'.303 [B] 83-24415
ISBN 0-8147-2991-6 vol. I.
ISBN 0-8147-2992-4 vol. II.
ISBN 0-8147-2993-2 vol. III
ISBN 0-8147-2994-0 vol. IV
ISBN 0-8147-2995-9 vol. V
ISBN 0-8147-2996-7 vol. VI
ISBN 0-8147-2989-4 (set)

MANUFACTURED IN THE UNITED STATES OF AMERICA

CLOTHBOUND EDITIONS OF NEW YORK UNIVERSITY PRESS BOOKS
ARE SMYTH-SEWN AND PRINTED ON PERMANENT AND DURABLE ACID-FREE PAPER.

The Collected Writings of Walt Whitman

THE PREPARATION OF THIS VOLUME,

AND COSTS ASSOCIATED WITH ITS PUBLICATION,

WERE SUPPORTED THROUGH GRANT NO. RP-*1726–80 FROM THE

Editing and Publication Programs

of the National Endowment for the Humanities,

AN INDEPENDENT FEDERAL AGENCY.

CENTER FOR
SCHOLARLY EDITIONS

AN APPROVED EDITION

MODERN LANGUAGE
ASSOCIATION OF AMERICA

CONTENTS

Preface

I have contracted so many debts in the course of the years that it is difficult to know where to begin acknowledging them.

My first acknowledgment must be to the General Research Fund of the University of Kansas, Grant Number 3361-XD-0038, which has supported this project for more years than I like to think of. I am also grateful to the Graduate Research Fund, the Faculty Development Fund, and the Small Grants Fund of the University of Kansas which provided funds for important but unanticipated expenses. Of course, behind these institutional labels are the colleagues who examined my research proposals and who voted their confidence in me. I am grateful to the staff of the Watson Library for support by acquiring books, locating other material, providing work space, and in general maintaining its tradition of service to scholarship. In recent years I owe a debt to Professor Alexandra Mason and the staffs of the Kenneth Spencer Research Library and of the Department of Regional History. I am grateful to two successive Chairmen of the Department of English, W. P. Albrecht and George Worth, Jr., who cooperated in scheduling and, when funds were available, in supplying assistance.

Although this has been a one-man project, I have been assisted by many students. I am grateful to all the graduates and undergraduates who loyally and meticulously transcribed my difficult material. I feel especially warm gratitude to Professor Marvin A. Carlson, now of Cornell University, and Mrs. Carol Ann Danks, who helped me set up a filing and indexing system that has served very well. Mrs. Danks also transcribed manuscripts in an exemplary fashion. Mr. Danny W. White, her successor, proved himself over a four-year period not only a splendid transcriber, but also something of an editorial wizard by locating in a sea of photographs the originals of unidentified material edited by my predecessors and by spotting necessary cross-references. In working through my folders I have recognized many notes in the writing of Professor Robert H. Deming, now of SUNY, Fredonia, and Professor Donald Yeats, now of the Western Australian Institute of Technology, who burrowed in the library stacks to good purpose. I have acknowledged assistance from members of my graduate seminar in individual notes. Professor Gene Edward Veith, now of Northeastern Oklahoma A & M College, first as a typist and then as editorial assistant, has skillfully helped put together Part I and made independent contributions to Part II.

Off campus, my greatest debt is to Sculley Bradley, who introduced me to Whitman studies and, as one of the general editors of *The Collected Writings,* made many helpful suggestions. Professor Gay Wilson Allen has also been of immense help. His generous trip from New York to Kansas was a practical and psychological boost when the project was stagnating. I have also been assisted by the late Professor Emory Holloway, who shared notes on and transcripts of manuscripts now vanished. Professor C. Carroll Hollis generously shared his research with me. Mr. Charles E. Feinberg extended the use of his great collection to me on several occasions.

The Committee on Editions of American Authors of the Modern Language Association of America, now Committee on Scholarly Editions, has twice supplied me with funds for typing expenses. The project was also supported in 1976–1977 by a fellowship for Independent Study and Research (#P76-58) from the National Endowment for the Humanities, an independent Federal agency.

I am indebted to the following librarians for assistance far beyond the call of duty: John C. Broderick, Assistant Librarian for Research Services, Library of Congress; Donald C. Gallup, Curator of American Literature, Beinecke Library, Yale University; Thomas M. Simkins, Jr., Curator of Rare Books, William R. Perkins Library, Duke University, and his successor John L. Sharpe, III; Miss Anne Freudenberg, Assistant Curator of Manuscripts, Alderman Library, University of Virginia; Mrs. Neda Westlake, Curator of Rare Books, Charles Patterson Van Pelt Library, University of Pennsylvania; Lewis M. Starke, Keeper of Rare Books, New York Public Library, and his successor Mrs. Maud D. Cole; H. C. Schultz, Curator of Manuscripts, and Alan Jutzi, Assistant Curator of Manuscripts, The Huntington Library. I am also grateful for various courtesies to the Adjutant General's Department, Commonwealth of Massachusetts; Professor Roger M. Asselineau; the late Miss Sylvia Beach; Professor Harold Blodgett; Butler County (Kansas) Historical Society; Center for Military History, Department of the Army; the late Mr. Ashley Trimble Cole; Columbia University Library; Professor William M. Gibson; Professor C. Carroll Hollis; The Houghton Library, Harvard University; Kansas State Historical Society; the late Mr. John S. Van E. Kohn; Professor James C. Meriwether; Mrs. James H. Minnick; Missouri Historical Society; Mrs. David Molinoff; Mr. Daniel Maggin; Mr. Edward Naumburg, Jr.; Charles Patterson Van Pelt Library, University of Pennsylvania; The John Rylands Library; Sheffield (England) City Libraries; Professor Esther Shephard; Professor Floyd Stovall; Professor William White; the late Mr. Walter Muir Whitehill, and many others whose courtesy I have acknowledged in the appropriate places.

I am indebted to the following persons and institutions for the kind permission to publish manuscripts in their collections: The Boston Public Library; Boston University Libraries; John Hay Library, Brown University; Mr. C. Waller Barrett; Mr. Richard G. Coker; Manuscript Division, Library of Congress; William R. Perkins Library, Duke University; The Huntington Library; Mr. Carl Haverlin; Kenneth Spencer Research Library, University of Kansas; The Pierpont Morgan Library; The Abernathy Library, Middlebury College; The Newberry Library; The Henry A. and Albert W. Berg Collection, The Manuscript Division and The Rare Book Division, New York Public Library; The Charles Patterson Van Pelt Library, University of Pennsylvania; Princeton University Library; Mills Memorial Library, Rollins College; Rutgers University Library; Mr. Rollo Silver; Edward

Lawrence Doheny Memorial Library, St. John's Seminary; Humanities Research Center, University of Texas at Austin; Mr. Robert Taylor; the late Justin Turner; The Alderman Library, University of Virginia; Wittenberg College Library; Mrs. Sidney L. Wright; Walt Whitman House, New Jersey Department of Environmental Protection; The Beinecke Library, Yale University.

Introduction

I

On December 7, 1882, Walt Whitman, in a letter to W. D. O'Connor about collecting documents bearing on the Boston censorship of 1881 *Leaves of Grass,* wrote:

> there is something quite preferable in this *collectanea* at first hand for a life, affair, even history, out of which the modern intelligent reader, (a *new* race unknown before our time) can take and adapt & shape for himself or herself—

Whether or not the modern intelligent reader prefers his documents straight, Whitman had a strong sense of the interest and value of "collectanea" and, aside from two occasions in 1873 and 1888 when, to put his affairs in order, he destroyed letters and manuscripts, he took pains to ensure that the reader could know him at first hand, even to "editing" the books of John Burroughs and Richard Maurice Bucke about him.

Close as these manuscripts bring the reader to Whitman, one is continually struck by their omissions and reticences. We have pencil sketches (not by Whitman) of him and other bohemians at Pfaff's, but almost no report of what went on. Whitman's Boston notebook of 1860 is full of the remarkable things he saw there, for he was impressed despite himself and was always a journalist who fancied the local color sketch, but there is no mention, for example, of his conversations with Emerson, or of his readiness with others to intervene by force if F. B. Sanborn, who had been implicated in the affairs of John Brown, were turned over to the federal authorities by the local courts. Even as memorandum books, as many of them might be more accurately described, they keep Whitman's secrets.

There was much of course that Whitman could not tell. The notebooks and miscellaneous documents of the 1850s do bring us close to him as he explores the Self which he had so recently discovered, but we do not discover the mystery of that Self or where it came from, probably because it was ineffable. He could not come closer to the experience than by metaphors of seduction or rape. Not only the early notebooks but the early fugitive scraps and leaves show this process of exploration and utterance, and the discoveries he was making in his new personality were often worked out in prose before they found their way into verse.

One of the most conspicuous features of the notebooks as they are now published complete is the number of men who are named and briefly identified by appearance or occupation. The lists seem to begin in 1856 or 1857, but no doubt they represent a habit of long standing, whether or not records survive. Obviously, as a newspaperman Whitman carried a notebook and collected material. Also obviously, the hospital notebooks, whatever else they may be, are the raw material for journalism as well as a kind of casebook. But what of the hundreds of other names? Many of them are totally unidentifiable. Some of them emerge, as one tracks down reiterated names, as people close to him. Fred Vaughan ruined himself in various ways and became for Whitman a monitory figure. The Baulsirs, Brooklyn ferrymen, remembered and respected Whitman as a friend and poet thirty years later. George Storms, a stage driver, was only one of a number of friends who named sons for him. Such is the impersonality (if one may use the word about Whitman) or furtiveness, as he put it, of the notebooks that the emotional significance of the names of Sergeant Thomas Sawyer, Peter Doyle, and Harry Stafford becomes clear only through the accidental survival of his letters. Some of Whitman's full references to Doyle and Stafford are, in fact, deliberately cryptic or coded. It dawns on one, finally, that whatever other reasons Whitman may have had for recording all these names, these men had poetic meaning for him, however brief the contact may have been. They were, as he said, metaphorically passengers on Brooklyn Ferry and participants in "orgies":

> as I pass O Manhattan, your frequent and swift flash of eyes offering me love,
> Offering response to my own—these repay me,
> Lovers, continual lovers, only repay me.

Other sides of Whitman also appear here. In addition to the great creative force we have the busy hack and the cultivator of his own reputation: sometimes distastefully, sometimes amusingly. For example, he repeatedly implied or more than implied that he had been in combat in the Civil War. As a journalist, Whitman was a poseur, with all the cocksure confidence of the half-educated free lance that he could be an instant authority on any subject. In LC (Feinberg) is an essay on French cooking (*Accent on Home Economics,* #10 [Wayne State University, 1962]), and in the MS of Part II we find "our own account" of the *Nibelungenlied,* with a translation lifted from a textbook. He was forever planning lecture series: on the history of religion, German philosophy, or literary history. Fortunately, the topics on which he could speak with authority were those that appear in *Leaves.* He was also an indefatigable self-promoter. It has long been known that he anonymously reviewed *LG* (1855), but in these manuscripts the reader will find evidence of a number of attempts to plant essays on himself that he wrote in the third person and tried to persuade his friends to sign. More amusingly, one finds accounts (in the third person) of strolls on Broadway or Pennsylvania Avenue in which the genial, bearded poet always heaves into sight.

The great poet is, happily, also present, and these manuscripts give us many insights into his creative process. The first thing that strikes one in surveying his manuscripts, even though one had already known it, is that both in prose and poetry he was a laborious writer. It was not major form for which he struggled. That seems to have come by a sort of precipitation—"struck from the float forever held in solution" as he put it in another context. What tormented him was the painful search for the right word or the right order of words. He could hardly write five words without changing three. Nothing could be more destructive to the image of the spontaneous genius and vatic poet than a glance at the laborious drafts of the startlingly frank, confessional passages of "Song of Myself," secs. 28–29, in "albot Wilson." Each line, almost each word, is revised until the page is an illegible tangle. Even more mysterious, because we have no intermediate steps, is the transformation of the melancholy drivel of "I am not glad tonight," a prose meditation in "Autobiographical Data," into an eerie scene of rebirth ("Song of Myself," sec. 49).

Second, we can also observe the curious way in which his poems did precipitate themselves, perhaps better when each manuscript is studied in its wild heterogeneity or in its context, than when each line is put into its slot in a variorum. In them on successive pages Whitman's mind moves from the far reaches of the Kosmos to the weekly omnibus receipts of London. He also kept his laundry lists in them. In "memorials," he tells himself "(verse in each picture illustrating a European Asiatic African," and immediately in the same page he notes the function of the singer in the ideal American opera. More seriously, Whitman apparently approached a poem in a variety of ways. Sometimes there was a topic, as indicated by the charming little scrap which reads only "Banjo Poem." The reader will find a good many prose suggestions for poems to be written (see especially Part II, Projected Poems), but it was equally characteristic, especially in the early years, for him to write without consideration of final use. Fragments of *LG* (1855), *LG* (1856), and even *LG* (1860) are scattered at random throughout the pre-1855 notebooks. A coherent description of sunset on the river in "memorials" contributes elements to "There Was a Child Went Forth" (1855) and "Crossing Brooklyn Ferry" (1856). Rather more magically, in a notebook he kept during his visit to Ocean Grove, N. J., in 1883, "Viccissini Sav," entries designed for a bit of newspaper self-puffing turn into "With Husky-Haughty Lips, O Sea!" before the reader's startled eyes. "When Lilacs Last in the Dooryard Bloom'd" can be traced from some notes on mourning displays in New York, through some notes on the habits of the hermit thrush that Whitman got from John Burroughs, through a list of appropriate words, and finally through a few scattered lines.

Whitman's prose is a stepbrother of his poetry. It is true that he possessed a gift of epigrammatic phrasing and has moments of genuine eloquence, and it is true that *Specimen Days* has yet to receive adequate criticism, but he was not a talented prose writer. His letters have an appealing directness and simplicity; in his formal prose he appears to be self-conscious. Much of the prose manuscript does present valuable insights (not always flattering) into his intellectual life. One has to keep reminding himself that poets need not be bookish, that they find what they need in strange ways. Because of the limitations of this project, no drafts for the prose of *Specimen Days and Collect* are presented here, but many manuscripts illumine their composition.

II

In their original plan these volumes were to present a scholarly edition of all Whitman's notebooks and all of his miscellaneous prose manuscripts left incomplete or unpublished, except those in the collection of Mr. Charles E. Feinberg (now in the Library of Congress). But publication of the Feinberg Manuscripts was limited to only a selection, *Daybooks and Notebooks,* ed. William White. Since some forty of the manuscripts left unpublished, especially those before 1865, are of striking importance, I have taken them on at the last minute as my responsibility. Since I had the pleasure of studying all the Feinberg manuscripts before they were stored for safety in bank vaults in the late 1960s and again in part after they arrived at the Library of Congress, I have been able to provide cross-references for these.

Certain limitations, however, have been intentionally observed. From the beginning the editors of *The Collected Writings* agreed that verse versions of poems or trial lines for poems belonged in the Manuscript Variorum *Leaves of Grass,* and there they will appear. Nevertheless, the editors agreed that the notebooks had a special character of their own beyond their interest as a source of variant readings and should be presented complete. Sketches for unwritten poems appear in Part II. The editors also agreed that treatment of variants to *Specimen Days and Collect,* on the scale used in the poetical notebooks, would be an extravagance. Prose manuscripts which are not actual variants but are related in content to published prose like *Democratic Vistas* or "The Tramp and Strike Question" are also included. Verbal relationship has been the shibboleth for exclusion. Other classes of manuscripts have been omitted: mere labels, illegible scraps, most trial titles (which are late and highly repetitive, see LC), the minutes of the Smithtown Debating Society and Whitman's official writings as a government clerk. Incidentally, the few official documents that are available, like "Case of General Dyer" (Morristown, N. J., National Historical Park), show that Whitman's job in the Attorney General's Office was that of a legal researcher and opinion-writer rather than of a mere copyist. Marginalia and contributions to Bucke's *Walt Whitman* and similar works are also excluded, although his brief suggestions to Kennedy have been kept. A number of WW's MS are notes on or even extracts from his reading, most conspicuously, perhaps, his notes on oratory and on hygiene, which were long taken to be original. All such have been included because he was interested enough to take those notes or laboriously transcribe those extracts. Manuscripts listed in auction catalogs but not otherwise available have not been noted. At one time, I contemplated a list of "lost" manuscripts from dealers' catalogs, but later realized that such a list would inevitably contain bibliographical ghosts. Manuscripts published by previous editors but since "lost" have been reprinted from the earlier text in default of a manuscript source.

I owe, of course, a great debt to my editorial predecessors, although none of them, with the exception of Emory Holloway, avoids the serious faults of not identifying his sources and of running manuscripts together. None of them pays more than passing attention to the existence of variant readings, which are of crucial importance. The most serious complaint against Holloway is that he did not print the rich notebook material at his disposal, but, of course, he had no way of knowing that ten notebooks (and a cardboard butterfly) were to disappear from the Library of Congress collection under circumstances still not satisfactorily explained. I have identified, described and located each manuscript. Variant readings have been recorded. I have tried to "reconstruct" the lost notebooks. The reader should remember that all LC manuscripts (except Feinberg) were mounted in large albums at some time in the past. Stubs and blank leaves from notebooks were preserved in envelopes, but it is impossible to reconstruct any notebook accurately, and none of these detached scraps has been included in my pagination. Subject to the limitations explained above, I believe that every manuscript known to me (except in the Feinberg collection) and all notebooks before 1865 are for the first time available in full. A number of notebooks from Feinberg, evidently pre-1855, appear in *Daybooks and Notebooks*.

Bibliographical descriptions in headnotes may not be as detailed as they might be, but in the long run a verbal description, however detailed and elaborate, is inadequate for the scholar whose case rests on comparison of minute physical details. He must consult the originals. Thus, systematic attention to the presence of pinholes has been neglected, for comparison of bound manuscripts in the same collection is almost impossible, not to mention comparison of manuscripts in different collections. Trimming by a dealer or collector has not usually been noted unless it affects the text. Mountings, bindings, and framings are not usually noted. The texts are based on photographs which I have annotated from the originals. The few manuscripts which I have not examined at least once have been examined for me by their learned custodians. Vertical dimensions are given first. All references to the text of Walt Whitman, unless otherwise noted, are to *The Collected Writings*.

I have been particularly full, perhaps to excess, in identifications and explanatory footnotes. Identification of books has usually been from the *National Union Catalog* or occasionally the British Museum *Catalogue*. Dates and biographical material are usually from the *Dictionary of American Biography,* the *Britannica* or some similar standard source. Less-routine sources have been indicated in the notes. I have been especially concerned to identify as many of the names listed in the notebooks as possible. City directories for Brooklyn, New York, and Washington have been searched for the appropriate years through 1873, and those of Philadelphia for later years. Unidentifiable names have been passed over in silence.

From the beginning my intention has been to present an uncluttered text, free of all symbols except necessary footnote numbers. Textual footnotes are in the same series as the explanatory notes, for, since the emendations noted are all Whitman's rather than his printer's or editor's, they should be conveniently located. One characteristic of many Whitman manuscripts has been obscured in editing, that is, his habit of writing almost at haphazard on the page. Examination of recent editions of Emerson and Whitman has convinced me that the values of attempting to reproduce this randomness typographically are overweighed by the facts that even a typographical arrangement cannot convey the subtle variations that give such a page of manuscript its effect on the reader, that the page is fatiguing to the eye and mind, and that such a practice uses a great deal of space. Since relatively inexpensive photocopies are now readily available for the scholar who needs to know the appearance of the page, it seemed more important to print as many manuscripts as possible than to print a smaller number of typographical semi-facsimiles. I should add, moreover, that to my mind the ideal edition of any manuscript would be a fully annotated photographic reproduction.

The reader will notice, further, that certain standardizations have been made. Whitman's often indeterminate paragraphing has been printed either with standard indentation or as a block paragraph. Prose paragraphs with hanging indentation are printed as blocks, but annotated. Lists and other short entries of a similar nature (e.g., people he met) in column are printed in a block, but annotated as to layout, and, if Whitman did not divide them by horizontal lines, they have been spaced by the editor. Horizontal lines separating entries, which range in length from a mere nervous flick of the pen to a line the width of the page, are all indicated by a slant line after the entry. If the length of the line seems functional, it is annotated. Whitman's eccentric spacing is noted. Prose lineation is disregarded except where it is clearly significant. Breaks in run-over lines of verse disregard Whitman's lineation. Whitman used "+" and "&" indiscriminately. All have been printed "&." Whitman was inconsistent in his use of double and single hyphens and in compounding (e.g., "to-day" throughout, but "good-looking," "good looking," etc.). When in doubt about end-line compoundings my practice has been to retain the hyphen. Like most writers he usually failed to cancel following punctuation when he cancelled a word, although he usually inserted following punctuation with an inserted word or phrase. This means I have omitted double punctuation. A number of examples were recorded, but, as they multiplied and his general practice became clear, no further examples were noted. One of his favorite graphic devices was the use of a brace, usually large, to support a number of subentries, usually in a column. These have been indicated in the text by a nonce symbol, [:], and noted. Another favorite device, the pointing fist or hand, is recorded in the footnotes, as are marginal lines or similar forms of emphasis. Conjectural readings are marked [?] and illegible words or passages rendered [*illeg.*]. [*Sic*] has not been used to mark his rare misspellings or the more frequent lapses in sentence structure in hastily written passages. Ditto marks are indicated by repeating the word in square brackets and italics. Whitman's infrequent square brackets, only half a dozen or so pairs, are printed and noted as his. Inscriptions in other hands and inserted clippings or calling cards are recorded in the notes.

The most difficult problem is that of words ending in "-ing." Despite examination of a large number of examples in the originals and in enlarged photographs, it is impossible to determine whether, in a given specimen, Whitman wrote "-ing," "-i'g" or "-'g." All, therefore, have been standardized to "-ing." Despite these standardizations, the scholar who compares the printed text and the manuscript will find (barring errors) that this edition presents literally what Whitman wrote, "warts and all," and should be able to follow the steps towards the final text.

Arrangement of the manuscripts has been a problem. A chronological arrangement or "log" was attractive, but dating proved too uncertain. A very elaborate system of coding physical characteristics of manuscripts on "McBee Keysort Selector" cards in the hope of determining dates was a massive waste of time. Paper is not very informative, for Whitman obviously supplied himself with paper in an informal way more often than he bought it. He used pink and green wove wrapper stock left over from *LG* (1855) for about a year. He probably was given the blue Williamsburgh tax blanks by a printer friend or a friend in the tax office after Williamsburgh became a part of the new Brooklyn in 1855, or, as Bowers suggests, he found them in the Brooklyn *Times* office in 1856. He seems to have exhausted this supply within a year or so. He took letterhead paper from government offices, but he was still using Attorney General's letterhead in the late 1870s. In the 1870s he began using something like a stenographer's notebook, but throughout his career he used commonplace, ruled white wove stock. I was unable to undertake an analysis of his handwriting similar to that made of Emily Dickinson's by Theodora Van Wagenen Ward, but it is clear that Whitman's writing (like most people's) changed several times in his career. A small neat hand seems characteristic of the 1850s, regardless of paper size; a more loose and flowing hand appears in the 1860s and 1870s. Even at its clearest after his stroke, his writing shows varying degrees of irregularity. The photostats of dated or dateable MS assembled for these volumes provide a useful basis for dating. Other peculiarities of materials are noted where relevant. Frequently a combination of subject, writing material, and writing has formed a reasonable basis for a conjectural date, but I am not dogmatic about my conjectural dates. It should be emphasized that since Whitman saved paper there is often no connection between the rectos and versos. His erratic manner of keeping notebooks is explained in headnotes.

Neither a strict chronological order nor, as it appeared, a topical order was feasible. Part I, which contains material more or less biographical, the history of the personality so to speak, is loosely chronological. The topical material is that which could be easily grouped together, such as his western trip in 1879. Notebooks, which range widely in content as I noted above, are inserted under the earliest date and in what seemed to be the proper sequence, and I have attempted to rearrange the entries in order of inscription. Part II is arranged according to more sharply defined topics, such as Projected Poems, Oratory, Politics, Explanations, and Words, with a considerable chronological range in each category. There is also considerable overlap among categories and even between Parts I and II. It was impossible, for example, to make a clear distinction between efforts at self-promotion, which are in Part I, and efforts to explain his aims, which are in Part II. Since the organization is not entirely satisfactory to me, I do not expect it will satisfy a reader. I hope that the abundant notes and the index of names will assist him.

ABBREVIATIONS[1]

Allen	Gay Wilson Allen, *The Solitary Singer* (1955)
—, *Handbook*	*Walt Whitman Handbook* (1946)
—, *New Handbook*	*The New Walt Whitman Handbook* (1975)
Asselineau	Roger Asselineau, *L'Evolution de Walt Whitman* (1954)
Asselineau (2)	Roger Asselineau, *The Evolution of Walt Whitman,* Eng. tr., 2 vols. (1960, 1962)
Barrett	Clifton Waller Barrett Collection, University of Virginia Library
Barrus	Clara Barrus, *Whitman and Burroughs, Comrades* (1931)
Bayley	William D. Bayley Collection, Ohio Wesleyan University
Berg	Henry W. and Albert A. Berg Collection, New York Public Library. Astor, Lenox and Tilden Foundations
Berkeley	Bancroft Library, University of California at Berkeley
Blodgett	Harold Blodgett, *Walt Whitman in England* (1934)
Blue Book	*LG* (1860) with WW's corrections, Oscar Lion Collection, Rare Book Division, New York Public Library, Astor, Lenox and Tilden Foundations. Arthur Golden, ed., *Walt Whitman's Blue Book* (1968)
Boston	Boston Public Library
Bowers	Fredson Bowers, *Whitman's Manuscripts, Leaves of Grass, 1860* (1955)
Brown	John Hay Library, Brown University
Bucke	Richard Maurice Bucke, *Walt Whitman* (1883)
Calamus	*Calamus: A Series of Letters Written during the Years 1868–1880 by Whitman to a Young Friend (Peter Doyle)*, ed. by R. M. Bucke (1897), also *CW,* VIII, vii–167
Coll W	*Collected Writings of Walt Whitman,* in progress: N.Y.U. Press, 1961–
Corr.	*Correspondence of Walt Whitman,* ed. by Edwin H. Miller, 6 vols. In *Coll W*
CPP	*Complete Poems & Prose of Walt Whitman,* 1855–1888 (1888)
CW	*Complete Writings of Walt Whitman,* ed by R. M. Bucke and others, 10 vols. (1902)
DA	*Dictionary of Americanisms*

1. The list of abbreviations does not include those in *MLA International Bibliography.*

DAB	*Dictionary of American Biography*
DN	*Daybooks and Notebooks,* ed. William White, 3 vols. (1977). In *Coll W*
Doheny	Estelle Doheny Collection, Doheny Memorial Library, St. John's Seminary, Camarillo, California
Donaldson	Thomas Donaldson, *Walt Whitman the Man* (1896)
DT	Whitman, *Drum-Taps* (1865–1866)
Duke	William R. Perkins Library, Duke University: Trent Collection
DV	Whitman, *Democratic Vistas* (1871)
Eby	Edwin Harold Eby, *A Concordance of Walt Whitman's Leaves of Grass and Selected Prose Writings* (1955)
EP&F	*The Early Poems and the Fiction,* ed. Thomas L. Brasher (1963). In *Coll W*
Faner	Robert D. Faner, *Walt Whitman and Opera* (1951)
FC&I	*Faint Clews and Indirections* (Trent *MS* Collection), ed. by Clarence Gohdes and Rollo G. Silver (1949)
Feinberg	Charles E. Feinberg Collection
Feinberg *Cat.*	*Walt Whitman: A Selection of the Manuscripts . . . Gathered by Charles E. Feinberg* (1955)
Francis and Lozynsky	Gloria Francis and Artem Lozynsky, comps., *Walt Whitman at Auction, 1899–1977* (1978)
Fulghum	W. B. Fulghum, Jr., "Walt Whitman's Debt to Joseph Gostwick," *AL,* 12 Jan., (1941)
Furness	Clifton J. Furness, *Walt Whitman's Workshop* (1928)
Furness *LG*	*Leaves of Grass* [facsimile], ed. by Clifton Joseph Furness (1939)
Furness *NEQ*	"Walt Whitman Looks at Boston," *NEQ,* 1 (July, 1928)
GBF	Whitman, *Good-Bye My Fancy* (1891)
Glicksberg	Charles I. Glicksberg, *Walt Whitman and the Civil War* (1933)
Glicksberg *AL*	"Walt Whitman in 1862," *AL,* 6 (Nov., 1934)
Hanley	T. E. Hanley Collection, Humanities Research Center, University of Texas
Holloway	Emory Holloway, *Whitman: An Interpretation in Narrative* (1926)
Houghton	Houghton Library, Harvard University
Huntington	Henry E. Huntington Library, San Marino, California
In Re	*In Re Walt Whitman,* ed. by Horace L. Traubel, R. M. Bucke, T. B. Harned (1893)
Johnston & Wallace	John Johnston, M.D. and J. W. Wallace, *Visits to Walt Whitman in 1890–1891* (1918)
LC	Library of Congress
LC *Cat*	*Walt Whitman: Catalog Based upon the Collections of the Library of Congress* (1955)

LG	*Leaves of Grass* (*LG, LG* [1860], etc.)
LG CRE	*Leaves of Grass, Comprehensive Reader's Edition*. In *Coll W*
LG Variorum	A Textual Variorum of the Printed Poems of *Leaves of Grass,* ed. Sculley Bradley, Harold W. Blodgett, Arthur Golden and William White. In *Coll W*
LGTR	*Leaves of Grass and Two Rivulets* (Centennial edition, 1876)
Lion	Oscar Lion Collection, Rare Book Division, New York Public Library. Astor, Lenox and Tilden Foundations
Morgan	Pierpont Morgan Library, New York City
N&F	*Notes and Fragments,* ed. by R. M. Bucke (1899): republished, *CW,* IX–X
NB	Whitman, *November Boughs* (1888)
NED	*New English Dictionary*
NYD	*New York Dissected,* ed. Emory Holloway and Ralph Adimari (1936)
NYPL	New York Public Library; see Berg; see Lion
NYPL (MSS)	New York Public Library (Manuscript Division), Astor, Lenox and Tilden Foundations
NYWG	New York *Weekly Graphic*
Pennsylvania	Charles Patterson Van Pelt Library, University of Pennsylvania
Rutgers	Rutgers University Library
Prose 92	*Prose Works 1892,* ed. Floyd Stovall, 2 vols. (1963–1964). In *Coll W*
SD	*Specimen Days* (1882)
SDC	Whitman, *Specimen Days & Collect* (1882)
Stovall, *AL*	Floyd Stovall, "Notes on Whitman's Reading," *AL,* 26 (Nov., 1954)
Stovall, *Foreground*	Floyd Stovall, *The Foreground of "Leaves of Grass"* (1974)
Texas	Library of the University of Texas: Hanley
Traubel	Horace Traubel, *With Walt Whitman in Camden,* 3 vols. (1906–1914); Vol. IV, ed. Sculley Bradley (1953); Vol. V, ed. Gertrude Traubel (1963)
TR	Whitman, *Two Rivulets* (1876)
Trent	Trent Memorial Collection; see Duke
Trent *Cat*	*Catalog of the Whitman Collection in the Duke University Library,* ed. Ellen Frances Frey (1945)
UPP	*The Uncollected Poetry and Prose of Walt Whitman,* 2 vols., ed. by Emory Holloway (1921)
Virginia	Alderman Library, University of Virginia
WDC	Whitman, *Walt Whitman's Diary in Canada,* ed. by William Sloane Kennedy (1904). In *DN,* III
WW	Walt Whitman
Yale	Yale Collection of American Literature, Yale University

CHRONOLOGY OF WALT WHITMAN'S LIFE AND WORK

1819 Born May 31 at West Hills, near Huntington, Long Island.

1813 May 27, Whitman family moves to Brooklyn.

1825–30 Attends public school in Brooklyn.

1830 Office boy for doctor, lawyer.

1830–34 Learns printing trade. In 1831 he was an apprentice for the Long Island *Patriot;* published "sentimental bits."

1835 Printer in New York City until great fire August 12.

1836–38 Summer of 1836, begins teaching at East Norwich, Long Island; by winter 1837–38 has taught at Hempstead, Babylon, Long Swamp, and Smithtown.

1838–39 Edits weekly newspaper, the *Long Islander,* at Huntington.

1840–41 Autumn, 1840, campaigns for Van Buren; then teaches school at Trimming Square, Woodbury, Dix Hills, and Whitestone. Early poems published in *Long Island Democrat.*

1841 May, goes to New York City to work as printer in *New World* office; begins writing for the *Democratic* Review. By 1848 had contributed to *Democratic Review, American* [*Whig*] *Review,* New York *Sun, Broadway Journal, Columbian Mazazine.*

1842 Spring, edits a daily newspaper in New York City, the *Aurora;* edits *Evening Tattler* for short time.

1845–46 August, returns to Brooklyn, writes for *Long Island Star* from September until March.

1846–48 From March, 1846, until January, 1848, edits Brooklyn *Daily Eagle.*

1847 Writes earliest mature poetry and prose.

1848 January, dismissed from *Eagle;* February, he and his brother Jeff leave for New Orleans to work on the *Crescent;* leaves May 27; returns via Mississippi River and Great Lakes

1848–49 September 9, 1848, to September 11, 1849, edits a Free Soil newspaper, the Brooklyn *Freeman.*

1850–54 Operates printing office and stationery store; does free-lance journalism; builds and speculates in houses.

1855 Early July, *Leaves of Grass* is printed by Rome Brothers in Brooklyn; father dies July 11; Emerson writes to poet on July 21.

1856 Writes for *Life Illustrated;* publishes second edition of *Leaves of Grass* in summer and writes "The Eighteenth Presidency!" Thoreau and Alcott visit him, and probably Emerson.

1857–59 From spring of 1857 until about summer of 1859 edits the Brooklyn

Times; unemployed winter of 1859 and 1860; frequents Pfaff's bohemian restaurant.

1860 March, goes to Boston to see third edition of *Leaves of Grass* through the press; rejects Emerson's objections to publishing "Children of Adam"; meets W.D. O'Connor and J.T. Trowbridge; attended trial of F.B. Sunborn.

1861 April 12, Civil War begins; George Whitman enlists.

1862 December, goes to Fredericksburg, Virginia, scene of recent battle in which George was wounded to find him, stays in camp two weeks.

1863 Remains in Washington, D.C., working part time in Army Paymaster's office; visits soldiers in hospitals.

1864 June 22 to January 23, 1865 in Brooklyn because of illness.

1865 January 24, appointed clerk in Department of Interior, returns to Washington; meets Peter Doyle; witnesses Lincoln's second inauguration; Lincoln assassinated, April 14, while WW was in Brooklyn; Doyle was present in theater; May, *Drum-Taps* is printed; June 30, is discharged from position by Secretary James Harlan but re-employed next day in Attorney General's office; autumn, prints *Drum-Taps and Sequel,* containing "When Lilacs Last in the Dooryard Bloom'd."

1866 William D. O'Connor publishes *The Good Gray Poet.*

1867 John Burroughs publishes *Notes on Walt Whitman as Poet and Person;* July 6, William Michael Rossetti publishes article on Whitman's poetry in London *Chronicle;* "Democracy" (part of *Democratic Vistas*) published in December *Galaxy; Leaves of Grass* (1867) published.

1868 Rossetti's *Poems of Walt Whitman* (selected and expurgated) published in England; "Personalism" (second part of *Democratic Vistas*) in May *Galaxy;* second issue of 1867 *Leaves of Grass,* with *Drum-Taps and Sequel* added; praised in Swinburne's *William Blake.*

1869 Mrs. Anne Gilchrist reads Rossetti edition and falls in love with the poet.

1870 July, is very depressed because of Peter Doyle; prints fifth edition of *Leaves of Grass,* and *Democratic Vistas* and *Passage to India,* all dated 1871.

1871 September 3, Mrs. Gilchrist's first love letter; September 7, reads "After All Not to Create Only" at opening of American Institute Exhibition in New York; letter from Tennyson; Swinburne's "To Walt Whitman in America"; Edward Dowden's "The Poetry of Democracy".

1872 June 26, reads "As a Strong Bird on Pinions Free" at Dartmouth College commencement; first letter from J.A. Symonds; T. Bentzon's article in *Revue des Deux Mondes.*

1873 January 23, suffers paralytic stroke; mother dies May 23; unable to work, stays with brother George in Camden, New Jersey.

1874 "Song of the Redwood-Tree" and "Prayer of Columbus."

1875 Prepares Centennial Edition of *Leaves of Grass* and *Two Rivulets* (dated

1876); *Memoranda During the War* published; visits Washington in November and attends dedication of Poe monument in Baltimore.

1876 Controversy in British and American press over America's neglect of Whitman; spring, meets Harry Stafford, and begins recuperation at Stafford farm, at Timber Creek; September, Mrs. Gilchrist arrives and rents house in Philadelphia.

1877 January 28, gives lecture on Tom Paine in Philadelphia; goes to New York in March and is painted by George W. Waters; during summer gains strength by sun-bathing at Timber Creek; Edward Carpenter visits; R.M. Bucke visits.

1878 Spring, too weak to give projected Lincoln lecture, but in June visits J.H. Johnston and John Burroughs in New York.

1879 April to June, in New York, where he gives first Lincoln lecture, and says farewell to Mrs. Gilchrist, who returns to England; September, goes to the West for the first time and visits Kansas and Colorado; because of illness remains in St. Louis with his brother Jeff from October to January.

1880 Gives Lincoln lecture in Philadelphia; summer, visits Dr. R.M. Bucke in London, Ontario.

1881 April 15, gives Lincoln lecture in Boston; returns to Boston in August to read proof of *Leaves of Grass,* being published by James R. Osgood; poems receive final arrangement in this edition; guest of Emerson; returns home in October.

1882 Meets Oscar Wilde; Osgood ceases to distribute *Leaves of Grass* because District Attorney threatens prosecution unless the book is expurgated; publication is resumed in June by Rees Welsh in Philadelphia, who also publishes *Specimen Days and Collect;* both books transferred to David McKay, Philadelphia.

1883 Dr. Bucke publishes *Walt Whitman,* a critical study closely "edited" by the poet.

1884 Buys house on Mickle Street, Camden, New Jersey.

1885 In poor health; friends buy a horse and phaeton so that the poet will not be "house-tied"; November 29, Mrs. Gilchrist dies.

1886 Gives Lincoln lecture four times in Elkton, Maryland, Camden, Philadelphia, and Haddonfield, New Jersey; is painted by John White Alexander.

1887 Gives Lincoln lecture in New York; is painted by Thomas Eakins.

1888 Horace Traubel raises funds for doctors and nurses; *November Boughs* printed; money sent from England; *Complete Poems and Prose of Walt Whitman.*

1889 Last birthday dinner, proceedings published in *Camden's Compliment to Walt Whitman; Leaves of Grass. With Sands at Seventy and A Backward Glance o'er Travel'd Roads.*

1890 Writes indignant letter to J. A. Symonds, dated August 19, denouncing

Symonds's interpretation of "Calamus" poems, claims six illegitimate children.

1891 *Good-bye My Fancy* is printed, and the "death-bed edition" of *Leaves of Grass* (dated 1891–2).

1892 Dies March 26, buried in Harleigh Cemetery, Camden, New Jersey. *Complete Prose Works*.

LIST OF TITLES

(Titles are given below in the order in which they appear in the four volumes of *The Notebooks and Unpublished Prose Manuscripts*. They also are listed alphabetically in the index in Volume IV.)

LIST OF ILLUSTRATIONS

The Collected Writings of Walt Whitman

The Manuscripts

I. Family Notes and Autobiography.

Whitman had a lively feeling for his family, not only for the immediate circle, but also for his scattered relatives, especially on his mother's side. Besides those recorded in the following manuscripts, a Mrs. Thomas Velsor (Mary) is named in "September & October 1863," a Rebecca Velsor and a Baily Van Velsor in 1862 or 1863 in "return my book," and one or more Joseph Velsors in "George Walker Edward Smithson," "D. W. Wilder," and *Corr.*, I, 280*n*. These manuscripts also reveal Whitman's great interest in his ancestors.

From July 28 to August 1, 1881, WW and Dr. Bucke visited the ancestral sites of Whitman's family on Long Island in search of background for *Specimen Days* and Bucke's *Walt Whitman*. While there they called on Henry Lloyd, of West Hills, whose information WW wrote down in "Genealogical Notes" (*DN*, I, 250*n*1297). Probably he had made inquiries about his New England ancestry earlier that summer at the New England Historic Genealogical Society in Boston to which he had a guest card (*Lafayette in Brooklyn*). "Daybook" ([210], *DN*, I, 265) gives a list of books he may have consulted and the names of genealogists in New York and Long Island.

His interest in his own biography was not so great. In 1855 or 1856 he made a record of his jobs and residences between 1826 and 1848 in "Autobiographical Data." The sketches here were written as self-advertisement, an art in which, as a later section shows, he was a master. For self-advertisements see "We suppose it will excite."

The manuscripts are arranged chronologically.

September 11, 12, 13—1850.

Manuscript in Virginia (Barrett) [*1–2*] and in Duke (40, #3) [*3–4*]. Leaf 1 [*1–2*] inscribed in black ink on recto and verso on white wove sheet 12¼″ x 7¹⁴/₁₆″ with blue rules ⁵/₁₆″ apart. Leaf 2 [*3–4*] is inscribed in green ink with emendations as noted in black ink, red ink, and black pencil on white wove sheet 12″ x 7⅜″ with blue rules ⁵/₁₆″ apart. A sales catalog clipping in Duke indicates that at one time [*3–4*] were accompanied by a clipping "Walt Whitman in Huntington" from the *Long-Islander,* August 5, 1881, endorsed by WW: "is in appendix to Dr. Bucke's W.W." The clipping was not found, nor is it in Bucke. On the basis of WW's statement in "The Old Whitman and Van Velsor Cemeteries" (*SD, Prose 92,* I, 5), Allen, 561, assigns the visit to 1853 or 1854. Obviously WW's memory was at fault in 1880 or 1881, although, curiously, he was able to find the MS in 1883 to note his stepuncle Alonzo's death [*1–2*] first printed in "Walt Whitman. Unpublished Notes and Letters," *Wake,* 7 (1948), 19–20; [*3–4*] first printed in *FC&I,* 44–46.

September 11, 12, 13—1850.

These three days, we have been on a visit, (father and myself,) to West Hills, the old native place.— We went up in the L.IRR., and so in the stage to Woodbury—then on foot, along the turnpike and "across lots" to Colyer's.— I plumped in the kitchen door.— Aunt S.[1] (father's sister)[2] was standing there—I knew her at once, although it is very many years since I saw her, and she looked very old and bent. (She is 74[3] years old.)—Hannah her daughter,[4] came in, after a moment. Their[5] appearance was peculiar; but both H. and Aunt S. made us heartily welcome—after the latter recovered from a momentary shock and surprise; for she didn't at first know what to think of it.—

Richard Colyer died about five years ago.— Hannah, the widow, is certainly[6] a clever hearted creature; she made us very welcome, and was evidently sincere about it.— Hard work, losing her husband, and some troubles among her children, have made her a little vaporish, and she complains of bad health.—

Andrew, the eldest son, is a good natured young man, and good-hearted as

1. Sarah Whitman. See "Nehemiah Whitman."

2. Parenthesis and the two words inserted in black ink on a line above and following "Aunt S."

3. Deleted: "72" ; "74" inserted in pencil above.

4. Preceding two words inserted in black ink.

5. Last two letters of "their" written over [*illeg.*].

6. Initial "c" written over [*illeg.*].

the world goes.— He married some three years since, but is separated from his wife.— His little boy is with him —being withdrawn from its mother.—

Charles, the other son is a boy of 16.— Harriet married Edgar Hewlett —he now lives (he died Sept '53.)[7] in New York—drives cart.— Sarah married Lemuel Carll —he lives on his father's place, at the Hills. In the summer of '51, he bought a farm,[8] at Woodbury and moved on it.[9]

Aunt S. is indeed an original. She has very little regard for dress; but is craving for money and property.— She has always shown a masculine, determined mind.— Soon after her marriage, (to one[10] Walters,) her husband took to drink; she separated from him, and [2] would never live with him afterward.— She had the daughter, Hannah.— Coming to Brooklyn as house-keeper, after a few years she returned with a singularly large sum of money; she and the daughter and the latter's husband[11] Richard Colyer settled down in the farm and were industrious and made money.—

Walters died some four or five years ago at the house of his brother, James Walters, the carriage maker, in Brooklyn.—

West Hills is a romantic and beautiful spot; it is the most hilly and elevated part of Long Island.— The "high hill" affords an extensive and pleasant view.—

I went down to the old native place, it is indeed a fine situation, and it seemed familiar enough to me, for I remembered every part, just as well as though only a day had passed since the times when I used to scoot around there a youngster

The old grave yard, on the Hill has some new graves.— The Whitmans must have been a race of[12] note; there are I should say as many as fifty graves there— and it is only their private family burying ground.— Besides this, many others[13] of them must have been buried at Huntington village, for I remember seeing numerous old grave stones that were brought from their graves, at the time of the Revolutionary war—for the British encamped on the Huntington hill, and took away grave stones for ovens and hearths, &c.—[14] The stones I saw were brought away, lest they might be despoiled, and somehow, when the war passed over, they were never returned.

The Whitmans appear to have been mostly of the Quaker notion, concerning [3] tomb stones; for on the old hill, at the native place, among all the numerous graves, there is not one inscribed grave stone, except Mahala Whitman, and I think I have heard that that was put up at the instance of a young man who was to have been married to her.—

7. Parenthesized words inserted in black pencil on a line above "lives"
8. Deleted: "and"
9. Entire sentence inserted in black pencil above the following "he" in "he lives"
10. Preceding two words inserted in black ink.
11. Preceding three words inserted in black pencil.
12. Deleted in black ink: "some" before "note;"
13. "Others" inserted in black ink on a line above "many"
14. Deleted word [*illeg.*] and following word smeared; "hearths" following "ovens"

The old house in which my father's grand parents lived, (and their parents[15] before them,) is still partly standing—a ponderous frame; it is now turned into a carriage house and granary.— The largest trees near it, that I remember, appear to have been cut down.—

The Whitmans were among the earliest settlers of that part of Long Island—West Hills, township of Huntington, county of Suffolk, New York.— They must have originally come from some[16] rural district of England—a stalwart, massive, heavy, long-lived race. They appear to have been always of democratic and heretical tendencies. Some of them are yet represented[17] by descendants in New England

My father's grandfather was quite a large territorial owner in that part of Long Island, and also on the southern shore of the town.— They all espoused with ardor the side of the "rebellion" in 76.

I remember when a boy hearing grandmother Whitman tell about the times of the revolutionary war. The British had full swing over Long Island, and foraged every where, and committed the most horrible excesses—enough to make one's blood boil even to hear of now.— My father's father I never saw.—

[4] Mother's family lived only two or three miles from West Hills on a solitary[18] picturesque road, that wound up from Cold Spring Harbor.— Her father was Major[19] Van Velsor, and her mother's name Naomi Williams.[20]— (Capt. Williams and his wife, her parents, fine old couple, exceedingly generous.)[21] I remember them both (my mother's parents)[22] very well. She was a mild, gentle, and sweet tempered woman, fond of children—remarkably generous and hospitable in disposition—a good wife and mother.— In dress she was rather Quakerish.— Her mother's[23] (my great grandmother's)[24] maiden name[25] was Mary Woolley, and her father, Capt: Williams, was owner of a vessel that sailed between New York and Florida.[26]

Major Van Velsor was a good specimen of a hearty, solid, fat old gentleman, on good terms with the world, and who liked his ease.— For over forty years, he drove a stage and market wagon from his farm to Brooklyn ferry, where he used to put up at Smith & Wood's old tavern on the west side of the street, near Fulton ferry.[27]— He was wonderfully regular in these weekly trips; and in those old fash-

15. Deleted in black ink: "probably" after "parents" ; inserted in black ink: "before them" on a line above.
16. The word "some" written over "the" in the line.
17. The word "represented" is written over [*illeg.*].
18. Deleted: "but" after "solitary"
19. [Cornelius] . WW left a space, probably to be filled in with "Cornelius"
20. Punctuation in black pencil.
21. Sentence inserted in black pencil on a line above "Williams.—"
22. Parentheses and words inserted in red ink under sentence in *n*21 to follow "both"
23. Possessive inserted in black pencil.
24. Parentheses and words inserted in black ink between lines.
25. Preceding two words inserted in black pencil after entry in *n*24 between lines.
26. Preceding seventeen words inserted in a small hand between lines in black ink.
27. Period deleted; comma and preceding three words inserted in black ink.

ioned times, people could almost tell the time of day, by his stage passing along the road—so punctual was he.— I have been up and down with him many times: I well remember how sick the smell of the lampblack and oil with which the canvass covering of the stage was painted, would make me.—

After my own[28] grandmother died, in 1826[29] the old man married again—[30] He had a son Alonzo, by this second marriage—now, (Sept. 1850;) in California. He is a good young man, I think, from what I know of him.

He[31] has[32] since returned from California with his "pile."[33] went into business in New York, and died[34] at Newark, N.J. July 22, 1883[35]

28. Preceding two words inserted in black ink.

29. WW questioned the date by crossing out "2" and writing "3" over "2" in pencil and then "?3" above it. "1826" is correct.

30. Deleted in pencil: "but did not make a very good investment.—"

31. In a darker ink over [*illeg.*]

32. Inserted in line above "He"

33. Sentence in a fainter black ink.

34. Deleted: "in" before "at"

35. Preceding fourteen words inserted in black ink without deleting the preceding period. The ink is much darker and the writing more irregular. *FC&I,* 45*n*4 notes the appearance of an obituary for Alonzo Van Velsor in the Newark *Daily Advertiser,* July 23, 1883. Alonzo was probably also related to Baily Van Velsor of Newark. See "return my book."

Nehemiah Whitman.

Manuscript in NYPL (Berg). One leaf white wove paper, 7¾" x 4". Faded rules ⅛" apart. Recto in green ink with insertions in black ink; verso in faded black ink with insertions in fresher black. The last eleven lines (commencing "Built in Skillman st . . .") in black pencil with insertions in the fresher black ink. "Sept 11, 12, 13—1850" and "*'Wants'*" are the only other MS in green ink that have been found. They are in a similar handwriting. Thus 1850 must be the approximate date of inscription for the recto. The date of death for Jesse Whitman, September 8, 1845, in green ink, establishes the earliest possible date. The date of sale of the two houses on Cumberland Street, March, 1853, establishes the earliest possible date of inscription for the verso. The date of building on Skillman Street, establishes 1854 for the earliest possible date for the pencilled inscription on the verso. The dates from 1855 to 1861 are in the fresh black ink. WW must have worked over this record at least three times between 1850 and 1861. See also "Autobiographical Data."

Printed in part in *UPP,* II, 88*n*.

Nehemiah Whitman,[1] descended from one of the[2] earliest English emigrants to America, was born and died on the old[3] homestead at West Hills—which was inherited by his son, His wife was Sarah[4] White—

(Sarah White born about 1713 [*WW's ditto* of her name] died 1801[5] see next page—bottom)[6]

Jesse Whitman, born Jan. 29, 1749[7] [*WW's ditto*] died Feb. 12, 1803

Hannah Brush, born Oct. 6, *1753*[8] [*WW's ditto*] died Jan. 6, 1834 [:][9] Married, April 22, 1775

1. WW's paternal great grandfather. Entry in hanging indentation.
2. There are at least three layers of writing in the preceding words (the first line of the MS). One is possibly pencil and one erased green ink. One at the very top seems to read: "—of NC, built the old house [?] [*illeg.*] born"
3. Inserted and deleted: [*illeg.*]
4. Originally "Phebe" ; deletion and insertion in black ink.
5. "1" over "2"
6. The entries in this paragraph were inserted at the right side of the page in black pencil by the top of the brace referred to in *n*9. The last four words are in black ink.
7. His paternal grandfather.
8. His paternal grandmother.
9. Brace to right of two preceding entries. Last notation is centered on the brace to the right.

The[10] Whitman and Brush families were among the most ardent of the[11] "Rebels" of '76, in Suffolk county.— See "*Reminiscences*".—[12] One of the latter, Maj. Brush, was often and angrily denounced by the British local[13] proclamations, and by the loyalists of Long Island. He was confined for a time in the "Provost" in New York, under the charge of the infamous Cunningham

Jesse Whitman, jr[14] born June 25, 1776 Died at Dix Hills, Sept. 8, 1845

Sarah Whitman, born Jan. 1, 1778 died Feb. 2, 1852[15]

Naomi Van Velsor died, February 1826[16]
Major Cornelius Van Velsor[17] born 1758.[18] died, August, 1837, aged 79
(He was son of Garret Van Velsor
Garret Van Velsor, died 1812 Phebe Akely[19] [:] parents of Major Van Velsor

One of the sons[20] of Nehemiah Whitman was a Lieutenant in Col. Josiah Smith's Regiment of the American Patriot[21] Army[22] of 1776 of Washington, (Lee[23] 1st edition Reminiscences of Long Island, vol. 2, page 28 or vol. 3, page 87)

He was in the disastrous battle of Brooklyn[24] the reg. having been ordered to place themselves under Gen. Greene, some days before that battle[25] by Brig. Gen. Woodhull, who[26] was also President of the N.Y. Convention.—

10. Paragraph begins a third of the way across the leaf and extends down right margin beyond "Sarah Whitman"

11. Redundant "the" not printed.

12. See below, *n*23. This book has not been located. The remainder of this paragraph is written in a column down the right edge of the leaf beside the three following entries.

13. Inserted: "local" on line above.

14. A paternal uncle.

15. Presumably a paternal aunt. The entry of her death is in faded black ink. Brace at right of entry. See "September 11, 12, 13—1850."

16. His maternal grandmother, *née* Williams.

17. His maternal grandfather.

18. Preceding two words and period inserted on a line above.

19. Deleted: "Jenny Kossabon" . The genealogical chart prepared by Bucke (Allen, 595–596) names Mary Kossabone as the wife of Garret Van Velsor. No other reference to Phebe Akeley has been found, but the name may have survived in that of Phebe Pintard, one of WW's maternal aunts. See "Oct. 29. '62." Brace connecting this entry and preceding at right.

20. An entry under these two words (written above the line) was obliterated by smearing the green ink.

21. Preceding two words inserted between the lines, above "the Army"

22. Deleted: "Under [*ins.*] chief command"; inserted: "of 1776" *FC&I*, 43*n*, notes that "The National Society of the Sons of the American Revolution possesses no record of a Lt. Whitman in Col. Smith's regiment. . . ."

23. Possibly "See" . This book has not been located.

24. Deleted: "Col. Smith's" after "Brooklyn" ; inserted: "the" above the deletion.

25. Deleted: ";—" .

26. Deleted: "had charge general charge on L. I.—" ; inserted: "was also President of the N.Y. Convention"

The L.I. regiment were hemmed in the lines [over][27]

[2][28] We moved to Brooklyn, (Front st.) in May, 1823. Moved to Cranberry st. (opposite the church,)[29] in '24.

[*WW's ditto (referring to* "Moved to")] Johnson st. May 1st 1825.— (Covert, the villain.[30]

[*WW's ditto*] Across the way, (Van Dyke's) were there 4th July 1826.

[*WW's ditto*] Adams st. lived there spring of '27

[*WW's ditto*] To Tillary cor. Washington, (Miller's) 1st May 1827

[*WW's ditto*] To own house in Nov. and lived there till Nov. 18[31]

Lived in Henry st. (near Cranberry,) the winter before the first cholera summer.[32]

Moved to Liberty st. Were there one of[33] cholera summers.— (The old Hardenburghs up stairs) (I was there alone in the house a while.) The miserable scoundrel Gil. Reid,[34] and the suffering he caused us all.— Graham the old devil, that owned the house.)

Moved from Liberty st. to Front st. (eastern part, and lived there in spring and early summer of 1833. mother very sick[35] (Mrs. Sibley.)

Family[36] Moved in the country.— Lived at Norwich in 1834 I remained in Brooklyn.[37]

· From there to Hempstead—were there 1835–6.— Moved from Hempstead to Babylon, Aug. 1836

[*WW's ditto under* "Moved"] to Dix Hills in May, 1840

27. Faded black ink at right below.

28. Except for entries noted and the final passage, "Built on Skillman st . . . owned very largely by Whitmans." which is in pencil, the entire page is in faded black ink.

29. The church is the First Presbyterian Church.

30. The 1826–1827 directory lists a Richard D. Covert, Adams near Johnson. The directory for 1829–1830 (1827–1829 is not available) lists Richard D. Covert, attorney, 87 Cranberry. In "A schoolmaster while intoxicated" (1848?–1852), WW sketched a short story involving a villainous lawyer named Covert who defrauds his wards and entertains "licentious" feelings toward one who is a female and told himself to "tell the story of Covert's father swindling, about the house on Johnson st — damn him." A Covert is also mentioned in "One Wicked Impulse" (1845), *EP&F,* 309ff.

31. Deleted: "31" from original "1831"

32. The first reference to the Whitmans in the Brooklyn directory, however, is to "Walter Whitman, carpenter, Henry near Fulton" in 1825–1826, when according to this MS, they were on Johnson or Adams. The first cholera epidemic occurred in New York in the summer of 1832 and recurred almost annually until the end of the century. Thus the winter they lived on Henry was 1831–1832 (but see preceding entry). The directory for the years 1829–1832 lists them at 41 Tillary. WW must have confused Henry and Tillary streets. The family does not appear in the directory annually.

33. The words "one of" are written over smeared: "the first"

34. A Gilbert Reid, saddle and harness-maker, is listed at 66 Fulton in 1832–1833. The Hardenburghs (above) and Graham (below) could not be identified.

35. Preceding three words inserted in black ink above "1833" . Mrs. Sibley could not be identified.

36. Word inserted in blacker ink above "Moved" . Capital on "Moved" not corrected.

37. Preceding four words inserted on a line above "in 1834"

[*WW's ditto under* "Moved"] from Dix Hills to Brooklyn Aug. 6, 1844 [:] I remaining in Brooklyn[38]

Moved into house in Prince st. in Dec. 1846[39]

I[40] built the place 106 Myrtle av. in winter of 1848–9,[41] and moved in, latter part of April '49

I Sold[42] the Myrtle av. house in May, '52, and built in Cumberland street, where we moved Sept. 1st, '52.

Sold the two 3 story houses in Cumberland st. March 1853. moved into the little 2 story house Cumberland st.[43] April 21st, '53[44] (lived there just one year exactly)

Built in Skillman st. and moved there May, 1854

Moved in Ryerson st, May 1855.— Lived in Classon from may 1st[45] '56, '7 '8 '9[46]

Lived in Portland av. from may 1st '59 '60 '61[47]

Sarah White, my great grandmother Whitman, lived to be 90 years old.— She was a large, strong woman, chewed tobacco, opium &c.— petted her slaves, and had always a crowd of little niggers about her.— She would sit with her feet up before the fire, just like a man—was every way decided and masculine in behavior[48]

The tradition of my grandfather, Jesse Whitman was that there were four brothers, Englishmen his remote ancestors[49] who came over here.— One settled on Long Island—West Hills was formerly inhabited and owned very largely by Whitmans.—

38. Four words written lengthwise at left in blacker ink with brace covering this and preceding two entries. In short, he remained in Brooklyn from 1834 to 1844?

39. The directory for 1845–1846 lists the Whitmans at Prince and Willoughby.

40. "I" inserted; "Built" not reduced to lowercase.

41. This was after his return from New Orleans. "Autobiographical Data" repeats information about these later moves. See also "albot Wilson" [inside front cover].

42. "Sold" written over smeared erasure, not reduced to lowercase.

43. Preceding two words inserted on a line above "house"

44. The remainder of the MS, including the parenthetical entry following this note, which is written in the right margin, is in black pencil, except as noted.

45. Preceding words inserted.

46. Sentence and initial dash in black ink.

47. Sentence inserted in black ink.

48. In "Isaac Joseph" WW says his paternal grandmother, Hannah Brush, described a similar scene at the home of her aunt, Vashti Platt.

49. Preceding three words inserted on a line above "Englishmen"

Isaac Joseph.

Manuscript in Duke (39, #2). Soft white wove paper, approx. 6¼" x 3¾". Inscribed in pencil. The writing suggests the 1850s. Printed in *FCI,* 43.

Isaac Joseph Stephen & Jesse (my grandfather)[:][1]sons of Nehemiah Whitman

Phebe—[2] [:] daughters

Hannah Brush,[3] daughter of Tredwell Brush & —— *Platt* Her parents died when she was quite young,[4] she[5] was adopted by her aunt Vashti Platt— This latter must have been mistress of quite an estate, for grandmother related that she has seen fourteen little niggers, belonging to the family, eating their supper at evening, all at once[6] in the kitchen.[7] Tredwell Brush, her brother, died a young man unmarried

1. Names in column behind a brace. A check mark in an unknown hand follows the first four names.

2. Names in column. The blank is possibly for Mahala Whitman, whose gravestone WW saw in 1850 ("September 11, 12, 13—1850.").

3. WW's paternal grandmother.

4. Deleted: "and"

5. Deleted: "went" ; inserted: "was" on a line above.

6. Preceding three words inserted on a line above beginning at "in"

7. See a somewhat similar anecdote about Sarah White Whitman his great grandmother, "Nehemiah Whitman." See also "Oct. 17, 1860."

Progenitors.

Manuscript in Duke (not in Trent *Cat.*). Inscribed in black pencil with black pen emendations on white wove paper, probably from a pocket ledger, 5⅞" x 3^5/16". Horizontal blue rules ¼" apart; vertical red line at ^{22}/32" from left, red double rule, 2^{22}/32", red single rule at 3¼". Bound, probably by a dealer, with "Capt John Williams," but clearly a distinct manuscript, not only because of repetitions but because of differences in paper. WW used pocket ledger paper as early as 1847, see "albot Wilson." The writing is also that of his earliest notebooks, the 1850s. See "Sept 11, 12, 13—1850."

Progenitors)[1] in the little house on the hill, Cold Spring

Capt. John Williams & Mary Woolley Cold Spring, LI [:] parents of Amy Williams mother's mother

They[2] (Capt. John & Mary) had 8 daughters and two sons—the men father & sons[3] all followed the water—were expert sailors—Capt. John was a wonderful man for his[4] friends,[5] hospitality good living &c.— Amy [6], (mother's mother)[7] when he came in from a voyage, would take one child in her arms and another by the hand, and go over the hills afoot to see her father.— He died aboard his vessel in N.Y. Mary (mother's grandmother)[8] was washing—when a vessel came up the Harbor with the flag at half-mast.— It brought the corpse;— a neighbor heard the news, came up to the little house on the hill—took the tub and set it away and told the death. Mary had been looking at the vessel with the spy glass.[9]

1. The first few lines are set out in characteristic braces and parentheses. This half-parenthesis separates "Progenitors," which was written as a centered title, from the following added upper right: "in . . . Spring" ; "Capt. John . . . L. I." is on a brace pointing to "parents . . . mother" . It would seem from the density of the pencil, that WW added "Amy Williams" first. What precedes and follows is darker.

2. Entry begins as a hanging paragraph, but by the last third of the page, inscription has drifted to the left margin set by initial "Capt."

3. Preceding three words inserted on a line above beginning over "men"

4. Inserted on line above following "for"

5. Deleted: "amiableness" ; inserted: "hospitality" on line above.

6. "Amy" written over [*illeg.*]

7. Parenthetical phrase inserted on a line above beginning over comma after "Amy"

8. Parenthetical phrase inserted on a line above beginning after "Mary" below; deleted: "the" ; inserted: "when" on a line above "a"

9. Preceding nine words cramped in at bottom of leaf in slightly darker pencil, probably the result of trying to fill the narrow space available at the foot of the page.

Capt John Williams.

Manuscript in Duke (not in Trent *Cat.*). Inscribed in black pencil and black ink on three leaves of white laid paper, 6¼" x 3¾" with heavy basket weave pattern in texture. Versos blank. In upper left embossed stamp of a London papermaker.

Had at one time been folded horizontally in three. Bound, probably by dealer, with "Progenitors." No similar paper has been noted, but the writing is that of the 1850s. See "Sept 11, 12, 13—1850."

[*1*] Capt John Williams, (his wife Mary Woolley)[1] my grandmother Velsor's father,[2] was a sailor & master of a vessel, went frequently to the West Indies, & the Spanish Main,[3] was a remarkably generous man, took more delight in giving & [4] when home in unstinted hospitality & charity to the poor than any thing else. His two sons mother's uncles[5] were also sailors, their names were John & Thomas —then there were eight girls besides, all lived to be either elderly or very old. One of them, Sally, is now (Nov '64) living in New York City, over 90 years of age she died in[6]

[2][7] ?Cornelius ?Caleb Van Velsor's parents (mother's grandparents)

Garret Van Velsor died aged 70[8] when mother was 18 years old

?Mary Kossabone died two or three years before mother was born & our great grand mother[9]

the Kossabones were a good family

the above two had six children, three boys & three girls & grandfather Van Velsor was the second son

1. Parenthetical phrase inserted on two lines above "Williams"

2. Deleted in black ink: "(her maiden [*ins. and del. in black ink*] name was Amy [*ins. and del. above in black ink*] Naomi Williams)"

3. Preceding four words inserted on a line above "Indies" ; "the" inserted above and before "Spanish".

4. Deleted: "in" following "&" ; inserted: "when . . . unstinted" *on a line above* "hospitality"

5. Preceding two words inserted on a line above beginning "after" "his"

6. "She died in" inserted on a line above in black ink beginning above "90" . Sarah Williams was alive as late as 1873. See "1873. Nov. 20."

7. Inscribed in black pencil on irregularly cut paper, 6¼" and 3½", like [*1*]. Pinholes at top as in following leaf ([3]). Another indescribable inscription. Lower half of leaf smeared.

8. Preceding two words inserted on a line above, beginning after "died" . Hanging indentation.

9. Preceding five words inserted on two lines aligned on "born" . Writing smeared. Hanging indentation.

——— our great grandmother Garretts wife, was a superior woman, much beloved, she died quite suddenly,— she was about going for some things to New York complained of a pain in her[10] [*3*][11] head, but continued talking about the things,[12] went & sat down on a bed in the room, spoke of the severity of the pain in her head, & in a few minutes it was evident she was in a dying condition

——— Garret Van Velsor lived some twenty years after,[13]— his trade was that[14] of weaver of cloth —mother, when a child, used to go & see him,[15] she remembered him at work at his loom, & also going to church,[16] wearing the white linen caps, turned up around, which old men wore

10. The writing is cramped in the last line.

11. Pencil on same paper as [*12*].

12. Deleted: "was compelled to sit" , "go" following "things" ; inserted: "went &" on a line above beginning after "things"

13. Deleted: "he was" following the dash.

14. Deleted: "a" before "weaver"

15. Deleted: "at" before "she"

16. Following words cramped in at bottom of leaf.

Hannah Brush, (My Grandmother.

Manuscript in Duke (39, #2). Blue wove paper approx. 3⅜" x 3¾". Lines 5/16" apart. Inscribed in pencil. Both entries with hanging indentation. The writing suggests the 1850s. Printed *FC&I,* 43.

Hannah Brush, (my grandmother Whitman) had only one brother, who died a young man—(the grave-stones[1] from his grave were among those I saw at the back door)

And only one sister who married ——— Scudder, father of old[2] Tredwell[3] Scudder, (on the South Side,) who was[4] father of Tredwell,[5] Walter,[6] Richard, Wilmot, Hannah & Julia Scudder.[7]

1. The gravestones are referred to in "Sept 11, 12, 13—1850."
2. "old" inserted on a line above "of"
3. Inserted and deleted: "Walter W" on a line above and before "Scudder"
4. Preceding two words inserted on a line above "father"
5. Deleted: "Wilmot"
6. Deleted: "Scudder &c"
7. For the Scudders, see "Hannah Brush," "Oct. 17, 1860," "Poem incarnating the mind."

Walter Whitman Married Louisa.

Manuscript in Duke (41, #6). White wove paper 14" x 7⅜". Blue lines 5/16" apart. Inscribed in black ink with pencil and red ink additions. Printed in *FC&I,* 47–48. On verso is a fragmentary account of his return from New Orleans in 1848, "is rougher than it was" ("New Orleans in 1848," *Prose 92,* II, 609–610). It seems probable that the manuscript was written after 1852, for the date of Hannah Louisa Whitman's marriage to Charles Heyde seems to be an original part of the manuscript. However, the fact that the newspaper obituary of Walter Whitman, who died July 11, 1855, pasted on the page, is both preceded and followed by written entries, suggests that at least what follows was written in 1855 or later. See "Progenitors" and "Capt John Williams."

Walter Whitman married Louisa Van Velsor June 8, 1816. Mary E. Whitman & Ansel Van Nostrand, Married, Jan. 2, 1840. Hannah Louisa Whitman & Charles Louis Heyde, married 16th[1] March 1852.

Walter Whitman born July 14th 1789.— died July 11th 1855: aged 66 buried at Evergreen Cemetery.[2] Louisa Van Velsor [*born*][3] Sept. 22, 1795 Jesse Whitman [*born*] March 2, 1818.[4] Walter Whitman Jr. born May 31, 1819 Mary Elizabeth Whitman [*born*] Feb. 3, 1821 Hannah Louise Whitman [*born*] Nov. 28, 1823 Infant born March 2d 1825[5] Andrew Jackson Whitman, born April 7th 1827 George Washington Whitman [*born*] Nov. 28th 1829. Jefferson Whitman, born July 18th 1833 Edward Whitman born August 9th 1835[6]

1. WW had originally written "early in" which he deleted to insert "16th" on a line above with a caret below the line and following "16th" . In the Bible which WW gave his sister Mary Van Nostrand in 1878 the date is given as April (Katherine Molinoff, *Some Notes on Whitman's Family* [Brooklyn, 1941], 7).

2. The date of death and place of burial added in pencil at right and aligned in two lines on "Walter Whitman . . ." entry; the age in red ink. The following ten entries are in column.

3. WW used dittos for *"born"* presented in brackets here.

4. In the Van Nostrand Bible the date is given as April 2, 1818 (Molinoff, *Some Notes,* 7).

5. In the Van Nostrand Bible the date is given as April 12, 1825. (Ibid.)

6. Newspaper obituary pasted to the manuscript following this entry. "DIED. In Brooklyn, on the night of July 11th, 1855, WALTER WHITMAN, senior, after an exhausting illness of nearly 3 years, from paralysis. Born at West Hills, town of Huntington, L. I., July 14th, 1789; was mostly a resident of New York city and Brooklyn; a carpenter. His death was easy and unconscious. Buried in the Cemetery of the Evergreens. Present: His widow, and a large family of sons and daughters." Whitman corrected the day in ink.

Infant died Sept. 14, 1825, aged 6 months & 12 days. Naomi or Amy Williams was daughter of Capt. Williams and his wife Molly Williams.[7] Besides two sons, they had eight daughters, Amy, Sally, Peggy, Hannah, Clara, Molly .— They lived in a little house high upon the hills at Cold Spring.— Aunt Molly, the mother was easy, good-natured, and inclined to let things go. Capt. Williams followed the sea.—

7. In "Progenitors" the name is given in the formal form, Mary.

In the Revolution.

Manuscript in Duke (39, #1). White laid paper, approx. 5¾" x 4¾". Blue rules 5/16" apart. Inscribed in black ink. Printed *FC&I,* 42. The relatively loose writing suggests a date in the 1860s.

In the Revolution, a squad of British cavalrey, on a raid on their own account, came to Kell Van Velsor's, (mother's father, "Uncle Kell,"[1]) then a youth,[2] and went to the barn, and were just taking away[3] a very fine young sorrel mare. Amy V. V.[4] and Kell's sisters, prevented him by force for a while[5] from going to interfere, but just as the British soldiers were leading the mare out, K. broke away from the women, made a rush, and seized the bridle from the thieves. They drew their sabres, and flourished them round his head, but he was resolute; and demanded to see their authority for pressing his horse. As usual, great courage,[6] will, and coolness, stood him in hand. The swords flourished and flashed around his head—the women[7] were in tears, expecting he would be killed; but he held on to the mare, and the upshot of it was, the British rode away without her.

Grandmother Whitman[8] tells that one day a British quartermaster's deputy, with some attendants, came out to her house, (the old house below the hill,) and ordered her to get ready the parlor and adjoining bedroom for an officer of rank, in a few days. She did so, but the officer never came.

1. "Uncle Kell," inserted on a line above "father" . Major Cornelius Van Velsor.
2. Preceding three words inserted on a line above, flush right.
3. "away" inserted on a line above "a"
4. Amy Williams Van Velsor.
5. Preceding three words inserted on a line above "force"
6. Deleted: "and" before "will"
7. Illegible correction in "women"
8. Hannah Brush Whitman.

Oct. 17, 1860.—Portland Av.

Manuscript in University of Kansas. Four white wove leaves, 8″ x 6¼″, originally two leaves torn and folded by WW. Fragment of embossed stamp: "Owen and H . . . So Lee Mass." WW used Owen and Hurlburt paper in the late 1850s also. See "What Name? *Religious* Canticles" and "Spring of 1859." Inscribed in black ink with emendations in black ink, from two different pens, and black pencil. The pencil emendations are from 1884; those with a broader point pen probably soon after the original inscription. The MS does not record a visit to the family sites, which he seems not to have visited between 1855 with his father and 1881 with Dr. Bucke. It is possibly a record of a conversation with his mother. This was written in 1860 and 1884.

Oct. 17, 1860.—Portland av.

Hannah Brush, (my grandmother Whitman, my father's mother—[1]) and her sister were orphans, brought up by their Aunt, Vashti Platt, who had a large farm in the east end of Suffolk County. Mother has told me that Grandmother Whitman, (H B)[2] when she was a girl, living with her aunt in the farmhouse, has counted as many as[3] sixteen little "niggers" in the kitchen[4] eating their meal of samp and milk.[5] Grandmother's sister married Tredwell Scudder,[6] (south side Long Island, east of Babylon,)—his son, Walter Scudder.

The Brushes, (Grandmother's father, brother, &c.) were buried on the old hill grave yard, in the village of Huntington. When the British, at the revolution ?(   ),[7] took possession of the [2] island,[8] and were at Huntington among the

1. Preceding three words and dash inserted above "Whitman . . . and" in black pencil, presumably in 1884.

2. Parenthesized initials inserted in black pencil above.

3. Preceding three words inserted in black ink above.

4. Preceding three words inserted in black ink above.

5. This anecdote appears in "Isaac Joseph," which is possibly a little earlier, and "Some Diary Notes at Random," *NB, Prose 92,* II, 580. The number of slaves differs. There is possibly some reference to it in "Two Old Family Interiors," *SD,* ibid., I, 8–9.

6. Tredwell Scudder (1778–1834). Born and died in Islip, Suffolk County, L. I. As WW notes later, he served in the House of Representatives in the 50th Congress (1817–1819). He did not stand for renomination. He was a member of the State Assembly several times, was town supervisor, and engaged in "agricultural pursuits" (*Biographical Dictionary of the American Congress, 1774–1927* Washington [1928] 1504). According to Mr. John W. Watson of the Long Island Historical Society, he was a Republican. See also "Hannah Brush."

7. Inserted in black pencil.

8. Deleted in black ink: "they"

rest, they used the grave-stones as building materials. So Grandmother had[9] the gravestones of her folks taken up, and carried to West Hills, to the Whitman homestead, intending to replace them when the British soldiers left. But they never were replaced. I saw them there, moss-covered & cracked[10] near the back door, summer after summer, when I was a little[11] boy, in 1829,[12] '30[13] and[14] '32—[15] they leaned up against the back of the house, all blue and gray and[16] covered with green scum and moss—but with the old[17] lettering as plain as ever. [*3*] Grandmother Whitman was a very fine needlewoman, first rate[18] at embroidery &c. She was a capital dressmaker, had learned the trade, and worked at at it. She also taught school several years. I remember her very well. She was very cheerful, sensible, lady like, healthy, good-looking woman, of the old school.

Tredwell Scudder, aforementioned,[19] was a member of the U.S. Congress, several terms, I believe.

I remember very well[20] the old house of the Whitmans, at West Hills—the one used for two or three generations previous to my father[21] and which my father was born in.[22] When I was a boy, I used to go into it I remember the great heavy timbers, low [*4*] ceilings, upper Chambers, &c—and the long kitchen, &c. It[23] had on one side a beautiful grove of black-walnuts, locusts, &c. and in the rear a small peach orchard. All was in great neglect, however, I remember the immense leaves of the[24] burdock plants,[25] &c. Under[26] these the turkeys used to make their nests, and hatch out their broods. [1884—It is still standing—used as granary coach-house, &c][27]

9. Deleted in black ink: "those" ; inserted in black ink: "the gravestones"
10. Preceding four words inserted in black ink above "I saw them there"
11. Inserted in black ink above.
12. "29" written over "30" in black ink.
13. "o" written over "2" in black ink.
14. Inserted in black ink above.
15. Deleted: [*illeg.*]
16. Preceding four words inserted in black ink, but apparently with a broader nib.
17. Inserted in black ink, but apparently with a broader nib.
18. Deleted in black pencil: "great" ; inserted in black pencil above: "first rate"
19. Deleted in black ink: "served"
20. Preceding two words inserted in black ink on a line above "the"
21. Deleted in black pencil: "—but" following "father" ; inserted in black pencil: "and" on a line above "but"
22. What may be a question mark in black pencil above.
23. Deleted: "was" following "It"
24. Preceding three words inserted in black ink on a line above "immense burdock"
25. Deleted in black ink: "bushes" ; comma not deleted, not shown here; inserted: "plants," above "bushes"
26. Delted in black ink: "In" ; inserted in black ink: "Under" on a line above "In"
27. Added in black pencil. The square brackets are WW's.

Oct. 29. '62.

Manuscript in Duke (39, #2). One leaf $7^{11}/_{16}'' \times 4^{7}/_{8}''$. White wove paper. Inscribed in pencil. Printed *FC&I,* 44.

Oct. 29. '62—Brooklyn Portland avenue

A visit from Sarah Mead, mother's aunt, (her mother's sister,[1]) She is 80 years of age, quite smart—lives with her daughter in New York.

Phœbe Pintard,[2] another of mother's aunts, aged 85, lives in New York.

Mrs Clara Avery, aged about 82, is also living.

Peggy Williams, (another) an old maid died about two years ago.

(The above are four of the eight daughters of Capt Williams, mothers maternal grandfather)

1. The folder in Duke also contains two clippings signed "W. H.," containing Aunt Sarah's reminiscences. In the first it is mentioned that she had seen Washington in 1790, that WW was her grandnephew and had written her in 1876. The second is endorsed by WW as coming from the New York *Evening Post* (February 22, 1878) and "death of Aunt Sarah Mead early in April '78." Her obituary appeared in the New York *Times,* April 12, 1878 (*FC&I,* 45*n*.). Aunt Sarah is also mentioned in *Corr.,* II, 202, 210, 211, 215, 264; III, 114–115, 443; and "*1873. Nov.* 20. Camden."

2. Aunt Phoebe is further referred to in *Corr.,* II, 210; "return my book"; and "*1873. Nov.* 20. Camden."

(Nov. 23d. 62 Portland Av.

Manuscript in Duke (40, #4). Leaf [*1*] on heavy white wove paper, 6¼" x 3⅝". Blue rules 5/16" apart; inscription in pencil. Leaf [2] on white wove paper 6¼" x 3¾"; inscription in pencil. Despite the difference in paper the leaves are foliated in what appears to be WW's hand. The writing is identical and the material reasonably related. On the verso of leaf [2] is a memorandum, "Vedder at Brother Jonathan." Printed in *FC&I,* 46–47, which, however, treats it as two separate manuscripts. The date is between 1861 and 1862.

(Nov. 23d. 62 Portland av.[1]

Jesse Whitman the youngest of the children[2] (my grandfather) had 2 (or 3?) brothers, older than himself, Stephen and Isaac; and one sister, Phebe.— She married Zaire Jarvis, ([3]he lived just west of Babylon, on the South road, in 1840)[4]

Isaac had a son *Jacob Whitman,* a carpenter,— of this Jacob[5] him my[6] father learnt his trade—[7]the first part of the time about Huntington, West Hills, &c. and the last portion of his apprenticeship, (? about —— years)[8] in New York city.—

Jacob Whitman, (above mentioned) worked as a sort of foreman[9] for a Venetian blind maker in New York—who died, and J. W. married the widow, and had two children by her— She died, and then J. W. married her daughter, and by her had quite a brood of children

[2]Father finished his apprenticeship in New York city, and then worked for some three years there—[10] I have heard him speak of boarding steady[11] for three years in New York in[12] one place. He then went up around the Hills,[13] and

1. At right with vertical line before and extending below date. The street may have been added later. "62" is clearly part of the date.
2. Preceding five words inserted on a line above "(my grandfather)"
3. Deleted: "on the" before "he lived"
4. MS paragraph has hanging indentation.
5. "this Jacob" inserted on a line above "of him"
6. "my" inserted on a line above, between "him" and "father"
7. Word deleted before "the first"
8. Parenthesis and words inserted on two lines aligned on "apprenticeship"
9. Preceding five words inserted; "worked" on line before "for a venetian blind maker" ; the rest on a line beginning after "worked"
10. Deleted: "he" before "I"
11. Inserted "steady" on a line above, at the end of "boarding"
12. Deleted: "the same" after "in"
13. Capital "H" written over lowercase.

South, Long Island, and took contracts at building. He was a first rate carpenter, did solid, substantial, conscientious work. I have heard mother say that he would sometimes lay awake all night planning out[14] some unusually difficult plan in his building arrangements.

14. "Out" inserted on line above.

1873. Nov. 20. Camden.

Manuscript in Duke (39, #2). White wove paper, approx. 5⁵⁄₁₆″ x 5″. Blue lines ⅜″ apart. Embossed Mercury with a caduceus in upper left corner. Inscribed in black ink. Aunt Sarah died at the age of 97 in April, 1878. See "Oct. 29. '62" and *Corr.,* III, 114. First printed *FC&I,* 44.

1873. Nov. 20. Camden.

Just rec'd word from N.Y., from mother's aunt, Mrs. Sarah Mead, (born Williams.) She is now[1] in her 92d year, having been born 24th Sept. 1782. On her 91st[2] birth-day, now just past, she rode in a carriage through Central Park, & took great interest & pleasure in the scenes. Her sister, Mrs. Phebe Pintard, died a few years since in N.Y.; must have been nearly a hundred years old.

1. "Now" inserted at the end of the line.
2. Deleted: "if" before "birth-day"

Kirkby Geo. Kill'd.

Manuscript in Virginia (Barrett). White wove scrap with blue lines ⅜" apart. Inscribed in pencil. "George" is the son of Andrew Whitman (d. December 3, 1863) and his wife Nancy. There is a Boonton in northeastern New Jersey. Mr. Kirkby is unidentifiable, although at the top of the page in another hand is "Wm Kirkby 61 Poplar St. Brooklyn." In June, 1878 WW was in New York City and visited John Burroughs in Esopus, N.Y. The date seems to be 1878.

Kirkby[1] Geo. kill'd at Boonton, NJ in Aug: '72[2] the extortions of the county physician—the chief of police—the RR wanted & took[3] $2 for carrying the body on to NY—Skinflints.— the RR kill'd[4] the little fellow one day & made us pay $2 the next for carrying the body on/[5] June '78 Mr K[6]/—saw Nancy 2 months[7] ago,

1. "Kirkby" inscribed in top margin. On first three rules in another hand in lighter pencil: "Wm Kirkby 61 Poplar St. Brooklyn"

2. "N J" written in under "Boonton." "in Aug: '72" on a short line at left with a hanging indentation.

3. Preceding two words inserted on a line above "for"

4. Further hanging indentation begins here. Short line opposite at left.

5. This short line at left and that following seem to set off the entry which is at left.

6. Next entry out to left margin.

7. "months" inserted on a line above "2 ago."

Marriages.

Manuscript in Missouri Historical Society. Two sheets white laid notepaper 9¹¹/₁₆" x 7¹¹/₁₆" folded in thirds from side to side. Inscribed in black ink and black pencil as noted. Entries are in column. The MS came to the Missouri Historical Society from the estate of Jessie Louisa Whitman, the younger daughter of Thomas Jefferson Whitman. The entries in WW's hand were conceivably made by him during his visit in St. Louis in the winter of 1879–1880. The others were probably made by Jessie Louisa after her father's death.

Marriages

Walter Whitman and Louisa Van Velsor [:][1] June 8, 1816 Ansel Van Nostrand and Mary E. Whitman [:] Jan 2, 1840 Charles L. Heyde and Hannah L. Whitman [:] March 15,[2] 1852 Thos. J. Whitman and Martha E. Mitchell [:] Feb. 23, 1859 George W. Whitman and Louisa Orr Haslam [:] March[3] 14, 1871

Births

Walter Whitman born July 14, 1789 Louisa Van Velsor Sept. 22, 1795 Jesse Whitman [WW used dittos for these entries: *born*] March 2, 1818 Walt Whitman [*born*] *May* 31, 1819 Mary Elizabeth [*born*] Feb. 3, 1821 Hannah Louisa [*born*] Nov. 28, 1823 Infant ——— March 2, 1825 Andrew Jackson April 7, 1827 George Washington Nov. 28, 1829 Thos. Jefferson—July 18, 1833 Edward Aug 9, 1835

[*3;2 blank*] *Deaths*

Infant died Sept. 14, 1825. aged 6 mos. 12 d. Walter Whitman [WW used dittos for these entries: *died*] July 11, 1855, buried in Evergreens cemetery Brooklyn. Andrew J. Whitman [*died*] Dec. 3. 1863 Jesse Whitman [*died*] March 21, 1870 Martha E. Whitman [*died*] Feb. 19. 1873 Louisa Whitman, May 23, 1873 Harleigh Cemetery[4] [*4*] Births / Deaths / Marriages.[5]

1. The entries are in column. WW used braces to connect pairs of names.
2. Bucke holograph in Trent (Allen, 596) gives date March 16.
3. Bucke holograph (Allen, 596) gives April 14.
4. In another hand, probably that of Jeff's daughter Jessie Louisa, in black ink except for the last entry in black pencil: "Walt Whitman March 26th 1892 [dittos below "Harleigh Cemetery" preceding] Louisa Orr Wife of G. W. Whitman August 9th 1892 [*dittos*] Thomas J. Whitman November 25th 1890 St Louis Mo Ed L. Whitman 1892 Harleigh Cem George W Whitman Dec. 1901 [*dittos*] Hannah L Heyde July 16 1908 [*dittos*] Mannahatta Whitman Sept 3 1886 St. Louis Mo. Mary Van Nostrand died 1899 Greenford, L. I." Bucke holograph (Allen, 597) gives 1888 for death of Mannahatta.
5. Outside cover on center fold of three.

Walt Whitman Said Lately.

Manuscript in Huntington (HM 492). Inscribed in "indelible pencil" on one sheet, 11″ x 8½″, and a scrap, 3″ x 8½″, both white wove showing part of watermark with date 1886. The scrap was pasted to the recto edge of the sheet and contains the sentence beginning: "She was of ordinary medium size. . . ." Descriptive detail courtesy of Huntington. Kennedy, to whom WW sent it to help him with a book (*Corr.*, IV, 40, 41, 42), used it with "It is curious" and "Going back far enough" in "Dutch Traits of Walt Whitman," *In Re*, 195–199. In *WDC*, 68, he omits the first two sentences, which are hard to explain except as an example of WW's irrepressible urge for publicity. See also *"Walt Whitman*, (from Holland." The date is obviously after 1886. First printed in *WDC*, 68–69.

Walt Whitman[1] said lately to one of his interviewers, "I consider myself an American, but[2] with the[3] traits of my far-back origin; among others English, Quaker and Hollandisk." It is the last department I will now speak of.[4] Whitman *favors* (as the old vernacular word had it) his mother, *nee* Louisa Van Velsor of Queens county, New York.

She was of ordinary[5] medium size (a little *plus*) of splendid physique and health,[6] a hard worker, had eight children, was[7] beloved by all who met her, good-looking to the last,[8] lived to be nearly 80; no tenderer and more invariable tie was[9] ever between mother and son than the love between her and W W.[10]

No one could have seen her, and her father Major Kale (Cornelius) Van Velsor, either in their prime or in their older age, without instantly perceiving their[11] plainly marked Hollandisk physiognomy, color, and body-build. Walt

1. Deleted: "himself" before "said"

2. "but" inserted on a line above "American, with"

3. Deleted: "other" before "traits"

4. Deleted: "and perhaps at random" after "speak of" . Following this, not printed here, is: "run in)" on a line above the period.

5. "ordinary" inserted on a line above "of medium"

6. Preceding two words and comma inserted on a line above "physique a"

7. "was" inserted on a line above between "children beloved"

8. Preceding four words and comma inserted on a line above.

9. Deleted: "ever" ; inserted: "was" on a line above.

10. Preceding sentence on small scrap inserted with arrow by WW. Over the arrow on the large sheet is written: "(take in" above "one could" . "No one" originally run in after "New York" above.

11. Deleted: "old"

Whitman has[12] all of it; he shows it in his old features now[13] his full flesh and[14] red color. The Van Velsors, (Walt's mother's family) were pure Low Dutch, of the third or fourth[15] remove from the original immigrants.[16] Few realize how this Dutch element has[17] percolated into[18] our New York, Pennsylvania, and other regions[19] not so much in ostensible literature and politics, but deep[20] in the blood and breed of the race,[21] and to tinge all that is to come. Like the Quakers the Dutch are very practical and materialistic and are great money-makers,[22] in the bulk and concrete of the ostent of life[23] but are yet[24] terribly transcendental and cloudy too. More than half the Hollandisk immigrants[25] to New York bay[26] became farmers, and a good portion of the rest[27] became engineers or sailors

12. Deleted: "it too and"
13. "now" inserted on a line above "his"
14. Deleted: "his"
15. Deleted: "descent" ; inserted: "remove" above .
16. Deleted: initial "e" ; inserted: "im" on a line above "e" to form "immigrants" . Deleted: "to New York [*illeg.*]" following "immigrants"
17. Deleted: "entered" ; inserted: "percolated" above.
18. Deleted: "the" ; inserted: "our" on a line above "the"
19. Preceding ten words inserted above the line "Few . . . not"
20. "deep" inserted on a line above "but in"
21. Preceding three words and comma inserted on a line above "breed and"
22. Deleted: "for" ; inserted "in" on a line above.
23. Preceding five words inserted on a line above "and concrete"
24. "yet" inserted on a line above "are terribly"
25. Deleted: initial "e" ; inserted: "im" on a line above to form "immigrants"
26. Preceding four words inserted on a line above "immigrants became"
27. Deleted: "were" ; inserted "became" on a line above.

It Is Curious.

Manuscript not found. Text from *WDC,* 69–70. Kennedy says that this MS was sent him for help in work on Whitman with "Walt Whitman said lately," which he prints (but not "verbatim") with this. He used it with the other MS in "Dutch Traits of Walt Whitman," *In Re,* 195–199. The date is probably 1886. First printed in *WDC,* 69–70.

It is curious how deep influences, elements, and characteristic-trends operate through races and long periods of time in practical events or palpably in long continued struggles of war and peace—and then sprout out eventually in some marked book, perhaps poem. Whitman himself is fond of resuming the history and development of the Low Dutch, and their fierce war against Philip and Alva, and the building of the dykes, and the shipping and trade and colonization from 1600 to the present, and the old cities and towers and soldiery and markets and salt-air, and flat topography, and human physiognomy and bodily form (not the Jewish seems to be more strictly perpetuated than these Hollandisk), and their coming and planting here in America, and investing themselves not so much in outward manifestations, but in the blood and deeds of the race; and the poet considers his "Leaves of Grass" to be, in some respects, spinally understood only by reference to that Hollandisk history and personality.

Going Back Far Enough.

Manuscript in Huntington (HM 492a). Inscribed in purple crayon on back of a request for an autograph signed by W. E. Mitchell. Description courtesy of Huntington. Kennedy, to whom WW gave it, used it with "It is curious" and "Walt Whitman said lately" in "Dutch Traits of Walt Whitman," *In Re,* 195–199. The date is probably 1886. First printed in *WDC,* 67–68.

Going back far enough[1] ancestrally Walt Whitman undoubtedly[2] comes meandering from a[3] blended tri-heredity stream of Dutch (Hollandisk) the original Friends (Quakers) and the Puritans of Cromwell's time. The first Whitman immigrant settled in Connecticut, 1635, and a son of his went over to Long Island, as farmer at West Hills, Suffolk county; and a young descendant five generations afterward marries a daughter of Cornelius and Amy Van Velsor (the last of Quaker training and *née* Williams.) This daughter was the mother of W W.— [4] Though developed and Anglofied and Americanized, she was Hollandisk from top to toe, and W W inherits her to the life, emotionally, full-bloodedness, voice, and physiognomy

1. Preceding three words inserted on a line flush left and extending above "Ancestrally" Uppercase "Ancestrally" not reduced.

2. Inserted above "Whitman comes"

3. Deleted in black pencil: "Heredity" . It appears that WW inserted "blended" above, before deleting "heredity" , then inserted "tri-heredity stream [*del.*] of" after "blended" on the same line above.

4. WW seems to have punctuated with a colon, then to have written over it the period and dash, then to have raised "though" to uppercase.

Lafayette in Brooklyn.

Manuscript in Huntington (HM 118a). P. [*1*] inscribed in blue pencil on white wove scrap with red ink corrections. Pp. [*2–7*] inscribed in black ink, with pencil corrections, on twelve white wove scraps (as noted) of a different quality, some with "Rand, Avery & Co., Printers" stamp on verso. The manuscript seems to date from 1881, when WW visited Boston to supervise the publication of the 1881 *Leaves* of which Rand, Avery was the printer. With the manuscript is a six-page essay MS by John Burroughs which was used for the edition published privately by George B. Smith, New York, 1905. At Yale is a typed and annotated copy of both the Whitman and Burroughs manuscripts which was apparently used for the 1905 edition.

No other reference to WW's having addressed the New England Historic Genealogical Society has been found. Nevertheless the Yale typescript notes that there were two meetings of the Society devoted to Lafayette in 1881: October 7 and December 7. Since, in a deleted phrase (*n* 2), WW says it was given "yesterday afternoon," it must have been in October. In December, of course, WW was back in Camden. Mr. Edgar Dean Packard, current Director of the Society, reports no record of WW's presence, but since he had a guest card ("Daybook," [*208*], *DN*, 262), it is possible that he was guest on October 7 and joined the discussion after the paper by the Reverend A. B. Muzzey of Cambridge. Since, according to Mr. Packard, the records of the Society are not kept in such a way as to provide a membership list for any given year, WW's host cannot be identified.

WW was apparently very fond of the recollection, for he refers to it in "Reminiscences of Brooklyn," *UPP*, II, 2–3; "Brooklyniana," ibid., II, 256–257; "My First Reading—Lafayette," *SD*, *Prose 92*, I, 13; "Old Brooklyn Days," ibid., II, 688; "Notes at End," *Complete Poems and Prose of Walt Whitman*, 1855–1888 [Philadelphia], 1888, [1–2] (separately paged). The incident of Lafayette's kissing him first appears in *SD*, where it is in a footnote attributed to Burroughs. He noted the destruction of the Library in May, 1858 (LC—Feinberg).

The use of Rand and Avery paper indicates a date of 1881 or a little later. First printed in *Lafayette in Brooklyn* (NY, George B. Smith), 1905.

Lafayette in Brooklyn
By WALT WHITMAN[1]

The following impromptu reminiscence of Lafayette's visit to this country in 1825, and his going over one day to Brooklyn, New York, was given[2] some time since

1. In black pencil at upper left, deleted in red ink: "follow copy in punctuation" ; deleted title in pencil: *"Walt Whitman on Lafayette"* ; present title inserted in red ink.

2. Deleted in black ink: "yesterday afternoon" ; inserted above in red ink: "some time since"

at a meeting of the[3] New England Historic Genealogical Society in Somerset street Boston.[4]

Walt Whitman

[2][5] It was in[6] 1824, (or '25, I am not certain which. I was a little "kid" of five or six years old.)[7] I remember it was an[8] exceptionally pleasant and sunny forenoon.[9] At that time the reception of a public man, or[10] other festival of the kind, was[11] very different from any thing of the[12] sort now—was[13] quite informal and old-fashioned, without the crowds, and blare and ceremony of the present day; but was full as hearty & far less tedious.[14] The people on this occasion[15] all turned out and formed[16] on both sides of a hollow lane nearly[17] two miles long, thickly[18] fringed with well-dress'd[19] humanity, women as well as men,[20] the children placed in front. That was about all, yet it was singularly effective.[21] Lafayette came over at Fulton[22] Ferry, (then called the Old Ferry) in a large canary-colored [3] open barouche, drawn by four magnificent[23] white horses. I think there was[24] no band of music, and I think[25] no speechifying, (or if so, only a few brief words)—but a marked[26] profusion of young children,[27] and old men,[28] (several of the latter were revolutionary soldiers,)[29] and a number of blacks freed from slavery by the

3. Deleted in red ink: "N E" ; inserted in red ink above the line: "New England"

4. "Boston" inserted in red ink. This and preceding changes suggest revision of a MS prepared for Boston publication.

5. "¶" and indentation in MS.

6. Deleted: "184" before "1824" . The incident occurred July 4, 1825.

7. Parenthesis and preceding eleven words inserted. Redundant end parenthesis not deleted, not shown.

8. Inserted: "exceptionally"

9. Inserted in ink: "At" ; inserted in pencil: "that time" ; "The" not reduced to lowercase in MS.

10. Deleted: "any" before "other"

11. Deleted: "very" ; inserted: "very" above.

12. Inserted and deleted: [*illeg.*]

13. Deleted: "very" ; inserted and deleted: "then" ; inserted: "quite" above.

14. Preceding period and nine words inserted; original period corrected to semicolon.

15. Preceding three words inserted.

16. Beginning of second pasted-on scrap. Deleted: "in" ; inserted: "on"

17. "nearly" inserted.

18. "thickly" inserted.

19. "well-dress'd" inserted.

20. Inserted and deleted: "with"

21. Preceding period and five words inserted in black pencil; original period corrected to comma.

22. Beginning of third pasted-on scrap.

23. "magnificent" inserted on line above.

24. Deleted: "no [*illeg.*] not a single" ; inserted: "no" on line above.

25. "I think" inserted on line above.

26. "marked" inserted in black pencil.

27. Deleted in black pencil: "many" ; inserted in black pencil: "and" on line above.

28. Deleted: "a number" ; first parenthesis inserted in black pencil; inserted: "several of" ; redundant "of" not printed; deleted in black pencil: "them" ; inserted in black pencil: "the latter were"

29. Parenthesis inserted in black pencil.

then late New York emancipation acts.[30] These diversified the main[31] assemblage which was composed of substantial Brooklyn citizens with their wives.[32]

Through[33] all, the carriage of the[34] noble Frenchman[35] was very[36] slowly driven. I remember that[37] the fine horses[38] [*4*] and their impatient action under the curb, attracted my attention fully[39] as much as the great visitor himself.[40] The whole thing was curiously magnetic and quiet.[41] Lafayette was evidently deeply pleased and affected. Smiles and tears contended on his homely[42] yet most winning features.[43] But the[44] principal incident in my recollection is[45] now to come. They were[46] at that time just commencing the foundation of the Brooklyn Apprentices Library, and Lafayette had consented to lay the cornerstone[47] with his own hands—that is to grasp it personally. Some half a mile or over[48] from the ferry, he stopt,[49] got out of the barouche, and in the midst of the crowd, with other gentlemen, assisted [*5*] in lifting the children,[50] amid the deep-cut[51] excavation and[52] heaps of stones,[53] to safe spots where they could see the[54] ceremony. Happening to stand near, I remember I was taken[55] up by Lafayette[56] in his arms[57] and held a moment—I[58] remember that he press'd my[59] cheek with a

30. Deleted: "But"

31. "These diversified" inserted; deleted: "pa[?]" before "assemblage"

32. Following text on a fourth pasted-on piece. Since the top of "¶" is obscured, it must have been inscribed before pasting. "¶" before indentation not printed here.

33. Redundant comma not printed here; deleted: "there" ; inserted: "all," above "following" "there"

34. Deleted in black pencil: "visitor" before "noble"

35. Preceding four words inserted in black pencil.

36. "very" inserted in black pencil.

37. "that" inserted.

38. Comma deleted.

39. "fully" inserted.

40. "himself" inserted with redundant period not printed here.

41. Sentence inserted.

42. Deleted: "but" ; inserted: "yet"

43. Beginning of fifth pasted-on scrap, which shows signs of trimmed-off inscription.

44. MS shows what appears to be a large "3" in black pencil.

45. Deleted: "to"

46. Beginning of sixth pasted-on scrap which shows traces of trimmed-off inscription at top. First two words on a tongue projecting above remainder of scrap at left.

47. Beginning of seventh pasted-on scrap. Following nine words inserted on both scraps after pasting. Redundant period not printed here.

48. Preceding two words inserted.

49. Deleted: "and"

50. Deleted: "to safe spots" following "children"

51. "the deep-cut" inserted on line above.

52. Beginning of eighth pasted-on scrap.

53. Deleted: "taking boys and girls [*three preceding words ins. and del.*] them up in his arms, and placing them"

54. Beginning of ninth pasted-on scrap.

55. Beginning of tenth pasted-on scrap.

56. Preceding two words inserted on a line above.

57. Comma deleted.

58. "I" inserted in black pencil.

59. Deleted: "head" ; inserted: "cheek" on a line above.

kiss as he set me down—the childish wonder and nonchalance[60] during the whole affair at the time,—[61] constrasting with the indescribable preciousness of the reminiscence since.[62]

I remember quite well[63] Lafayette's looks, tall, brown, not handsome in the face, but of[64] fine figure[65] & the pattern of good-nature, health, manliness and[66] human attraction.[6][67] (A[68] life size full length oil-painting exhibited[69] years ago in Philadelphia, in 1877 I think,[70] seems to me an admirable likeness as I recollect him at the time.)[71]

That beautiful sunshiny day,[72] sixty years since, the[73] spontaneous effusion of all stages of[74] humanity, and the occasion,[75] made[76] a picture,[77] which time has[78] continued to set deeper and deeper in my recollection.

60. Deleted: "at" ; inserted: "during" above.

61. Deleted: "that and" ; inserted: "contrasting"

62. Beginning of eleventh pasted-on scrap. "¶" before indentation not printed here.

63. Deleted: "his books" ; inserted in black pencil above: "Lafayette's looks at the time [*preceding three words deleted*]" . Comma following deleted "books" not deleted, not printed.

64. Deleted: "good" ; inserted: "fine" on line above "but"

65. Preceding three words inserted.

66. Deleted: "very attractive" ; inserted: "human attraction." Redundant period not deleted, not printed.

67. Deleted: "A P"

68. Deleted: "large [*illeg.*]" ; inserted above: "life size"

69. Deleted: "four or five" before "exhibited"

70. Preceding four words inserted on line above.

71. Deleted: "I" ; "¶" before following indentation not printed here; beginning of twelfth scrap; deleted: "The" ; inserted: "That" following "¶" sign.

72. Inserted and deleted: [*illeg.*]; inserted: "sixty years since,"

73. Deleted: "occasion and [*illeg.*]"

74. Preceding three words inserted on line above.

75. Comma and preceding three words inserted on line above. Redundant comma not deleted, not printed.

76. Deleted: "something"

77. Deleted: "an impression only that" ; inserted: "which" on a line above "that"

78. Deleted: "so"

Biographical Note.

Manuscript in Virginia (Barrett). Inscribed in black pencil on three sheets of cream wove foolscap paper, 11" x 8⅜", watermarked "L. L. Brown." Pages numbered by WW on rectos. Versos are blank. The data are not entirely consistent with those given by WW in earlier accounts or established by biographers. The Whitmans moved to Brooklyn May 27, 1823; WW was sent to school in 1825 and remained for six years. He was employed in the law office of James B. and Edward Clark at age 11 (1830 or 1831) and in 1831 entered the printing office of the Long Island *Patriot.* He began teaching school in 1836 and edited the *Long Islander* in 1838 and 1839. He returned to New York in May, 1841. His travels "south and southwest" were confined to his voyage on the Mississippi to New Orleans and back. Cf. Allen, 1–100, "Nehemiah Whitman," "Autobiographical Data," "Autobiographic Note," Memoranda and revised version of 1889, LC (Feinberg). First published in facsimile in *Leaves of Grass Including a Facsimile autobiography variorum readings of the poems and a department of Gathered Leaves* (Philadelphia, 1900), after p. x. The date is obviously 1888.

Biographical Note of Walt Whitman

1819—May 31

Born at West Hills, Long Island, State of New York—second child of Walter and Louisa, (born Van Velsor) Whitman. 1820, '21, '22 and '23 continued at West Hills.

1824

Moved to Brooklyn. Went to Public School, 1831, tended in lawyer's office. Then a doctor's. In 1834 went into printing office to learn type-setting.[1]

1838

Teaching country[2] schools in Suffolk county. Continued[3] at it, partly in Queens county, for three years. Then starts a weekly paper "the Long Islander" at Huntington, L. I.

1. Deleted: "&c."
2. Deleted: "sh" before "schools"
3. Change from present tense to past.

1840

Back in New York City working at printing and journalistic writing. In 1846 and '7 edits the "Eagle" newspaper in Brooklyn.

1848

Goes[4] to New Orleans as an editor on the Staff of "the Crescent" newspaper. Afterward travels south and south west.

1850

Returns north. Publishes "the Freeman" news paper in Brooklyn. Then works at building houses and selling them

1855[5]

Issues "Leaves of Grass," first edition, small quarto[6] 95 pages. In 1856, 2d edition, 16 mo. 384 pages. 1860, third edition,[7] 456 pages, 12 mo. Boston.

1862

Goes down to the Secession War Fields. Begins his ministrations to the wounded[8] in the hospitals and after battles, and continues at them steadily[9] for three years. In 1865 gets an appointment as Department Clerk

1867

Publishes 4th edition "Leaves of Grass" including "Drum Taps." In 1871 fifth edition

1873

Prostrated by paralysis at Washington. Starts for Atlantic sea-shore by order of the physician. Breaks down badly at Philadelphia, and takes up quarters in Camden, New Jersey; where he has remained up to date; for over fifteen years.[10]

4. Deleted: "to"
5. Deleted: "1855 1855" following date entered.
6. Preceding two words inserted on a line above.
7. Deleted: "42"
8. Preceding three words inserted on a line above.
9. Inserted above "them"
10. Preceding four words inserted on a line above.

1876

Sixth or Centennial[11] issue of L. of G. with another Volume, "Two Rivulets," of prose and poems alternately. In 1881, seventh issue of L. of G. pub'd by Osgood & Co. Boston.

1882

Eighth issue of "Leaves of Grass" pub'd[12] by David McKay, Philadelphia. Also "Specimen Days" a prose and autobiographic Volume.

1888

Mr Whitman is now in his 70th year. He is almost entirely disabled physically, through the paralysis from his persistent army-hospital[13] labors in 1863 and '64;[14] but[15] is now[16] just printing, we hear, a little volume of additional prose and verse called "November Boughs." He resides in Mickle street, Camden, New Jersey.[17]

11. Preceding two words inserted on a line above.
12. Inserted above "by"
13. Inserted: "army-"
14. Preceding four words inserted on a line above. He also made visits in 1865.
15. Deleted: "B"
16. Inserted above.
17. Cancelled paragraph near bottom of the page: "these three pages MS can be put in *one page* or *two pages* type, for the book as you choose — (not more than two pages)"

Walt Whitman.

MS not found. Text from facsimile in Appleton's *Annual Encyclopedia* for 1892 (NY, 1893) between pp. 796–797. Described by Arthur Stedman in the *Encyclopedia* sketch as "on the back of a blue letter sheet on which someone had written for his autograph." The facsimile measures 11¼" x 8½", apparently written in black ink. Thinking that he "might be itemized or briefly biographized" in Appleton's *American Cyclopedia,* WW volunteered "some authentic statistics" to the associate editor, Robert Carter, May 7, 1875 (*Corr.,* II, 332). WW's "statistics" were not used in the *Cyclopedia,* but when Stedman, the son of WW's friend Edmund Clarence Stedman, wrote the long and friendly sketch for Appleton's *Annual Encyclopedia* (for 1892) the MS came into his hands and he printed it in facsimile (Hubert Hoeltje, "Whitman's Letter to Robert Carter," *AL,* 25 [November, 1953], 359–362).

Walt Whitman

Born in New York state, (West Hills, Suffolk Co., L. I.,) May 31, 1819. Parentage on the father's side English, on the mother's[1] (Van Velsor.) side,— Holland Dutch. From early childhood[2] lived in Brooklyn and New York cities—went to the public schools several years—then learn'd the trade of printer & worked (1836[3]–'45)[4] during summers as school-teacher on Long Island, & winters[5] as compositor in N.Y. & Brooklyn offices. Also as editor and Magazine writer.[6] In 1847, '8, and '9, he[7] made a leisurely tour through the United States, stopping in the various cities &[8] visiting nearly every[9] section, especially on the Mississippi,[10] Missouri, & Ohio rivers, & also[11] Canada. Was in New Orleans a year, as editor.[12] Returning to

1. Deleted: "side"
2. Deleted: "to age of 26" ; inserted: "lived"
3. "6" written over "5[?]" His alternation between school teaching and printing was not so symetrically seasonal as he claims. He did not return to "N.Y. & Brooklyn offices" until 1841 (Allen 27, 42).
4. Deleted: "in" ; inserted: "during"
5. Preceding eleven words inserted.
6. His earliest known writings were printed in 1840.
7. Inserted on a line above.
8. Preceding six words inserted on a line above "states"
9. Deleted: "one" ; inserted: "section" above.
10. "ssi" inserted above.
11. Inserted above "Canada"
12. The account of his travels is rather expansive. He left for New Orleans in February, 1848 and returned May 27. His travels were on the Mississippi and Ohio (but not the Missouri), and on the Great Lakes. His lake boat may have touched Canada.

Brooklyn, (1851, '3, '4) went into carpentering & building. In 1855 published the first instalment of *"Leaves of Grass,"* ([13] Since [?] increased by five other cumulative issues, making the work, in its now[14] finished state, a book of about 380 ordinary pages.) During the war, from[15] 1862 to '65,[16] he became personally engaged[17] among the armies, on the field in Virginia, especially[18] in the camps' hospitals &[19] in[20] the numerous ones[21] of Washington City, as a volunteer aid & nurse to the[22] wounded & sick of[23] both North & South. In 1865 was appointed to a clerkship in Attorney General's office, Washington, which he held till 1874. Was of remarkable bodily health & physique, till 1873, when he had a stroke of paralysis,[24] by which he is still disabled. His writings, in their latest form, & as completed, consist of the before-mentioned *"Leaves of Grass,"* and another volume of about the same size[25] called[26] *"Two Rivulets,"* a varied collection of pieces in prose & poetry. Of the "Leaves" it has been said,[27] "probably the whole of these unrhymed songs, if not all Whitman's writings, only ring the changes[28] on the ejaculation, How vast, how eligible, how joyful, how real, & how immortal, is a human being, body as well as soul,[29] in himself or herself!" Whitman is unmarried, is now, (1875) in his 57th year, & lives in seclusion at Camden, New Jersey.

13. Deleted: "to which there have since been" ; inserted: ("Since increased" . Redundant single parenthesis not deleted, not shown here.

14. Inserted.

15. Written over "f" of "of"

16. Deleted: "was" following " '65" ; inserted: "he became [*del.*] steadily personally" on line above.

17. Deleted: "constantly"

18. Inserted on a line above "in"

19. Deleted: "especially" before "in"

20. Deleted: "the" before "the"

21. Deleted: "in" ; inserted: "of" above.

22. Inserted on a line above.

23. Deleted: "the armies" following "of"

24. Deleted: "from" ; inserted: "by" above.

25. Preceding five words inserted on a line above "volume called"

26. Deleted: " 'Two"

27. Deleted: "by" before "probably"

28. Deleted: "in some sort"

29. Preceding five words inserted on a line above.

Walt Whitman, (from Holland.

Manuscript in Yale. Inscribed in black ink on white wove paper, 10⅝" x 8¼". WW was rapidly declining in health, but had a period of strength in the spring of 1890. The writing is remarkably firm and most unlike that of other MS of his last years. See "Walt Whitman said lately." Printed in part in Dixon Wecter, "Walt Whitman as Civil Servant," *PMLA,* 58 (December, 1943), 1106*n*.

Walt Whitman, ([1]from Holland and English immigration-stock son of Walter Whitman, farmer and carpenter, and his wife, *nee* Louisa Van Velsor,) was born May 31, 1819, about 30 miles from New York City, at West Hills, Suffolk co., N.Y. state; but moved very early to Brooklyn and New York[2] cities where he grew up through boy hood and young manhood, had a plain education in the public schools, learned the trade of printer, edited newspapers, then went off for two years on a working and journeying tour, through nearly every one of the Middle,[3] Southern and Western States, and to Louisiana and Texas, (during the Mexican war of 1848 and '9.)[4] Returning[5] leisurely up the Mississippi and northern Lakes back[6] to New York City, he lived and worked there till 1862 when he left for Washington City and "the front" of the Secession war. His intense and continued personal occupation, day and night, for over two years following, in nursing the army wounded and sick, northern and southern alike, resulted in a severe prostration and paralysis at the end of the contest, which he has suffered under since, though his mind remains unimpair'd and he still writes. He is author of "Leaves of Grass," a book of poems, "Specimen Days and Collect" a prose autobiography, notes of the war-hospitals, and collection of various essays, and "November Boughs" an old age compilation only yet perhaps partly completed.[7] It remains to be said that W.W. is perceptibly of Quaker stamp, has been and is of buoyant and robust physique, and yet lives (May, 1890), in Camden, New Jersey.

1. Deleted: "of" ; inserted: "from" on line above.
2. Deleted: "and Brookl" ; inserted: "cities where" above.
3. "Middle," inserted on line above.
4. WW was in New Orleans between February 11 and June 15, 1848. No earlier claim to having visited Texas has been noted.
5. Deleted: "leisurely" before "leisurely"
6. Inserted on a line above "Lakes to"
7. *November Boughs* had been published in 1888. Possibly WW projected a sequel.

II. Brooklyn and New York 1841–1862.

The manuscripts in this section are arranged in a roughly chronological order and cover a wide range of material, from his visits to elementary schoolrooms in Brooklyn to the visions of the first three editions of *Leaves of Grass*. In time they range from his school teaching days on Long Island in 1841 to a memorandum for an appointment in November, 1862, a month before his hasty departure for Washington in search of his wounded brother.

Although, as I suggested in the Introduction, a serious and prolonged attempt to date the manuscripts by paper and writing materials has been a failure, the evidence of paper is sometimes useful in dating manuscripts of this period. Aside from the indistinguishable papers that Whitman picked up, two kinds appear which he used in relatively well defined periods. The first is a pink, green or yellow wove wrapper stock from *Leaves of Grass* (1855), which was issued in a paperbound state as well as the famous green cloth. The other paper is a blue wove paper on which is printed either tax forms or election forms from the City of Williamsburgh. Williamsburgh, the part of Brooklyn in which Whitman lived, became part of the modern Borough of Brooklyn January 1, 1855.

The pink paper is much more common than the green or yellow. Bowers (xli) says that the earliest use he has seen of pink paper is dated January, 1856 ("*Goethe's* Complete Works"), the latest dated March 1, 1857 ("Dr. Priestly"). Because of fading I am not certain that any of the manuscripts printed here as being on green wrapper paper are actually so, since the most famous example of a paperbound *Leaves* is Whitman's own copy now in the Berg Collection, New York Public Library, the cover of which has faded to a muddy brown.

Bowers (xli), plausibly assuming that the Brooklyn *Times* had the printing contract for the City of Williamsburgh, suggests that Whitman found a supply of the obsolete forms in the *Times* printshop when he became editor in February, 1857. He used this paper from 1857 to 1860.

In addition to the notebooks printed here, a notebook or scrapbook dealing with words began after 1856, and fifteen other notebooks, the first six of which date from before 1860, are printed in *DN,* Vol. III.

Jan 12. Walter Whitman.

Text from photograph of visitors' book Public School #13, Borough of Manhattan, NYC, facing p. 33, Florence B. Freedman, *Walt Whitman Looks at the Schools* (NY, 1950). In January, 1841 WW was teaching at Whitestone, L. I. See other writings on education in Part II.

Jan 12. Walter Whitman, Examined the Arithmetic classes and found them quite proficient

Walter Whitman, of Suffolk Co.

Text from photograph of visitors' book, Public School #13, Borough of Manhattan, NYC, facing p. 32, Florence B. Freedman, *Walt Whitman Looks at the Schools* (NY, 1950). Suffolk County forms the eastern part of Long Island, where WW was teaching. See other writings on education under that heading below.

Walter Whitman, of Suffolk co. L. I. spent two hours at School No 13 examined the classes in Grammar and Arithmetic and was highly gratified by the promptness and the understanding spirit which marked [?] the pupils. Visitted several schools and upon the whole considers [*illeg.*] to be the best managed of any he has seen as yet. Sept 3d—1841

Of a Summer Evening.

Manuscript in Duke (18, #2). Inscribed in blue ink on five leaves of light brown wove paper, so thin that flecks of pulp can be seen when it is held against the light. Approximate dimensions: [*1*] 8¼" x 6⅝" (actually two scraps, 1" x 6⅝" and 7¼" x 6⅝", pasted on backing by WW?), upper right corner trimmed; [*2*] 4" x 6¾"; [*3*] 7⅝" x 6⅝", upper left, lower left, and lower right corners trimmed; [*4*] 7⅝" x 6⅝"; [*5*] 4 5/16" x 6¾", upper left and lower right corners trimmed. Foliation by an unknown hand. Emendation in blue ink with a finer pen, black ink, black pencil. Blue ink is unusual, but does not suggest a date. The small, clerkly hand suggests an early date, probably of the late 1840s. It is, however, more "flowing" than that of the early notebooks. The MS seems related to the verse lines, "I am that half-grown boy, fallen asleep" (*CW,* III, 280; see MS Variorum). First published *N&F,* 122 (Pt. III, #136; *CW,* IX, 146–147). WW's last published story was "The Shadow and Light of a Young Man's Soul," June, 1848 (*EPF,* 338). See also notes for novels in "med *Cophosis,*" *DN,* III, 774–775. He apparently turned his mind again to fiction in 1852 ("A schoolmaster while intoxicated") and even later. See "A prostitute," "A new Love Story," and the very late "Summers and Winters were."

[*1*] Of a summer evening a boy fell asleep with the tears of foolish passion yet undried upon his cheeks.— And there he dreamed a dream.— Years, with all their chequered events of pain and joy, rolled away. Many were spent in travel—some in the pursuit of power and[1] wealth—which pursuit was successful.— At an advanced age, and sobered down from the hot-brained fever of[2] youth, a message came that his mother was nigh to death, and desired his presence.— Swift wheels rattled then—and the patter of horses' hoofs sounded rapidly on the road—but the beatings of the traveller's heart were more rapid still.— When he arrived at his early home, he found his mother dead. He stood and looked upon her face, and then[3] went aside.— And many [*2*] a time again approached he to[4] the coffin, and held up the white linen, and gazed and gazed.— He came in the day, when crowds were in the rooms—though all to him was a vacant blank—all but the corpse of his mother.— And at last he came in the silence of the midnight before the burial, when the tired watchers were asleep.— Long—long—long—were his eyes rivetted on the features of[5] that dead corpse, with an expecting look, as if he

1. Preceding two words inserted above "of wealth"
2. Deleted: "his"
3. "then" inserted with pencil on a line above.
4. Deleted in black pencil: "to"
5. Deleted with finer-nibbed pen: "the dead one," ; inserted: "that dead corpse" on a line above.

waited something.— He bent down his ear to the cold blue lips and listened—but the cold blue lips were hushed for ever.— Now for two little words, *I pardon,* that proud rich man would almost[6] have [3] been willing to live in[7] poverty for ever: but the words came not.— From the moment when he first saw[8] his mother's face, and whenever he looked at her, a wondrous faculty had awoke within him.— All that was present—every thing, connected with his business,[9] his schemes of ambition,[10] his worldly gains, his friendships, and his plans of life, seemed entirely melted from his thought.— A doubly refined memory called up before him and around him, all he had ever done in his life that seemed directly or indirectly unfilial toward his mother.— Each word, each look, each action,[11] returned; not the minutest trifle connected with them but stood in[12] brilliant [4] light before him.— He remembered how on such a day in boyhood[13] he ran from home—how once in vicious spite[14] he terrified her by a[15] plot to make her believe he was drowned—how at such a time he had mocked her words—and again how he had[16] many times denied her authority.—[17] And[18] strangely[19] distinct was the remotest, the tiniest, of all circumstances involved in these memories.— O, Crucified! who meekly at the command of thy parents went down from the temple at Jerusalem, and was ever gentle to her that gave thee birth—thy dreary death-agonies alone—so it seemed to him—[20]outdid the pangs of that[21] gazer on the dead!

[5] And this was the boy's vision. Ah, happy that boy to wake and find it indeed but a dream!— Covered with huge drops of sweat, and trembling in every limb, the youth raised himself from his horrid slumber, and blessed God that the path of the future years[22] yet lay before him.[23]

6. Inserted with finer-nibbed pen on a line above "have"

7. Deleted: "disgrace and" following "in"

8. Deleted: "her" following "saw" ; inserted with finer-nibbed pen: "his mother's" on a line above.

9. Deleted: dash.

10. Deleted: dash.

11. Deleted: "swarmed there" ; inserted with finer-nibbed pen: "returned" on a line above "swarmed"

12. Deleted: "bold"

13. Preceding two words inserted in black ink on a line above.

14. Preceding three words inserted with a finer-nibbed pen on a line above.

15. Deleted: "rranging a" . Initial "a" in "arranging" left undeleted.

16. Deleted: "openly" ; inserted with a finer-nibbed pen: "many times"

17. Deleted: "over him"

18. Deleted: "it was"

19. "ly" added; deleted: "how" before "distinct" . All in black ink.

20. Preceding five words and dashes inserted with finer pen on a line over "alone" ; deleted in black ink: "were sharper" ; inserted in black ink: "outdid" on a line over above the deleted "over"

21. Deleted in black pencil: "dream—" before "gazer"

22. Deleted: "was yet" ; inserted with finer-nibbed pen: "yet lay" on a line above.

23. Deleted: "and that he had yet [*ins. and del. in finer-nibbed pen on a line above:* "there was still"] time to avoid the fearful consummation which had come to him in fancy!—"

Distinctness Every Syllable.

Manuscript in Duke (18, #1). Inscribed in pencil on white wove paper approx. 10$^{7}/_{16}$" x 7¾", brown rules ⅜" apart, vertical chain lines, embossed "LONDON" with curlicues at upper left. First printed Bucke (*N&F,* 115–116 [Pt. III, #109]; *CW,* IX, 132–133). Bucke dates it as from the " '40's or early '50's."

distinctness every syllable the flounderer spoke, up to his hips in the snow, and blinded by the[1] sharp crystals[2] that made the air[3] one opaque white.— He swore, prayed, howled, and[4] wept.—[5] Pete was terrified himself.— It was the[6] blackest and bitterest[7] night, and by far[8] the wildest storm he had ever known.— The snow lay deep, and[9] had many huge drifts.— He went[10] aloft in the garret and gave the[11] farm laborer a dollar[12] cash in hand[13] to get up and go with him in search of the tipsy friend.— While they stood inside the door, listening more clearly for the point whence the poor[14] fellow's cries proceeded, they could hear every word[15] with the minutest clearness; but when[16] one rod from the stoop, and standing[17] in the storm, of[18] not one sound[19] were they conscious except the soughing storm,[20] strained they ever so[21] hard.— For an hour they plunged through

1. Deleted: "cutting" ; inserted: "sharp" above; inserted and deleted: "white" following "sharp"
2. Deleted: "[*illeg.*] making" ; inserted: "that made" above.
3. Deleted: "densely" ; inserted: "one opaque" above; deleted "one" and then reinserted "one" above the deleted "one"
4. Inserted.
5. Deleted: "The"
6. Deleted: "dark"
7. Preceding two words inserted on a line above "blackest night"
8. Preceding two words inserted on a line above "and . . . the"
9. Deleted: "in" following "and" ; inserted: "had" on a line above.
10. Deleted: "up" ; inserted: "aloft" on a line above.
11. Written over [*illeg.*]. Deleted: "young" ; inserted: "farm" on a line above.
12. Deleted: "in"
13. A dense blot obscures preceding two words. Reading from *N&F,* 115.
14. Deleted: "young"
15. Preceding two words inserted on a line above "hear with"
16. Deleted: "they reach"
17. Written over "stood"
18. Inserted on a line above and before "not"
19. Deleted: "could they"
20. Deleted: "though they"
21. Preceding three words inserted on a line above "hard—."

the drifts, guiding themselves as well as they could by well known trees and fences. Pete[22] had been satisfied, while listening in the house, that the drunken youth was stuck in a certain field,[23] usually a shorter cut across the road.— So they went heading to and fro over that[24] ground, feeling as well as they could with their feet; and sure enough, at last, there they[25] hit him, under the snow, perfectly[26] stiff and still.— They[27] carried him back to the house, and had a good time fighting the death in him the whole night. But they saved him.—

Coarse, wild, sensual, and[28] strong, was this young man's nature;[29] for coarse wild and strong had been his life.— He[30] has large and ugly qualities enough, but[31] he[32] is self complete, and his very grossness and dishonesty are noble, from their[33] candor.[34] The[35] castrated[36] goodness of schools and churches, he knew nothing of

22. Deleted: "had" before "had" now in text.
23. Deleted: "just"
24. Deleted: "field"
25. Deleted: "felt" ; inserted: "hit" on a line above.
26. Inserted on a line above "snow" . . . "stiff"
27. Deleted: [*illeg.*].
28. Deleted: "st"
29. Deleted in pencil: "and" ; inserted in pencil: "for" on a line above.
30. Deleted: "had" ; inserted: "has" on a line above.
31. Written over [*illeg.*]; deleted: [*illeg.*]
32. Deleted: "was" ; inserted: "is" on a line above.
33. Inserted on a line above "their . . . candor"
34. Deleted: "[*illeg.*] All"
35. Capitalized over lowercase.
36. Deleted: "cant" ; inserted: "goodness" on a line above.

This Singular Young Man.

Manuscript in Duke (18, #3). Inscribed in black pencil on two leaves of white laid paper with vertical chainlines and brown rules 5/16" apart. Each leaf consists of two irregular scraps pasted together. Approximate measurements: [*1*] 5" x 7⅞" and 6¾" x 7¾"; [*2*] 6¾" x 7¾" and 4⅝" x 7¾". Leaf [*1*] torn and heavily stained at left corners; leaf [*2*] less stained. Bucke assigns it to the 1840s. First published *N&F,* 116–117, 114–115 (Pt. III, #111, 108; *CW,* IX, 130–132, 135) as two detached items.

This singular[1] young man was unnoted for any strong [*illeg.*] qualities; and[2] he certainly had no bad qualities [*illeg.*][3] possessed very little of what is called education.— He remained [*?*] much[4] by himself; though he had many brothers, sisters, and[5] relations and acquaintances.— He did no work, like the rest.—[6] By far the most of the time he remained silent.— He was not eccentric,[7] nor did any one[8] suspect him[9] insane:— He loved, in summer, to sit[10] or[11] lean on the rails of the fence, apparently in[12] pleasant thought.— He was rather less than the[13] good size of a man: his figure and face[14] were full, his complexion without much color, his eyes, large, clear, and black.— He never drank rum, never went after women,[15] and took no[16] part in the country frolics.—[17]

He certainly had the power of a foreseer.— He very often knew,[18] days beforehand, of a death that[19] should happen and who it was, and how it was to be.— This terrible consciousness came to him, irrespective of place or occasion.—

1. Deleted: "being" ; inserted: "young man" on a line above.
2. Deleted: "still"
3. Deleted: "had" ; inserted: "possessed" on a line above and before "very"
4. Deleted: "with"
5. Deleted: "oth"
6. Deleted: "He was" "Th"
7. First "c" written over "x"
8. Deleted: "th"
9. Deleted: "of"
10. Written over [*illeg.*].
11. Written over "on"
12. Written over [*illeg.*].
13. Deleted: "full" ; inserted: "good" above.
14. Preceding two words inserted.
15. Deleted: [*illeg.*]; inserted: "and" on a line above.
16. Inserted on a line above "took . . . part"
17. End of first scrap.
18. Deleted: "week"
19. Deleted: "was to" ; inserted: "should" on a line above.

Sometimes it came to him at night[20] while he lay[21] sleeping in bed;[22] sometimes while he was eating at the table.—[23] When it came he would rise up,[24] and[25] prepare himself, without[26] speaking not a word,[27] walking straight[28] for the grave yard of the village.—[29] There he would remain[30] a short time, like one[31] with a vision. He would then sometimes see, mistily, the whole of the[32] soon coming[33] funeral.— The[34] procession would arrive, and the minister. The coffin would be brought in, and placed on the[35] trestles, and the lid would be silently[36] taken off,[37] and he with the rest would look on the face of the corpse.— Then they[38] would screw the lid on for the last time,[39] and the minister would pray, and[40] then the burial; and then a pause, after which the people would [*illeg.*] leave and with return home and [2][41] where he[42] withdrew for a long time to a solitary part of the house.—

In this manner,[43] just after commencing his dinner one day he felt the horrible touch[44] quicken the pulses within him;[45] and knew the sign well.— He[46] stopped, pushed back the plate from[47] under his mouth and rose to go.— Mother nor any one else spoke a word to him.— Something more[48] ghastly and blear than ever seemed this time to ride upon his[49] galloping heart.—[50] Swiftly he sped

20. Preceding two words inserted on a line above "while"
21. Deleted: "asleep" ; inserted: "sleeping" on a line above.
22. Deleted: [*illeg.*]
23. Deleted: "Then" ; inserted: "When it came" on a line above "Then he"
24. Word and comma inserted on a line above "rise . . . and"
25. Deleted: "dress himself"
26. Inserted on a line above "speaking"
27. Deleted: "but"
28. Deleted: "way"
29. Written over "town"
30. Written over "rep"
31. "one" written over [*illeg.*]. Deleted: "in" ; inserted: "with a" on a line above.
32. Deleted: "future"
33. Preceding four words and deletion inserted on a line above "funeral.— The"
34. Capitalized over lowercase "t"
35. Deleted: "tressels"
36. Inserted on a line above "silently . . . taken"
37. Deleted: [*illeg.*]
38. Inserted over [*illeg.*].
39. Preceding five words and comma inserted on a line above "on . . . and"
40. Deleted: "they"
41. Deleted: "retiring"
42. Inserted and deleted: "was" above "he" ; deleted: "retired" ; inserted: "withdrew" on a line above.
43. Deleted: "while at" ; inserted: "just after commencing" on a line above.
44. Deleted: "motion" ; inserted: "touch quicken the pulses" on a line above "within him;"
45. Deleted: period; inserted: semicolon; inserted and deleted: "He" ; inserted before deletion: "and" ; inserted: "knew the sign well;"
46. Deleted: "paused"
47. Deleted: "before him—" ; inserted: "under . . . go" on a line above.
48. Deleted: "than usually wretched and" ; inserted: "ghastly and blear than ever [*del.*] before" before "seemed"
49. Deleted: "flying" ; inserted: "galloping" on a line above "flying"
50. Deleted: "He knew the sign well; and the thought came to him"

from the house, and along the road to the grave yard, and threw himself flat on his belly[51] on the[52] earth,— and folded his arms[53] under his[54] open eyes.—[55]

Then the world receded from him.— And as it[56] became dim in the distance, he plainly heard the bell of the church tolling the burial[57] toll.— Presently he saw afar off, the funeral ranks approaching.— Slow: how slow, and how long.—[58] How noiseless, entering the old gate and treading on[59] that never mowed grass.—[60] They set down the coffin, and[61] a cry of despair went[62] from him, when he saw that the black dressed mourners who stood nearest were his own folks.— Perhaps it was himself he should see in the linen shroud there.— They lifted the lid and he looked on the dead[63] face of his sister, who[64] was that minute at home with the others at the table, and in ordinary health.— Yet it all came to pass as the young man beheld it.—

51. Preceding four words inserted on a line above "himself . . . on the"
52. Deleted: "grass" ; inserted: "earth" on a line above.
53. Deleted: "over" ; inserted: "under" on a line above.
54. Deleted: "close"
55. End of scrap.
56. Deleted: "was gone" ; inserted: "became dim" on a line above.
57. Written over [*illeg.*].
58. Deleted: ", and" ; inserted: ".— How" on a line above.
59. Deleted: "the thick unmow" ; inserted: "that" above "unmow"
60. Cf. "Song of Myself" (1855), sec. 6, l. 110.
61. Deleted: "the knife" ; inserted: "a cry" on a line above.
62. Deleted: "through his side" ; inserted: "from him" on a line above.
63. Inserted on a line above "face"
64. Deleted: "sat" "had been"

albot Wilson.

The original manuscript has disappeared. The present text is based on a microfilm of the original in LC (#80) which was made there for Floyd Stovall sometime in the summer of 1934 before the manuscript disappeared and loaned by him to the Library in the 1950s so that copies could be made. (Floyd Stovall, "Dating Whitman's Early Notebooks," *SB,* 24 [1971], 197.) It is not listed in LC catalog; #80 is a collection of photostats of individual pages. The microfilm presents several problems, possibly because of carelessness in photography or the condition of the notebook at the time, which are mentioned in the footnotes. The notebook has been described in *UPP,* II, 63, *n*6 and in *Ten Notebooks,* 6. The following summary is based on these sources, on Stovall, and on examination of the microfilm.

Pages of this notebook were 5½" x 3½"; with slight variations. It appears to have been commercially manufactured. Holloway, in *UPP,* reports that it locked "with a pencil thrust through three improvised leather loops." Neither the pencil nor the loops are visible in the microfilm. Stovall (198) reports that the loops "were fastened, presumably pasted, to the outside and inside edges of the covers, the middle one to the front cover and the upper and lower ones to the back. Thus, a pencil thrust through these three loops parallel to the backstrip would keep the book closed." The binding was green board with a leather backstrip. The pages were vertically ruled for accounts as follows: a single line about ⅝" from the left margin, a double line about ¾" from the right margin, and a single line ⅜" from the right margin. There are extremely faint traces of horizontal rules. Before converting the notebook to literary use, WW had used it for accounts, traces of which are visible on the stubs of cut-out pages. After he began composing in it, he made a number of miscellaneous, but significant, memoranda, two of which are discussed below.

The problem of dating the notebook has proved to be difficult. Holloway dated it 1847 on the basis of dates on pages [*17*] and [*63*]. WW himself or his intimates gave contradictory accounts of the beginning of *Leaves.* John Burroughs, or more likely WW himself, said (in Burroughs' *Notes on Walt Whitman as Poet and Person,* [NY, 1867], 83): "It is at this period (1853 and the seasons immediately following) that I come upon the first inklings of *Leaves of Grass.*" The pompous obscurity of this sentence can be taken to mean that WW began *Leaves of Grass* in 1853. In 1863 or 1864, he had told J. T. Trowbridge (*My Own Story* [Boston, 1903], 336–367) that he began in 1854, after Emerson had brought him to a boil. (This information does not appear in Trowbridge's MS diary.) In the 1872 Preface WW wrote, however, "I commenced, years ago, elaborating the plan of my poems, and continued turning over that plan, and shifting it in my mind through many years (from the age of twenty-eight [1847] to thirty-five [1854]) experimenting much, and writing and abandoning much. . . ." (*Prose 92,* II, 461). It was very likely in 1854 that he "came to a boil" or, to shift the figure, that individual poems and the volume itself precipitated themselves from what his notebooks show to be his very random notes.

This notebook was used from 1847 to the early 1850s, as Esther Shephard showed

("Possible Sources of Some of Whitman's Ideas in *Hermes Mercurius Trismegistus* and Other Works," *MLQ*, 14 [March, 1953], 66–67*n*13), and such a long time span is characteristic, in that Whitman kept his notebooks in as disorderly a fashion as he kept his room in Mickle Street. A study of his notebooks written between 1862–1863 shows, for example, that in 1863 he kept seven overlapping notebooks, one of which he had been using on and off since 1857 ("return my book").

In "Walt Whitman's Earliest Known Notebook" (*PMLA*, 83 [October, 1968], 1453–1456) I analyzed the evidence for dating and concluded that WW had used the notebook for prose and poetry connected with the *Leaves* as early as 1847 and as late as 1854. The evidence is detailed in the footnotes to the MS. He was, of course, keeping five other notebooks in 1854.

Stovall, in his *SB* article in reply to mine, rejects this early dating in favor of 1854. He finds significance in the fact that other surviving early notebooks, that is, LC #83, "the regular old followers," #84, "memorials," #85, "Poem incarnating the mind," and #86, "You know how the one brain" are of that year. He does not mention "I know a rich capitalist," which is not LC but is also 1854. Since we know that late in life WW destroyed a quantity of his papers, the mere scarcity of datable MS before 1854 in LC or elsewhere is no proof that they did not exist or that the present notebook is not earlier than that date. WW's curious and characteristic warning to himself in 1846 not to fall into Ossianism ("An Ossianic ¶") indicates that even before writing in this notebook he was searching for a new mode of utterance.

Stovall further finds it "incredible" that WW should have taken eight years to publish such magnificent verse. Perhaps "remarkable" would have been a sufficiently emphatic term, for there is a considerable distance between the scattered and unorganized, if incandescent, passages of the notebook and the subtle structure of "Song of Myself"—not to mention the composition of the Preface and the eleven other poems of *LG* (1855).

More importantly, he also rejects the most crucial evidence of the 1847 date. At the top of page [*17*] is a memorandum, possibly cancelled, of a payment to a mason on April 19, 1847. This is preceded and followed by prose of a consistent style. The other passage is at the top of page [*63*], a memorandum of a payment by a Mr. V. A. in 1847, which is preceded and followed by verse. It is not surprising to find such mundane matters intermingled with intense private outpourings, for WW put everything and anything into his notebooks (or memorandum books). Stovall does not comment on the first passage other than to mention it, but he finds the time relationship between personal finance and poetry in the second more questionable. To his eyes, the writing of the verse line is "much brighter [than the memorandum] and must . . . be of a later date." The brighter quality of the verse, such as it is, may well be the result of the poor photographic reproduction of the memorandum. It is entirely possible, in fact probable, that the verse was entered at a somewhat later date—but not necessarily as late as 1854. On the evidence of his practice in other notebooks, what happened is probably as follows. WW, who was a paper-saver, salvaged an old notebook by cutting out obsolete entries. It is unlikely that he would keep two such entries while disposing of others. When he paid the mason and received the money from Mr. V. A. he entered these currently important facts on random blank pages and later wrote around them. The entries must have been of current value in 1847 or have been made almost concurrently with the writing of the literary material. In either case, the date of these parts of the notebook must be 1847 or very close to it.

A hitherto undiscussed passage of January, 1854 in a notebook of 1853–1854 ("Poem incarnating the mind") complicates the problem further. One of the most striking characteristics of "Song of Myself" and other poems of *LG* (1855) is the use of the generic or cosmic or transcendental "I." This "I" is used throughout the present notebook. In "Poem incarnating the mind," however, the draft of Sec. 33 of "Song of Myself" was originally written in the third person (e.g., "He is the man; he suffered, he was there") and later revised to the first person. The significance of this passage of course goes beyond the question of dating manuscripts. When did WW develop his sense of cosmic unity? On the evidence of the present notebook, one would say 1847. From "Poem incarnating the mind" the conclusion is 1854. However, it is quite possible that the development of his cosmic sense was slow. The "I" of the present notebook does not conspicuously relate itself to others except as teacher or healer. The suffering it feels is internal and personal, whereas the "I" of "Poem incarnating the mind" identifies itself with others. Possibly it is a question of psychic development. Therefore, to return to the question of dating MS, it does not inevitably follow that the third-person passages of 1854 antedate the first-person passages of 1847. The situation is not tidy, but I have felt that dating this notebook to a period between 1847 and 1854 is still valid and have given it pride of place.

Allen, 134–135, discusses the emotional and intellectual content of this and other early notebooks. See also Arthur Wrobel "Whitman and the Phrenologists. The Divine Body and the Sensuous Soul," *PMLA,* 89 (January, 1974), 17–23.

The notebook was first published by Holloway in *UPP,* II, 63–76. Photographic reproductions can be found in LC #80 (photostats #3300–#3312); *UPP,* II, facing 70; *Ten Notebooks,* 7; Esther Shephard, "The Inside Front and Back Covers of Whitman's Earliest Known Notebook: Some Observations on Photocopy and Verbal Descriptions," *PMLA,* 87 (October, 1972), 1119–1121, and in the present edition.

[*Inside front cover*] albot[1] Wilson st go to corner Division ave. & 7th st.[2] 466½ avenue Brooklyn/ Mr. Stebbins 110 Broadway Room 8 over the Metropolitan Bank

[*1*] Jeffs. [*illeg.*] Joseph Pemberton maker Liverpool No 41,303 Lever cover [*illeg.*]/[3] W Quartier Au[*illeg.*] Swisse No 51,575/[4]

1. Upper left-hand corner damaged. Probably the artist, Jesse Talbot, who is listed on Wilson Street in the Brooklyn Directory for 1854–1855. See inside back cover, "Mr. & Mrs. Fitz"[*991Vn*], "return my book," and "[*illeg.*] Dick Hunt." In 1857 WW owned Talbot's painting, "The Christian and the Cross," a scene from *Pilgrim's Progress* (a surprising choice), which was seized by James Parton as part payment on a loan (Allen, 209–210; *Corr.,* II, 90.) Joseph Jay Rubin, *The Historic Whitman* (University Park, 1973), 263, quotes WW's criticism of Talbot's work. See illustrations.

2. The following deleted entries are on the inside cover: "Walter Whitman 71 Prince street and 30 Fulton st Brooklyn 106 Myrtle" "466 ½" is to the left as if a correction of "71", and "avenue Brooklyn" is below preceding "Mr. Stebbins . . ." The Prince Street residence was bought by Walter Whitman Sr. in 1844 and sold to WW on May 25, 1847. The Myrtle Avenue property was bought by WW on October 30, 1848. He built a house that winter, moved into it in the latter part of April, 1849, and sold it in May, 1852. See "Nehemiah Whitman." The Fulton Street address is that of the Brooklyn *Eagle.* "466 ½" has not been identified. Line below almost from side to side.

3. Line across leaf.

4. After "W" deleted: "watch" . Probably the entire entry refers to a watch, possibly the silver watch WW bought for $10 in 1846. See Charles F. Feinberg, "A Whitman Collector Destroys a Whitman Myth," *PBSA,* 52 (1958), 76. A line across leaf overwritten with curved flourishes.

[*3; 2 blank*] Be simple and clear be not occult.[5]

True noble expanding American character is raised on a far more lasting and universal basis than that of any[6] of the characters of [7] the "gentlemen" of aristocratic life, or of novels, or under[*?*] the European or Asian[*?*] forms of society or government.—[8] It is to be illimitably proud, independent[*?*], self-possessed[9] generous and gentle.— It is to accept nothing except what is equally free and eligible to any body else.[10] It is to be poor, rather than rich—but to prefer [*4*] death sooner than any mean dependence.—Prudence is part of it, because prudence is the right arm of independence.[11]

Every American young man should carry himself with the finished and haughty bearing of the greatest ruler and proprietor—for he is[12] a great ruler and proprietor—[13] the greatest.

Great latitude must be allowed to others

Play[14] your muscle, and it will be lithe as[15] [5] caoutchouc and strong as iron—I wish to see American young men the workingmen, carry themselves with a high horse[16]/

[5] Where is the being of which I am the inferior?—It is the of the[17] sly or shallow to divide men like the metals into those more precious and others less precious, intrinsically

I never yet knew[18] how it felt to think I[19] stood in the presence of my superior.—[20] *If the presence of*[21] God were made visible immediately before me,[22] I could not abase myself.— How do I know but I shall myself

[7] I will not be[23] the cart, nor the load on the cart, nor the horses that draw the cart; but I will be the[24] little hands that guide the cart.—

5. Cf. 1855 Preface, 717, ll. 270–290. (All further line and page references for the Preface are to *LG CRE*.) This sentence has the appearance of a later entry jammed in at the top of the page.

6. From this point the left margin is about three characters further left.

7. Deleted: "of"

8. Cf. 1855 Preface, 710, ll. 51ff.

9. Deleted: "and"

10. Cf. "Song of Myself" (1855), sec. 24, l. 507.

11. See [*17, 18, 52, 74*]; "I know a rich capitalist" [*1, 20, 22–23*]; "human feet, awaits us"; "The regular old followers"; 1855 Preface, 723–724, ll. 480–509; "Song of Prudence" (1856). See also "Sun-Down Papers," #7, #9, "Motley's Your Only Wear," "Morbid appetite for Money," *UPP*, I, 37–38, 47, 111, 123.

12. Deleted: "then"

13. Deleted: "the"

14. Deleted first word: "Bring"

15. Deleted: "will [*illeg.*]" at foot of page.

16. Short line from left under this line.

17. Inserted on a line above "the . . . sly"

18. Deleted: "what it was to feel"

19. Preceding two words inserted on a line above "to"

20. Deleted: "I could now abase myself if God"

21. Deleted: "God were" . Cf. "Song of Myself" (1855), sec. 48, ll. 1269–1271.

22. Inserted on a line above "before . . . it"

23. Deleted: "have" ; inserted: "be" on a line above.

24. Deleted: "pair of little" ; inserted: "little" on a line above "the"

[*8*] Ask Mr. Dwight about the highest numeral term known[25]

[*10; 9 blank*] Different objects which decay, and by the chemistry of nature, their bodies are into spears of grass—[26]/

America[27] receives with calmness the spirit of the past[28]/

[*11*] Bring all the art and science of the world, and baffle and humble it with one spear of grass[29]/

Liberty is not the[30] fruition but the dawn of the morning of a nation.—

The night has passed and the day appears when people walk abroad—to do evil or to do good

[*12*] The soul or spirit transmutes itself into all matter—into rocks, and can [*illeg.*] live the life of a rock—into the sea, and can feel itself the sea—into the oak, or other tree—into an animal, and feel itself a horse, a fish, or a bird—into the earth—into the motions of the suns and stars—

A man only is interested in any thing when he identifies himself with it—he must himself be whirling and speeding through space like the planet [*13*] Mercury.— he must be driving like a cloud—he must shine like the sun—he must be orbic and balanced in the air, like this earth—he must crawl like the pismire—he must[31] —he would be growing fragrantly in the air like[32] the locust blossoms—he would rumble and crash like thunder in the sky—he would spring like a cat on his prey—he would splash like a whale in the[33]

25. The Brooklyn City directories from 1846–1847 to 1854–1855 list a Benjamin W. Dwight as a clergyman or teacher. Fr. John E. Bernbrock gives his dates as 1816–1889 and says he conducted Dwight's High School, 1846–1888, and wrote *Modern Philology: Its Discoveries, History and Influence* (NY, 1859) and *Modern Philology: First and Second Series* (NY, 1864) ("Walt Whitman and Anglo-Saxonism," Diss. Univ. NC, 1961, 7*n*). WW's interest in numeration was not casual, for the higher terms are conspicuous in the 1855 poems and almost nowhere else. Millions and billions are used generally throughout the 1855 poems. (Unless otherwise noted, all citations are of "Song of Myself.") *TRILLIONS:* (ll. 1138–1139); above [*63*]. In an early draft in NYPL (Berg), the reading is "billions". See *LG MS Variorum*. *QUADRILLIONS:* (sec. 45), l. 1194. *QUINTILLIONS:* (sec. 33), l. 799; "I Sing the Body Electric" (1855), sec. 7, l. 99. *SEXTILLIONS:* (sec. 31), l. 669; cf. [*63*] above and *"TRILLIONS,"* above. *OCTILLIONS:* (sec. 45), l. 1194. *DECILLIONS:* (sec. 22), l. 473; "Who Learns My Lesson Complete?" (1855), l. 14 (reduced to "billions" in 1867). See also "Cheap looking glasses," "Poem incarnating the mind."

26. Line almost from side to side below. Cf. "Song of Myself" (1855), secs. 6, 49, 52, ll. 110–130, 1294–1296, 1339–1340.

27. "American" changed to "America" ; deleted: "under takes" ; inserted: "receives" on a line above.

28. Short line below "past" . Cf. 1855 Preface, ll. 2–3, 709.

29. Line three-quarters across from left.

30. Deleted: "head[*?*]" ; inserted: "fruition" on a line above.

31. Space in MS is almost a full line long.

32. Deleted: "a"

33. Last word possibly "blue" . Cf. 1855 Preface, 711–712, ll. 61–110; "Song of Myself" (1855), secs. 13–14, ll. 232–252; secs. 31–32, ll. 670–709; "The Sleepers" (1855), sec. 1, ll. 42–49; "There Was a Child Went Forth" (1855); [*57–58*] post. Other passages might be cited.

[*14*] The mean and bandaged[34] spirit is perpetually dissatisfied with itself— It is too wicked, or too poor, or too feeble

[*15*][34a] Never speak of the soul as any thing but intrinsically great.— The adjective affixed to it must always testify greatness and immortality and purity.—

[*16*][35] The effusion or corporation of the[36] soul is always under the beautiful laws of physiology—I guess the soul itself can never be any ? thing but great and pure and immortal; but it[37] makes itself visible only through matter—a perfect head, and[38] bowels[39] and bones to match[40] is the easy gate through which it comes from its[41] embowered garden, and pleasantly appears to the sight[42] [*45; 44 blank*][43] of the world.— A twisted skull, and blood[44] watery or rotten by[45] ancestry or gluttony, or rum or bad disorders,—they are the darkness toward which the plant will not grow, although its seed lies waiting[46] for ages.—[47]

[*17*][48] 1847
April 19th Mason commenced work on the basement
rooms
paid mason in full/[49]

I know the bread is[50] my bread, and that on it[51] must I dine and sup.[52] I know[53] I may munch,[54] and not grit my teeth against the laws of church or state.

34. Deleted: [*illeg.*]; "spirit" written in on a line above.
34a. This page and part of [*14*] shown on LC photostat, sheet [*3300*]
35. Page shown on LC photostat, sheet [*3305*], *Ten Notebooks,* 7 and in the present edition.
36. Inserted above: "effusion . . . the"
37. Deleted: [*illeg.*]
38. Deleted: [*illeg.*]
39. Inserted: "and bones"
40. Deleted: "will"
41. Deleted: "wonderful" ; inserted: "embowered"
42. The text of this passage is continued on [*45*] which is here inserted for the sake of continuity on the assumption that the insertion follows the order of inscription.
43. Page shown on LC photostat, sheet [*3301*].
44. Deleted: "made then" ; inserted and deleted: [*illeg.*]; inserted: "watery" on a line above.
45. Inserted: "ancestry or" on a line above "ancestry . . . or"
46. Written over an illegible word.
47. "The Sleepers" (1855), sec. 7, ll. 154–160.
48. Page shown on LC photostat, sheet [*3305*], *Ten Notebooks,* 7 and in the present edition.
49. Charles E. Feinberg, *PBSA,* 52 (1958), 77, notes a receipt dated May 1 for a $56 mason's bill. The day of the month is overwritten and the entry appears to have been cancelled by a diagonal line.
50. Deleted: "mine, I have not a dime more" ; "fip" previously deleted and "dime" inserted. A "fip" was originally a Spanish silver coin worth six cents; it was also called a "half-dime."
51. Inserted: "that on it"
52. Deleted: "for the dime that bought it was my last" . Following period and dash not deleted, not printed.
53. Deleted: "the"
54. Deleted: "and munch"

What is this then that balances itself upon my lips and wrestles[55] as with the knuckles of God, for (3) [*38*] (3)[56] every bite, I put between them, and if[57] my belly is[58] victor, can't[59] even then be foiled, but follows the[60] innocent food down[61] my throat and[62] turns it to fire and lead within me? What[63] angry snake[64] hisses at my ear,[65] [*39*][66] And what is it[67] but my[68] soul that hisses like an angry snake,[69] Fool! will you stuff your greed and starve me? [*38*] O fool will you stuff your greed and starve your soul?[70]

[*18*] The[71] ignorant man is demented with the madness of owning things— of having[72] by warranty deeds and[73] court clerk's records, the right to mortgage, sell,[74] give away or raise money on certain possessions.— But the wisest soul knows that[75] no object[76] can really be owned by one man or woman any more than another.—[77] The orthodox proprietor says This[78] is mine. I earned or received or paid for it,— and by[79] positive right of my own, I will put[80] a fence around it, and keep[81] it exclusively to myself—. . . . . . Yet[82]—yet—what cold[83] drop is

55. Deleted: "like"

56. The text of this passage is continued on [*38*] and is here inserted for the sake of continuity on the assumption that the insertion follows the order of inscription. It is not known why WW used "3)" as a catchword.

57. Deleted: "I"

58. Deleted: "the"

59. Deleted: "it that will not then" and several illegible words; inserted above: "can't"

60. Deleted: "crust" ; inserted: "innocent food"

61. Deleted and inserted: "my throat"

62. Successively deleted: "as" "like" "makes it" ; inserted above: "turns it to"

63. Deleted: [*illeg.*]; inserted: "angry snake"

64. Deleted: "that hisses whistles softly"; inserted: "hisses"

65. Deleted: "as saying, deny your greed and this night your soul shall"

66. Sentence written on [*39*] but a brace indicates that it is to be read as part of [*38*].

67. Inserted.

68. Deleted: "soul"

69. Deleted: "O" ; "Fool" capitalized.

70. Cf. "Who was Swedenborg," *UPP,* II, 16.

71. Deleted: "world" ; inserted: "ignorant man" on a line above "world . . . is"

72. Deleted: "like[*?*]" ; inserted: "by warranty" on a line above.

73. Deleted: "lawful possession and [*illeg.*] perfect" ; inserted: "court clerk's records" on a line above; inserted: "the"

74. Deleted: "dispose of" ; inserted: "give away"

75. Deleted: "nothing" ; inserted: "not one object" on a line above; then deleted: "not one" ; inserted: "no" before "not one"

76. Deleted: "in the vast universe" on the line following the deleted "nothing"

77. Deleted: "meddlesome[*?*] fool who [*ins. and del.*] who fancies that" ; inserted: "orthodox proprietor" on lines above.

78. "T" in "this" capitalized.

79. Inserted above: "by [*del.*] a positive right of my own, I"

80. Deleted: "this" ; inserted above: "a"

81. Deleted: "the"

82. Uppercase "Y" over lowercase.

83. Inserted on a line above "what . . . drop"

[*19*][84] that[85] which slowly patters, patters[86] with sharpened[87] poisoned points, on the skull of his greediness, and go whichever way he[88] may, it still hits him,[89] though he see not whence it[90] drips nor what it is?—[91] dismal and measureless fool not to[92] see the hourly lessons of[93] the one eternal law,[94] that he who would grab blessings to himself,[95] as by right, and deny others their equal chance and will not share with them every thing that he has[96]

[*20*] He cannot share[97] his friend or his wife because[98] of them he is no owner,[99] except by[1] their love, and if any one gets that away from him,[2] lets[3] wife and friend go, the tail with the hide[4]

[*23; 21 and 22 torn out*][5] The ignorant think that to the entertainment of life[6] they will be admitted by a ticket or check, and the[7] dream of their existence is to get the money that they may buy this[8] wonderful card.— But the wise soul[9]

[*25; 24* [10]] Every soul has its own individual language, often unspoken, or lamely feebly haltingly[11] spoken; but a[12] true fit for[13] that man, and perfectly

84. Deleted: "that it"
85. Inserted: "which slowly" on a line above "that"
86. Deleted: "like" after "patters" ; inserted and deleted: "pin points cold" ; inserted and deleted: "with" on a line above "pin points" ; inserted: "with" following on line above.
87. Deleted: "specks of water down" ; inserted: "poisoned points" on a line above.
88. Deleted: "will" ; inserted: "may" on a line above.
89. Deleted: "so"
90. Deleted: "comes" ; inserted: "drips" on a line above.
91. Deleted: "How can I be [*previously del.*] a that" on a line above "a" . *UPP,* I, 67, reads "that dismal . . . ," but "that" is clearly deleted.
92. Deleted: "understand" ; inserted: "see" on a line above.
93. Deleted: "an[?]" ; inserted: "the" on a line above "an" (at the end of the line) and "one" on a line above "eternal" at the beginning of the line following.
94. Deleted: "which"
95. Deleted: "and"
96. Text breaks off two-thirds of the way across the page.
97. Deleted: "with them"
98. Deleted: "no man owns those" ; inserted: "of them" on a line above.
99. Deleted: "except of He"
1. Deleted: "of" ; inserted: "by" on a line above.
2. Deleted: "he had should"
3. Deleted: "wife and friend the whole"
4. Another version on [*59*].
5. Deleted: "While the" on a separate line at the top of [*23*]. Possibly a vertical waved line from the top of the leaf to "existence"
6. Deleted: "you are" ; inserted: "they will be" on a line above.
7. Deleted: [*illeg.*]
8. Illegible fragment of word deleted.
9. See [*3, 59, 60*] for further references to ownership.
10. For reasons not clear, perhaps lack of care by the photographer, [*24*] duplicates [*20*]. The photograph seems to show a stub between [*24*] and [*26*] which, because of the confusion caused by the duplication, has not been counted in the pagination. See also LC photostat, sheet [*3300*].
11. The word "feebly" inserted on a line above "lamely" ; "haltingly" on a line below.
12. Deleted: "perfect" ; inserted: "true" on a line above.
13. Deleted: "[*illeg.*] and"

adapted to[14] his use.— The truths I tell to[15] you or any other, may not be[16] plain to you,[17] because I do not translate them[18] fully from my idiom into yours.— If I could do so, and do it well, they would be as apparent to you as they are to me; for they are[19] truths.—No two have exactly the same language,[20] and the great translator [*26*] and joiner of[21] the whole is the poet,[22] He[23] has the divine grammar of all tongues, and[24] says indifferently and alike[25] How are you friend? to the President in the midst of his cabinet, and Good day my brother, to Sambo, among the[26] hoes of the sugar field, and both understand him and[27] know that[28] his speech is[29] right.—

[*27*] The universal and fluid soul impounds within itself not only all the good characters and heros but the distorted characters, murderers, thieves[30]

[*28*][31] I said to my soul When we become the[32] enfolders[33] of all these orbs,[34] and open to the life, and delight and knowledge of every thing in them, or of them, shall we be filled and satisfied? and the answer was[35]   No, when we fetch that height, we shall not be filled and satisfied but shall look as high beyond.[36]

14. Originally "for" ; "to" written over.

15. Inserted on a line above.

16. Deleted: "apparent" ; inserted: "plain" on a line above.

17. Inserted and deleted: "or that other" on a line above following "you"

18. Deleted: "well" ; inserted and deleted: "rightly" on a line above; inserted: "fully" on the same line following the deleted word "rightly"

19. Deleted: "eternal"

20. Deleted: "but" ; inserted: "and" on a line above.

21. Deleted: "all" ; inserted: "The whole" on a line above the deleted word "all" and "is"

22. Deleted: "because" ; comma not changed to period. See [*48*] for another version. Esther Shephard, in *Walt Whitman's Pose* (NY, 1938), 177–178, first pointed out the striking similarity between this and a passage WW marked in George Sand's *The Countess of Rudolstadt* (trans. 1847) and copied out. See also Shephard, "Whitman's Copy of George Sand" *WWR*, 9 (June, 1963), 34–36, 37 and Grier, "Walt Whitman's Earliest Known Notebook," *PMLA*, 83 (October, 1968), 1456. For WW's other MS transcript, see "the unknown refused."

23. Deleted: "enters into the"

24. Deleted: "what"

25. Inserted: "indifferently and alike" on a line above "says . . . are"

26. Deleted: "black slaves" ; inserted and deleted on a line above the deleted word "black" : [*illeg.*]; "hoes" inserted on a line above the deleted word "slaves"

27. Inserted: "understand him and" on a line above "both . . . that"

28. Deleted: "his" before "his speech"

29. Deleted: "well for him hi" ; inserted and deleted: "rightly" ; inserted: "right" on a line above. End punctuation is a tangle of period over comma, inserted period, inserted dash. Cf. "Song of the Answerer" (1855), sec. 1, ll. 34–36.

30. See [*12*] and [*29*].

31. The top half of the page is blank. Deleted: "and" written flush left at the beginning of the sentence; inserted: "I" above the deleted word "and"

32. Deleted: "god"

33. "enfolding[*?*]" emended to "enfolders" ; inserted: "of"

34. Inserted on a line above "these . . . and"

35. In the MS the space is half a line long.

36. Cf. "Song of Myself" (1855), sec. 46, ll. 1220–1222.

[29] *Dilation* [37]

I think the soul will never stop, or attain to any[38] growth beyond which it shall not go.—[39] When I walk[40] at night by the sea shore and looked up[41] at the[42] countless stars, I ask[43] of my soul whether it would be filled and satisfied when it[44] should become the god enfolding[45] all these, and open to the life and delight and knowledge of every thing in them or of them, and the answer was plainer to[46] me— [30][47] at the[48] breaking water on the sands at my feet; and[49] the answer was, No, when I reach there, I shall want[50] to go further still.—

[*32; 31 blank*] The run of poets and the learned have

When[51] I see where the east is greater than the west,—[52] where the sound[53] man's part of the[54] child is greater than the sound[55] woman's part—[56] or where[57] a father [58] is more needful than a mother to produce me—then I[59] guess I shall see how spirit is greater than matter.—[60] Here[61] the run of poets and the learned always*[62][*33*][63] *always strike[64] and[65] here shoots the ballast of many a grand

37. See P. Z. Rosenthal, "'Dilation' in Whitman's Early Writing," *WWR*, 20 (March, 1974), 3–15. See also [56] following.

38. Deleted: "its" before "growth"

39. Originally: "go no further" ; "no further" deleted ; "not" inserted on a line above "go" Period and dash not deleted after "no further"

40. In preceding phrase, deleted: "have sometimes when I" ; inserted on a line above initial "I" : "when" ; "walked" emended to "walk"

41. Deleted: "to" ; inserted: "at" on a line above.

42. Deleted: "stars"

43. Deleted: "and" ; inserted and deleted: [*illeg.*]; inserted: "I" ; on a line above deleted "and" ; "asked" emended to "ask"

44. Deleted: "was" ; inserted: "should become" on a line above.

45. Deleted: [*illeg.*]

46. Deleted: "my under-" ; inserted: "me" on a line above.

47. Deleted: "than [*illeg.*]" ; inserted: "at" on a line above.

48. Deleted: [*illeg.*]

49. Deleted: "it" ; inserted: "the answer" on a line above "the was"

50. Deleted: "more[?]"

51. Deleted: "you show me how" ; inserted: "I inquire" on a line above; [*del.*] "inquire" [*ins.*] "see" [*ins.*] "where" on a line above.

52. Deleted: "how" ; inserted: "where" on a line above.

53. Inserted on a line above "the . . . man's"

54. Inserted and deleted: "new born" on a line above "child"

55. Inserted on a line above "the . . . woman's"

56. Deleted: "how"

57. Deleted: "the" ; inserted: "a" on a line above.

58. Deleted: "than[?]" after the space.

59. Deleted: "know" ; inserted: "guess" above.

60. Cf. "Song of Myself" (1855), sec. 3, ll. 52–54, sec. 5, ll. 82–83, sec. 48, ll. 1269–1270; "I Sing The Body Electric" (1855), sec. 1, ll. 7–8.

61. Original beginning: "On" ; "Here" inserted above; "The" not lowercased.

62. Deleted: "usually stub their toes here, and generally fall and* sh" ; inserted: "always" on a line above "usually"

63. Passage from [*33*] inserted here according to WW's asterisks. Deleted: [*illeg.*]; inserted: "always" Page shown in LC photostat sheet [*3303*].

64. Deleted: "here"

65. Inserted and deleted: "it[?]" above "and" ; inserted: "here" above, between "it" and "and"

head.— My life is a miracle and my body which lives is a miracle;[66] but of what I can nibble at the edges of the limitless and delicious wonder I know that I cannot separate[67] them, and call one superior and the other inferior, any more than I can say my sight is greater than my eyes.—*

You have been told that[68] mind is greater than matter[69]

[34][70] I cannot understand the mystery, but I am[71] always[72] conscious of myself as two—as my soul and I; and I[73] reckon it is the same with all[74] men and women.—[75]

[35][76] I know that my body will[77]

[36][78] whose sides are crowded[79] the rich cities of all living philosophy, and oval gates[80] that[81] pass you in to[82] fields of clover[83] and landscapes[84] clumped with sassafras, and orchards of good apples, and[85] every breath through your mouth[86] shall be of a new perfumed,[87] and elastic air, which is love.—

But I will take[88] each man and woman of you to the window and open the shutters and the sash, and my left arm shall hook[89] you round the waist, and my right shall point shall point you to the[90] endless and beginningless road up along[91]

66. Cf. 1855 Preface, 719, ll. 350–351; "Song of Myself" (1855), sec. 24ll. 523; "Miracles" (1856). The theme is a frequent one.

67. Deleted: "the" before "them"

68. Deleted: "intellect" before "mind"

69. The intended order of inscription is not clear. "You . . . matter" is the first entry on [33], but WW connected "Here . . . always" [32] and "always . . . eyes" by asterisks. The passage is therefore rearranged.

70. Page shown on LC photostat, sheet [3303].

71. Inserted: "am" on a line above "I . . . always"

72. Deleted: "think" ; inserted: "conscious" on a line above.

73. Deleted: "gue"

74. Deleted: [*illeg.*]

75. Cf. "Song of Myself" (1855), secs. 2, 5, ll. 52–54, 82–83.

76. Page shown on LC photostat, sheet [3303].

77. Deleted: "decay"

78. No related passage precedes this, and, as far as one can tell from the microfilm, there are no missing pages. See, however, [49].

79. Deleted: "with"

80. Deleted: [*illeg.*]

81. Deleted: "let" ; inserted: "pass" on a line above.

82. Deleted: "immortal gardens landscapes of hill sides and"

83. Inserted above and deleted: "and [*illeg.*]" on a line above "clover . . . and"

84. Deleted: "of"

85. Deleted: "of your" ; inserted: "every" on a line above "your"

86. Preceding three words inserted on a line above "breath . . . be"

87. Deleted: "immortal[*?*]"

88. Deleted: "every man or woman" ; inserted: "each" on a line above "every" ; inserted and deleted on a line above "man" : [*illeg.*]; inserted and deleted above "or" : "and" ; finally inserted: "man and woman of you" on a line above.

89. Deleted: "him" ; inserted: "you" on a line above "him"

90. Deleted: "road" before "endless"

91. "Up" with a caret and circled at foot of the page, but nothing precedes and there is no evidence of a missing leaf. See, however, [49–50]. Cf. "Song of Myself" (1855), sec. 46, ll. 1207–1209. See also [49–50].

[*38;37*[92]] the sidewalks of eternity they are[93] the freckles of Jupiter

[*40*][94] The being I want to see you[95] become

If I walk with Jah in Heaven and he[96] assume to be intrinsically greater than I, it offends me; and I[97] shall certainly withdraw[98] from Heaven,—for the[99] soul[1] prefers freedom in the[2] prairie[3] or the[4] untrodden woods—and there can be no freedom where[5]

[*41*] Why can we not see beings[6] who by the[7] manliness and transparence of their natures, disarm[8] the[9] entire world, and brings[10] one and all to his side, as friends and believers?—[11] Can no father beget or mother conceive a man child[12] so entire and so elastic[13] that whatever action he do or whatever syllable he[14] speak, it shall be melodious to all[15] creatures, and none shall [*42*] be an exception to the universal and affectionate[16] Yes of the earth.

The[17] first[18] inspiration of real[19] wisdom in[20] our souls lets us know that[21] the[22]

92. For reasons not clear, perhaps lack of care by the photographer, [*37*] duplicates [*23*]. There is no sign of a stub between [36] and [*37*]. See [*24*]*n*10 for a similar situation.

93. Inserted: "they are" in the margin before "the"

94. [*38–39*] inserted after [*17*] in accordance with WW's directions: "(3 every bite . . . soul?" on [*38–39*].

95. Deleted: "develope"

96. Original reading: "If God himself assume" ; inserted: "If I . . . and he"

97. Deleted: "will" ; inserted: "shall certainly" on a line above "will . . . withdraw"

98. Deleted: "myself"

99. Deleted: "great"

1. Deleted: "will"

2. Deleted: "lonesomest"

3. Deleted: "to to"

4. Deleted: "woo"

5. Cf. [*3–7*]

6. Deleted: "Shall we never see a being" ; inserted: "Why . . . beings"

7. Deleted: "majesty" ; inserted: "manliness" on a line above "majesty"

8. "s" deleted from "disarms" ; deleted: "all criticism and"

9. Deleted: "rest of the" ; inserted: "entire" above "the . . . world"

10. WW omitted to delete final "s" ; deleted: "them"

11. Three false starts: [*illeg.*] ; "Are we never to" ; "I would see that" Inserted: "Can . . . conceive a" on lines above. Illegible word deleted after "father"

12. Inserted on a line above "so"

13. Deleted: "the and so free from all discords"

14. Deleted: "utt"

15. Deleted: "man" ; inserted: "creatures" on a line above.

16. Preceding two words inserted above "universal of"

17. Uppercase written over lowercase.

18. Deleted: "effusion"

19. Inserted on a line above "wisdom"

20. Deleted: [*illeg.*]

21. Deleted: "all human beings"

22. Deleted: "selfishness and malignity that happen" ; inserted: "self . . . thought" on a line above.

self will and wickedness we thought so[23] unsightly in our race[24] are [*43*][25] by no means what we were told, but something far different,—and not amiss to[26] except to the spirit of the[27] feeble and[28] the shorn.—[*42*][29] as the freckles and bristley beard[30] of Jupiter[31]—to be[32] removed by washes and razors,[33] under the judgement of genteel squirts,[34] but[35] in the sight of the great master, proportionate and essential and sublime.—[36]

[*47; 46 blank, 44–45*][37] Wickedness is most likely the absence of freedom and health in the soul.— If a man babe[38] or woman babe[39] of decent progenitors should grow up without restraint or starvation or

[*48*] Every soul has its own language,[40]

The reason why any truth[41] which I tell is not apparent to you, is mostly because I fail to translating it from my language into[42]

23. Deleted: "vast" ; inserted above: "unsightly"

24. Deleted: [*illeg.*]; inserted and deleted: [*illeg.*] on a line above.

25. There are traces of a bracket on the inside of [*43*] opposite the words "unsightly in our race are" which end the MS line on [*42*]. It has therefore been inserted in the text on [*42*], despite its end punctuation. It may, however, be an alternate reading. Deleted: "not" ; inserted: "by no means" on a line above "not . . . what" with which WW started the leaf.

26. The emendations are so complex as to be difficult to record. There were several stages of deletions and a few words were retained to form part of the present reading. The following can be deciphered: "and better [*following* "different," *period and dash not del.*] These are and an essential part of the universe [*illeg.*] which cannot and must not ungrateful [*ins.:* "amiss to" *on a line above* "ungrateful"] to the [*illeg.*] accomplished any [*illeg.*] but"

27. Inserted: "the spirit of the " on a line above "feeble . . . and"

28. Deleted: "the shaved" ; inserted: "the shorn—" on a line above. Deleted: "spirits [*illeg.*] spirits" following the deleted "the shaved"

29. Deleted: "but" ; inserted: "as"

30. Inserted: "and bristley beard" on a line above "freckles . . . of"

31. A gap and two illegible deleted words follow. There may have been an inscription in the gap.

32. Inserted: "to be" on a line above the gap.

33. Deleted: "from the if" Cf. "Song of Myself" (1855), sec. 22, *LG* (1855), 28: "Washes and razors for foofoos . . . . for me freckles and a bristling beard." Dropped in 1881.

34. Deleted: "and"

35. Inserted: "in the sight of the great master" on a line above.

36. Deleted: "in the sight of the master grand great master" There were internal deletions before the whole phrase was stricken.

37. [*45*] inserted in context after [*16*]. [*46–47*] shown on LC photostat, sheet [*3302*].

38. Inserted on a line above "man" in the outside margin.

39. Inserted on a line above "woman . . . of"

40. Inserted at the top of the page. Page shown on LC photostat, sheet [*3304*].

41. Deleted: [*illeg.*]

42. Cf. [*25–26*].

[*49*][43] I will not be a great philosopher, and found any school, and[44] build it[45] with iron pillars, and gather the young men[46] around me. and make them my disciples[47] that[48] new superior[49] churches and politics[50] shall come.— But I will[51] open the shutters and the[52] sash, and[53] hook my left[54] arm around your waist till I point you to the road along[55] which[56] are the cities of all living philosophy and[57] pleasure.—Not I[58]—not God—can travel [*50*][59] this road for you.— It is not far, it is within[60] the stretch of your[61] thumb; perhaps you shall find you are on it already and did not know.— Perhaps you shall find it every where over[62] the ocean and over[63] the land, when you once have the vision to behold it.—[64]

[*52; 51 blank*][65] I am hungry and with my[66] last dime get me some meat and bread, and[67] have appetite enough to[68] relish it all.— But then[69] like a phantom at my side suddenly[70] appears a starved face, either human or brute, uttering not a word.[71]

43. Page shown on LC photostat, sheet [*3304*].
44. Deleted: [*illeg.*]
45. Deleted: "on" ; inserted: "with" on a line above "on"
46. The MS has "me" rather than "men" printed here.
47. Deleted: "and found a"
48. Inserted on a line above "and"
49. Inserted: "-es" added to "church"
50. Inserted: "shall come" on a line above "—But"
51. Deleted: "Show every man, [*illeg.*] the sh" One of WW's characteristic fists with extended index finger is inserted above "every" but points left.
52. Deleted: "window" ; inserted: "sash" on a line above.
53. Deleted: "you shall stand at my side, and I will show" ; inserted: "hook . . . point" on line above.
54. Deleted: [*illeg.*]
55. Inserted on a line above "road . . . which"
56. Deleted: "leads to all the learning [*del.*] knowledge [*ins.*] and truth and pleasure" ; inserted: "are . . . living" on lines above.
57. Deleted: "all"
58. Deleted: [*illeg.*]
59. Page shown on LC photostat, sheet [*3306*]. Deleted: "it" ; inserted: "this road" on a line above at the top of the leaf, in left margin.
60. Deleted: "the reach[*?*]" ; inserted: "the stretch" on a line above.
61. Deleted: "arm" ; inserted: "thumb" on a line above.
62. Deleted: "on" ; inserted: "over" on a line above.
63. Inserted on a line above "the"
64. Cf. [*36*].
65. Deleted: "If"
66. Deleted: "money buy a loaf of" ; inserted: "last . . . and"
67. Deleted: "would" on a line above "money . . . bread"
68. Deleted: "eat" ; inserted: "relish" on a line above.
69. Inserted on a line above "But . . . like"
70. Inserted on a line above "appears"
71. Deleted: "but with ["both" *del.*]" ; "Am I a"; inserted and deleted: "Have I a Have I then the passionless squid or clam–shell [*?*], not I feel in my heart that nor [*del.*] I or[*?*] it were my"

Now do I talk of mine and his? — Has[72] my heart no more passion than[73] a squid or clam shell had?

[53] I will not descend among professors and capitalists,[74]—I will turn up the ends of my trowsers[75] around my boots, and my cuffs back from my wrists, and go[76] with drivers and boatmen and men[77] that catch fish or[78] work in the field. I know[79] they are sublime

[54][80] I am the poet of slaves and of the[81] masters of slaves
I am the poet of the body
And I am[82]

I am the poet of the body
And I am the poet of the soul[83]
I go with the slaves of the earth equally with the masters[84]
And I will stand between the masters and the slaves,
Entering[85] into both[86] so that both shall understand me alike.

[55][87] I am the poet of Strength[88] and Hope[89]
Where is the house of any one dying?
Thither I speed and[90] turn the knob of the door,
Let[91] the physician and the priest[92] timidly withdraw

72. Original opening: "It" ; inserted on a line above: "Has"
73. Deleted: "the" ; inserted: "a" on a line above "the"
74. Deleted: "and good society"
75. Deleted: "up" Cf. "Song of Myself" (1855), sec. 10.
76. Deleted: "among the rough" ; inserted: "with" on a line above "among"
77. Deleted: "who" ; inserted above: "that"
78. Deleted: "hoe corn" ; inserted: "work . . . field" on a line above.
79. Deleted: "that"
80. Holloway, *UPP,* II, 69, reports several blank pages between the prose and verse. No trace of these pages is to be seen on the microfilm. [54] reproduced *UPP,* II, facing 70.
81. Inserted on a line above "the . . . masters"
82. Entire passage cancelled with a diagonal slash. There is a gap of approximately three lines' width between this passage and the next.
83. Cf. "Song of Myself" (1855), sec. 21, l. 422.
84. Original reading "Thus[?] the slaves are mine [*comma not del.*] and the masters are equally mine "; "the slaves" "masters" "mine" retained.
85. Deleted at beginning of line: "And I" ; "Entering" capitalized.
86. Deleted: "and"
87. Page reproduced *UPP,* II, facing 70. This and the following three pages are almost indecipherable because of heavy emendation. "I" is perhaps written over "I"
88. Capitalized over lowercase "s"
89. Following this line is a deleted fragment: "Swiftly pass I" on a separate line. WW used the thought two lines later.
90. Deleted: "raise[?]"
91. WW made two false starts, beginning with "Let" then inserting "And" on a line above, and then reinserted "Let" before "And," . Since the lowercase letter on "the" was changed to a capital, he may have thought of beginning the line with that word.
92. Deleted: "stand apart" ; inserted: "timidly withdraw" on a line above.

That[93] I seize on the[94] ghastly man and raise him with resistless will;
O[95] Despairer! I[96] tell you, you shall not[97] go down,
Here is my[98] arm, press your whole weight upon me,
[56][99] With tremendous[1] breath I force him to dilate,[2]
Every room of[3] your house[4] do I fill with armed men
Lovers of me,[5] bafflers of hell,
Not doubt not fear not death[6] shall[7] lay finger[8] you[9]
For[10] I have you all to myself
Sleep![11] for I and they stand guard this night,
And when you rise in the morning you find[12] what I told you is so.[13]

93. Inserted on a line above "I"

94. Deleted: "despairer" ; inserted: "ghastly man" on a line above.

95. Deleted: "ghastly man" ; inserted: "Despairer" on a line above "ghastly man" ; deleted: "you shall"

96. Deleted: "say" ; inserted: "tell you" on a line above "I . . . you" . Redundant inserted "you" here omitted.

97. Deleted: "die" ; inserted: "go down" following on the same line.

98. Deleted: "hand" "sink" ; inserted: "arm" on a line above.

99. WW experimented with a number of openings: "O" "Lo!" "In my" [*he did not delete* "In"], "with" "With"

1. Deleted: "will" ; inserted: "breath" on a line above.

2. See [24] above. The following fragmentary lines are deleted: "I will not" "Doubt and fear" "Will Treading" "Baffling doubt and" "I shall[?]" "Doubt shall not" The last is marked "Take up" in the left margin. Two lines following have been transposed up according to WW's "tr. up."

3. Deleted: "the" ; inserted: "your" on a line above.

4. Deleted: "will" ; inserted: "do" on a line above.

5. Deleted: [*illeg.*]

6. Deleted: "itself"

7. Deleted: "lay"

8. Deleted: "on [?]"

9. An illegible deleted passage, part of this line, follows, of which only an undeleted "I" is legible. An illegible line in a cramped hand was inserted and deleted between this and the following line.

10. "For" may belong to the inserted and deleted line mentioned in *n9*. The microfilm and the photostats are almost illegible because of WW's vigorous emendations. *UPP,* II, 69 gives the defensible reading: "And you are mine all to myself."

11. This and the following line are written on the inside margin of the page near the top. Since there are no definitive indications as to where they fit, they might possibly follow line 1 on this page, but it was assumed that the lines marked "tr up" (*n2* above) should precede them. Holloway made the same decision in *UPP,* and the lines are in this order in *LG:* "Song of Myself" (1855), sec. 40, ll. 1008–1020. Further MS versions [*64*], [*73*], following.

12. Deleted: "that I told you"

13. Three fragmentary lines: "Keep back"
"And while"
"The[?]" have been deleted.

[57] I am the poet of reality,[14]
I say the earth[15] is not[16] [*illeg.*][17] echo;
Nor man an apparition[18]
But that all the things seen are real[19]
The[20] witness and albic dawn of[21] things equally real not yet[*?*][22] seen
I[23] have split the earth and the hard coal and rocks and the solid bed of the sea[24]
And went down to reconnoitre there a long time,[25]
And bring[26] back[27] a report[28]
[58] And I understand that those are[29] positive and dense every one
And that what it seems to the child they are[30]

14. Cf. "Song of Myself" (1855), sec. 23, l. 483.

15. The first half of the line is almost illegible. Apparently WW began "The earth" and later added "I say" to the left. "T" in "The poet" was not lowercased and is not printed. Deleted additions above the line are illegible.

16. "not" is written over an illegible word.

17. Inserted: [*illeg.*] The word does not seem to be "an" *UPP,* II, 69 inserts "an" Cf. "To Think of Time" (1855), sec. 6, l. 69.

18. On the microfilm the line reads: "Man [*illeg. del.*] Nor man an apparition" WW possibly neglected to delete the first "Man"

19. The original deleted line, with the exception of "real" is illegible. Deleted: "I see" may be part of the original line or present line after "all" ; "things seen" written above "[*del.*] I see"

20. WW originally wrote "Here is the" ; deleted "Here" , and inserted "it" which he then deleted and capitalized "the"

21. Deleted: "of health[*?*] [*illeg.*]" ; inserted: "things equally real" on a line beginning above "dawn"

22. Four deleted illegible words precede these three words. In the MS WW inserted "but" or "yet" after "not" Three partially deleted trial lines follow: "But which are [*four words ins.*] I know to be equally real. I know"

"I know you too, solid [*del.*] earth [*ins. and del.*] hills ground and and rocks"

"I have been"

23. The line is marked in the left margin by a paragraph sign. The original opening phrase was: "I believe in" over which "have split" has been written on a line above.

24. Preceding seven words inserted in a cramped hand below the line.

25. Original line, partly deleted, partly illegible, seems to have been: "And have sent my soul to take board there a long time" "went down" written on a line above "to" and before "reconnoitre" written on the same line above the deleted "take board"

26. Inserted above three deleted illegible words.

27. Deleted: "its" ; inserted: "a" above.

28. Cf. "Song of Myself" (1855), secs. 31–32, 44, ll. 670–695, 1148–1169; [*12*] ante.

29. Original reading: "And now I know that it is what the it is all" with "understand" written on a line above "know" ; "everyone" inserted on a line above "and dense"

30. Original reading: "And that what they [*?*] seems to the child it is" . Five deleted lines follow:

"And that"
"For [*illeg.*] [*del.*] God [*ins.*] it does not joke"
"Nor is any [*del.*] thing [*ins.*] [*illeg.*] there any sham in the universe."
"And the world is no joke,
Nor any [*del.*] the part of it a sham" . Line from left one-third of the way across the leaf.

I am[31] for sinners and the unlearned[32]

[59][33] it is best not to curse, but quietly call the offal cart to his door and let physical[34] wife or friend go, the tail with the hide.—

[60] The dismal and measureless fool called a rich man, or thriver,[35] or some dismal and measureless fool, who leaves untouched those countless and every[?][36] spread tables[37] thick in immortal dishes,[38] heaped with the meats and drinks of God, and[39] fancies himself smart because he tugs and sweats[40] among cinders, and parings, and slush[41]

[61][42] I am the poet of little things and of babes[43]
Of each gnat in the air, and[44] of beetles rolling[45] balls of dung,[46]
Afar in the sky[47] was a nest[48]
And my soul[49] flew thither, and squat, and looked[50] out,
And saw[51] the journeywork of suns and systems of suns,

31. Deleted: "the"

32. Cf. "Song of Myself" (1855), secs. 16, 19, 22, ll. 330–348, 372–377, 463–467. The citations could be extended indefinitely.

33. Originally began: "may so well be. . . ." The passage is on a bracket pointing to the left, but has no connection with [58]. It closely repeats a passage on [20].

34. Inserted on a line above "wife"

35. "The dismal . . . thriver" inserted at the top of the page, above the following deleted: "What folks call a thriving or rich man is [*del.*] most likely"

36. [*Illeg.*] . *UPP,* II, 68 reads: "ever" conjecturally.

37. Original reading for preceding seven words: "leaves the fields ["previously" *del.*] leaves untasted the immortal[?] [*both preceding words del. The inserted words, also del., are illegible*] tables spread"

38. WW began "thick with" and deleted "with" ; inserted: "in the" and deleted "the" ; deleted: "every one"

39. Deleted: "thinks him"

40. Deleted: "in the slush after"

41. See [17–23].

42. Cf. "Song of Myself" (1855), sec. 31, ll. 663–668. The shift from prose to poetry here is puzzling, as is the reverse situation above, especially because here the leaves are clearly conjugate on the film. Possibly this is another example of WW's random use of pages.

43. WW made several false starts of the next line: "I [*illeg.*] "The" "Of the [*illeg.*] ants[?]"; "each" is inserted above.

44. "s" deleted from "gnats" . Originally: "the" which was deleted and replaced by an illegible word ("every[?]") above the line which in turn was deleted; "of" was then inserted on the same line above.

45. An illegible word, which may or may not have been deleted, is inserted above the line. "of dung" written on a line above "balls"

46. Cf. "Song of Myself" (1855) sec. 24, ll. 515.

47. Deleted: [*illeg.*]

48. Deleted: "built a nest in the" before "was a" ; deleted following : "sky" , "I" at the beginning of the sentence, before "Afar" , was not deleted, not printed.

49. Deleted: "stood there to [*illeg. ins. and del.*] reconnoitre" ; inserted: "flew thither" on a line above "stood there"

50. Deleted: "long upon the universe" ; inserted: "out" on a line above "long"

51. Deleted: "millions" ; inserted: "the journeywork of" on a line above. A redundant "of" here omitted.

And that a leaf of grass is not less than they[52]
[62] And that the pismire is equally[53] perfect, and all[54] grains of sand, and every egg of the wren.[55]
And the[56] tree-toad[57] is a chef' d ouvre[58] for the highest.
And the running-blackberry[59] would adorn the[60] parlors of Heaven
And the cow crunching with depressed neck surpasses[61] every statue,
And[62] pictures great and small crowd the rail-fence, and hang on[63] its[64] heaped stones and[65] elder and poke-weed.*[66]

[63] Amount rec'd from Mr. V. A.[67]
1847

I am the poet of Equality

*And a mouse is miracle enough to stagger[68] trillions of infidels.[69]
And I cannot put my toe anywhere to the ground

52. WW made two false starts: "And has known since that" and "And now I know that each" In the latter "now I know" and "each" were then deleted.
53. Inserted on a line above "perfect"
54. Inserted above and before two illegible words deleted.
55. A deleted half-line follows: "And that"
56. A deleted word is illegible, but conjecturally is "king"
57. Inserted: "tree" on a line above the deletion. The first letter of "toad" appears to have been written over another letter.
58. WW partially corrected the misspelling in *LG* (1855).
59. Deleted: "mocks the ornaments of"
60. Deleted: "house" ; inserted: "parlors" on a line above "house"
61. Deleted: "all statues" ; inserted: "every statue" on a line above.
62. WW began: "And the rail-fence" He deleted "the" and inserted "a thousand pictures [*illeg.*] crowd the" above "rail-fence" He then deleted "a thousand" and the illegible word and inserted "great and small" on a line above the illegible word. Cf. "Pictures," *LG CRE,* 642–649.
63. The deletions which led to the present reading "and hang on" are illegible.
64. Deleted: "loose" ; inserted: "heaped" on a line above.
65. Deleted: [*illeg.*]
66. WW began another line, but deleted it without finishing it: "Is picture enough" . Cf. "Song of Myself" (1855), sec. 5, l. 98. Since the prose entry at the top of [63] is important in the dating of the notebook, it has been left in the original position. As the asterisks indicate, however, WW intended the verse to be read continuously.
67. "Amount rec'd . . ." is at the head of this page and "1847" is lower and at the left in the first printed column on the page. (It will be remembered that the notebook is ruled for accounts.) Stovall (*SB,* 24, 199) detects some illegible erased lines of text below the entry) Professor Holloway has suggested to me that "Mr. V.A." was Isaac Van Anden, the publisher of the Brooklyn *Eagle.* Examination of Brooklyn city directories of the 1840s showed that Van Anden was the only person who could be "V.A." It seems probable that at the time he was writing the lines which precede and follow, WW was settling his accounts with Van Anden before leaving for New Orleans. The memorandum cannot be much later than early 1848, otherwise it would have had little meaning. WW received $10.00 by mail from Van Anden, possibly for his hospital work, April 15, 1863 (*Corr.,* I, 87). See reproduction.
68. Deleted: "an infidel" following "stagger" Last three words of line probably added after deletion of "an infidel" . This revision permits the first use of a high number in this notebook, but see his interest noted earlier, [8].
69. Cf. "Song of Myself" (1855), sec. 31, l. 669.

But it[70] must touch numberless and curious books
Each one scorning all that schools and science can do fully to translate them*[71]

[*66; 65 blank*] *[72] And the salt marsh and creek[73] have[74] delicious odors,
And[75] potato and ears of maize make a fat breakfast,[76]
And[77] huckleberrys from the woods[78] distill[79] joyous deliriums./

[*64*][80] I dilate you with tremendous breath,—
I buoy you up,
Every room of your house do I fill with armed men
Lovers of me, bafflers of hell,
Sleep! for I and they stand guard[81] this night
Not doubt, not fear, not Death shall lay finger upon you
I[82] have embraced[83] you, and henceforth possess you all to myself.[84]
And when you rise in the morning you shall find it is so.—[85]

[*66*] God and I are now here
Speak! what would you have of us?[86]

[*68; 67 blank*] I am the Poet[87]

[*69*][88] Have you supposed it beautiful to be born?
I tell you[89] I know it is[90] just as beautiful to die;

70. Deleted: "shall" ; inserted: "must" on a line above.

71. WW orginally wrote: "Each one above all that science of schools and" . He deleted "above" and inserted "scorning" and deleted "science of" . He then continued: "science of the world can do fully to read them" then deleted "of the world" and "read" and inserted "translate" on a line above "to read them" . Cf. "Song of Myself" (1855), sec. 14, ll. 253–254.

72. This passage has been transferred to precede [*64*] in accordance with WW's asterisks. Earlier line partly deleted: "*And the odor of the salt marsh is [*ins. on a line above* "is . . . perfume" delicious perfume enough" . Marked in left margin with WW's characteristic pointing hand. [*64*] follows. See illustration.

73. Two preceding words inserted on a line above "marsh . . . have"

74. Deleted: "a" before "delicious"

75. Deleted: "a"

76. Deleted: "who [?] [*illeg.*]"

77. Deleted: "a handful of"

78. Preceding three words inserted on a line above "huckleberries"

79. Deleted: "[*illeg.*] a"

80. Cancelled line at top of page: "Buoyed with tremendous breath shall you be, and dilated"

81. Deleted: "all" ; inserted: "this" on a line above.

82. The line originally began: "God and"

83. Inserted above "you"

84. WW originally wrote "ourselves" . He then wrote "my" over "our" but did not change "selves"

85. Cf. "Song of Myself" (1855), sec. 40, ll. 1008–1020. Cf. also [*55–56*].

86. This passage in lighter script seems to have no connection with the preceding three lines transferred to follow [*63*] and is separated from them by a line across the page. See "Poem incarnating the mind of an old man" [*867V*], where the repetition is almost verbatim.

87. See [*54, 55, 57*].

88. Deleted: "Do" ; inserted: "Have" above.

89. Deleted: "it" ; inserted: "I know" on a line above.

90. Deleted: one illegible word; inserted: "just as" above.

For I take my death with the dying
And my birth with the new-born babes[91]

[70] I am the poet of sin,
For I do not believe in sin
    In the silence[92] and darkness[93]
Among murderers and cannibals and traders in slaves
Stepped my[94] spirit with light feet, and pried among[95] their heads and made[96] fissures[97] to look through
And there[98] saw folded fœtuses of twins[99] like the fœtuses of[1] twins in the womb,[2]
Mute with bent necks, waiting to be born.—[3]
And one was Sympathy and one was truth.

[72; *71 blank*] I am the poet of women as well as men.
The woman is not[4] less than the man
But she is[5] never the same,

I remember I stood one Sunday forenoon,[6]

(the Peacemaker)[7]

[73] Strength

Where is one abortive, mangy, cold—[8]
Starved of his masculine lustiness?

91. Cf. "Song of Myself" (1855), sec. 7, ll. 131–133.
92. Deleted: "of"
93. The verse is indented because WW marked it with a paragraph mark, but there is no space between it and the preceding line in the notebook.
94. Deleted: "soul"
95. Deleted: "them" ; inserted: "their heads" on a line above "them . . . and"
96. Deleted: [*illeg.*]; inserted: "made" above.
97. Deleted: illegible phrase; inserted: "to look through"
98. Deleted: one illegible word; inserted: "saw folded" on a line above the illegible word and "fœses"
99. Two lines deleted:
"And not [*illeg.*] a [*illeg.*] there in [*illeg.*] of the earth"
"Saw truth and sympathy lay folded,"
1. Preceding two words inserted on a line above "womb"
2. Inserted: "in the womb," on a line above "like . . . twins"
3. Originally written as two verses, but marked by an arrow as a single verse by WW. He did not reduce "Waiting" to lowercase.
4. Deleted: "the same" ; "as" by oversight not deleted after "same" ; inserted: "less than the man" on a line above "the same as"
5. Deleted: "not less" ; inserted: "never the same," on a line above. Cf. "Song of Myself" (1855), sec. 21, ll. 425–427; "A Song for Occupations" (1855), sec. 2, ll. 33–35.
6. Cf. "Song of Myself" (1855), sec. 5, l. 87.
7. *DV, Prose* 92, II, 401, ll. 1187–1198. In lighter script. There is a remote chance that the entry may refer to a cannon called "The Peacemaker" which, on February 29, 1844, exploded on the U.S. Steamer *Princeton,* in the Brooklyn Navy Yard, killing the Secretary of the Navy and several other people.
8. Originally a question mark. Possibly the dash is a mark of deletion.

Without core[9]
Loose in the knees,[10]
Clutch fast to me, my[11] ungrown brother,
That[12] I[13] infuse you with[14] grit and jets of[15] life
I[16] am not to be denied—I compel;[17]
*It is quite indifferent to me who you are.[18]
*I have stores plenty and to spare
And of[19] whatsoever I have I[20] bestow upon you
And first I bestow of my love.[21]

[74][22] It were easy to be rich owning a dozen banks
But to be rich/
It were easy to grant offices and favors being President
But to grant largess and favor/
It were easy to be beautiful with a fine complexion and regular features
But to beautiful/
It were easy to[23] shine and attract attention in grand clothes
But to outshine ? in sixpenny muslin

[79; 75–78 *cut out*][24] One touch of a tug of me has[25] unhaltered all my[26] senses[27] but feeling

9. Deleted a one-word line: "Weakened" . The present verse was deleted from the end of the following line and brought up here.

10. Deleted: "without core?" ; inserted and deleted: "and [*not del., not printed*] [*illeg. del.*] [*ins.*] grit and" on a line above "without core" ; "and grit" written below "without core" and deleted.

11. Deleted: "my" before "my"

12. Deleted: "And" ; inserted: "That" on a line above.

13. Deleted: "will"

14. Inserted: "grit and" on a line above "jets"

15. WW deleted "new," inserted and deleted "grit" above "new" which he apparently then inserted two words back in the line (*n*14).

16. Deleted: [*illeg.*]

17. The entire line is an insertion between the preceding and following lines.

18. Deleted and inserted: "are" on a line above. This line is the last line on [73] but it is marked by the asterisk to indicate that it should be moved up. Whether it should precede or follow "*I have stores plenty and to spare" is unclear. *UPP,* II, 72 has been followed.

19. Inserted on a line above "And . . . whatsoever"

20. Deleted: "share fully with" ; inserted: "bestow upon" on a line above "share"

21. Cf. "Song of Myself" (1855), sec. 40, ll. 994–1000 and [55–56, 64].

22. Shown in LC photostat, sheet [3307]. Short lines from left separate each pair of lines.

23. Deleted: "be"

24. Shown on LC photostat, sheet [3307]. The entire page is cancelled by a vertical line. There are two stubs: [75–78]. [76] shows only a column of double zeros. On [77] are the beginnings of four widely spaced entries which may have named months: October through December. Like most of the stubs, they seem to have contained accounts. See [85].

25. Deleted: "made" ; inserted: "unhaltered" on a line above.

26. Deleted: "other"

27. Deleted: "run"

That pleases the rest so, they have [28] given up to[29] it[30] in submission
They are all emulous to swap themselves off for what it can do to them,
Every one[31] must be a[32] touch.—
Or[33] else she will abdicate and nibble only at the edges of[34] feeling.
They move caressingly up and down my body[35]
[80][36] They[37] leave themselves and[38] come with bribes[39] to whatever part of me touches.—
To[40] my lips,[41] to the palms of my hands, and whatever my hands hold.
Each brings the best she has,
For each is[42] in love with touch.[43]
[85; *81–84 cut out*][44] I do not wonder that one feeling now, does so much for me,[45]
He is[46] free of all the rest,— and[47] swiftly begets offspring of them, better than the dams.

A touch now[48] reads me a library of[49] knowledge in an instant,[50]
It smells for me the fragrance of[51] wine and lemon-blows,

28. Inserted on a line above.
29. Preceding two words inserted on line above.
30. Deleted: "for thanks"
31. Deleted: "wants to" ; inserted: "must" on a line above.
32. Deleted: "feeling" ; period and dash not deleted; inserted: "a touch" on a line above.
33. Deleted: "if that cannot be they" ; inserted: "else she" on a line above.
34. Deleted: "a touch" ; inserted: "feeling." on a line above.
35. The revisions are complex. WW apparently began: "They bring gifts to the" , deleted "the" and then recast the line, deleting "bring gifts to" and continued "come caressingly all down my body" . He then deleted "come" "all" and "down" and inserted "more" and "up and down" above.
36. Page shown on LC photostat, sheet [*3307*]. The entire page is cancelled with a vertical line. An entire line at the top of the page has been deleted: "They stand on [*del.*] my each finger [*preceding two words ins. above*] and promontory,"
37. Deleted: "have left" ; inserted: "leave" on a line above.
38. Deleted: "brought all their" ; inserted: "come with bribes" on line above.
39. Deleted: "to whatever" ; inserted on line above and deleted: "their store then[?]" ; inserted on line above: "to whatever"
40. Deleted: "Sometimes" ; "to" capitalized.
41. Deleted: "and and"
42. Deleted: "now"
43. Fragmentary line deleted: "Each would be too"
44. Shown on LC photostat, sheet [*3308*]. The entire page is cancelled with a vertical stroke. Stubs of two leaves are visible. The first, [*81*], apparently contained accounts. "Feb" "Mar[?]" "23[?]" "3" "Apr[?]" May[?] are visible. See [*77*].
45. Photostat unclear. WW apparently first wrote: "Now I do not wonder a touch does so much for me now" ; then revised to "I do not wonder [*del.*] as when feeling does so much for me" ; then revised to the present reading.
46. Deleted: "recruited from" ; inserted: "free of" on a line above.
47. Deleted: "improves" ; inserted: "swiftly" on a line above.
48. Deleted: "shows me how" ; inserted: "reads me" on a line above.
49. Deleted: "delight can be read" ; inserted: "knowledge" on a line above.
50. Following fragmentary verse deleted: "It shows me how"
51. Deleted: "roses" ; inserted: "wine and lemon-blows." on a line above.

It tastes for me ripe strawberries and melons.—
[86][52] It talks for me with a tongue of its own,
It finds an ear wherever it[53] rests or taps,
It brings[54] the rest around it,[55] and enjoy them[?] meanwhile and then they all[56] stand on a headland and mock me[57]
The[58] sentries have deserted[59] every other part of[60] me[61]
They have all come to the headland to witness and assist against me.—[62]
They have left me helpless to the torrent of touch
[87][63] I am given up by traitors,
I talk wildly I[?] am surely out of my head,[64]
I am myself the greatest traitor
I[65] went myself first to the headland/[66]

Unloose me touch[67] you are taking the breath from my throat
Unbar your gates—[68] you[69] are too much for me.—[70]

52. Shown also on LC photostat, sheet [3309]. The entire page is cancelled by a vertical stroke.

53. Deleted: "taps or" ; inserted: "rests" on a line above.

54. Deleted: "all"

55. Deleted: "and" ; inserted: "and" above; inserted above and deleted: "to" ; inserted between lines: "enjoy them[?] meanwhile and then they [*ins. above*] all stand on a headland and mock me" *UPP,* II, 73, which was made from the holograph, reads: "It brings the rest around it, and they all stand on a headland and mock me" The reading offered here is open to question, but it accounts for all the words visible on the photostat.

56. Inserted above line.

57. Deleted: "but [*illeg.*]" The two following verses deleted:
"I am all [*del.*] given up by traitors"
"A [*del.*] I am myself the greatest traitor"
Both lines were used in [87].

58. Deleted: original beginning: "All" ; inserted above line: "The sentries" . Lowercase "the" capitalized.

59. Deleted: "and take"

60. Deleted: [*illeg.*]

61. Deleted: "but [*illeg.*]"

62. This verse brought up from the bottom of the leaf on an arrow. The last seven words are on the bottom of [86]. Two verses deleted:
"I roam about drunk and stagger"
"They have left me to touch and [*del.*] gone taken [*preceding three words ins. above*] to be their place on a headland the better to witness"

63. Appears also in LC photostat, sheet [3309]. The entire page is cancelled with a vertical stroke. Between this and the preceding page appear stubs identical with those between [80] and [85]. They have not been counted in my pagination.

64. The line, which is cramped between the preceding and following, is a later insertion.

65. The line originally began with "For"

66. Although the film is indistinct, there seems to be a line across the page following this verse. The following space is in the MS.

67. Deleted: "I can stand it no longer" ; inserted above line: "you . . . throat"

68. Deleted: "can hold" . WW did not delete "I" , not printed here. Inserted and deleted: "would keep" on a line above "can hold"

69. Deleted: "no longer for if I do you will kill me" ; inserted above: "are . . . me"

70. Three succeeding verses were deleted: "Pass out of me" "Pass as you will"
"Gods! will"
The idea was reworked on [88] and [89].

[*88*][71] Fierce[72] Wrestler! do you keep your heaviest[73] grip for the last?
Will[74] you sting me most even at parting?
Will you struggle even at the threshold with[75] spasms more delicious than all before?[76]
Does[77] it make you ache so to leave me?
Do you wish to show me that even what you did before was nothing to what you can do[78]
Or have you and all the rest combined to see how much I can endure
[*89*][79] Pass as you will; take drops of my life[80] if that is what you are after
Only pass to some one else, for I can contain you no longer.
I held more than I thought
I did not think I was big enough for so much exstasy
Or that a touch could take it all out of me.[81]

[*90*][82] I am a Curse:
Sharper[83] than[84] serpent's eyes or wind[85] of the ice-fields![86]

O topple down[87] Curse! topple more heavy than death!
I am lurid with rage![88]
I invoke Revenge to assist me.—
I

[*91*][89] Let fate pursue them
I do not know any horror that is dreadful enough for them—
What is the worst whip you have

71. Shown also on LC photostat, sheet [*3310*]. The entire page is cancelled with a vertical stroke.

72. "Fierce" is written small and is probably a later insertion.

73. Deleted: "strike" ; inserted: "grip" on a line above.

74. The line originally began: "Gods! will" (see [*87*] *n*70). WW deleted "Gods!" in favor of "Wrestler!" which he deleted. He then capitalized "will"

75. Deleted: "gigantic" ; inserted on line above and deleted: "delicious"

76. Deleted: "Will you renew this and"

77. Deleted line: "[*del.*] W Even as you fade and withdraw"

78. This verse, which occupies four lines with hanging indentation, is marked on the left margin by a single large parenthesis.

79. Shown on LC photostat, sheet [*3310*]. The entire page is cancelled with a vertical stroke.

80. Deleted: "only go, or is"

81. Cf. "Song of Myself" (1855), sec. 28–29, ll. 619–643.

82. Page shown on LC microfilm, sheet [*3311*]. See related lines in *N&F,* 19, and *LG MS* Variorum.

83. "Sharper" was not originally capitalized.

84. Deleted: and

85. "d" appears to have been written over a faulty letter.

86. The spacing between this line and the next is quite wide.

87. Deleted: "like"

88. The spacing between this line and the next is quite wide.

89. Shown on LC photostat, sheet [*3311*]. At the top of the page: "A divine fa [*fate?*]; [*two preceding words del.*]"

May the g-------[90] that begat them rot
May the womb that begat

[*92*][91] I will not listen
I will not spare
They shall not[92] hide themselves in their graves
I will pursue them thither[93]
Out with them coffins—[94]
Out with them from their shrouds!
The lappets of God shall not protect them/[95]

This shall be placed in the library of the laws
And they shall be placed in the childs—doctors—songwriters

[*93*][96] Observing the summer grass[97]/

In vain[98] were nails driven through my hands,[99]
I remember[1] my crucifixion and[2] bloody coronation
The sepulchre and the white[3] linen have yielded me up[4]
I[5] remember the mockers and the buffeting insults[6]
I am[7] alive in New York and San Francisco,[8]
Again I tread the streets after two thousand years[9]

90. Originally "genitals" , then erased and long dash inserted. The erased word is quite clear.

91. Page shown on LC photostat, sheet [*3312*].

92. Inserted on a line above "shall . . . hide"

93. This word is in heavier pencil and in a cramped hand, as if in an afterthought.

94. Original reading: "Out with them from" ; "coffins" inserted. WW did not correct "them" to "their"

95. Separated from the following verse by a line drawn across the page. Cf. excluded lines from "The Sleepers" (1855), *LG CRE,* 627–628, or "Respondez" (1856), ibid., 591–594, for a similar mood.

96. Shown on LC photostat, sheet [*3313*].

97. A line across the page separates this verse from the next. Cf. "Song of Myself" (1855), sec. 1, l. 5.

98. Deleted: "the" ; inserted: "were" on a line above.

99. Deleted: "and my head my head mocked with a prickly"

1. Deleted: "I am here after" ; inserted: "I remember" on a line above.

2. Deleted. "my"

3. Deleted: "[*illeg.*] shroud"

4. This verse is at the top of the page and is moved here following WW's marginal arrow point and asterisk. It is followed in its original position by "Observing the" deleted in a sprawling hand. Apparently he then made a new start at the top of the page: "The sepulchre" . This was deleted, and he began again below and to the right, above and below the original "Observing the summer grass/"

5. Originally "the" ; inserted: "I" above.

6. The last four words are written up the right margin. The entire verse appears to be a later insertion.

7. Deleted: "just as"

8. Deleted: "after two thousand years"

9. Cf. identification with Christ in "Song of Myself" (1855), sec. 38, ll. 963–965.

[94][10] Not all the traditions can put vitality in[11] churches
They are not alive, they are cold[12] mortar and brick,
I[13] can easily build as good, and so can you.
Books[14] are not men—[15]/

In other authors of the first class there have been celebraters of ? (low life)[16] and characters—holding it up as curious observers—but here is one who enters in it with love[17]

[95][18] I follow (animals and birds,)[19]
Literature is full of perfumes[20]
(criticism on *Myself*)[21]

[96][22] The highway
The road/[23]
It seems to say sternly,[24] Do not leave me
—Loss — — is our[?]
O road I am not [*illeg.*][25]

[97][26] These are the thoughts of all men in all ages and lands—
They are not original with me—they are mine—they are yours just the same
If these thoughts are not for all they are nothing
If they do not enclose everything they are nothing
If they are not the school of all things physical, moral and mental they are nothing[27]

10. The first entry on the page is deleted: "Nothing"
11. Deleted: "[*illeg.*] built"
12. Inserted on a line above "mortar"
13. Deleted: [*illeg.*]; inserted: "can" above.
14. The verse originally began: "The books"
15. Cf. "A Song for Occupations" (1855), sec. 6, l. 147. Two deleted fragmentary continuations follow: "all the" "they but" For last line cf. "So Long!" (1860), ll. 53–54. A line drawn halfway across the page separates this passage from what follows.
16. Circled in MS.
17. Cf. 1855 Preface, *LG CRE,* 715, ll. 216–231.
18. Lower third of leaf torn out.
19. Cf. "Song of Myself" (1855), secs. 13–14, 32, ll. 234–253, 684–709.
20. This line may be either underlined or deleted. Cf. "Song of Myself" (1855) sec. 2, ll. 14ff.
21. On the basis of this line Esther Shephard, *MLQ,* 14, 66–67 *n* 13, argues for a date of 1854 for this notebook. See further discussion in headnote. A cancelled verse follows: "the torn trousers [*ins. over illeg.*] the lodge but in the woods the stillhunt" . The lower third of the leaf is torn out. Line across at right.
22. The entire page is concelled by a vertical line. Lower third cut off.
23. The two preceding entries are separated by a short line from what follows. Possibly they are titles.
24. Deleted: "Back"
25. Cf. "Song of Myself" (1855), sec. 46, ll. 1202–1219, and "Song of the Open Road" (1856).
26. The entire page is cancelled by a vertical line.
27. Cf. "Song of Myself" (1855), sec. 17, ll. 355–358.

[*98*] Test[28] of a poem/

How far it can elevate, enlarge, purify,[29] deepen, and make happy the attributes of the[30] body and soul of a man/[31]

[*99*][32] Justice[33] is not varied or tempered in the passage of[34] laws by legislatures.—[35] legislatures cannot[36] alter it any more than they can[37] love or pride or the attraction of gravity.[38] The quality of justice is in the soul.— It is immutable . . . . it remains through all times and nations and administrations . . . . it does not depend on majorities[39] and minorities . . . . Whoever violates it[40] pays the penalty just as certainly as he who violates the attraction [*100*][41] of gravity . . . . whether a nation violates it[42]. . . . or an individual, it makes no difference.

The[43] consciousness of[44] individuals is the test of justice.— What is mean or cruel for an individual is so for a nation./[45]

I am not so anxious to give you the truth. But I am very anxious to[46] have you understand that all[47] truth and power are feeble to you except your own.—[48] Can I beget a child for you?

[*101*][49] This is the common air . . . . it is for the heroes and sages . . . . it is for the workingmen and farmers . . . . it is for the wicked just the same as the righteous.

I will not have a single person left out . . . . I will have[50] the prostitute and the thief invited . . . .

I will make no difference between them and the rest.[51]/

28. Short line from left under "Test"

29. Inserted on a line above "deepen"

30. Inserted: "attributes of the" on a line above "the body . . . and"

31. This passage is followed by a line across the page. The succeeding prose has been transfered to [*104*] in accordance with WW's marginal asterisks.

32. The entire page is cancelled by two vertical lines.

33. Deleted: "does not depend upon" ; inserted: "is not . . . in" on line above.

34. Deleted: "a"

35. Deleted: "The"

36. Deleted: "settle[?]" ; inserted: "alter" above.

37. Deleted: "settle[?]"

38. Preceding five words inserted on a line above "love or pride" . Period and dash not deleted after "pride"

39. Deleted: "and" before "and"

40. Three words deleted: [*illeg.*] "shall" "full"

41. Not cancelled.

42. Preceding two words inserted on a line above "or an"

43. The original beginning of the sentence has been deleted: "The test of justice is" . "The" capitalized over lowercase.

44. Deleted: "an[?]" ; "s" added to "individual"

45. A line is drawn across the page after this paragraph.

46. Deleted: "see[?]" ; inserted: "have"

47. Inserted on a line above "that . . . truth"

48. Deleted: "You" ; inserted: "Can I beget"

49. The following two verses are cancelled with a vertical line.

50. Inserted on line above.

51. Cf. "Song of Myself" (1855), secs. 17, 19, ll. 360, 374–375. Line across the leaf.

Let every thing be as free as possible.— There is always danger in constipation.— There is never danger in no constipation.— Let the schools and hospitals for the sick and idiots and the aged be perfectly free

[*102*] No matter what stage of excellence and[52] grandeur a nation has arrived to, it shall be but the start to further excellence and grandeur.— It shall enlarge the doors.— If it once settle down, placidly, content with what is, or with the past, it begins then to decay[53]/

There are many pleasant

Man has not art enough to make the truth[54] repulsive—nor of all the beautiful things of the universe is there any more beautiful than truth.

[*103*] In the earliest times (as we call them—though doubtless the term is wrong,) every thing written at all was poetry.— To write any how[55] was a beautiful wonder.— Therefore history, laws, religion, war, were[56] all in the keeping of the poet.— He was literature.— It was nothing but poems. Though a division and subdivision of subjects has for many centuries been made since then, it still prevails very much [*104*] as in those early times, so called.— Every thing yet is made the subject of poetry—narratives, descriptions, jokes, sermons, recipes, &c &c[57]/

vast and tremendous is the scheme! It involves no less than constructing a[58] nation of nations—a[59] state whose grandeur and comprehensiveness of territory and people make the mightiest of the past almost insignificant and (back *)

*[60] the people of this state[61] instead of being ruled by the old complex laws, and the involved machinery of all governments hitherto, shall be ruled mainly by individual character and conviction.— The recognised character of the citizen shall be so pervaded by the best qualities of law and power that law and power shall be superseded from this government and transferred to the citizen.

[*105*] Could we imagine such a thing—let us suggest that before a manchild or womanchild was born it should be suggested that a human being could be

52. Deleted: [*illeg.*]
53. Line across the leaf.
54. Deleted: [*illeg.*]
55. Inserted: "any how" on a line above "was"
56. Inserted on a line above "war, all"
57. Line across the leaf.
58. Deleted: "state"
59. Deleted:"state whose integral" . Cf. 1855 Preface, l. 16, *LG CRE*, 709.
60. Transferred here from [98] according to WW's asterisks.
61. Deleted: "should[?]"

born—imagine the world in its formation—the long rolling heaving cycles—can man appear here?— Can the beautiful[62] vegetable and animal life appear here?

[*106*][63] Washington House Central st. Lowell [64]/ No 11[65] Massachusetts Corporation[*?*] Jane & Rebecca Horton[66]/ John I Storms[67] Big Creek P. O. Shelby county Tenn.

[*Inside back cover;* [68] *107–108 cut out*] Chapman 147. Atlantic st bet Henry & Clinton[69] 102 Reade st[70] Talbot[71] Wilson st. between Lee & Division av. two squares east of Bedford av.

62. Deleted: "animal"

63. All entries are separated by lines across the page. The notebook was turned sideways, so that the left edge is now the top of the page.

64. Line across right three-quarters of leaf.

65. In a circle at the left edge of this entry, WW wrote: "or 13 or 25"

66. Line across leaf.

67. Stovall, *SB,* 200, suspects that this person is identical with George I. Storms, an omnibus driver and a long-time friend, who named his son after WW. Since we do not know the date of this entry nor when WW and Storms met nor whether Storms had any connection with Tennessee, the identification is doubtful. For George I. Storms see "D. W. Wilder"

68. Since there are no ruled lines visible on the microfilm, this has been taken to be the inside back cover.

69. The notebook has been turned rightside up for this entry. Possibly the artist, Frederic Chapman, 1818–1891, who is listed as living at 147 Atlantic Ave. in the Brooklyn directories for 1854–1856.

70. The notebook has been turned sideways for this and the following entry.

71. See [*1*]*n1*.

"The Unknown Refused."

Manuscript in Virginia (Barrett). Inscribed in pencil on white wove paper, 5″ x 8½″. WW was fond of this passage from George Sand's *The Countess of Rudolstadt* (part II of *Consuelo*) and quotes and paraphrases it in his earlier known notebook ("albot Wilson"). The date is the late 1840s or early 1850s. First printed *N&F,* 62 (Pt. II, #34; *CW,* IX, 19).

"The unknown refused to explain himself. 'What could I say to you that I have not said in another (my own) language? Is it my fault that you have not understood me? You think I wished to speak to your senses, & it was my soul spoke to you. What do I say! It was the soul of the whole of humanity that spoke to you through mine'."—*George Sand. Consuelo.* Vol 5, page 264

Wooding at Night.

Manuscript in Duke (50, #38). Inscribed in black pencil on one side of three leaves of gray, thin, wove paper in which a vertical texturing and flecks of pulp (?) are faintly visible. The leaves are irregular in size and have been trimmed, but the approximate size of each is 9½" x 7¼". There are pinholes. Since the contents deal with WW's return voyage from New Orleans it is inserted here. Since the handwriting, an irregular scrawl, differs from that of "1848 New Orleans / March 18th," it was not part of the same manuscript. WW narrated his return voyage in "New Orleans in 1848," *Prose 92,* II, 604–610, but did not use any of the material in these notes. First published *FC&I,* 57–58.

wooding at night—the 20 deck hands at work briskly as bees—in going up the river the flat-boat loaded with wood was attached to the side of our steamer and taken along with us, until the wood was transferred—

Spectacle of the men lying around in groups on the forward part of the lower deck at night—some asleep some conversing—glare of the fire upon them—Some emigrants on their way "up country"—young fellow and his stout young German wife.— Gruffness of the mate to the boat hands—(*Life,* lot appearance, characteristics, pay, recklessness, premature deaths, etc etc of the western boat-hands.)

Expressions of the mate.— "Step-along,[1] bullies!" Come bullies, hop, now! hop now!"

Mixture of passengers.— A couple of those respectable[?] old gentlemen who are sent to great "Conventions.— Our two were on the [2] way to Philadelphia.—[2] At the place where we took one of them up (describe his appearance, his silver mounted cane etc,) he had about two-score hands to shake, and as many "good-byes" to utter.—

"Now, Uncle Daniel,[3] you must nominate Clay," said one.—

"Taylor, Uncle Dan" sang out another

(Had there been time, we should no doubt have had an argument; but western steamboats, like wind and tide, wait for [*no?*][4] man, on certain occasions; and this was one of them.— (Describe this old gentleman's[?] manner on the boat his kid gloves.)

1. Deleted: "my"

2. The convention referred to was the Whig convention at Philadelphia on June 7. Zachary Taylor was nominated.

3. Preceding comma and two words inserted.

4. *UPP* insertion.

The other convention man, seemed to be generally known too.— he was called "Doctor"; wore a white cravat; was deaf, tall, apparently rhumatic, and slept[?] most of the passage—except about meal

[3] Cookery of the boats bad.— raw strong coffee—too much grease—haste of the people to get to the table—would rush in and seize their chairs, ready to spring into their places the moment the bell rang.—

Long monotonous stretch of the Mississippi—Planter's dwellings surrounded with their hamlets of negro huts—groves of negro men women and children in the fields, hoeing the young cotton

Our competition, or race, with the "Grand Turk"—continued from day to day.— Deceptiveness of the steamboat officers as to time of starting, etc.— Gallantry toward the females.— Painful effect of the excessive flatness of the country.—

1848 New Orleans.

Manuscript not found; present text from *UPP,* II, 77–78, which does not describe the manuscript. The manuscript was the property of Dr. Bucke and is listed as no. 51 in *Catalogue of Important Letters, Manuscripts and Books . . . the Property of the Late Richard Maurice Bucke, to be sold . . . by Southeby & Co.,* London, 1935, but is not listed in *Manuscripts, Autograph Letters, First Editions and Portraits of Walt Whitman . . . ,* New York, 1936 (American Art Association Anderson Galleries). WW wrote about his experiences in "New Orleans in 1848" *Prose 92,* II, 604–610, 773, but the material about his difficulties with the publishers does not appear, despite his remark "(I am transcribing from my notes written at the time)." See "wooding at night" and "is rougher than it was" (Duke) (used in ibid., II, 609–610) for closely related material.

1848 New Orleans/ March 18th. We have now been publishing "the *Crescent,*" two weeks;[1] and it seems to be going ahead handsomely. My situation is rather a pleasant one. I get through at evening much earlier than I had anticipated, which I like, of course, very well. There are many peculiarities in New Orleans that I shall jot down at my leisure in these pages. It seems somewhat strange that I have not heard from home. It is now over a month, and no letter yet.

(I arrived in New Orleans, on the night of Friday Feb. 25th; and left it Saturday afternoon, May 27th, '48.)[2]

On board steamer *Griffith* Upper part of Lake Huron, Saturday morning, June 10th, 1848.

For a few weeks after I commenced my duties at New Orleans, matters went on very pleasantly. People seemed to treat me kindly, particularly H.[3] and M'C.[4] My health was most capital; I frequently thought indeed that I felt better than ever before in my life. After changing my boarding house, Jef. and I were, take it altogether, pretty comfortable. We had good beds, and though the noise was incessant, day and night, we slept well. The plan of going to dinner when we liked, and calling for what we wanted, out of a variety of dishes, was more convenient than the usual way of boarding houses.

Through some unaccountable means, however, both H. and M'C, after a

1. See Allen, 91, 94–100 for details of WW's experiences in New Orleans. The first issue of the *Daily Crescent* was on March 5.

2. It would seem that this sentence and the remainder of the narrative were written after WW's return to New York, whereas the first paragraph was written on the spot.

3. "H." is probably A. H. Hayes, one of the publishers.

4. "M'C." is probably J. E. McClure, another publisher, who employed WW in New York.

while, exhibited a singular sort of coldness, toward me, and the latter an irritability toward Jef., who had, at times, much harder work than I was willing he should do.

The arrangements of the office were in this wise: I generally went about my work about 9 o'clock, overhauling the papers rec'd by mail, and "making up the news," as it is called, both with pen and scissors. A Mr. Larue (a good writer,) generally prepared the leading editorials; Mr. Reeder, (an amiable-hearted young man, but excessively intemperate) was the "city news" man; (poor Reeder is dead, since)[5] and a young fellow named Da Poute,[6] officiated as translator of Mexican and foreign n—items; factotum in general. I had been accustomed to having frequent conferences, in my former situations with the proprietors of newspapers, on the subject of management, etc. But when the coldness above alluded to broke out, H. seemed to be studiously silent upon all these matters. My own pride was touched—and I met their conduct with equal haughtiness on my part. On Wednesday May 24th I sent down a note requesting a small sum of money. M'C returned me a bill of what money I had already drawn, and stated that they could not make "advances." I answered by reminding them of certain points which appeared to have been forgotten, making me *not* their debtor, and told them in my reply I thought it would be better to dissolve the connection. They agreed to my plan (after some objections on the part of me);[7] and I determined to leave on the succeeding Saturday.

Accordingly on Friday I packed up my traps, and[8]

5. Holloway notes that this parenthesis is added in pencil.
6. Possibly "da Ponte"
7. Holloway notes that this parenthesis is added in pencil.
8. Holloway notes that the manuscript is here torn.

"Wants."

Manuscript in Duke (24, #26). Inscribed on seven leaves of faded white wove paper, approx. 9¾" x 7½". Each leaf, for reasons not clear, has been carefully cut across in half so as to miss words. Upper and lower right corners of [*1,3,4,7*] are trimmed. [*1*] is inscribed in black ink (now faded), with corrections in black ink and pencil. The others are inscribed in green ink with corrections in green ink, black ink and black pencil. WW numbered the leaves from [2] to [7] at top center. The manuscript is obviously a piece of journalism destined for an unknown paper. *FC&I,* 23, suggests a date between 1841 and 1860, although 1862 is a possible terminal date since WW was writing for the Brooklyn *Standard* in 1861–1862 and the New York *Leader* in 1862. *FC&I* also suggests it may be part of the unlocated "Plaza Sketches" (*NYD,* 227). The curious use of black and green ink is matched only in "September 11, 12, 13—1850" and "Nehemiah Whitman." The latter was written between 1845 and 1853. Therefore a date near 1850 seems possible. The insertion of "New York" before "Fulton street," p. 5, suggests that he might have been writing for a Brooklyn audience. A Manhattanite would probably never think of Fulton Street in Brooklyn. First printed *FC&I,* 23–28.

"Wants."

Our daily papers, in New York, show that the "wants" of the human race, hereabout,[1] are by no means those few[2] which philosophers[3] have long been in the habit of recommending.— Every morning, there they appear—[4] stretched columns of them— of one general character, and stereotyped phrase—but still with a certain variety that marks the difference of nation, taste, or circumstance.—[5]

Life, to both poor and rich, in great cities, is an excitement and a struggle!— Those of our readers, in the country, who jog along[6] their solid, easy way, and are not in danger of[7] falling on[8] slippery places, know very little of the shifts and frequent[9] desperations[10] of the[11] existence of the poor in[12] cities—which go far

1. Inserted on a line above "race"
2. Deleted: quotation marks before and after word.
3. Deleted: "are" ; inserted: "have long been" on a line above "are . . . in"
4. Deleted: "long" ; inserted: "stretched" on a line above.
5. End of scrap.
6. Deleted: "in their" ; inserted: "their" on a line above.
7. Deleted: [*illeg.*]
8. Deleted: "dangerous" ; inserted: "slippery" on a line above.
9. Inserted on a line above "and . . . desperations"
10. Smeared out: "of" before "of"
11. Deleted: "life" ; inserted: "existence" on a line above.
12. Deleted: "great"

to counterbalance the supreme advantages that, (reasoners[13] may say what they like,) make the city so attractive and fascinating.

These "wants" in the news papers are illustrative of the precarious nature of employment and existence here.— The[14] merchants and prosperous[15] mechanics do not appear in their columns—[16] 2 [17] Happily, as to the latter class, in this country, work is not yet[18] so hard to get, or employers at present[19] so lordly, as to make it necessary for the carpenter or mason to run around and look to[20] intermediate agencies for a situation.—[21] And among the commercial part of the community, there is a prejudice against filling even a subordinate clerkship through the means of the "want" column, or[22] Intelligence office.—[23]

The vast majority of those who have to do with[24] the "Wants" department, are, domestic[25] servants who[26] need places and mistresses who[27] need "help".— Most of the females of the former class are Irish women and girls.— Generally,[28] when they come to the office with their little advertisements, they appear decently dressed, some indeed with quite costly attire—a large proportion having been to service, and[29] many of them left of their own accord.—[30] They are stout, square shouldered women, with the well-known Milesian features.— Not a few of them are really good looking; although, as a general thing, the best part of their countenances is[31] an expression of patience, honesty,[32] and good nature.

At the office of the[33] Irish Emigrant Society, may be seen a somewhat differ-

13. Written over smeared out "writers"

14. Deleted in black pencil: "vast majority of the"

15. Inserted in black pencil on a line above "and . . . mechanics"

16. Deleted in ink: "indeed rarely in their" ; inserted and deleted in black pencil: "rarely in their"

17. Deleted in black pencil: "lives ever enter [*illeg.*]" . Period and dash not deleted.

18. Underlining below "yet" deleted in black pencil.

19. Underlining of preceding two words deleted in black pencil.

20. Deleted in black ink: "all"

21. Deleted in black pencil: "As to" ; inserted in pencil: "And among" on a line above "As to . . . the commercial"

22. Preceding three words inserted in black ink on a line above "the . . . Intelligence"

23. End of scrap.

24. Deleted in black ink: "Intelligence offices," ; inserted in black ink: "the 'Wants' department," on a line above.

25. Inserted on a line above "servants"

26. Deleted in black ink: "want" ; inserted in black ink: "need" on a line above.

27. Deleted in black ink: "want" ; inserted in black ink: "need" on a line above.

28. Deleted in black ink: "at the Intelligence office" ; following comma not deleted; inserted in black ink: "when they come . . . advertisements," above.

29. Deleted in black pencil: "either" ; inserted in black pencil: "many of them" on a line above "either . . . left"

30. Deleted in black pencil: "or been discharged" ; comma in preceding comma-dash punctuation altered to period; succeeding period-dash not deleted.

31. Deleted in black pencil: "its" ; inserted in black pencil: "an" above.

32. Word and comma inserted in black ink on a line above "patience . . . and"

33. Deleted in black ink: "Commissioners of Emigration" ; comma not deleted not printed; deleted in black ink: "(we believe it is,) on the west side of Spruce street" ; initial parenthesis not deleted, final comma not deleted; inserted in black ink: "Irish Immigrant Society," on a line above "of Emigration"

ent class, too short of cash to pay even for a "want" advertisment;[34] seeking also domestic employment.— They are females "just from Ireland".— Hot as the day may be, any time[35] 3 from June to August, many of them will be sweltering in thick woolen cloaks or shawls; and the whole[36] crowd[37] standing shoulder to shoulder, with red faces, and much panting.— In dress, the substantial is altogether ahead of the graceful, or the seasonable.— Their feet have thick, well nailed, shoes, evidently made to last—the very extreme, against the smart patent leather, delicate soled article, which even our hardy young city[38] workingmen now usually wear in summer.— The bonnets of the women are stout Leghorn, well used by their thrifty mothers or grand-mothers, in some cases—and therefore, as may be supposed, without much pretension to style.—[39]

Although, in looking over the miscellaneous collection at the office of the[40] Irish Emigrant Society, a stupid and stultified[41] face[42] may now and then be seen, yet the general run is that of persons of fair natural capacity, although brought up under circumstances that render the traits and usages of intelligent life in the city, at first[43] altogether strange to them.—

At any rate, we never look upon one of these collections of poor creatures, without feelings of sympathy and a devout[44] hope that they may have good luck.— Born in a land, which furnishes to modern times the most appaling instance of how partial and bad government must 4 at last result in wide-spread individual ruin,—[45] portions of the men and women[46] of that land literally starving to death every year— the immense product of their naturally fertile island, monopolized in the hands of a few, and mostly sent to foreign markets, while they emaciate and die—wages at the lowest figure, and employment hard to be had at that—all the honorable places and civil and religious berths occupied by their[47] tyrants—the numerous passionate struggles they have made for relief, at last tacitly given up in despair—with a sort of horrid contentment under the despotism,[48] insult, poverty and starvation that seem to be their destined fate for ever—[49] how can one help

34. Preceding eleven words and semicolon inserted on a line above "different class . . . domestic"

35. Inserted in black ink on a line above "any"

36. Inserted in black ink on a line above "the . . . crowd"

37. Deleted in black ink: "will be"

38. Inserted on a line above the word space between "young" and "workingmen"

39. End of scrap.

40. Deleted: "Commissioners"

41. Deleted: "looking"

42. Comma deleted.

43. Preceding two words inserted on a line above "altogether"

44. Inserted in black pencil on a line above "a"

45. Deleted in black pencil: "large" ; inserted: a dash after the deleted word. One dash omitted here.

46. Deleted: "around them" ; inserted: "of that land" on a line above.

47. Deleted in black ink: "conquerors and" ; inserted and deleted in black ink: "oppressors" on a line above.

48. End of scrap.

49. Deleted in black ink: "what"

feeling[50] a deep sympathy for these poor[51] men and women, ignorant and awkward as they are?—[52]

Then, did you ever notice, the Intelligence offices, scattered about the city?— Those illustrate the "wants" advertised in the papers.— Sometimes, the low basement rooms will be crowded with Irish girls, seated around on long benches, and holding their linen handkerchiefs and fans in their hands.— Some of them are dressed in real fashion, and, when they go out, will draw on their kid gloves and hoist their 5 parasols.— Yes, a close jam of stalwart female humanity, our eyes often catch in those basements, as we pass.—[53] There they are, perpetually standing or seated in that way,[54] waiting for some master or mistress to come along and give them a "call".—[55] Probably,[56] also, many of them dress up and go to the Intelligence Office,[57] from[58] motives like those of the fashionable lady who dawdles a morning through the shops and pavement of Broadway.— To the Irish girl, out of a situation, the Intelligence Office is a place of public seeing and being seen.— She makes acquaintance with many Bridgets and Bettys; and notes are compared, and much interesting kitchen[59] news passed from[60] mouth to ear.—[61]

You will[62] notice, at these offices, hardly any Americans; probably none.— At the places we have[63] beheld in our daily walks, we[64] do not yet remember seeing[65] a single American, of either sex.— The same fact applied generally to

50. Deleted in black ink: "kindly toward" ; inserted in black ink: "a deep sympathy for" on a line above.

51. Deleted: "Irish"

52. The next paragraph originally began: "But at the usual Intelligence Offices, there is, as we have intimated," This was deleted in black pencil and the following inserted in black ink and deleted: "the 'Want' columns of the morning papers represent what may be called" The original continued and was deleted: "a somewhat higher range of people [*ins. in black pencil:* "than those at the Emigration office"] wanting employment." The original continued: "(run on) There is one office in Nassau street, toward John, which we pass often" [*all del.*]. Inserted:

"¶Then Reader [*del.*], did you ever . . . in the paper." on lines started above "street" and ended before "Sometimes"

53. Deleted: "Why are they" ; inserted: "There they are, perpetually" inserted on a line above the deletion and "standing"

54. Deleted in black ink: "?—Are the" ; inserted in black ink: comma.

55. Deleted: question mark; inserted: period.

56. Deleted in black ink: "however, [*comma not del.*] they" ; inserted in black ink: "also, many of them" inserted on a line above "they . . . dress"

57. Deleted: "much" ; inserted and deleted: "partly" on a line above.

58. Deleted: "the same motives as those of" ; inserted: "motives like those of" on a line above "the . . . motives"

59. Inserted on a line above "news"

60. Deleted: "hand"

61. Paragraph cancelled in black ink: "It is said that some of the New York Intelligence offices are made subsidiary to the basest purposes of men of licentious passions.— To the credit of humanity, we hope that, if this be a fact at all, it is the very rare exception—and we are inclined [*del.*] to [*ins. on line above*] think believe that it is only so.—"

62. Deleted in black ink: "see" ; inserted in black ink: "notice" on a line above.

63. Deleted in black ink: "notice" ; inserted in black ink: "beheld" on a line above.

64. Deleted: "ha"

65. Deleted in black ink: "an" ; inserted in black ink: "a single" on a line above.

the "want" columns.—[66] Indeed, there is something utterly repugnant, in the American character, to[67] the station of a servant.— The nearest we ever came to being in danger from[68] a fight, was, one unfortunate 6 day when we accompanied a newly arrived[69] Swiss gentleman, who had resided some time in England, to dine at one of the New York[70] Fulton street eating houses.— A good looking, democratic, young[71] American, in his shirt sleeves, was rather peremptorily accosted by our Swiss friend, as "Waiter."—

The young chap's face turned as red as fire, and he was ready for a scrimmage in a moment.—

Around the doors of the larger intelligence offices,[72] stand and lounge the lads and men who[73] wish work.— They are Irish and English, mostly.— Every[74] well dressed passer, who comes along, is examined by their[75] eyes, with an anxious, appealing sort of look.— The English have ruddy healthy faces, and their square shoulders and large arms look the right sort for labor.— We should think these chaps invaluable upon well conducted farms. They are evidently intelligent, and of a sort who would take pride in doing their work well.—

The Irish boys are ready for anything—but mostly prefer, what indeed they are at first[76] best fitted for, to wield the pick axe or the spade.— They will generally[77] make a florid description of their capacities, by no means doing injustice to themselves, and winding up with a strong appeal to your personal benevolence, and the special virtue of giving them the preference.—

7 The Englishman, on the contrary, is a man of few words, and rarely claims more than he deserves.— Nor does he press himself upon you.—

Now and then, should you be looking[78] at the scenes in one of these offices, you will see a mistress come after a servant.— Perhaps she is the keeper of a boarding house—a place, by the by[79] where the servants are apt to[80] get plenty of hard work and rough usage.— Her cold[?] eye ranges over the whole crowd [?] and[?] at once rejects all the good-looking[?][81] girls.— There is always

66. Preceding sentence inserted in black ink on a line above "sex . . . something"

67. Deleted: "being" ; inserted: "the station of" on a line above "being . . .a"

68. Preceding four words inserted on a line above "to . . . a fight"

69. Preceding two words inserted on a line above "a . . . Swiss"

70. Preceding two words inserted in black pencil on a line above "the . . . Fulton"

71. Deleted in black ink: "fellow" [*comma not del.*]; inserted: "American," on a line above "fellow" ; deleted in green ink: "with" following deleted "fellow"

72. Inserted in black ink, deleted in black pencil: "which are a sort of tangible "want" advertisement" on a line above "offices . . . lounge" . Succeeding dash not deleted.

73. Deleted: "want" ; inserted: "wish" on a line above.

74. Deleted: "one" ; inserted: "well dressed passer," on a line above the period and dash and "one"

75. End of scrap.

76. Deleted in black ink: "most" ; inserted in black ink: "best" on a line above.

77. Deleted: "give" ; inserted: "make" on a line above.

78. Deleted: "after"

79. Preceding three words inserted on a line above "place"

80. Preceding three words inserted on a line above "get"

81. End of scrap.

trouble[?] in[?] a boarding house where[82] happens[?] to[?][83] be a plump, handsome Biddy.— It is very strange.—

The good lady inquires and examines, and ponders and looks sharp.— She thinks well of this one's broad shoulders, but fears that she may be a trifle too fond of whiskey: isn't that the inference from her face?— In the mean time, the poor girls are quite in a state of excitement and emulation;—[84] until the successful competitor marches off with her new mistress[85] as proud as a peacock.—

All these girls, likely, have some friend—some cousin, aunt,[86] or one "whose mother lived near, in the old[87] country"—in whose domicile they are furnished with a shelter, while waiting to get a place.— The kindness of the Irish to each other, of which this is one specimen, puts to the[88]

82. Deleted in black pencil: "there"
83. MS torn at right bottom of first scrap and right top of the second.
84. Deleted: "and" ; inserted: "until" on a line above.
85. Preceding four words inserted on a line above "marches . . . as proud as"
86. Inserted on a line above "or"
87. Originally: "ould" ; "u" deleted.
88. Remainder missing.

Nerve.—A Frenchman.

Manuscript in LC (not in *Cat.;* gift of American Institute of Aeronautics). Inscribed in black pencil on scrap of white wove paper, 3 13/16" x 7⅞", irregular left edge, with blue rules 5/16" apart. On verso: "Whitman mss—in pencil This piece of mss. is entirely in the holograph of Walt Whitman. It was written about 1850—Whitman made other comment on the Brooklyn Military Gardens. These bits were written for Brooklyn newspapers, Times, Eagle Star etc—Alfred Goldsmith—June 17–32." No publication has been found. The writing and topic support Goldsmith's date. I am indebted to Dr. John C. Broderick, Manuscript Division, LC, for calling the manuscript to my attention and supplying data.

Nerve.— A Frenchman named ————[1] a voyager in a balloon[2] from the Military Garden in Brooklyn, rested simply on a narrow triangle with cross pieces of sticks.— On these, away up in the air and even[3] when we could only see him well by the aid of glasses, he would swing down like a monkey,[4] in that vast emptiness, holding on merely by his hands, and drawing himself up again, and turning somersets as nimbly as a cat.—

W

1. WW used a waved line.
2. Deleted: "that went"
3. Preceding two words inserted on a line above "when"
4. Deleted: "holding on"

(Of the Great Poet.)

Manuscript in Duke (20, #10). Inscribed in black pencil on three irregular leaves with trimmed corners of soft-textured brown or tan wove paper: [*1*] 9½" x 5½", [*2*] 9" x 5", [*3*] 8 15/16" x 5½". All leaves have a printed offset on verso. Bucke prints them separately, and divides [*2*] into two items. He sees a resemblance between [*1*] and "Poem of the Singers, and of the Words of the Poem" ("Song of the Answerer," ll. 73–83) (*LG* 1856, 264). Stovall (*Foreground,* 269*n*) traces [*3*] to WW's reading of H. N. Hudson's "Thoughts on Reading," *American Whig Review,* 1 (May, 1845), 483–496 (Bucke's clipping no. 439), which he clipped and annotated. The writing is certainly that of WW's early period. The thought and language clearly anticipate Preface (1855). Printed *N&F,* 68 (Pt.1, #49; *CW,* IX, 30–31), 129 (Pt. 3, #s 166, 167; *CW,* IX, 160–161), 130 (Pt.3, #171; *CW,* IX, 162).

(Of the great poet.) (Finally) For preface.

It is not that he gives his country great poems; it is that he gives his country the spirit which makes the greatest poems [1] and the greatest material for poems.—/

(He could say) [2] I know well enough the perpetual myself in my poems—but it is because the universe is in myself,—it shall all pass through me as a procession.— I say nothing of myself, which I do not equally say of all others, men and women.

—? (or) (Finally) (It is not that he gives you his country)

He [3] does not give you the usual poems and metaphysics.— He gives you [4] materials for you to form for yourself [5] poems, [6] metaphysics, [7] politics, behavior, [8] histories [9] romancés, [10] essays and every thing else.— [11]

[*2*] [12] One having attained [13] those insights and contents which the [14] universe

1. Deleted: [*illeg.*]
2. Written above "I know" . Line through or under first three letters.
3. This paragraph is entirely indented about five spaces.
4. Deleted: "the"
5. Inserted and deleted above "yourself": "the"
6. Deleted: "and"
7. Deleted: "and" before "metaphysics" ; preceding two words and commas inserted.
8. Deleted: "and" between "politics, behavior" on a line above "and histories"
9. Deleted: "and"
10. Deleted: "and"
11. Erased: "that literature can [*ins.*] embody"
12. Deleted above opening of first line: "Here" ; deleted opening of first line: "He is as"
13. Deleted: "to"
14. Deleted: "study of the"

gives to[15] men capable of comprehending it,[16] would publish the same, and persuade[17] other men and women to the same.— The conditions are simple, spiritual, physical, close at hand. . . . they are long and arduous and require faith,[18] they[19] exist altogether with the taught, and not with the teaching or teacher.—[20]/

What is wanted is not[21] inquiries and reviews and

—We want satisfiers, joiners,[22] lovers.— These[23] heated, torn, distracted ages are to be compacted and made whole.—[24]

[*3*] It is not enough of these states that they are to hold away over physical objects, over[25] armies, navies, wealth,[26] and[27] manufactures and all[28] substantial objects.—[29] They must be eminent leaders[30] of the mind and imagination.— Here must arise the great poets and orators[31] that all new centuries continually wait for.—

15. Deleted: "those" ; inserted: "men" on a line above.
16. Deleted: "is not"
17. Deleted: "all" ; inserted: "other" on a line above.
18. Preceding eight words inserted.
19. Deleted: [*illeg.*] [*illeg.*] [*illeg.*]; inserted: "exist" on a line above the last deletion.
20. A blank space occupying the space of about three lines follows.
21. Deleted: "questioning"
22. Deleted: "compaction" ; comma not deleted, not printed.
23. Written over [*illeg.*]
24. Bucke (*N&F,* 129; *CW,* VI, 161) adds: "These frothing, maddening waves are to be" which is not visible in the MS.
25. Deleted: "those"
26. Deleted: "population"
27. Deleted: "all"
28. Inserted.
29. Deleted: "They" before the "They" printed here.
30. Deleted: "and"
31. Deleted: "of the" ; inserted: "that all" on a line above.

A Schoolmaster.

Manuscript in LC (#82). Red paper-covered notebook, ruled for accounts, 5" x 3". Cover now removed and mounted as item [*832*]. White wove paper. Blue lines ¼"; apart. Margin of ¾" at bottom; vertical red lines from the left: single, ½"; double, ¾"; single, 2 7/16". The hinge is at the left. Obviously WW was using the notebook upsidedown and backward. Inscribed in black pencil with entries in black ink as noted. WW published stories as late as 1848, but the inscription on [*836 R*] suggests a date for this MS as late as 1852.

[*833R; 832 front cover* [1]] a schoolmaster (while intoxicated,)[2] was married to a woman, by certain persons to cover their own guilt./

Money (bills) taken from a person who was down (died) of the small pox, carried the contagion; and those who took it died of the dis./

horrible effects of the taking of *mercury*—the swelled tongue/

[*833V*] Introduce a character (pick-pocket—bad) who goes to California in haste, to escape detection and punishment for crime—After a short while they received a letter—or read in a newspaper—an account of his being hung/

? make the pickpocket the husband of a worthy woman who has been inveigled into marriage with him.—

[*837V; 836R* [3]*; 836V blank; 837R blank*] Introduce Jack's friends—two or three—/

An elderly woman[4] comes to the office to secure Covert's[5] services[6] in behalf of her son, who is arrested for

1. The entire cover is numbered [*832*] by LC.
2. Parentheses and enclosed words inserted on a line above.
3. [*834R* and *835R*] are newspaper clippings pasted on [*836R*]. The first relates a heroic rescue of a mother and children from a burning house in Cambridge, Mass., the second the sale of the children of a free father and slave mother in Goldsboro, N.C. The latter is endorsed "Tribune, March 1852." Esther Shephard, *Walt Whitman's Pose,* facing p. 94, reproduces [*833V–836R*].
4. Deleted: "man[?]" ; inserted: "woman" on a line above.
5. See *n* 13 below.
6. Deleted: "fo" ; before inserted : "in"

[*838V; R blank*] Martha, is the ward of Covert, inheriting property, so situated as to require the services of a limb-of-the law. (Her[7] aunt, the old Quaker lady) is dead—and Martha lives in Covert's house, in the situation of half servant—[8]

Jack, on going to Covert's house, one evening[9] recognizes the[10] portrait of the old lady—it affects him to tears

[*839R*] Make Wigglesworth[11] Some remarks about the villainy of lawyers—tell the story of Covert's father's[12] swindling, about the house in Johnson st—damn him[13]

Make Wigglesworth tell Jack a good long account of Covert and his character and villainies

(Covert[14] to effect a marriage with her—also for the sake of her property. [*839V*]—He is divided in his libidinous feelings between Martha and Miss Lehging[*?*]

[*840R*] —The main hinge of the story will be Covert's determination to embezzle Martha's property—by means of withholding deeds, wills documents, &c &c—and Jack Engle, who early discovers that intention—being pervaded by a determination[15] to foil him—

With this view, he applies himself with zeal to study law and watches with great sharpness—

[*840V*]The story of Martha[16] is that her[17] Uncle, wealthy who had adopted her a fine hearted man, (but possessed of a frightfully passionate temper,)—under the influence of this passion, commits homicide—(the victim is Jack's father)
—He is arrested the shock is too much for him—while in prison,—he[18] makes a will, [*841R*] dividing his property equally between Martha and the offspring of his victim—or the latter failing, it was all to go to Martha.—

7. Deleted: "mother" ; inserted: "aunt" on a line above.

8. Preceding fourteen words written at bottom of page and connected by a line.

9. Preceding two words inserted on a line above "recognizes."

10. Deleted: "like"

11. Jammed in at top of page and connected by a line to the entry on Wigglesworth below.

12. Inserted on a line above "swindling"

13. Professor Holloway points out in a letter that in "Nehemiah Whitman" is the entry "[*moved to*] Johnson st. May 1st 1825.— (Covert the villain." The Brooklyn directory lists a lawyer, Richard D. Covert. A Covert is also mentioned in "One Wicked Impulse" (1845). *EP&F,* 309 ff.

14. Deleted: "has licentious feelings toward Martha and wishes"

15. Deleted: "the"

16. Deleted: "shall be"

17. Deleted: "father" ; inserted above: "uncle, wealthy who had adopted her"

18. Deleted: "divides his"

The widow left Philadelphia, (where these sad events happened,) and came on to New York. In consequence of the nature of the affair, she gradually withdrew from all her relations and[19] former friends. (she was extra [*841V*] sensitive) and lived with Martha, shut out from the world and/
Introduce some scene in a religious revival meeting—[20]/
Make a character of a ranting religious exhorter—sincere, but a great fool.

Make Wigglesworth "get religion," through Calvin Peterson
[*842R*][21]Don't forget Seligny
(describe Tom Peterson fine young fellow
Smytthe/ Pepperick Ferris

[*843R*[22]*; 842V blank*] "The cup goes round,
And none so artful as to put it by."

O, earth how coulds't thou rudely push him back when he had but just crossed thy threshold?

[*843V–844V blank*]

19. Preceding two words inserted on a line above "her . . . former"
20. Remainder of this page in black ink.
21. This page in black ink.
22. This page in black ink. The two quotations have not been identified.

35 Lispenard.

Manuscript in Duke (41, #7). On verso of cover, 12½" x 6¾", twice inscribed as Jefferson Whitman's writing book (once in ink). Inscribed in pencil with the exception of "35 Lispenard." There are a number of figures, either addition or division. The total of one is $513.02, whereas it should be $613.02. The first two entries are at the top, the others at the bottom. Printed *FC&I,* 49.

35 Lispenard[1]
Carpenters risk expires Jan 13th

July 31st 1852—Mr Schofield[2] owes W.W. for eleven days work

Aug 14 Inclusive of to-day—Half a day for the week ending Aug 7th)—six days and a half—altogether 17 days

Aug 21—Made full week the past week (Schofield owes for 23 ½ days) $26.42

1. No other record has been found of Whitman's connection with housebuilding on Lispenard Street.

2. Charles E. Feinberg, "A Whitman Collector Destroys a Whitman Myth," *PBSA,* 52 (1952), 83–86 records a number of other transactions with Scofield, who, contrary to the implications of this memorandum, appears to have been employed by WW. Scofield is probably Minard S. Scofield, carpenter, Bond corner of State, as listed in the 1851–1852 Brooklyn City Directory. See the numerous receipts in LC (Feinberg).

Rules for Composition.

Manuscript in Duke (48, #43). Inscribed in black pencil on three scraps of white laid paper with blue rules ⅜″ apart; pasted down together. Scrap 1 approx. 3″ x 7¾″; scrap 2 approx. 4 13/16″ x 7¾″; scrap 3 approx. 2½″ x 7¾″. Most corners clipped, although scraps fit along upper and lower edges. The mounting is a dealer's. Since the hand is a small, regular hand like that in early drafts of *LG* 1855 and carefully written parts of the early notebook "albot Wilson," Bucke's conjectural date of the early 1850s is probably correct. Reproduced in Trent *Cat.* facing 36. First printed *N&F,* 70 (Pt. II, #58; *CW,* XI, 34–35).

Rules for Composition

A perfectly transparent plate-glassy style, artless, with no ornaments, or attempts at ornaments, for their own sake,—they[1] only[2] looking well when like the beauties of the person or character, by nature and intuition, and[3] never lugged[4] in to show off, which[5] nullifies the best of them, no matter[6] when and where.[7]

Take no illustrations whatever from the ancients or classics, nor from the mythology, nor Egypt, Greece,[8] or Rome—nor from the royal and aristocratic institutions and forms of Europe.— Make no mention or allusion to them whatever, except as they relate to the New, present things—to our country—to American character or interests.— Of specific mention of them, even for[9] these purposes, as little as possible.—[10]

Too much attempt at ornament is the clur upon nearly all literary styles.[11]

Clearness, simplicity, no twistified or foggy sentences, at all—the most translucid clearness without variation.—[12]

Common idioms and phrases—Yankeeisms and vulgarisms— cant expressions, when very pat only.—[13]

1. Inserted on a line above "only"
2. Deleted: "coming in where" ; inserted and deleted: "answering" on a line above "coming" ; inserted: "looking well when" on a line above "in . . . like"
3. Inserted on a line above "never"
4. Deleted: "in" ; inserted and deleted: "in by the colla" ; on a line above the deleted "in" and "to show" . Inserted: "in" on the line before "in . . . colla"
5. Deleted: "founders" ; inserted: "nullifies" above.
6. Deleted: "under"
7. Deleted: "or [*del.*] with [*ins. above* "with"] of the most favorable cases." Period inserted, end of scrap 1. Margins at bottom of scrap 1 and top of scrap 2 make a wide gap between paragraphs.
8. Word appears to have been circled.
9. Written over [*illeg.*]
10. Written larger than remainder of text.
11. This sentence gives the visual impression of having been written in here hastily.
12. End of scrap 2. Wide space between paragraphs because of top margin of scrap 3.
13. Paragraph deleted: "Mention not God at all"

Poem Incarnating the Mind.

Manuscript in LC (#85). A brown paper-covered notebook, leaves 5⅞" x 3¾". MS was dissassembled by LC and leaves mounted separately. No inscription on cover; present label apparently affixed later. Blue (?) horizontal lines 5/16" apart. Ruled vertically in red as for accounts: single approximately ½"; double approximately 2½"; single 3½" from left edge. Inscription in black pencil of varying density. First published by Holloway in *UPP*, II, 79–83 as "Manuscript Notebook—2."

The date is obviously prior to 1855, and the repetition between [*867V*] of this notebook and [*66*] of "albot Wilson" suggests that it is one of the earliest surviving. WW's change of third person pronouns and verb forms to first person, [*865V–866R*], also suggests an early date, although he had used first person forms in "albot Wilson." This notebook may therefore antedate "albot Wilson," and it certainly raises questions about the role of the generic "I" or Transcendental ego in WW's most egoistic poetry. See also "He is the brave boy that saved them too" (*n* 64). These lines could not have been written before January, 1854. There are many lines which found a place in *LG* 1855, but it should be noted that there are lines which were used in "Miracles" and "A Song of the Rolling Earth" in 1856. One passage which finally was used in "Miracles" is combined with one which was used in the 1855 Preface [*864 R&V*].

The MS text has been rearranged here as noted to follow order of inscription.

I am much indebted to Professor Joseph E. Geist, of Central Methodist College, for valuable assistance with the notes.

[*857R*] Poem incarnating the mind of an old man, whose life has been magnificently developed—the wildest and most exuberant joy—the utterance of hope and floods of anticipation—faith in whatever happens—but all enfolded in Joy Joy Joy, which underlies and overtops the whole effusion[1]/

Why are you cautious[2] of the ? and[3] of your eyes? I guess it is because they incarnate to me the

[*857V*] Crossing the Fulton ferry[4] to-day,[5] I met an old acquaintance,[6] whom I had missed from the city these three years.— He told me his experience that

1. Cf. "A Song of Joys" (1860), ll. 86–88 and "[*illeg.*] Dick Hunt" [*183*]. Line across leaf.
2. Deleted: "and"
3. Inserted on a line above the word space between "the . . . of"
4. Between Brooklyn and Manhattan.
5. Preceding five words inserted on a line below the first line, "Crossing . . . to-day,"
6. Deleted: "to-day"

time.— He had been[7] at Albany and Washington employed as reporter and lobbyer.—[8] He corresponded with newspapers and received pay.—[9] When dull legislators made dull speeches, he licked them into sleekness, and so had synopses of them put in print, and received pay.— He took hold of some scheme or claim[10] upon the legislature, and lobbied for it;—he helped men who were office seeking; he put *[*859R*]*[11] greenhorns through their noviciate; he manufactured public opinion at a distance, and so forth, and so forth. For all these he duly received pay.—/

[*858R*] with merchants[12] and factors the point of honor is to pay notes punctually,—to pay off the men every Saturday night,—to[13] permit no demands which they cannot satisfy at an appointed day.—/

Concerned in the make of a grand steam ship[14] we cannot sleep nights for thinking on the pennant halyards,[15] and the gaskets, but[16] feel no speck of anxiety about the style and strength of the engines.—

[*859V; 858V; 859R*[17]] But the spirits, effusing mind, character

No man and no woman can[18] gash or starve or overburden[19] or imbibe[20] rotten stuff in[21] that superior nature of his or her's, any[22] more than one can poison or starve his body.—[23]

[*860R*] story of Julia Scudder whose husband left her.[24]/

7. Deleted: "reporting and lobbying" on a line above "Washington . . . corresponded"

8. Preceding five words inserted. Period and dash after "Washington" not deleted.

9. Deleted: "He"

10. Deleted: "before" ; inserted: "upon" on a line above.

11. First entry on [*859R*] inserted here following WW's asterisks.

12. Deleted: "and tradesmen" ; inserted: "and factors" on a line above.

13. Deleted: "have" ; inserted and deleted: "receive" above; inserted: "permit" following "receive"

14. Entry originally began: "We cannot sleep" ; inserted above and deleted: "We are" before "Concerned" ; inserted: "Concerned in the make of [*del.*] the [*ins.*] a grand steam ship" Last three words crammed into two lines at right over an erasure. Line across leaf above entry.

15. Deleted: "of the steamer" ; inserted: "and the [*del.*] little gaskets," on a line above.

16. Deleted: "we"

17. [*859R*] has been placed elsewhere in the text to follow the order of inscription. [*858V*] and the second entry, in verse, on [*859R*] are in a darker and more irregular inscription and appear to have been used to continue [*865V*] ff. All of [*859V*] is cancelled by a diagonal slash.

18. Deleted: "[*illeg.*] bruise" ; inserted on a line above "bruise" : "gash"

19. Deleted: "or pollute"

20. Deleted: "bad" ; inserted: "rotten" on a line above.

21. Deleted: "the" ; inserted on a line above "the . . . her's" : "that superior nature of"

22. Written over: "and"

23. Cf. "I Sing the Body Electric" (1855), sec. 1, l. 5; sec. 8, l. 127. Line deleted: "What minutes of damnation" Following line inserted at end of verse sequence [*859R*] in accordance with WW's instruction on that page.

24. WW had a remote cousin Julia Scudder, the daughter of his paternal grandmother's sister and sister of Tredwell Scudder. Nothing is known of her marriage. See "Hannah Brush" and "Oct. 17, 1860." The entry is in a darker hand than that of the other prose as if written in haste. Line across the leaf below.

It is not the faculty of sight better than the ? of the eye? Is not the human voice more than the rings of the windpipe?[25]

No man[26] means to[27] deform or sicken the body. For[28] that wonderful and beautiful vessel, we[29] make[30]

[*860V*] *Lotos*—the water lily of the Nile honey-lotus—honey-clover

Amelioration is the blood that runs through the body of the universe.—[31] I do not lag—I do not hasten—[32] I bide my[33] hour over billions of billions[34] of years—I exist in the[35] void that[36] takes uncounted[37] time and coheres to a nebula?,[38] and in further[39] time cohering[40] to an orb,[41] marches,[42] gladly round, a beautiful[43] tangible creature, in her[44] place in the[45] processions of God,[46] where new comers have been falling in the ranks for[47] [*861R*] ever, and[48] will be so always—I could be balked no how, not if all[49] worlds and living beings[50] were[51] this minute reduced back into the[52] impalpable film of chaos—I should surely bring up again where we now stand, and go[53] as much further and[54] thence on

25. "rings . . . windpipe" inserted in a small hand above the following entry.
26. Deleted: "and no woman will"
27. Deleted: "stab
28. Deleted: "Of" ; inserted: "For" above.
29. Deleted: "are pro"
30. The remainder of the page is blank.
31. Deleted: "I grow"
32. Cf. "A Song of the Rolling Earth" (1856), sec. 1, ll. 17–18. Inserted and deleted: "—it appears to say—" on a line above "hasten . . . hide" . Dashes not deleted.
33. Deleted: "time" ; inserted above and deleted: "day" ; inserted: "hour" after "day"
34. Preceding two words inserted. Note WW's use of higher number here and later [*861R*, *864V*]. Cf. "albot Wilson" [*8*].
35. Deleted: "formless"
36. Deleted: "through" ; inserted and deleted: "asks for" on a line above; inserted "takes" after "asks for"
37. Deleted: "ages forms" ; inserted: "time and coheres to" on a line above.
38. The question mark is above "Nebula"
39. Deleted: "ages" ; inserted: "time" on a line above.
40. Written over "es" in "coheres" : "ing"
41. Cf. "Song of Myself" (1855), sec. 44, l. 1164. Deleted: "and"
42. Deleted: "like" ; inserted: "gladly round" on a line above.
43. Inserted on a line above "a . . . tangible"
44. Written over "its"
45. Deleted: "new"
46. Deleted: "whither the troops are hastening for" ; inserted on a line above: "where new accessions have been" ; deleted: "accessions" ; inserted: "comers" above "accessions"
47. Entire preceding entry cancelled by an "X."
48. Deleted: "now"
49. Deleted: "the"
50. Deleted: "in"
51. Deleted: "turned" ; inserted on a line above "were turned" : "this [*del.*] hour [*ins.*] "minute" [*on a line above* "hour"] reduced"
52. Deleted: "fog" ; inserted: "impalpable film" on a line above.
53. Deleted: "on"
54. Deleted: "still" ; inserted: "thence" on a line above.

and on—[55] my right hand is time, and my left hand is space—both are ample—a few[56] quintillions of cycles, a few sextillions of cubic leagues, are not of[57] importance to me—[58] what I[59] shall attain to I[60] can never tell, for there is something that [*861V*][61] underlies[62] me, of whom I am[63] a part and instrument.—[64]

such is the

Tongue of a million voices,[65] tell us[66] more.[67] Come,[68] we listen, we listen with[69] itchings of desire,[70] to hear your tale of the soul.—

Throb[71] and wait, and lay our[72] ears to the wall[73] as we may, we throb [*862 R*] and wait for the god[74] in vain.— I am vast—he seems to console us with[75] a whispering undertone in lack of an answer—and my work[76] is wherever the universe is—but[77] the Soul of man! the Soul of Man!—[78]

[*863R; 862 V blank*][79] Of all the plenty[80] there is, no plenty is comparable to the plenty of time and space.— Of these there is ample store,— there is no limit

55. Deleted: "I think a few so"
56. Written over [*illeg.*]
57. Inserted on a line above "of" and deleted: "special"
58. Deleted: "I"
59. Deleted: "attain"
60. Deleted: "do not know" ; inserted: "can never tell" on a line above.
61. First entry cancelled with "X"
62. Deleted: "and overtakes"
63. Deleted: "an effusion" ; inserted and deleted: "an[?] attribute" on a line above "effusion" ; inserted: "a part" before "an attribute"
64. Cf. "Song of Myself" (1855), sec. 45, ll. 1190–1195. From "Amelioration is the blood" [*860V*] to this point has been cancelled, probably because it was used in "Song of Myself."
65. Opening deleted: "And will you" ; inserted: "Tongue of a million voices," on a line above [*del.*] "And will"
66. Deleted "no"
67. Deleted: "of" "tongue of a million voices" Question mark and dash not deleted, not printed.
68. Deleted: "we listen O mouth of mystery"
69. Deleted: "desiring stretched pangs" ; inserted: "itchings" on a line above "pangs"
70. Deleted: "for" ; inserted: "to hear" on a line above.
71. Opening deleted: "We" ; "Throb" capitalized.
72. Deleted: "your" ; inserted: "our" on a line above.
73. Deleted: [*illeg.*]
74. Preceding three words inserted on a line above "wait . . . in vain.—"
75. Deleted: "instead" ; succeeding five words inserted on a line above "with . . . of an answer—"
76. Deleted: "s" from "works" "are what" ; inserted: "is wherever" on a line above.
77. Deleted: "we are only the morning wakers to the soul of man"
78. Deleted with two diagonal slashes: "To that, we do the office of the servants who wake their master at the dawn." Originally: ". . . servant . . . wakes his . . ."
79. Entire page deleted with an "X" Lower two thirds of leaf blank.
80. Deleted: "in nature"

[*863V*][81]All truths lie[82] waiting in all things.— They neither urge the opening of themselves nor resist it.—[83]

For their birth you need not the obstetric or forceps[84] of the surgeon.[85] They[86] unfold to you and emit themselves,[87] more fragrant than roses from[88] living buds,[89] whenever you fetch[90] the[91] spring sunshine[92] moistened with summer rain.— But it must be in yourself.— It shall come [*864R*] from your soul.— It shall be love.— / [*863V*][93] (The heart of man alone is the one unbalanced and restless thing in the world)

[*864R*][94] We hear of miracles.— But what is there that is not a miracle?[95] What[96] may you conceive of or[97] name to me in the future, that[98] shall be beyond the least thing around us?—I am looking in your eyes,—tell me[99] then, if you can, what is[1] there in the immortality of the soul more[2] than this[3] spiritual and beautiful miracle of sight?—[4] By the equally subtle one of[5] Volition,[6] I open[7] two pairs of lids, only as big as[8] peach pits[9], when lo! the unnamable variety and

81. Entire page cancelled with a diagonal slash. Cf. "Song of Myself" (1855), sec. 30, ll. 648–650.

82. Deleted: "hidde"

83. Deleted beginning of next paragraph: "And the"

84. Written over "or[?]"

85. Cf. "Song of Myself" (1855), sec. 30, l. 650. Deleted: "Approach them with love"

86. "y" written over an illegible letter; inserted and deleted: [*illeg.*] above "unfold"

87. Inserted: "selves" on a line above the word space between "them . . . more"

88. Deleted: "there" ; inserted: "living" above.

89. Deleted: "if" ; inserted: "whenever" on a line above "if . . . you"

90. Deleted: "in yourself"

91. Final "e" written over [*illeg.*]

92. Deleted: "and" ; inserted: "moistened with" on a line above "and . . . summer"

93. Parenthetical sentence placed here following WW's markings, which are not entirely clear but accepted by Holloway. Cancelled as is rest of page. Line across leaf below.

94. Entire page cancelled with an "X"

95. Cf. "Miracles" (1856), ll. 1–2. Deleted successively: "What" "Of" ; present "What" capitalized.

96. Deleted: "can" ; inserted: "may" above.

97. Deleted: "propound" ; inserted: "name" above.

98. Deleted: "were a greater miracle than [*illeg.*] any" ; inserted: "stranger and subtler shall be beyond [*ins. under* "shall"] all or the least" on lines above; deleted: "stranger and subtler" "all or"

99. Deleted: "O"

1. Inserted between lines: "there . . . soul"

2. Deleted: "incomprehensible"

3. Deleted: "curious" ; inserted: "spiritual" above.

4. Cf. "Who Learns My Lesson Complete?" (1855), ll. 18–19.

5. Preceding six words inserted on a line above "—Volition . . . is an" which was deleted before "open"

6. Deleted: "is an"

7. Deleted: "to almond sized" ; inserted: "two pairs of" above.

8. Deleted: "a"

9. Final "s" added.

whelming splendor*[*864V*]*[10] of the whole world[11] come to me[12] with silence and with swiftness.— In an instant make I fluid and draw to myself,[13] keeping each to its distinct isolation, and no hubbub or confusion, or jam, the whole of physical nature, though rocks are dense and hills are ponderous, and the stars are[14] away off sextillions of miles.[15]— All the years of all the beings that have ever[16] lived on the earth,*[*867V*][17] with all the science and genius,[18] were nobly occupied in[19] the employment of investigating this[20] single[21] minute of my life

[*864V*] We know that sympathy or love is the law[22] over all laws, because nothing else but love[23] is the soul conscious of pure happiness, which[24] appears to be the ultimate resting place[25] and point of all things.—/

[*865R*] If the light of a half day dawn were arrested, and held so for a thousand years[26]

The thin swift passing clouds like lace, blown overhead during a storm are called the *flying scud*[27]/

Let[28] us suppose[29] that all the most rational people of the world had gone no further than children of twelve years old—or, as this seems forced, suppose the utmost advance yet made was the advance of the Camanches and kindred peoples [*illeg.*][30]

10. On lower half of the page. The asterisks are WW's. The entire leaf is cancelled with an "X"

11. Deleted: "to"

12. Deleted: "I make then" ; inserted: "with silence . . . instant"

13. Deleted: "however dense," ; inserted: "keeping each to its distinct isolation, and no hubbub or jam [*del.; redundant* "or" *not del., not printed*] confusion or jam,"

14. Deleted: "far" ; inserted: "away" on a line above.

15. Cf. 1855 Preface, 714, ll. 168–175.

16. Deleted: "life"

17. Passage inserted here following WW's asterisks. Line across leaf below.

18. Deleted: "for implements, were"

19. Deleted: "single" ; inserted: "the" on a line above.

20. Deleted: "one"

21. Deleted: "abstract one minute" ; inserted: "minute" on a line above.

22. Deleted: "of" ; inserted: "over"

23. Deleted: "does" ; inserted: "is" on a line above.

24. Deleted: "is" ; inserted: "appears to be" on a line above.

25. Deleted: "of"

26. In very small script. Following verse passage transferred to [*865V*] according to WW's instructions: "And chalked on a board . . ."

27. Also in very small script. Line across leaf below.

28. Originally preceded by "If"

29. Deleted: "for fo"

30. Also in very small script.

[*865V*][31] The Poet
All the[32] large hearts of heroes,
All the courage of olden time and new[33]
How[34] spied the captain and sailors[35] the great wreck with its drifting hundreds,[36]
How they waited,[37] their craft shooting[38] like an arrow up and down[39] the storm.
How they[40] gripped close with Death there[41] on the sea, and gave him not one inch, but[42] held on day and night[43]* (overleaf)[44]
[*865R*][45]And[46] chalked on a[47] board, *Be of good cheer, we will not desert you,* and held it up[48] and did it;
[*865V*] How the lank[49] white faced women looked[50] when ferried[51] safely at last as from the sides[52] their[53] prepared graves
How the children, and the lifted[54] sick, and the sharp-lipped, unshaved men;

31. Entire page cancelled with an "X" . The following sequence of verse lines has been rearranged in what appears to be the order of inscription, following WW's directions and the sequence of the received text. Cf. "Song of Myself"(1855), sec. 33, ll. 822–843. As in other notebooks WW here used pages at random. The verse entries were either made with a softer pencil than the others, or, more likely, WW was exerting more pressure in his excitement.

32. Deleted: "greatness and bea" ; inserted: "large hearts of heroes" on a line above.

33. The following verses are based on the wreck of the streamer *San Francisco* and the rescue of the passengers by Capt. Creighton of the *Three Bells of Glasgow* between December 24, 1853 and January 4, 1854, which attracted wide attention. There was even a Currier and Ives print of the subject. See Harry T. Peters, *Currier and Ives* (Garden City, 1942), plate 20. WW collected six clippings from the N.Y. *Tribune* (Trent *Cat.*, 69). On two of them, is bracketed the passage paraphrased in the poem. See "The regular old followers" and "I know a rich capitalist."

34. Original beginning deleted: "What" ; inserted: "How spied" between lines.

35. Before the insertion just noted the line continued: "did where they" WW, however, deleted these three words and began a *new* verse by inserting: "How they waited, their craft" between lines.

36. Inserted between lines: "the [*illeg. del.*] [*ins. above*] great wreck with its [*del.*] helpless drifting hundreds,"

37. See *n* 35, above.

38. Deleted: "madly" ; inserted: "like an arrow" on a line above.

39. Deleted: "in"

40. Two preceding words inserted on a line above "How" in a lighter hand.

41. Inserted on a line above.

42. The preceding seventeen words of this verse were inserted between lines.

43. This verse is a revision, apparently in several steps, of the following, above which it was written: "And in that deadly sea waited for days and nights near the helpless ragged [*ins.*] great [*ins.*] wreck" ; "days and nights" was altered to the singular and left as the conclusion of the new line. "And" was not deleted, apparently through oversight.

44. In left margin.

45. Deleted: "Th[?]" . Verse cancelled with an"X"

46. Deleted: "wrote"

47. Deleted: "great"

48. Deleted: "as they to against the"

49. Inserted on a line above.

50. Deleted: "as they" ; inserted: "when"

51. Deleted: "them"

52. Preceding two words inserted above.

53. Deleted: "waiting" ; inserted on line above: "prepared"

54. Inserted above.

All this[55] I[56] swallow in[57] my soul, and it becomes[58] mine, and[59] I likes it well,
I am[60] the man;[61] I suffered,[62] I was[63] there:[64]
All the beautiful disdain and calmness of martyrs
[866R][65] The old woman that was chained and burnt[66] with dry wood, and her children looking on,[67]
The great queens that walked serenely to the block,[68]
The hunted[69] slave[70] who flags in the race at last, and[71] leans up by the fence,[72] blowing and covered with sweat,[73]
And[74] the twinges that sting like needles his breast and neck
The murderous buck-shot[75] and the bullets.
All this[76] I not only[77] feel and see[78] but am.[79]
I am[80] the hunted slave
Damnation and despair are close upon me[81]
I clutch[82] the rail of the fence. *(back

55. Deleted: "he" ; inserted: "I"
56. Deleted: "drinks" ; inserted above: "swallows" ; final "s" of "swallows" deleted.
57. Deleted: "his" ; inserted above: "my"
58. Deleted: "his" ; inserted above: "mine"
59. Deleted: "he" ; inserted above: "I" WW forgot to correct following MS "likes" to "like"
60. Deleted: "He is" ; inserted above: "I am"
61. Deleted: "[*illeg.*] he" ; inserted above: "I"
62. Deleted: "he" ; inserted: "I"
63. Deleted: "And more:" ; inserted: "there" . "And more" may have been the beginning of a new verse.
64. Verse inserted between lines and deleted: "He is the brave boy that saved them too"
65. Page cancelled with an "X"
66. Three preceding words written over an erasure.
67. Cf. also "Pictures."
68. Cf. "Pictures."
69. Inserted.
70. Deleted: "that stood could run no longer" ; inserted: "who flags in the race at last"
71. Deleted: "then stood by" ; inserted: "leans [*del.*] leaned up by"
72. Deleted: "panting" ; inserted to left: "blowing"
73. Deleted verses:
"And his eye [*del.*] shoot [*ins.*] that [*ins.*] burns defiance and desperation hatred
And the buck shotwere"
Comma after "shot" not deleted, not printed.
74. Deleted: "the how"
75. Deleted: "planted like terrible" ; inserted: "and the bullets."
76. Deleted: initial "This" ; inserted: "All" . Present "this" written over [*illeg.*]. Deleted: "he" ; inserted: "I"
77. Inserted: "feels and" ; terminal "s" deleted from "feels" . Evidently the change in pronouns was a late revision.
78. Terminal "s" deleted from "sees" . WW inserted "and feels" at this point and only partly deleted it after inserting it earlier in the line.
79. The word is written above the line between "see" and "but" . The page is very cluttered at this point; "is" which might be expected as a deletion, is not to be found.
80. Deleted: initial "He is" ; inserted: "I am
81. Line inserted in very small script. Deleted: "him" ; inserted: "me"
82. Deleted: initial "He" ; inserted: "I" ; terminal "es" deleted from "clutches"

[*858V*][83] My gore[84] presently[85] trickles[86] thinned with[87] ooze of my skin[88] as I[89] fall[90] on the reddened[91] grass and stones,
And the hunters haul up close with their unwilling horses,
Till[92] taunt and[93] oath swim away from my[94] dim[95] dizzy[96] ears[97]
What the rebel,[98] felt gaily adjusting his neck to the rope noose,[99]
What the[1] savage, lashed to the stump,[2] spirting yells and laughter[3] at every foe[4]
What rage of hell[5] urged [*859R*][6] the lips and[7] hands of the[8] victors.
How fared[9] the young captain[10] pale and flat on his own[11] bloody deck

83. Entire page cancelled with an "X"

84. Deleted: initial "His blood" ; inserted above: "My gore"

85. Deleted: [*illeg.*]; inserted: "trickles" on a line above.

86. Inserted and deleted: "[*illeg.*] some of" on a line above "trickles" , then, [*illeg.*] following "trickles" Four illegible words, one inserted above the third also deleted.

87. Deleted: "the plentiful sweat," ; inserted: "[*del.*] salt ooze of my skin" on a line beginning above [*del.*] "sweat"

88. MS almost indecipherable. Deleted: "see how it" "and trickles down the black skin" ; inserted: "as" ; deleted: "See how it" was brought into the second fragment after "and" by a caret before deletion.

89. Deleted: initial "He slowly" ; inserted at beginning: "I" ; then "fall . . ." is continued on the same line following the deleted "He slowly"

90. Final "s" deleted.

91. Inserted on a line above "the . . . grass"

92. Original opening deleted: "And the" ; inserted: "Till" on a line above.

93. Deleted: "curse dark" ; inserted: "oath swim" on a line above.

94. Preceding three words inserted on a line above beginning in the left margin and ending after "from"

95. Deleted: "and"

96. Deleted: "in his" ; inserted and deleted: "away from my" on a line above. To sum up in part, WW's first intention seems to have been: "taunt and curse dark dim and dizzy in his ears" . When he changed from third to first person, after trying "away from my" before "ears" he moved it to precede "dim dizzy"

97. Cf. *Pictures*. Deleted verse: "What Lucifer [*del*] felt, [*ins.*] cursed [*ins.*] when [*on a line above*] tumbling from Heaven" WW marked this to be transposed to follow the next verse ("What the rebel . . ."), deleted the asterisk before "rope noose" in that verse, but forgot to delete "tr*" above "What Lucifer . . ." Cf. omitted passage from 1855 "The Sleepers," "Now Lucifer was not dead . . . ," and notes thereon, *LG CRE,* 627–628. Cf. "Song of Myself" (1855), sec. 33, ll. 834–843.

98. Deleted: "When he" ; inserted above: "felt"

99. Cf. "Song of Myself" (sec. 33), *LG* (1855), 42: "What the rebel said gaily adjusting his throat to the rope-noose," Line dropped in *LG* (1867). The word "noose," written over [*illeg*].

1. Deleted: "red" ; inserted and deleted: "brown" on a line above.

2. Deleted: "but yelling still" ; inserted and deleted: "launching" on a line above; inserted: "launching" before the deleted: "spirting" ; "yells and" added before "laughter" . As so often, these emendations represent more pains by WW than any description can suggest.

3. Deleted: "to"

4. "Song of Myself" (sec. 33), *LG* (1855), 42: "what the savage at the stump, his eye-sockets empty, his mouth spirting whoops and defiance," Line dropped in *LG* (1867)

5. Deleted: "of" "spirted" ; inserted below: [*del.*] "is urged"

6. Text cancelled with with an "X" through "(overleaf" Deleted "from" before "lips"

7. Deleted: "fingers" following "and" ; inserted: "hands" following the deletion.

8. Deleted: "vict captors"

9. Preceding inserted on a line above "The young" . Capital on "The" not corrected.

10. Deleted: "that lay dying" ; inserted: "pale and [*del.*] ebbing" "[*illeg. ins. and del.*]" [*ins. and del.*] "pale" ; inserted: "flat" on a line above "on"

11. Inserted on a line above the word space between "his . . . bloody"

The pangs of defeat[12] sharper than[13] the green edged wounds of his side
What choked the throat of the general when he surrendered[14] his army (over leaf[15]
What heightless dread falls[16] in the click of a moment

[*866V*][17] All around me I hear how great is Adam or Eve—how[18] significant the illustrious Greeks, or later Italians and Germans, and modern[19] celebrities of England and France.— Yes Christ was[20] large and[21] Homer was great;[22] and so Columbus and Washington and Fulton. But greatness is the other word for developement,[23] and in my soul[24] I know that I am[25] large and strong as any of them, probably[26] larger.

Because all that they did I feel that I too could do, and more[27] and that multiplied; and after none of them or their achievements [*867R*] does[28] my stomach say enough and[29] satisfied[*?*][30] Except[*?*][31] Christ; he alone[32] brings the perfumed bread,[33] ever vivifying and clean, to me,—ever fresh and plenty every welcome and to[34] spare.—

Not even God[35] is so great to me as Myself[36] is great to me.—[37] Who knows but I too shall in time be a God as pure and prodigious as any of them.—[38]

12. Deleted: "more" ; inserted: "sharper" on a line above.
13. Deleted: "death to his hearts breast" ; inserted: "the green edged wounds [*del.*] of of his side" on a line above.
14. Deleted: "with all"
15. Passage apparently continues on [*859R*]. Deleted line: "What minutes of damnation"
16. Inserted.
17. Cf. "albot Wilson" [*6*].
18. Deleted: "illustrious are" ; inserted: "significant" on a line above "illustrious"
19. Deleted: "En–"
20. Deleted: "Great [*written over illeg.*]" ; inserted: "large" on a line above.
21. Deleted: "so was"
22. Preceding two words inserted on a line above "and"
23. Deleted: "to me" . Cf. "Song of Myself" (1855), sec. 21, l. 430.
24. Preceding twelve words inserted between lines.
25. Deleted: "great" ; inserted: "large and strong" on a line above "great"
26. Deleted: "greater" ; inserted: "larger" on a line above "greater"
27. Deleted: ", and" ; inserted: "and that multiplied; and [*del.*] when [*ins.*] after" on a line above "and"
28. Written over "is"
29. Deleted: "fully" ; preceding three words inserted on a line above "fully"
30. Upper right hand corner of leaf missing. Deleted: "fully satisfies me" . Period and dash not deleted.
31. Upper right hand corner of leaf missing.
32. Deleted: "is the" ; inserted on a line above "is" : "brings the"
33. Deleted: "fol" ; inserted above and deleted: "up to" ; deleted: "my soul" ; inserted: "ever . . . me,—" above "ever fresh"
34. Deleted: "sufficient" ; inserted: "to spare on a line above "sufficient"
35. Deleted: "that dread ?"
36. Uppercase "M" written over lowercase.
37. Cf. "Song of Myself" (1855), sec. 48, l. 1271.
38. Sentence beginning with "Who knows . . ." inserted between lines.

Now[39] I[40] stand here, a personality in the Universe,[41] a personality perfect and sound;[42] all things and all other beings as an audience at the play-house[43] perpetually and perpetually calling me out from[44] behind[45] curtain.—[46]

[*867V*] shall we sky-lark with God

The poet seems to say to the rest of the world
Come, God and I are now here
What will you have of us.[47]/

[*868R*] *Blacksmithing*
when they have a *great heat* in the fire.—
Five or six blacksmiths swing their sledges[48] *over*hand *over*hand *overhand.*—[49]

It would be as though some publisher should reject the best[50] poems ever written in the world because he who brings them to be printed has a[51] shabby umbrella, or mud on the shank of his boot.

[*868V*] The creek on Long Island when the boating party were returning and capsized, and the young man saved his sweetheart and lost his sister/

One[52] grand faculty[53] we want,—and that is the power to pierce[54] fine clothing and thick coated[55] shams, and settle for sure what the reality of the thing clothed and disguised is, and what it weighs stark naked; the power of[56] slipping like an eel[57] through all blandishments and graspings[58]

[*869R, inside back cover*] of convention: the power

39. Inserted on a line above "stand"
40. Deleted: "an existence"
41. Inserted and deleted: "isolated" ; inserted: "a personality"
42. Cf. "Song of Myself" (1855), sec. 44, l. 1168. Deleted: "is isolated" "all" ; inserted: "to"
43. Preceding six words inserted on a line above.
44. Deleted: "my recesses"
45. Deleted: "the" ; inserted: "my" on a line above.
46. The entire paragraph cancelled with an "X" The last twenty-two words may have been previously cancelled with two long question marks written on the text.
47. Cf. "albot Wilson" [*66*]. Third entry below rule transferred to follow [*864R*] following WW's asterisks. Remainder of page on [*864V*] following WW's asterisk.
48 Deleted: "in"
49. Cf. "Song of Myself" (1855), p. 20; sec. 12, ll. 219–224.
50. Deleted: "and"
51. Deleted: "worn"
52. Original first word deleted: "I"
53. Deleted: [*illeg.*]
54. Deleted: "all" ; inserted: "fine" on a line above.
55. Preceding two words inserted on a line above "shams,"
56. Deleted: "eluding and"
57. Deleted: "from" ; inserted on a line above "through all" : "through"
58. Deleted: asterisk and [*illeg.*]

The Regular Old Followers.

Manuscript in LC (#83, sheets 845–855). Brown paper covers. On front (actually back, see below), white label in another hand: "Notebook Walt Whitman." Inscribed in black pencil and ink on white pages ruled for accounts, 5⅞" x 3¹¹/₁₆". Blue lines ⅛" apart. Vertical red rules: single, ⁵/₁₆" from left edge; double, 2¹¹/₁₆" from left, single, 3³/₁₆" from left. The vertical red rules on the pages with literary entries read in the reverse of that above—that is, the reverse of the customary ruling for account books. It is probable that they were made starting from the back with the notebook turned upsidedown. Leaf [*855V*], specifications of a building, is thus entered in the normal manner and may well have been entered first. The references to the *San Francisco* disaster (*850V ff.*) could not have been made before January, 1854, and other entries as noted were used in poems of 1855. The date is probably between late 1853 and 1855. I am indebted to Professor Joseph E. Geist, of Central Methodist College, for valuable contributions to the notes.

[*846R; inside back cover blank*] The regular old followers of the law and traditions as plainly first expounded among the Mahometans are called Loonees[1]/

[*846V*] [*illeg.*] wonders[1a]

[*847R*] What is it to own any thing?—[2] It is to incorporate it into yourself, as the primal god swallowed the five[3] immortal offspring of Rhea,[4] and accumulated[5] to his life and[6] knowledge and strength all that would have grown in them.—[7]

1. Short line from left below.

1a. A caret precedes [*illeg.*] and another is written through "wonders"

2. The nature of property and ownership deeply concerned WW prior to 1855. Although none of these passages appear directly in the poetry, there is an inner relationship with "A Song for Occupations" and "Crossing Brooklyn Ferry." For other comments see "albot Wilson," "I know a rich capitalist," "such a thing as ownership," "memorials," "human feet, awaits us," "I tell you greedy smoucher!", "Do you know what music does," "The only way in which anything can be owned," "The money value of real and personal estate," "The noble soul." See also "Sun-Down Papers," #'s 7, 9, "Motley's Your Only Wear," "Morbid Appetite for Money," *UPP,* I, 37–38, 47, 111, 123, 1855 Preface, ll. 437, 479–532, *LG CRE,* 721, 723–724, "Thoughts—4: 'Of Ownership . . . ,'" *LG* (1860), *CRE,* 611, and Notebook 2 [3–4, 20–21] *DN,* III, 761, 763. This paragraph first printed in Furness, 45.

3. Deleted: "twelve" ; inserted: "five" on a line above.

4. Deleted: "Gaea" ; inserted: "Rhea" WW was understandably confused by the bewildering genealogy of the gods.

5. Deleted: "added" ; inserted: "accumulated" on a line above "added to"

6. Deleted: "stren"

7. [*847V*] placed in order of inscription following [*848R*] as indicated by sense and by WW's asterisks.

[*848R*][8] into the soul and is the[?] strength and life and knowledge they evoke there.—

I will not envy a man who possesses[9] sides of beef and barrels of apples or cubic rods of good coal *[*847V*]* if he merely have all the care and[10] hauling and[11] lowering and hoisting of them, and so goes on for a lifetime, and they never serve[12] his sinews and blood and senses for food or for warmth.—[13] The more of these he has, the more books to keep, the more he[14] stays indoors, the more he demeans and wilts[15] and shins[16] it, and deforms himself into the crooked. Will it pay?—[17]

Just as much as the care-taker of beef and apples and[18] coal which never warm him nor enrich [*849R; 848V blank*] him

[*849V*] *Faith.*—Becalmed at sea, a man refreshes himself by swimming round the ship.—A[19] deaf and dumb boy his younger brother is looking over the and the swimmer,[20] floating lazily on his back, smiles and beckons with his head[21]

Without[22] waiting a moment the young child, laughing and clucking springs into the [*851R*][23] sea, and as he rises to the surface[24] feels no fear but laughs and though he sink and drown he feels it not for the man is with him there

[*850R*] *Death Song*

Joy Joy! O full of Joy[25]
Away becalmed at sea[26] One day
I saw a babe, laughing kicking, &c &c

And as a swimmer[27] floated[28] in the waves, he called the child.—Laughing it sprang, and there [29]

8. Apparently a leaf is lacking. The lower two-thirds of this leaf have been trimmed.
9. Illegible mark deleted.
10. Deleted: "lifting" before "hauling"
11. Deleted: "hoisting" before "lowering"
12. Deleted: "to"
13. Inserted: "for . . . warmth." on a line above "senses.—" and into right margin.
14. Deleted: "must"
15. Deleted: "himself"
16. Either "to hit or kick a person in the shins" or "attempt to borrow money." *DAE,* IV.
17. This paragraph first printed in Furness, 46.
18. Deleted: "who never eats thereof" ; inserted: "and coal" on a line above "who never"
19. Deleted: "little child [*illeg.*]" on a line above [*illeg.*] ; inserted: "deaf . . . brother" on a line below.
20. Deleted: "lazily"
21. Deleted: "for the babe to come.— "
22. Illegible mark deleted.
23. Placed here in order of inscription.
24. Inserted: "to the surface" on two short lines above "rises" and into the right margin.
25. WW may have intended to delete this line, but the placement of the cancelling line is not clear.
26. Deleted: "On the sea shore" beginning a new line following "Joy" ; inserted: "Away becalmed at sea" on a line above "On . . . One day"
27. Deleted: "passed"
28. Deleted: "idly"
29. See [*852V*], below.

[*850V*] Black Bob and the young girl/

When the[30] ship strikes, who thinks of a gold watch or earrings?—/[31]

When the San Francisco was wrecked, the most valuable jewelry lay about the cabin unnoticed on the floor/[32]

[*851V*][33] Disaster, and temptation, are the examiners[34] of a[35] man.— They take his weight and density; and thenceforward he can be labeled or stamped at so much value.

Agitation is the test of the goodness and solidness of all politics and laws and institutions[36] and religions.— If they cannot stand it, there is no[37] genuine life in them, and shall die.[38]

[*852R*] Where others see[39] a[40] slave a pariah an emptier of privies the Poet beholds what[41] when the days of the soul are accomplished shall be[42] peer of god.

Where others are scornfully silent at some[43] steerage passenger from a foreign land, or black[44] the poet says, "My[45] brother! good day!"

And to the great king "How are[46] you friend?"[47]

30. Deleted: "passengers"

31. Line two-thirds across leaf from left below.

32. Line two-thirds across leaf from left follows entry. He is possibly resuming the theme of ownership (see [847*V*], [848*R*] above), but he used it in the "heroes" sequence of "Song of Myself" (1855), sec. 33, ll. 822–832, Cf. "Poem incarnating the mind" and "I know a rich capitalist."

33. Deleted: "The Death" ; "Disaster" capitalized. Paragraph first printed in Furness, 45.

34. Deleted: "and measurers"

35. Inserted on a line in the word space above "of . . . man"

36. Illegible mark deleted.

37. Deleted: "life"

38. Parallels in "Song of Myself" (1855), sec. 23, l. 496, and "Myself and Mine" (1860), l. 12. Paragraph first printed in Furness, 45.

39. Deleted: "some"

40. Deleted: "dolt, a clown, rags" ; inserted: "a slave . . . privies" on lines above. Redundant "a" following deleted "some" under "slave" not printed. Four-dot ellipses below "privies".

41. Deleted (except for second "be"): "shall be one day be a mate for" ; inserted: "when . . . accomplished" on a line above.

42. Deleted: "a mate for the greatest gods" ; inserted: "shall be" on a line under "the days" ; inserted: "the peers of god." on a line above "greatest gods" and into right margin; "the" before "peers" deleted.

43. Deleted: "one" ; inserted: "steerage passenger" on a line above "one from"

44. Inserted and deleted: "or emptier of privies" on a line above "the poet says" . WW evidently decided to use it at the top of the leaf.

45. Deleted: " 'Good Day" ; "My" capitalized.

46. Written over an illegible word.

47. Entire page cancelled with an "X" See "Song of Myself"(1855), sec. 40, ll. 1003–1005, "Song of the Answerer" (1855), sec. 1, ll. 34–36, "I Sing the Body Electric" (1855, 1856). First printed Furness, 83.

[*852V*][48] You have timidly waded close to the shore,[49] holding a board

Come with me, that[50] I teach you that you be a bold swimmer, and leap from the into the[51] unsounded sea, and, come up, and[52] shout, and laughingly shake the water from your hair.—/[53]

The poet is a recruiter He goes forth beating the drum.— O, who will not join his troop?[54]

[*853R*] The boat starts out from her ship, and finds a vast cake of ice reaching from one shore to the other. Five times she drives into it, and five times recoils and has to put back.— The sixth time she plunges[55] desperately on, the ice opens a crack as she advances, and so makes a chance for her just the very way she most wants to go.—

[*853V*] When a grand and melodious thought is[56] told to men for the first time,[57] down and within their hearts[58] each one says,[59] That music! those large and exquisite passages! where have I heard them before?[60]

[*854V; 854R blank*] a noble soul[61] often illustrates itself in what the world rates as trivial; the grandeur and beauty of the spirit making the commonest action more luminous than the sun.—[62] I knew of a[63] woman, in a little farm house in the country, who took a pair of her[64] home-knit stockings and exchanged them at the store for tea.— Coming home she stopped at her nearest neighbor's gate, and called

48. [852] shows the stub of about two-thirds of a conjugate leaf at right on which the opening letters of thirteen lines are visible. WW apparently cut it out himself. The lower third is also cut out, but without leaving a stub. Deleted: "Have"

49. Deleted: "wading"

50. Deleted: "I [*illeg.*] learn" ; inserted: "that I" on a line above [*illeg.*]; deleted on next line: "learn" ; inserted: "teach" above.

51. Deleted: "open" ; inserted and deleted: "plain seas" on a line above "sea,"; inserted: "unsounded" following the deleted "plain sea"

52. Deleted: "laugh"

53. Line across below. Short line in middle of leaf above "the poet is." Entire passage cancelled with an "X" See [*849V*], [*851V*], [*850R*] ante and "Song of Myself" (1855), sec. 46, ll. 1231–1233.

54. First printed in Furness, 66, 83. See "Poem of the Drum"

55. Deleted "far"

56. Deleted: "taken"

57. Deleted: "the" ; inserted: "down and within" on a line above "the their hearts"

58. Inserted: "they each one" on a line above "says" ; deleted: "they"

59. Deleted: "in it down and within" ; "s" added to "say"

60. Paragraph first printed in Furness, 65.

61. Deleted: "shows" ; inserted: "[*del.*] off often illustrates" on a line above "shows itself"

62. Sentence first printed in Furness, 45, who omits the rest of the passage although it illustrates the abstract proposition.

63. Deleted: "farm"

64. Inserted: "her" on a line above the word space between "of . . . home"

to her that she had something good;[65] and the neighbor must[66] fetch out a cup and go [*855R*][67] halves; for both loved tea,[68] and were without for[69] some days, and had no money.—

[*855V; inside front cover blank*][70] Front windows on first floor,—lights 13 X 17— Window five lights high—

A sash of two lights across top—The other eight lights made in two door-sides, hung each with hinges

65. Deleted: "tea" ; inserted: "something good;" on a line above "tea and"
66. Illegible mark deleted.
67. Deleted: "half"
68. Deleted: "and had no money"
69. Illegible mark deleted.
70. Notebook turned upsidedown. Leaf cancelled with vertical stroke. As explained in the headnote, there is a strong probability that this is the earliest entry.

The Only Way.

Manuscript in Rutgers. Inscribed in pencil on white laid paper, 4⅜" x 7¾"; with vertical chain lines and faded blue rules recto and verso ⅜": Corners clipped, cut at the bottom and possibly the left edge. Numbered "6" at top center in another hand. Date is probably before 1860. Printed in *N&F,* 125 (Pt. III, #147; *CW,* IX, 153). Cf. "Thoughts—4: 'Of Ownership." For references to other of WW's thoughts on ownership see "The regular old followers."

The only way in which any thing can really be owned, is by the infusion or inspiration of it in the soul—[1] Can I dully suppose that[2] I may attain to certain possessions,—as houses or stocks or lands or goods; and[3] when[4] I have paid the money[5] and[6] taken the receipts and warranty deeds,—then such property will be[7] mine to enter upon and enjoy.—Yes, may-be[8] as[9] people stone blind from their birth,[10] enjoy the exhibitions of pictures and sculpture.—[11]

1. Deleted: "The ignorant" ; inserted: "Can I" on a line above "[*del.*] ignorant dully"
2. Deleted: "they may" ; inserted: "I may" above.
3. Deleted: "that such property will be theirs,"
4. Deleted: "they" ; inserted: "I"
5. Preceding two words inserted in the right margin.
6. Deleted: "got" ; inserted: "taken" above.
7. Deleted: "theirs," ; inserted: "mine"
8. Inserted on a line above "as"
9. Deleted: "these" ; inserted: "people" on a line above and following "may-be"
10. Deleted: "enter[*?*]" ; inserted: "enjoy" above.
11. Erased: "But the true owner of the library[*?*]" The reading "library" is from *N&F.*

The Money Value.

Manuscript at Rutgers. Inscribed in black pencil on white laid paper. Faded rules ⅜". recto and verso. Corners trimmed. Numbered "7" top center probably not by WW. On verso "ground where you can rest yourself," a prose passage which leads to "Song of Myself," sec. 46, l. 1266ff. The verso, the writing and topic suggest a date before 1855. Cf. "The regular old followers." First published *N&F,* 126 (Pt. III, #148; *CW,* IX, 153–154).

The money value of real and personal[1] estate in New York city is somewhere between five hundred millions and[2] a thousand millions of dollars.—Now what is all this in itself?— Though it seems to be the of all men and all women to,—though for its security the laws are made and the police drilled—though — yet in its positive intrinsic it is all nothing of account.— The whole of[3] it is not of so much account as a pitcher of water, or a[4] basket of fresh eggs,—[5] The only way we attach it to our feelings is by[6] identifying it with the[7] human spirit,—through love, through pride, through our craving for beauty and happiness.

1. Deleted: "property"
2. Deleted: "an" ; inserted: "a"
3. Preceding three words inserted on a line above "It is" ; "I" in "It" not reduced in MS.
4. Deleted: "dozen [*illeg.*]"
5. Deleted: "I will"
6. Redundant "by" not deleted; deleted: "attaching it" following the redundant "by"
7. Inserted in word space above "with humans"

Such a Thing As Ownership.

Manuscript not found. Text from Furness, 45. Presumably the original was in LC. Since the idea expressed is one that occupied WW's mind while he was preparing *LG* 1855 and the MS may have been part of an early notebook, it is placed with the notebooks of that period. See "The regular old followers." Furness notes (*n* 307) that "The arrangement of material in MS. doubtful" and inserts "[There is no]" at the beginning.

such a thing as ownership here anyhow—one of the laws being that from the moment a man takes the smallest page exclusively to himself, and tries to keep it from the rest, from that moment it begins to wither under his hand and its immortal hieroglyphics presently fade away and become blank.

The Noble Soul.

Manuscript in Duke (5, #6). Inscribed in black pencil on white laid paper, approx. 6¾"· x 7¾"; horizontal chain lines ¼": Top and right edges trimmed. Recto has verses against conventional religion probably related to "Song of Myself," sec. 41. For this MS, cf. "Song of Myself," *LG* (1855), sec. 24, l. 507. First printed *N&F,* 122 (Pt. III, #134; *CW,* IX, 145). Bracketed words are those apparently trimmed off the extant MS but printed by Bucke. For other notes on property see "The regular old followers." The date is before 1855.

[1]The noble soul[2] steadily rejects[3] any liberty[?] or[4] privilege[5] or wealth that is not[6] open on the same terms to every other man and every other woman on the face of the earth[?] Meanwhile[?][7] it[8] is the[9] endless delusion of[10] big and little smouchers,[11] in all their varieties,[12] whether usurping the rule of an empire, or thieving a negro and selling him,—[13] whatever and whichever[14] of the ways[15] that legislators, lawyers,[16] the priests and the[?] educated[17] and pious,[18] prefer

1. Fragments of writing visible at top edge. Following thirty-three words brought up from the bottom of the leaf with asterisks and the notation "tr up"

2. Deleted: "sternly" ; inserted and deleted: "always" on a line above; inserted: "steadily" following the deleted "always"

3. Deleted: "any" ; inserted and deleted: "any" on a line above; inserted: "any" after "any" deleted above the original deletion.

4. Deleted: "favor that" ; redundant "or" not deleted, not shown.

5. Deleted: "of" ; inserted: "or" above.

6. Deleted: "equall"

7. Inserted: "The noble . . . from bottom" according to traces of writing at the top, which has been trimmed.

8. Uppercase "It" not reduced in MS.

9. Deleted: "perpetual"

10. Deleted: "the"

11. Deleted: "of the at"

12. Deleted: "circumstances and degre what-not of their greediness"

13. Deleted: "or slyly pocketing a roll of rolled ribbon from the counter" ; inserted: "whatever and whichever" on a line above "slyly pocketing"

14. Deleted: "any[?]"

15. Deleted: "in which" ; inserted: "that legislators," on a line above "in which lawyers"

16. Deleted: "and" ; inserted: "the" above.

17. Inserted: "and pious," on a line above.

18. Deleted: "classes, under the"

certain[19] advantages to themselves, over[20] the vast[21] retinues of the poor[?] the laboring, ignorant man, black men, sinners, and[?] so on—to suppose[22] they have succeded when the documents are signed and sealed, and they enter in possession of their gains.—[23] Shallow driblets ? of a[24] day![25] are[26] less in[27] their high success, than the[28] dullest of[29] the people they would overtop[30].

19. Inserted and deleted: "political" on a line above "certain"

20. Deleted: "equal"

21. Deleted: "armies" ; inserted: "retinues" above.

22. Deleted: "that"

23. Inserted and deleted: "These" on a line above ".—" ; "Shallow" following "These" ; capital "D" in "Driblets" changed to lowercase.

24. A second question mark over "a"

25. A second "!" deleted. Deleted: "you [*illeg.*]"

26. Deleted: "worse" ; inserted and deleted: "shallower" on a line above; inserted: "less" following "shallower"

27. Deleted: "your" ; inserted: "their" on a line above.

28. Deleted: "lowest" ; inserted: "dullest" on a line above.

29. Deleted: "those you have" following "of" ; inserted: "the" on a line above "those" ; inserted and deleted: [*illeg.*]; inserted: "people they would" on a line above "those you have"

30. "ped" deleted in "overtopped." Superscript "2" written above final dash. Deleted: "If there be Whatever it be, liberty [*illeg. del.*] or wealth or knowledge privilege" . At bottom of the leaf, centered, is the notation "over" enclosed with a curved line. The text, however, is not continued on verso.

I Tell You Greedy Smoucher!

Text from *N&F* and Duke (16, #39). Manuscript lacks first paragraph; *N&F* text lacks final sentence. No clipped ascenders, however, show at the bottom of the leaf. MS inscribed in black pencil on white wove scrap approx. 4¾" x 7½". Brownish rules ⅜", corners clipped. Bucke calls attention to the relationship between the first paragraph and "Song of Myself" (1855), sec. 24, 1. 507. See also "The noble soul." First printed *N&F,* 204 (Pt. III, #204; *CW,* IX, 203). See "The regular old followers." The date is before or early in 1855.

I tell you greedy smoucher! I will have nothing which any man or any woman, anywhere on the face of the earth, or of any color or country cannot also have.

Remember that the clock and the hands of the clock, only tell the time—they are not themselves the aggregated years.—[1] Which is greatest—time, which baffles us, or its indexes, made[2] of wood and brass,[3] by a[4] workman at ten dollars a week?— Time itself knows no index it is merely[5] to stand us a little in help that[6] we combine sets of springs and wheels and arbitrarily divide[7] by hours and quarters—and call[8] this[9] measuring[10] time.—[11] But that stunning, swimming puzzle envelops[12] the soul itself and the Elder Brother of the soul and[13] had no beginning and can never cease

1. Deleted: "Time"
2. Deleted: "by"
3. Deleted: "at"
4. Inserted on a line above the wordspace between "by . . . workman"
5. Deleted: "for"
6. Following seven words inserted on a line over "in help . . . combine" ; deleted: "are"
7. Inserted and deleted: "it"
8. Deleted: "these miserable"
9. "is" inserted over "e"
10. "ing" inserted over "e" ; deleted: "of"
11. Deleted: "Contemptible enough indeed" on a line above "enough" [*ins. not del., not printed*] "are they such measuring [*two words ins. and del.* on a line above "such measuring"] they all compared with that vast" ; inserted: "But that stunning, swimming"
12. "s" inserted over "ing" ; deleted: "God him ["self" *not del.*]" ; inserted: "the soul it [*before* "self"]"
13. Preceding eight words inserted on a line above "which" ; deleted: "which"

You Know How the One.

Manuscript not found. LC (#86) has six photostated pages (LC item #'s *3317–3319*). LC *Cat.,* 17, gives 5¾" x 3⅝" as dimensions. Holloway, *UPP,* II, 83, *n*6, describes it as very badly blurred in places and generally like his "Manuscript Notebook—2," "Poem incarnating the mind." It is probably a homemade notebook written in pencil. The text here given follows *UPP,* II, 83–86, and the available photostats. The date is before 1855.

You know how the one brain includes those beautiful wonders the perceptions or senses—includes also the subtle processes of thought and reason and causality, and an infinite variety else, so diverging and converging as to either make much of the finest thread of silk or wind its fingers round the world.— Well the one duty under which a man or woman is bound to himself or herself is the enfolder of every bit that follows.— That is the only independent, living entire obligation.— As small pipes from the aqueduct main, the rest are parts that flow out of it. They come not thence, they are only so many dead arms or legs, ghastly perhaps galvanised into a little motion, but having no vitality from the heart.

You have for instance been warned through your whole life, week days and Sundays, to pay your devoir[?][1] to God.[2] Religion the original and main matter. Really there is no such thing.— What is called such, even accepting the most florid and large description of it, is but one little item in the sum of that boundless account which a man should be always balancing with his own soul. I have seen corpses shrunken and shriveled— I have seen dismal mannikins of abortions, still-births so small that the doctors preserved them in bottles— But no corpse have I seen—no minnied[3] abortion— that appears to me more shrunken, from comparison to the fullest muscular health of some fine giant—more inert and blue and fit for the swiftest burial—more awfully a corpse because a perfect shaped and affectionate youth, in living strength and suppleness, stands ready to take his room, when the hearse carries the defunct away—than the whole and the best of what over this great earth has been called, and is still called, Religion, seems to me in comparison with the devotion ? loving in a sort worthy that immeasurable love, stronger than the propulsion of this globe, ecstatic as the closest embraces of the god that made this globe—fiercer than the fires of the sun around which it

1. Holloway's query.
2. Cf. other MS on religion post.
3. Holloway suggests "mummied"

eternally swings—more faithful than the faith that keeps it in its company and place—divergent and vast as the space that lies beyond—which belongs to any well developed man which is the great law whence spring the lesser laws we call Nature's.

Of the Poet[4]

From each word, as from a womb, spring babes that shall grow to giants and beget superber breeds upon the earth.[5]

He drinks up quickly all terms, all languages, and meanings.[6] To his curbless and bottomless powers, they be like ponds of rain water to the migrating herds of buffalo, who make the earth miles square look like a creeping spread. See! he has only passed this way, and they are drained dry.

You break your arm, and a good surgeon sets it and cures it complete; but no cure ever avails for an organic disease of the heart.

Your mighty religions and political improvements—good enough as far as they go—are still but partial reforms—a good back—a well shaped foot—a fine head of hair—a nice ear for music—or a peculiar faculty for engineering. I would give you the entire health, both of spirit and flesh, the life of grace and strength and action, from which all else flows.— What I give you, I know, cannot be argued about, and will not attract men's enthusiasms and interests.

[*3319L*][7] I[8] want[9] a ? [10]sublime of Hymn[11] Chorus and orchestrium[?],[12] wide as the[13] orbit of suns, reliable[?][14] as immortality and[15] and filling all my capacity to receive the kisses as the sea fills scooped out valleys.[16] Tenor[17] clean and fresh

4. Not in *UPP*; inserted on authority of a set of typed notes made by Holloway when the MS was still in the possession of Thomas B. Harned.

5. "Song of Myself" (1855), sec. 40, ll. 1006–1007.

6. Cf. "Song of the Answerer" (1855), ll. 32, and "albot Wilson."

7. Despite LC item number these pages are obviously primitive versions of [*3317L, 3317R, and 3318*]. The entire page is cancelled with an "X"

8. Originally "We" ;"I" inserted above.

9. Deleted: "the" ; inserted above: "a"

10. The question mark is above "sublime"

11. Deleted: "out some vast"

12. Deleted: "whose strain is"

13. Deleted: "world" ; inserted: "orbit of suns," on a line above "the world"

14. Deleted: "pure as Jesus" ; inserted above: "[*del.*] sure as immortality

15. Deleted: "sweet as the"

16. It is impossible to distinguish more than a few scattered words. Professor C. Carroll Hollis, who kindly checked my readings of this MS, and I do not always agree on them. An unintelligible "tr*" here. Inserted: "boundless"

17. Deleted: "[*illeg.*] [*ins.*] which swell"

as the Creation[18] whose vast pure volume floods my soul I want the Soprano[19] that over-leaps[20] the stars. +[21]

[*3319R*] For this huge[*?*] harmony to give us but one feeble note, and that a false one?[22]

The ox is too tired[*?*] — he rests standing

The attraction of gravity is the law upon which you make your house plumb [*illeg.*] but thats not what the law is specially made for

[*3317L*][23] I want that tenor, large and fresh as the creation, the orbed[24] parting of whose[25] mouth shall lift over my head the sluices[26] of all the delight[27] yet discovered for our race.—[28]

I want the soprano that lithely[29] overleaps the stars, and convulses me like the love-grip of her in whose arms I lay last[30] night.— I want[31] an infinite chorus and orchestrium, wide as the orbit of[32] Uranus[33] true as the hours of the[34] day,[35] and filling my capacities to receive, as thoroughly as the sea fills its scooped out[36] sands.—I want the chanted Hymn whose tremendous sentiment, / * (back[37] [*3317R*] shall[38] uncage in my heart a thousand new strengths, and unknown ardors and terrible extasies—making me enter intrinsically into all passions—dilating me beyond time and space—calmly sailing me down and down the broad

18. Following seven words inserted between lines.

19. Deleted: "that that thrills me like kisses of heaven of that" ; inserted: "that over-" on a line above "[*del.*] that leaps"

20. Deleted: "unfaltering to"

21. May be indication to transpose up to the top, which is the final order, [*3317*].

22. This sentence cancelled with an "X"

23. The entire page is cancelled with an "X"

24. Inserted on a line above "the parting"

25. Deleted: "orbed"

26. Deleted: [*illeg.*]

27. Deleted: "there is." ; inserted after deletion: "yet . . . race."

28. This version is the third of three drafts by WW including [*3319*]. After the first attempt he made another in the upper margin of the page which he deleted and is almost entirely illegible. The present (third) version was written between lines of the first, which read: "I want that [*illeg.*] tenor clean and fresh as the Creation, whose vast pure volume floods [*illeg.*]"

29. Inserted on a line above "over" (*in* "overleaps").

30. Preceding two words written over [*illeg.*]

31. Deleted: "a sublime" ; inserted: "an infinite" on a line above.

32. Deleted: "the farthest" ; inserted "Uranus" above. A question mark, WW's reminder to look up the name of the planet, is uncancelled.

33. Deleted: "reliable as immortality falling in truly" ; inserted: "true" on a line above "truly"

34. Inserted on a line above "of day"

35. Deleted: "and night,"

36. Deleted: "valleys." ; inserted: "sands." on a line above.

37. A later addition, for WW obviously continued on the facing page as well as on [*3318L*], which may or may not be earlier than [*3317L*].

38. Deleted in several stages: "put one through [*illeg.*] paces and powers" ; inserted in upper margin: "uncage . . . extasies"

supreme river,—startling me with the overture to some undreamable horror—stabbing me with myriads of forked distractions more furious than hail and lightnings.[39] lulling me drowsily with honeyed morphine opium—[40] writhing around me the[41] coils of collapsing death, and awakening me again to know, by that comparison, the only positive wonder in the world, and that, what we call life. [*3318L*][42]* shall uncage in my breast a thousand[43] wide-winged strengths and unknown ardors and terrible extasies—putting me through the[44] flights of all the passions—dilating me beyond time and[45] air—startling me with the overtures of[46] some unnamable horror—calmly sailing me all day on a[47] bright river with lazy slapping waves—[48]stabbing my heart with myriads of forked distractions more furious than hail or lightning—lulling me drowsily with honeyed[49] morphine—[50] tight'ning the[51] fakes of death about my throat, and awakening me again to know by that comparison, the[52] most positive wonder in the world, and that's what we call life.[53]

All the vastness of Astronomy—and space—systems of suns carried in their computation to the farthest that figures are able or that the broadest mathematical ? faculty can hold—and then multiplied in geometrical progression ten thousand billion fold do not more than symbolize the reflection of the reflection, of the spark thrown off a spark, from some emanation of God.— Even these the greatest of the great men of the world, can in their best moments

The air which furnishes me the breath to speak is subtle and boundless—but what is it compared to the things it serves me to speak—the meanings—

39. Preceding thirty-one words almost illegible. Original version: "[*illeg. del.*] [*ins.*] lulling [*ins.*] one with the sleep of honeyed tearing me with the wild [*illeg.*] of hail and lightnings [*del.*] that leap"

40. Written above the preceding word. Deleted: "and [*above line*] uncaging [*del.*] waking in my heart [*del.*] all a [*ins.*] thousand terrible [*ins. and del.*] ne strengths and ardors and [*illeg. ins.*] ecstasies."

41. Deleted word illegible but it is not "fakes" of the revision on [*3318L*]; inserted: "coils" above the deletion.

42. The page is cancelled with "X"

43. Deleted: [*illeg*]; inserted above and deleted: "[*illeg.*] winged broad" ; inserted: "wide-winged" following on the same line.

44. Deleted: "phases[*?*]" ; inserted: "flights" on a line above.

45. Deleted: "space" ; inserted: "air" above.

46. Written over illegible word.

47. Deleted: "broad"

48. Preceding four words inserted on a line above "river—stabbing"

49. Deleted: "opium" ; inserted: "morphine" above. Cf. [*3317R*] above.

50. Deleted: "writhing" ; inserted: "tightning" above.

51. Deleted: "coils" ; inserted: "fakes" above.

52. Deleted: "only" ; inserted above: "most"

53. Cf. "Song of Myself" (1855), sec. 26, ll. 601–610. *UPP* text resumes.

I Know a Rich Capitalist.

Manuscript in NYPL (Lion). Inscribed in black pencil in what appears to be a commercially made account book approx. 5¾" x 3½". Faint horizontal blue lines approx. ¼" apart throughout; ruled vertically in red for accounts. The red rules are not consistent: on two representative facing pages, the left page is ruled 5/16", double rule 13/16" and 2¾" from the left edge; on the right ⅝", double 1⅛", 3 3/16" from the left edge. WW turned the book upside down. Stitched into brown paper covers, which Dr. Lewis M. Stark, former Chief, Rare Book Division, NYPL, believes were supplied when the MS was in the possession of Oscar Lion. Although there are five entries on the nature of poetry which are connected by asterisks, [*16, 17, 18, 20, 22*], they do not seem to have been inscribed continuously nor are the texts continuous. Therefore they have not been rearranged. The date is 1854, the church referred to on [*1*] having been identified by Emory Holloway as the Marble Collegiate Church which was opened that year. The news of the wreck of the *San Francisco* was received in January of that year. Published by Holloway, "A Whitman Notebook," *Am Merc,* III (December, 1924), 476–480.

I know a rich capitalist who, out of his wealth, built a marble[1] church, the most splendid in the city; and when it was opened, he stood at the door, the first Sunday, and helped the sexton show people to seats.— He was the meanest looking person in the place, and proud[2] of his building and wealth.[3]

[*2*] The Elementary Laws do not get excited and run and bawl to vindicate themselves.[4]— The[5] doctors might all deny the attraction of gravity, and that sublime[6] power would never complain.— Be you[7] like the grand powers.—[8]/

Exist.[9]—Do not trouble yourself to soothe[10] sputterers and[11] infidels?.—[12] (Manure

1. Inserted on a line above "a church"
2. Deleted: "at"
3. See "albot Wilson," [*18–23,* 59–60]. For WW's objections to fashionable churches see *NYD,* 43–48.
4. Cf. "Song of Myself" (1855) sec. 20, ll. 410–411.
5. Deleted: "Priests and" ; inserted: "The" on a line above "and"
6. Deleted: "law"
7. Deleted: "thou" ; inserted above: "you"
8. "The Elemental . . . grand powers" cancelled with an "X." Line drawn across the page below entry.
9. Deleted: "The soul is larger than the"
10. Deleted: "set" following "to" "satisfy" "soothe" on a line above "to set" ; inserted: "soothe" on the same line above preceding the deletion.
11. Deleted: "babb"
12. Question mark above "infidels"

the[13] fields of the heart, for it brings great crops.—)[14] Sure as the [3] most certain sure[15]—[16]reliable as Immortality—[17]the effects[18] apper after the causes[19] are born.[20]/

I see on the Egyptian head-rests the most hideous forms and combinations of groups as if they intended to scare away unrest[21]

[5; *4 blank*] The genuine Man is not, as would have him, like one of a block of city houses, that can't stand except as it is upheld in the midst of the rest.[22]/

Greater than[23] wires of iron, or treaties, or even strong mutual interests is[24] Smpathy.—When Creighton[25] hove[26] to for many days and nights and rescued the wrecked thosand on the San Francisco[27]

[6] If a man spatter mud on his new clothes, by lifting[28] a child or an old woman over the slush[29] let him nevertheless be content.— Mud like that strikes in and makes beauty spots

[7] *Pride of birth*—
There is nothing in[30] the eminency of any office of President or Governor or Mayor, nothing[31] royal blood, or the inheritance[32] through a direct line of the[33] name of the most historical[34] heroes, or[35] that should make us carry our heads so

13. Deleted: "thy soul," ; inserted above: "the fields of the heart," "the" above "thy" , "fields . . . heart" above "soul, [*del.*] for it"
14. Deleted: "As" ; "Sure" capitalized.
15. Cf. "Song of Myself" (1855), sec. 3, l. 49.
16. Deleted: "as"
17. Deleted: "you"
18. Deleted: "come when" ; inserted: "apper after" written on a line above.
19. Deleted: "appear" ; inserted: "are born." above.
20. Rule across leaf.
21. Cf. "memorials."
22. Rule across leaf.
23. Deleted: "b"
24. Deleted: "the"
25. Caret inserted, but no other insertion.
26. Written over [*illeg.*]: "hove" ; deleted: "too"
27. See "Poem incarnating the mind."
28. Written over illegible word: "lifting"
29. Deleted: "gutter" ; inserted above: "slush"
30. Inserted. Following twelve words brought up from further down page, after "heroes, or . . ." Marked with "tr" , parentheses and asterisks by WW.
31. Inserted above "royal" : "nothing"
32. Deleted: "succession" ; inserted above: "inheritance"
33. Inserted: "name of the" on a line above "most"
34. Written over illegible word above "heroes,"
35. WW probably intended to delete "or" . Deleted: "in [*illeg.*]" ; "the . . . Mayor" transferred up according to WW's indications (see *n* 30); "that begins to" after transposed phrase deleted; followed by space; deleted at beginning of new line: "but [*illeg.*]"

high, and so fill us with[36] bulging pride, as the consciousness that we are[37] human souls.—[38] Office, however[39] exalted, and wealth, however capacious,[40] often show[41] a mean and starved nature

[*8*][42] The best of such distinctions abstractly amounts to little.—

Toiled for, suffered for, lived for, as they are by the[43] majority of men, their only real[44] charm is that they[45] symbolize[46] afar off the unspeakable haughtiness and nobleness[47] which[48] the[49] personality of[50] man carries well, if he[51] once take the hint of his[52] own birthright.

[*9*][53] Love is the cause of causes.— Out[54] of the first Nothing—[55] out of the[56] black fog[57] of the nostrils of Death which hung ebbless and floodless in the spread of space—it asked[58] of God with undeniable will, something to satisfy[59] itself.—[60]

By it then Chaos was staid with.—[60a] Like a brood of beautiful children came from them[61] the Laws of Nature.—

36. Deleted: "more than imperial pride," ; *inserted on a line above:* "than imperial bulging pride" ; *inserted and deleted* "than ever" *on the line following* "bulging pride" ; *also inserted and deleted on a separate line:* "spread itself in capitals or courts,"

37. Deleted: "hum"

38. Cf. 1855 Preface, l. 265, *LG CRE,* 716, and "Song of Prudence" (1856), l. 43.

39. Deleted: "high" ; inserted: "exalted" above.

40. Inserted: "may but often" on a line above "show" ; deleted: "may but"

41. Deleted: "many"

42. Deleted at top of page: "for their dogmas[?] ; as the"

43. Deleted: "vast"

44. Inserted: "only real" on a line above "their . . . charm"

45. Deleted: "but faintly"

46. Inserted: "afar off" on a line above "the"

47. Written over "nobility"

48. Deleted: "[*illeg.*] grace"

49. Deleted: "soul" ; inserted above: "personality"

50. Deleted: "every"

51. Deleted: "but" ; inserted above: "once" on a line above the word space between "his . . . inalienable"

52. Inserted: "own" ; deleted: "inalienable"

53. Entire leaf cancelled with "X" rewritten in verse on [*12*].

54. Deleted before "Out": "W"

55. Deleted: "and" ; inserted above: "out of"

56. Inserted: "black" on a line above "fog"

57. Deleted: "of primeval or original Vacuity, that vast and sluggish" ; inserted above: "of the nostrils of death which hung ebbless and floodless"

58. Inserted: "of God" on a line above "asked . . . with"

59. Deleted: "and itself" ; inserted: "itself" above "and" ; inserted and deleted: "and . . . its" on a line above "immortal longings—.

60. Deleted: "[*illeg.*] its"

60a. Deleted: "The like a family" ; inserted above: "Like a brood

61. Inserted and deleted: "whom we call" on a line above "them the"

[*10*] Yes he is like a small boy who raises a big kite, and it pulls entirely too hard for him.— He had better let it go ere it carry him entirely[62] up in the air and out of sight[63]/

A coffin swimming buoyantly on the swift flowing current of the river[63a]

[*11*] Yes I believe in the Trinity—God Reality—God Beneficence or Love—and God Imortality or Growth.[64]/

He dives in the water for a[65] drowned man and sees the body[66] with open staring eyes, and the hair floating out and up from his head

[*12*][67] Love is the cause of causes,
Out of the vast, first Nothing[68]
The ebbless and floodless vapor from the nostrils of Death,
It asked of God with undeniable will,
Something to satisfy itself.—
By it then Chaos was staid with
And duly came from them a brood of beautiful children
Whom we call the laws of nature

[*13*] There are two ?[69] of the soul, and both are illimitable, and they are its north latitude and its south latitude.— One of these is Love. The other is Dilation or Pride.[70] There is nothing so inconceivable haughty as the

The style of the most magnificent heroes or rulers is
[*14*]Nature ?[71] is always plumb

Loyalty of some flatterer of royalty who (latter)[72] is broght to the scaffold

62. Deleted: "out
63. Rule across leaf.
63a. Cf. "Pictures. "64. Rule across leaf.
65. Deleted: "dead" ; inserted over: "drowned"
66. Deleted: "and"
67. Entire entry cancelled by "X" Cf. [9].
68. Cf. "Song of Myself" (1855), sec. 44, l. 1153.
69. Deleted: "attributes" ; question mark inserted above.
70. Cf. "Song of Myself" (1855), sec. 21, l. 428, "Our Old Feuillage" (1860), l. 47, and "Feuillage," an 1856 MS (Bowers, 130). Cf. also "albot Wilson" [5].
71. "Nature " on line by itself; question mark below on level with remainder of line. Next entry at foot of leaf.
72. Probably WW meant "later"

[*15*][73] Why do we[74] look back, as[75] century after century adds to the length of the road between us,—why do we always[76] turn with[77] pleasure and curiosity to the sayings and doings[78] thirty centuries ago, of wandering Jewish tribes, of little Greek communities, of half savage Rome, and of Ethiopia and Persia? There is something in those sayings and doings that effuses directly from the soul— Raw and bungling as they send it out, They[79] do not[80] send it out at second hand, but fresh and alive.—[81]

[*16*]*[82]This Poetry, or aliment of the Soul, we must have.— It is clamored for with the most irresistible longing.— Accordingly it is everywhere and[83] each[84] and all that our senses can?

Children and simple people often[85] make speeches that illustrate[86] some of these relations, better

[*17*][87]Much the largest portion of what rides jauntily through the[88] literary[89] avenues as poetry, and keeps the saddle for scores, perhaps fifties of years, is awkward and ill paced[90] enough;—[91] such as Love-[92]shambles, in long metre or short,[93] some of them ardent,[94] but most of them very dismal and spavined,—[95] both styles always[96] on the road,— and

73. Deleted: "The reason that the" ; inserted: "Why do" on a line above "reason that"

74. Deleted: "turn of" ; inserted: "look"

75. Inserted on a line above "c" in "century"

76. Inserted on a line above "we turn"

77. Deleted: "living"

78. Inserted: "thirty centuries ago," on a line above "and doings of"

79. Changes in punctuation and capitalization in the preceding ten words are not clear nor apparently consistent.

80. Deleted: "give it fort"

81. Cf. 1855 Preface, ll. 1–10, 255–257, *LG CRE,* 709, 716.

82. Cf. [*17*], [*18*], [*23*], especially the latter, which is probably a continuation.

83. Deleted: "upon"

84. Deleted: "object[*?*]"

85. Deleted: "touch the [*illeg.*] tune"

86. Deleted: "this relation with"

87. Inserted: "Much" on a line above "the" ; "the" reduced to lowercase.

88. Deleted: "world"

89. Deleted: "world" following "literary" ; inserted: "avenues" on a line above the deletion.

90. Deleted: "ill-bouncing[*?*]" ; "balding[*?*]" inserted above "bouncing" and deleted; inserted above deletions: "ill paced"

91. Semicolon written over period; dash not deleted. Deleted: "jingling" ; inserted above: "such as"

92. "L" in "Love" is written over lowercase. Deleted: "songs" ; inserted above: "shambles"

93. Deleted: "some very"

94. Deleted: "and"

95. Illegible punctuation deleted; inserted: "—" ; deleted: "make up having "; inserted: "both styles" on a line above "make up"

96. Deleted: "been ready and numerous"

[*18*]*[97]What stuff passes for poetry in the world[98]
What awkward and ill-bouncing riders[99]/
What is printed in books or what not, and has rhymes attached to its tails, is but a very small portion of the poetry of /[1]

Case of the driver who came in looking as natural as life, but was frozen dead and hard

[*19*]A lawyer who had put off his case once, came in court and asked further delay,[2] with tears in his eyes stating the death of his Mother. The Judge was just granting his request, with great commiseration, when an old lady from the gallery Cries out "O ———— my son! how often have I whipped you for lying."

[*20*] pork and pound cake[3] and[4] products that can be stewed or worn[5] put in the bank.—[6]

All[7] that makes clear this relation, and[8] defines the road[9] betwen[10] conceivable objects and the human spirit,[11] and explains what those objects mean, is poetry, coarse or fine.—[12] Even if the explanation[13] be[14] two or three removes[15] off, as most are, or distantly suggested,[16] folks take them and relish them well;

97. Cf. [*16*], [*17*], [*23*].
98. There is a gap of two ruled lines' width between this verse and the following.
99. Rule across leaf.
1. Cf. 1855 Preface, 714, ll. 186–189, *LG CRE,* 714. Line across leaf.
2. Deleted: "in a tearf"
3. Deleted: "and things"
4. Deleted: "things" ; "products that can be" inserted on a line above "things"
5. Inserted above "put"
6. The order of inscription is difficult to determine on this leaf and the next. Since [*21*] also begins with "pork" , the present passage has not been transposed. Possibly WW wrote the present passage first and then, as it were, wrote up to it. See also [23] and the metaphor of eating which begins on [*16*].
7. Deleted: "expr"
8. Deleted: "tracks"
9. Deleted: "betwen" . The misspelling is WW's.
10. Deleted: "any thing" ; inserted above: "conceivable objects"
11. Inserted above "is poetry . . . or fine" : "and . . . mean"
12. Cf. 1855 Preface, ll. 177–180, *LG CRE,* 714.
13. Inserted above "be [*del.*] done" : "the explanation"
14. Deleted: "done at second and third [*del.*] hand, remove and" ; inserted above "at second and" : "two or three removes"
15. Deleted: "and" ; inserted above: "off, as most are, or"
16. Deleted: "we are thankful" ; inserted above: "folks take them and relish them well"

for we are greedy of this sort of[17] diet, and[18] never get[19] tired of stuffing* [*21*] pork

Friends

I discover that among people whose company is pleasant to me, I almost invariably grow fonder and fonder of those[20] who[21] constantly like me and are not afraid to show it[22] and who[23] good natured, have no notably offensive ways,[24] (They may be[25] ugly in the face; simple or slack in mind; and of common[26] employment.—tr)[27]

[*22*][28] You shall go in some rich man's house, where the long suite of parlors[29] has been attacked and taken possession of by artists, ornamenters, makers of carpetry, marble mantels,[30] curtains,[31] soft seats, and[32] morocco binding for books.—[33] What can be unbrought; for the place yet looks very beggarly.[34] The[35] gentleman who[36] footed the bills,[37] has surely[38] forgotten something.—[39] We remember that first of April[40] at the post office, when the young man in the linen jacket[41] blotched with ink handed[42] through the window a [*23*] very rare envelope, promising great things,[43] and we found nothing at all inside but a piece of blank paper.—/[44]

17. Deleted: "feeding" ; inserted above: "diet"
18. Deleted: "exceedingly voracious"
19. Deleted: "weary "; inserted above: "tired"
20. Deleted: "who without any"
21. Deleted: "evidently" ; inserted above: "constantly"
22. Inserted above "and" and deletions: "and are not afraid to show it" Deleted: "are" possibly in error; inserted above and deleted: "steady"
23. Inserted above "good" : " who"
24. Deleted: "[*illeg.*]" "and don't blow hot and cold"
25. Deleted: "plain" ; "ugly" inserted above.
26. Deleted: "po [*illeg.*]"
27. There seems to be no place to which this entry can be transposed, but it is related to [*1, 5, 6, 7, 8*].
28. On separate line at top of page, deleted: "Pile up your"
29. Deleted: "have" ; inserted above: "has"
30. Preceding two words inserted above "carpentry, curtains"
31. Deleted: "good"
32. Inserted above "morocco"
33. Deleted: "and marble mantels"
34. "What . . . beggarly" inserted above and below "The worthy [*del.*] gentleman who"
35. Deleted: "worthy"
36. Deleted: "has"
37. Deleted: "for all these"
38. Deleted: "omitted" ; inserted above: "forgotten
39. Cf. 1855 Preface, ll. 444–450, *LG CRE,* 722.
40. Deleted: "hour" ; inserted above and deleted: "moment" ; inserted above: "first of April"
41. Inserted above "jacket, handed" : "blotched with ink"
42. Deleted: "us out of" ; inserted above: "through"
43. Deleted: "when"
44. Line across leaf.

*[45] It is this which is the source of all Poetry; for there is in[46] men an instinct of the truth.[47] We have a saw toothed appetite[48] which restlessly hankers for[49] food out of this immense and varied earth[50] more[51] satisfactory than

[24] where the Congress meets is the sacred?[52] place.—If they adjourn from there to some log house or shed of hemlock boards

The[53] kernel of every object[54] thing[55] can be seen or[56] felt or thought of has its relation to the soul, and is significant of something there.—[57] He who can[58] tear off all husks and skins[59] and[60] pierce[61] straight through every stratagem of concealment,[62]*

45. Relates to other passages on poetry, [*16*], [*17*], [*18*], [*20*], but the asterisk probably indicates no more than a general connection.

46. Inserted above "is an" : "in all men" ; deleted: "all"

47. Deleted: "in all men" "There is a file" ; inserted above: "We have a saw"

48. Inserted and deleted: "with" on a line above "appetite which"

49. Deleted: "some satisfactory"

50. Deleted: "beyond mere something"

51. Inserted: "satisfactory" on a line above "more than"

52. Question mark above "sacred"

53. Deleted: "heart" ; inserted above: "kernel"

54. Deleted: "ever" . The first five words of this sentence are written above. WW began "Ever thing . . ." He probably intended to delete "thing"

55. Deleted: "that"

56. Inserted: "I felt or" on a line above "or"

57. Deleted: "This is this"

58. Deleted: "put" ; inserted on a line above "put all" : "tear off"

59. Deleted: "aside and"

60. Deleted: "find the" ; inserted above: "pierce [*del.*] on"

61. Inserted above: "straight through every" on a line above "strategem of concealment"

62. Deleted: "and goes to the actual" Cf. "Song of the Open Road" (1856), sec. 6, ll. 88–90. See [*16, 17, 18* above].

The Power By Which.

Manuscript in NYPL (Berg). Inscribed in black pencil on white wove scrap, 1⅝″ x 7⅞″. The writing suggests a date in the 1850s.

The power by which the carpenter plumbs his house, is the same power that dashes his brains out if he fall from the roof.—

There Is Some.

Manuscript in NYPL (Lion). Inscribed in black pencil on white wove paper, 3¾″ x $3^{15}/_{16}$″. Blue rules recto and verso. On it is mounted a printed quotation about the limited number of good conversationalists attributed in WW's hand in black ink to "Prince Metternich." The writing suggests a date in the 1850s.

There is some[1] dry wit yet in London *Punch.*— In the last number I read he says: "On Victor Hugo's forthcoming anniversary birth-day, he is to be re-christened Victor Ego."[2] Again: "Britain—a land on whose demesne the sun never sets—and on the[3] principal territory seldom rises"

1. Deleted: "real" ; inserted above: "dry"
2. Deleted: "And"
3. Deleted: "real" ; inserted above: "principal"

Memorials.

Manuscript missing, formerly in LC (#84), which has photostats of eight pages (item #'s 3313–3316). Text based on microfilm made during the 1930s by Floyd Stovall. Original described on film as: "64 pages about 4½ x 7, some blanks. Unbound and tied with green ribbon." The leaves are ruled horizontally, probably in blue, and according to a rule photographed on the film are 5/16" apart. The inscription appears to be in pencil. Page numbering is by the editor. Various entries first published in Furness as noted. The reference to the siege of Sevastopol [*91*], which began in October, 1854 and attracted world-wide attention, indicates that most, if not all of the notebook was written prior to 1855. The literary entries, however, indicate that WW not only used the notebook for *LG* 1855 but was generating the Adamic ideas of *LG* 1860. Two lines of "Debris" (1860) are also here. These Adamic entries suggest a late date in the series. See Floyd Stovall, "Dating Whitman's Early Notebooks," *SB,* 24 (1971), 201–204. I am indebted to Professor Joseph E. Geist, Central Methodist College, for valuable assistance with the notes.

[*1 blank; 2 illeg.*[1]; *3 illeg.*[2]]
[*4*] memorials—if the very timid and receptive he[3] made his chisels cut the granite with[4] tokens[5] feminine. He is the first after[6] Osiris.[7]

[*5*][8] Troy taken 1184 B.C. p. 295[*?*][9]

Dr. Abbott[10] tells us that Persians[*?*] told him of finding monuments [*illeg.*] Ethiopia with inscriptions and astronomical signs upon them.

1. Contains a few lines of prose; appparently several names and dates of the Prechristian era. Only "Joseph" and "Abraham" are legible.
2. The lower two-thirds of [*3–4*] has been clipped.
3. Deleted: "had"
4. Deleted: "the"
5. Deleted: "of"
6. Written over: "of"
7. Cf. "Song of Myself" (1855), sec. 41, l. 1030. Cf. also "Religions—Gods."
8. Lower two-thirds of [*5–6*] has been clipped.
9. See *n*40, below.
10. Dr. Henry Abbott, proprietor of the Museum of Egyptian Antiquities, helped WW in his Egyptian studies. See *NYD,* 27–40; and "I know a rich capitalist," "Abraham's visit to Egypt," "Moses of course was born," "Bunsen. The native name," "Immortality was realized," "Religions—Gods," "Egyptian religion," "Egypt (and probably," "Birth of Hercules."

[6] be sure of the district[11] where the trouble is—they wait thus perfectly still and in splendid postures

The childrens[12] dancing school at Dodworth's[13]

[7] The difference is only the baffling[?] difference of an inch.—But it is the difference between cutting[14] the rope[15] we cling to[16] 100 feet above the land.—whether we cut it an inch above or an inch below where our hands hold on for life [*illeg.*][17]

[8] WW.[?] Winel.[18]
A prince in Polish Austria near Hungary[19] on his estate on the highway, puts up a perpetual inn where all wayfarers are entertained free of charge; this he keeps always open, and gives meat and bread and lodgings—and sometimes comes to amuse himself with the guests.

[9][20] I have been asked, Which is the greater, the man or the woman?— Yes, I tell you, with the same answer that I tell whether Time is greater than space—and[21] [*illeg.*]

[*10*] The life of man on earth is the chef d'ouvre of all things.— What then! is it a suck? Has God[22] conceived a joke, and tried it on, and is it a small one?

[*11*][23] Of the poet.
He walks with perfect ease among a congress of kings,
And one king says[24] to another, Here is our equal, a prince[25] whom we knew not before
Then the great authors take him for an author
And the great soldiers for a captain

11. Inserted: "of the district" on a line above "where"
12. Inserted on a line above "The dancing"
13. Allan Dodworth conducted a well-known dancing school on Broadway.
14. Deleted: "of"
15. Deleted: "that holds us"
16. Written over [*illeg.*].
17. Four illegible lines.
18. Unidentifiable.
19. Inserted: "near Hungary" on a line above "on his"
20. The lower two-thirds of [9–*10*] have been torn out.
21. Inserted.
22. Deleted: "tried"
23. [*11*] cancelled with two vertical strokes. Ultimately joined to a passage from "albot Wilson" [26] to become the seventh poem of *LG* 1855, "A young man came to me . . . ," and in 1881, "Song of the Answerer," sec. 1, ll. 34–45, 48.
24. Deleted: [*illeg.*]; inserted above: "says"
25. Inserted: "a prince" on a line above "whom"

The sailors know that he has followed the sea,
The English believe that comes of Saxon stock
[*12*] And the Italians [*illeg.*]

This

O laugh when my eyes settle the land[26]
The bluey[27] spoon-drift, like white race-horse of brine, speeds before me

[*17; 13–16 torn out.*][28] such a thing as ownership here any how.— One of the[29] laws [*illeg.*][30] that[31] from the moment a[32] man takes the smallest page exclusively to himself and tries to keep it from the rest From[*?*] that [*illeg.*][33] moment it begins to wither under his hand[34] and[35] its immortal hieroglyphics presently[36] fade away and become blank.—[37]

stonecutter's tools
tooth-chisel—jib for the thumb[38]

[*18*] Of writers there are plenty who pay all demands upon them, if folks are willing to take notes, or paper acceptances of any sort; but only one out centuries who gives ready solid[39] cash.—

[*19*] It is a terrible sign of the human soul that it will not own any limit, even the widest.— The moment we knew the diameter of the earth to be eight thousand miles, it became no great thing to us.— With all the appalling grandeur

26. Cf. "Song of Myself" (1855), sec. 10, l. 181. Just above the following line, centered on the page, is what looks like a capital "T"

27. Inserted on a line above "spoon-"

28. Illegible word deleted before "such" . See "The regular old followers" for further notes on ownership.

29. Deleted: "The chief [*and six illegible words*]" ; inserted: "one of the" on a line above and preceding "laws"

30. Inserted on a line above "laws . . . that"

31. Deleted: [*illeg.*]

32. Deleted: "any" ; inserted above "a"

33. Deleted.

34. Preceding three words inserted on a line above "wither . . . and its"

35. Inserted and deleted: [*illeg.*] on a line under "hand" between "and its"

36. Inserted on a line above the end of "hieroglyphics" and over "fade"

37. Deleted: "[*illeg.*] and dead" Line from left one-third of the way across the leaf.

38. Cf. "A Song for Occupations" (1855), sec. 5, l. 111 and [*49*] of this notebook. The line, however, first appeared in *LG* 1856.

39. Inserted on a line above "cash"

of astronomy, if we could fix the line beyond which there was no more material universe, our soul, I think, would pine and begin its death sickness

[20] Remeses the Great, over 30 centuries ago
Solomon born 1032 B.C. [*Solomon*] ascended throne, 1015
Pharaoh, from phre or phra the *sun* Wilkinson[40]
Moses born 1571 B.C.
Exodus of the Israelites from Egypt 1491 B.C. 430 years after the arrival of Abraham in Egypt.—
Homer about 907 B.C.
Rome founded 753 B.C.

[*21*][41] The mirror that Nature holds and [*illeg.*] is deep and floating and ethereal and faithful.[42] If[43] a man always sends and[44] sees himself in it—from himself[45] he reflects the fashion of his[46] gods and all his religions and politics and books and art and social and public institutions—[47]ignorance or knowledge—kindness or cruelty—[48] grossness or refinement—definitions or chaos—each[49] is unerringly sent back to him or her who curiously gazes.

[22] There[50] is a fullsized[51] woman of calm and voluptuous beauty , . . .[52] the[53] unspeakable charm of the face of the mother of many children[54] is the charm of her face . . . she is clean and sweet and simple with immortal health . . . she holds always before her[55] what has the quality of a mirror, and dwells serenely behind it.—[56]

40. Stovall, *AL,* 347, calls attention to WW's use of Sir John Gardiner Wilkinson's *Manners and Customs of the Ancient Egyptians,* 5 vols., London, 1836–1840.

41. At top of leaf appear a pointing hand and "Over Leaf." The entry on [22], however, does not seem to be related.

42. WW began: "The [*del.*] rich nature is an etherial mirror deep deep and floating in it" He deleted this and inserted present reading above. "and [*illeg.*]" inserted on a line above "is deep" in present reading.

43. "If a" inserted over "A"

44. Preceding three words inserted on a line above "man . . . sees"

45. Deleted: "it" ; inserted "himself" on a line above "it . . . he"

46. Deleted: [*illeg.*]; preceding four words inserted on a line above "[*illeg.*] gods and"

47. At this point the writing becomes markedly more regular and darker. Possibly WW changed to ink. The same dark and more regular writing continues on [22]. [*23*] reverts to the somewhat irregular, lighter writing of the rest of the notebook. The reader, however, should realize that these differences, although noticeable, are relatively slight and that, in any case, writing material can never be determined from a photograph.

48. Dash over four dots.

49. Deleted: [*illeg.*]

50. Illegible mark above "is"

51. Inserted on a line above "woman"

52. Deleted: [*illeg.*], possibly continuation of ellipses.

53. Deleted: "unspeakable" preceding "unspeakable"

54. Cf. "Faces" (1855), sec. 1, l. 8.

55. Deleted: [*illeg.*]

56. Cf. "I Sing the Body Electric" (1855), sec. 5, ll. 68–71.

[23] When out of a feast[57] I eat only corn[58] and roast potatoes[59] for my dinner, through my own voluntary choice it is very well and I much content,[60] but if some arrogant head of the table prevent me by force from touching any thing but corn and potatoes then is my anger roused.—[61]/

Everyone that[62] speaks his word for slavery is himself the worst slave—the spirit of a freeman is not light enough in him to show that all the fattness of the earth were bitter to a bondaged[?][63] neck.—[64]

[24][65] In the respect of happiness or extasy, the beautiful gas[66] pervades the air continually, and we only need to be rightly tuned and conditioned, in order that it may catch to us ? ? (like gunpowder catches to fire,) and[67] flow into us like one river into another.[68]/

The schooner is[69] hoisting her sail[70] she will soon be down the coast.[71]/

river pirate old junk[?] shop

[25] I do not seek those that love me, I would rather seek[72] after some that hate me[73]

The village on the highland, seen from afar at sunset—the sun shining[?] on the red white [*illeg.*] or brown[74] gables, red white or brown[75]

57. Inserted: "out of a feast" on a line above "When . . . eat"
58. Deleted: "bread" ; inserted above: "corn" ; deleted: "for" before "for my dinner"
59. Cf. "albot Wilson" [66].
60. Inserted: "and I much content" on a line above "very well . . . but"
61. Line from the left halfway across the leaf.
62. Two illegible marks deleted.
63. Deleted: [*illeg.*]
64. For further notes on slavery see "Slavery—The slaveholders." Sentence printed by Furness, 75. See "As of the orator."
65. See "Song of the Open Road" (1856), sec. 8.
66. Deleted: [*illeg.*]
67. Deleted: "pass" ; inserted above: "flow"
68. Line from the left halfway across the leaf.
69. Deleted: "reefing" ; inserted above: "hoisting"
70. "s" deleted from "sails"
71. See *n*78 below. Line from the left one-third of the way across the leaf.
72. Deleted: "out"
73. Line from left. The remainder of this page has been cancelled by a vertical stroke. See "There Was a Child Went Forth" (1855), ll. 33ff. There are perhaps some echoes in "Crossing Brooklyn Ferry."
74. Inserted and deleted: "red" on a line above the word space between "the . . . white" ; inserted: "or brown" on a line above "gables"
75. The three preceding words appear to have been jotted down as an afterthought following "gables" . Cf. "There Was a Child Went Forth" (1855), l. 33. Short line below from left.

the ferry boat ever[76] plying[77] ever over the river[78]/
the schooner sleepily dropping down the tide the[79] [*illeg.*][80]astern towed by the rope.[81]

[26][82] In the open market[?] place[?] the barrels of apples, the flour and meat, and fat[83]? in bunks and bins./

The deckhand of the steamboat in his[84] red shirt,[85]/

The hayboat and barge—[86] the tug boat[87] bring her bearing of barges down the river[88]

the

[27] picture of the New York customs[?]/[89]

passage in poem middle?[90]-aged ? single[91] woman ? seeing from day to day for many years a man whom she deeply loves—never flagging—and eventually dies.—[92]/

The test of the goodness or truth of any thing is the soul itself—whatever does good to the soul, soothes, refreshes, cheers, inspirits, consoles, etc.—that is so, easy enough— But doctrines, sermons logic ??[93]

[28] Do you know what I well know

76. Inserted on a line above "boat flying"
77. Deleted: "forever and"
78. Cf. "Crossing Brooklyn Ferry." Short line below from left.
79. Deleted: "ketch"
80. The word is clearly not "boat"
81. Cf. [24].
82. Entries on this page not cancelled.
83. Deleted: "products" ; inserted: "fat" in left margin on a line above and before "products" . Question mark in blank space.
84. A caret stands above "his" and below "of" in "deckhand of the" written on the line above.
85. "shirt" written on a short line below from left.
86. Deleted: "flee"
87. Deleted: "with"
88. Cf. "Crossing Brooklyn Ferry" (1855), sec. 3, l. 46. Short line below from left.
89. Line across leaf from left.
90. This question mark is written above "aged" ; second mark is written following "woman"
91. Inserted on a line above "woman"
92. Line two-thirds of the way across the leaf.
93. Cf. "Song of Myself" (1855), sec. 30, ll. 653–654.

Do you [*know what*][94] it is to be loved as you pass in the street?
Do you know what it is to
Do you know what it is to have men and women crave the touch of your hand and the contact of you?[95]/

Not[96] must be the poets I would have The poets I would have must be a power in this state, and an engrossing power in the state.[97]

[*30; 29 blank*] If you have sons[98] custom them to be drivers of horses

I knew six brothers drivers of horses[99]

Why should I do much[1]

The capitol, the president, the laws,
I [*illeg.*]
There was never any more inception than there is now
Nor any more youth or age
And will never be any more perfection
Nor any more heaven or hell[2]

[*31*] The few who write the books and preach the sermons and?[3] keep ? the schools—[4] are they so much more than those who do not teach or preach, or write[5] This we call literature and science, is not so very much—there is enough of unaccountable importance and beauty in every step we tread and every thought of [*illeg.*][6]/

Literature to these gentlemen is a parlor in which no person is to be welcomed unless he come attired in dress coat and observing the approved decorums with the fashionable

94. WW used ditto marks.

95. Cf. "I Sing the Body Electric" (1855), sec. 4, "A Song for Occupations" (1855), sec. 1, l. 19; in 1856, "Song of the Open Road," sec. 7 and "Crossing Brooklyn Ferry," passim. Line from left two-thirds across leaf.

96. "The" deleted before "Not"

97. The thought is central in the 1855 Preface and *Democratic Vistas*.

98. Deleted: "habit" ; inserted: "custom" on a line above.

99. Between 1854 and 1856 WW seems to have thought driving horses was one of the ideal masculine occupations. Cf. 1855 Preface, l. 183, "Song of Myself" (1855), sec. 14, l. 257, "Myself and Mine" (1860), l. 2, "Understand that you can have," "Book-learning is good," "The Eighteenth Presidency!" "George Walker"

1. Written in a cramped hand closely above the following line of verse.

2. These four lines are cancelled with a vertical stroke. Cf. "Song of Myself" (1855), sec. 3, ll. 40–43.

3. Question mark before and above "keep"

4. Deleted: "I do not think that"

5. Deleted: "All" ; "This" capitalized.

6. A line separates this paragraph from that following.

[32] Poem—illustrating (*Good moments*)
soul in high glee all out (exquisite state of feeling of happiness—some moments at the opera[7]—in the woods[8]/

Criticism

He leaps over or dives under for the time, all the reforms and propositions that worry these days, and goes to the making of powerful[?] men and women.— With[9] these he says, all reforms, all good, will come.— Without these all reforms all good, all outside effects, are useless and helpless.—

[33][10] Poem

"The Bridegroom" ? for recitation (tremulous with joy. Mario's[11] voice quivering)[12]

(bring in a *death*[13]

We want no *reforms* no *institutions,* no *parties*— We want a *living principle* as nature has, under which nothing can go wrong—This must be vital through the United States, fit for the largest cases and actions and the [*illeg.*]

[34][14] Do you think I have written all this for my own good? Well, perhaps[15] I have. . . . but not in the you[16] imagine,[17]/

No one can realise anything unless he has it in him . . . . or has been it.
It must certainly tally[18] with what is in him . . . . other-wise it is all blank to him.
The animals[?] the past, light, space, if I have them not in me, I have them not at all
The future is in me as a seed or nascent thought.

7. See [33] of this notebook.

8. This entry is in a large, sprawling hand. See 1855 Preface, l. 21 and "Song of Myself" (1855), sec. 2, ll. 21–29. Two short lines from left below.

9. WW originally began the next sentence "These" ; deleted "These" and inserted "With" on a line above.

10. Cf. [48] in this notebook. The entire entry is in a large, sprawling hand.

11. Giovanni Mario, the great tenor, made his NY debut on September 4, 1854. See "A Visit to the Opera."

12. The final parenthesis extends down to the right of the preceding entry.

13. The whole entry is in a large sprawling hand.

14. Hanging indentation for both this and the following verse. WW began "If the" ; deleted the entry and began on a new line. Furness, 46, reprints the following verses, with the exception of the first two.

15. Deleted: "it is"

16. Deleted: "you think" following "you"

17. Cf. "Song of Myself" (1855), sec. 47, ll. 1247–1249. Short line from left below.

18. Inserted: "certainly" on a line above "tally"

[35] If the general has[19] a good army in himself, he has[20] a good army. . . . otherwise he has no[21] army worth mentioning[22]
If you[23] are rich in yourself you are rich . . . . otherwise you are wretchedly[24] poor
If you are located in yourself you are well located . . . .[25] you can never be[26] dislodged or moved thence
If you[27] are happy out of yourself you[28] are happy . . . .[29] but I tell you cannot be happy[30] by others any more than you can beget a child[31] by others. . . . or conceive a child[32] by others[33]

[36] I write not the[34] hymns
I see the building churches to God . . .
If I build a church it shall be[35] a church[36] to men and women
If I write hymns they[?] shall be all to men and women
If I become a devotee it shall be to men and women.

[37] [*illeg.*][37] Shorty[?] Brownie Dead bodie Hamlet's[?] Ghost Let-loose Graball Punch 4th of July Christmas Johnny Doughnuts Paggy—Shortey Pochuck Bonehardener Codmouth Black Jack Broadway Jack Dressmaker Harlem Charley Blow Bell [*illeg.*] [38] Dry Dock John Raggedy Jack Smith's Monkey Emigrant Wild man of Borneo Steamboat Elephant Buffalo Santa Anna Blind Sam Rosy Baltimore Charley Long Boston Short Boston Manneyunk Pretty Ike Jersey Mountaineer.

19. Deleted: [*illeg.*] ; inserted above: "a good"
20. Deleted: [*illeg.*] ; inserted above: "a good"
21. Deleted: "poor[?]"
22. ". . . . otherwise . . . army" is almost illegible and appears to have been added as an afterthought, and "worth mentioning" a still later afterthought. The line appears in "Debris" (1860), l. 4, *LG CRE,* 605.
23. Deleted: [*illeg.*]
24. Inserted on a line above "are . . . poor"
25. Deleted: "if not"
26. Deleted: [*illeg.*]
27. Deleted: "could be" ; inserted above: "are"
28. Deleted: "can be" ; inserted: "are" on a line above "be"
29. Deleted: "for" ; inserted above: "but"
30. Deleted: "through" ; inserted above: "by"
31. Deleted: "through" ; inserted above: "by"
32. Deleted: "through" ; inserted above: "by"
33. This line appeared in "Debris" (1860), ll. 5–6, *LG CRE,* 605, following the first line on this page.
34. Deleted: "these" ; inserted above: "the"
35. Deleted: "the" ; inserted: "a" following.
36. Deleted: "of" ; inserted above: "to"
37. [37–38] written in column in a large, loose hand. In an unpublished memorandum Emory Holloway identified these as nicknames of omnibus drivers. The real name of Graball was Patrick McMakin ("return my book"). WW mentioned some of these men in "Omnibus Jaunts and Drivers," *SD, Prose 92,* 19. For Broadway Jack Flood see *Corr.,* II, 69, 74–75, 118–119, "D.W. Wilder."

[39] It is not a labor of clothing or putting on or describing—it is a labor of clearing away and[38] reducing—for every thing is beautiful in itself and perfect—and the office of the poet is to remove what stands in the way of our perceiving the beauty and perfection[39]/

My final aim

To concentrate around me the leaders of all *reforms*—transcendentalist, spiritualists, free soilers

[40][40] flawless truth and put it in the windows of your brain[41]

A Man at Auction[42]

How much for the man
He is of ? value
For him the earth lay preparing billions of years without one animal or plant
For him the things of the air, the earth and the sea
He is not only himself
He is the father of other men who shall be fathers in their turn.

[41][43] *A Woman at Auction*

How much for the woman?
For her all
She[44] is not only herself, she is the bearer of of other woman, who shall be mothers,
She is the bearer of men who shall be fathers[?]

[42] For him all sentiments[45]
In his appointed day he becomes a God
In his appointed time he reaches his ecstasy
He is the one loved
He is the master

[43] (verse in each
picture illustrating a European Asiatic African/[46]

38. Deleted: "not"

39. Line from left across leaf.

40. The entire leaf is cancelled with a vertical stroke. The writing is a scrawl, but there are no emendations in the manuscript.

41. Preceding three words inserted below "the windows" The whole passage is cramped at the top of the leaf.

42. Cf. "I Sing the Body Electric" (1855), sec. 7.

43. The lower third of this leaf [41–42] has been cut off. The leaf is cancelled with a vertical stroke. Cf. "I Sing the Body Electric" (1855), sec. 8, ll. 118–120.

44. Deleted: "can"

45. Deleted verse: "for him"

46. Possibly the first suggestion of "Salut au Monde!" (1856). Proper nouns in column. Line from left below halfway across leaf.

American opera[47]

when a song is sung the accompaniment to be by only one instrument or two instruments the rest silent the vocal[48] performer to make far more of his song, or solo part, by by-play, attitudes, expressions, movements, &c. than is[49] at all made by the Italian opera singers—/

The American opera to be far more simple, and give far more scope to the *persons* enacting the characters

[*44*][50] Fiercely and with screaming energy

This great earth that rolls in the air, and the sun and moon, and men and women—do you think nothing more is to be made of than storekeeping and books and produce and drygoods and something to pay taxes on?

[*45*] Who are the[51] three old men going slowly with their arms about each others' necks[52]

Who are

[*46*][53] This great round globe with its rolling circles—and time—and perpetual motions—and all the moving animals—men and women—the sea and soil—the plants—the curious emanations

Have you in you the enthusiasm for the battles of[54] Bunker Hill and Long Island and Washington's retreat?—Have you the heroic feeling for—[55]

—Look forth then for there is still occasion for courage and devotion

—Nature is not so poor but there is always occasions for courage and determined power and defiance[?]

47. See [*56*] post, and "A Visit to the Opera." [*43*] and [*56*] first published by Furness, 201, *n*37.

48. Inserted on a line above "the . . . performer"

49. Deleted: "usual in the" ; inserted: "at all" on a line above "usual"

50. Paragraph with hanging indentation. Printed by Furness, 46, the source of the final five words. In MS "Fiercely" is circled. Like a number of passages in this notebook and others, this entry seems to have been written for oratorical delivery. See "restrain gesture."

51. Preceding three words inserted on a line above "Three old" Capital "Three" not reduced to lowercase in MS.

52. The old men appear in "Salut au Monde!" (1856), sec. 1, l. 10, and in "Debris" (1860), l. 30, *LG CRE*, 607.

53. Cf. [*44*]. Paragraph with hanging identation. On LC [*3315R*].

54. Deleted: "Washington's Re" ; inserted: "Bunker Hill and" on a line above "Washington's Re . . . Long Island"

55. First published in Furness, 59.

[47][56] Always any great and original persons, teacher, inventor,[57] artist or poet, must himself make the taste and by which only[58] he will be appreciated, or even received.[59]/

for oration

must[60] we be unchecked, [*illeg.*] , unmastered.— What real Americans can be made out of slaves? What real Americans can be made out of the masters of slaves?[61]/

Then you can say as[62] to Nature this words—lend us O Nature as much[?] as you like.— Lend us the children of the poor, the ignorant, and the depraved— We are ready for them—we can receive them—for them also we have preparation and welcome— We have not, only welcome for the healthy[?][63]

[48] (Poem)[64]

Bridalnight,

A[65] One quivering jelly of love limpid transparent—
Limitless[66] jets of love, hot and enormous
Arms of love[67] strong as attraction reach as wide[68] and large as the air
Drunken and crazy with love, swing in it's in the plumetless sea
[49][69] Loveflesh swelling and deliciously[70] aching whiteblood of love/

in dream[71] the architect that comes among the stonecutters and the heaps of cut stone

56. Original beginning: "A truly" deleted; "the" inserted and deleted above "truly" ; "Always any" inserted on a line above the deleted "A truly the" On LC [*3315L*].

57. Deleted: "poet or"

58. Inserted on a line above the wordspace between "which . . . he"

59. First printed in Furness, 66–67. Line from left one-third of the way across leaf.

60. Deleted: "shall" ; inserted above: "must"

61. First printed in Furness, 74. See "As of the orator." Furness (226) comments: "Cf. one of the early passages prepared for *Leaves* (Holloway, *Whitman* (1926), 116). The more tolerant tone of that utterance would seem to indicate that this note *For Oration* must date from a considerably earlier period." His argument is not clear. Line from left halfway across leaf.

62. Inserted on a line above "to"

63. First printed in Furness, 59.

64. See [*33*] in this notebook and "I Sing the Body Electric" (1855), sec. 5, ll.59–63. The two manuscript lines which are most clearly repeated in the poem were used in reverse order. The writing in the notebook is very ill-formed and suggestive of a hasty jotting. The passage is not cancelled. On LC [*3316R*].

65. "One" is inserted above "A" , but WW did not delete the original "A" .

66. An illegible word inserted and deleted on a line above and before "Limitless"

67. Deleted: [*illeg.*]

68. Preceding three words inserted on a line above "and large"

69. "Body" deleted before "Loveflesh" . On LC [*3316L*].

70. Deleted: "throbbing" ; inserted above; "aching"

71. Inserted: "in dream" above "the architect" ; "The" corrected to lowercase.

poem describes how the workman, possessed with an indescribable faith, go on age after age in their work—and at last came architects and used each in its place the stones they had cut[72]

[50] Poem of a road[73]

The snowstorm or rainstorm bunkroom stringteam the counterfeit detector the directory of the census returns, the Presidents mean[?] and the conference[?][74]
the blows of the fightingmen—the uppercut and onetwothree

The bugle calls in the ballroom—[75] the gentlemen go for their partners — the playing begins — the dancers bow to each other.[76]

[*51*] The swimming-bath
The stinggah

The dishes on the daily table —[77] the roast meat — the oysters — the coffee cornbread and rye and wheatbread,[78]

Message and the message of the Mayor and the message of the chief of Police/[79]
The questions are such as these
Has his life shown the true American character?
And does it show the true American character?
Has he been easy[?] and friendly with his workmen? —Has he been the stern master of slaves?
Has he been for making ignominious distinctions? —Has he respected the literary classes and looked on the ignorant classes with [*illeg.*]

72. Stone cutting, like horse driving, seems to have caught WW's interest in this period. Joseph Jay Rubin, *The Historic Whitman* (University Park, 1973), 261, suggests the influence of Horatio Greenough's *Travels . . . of . . . a Yankee Stonecutter* (1852), which had appeared in the *Democratic Review*. This passage develops into "A Song of the Rolling Earth" (1856), sec. 4, ll. 125 ff., but cf. also [*17*] of this notebook, 1855 Preface, ll. 115–117, *LG CRE,* 712, and "Song of Myself" (1855), sec. 13, l. 226.

73. This note suggests "Song of Myself" (1855), sec. 46 and "Song of the Open Road" (1856).

74. Inserted: "the census . . . conference[?]" on lines above "blows . . . fightingmen"

75. Deleted: "dancers lead out" ; inserted above: "gentlemen go for"

76. These two paragraphs cancelled by lines through first and last lines and by a vertical stroke. Although they suggest the catalogs of "Song of Myself," they were used there only in sec. 15, l. 287.

77. Deleted: "—the coffee"

78. This passage cancelled with a diagonal stroke as if it had been used elsewhere, but does not appear in *LG*. The writing is loose, like the passage on [50], of which it is probably a part.

79. These two lines are crammed in on six lines at left side of page in small writing beside the three lines: "oysters . . . wheatbread" , circled and cancelled as if used elsewhere. Line across leaf, below. Cf. a similar passage in "[*illeg.*] Dick Hunt," [*16*], which seems to be a reference to the Police Riots of 1857.

[52][80] If there be[81] some brute that is very sagacious and intelligent
And if being of our human race no more sagacious and intelligent than that animal — is one preferred to the other?[82]/

Equality of all rights[?] and persons is imperiously demanded by selfpreservation.—[83]

The cause of the ruin of all states that have been ruined has been that the whole body of the inhabitants without exception were not equally interested in the preservation of those states or cities — or that a portion was degraded[84]

[53] form of a poem or the composition in which the opinions are expressed by different wise men or youths, as 1st wise men, 1st youth 1st woman.— or as expressed by Socrates, Christ[85]/

The expression of[86] a perfect made man appears not only in his face—but in his limbs—the motion of his hands and arms[87] and all his joints—his walk—the carriage of his neck—and the flex of his waist and hips Dress does not hide him The [54][88] quality he has and the[89] strong sweet[90] supple[91] nature he has[92] strike through[93] cotton and woolen.— To see him walk[94] conveys the impression of hearing a beautiful poem.— To see his back and the back of his neck and[95] shoulderside is a spectacle.[96] Great is the body!— There is something in the[97] touch of any[98] candid clean person,—what it is I do not know . . . . but it fills me with wonderful and exquisite sensations. It is enough to be with him or her.—[99]

80. On LC [*3313R*].
81. Deleted: "animal" ; inserted above: "some brute
82. First printed in Furness, 60. Line across leaf below.
83. Crammed in above the following paragraph.
84. This and the preceding paragraph first printed as one paragraph in Furness, 58.
85. Line across leaf.
86. Deleted: "well" ; inserted above: "perfect"
87. Preceding two words inserted on a line above "and" preceding "his joints"
88. On LC [*3314R*].
89. Deleted: "clean"
90. Inserted on a line above "supple"
91. Deleted: [*illeg.*] ; inserted above: "nature"
92. Deleted: [*illeg.*]
93. Deleted successively: "his" "the"
94. Deleted: "is a spectacle [*del.*] or [*ins.*] to a" ; inserted: "conveys . . . beautiful" on lines above.
95. Preceding six words inserted on a line above "shoulderside . . . is a"
96. Cf. "I Sing the Body Electric" (1855), sec. 2, ll. 12–14, 28.
97. Deleted: "close presence" ; inserted: "touch" on a line above "presence"
98. Deleted; "human being" ; inserted: "candid and clean" on a line above "human" ; "person" inserted on next line above "being" ; deleted: "and" between "candid" and "clean"
99. The entire passage beginning with "The expression" halfway down [53] is cancelled with a simple vertical stroke.

[55][1] describe the perfect male body—pancratist—perfect in all gynasia[2]/

Poem of the Wrestlers[3]

My respiration and inspiration . . . . the beating of my heart . . . . the passing of blood and air through my lungs.[4]/

Addresses on Literature[5]

Though it have all the learning and art of the schools if it has not life it is nothing.[6] When you read or hear if it does[?] not call the blood leaping and flowing—of

—We do not fall in love with statues—we have healthy love for them

[56] *American opera.*[7]—put three banjos, (or more?) in the orchestra—and let them accompany (at times exclusively,) the songs of the baritone or tenor—[8]/

Let a considerable part of the performance be instrumental—by the orchestra only.—[9]

Let a few words go a great way—the plot not complicated but simple—Always one leading idea—as Friendship, Courage, Gratitude, Love
—always a distinct meaning[10]/

The story and libretti as now are generally of no account.—[11]/

In the American Opera the story and libretto must be the *body* of the performance.

[57] The fingers of the pianist playing lightly and rapidly over the keys.[12]

illustration

a man placing his ear To place the ear flat on the breast of the motionless body to see if it has any life in its heart./

1. Possibly an anticipation of sec. 9 (1856) of "I Sing the Body Electric." On LC [*3314L*].
2. Short line from left below.
3. See "I Sing the Body Electric" (1855), sec. 2, ll. 25–27. Short line from left below.
4. Cancelled with a diagonal stroke. See "Song of Myself" (1855), sec. 2, l. 23. Line across leaf.
5. Crammed in above the paragraph.
6. Deleted: "If"
7. See [*43*] ante. First entry with hanging indentation. First printed in Furness, 201.
8. Line across leaf.
9. Line across leaf.
10. Line from left two-thirds of the way across leaf under "always . . . meaning"
11. Short line from left above "In" . Block paragraph.
12. WW usually dismissed piano music as trivial and decorative, probably in reaction to the salon music of the time or even, perhaps, to the compositions and performances of Sigismond Thalberg or Louis Moreau Gottschalk, whom he might have heard perform. See, e.g., "America needs her own poems" and "To a Certain Civilian" (1865). First printed by Furness, 234*n*131. Line from left two-thirds of the way across the leaf under the passage.

Poem
The land where woman[?]
The land where

[58] The poor despiesed[?] Irish girls and boys[13] immigrants just over/[14]

A fierce protective sweep around shielding them
I am the poet of the shallow and flat and despised[?]
Any one[15] may know that the great heroes and poets are divine
But/

The woodman that takes his axe and jug with him shall take me with him all day,[16]

[59] Poem What endures
I have no mockings and laughter? [17]
I have only to be silent? [18] and/[19]

Men and women at auction./[20]
I see Here is[21] —Adam and Eve again[22]
I see the old myths
—the/

poem picture of war
—(the hospital at Sebastopol,)[23] then the opposite—the inferences and results—what war does to develope and strengthen and make more energetic and agile humanity—and what it contributes to poetry, oratory, &c.—

13. Two preceding words inserted on a line above "immigrants."

14. Line from left halfway across leaf.

15. Deleted: "can know" ; inserted: "may know" above. See "Song of Myself" (1855), sec. 24, ll. 513–514. Line halfway across the page under "But"

16. See "Song of Myself" (1855), sec. 47, l. 1258. Cancelled with a diagonal stroke.

17. Question mark above "laughter"

18. Question mark above "silent"

19. WW wrote the instruction "Modify" circled above the two preceding lines. See "Song of Myself" (1855), sec. 4, l. 81. Both lines cancelled by a vertical stroke. Line halfway across the page under "I have . . . and"

20. See "I Sing the Body Electric" (1855), sec. 7–8.

21. "Here is" written above "I see"

22. In the 1855 *Leaves,* Adam and Eve are mentioned only in "Great Are the Myths." It is, however, possible that WW was beginning to think of "Children of Adam."

23. The siege of Sevastopol in the Crimea lasted from October, 1854 to September, 1855. The work of Florence Nightingale in reorganizing the inadequate British military hospitals at Scutari rapidly became world famous. She arrived in the Crimea November 4, 1854.

[60][24] he does not lose by comparison with the orange tree or magnolia or with[25] fields that nourish the sugarplant or the cottonplant . . . .[26] what strengthens or clothes[27] adorns or is luscious can be had through subtle[28] counterparts[29] from him— from him[30] magnolia and orange[31] and sugarplant and cottonplant and all fruits and flowers and all the sorts and productions of the earth.—[32]

[*61*][33] Poem—addressed to a young man who has come of age and is[34] in possession of immense wealth.—[35]/

address on literature/

you must become a force in the state—and a real and great force—just as real and great as the president and congress—greater than they.

[62] I am an old artillerist
I tell of some[36]

On South Fifth st (Monroe place) 2 doors above the river from Sixth street—going toward Greenpoint—[37] On Wilson st[38]/ Green corner Fifth & Grand[39]

[*64; 63 blank*] blatherers[40]

24. Deleted at top of page: "all that"
25. Deleted: "the"
26. Deleted: "all that" ; inserted above: "what"
27. Inserted: "clothes" above "adorns"
28. Inserted: "subtle" above "through counterparts"
29. Inserted: "through counterparts" above "be had . . . from"
30. Illegible word inserted and deleted above "him"
31. "magnolias" and "oranges" reduced to the singular. These two trees do not appear in 1855 Preface, but do appear in "By Blue Ontario's Shore" (1856), l. 79. Cf. *n*41 below.
32. Cf. 1855 Preface, ll. 60 ff., *LG CRE,* 711–712.
33. The film shows what may be an irregularly torn stub which covers the five bottom lines on this leaf, but since the film is so indistinct, the stub has *not* been counted in numbering the pages. Dark lines and shadows across the upper left corner suggest that this and the next three lines may have been dog-eared at one time.
34. Preceding four words inserted on a line above "in po"
35. Line from left halfway across leaf.
36. Cf. "Song of Myself" (1855), sec. 33, ll. 858–859. Not cancelled. Line across leaf.
37. Line from left two-thirds of the way across the leaf above "On Wilson st"
38. Short line from left under "On Wilson"
39. The locations are in Brooklyn.
40. Cf. "By Blue Ontario's Shore" (1856), sec. 6, l. 90. The word was not used in 1855 Preface. Cf. *n*31, above.

The[41] affluent man is he who[42] confronts the grandest show or sees[43] by[44] an equivalent or more than equivalent[45] from[46] the[47] grander wealth of himself.—[48]

Insouciance[49]

een soo se áwnz /[50]

or the mettlesome action of the blood horse/[51] and the unimpeachableness of the sentiment of trees/[52] & jealous and haughty instinct[53] [65 *blank*.]

41. Deleted: "wealthy" ; inserted above: "affluent" .Printed in Furness, 45.

42. Deleted: "answers all the wealth" ; inserted above "confronts whatever the grandest show" ; deleted: "whatever"

43. Deleted: "or[?]"

44. Deleted: "its"

45. Preceding four words inserted on a line above ". . . lent . . . [*del.*] depths"

46. Illegible word deleted; "from" inserted below.

47. Deleted: "depths" ; inserted and deleted below: "bottomless riches[?]" ; inserted to left: "grander"

48. Cf. "The regular old followers."

49. Capitalized over "i"

50. WW used this in his French "dictionary" appended to "America's Mightiest Inheritance," *Life Illustrated* (April 12, 1856), *NYD*, 51–65. Short line from left. Printed in Furness, 208–43.

51. Line across leaf.

52. Line across leaf. Deleted: "haughty" preceeding " & jealous"

53. See 1855 Preface, ll. 280–281, *LG CRE*, 717. Printed by Furness, 51.

? Seems Perpetually Goading.

Manuscript not found. Text from *N&F,* 122 (Pt. III, #135; *CW,* IX, 145–146). For first printing see "The regular time for baking." This probably was written in the 1840s or early 1850s.

? seems perpetually goading me—the soul—If all seems right—it is not right—then corruption—then putridity—then mean maggots grow among men—they are born out of the too richly manured earth.

It Seems to Me.

Manuscript in Duke (17, #40). Inscribed in black pencil on small scrap of white wove paper. The date is not known, but it seems safe to date this sort of elementary advice between 1847 and early 1855. First printed *N&F,* 57 (Pt. II, #13; *CW,* IX, 6).

It seems to me—to avoid *all* poetical similes—to be faithful to the perfect likelihoods of nature—healthy, exact, simple, disdaining ornament.

"Every Accession."

Manuscript in NYPL (Berg). Inscribed in black ink on white paper, 2 13/16" x 3 13/16", corners trimmed. Rectangular mark of glossy brown substance, possibly mucilage. The quotation is from John Forster (1812–1876), English man of letters and biographer, *Statesmen of the Commonwealth of England,* 5 vols. (New York: Harper & Bros., 1846). Thomas L. Brasher, *Whitman as Editor of the Brooklyn "Eagle"* (Detroit, 1970), 240, says WW reviewed the work July 27 and September 7, 1846 in the Brooklyn *Eagle,* which may be an indication of the date of this MS. It clearly was written before or early in 1855. Printed in *N&F,* 176 (Pt. IV, #113; *CW,* X, 30).

"Every accession of originality of thought," says the author of *Statesmen of the Commonwealth of England,* "brings with it necessarily an accession of a certain originality of style."

Make No Quotations.

Manuscript in Duke (17, #40). Inscribed in black pencil on irregular scrap of white laid paper, 2½" x 7⅛". Corners clipped. Brownish rules ⅜" apart. First printed *N&F,* 56 (Pt. II, #7; *CW,* IX, 4–5). The date of such elementary advice must be between 1847 and early 1855.

Make no quotations, and no reference to any other writers.—[1]

Lumber the writing with nothing—let it[2] go as lightly as a bird flies in the air—or a fish swims in the sea

Be careful to temper down too much[3]

1. A dash following the dash deleted.
2. Deleted: "fly" ; inserted above: "go"
3. Deleted: "personality" . Cf. the much later advice, "To change the Book."

In the Present State.

Manuscript in NYPL (Berg). Inscribed in pencil on heavy white wove paper, 2 15/16" x 4 5/16". Corners trimmed. Printed in *N&F,* 146 (Pt. III, #193; *CW,* IX, 196–197). The small neat writing suggests this was written in the 1840s or early 1850s.

In the present state of[1] society & literature nothing is more singular than to be without singularity,[2] nothing more eccentric than to be entirely sane & without exentricity

1. Deleted: "Nothing is" on a line below "the present" (probably a false start); preceding five words inserted above.

2. Deleted: "[*illeg.*] and"

Cheap Looking Glasses.

Manuscript not found. Text from *N&F,* 143 (Pt. III, #188; *CW,* IX, 191–192). "Superb and infinitely manifold . . . mind of man or woman" is in MS in NYPL (Berg) from which it is transcribed. Inscribed in black pencil on white laid scrap, 2⁹⁄₁₆" x 7½". Brown rules ⅜" apart. It probably became separated from its context when the Bucke collection was put up at sale. No doubt the remainder of the original MS is in two scraps in unknown collections. The order of *N&F* is followed here. The writing, the paper and the word "octillion" (see "albot Wilson") indicate a date in the 1850s, probably before or early 1855.

Cheap looking glasses and nearly all pictures distort things from the unerring harmony and equilibrium of nature.

Superb and infinitely[1] manifold[2] as[3] natural objects are—[4]each foot out[5] of the[6] countless octillions of the cubic leagues of space[7] being crammed full of[8] absolute or[9] relative wonders,— not any one of these, nor the whole of them together, disturbs or seems awry to the mind of man or woman.— When one is sick or old or irritable and the richest parlors and costliest ornaments appear unsightly and . . .

1. Inserted on a line above "and man"
2. Inserted: [*illeg.*] on a line above and before "as"
3. Deleted: "the" ; inserted above: "natural"
4. Deleted: "not a so cubic solid" ; inserted on a line above the deleted "not a" : "each"
5. Inserted above the wordspace between "foot . . . of"
6. Deleted: "numberless" ; inserted above: "countless"
7. Deleted: "but has its positive [*illeg.*] ho is" ; inserted: "being" on a line above the deleted "is"
8. Deleted: "positive" ; inserted above: "absolute"
9. Deleted: "direct" ; inserted above: "relative"

Speaking of Literary Style.

Manuscript in NYPL (Berg). Inscribed in faded black ink on white faded wove paper, 2³/₁₆" x 7½", with blue rules ⅜" apart. An unknown hand has written "54" on the mounting sheet. Since on the recto of this scrap are lines anticipating the defeat passages in "Song of Myself" this probably was written in 1854 or early 1855. The source of the quotation from Voltaire has not been found. Printed in *N&F,* 143 (Pt. III, #186; *CW,* IX, 191).

Speaking of literary style in poems, "nothing is more easy," said Voltaire, than to do violence to nature—nothing more difficult than to imitate her."

verse was the first writing of all we know Greek,[1] the Old Testament

1. Deleted: [*illeg.*]

For Example, Whisper.

Manuscript not found. Text from *N&F,* 168 (Pt. IV, #60; *CW,* X, 17). Bucke describes the paper as "torn and almost falling to pieces" and points out the similarity of the text to "Song of Myself" (1855), sec. 43, ll. 1096–1110. The date is undoubtedly before 1855.

For example, whisper privately in your ear . . . the studies . . . be a rich investment if they . . . to bring the hat instantly off the . . . all his learning and bend himself to feel and fully enjoy . . . superb wonder of a blade of grass growing up green and crispy from the ground. Enter into the thoughts of the different theological faiths—effuse all that the believing Egyptian would— all that the Greek—all that the Hindoo, worshipping Brahma — the Koboo adoring his fetish stone or log—the Presbyterian—the Catholic with his crucifix and saints—the Turk with the Koran.

Mocking All the Textbooks.

Manuscript in NYPL (Berg). Inscribed on white laid paper, 2⅛" x 3¾", vertical chain lines, rules ⅜" apart on recto and verso. Cut up by WW. The bracketed lines are printed by Bucke (*N&F,* 58 [Pt. II, #22; *CW,* IX, 10]) but are not present in the existing MS which was probably trimmed. On verso is "is wider than the west." This was probably written before or early in 1855.

Mocking[1] all the textbooks and professors' expositions and proofs and diagrams and practical show, stand or lie millions of the[2] all the most beautiful and common facts.[3] [We are so proud of our learning! As if it were anything to analyze fluids and call certain parts oxygen or hydrogen, or to map out stars and call . . .]

1. Deleted: "Behind" "Eluding" ; inserted: "Mocking"
2. Deleted: [*illeg.*]
3. MS cut off.

Rule in All Addresses.

Manuscript in LC (Feinberg #1104–1107). Inscribed in pencil, except where noted, on both sides of a sheet of white wove paper, 12⅝" x 7⅝", rules ¼" apart, ¾" margin at top, torn out of a large bound notebook. The torn left edge indicates that [2] was the recto and may have been inscribed first. On [*1*] are lines for "Song of Myself" (1855), and on [2] are lines used in "Crossing Brooklyn Ferry" (1856). Whether the latter entries were made before *LG* 1855 or whether WW made the entries over a period of time before and after 1855 is not clear, although the plans for poems on [2] suggest that WW may have been thinking of a new edition. However, the physical evidence of the torn edge of the leaf may indicate that, despite the textual evidence used above, WW did begin to write on what is here called [2]. The date of the earliest drafts of "Crossing Brooklyn Ferry" may well have been before 1855. Cf. "memorials" in which 1860 poems appear in an 1854 notebook. The "poem descriptive of a good wife" *may* be related to early notes on housekeeping (see "The regular time for baking bread"). The date is probably before and shortly after 1855. (Gene Edward Veith, Jr.)

[*1*] *Rule in all addresses—and poems and other writings, etc.*— Do not undertake to say any thing however plain to you, unless you are positive[1] are making it perfectly plain to those who hear or read.— *Make* it plain.—[2]

Unhappy character.— One who depends mostly upon others for his or her happiness, will never have any at all.— To be constantly watching the changes in people you love.

One must be contained within himself— otherwise the world is all in vain.—

I say to my own greatness, Away!
I will not be a leader of men, I will always be their mate and companion.[3]
I do not desire eminence, I desire equality.—
I will[4] break up this[?] demention that man is the servant of God, or of many gods;[5]

1. Deleted in pencil: "it will be" ; inserted in pencil above: "are making it"
2. Preceding entry in ink. See later section on Oratory.
3. "Mate and companion" echoed in "Song of Myself" (1855), sec. 7, l. 137.
4. "will" circled.
5. Cf. "Song of Myself" (1855), sec. 20, l. 398; sec. 48, l. 1271.

I say that[6] every man is great to himself and every woman to herself;
And that to take an inferior[?] place or be humble is unbecoming /[7]

A mother as well as father, a child as well as a man;[8]
Not only an American, .but an African, Europeand, and Asiatic,[9]
A farmer, a carpenter, a blacksmith,[10] a cook
A lawyer, a doctor, a priest, a[11] sailor, an artist.[12]
Capable of all that is ugly and mean, and capable of[13] all that is pure and heroic,
Ignorant and accomplished, a chaos and[14] an answering purpose.[15]
Elasticity[16] I am—and I am the[17] dense rock—and[18] I this invisible[19] gas of the air—

Scheming, storming, planning, loving, cautioning[20]
Laughing and weeping, Backing and filling, appearing and disappearing
I travel day and night[21] these eternal roads[22]/[23]

Don't forget the bombardment[24]

In me are the old and young the fool[25] and the wise[26] thinker[27]
I enclose the heroic, and I enclose the mean and vicious.—

6. Deleted: "nothing [*illeg.*] he" ; inserted above: "every man"

7. The following eleven lines are cancelled by a vertical stroke and a large loop. Deleted false start: "A father" The false start and the first line, "A mother . . . a man;" seem to have been inserted.

8. "Song of Myself" (1855), sec. 16, l. 331.

9. See "The Sleepers" (1855), sec. 8, l. 163. The following line, originally the last part of the line "A lawyer . . . an artist," is transferred here by asterisks and WW's notation "tr up" in ink. Inserted in ink: "A farmer, a"

10. Deleted in ink: "a sailor,"

11. Deleted in ink: "farmer" ; inserted in ink: "sailor"

12. For the preceding two lines, cf. "Song of Myself" (1855), sec. 16, l. 347–348.

13. Preceding two words inserted on a line above "all that"

14. Deleted: "a perfect syste" ; inserted above: "an answering purpose"

15. The lines "Elasticity . . . air—" marked by curved line and WW's notation in ink: "? out" in the left margin.

16. The word is used in "Song of Myself" (1855), sec. 45, l. 1169. Deleted: "in"

17. Deleted: "solid" ; inserted above and deleted: "palpable" ; inserted below: "dense"

18. Deleted: "I the" ; inserted: "I this" on a line above the wordspace between "[*del.*] I the . . . invisible"

19. Inserted and deleted: "as the" on a line above the wordspace between "invisible gas" and "gas"

20. Deleted false start of next line: "Appearing and d" ; inserted above: "Laughing and weeping,"

21. Deleted: "such [*illeg.*]" ; inserted below: "these eternal roads"

22. For these three lines see "Song of Myself" (1855), sec. 33, ll. 795–797.

23. A curved line written across the page and through the following line, which WW thus may have intended to delete.

24. WW probably means the bombardment of the "old artillerist" in "Song of Myself" (1855), sec. 33, ll. 858ff. The following three lines are in ink.

25. Deleted: "—ish"

26. Deleted: "observer" ; inserted: "thinker"

27. See "Song of Myself" (1855), sec. 16, l. 330.

Life in the universe—a vast[28] circular procession whose ? rings expand outward and outward[29]

[2] Depressions

Every thing I have done seems to me blank and[30] suspicious.— I doubt whether[31] my greatest thoughts, as I had supposed them, are not shallow—and people will most likely laugh at[32] me.—[33] My pride is impotent, my love gets no response.— The complacency of nature is hateful—[34] I am[35] filled with restlessness.— I am[36] incomplete.—

We do not so much care what people say—we are deeply interested in what they do.— If we can imagine nothing left of a man but talk,— would not that be a ridiculous remnant?— Yet a deaf and dumb person might still be one of the heroes.—

It is only the shallow who Do you suppose I[37] would lift themselves myself[38] out of their race by something eminent and specially attractive.—

I am not quite such a fool as that
I am too great to be a mere President or Major General
I remain with my fellows,— with mechanics and farmers and common people;
I remain with them all on equal terms

There are many great painters— they paint scenes from[39] books, and illustrate from what the romancer and rhymster has prepared before them.— This artist does not illustrate or paint any such scenes or groups or characters.— He delineates[40] from himself.— Do you not like this magnificent disdain?[41]—[42]

Poem descriptive of a good wife (housekeeper, cook, Mother of many children.)/[43]

Poem

What is Beauty?
Beauty is simply health.

28. Inserted on a line above "circular"
29. See "Song of Myself" (1855), sec. 45, 1185–1186.
30. Deleted: "shallow and"
31. Inserted and deleted: "who" on a line above the wordspace between "whether my"
32. Deleted: "them.— —"
33. See "Crossing Brooklyn Ferry" (1856), sec. 6, ll. 68–69.
34. Deleted: "for"
35. Deleted: "so"
36. Deleted: "so"
37. Preceding four words above "only the shallow who"
38. "myself" written on a line above "themselves"
39. Deleted: "the"
40. Deleted: "for"
41. Deleted: "of"
42. Remaining entries in ink.
43. Hanging indentation. *LG* 1856 contained "Poem of Women" ("Unfolded Out of the Folds"). See also "George Walker" and "Song of the Broad-Axe" (1856), sec. 11.

Is Wider Than the West.

Manuscript in NYPL (Berg). Inscribed on white laid paper, approx. 2⅛" x 3¾". Vertical chain lines. Blue rules ⅜" apart on recto and verso. Cut up by WW? The first two entries are not in Bucke. The bracketed lines are printed by him in *N&F*, 58 (Pt. II, #23; *CW*, IX, 10) but are not in the MS. On recto is *"Mocking all the textbooks."* Since the second entry suggests "The orbic flex of his mouth is pouring and filling me full" ("Song of Myself" (1855), sec. 26, l. 602), this probably was written before or early in 1855.

is wider than the west.—

The orbed opening of whose mouth

Nature is rude at first—but once begun never tires Most works of [art tire. Only the Great Chef d'OEuvres never tire and never dazzle at first.]

How Gladly.

Manuscript in Duke (16, #39). Inscribed in faded black ink with pencil insertions on two pieces of irregular white paper approx. 4⅝" x 7¾" and 4⅞" x 7¾". Corners clipped. Brownish rules 5/16" apart. The two are not necessarily one piece, but matching pinholes show that they were once pinned together and Bucke, who probably had them in the original pinned state, prints them as one item (though in reverse order). This anticipates several passages in "Song of Myself" (1855), particularly sec. 11, ll. 182–183 and sec. 14, ll. 255–258, which suggests WW wrote this before or early in 1855. *N&F,* 125 (Pt. III, #145; *CW,* IX, 151–152).

[1]How gladly we leave[2] the best of what is called learned and refined society, or the company of[3] men from[4] stores and offices,[5] to sail all day on the river amid [*?*][6] a party of[7] fresh and jovial boatmen, with no coats or suspenders, and their trowsers tucked in their boots.—[8] Then[9] the quick[10] blood within[11] joins[12] their gay blood and[13] the twain dances[14] polkas from the[15] bottom to the top of the house,[16] long constraint in the respectable and money-making dens of existence,[17] a man emerges[18] for[19] a few hours[20] and comes up like a whale to

1. Paragraph symbol. There are traces of writing at top of the leaf, which has been trimmed.
2. Inserted in pencil: "the best . . . society, or" on a line above "we leave . . . [*del.*] lawyers"
3. Deleted in pencil: "lawyers and book-factors and"
4. "from" written over [*illeg.*]; deleted: "the"
5. Inserted and deleted in pencil: "from [*illeg.*] the best of what is called intellectual society" on a line above "to sail . . . river"
6. Bucke's reading. Heavily smeared and written over in MS.
7. Deleted: "pilots and" ; inserted above in pencil: "fresh and jovial"
8. Deleted: "what polkas are danced" ; following nine words inserted on a line above.
9. Deleted in pencil: "How" ; inserted in pencil before "how" : "Then"
10. Inserted on a line above "blood"
11. Deleted: "us"
12. Deleted in pencil: "other" ; inserted above in pencil: "their"
13. Inserted in pencil: "the twain" on a line above "dances"
14. Deleted: "swift"
15. Deleted: "top to the"
16. Plural "s" inserted and deleted in pencil; deleted in pencil: "when, [*ins.*] ? after"
17. Deleted: "we" ; inserted above: "a man" ; "s" added to "emerge"
18. Deleted: "for a few hours"
19. Written over "into[*?*]"
20. Following sixteen words inserted on a line above "for [*del.*] a . . . free and [*del.*] beautiful"

spout and breathe.— One glimpse then of the eternal[21] to[22] the[23] realities of[24] things—the real[25] sun, burning and dazzling—the old, forever young[26] and[?] solid earth—real men[27] and women refreshing,[28] hearty, and wicked.—[29]

Outdoors is the best antisep[tic][30] yet.— What a charm[?][31] there is[32] in men that have lived mainly in[?][33] the open air—among horses—at sea—on the canals[?][34]—digging clams—timbers[35]—rafters[36] and steamboaters,[37]— or[38] framers of houses—and mechanics generally.— Cleanly shaved and[39] grammatical folks I call Mister, and lay the tips of my fingers inside their elbows[40] after the orthodox fashion, and discuss whatever had the biggest headline in the morning papers, and pass the time as comfortably as the law allows.— But for the others, my arm leans over their shoulders, and around their necks.—In them nature justifies herself.—[41] Their indefinable excellence[42] gives[43] out something as[44] much[45] beyond the special[46] productions[47] of colleges and pews and parlors as the morning air of the prairie or the sea-shore outsmells the costliest scents of the perfume shop.

21. Deleted: "ly" in "eternally"
22. Deleted: "in" in "into"
23. Deleted: "free and beautiful"
24. Deleted: "the worl"
25. Inserted above "sun"
26. Written over a smaller "y" Inserted: "and[?] solid" on a line above "earth"
27. Inserted: "and women" on a line above "men . . . refreshing"
28. Deleted: "strong" ; inserted above: "hearty"
29. End of first leaf. Beginning of next leaf, upper left corner, badly smeared and damaged.
30. Tear in MS.
31. Tear in MS.
32. Deleted: "about" ; inserted: "in"
33. Tear in MS.
34. Tear in MS.
35. Deleted in pencil: "cutting timber" ; inserted above in pencil: "timberers"
36. Deleted in pencil: "rafting" ; inserted above in pencil: "rafters"
37. Suffix "ers" and comma written in pencil over "steamboating" ; remainder of sentence, to "mechanics generally" , inserted in pencil on a line above "— . . . gram"
38. Deleted in pencil: "house" before "framers"
39. Deleted: "more"
40. Deleted and smeared out: [*illeg.*] ; inserted above: "after"
41. Deleted: "and in [*capital* "I" *written over* "in" *and deleted*] [*ins. and del. in pencil*] in " ; punctuation changed to ".—" ; capital "T" written in pencil over lowercase in "their"
42. Deleted in pencil: "giving" ; inserted above in pencil: "gives"
43. Deleted: "us[?]" ; inserted above: "out"
44. Deleted: "superior[?] to all" ; inserted: "much beyond"
45. Deleted: "above" before the inserted "beyond"
46. Inserted on a line above "prod"
47. Remaining twenty-four words are not in the MS, which does have traces of writing that has been clipped off. Text from Bucke.

And to the Soul.

Manuscript in LC (#63, sheet #295R). Inscribed in black ink and pencil on laid paper, 12⅞" x 8¼", vertical chainlines 1¹/₁₆" apart. Faded rules ⅜" apart. The paper is identical to that of "human feet, await us," dated 1855 or earlier. The second paragraph is printed in Furness, 60.

And to the soul every feeble and helpless creature is its child

[1]Clergymen? get their two or ten thousand a year, and members of Congress their eight dollars a day; and certainly it is right enough[2] by the moral[3] theory that floats on the surface[4],—Which is exactly the same as the paper money theory; every body knows that it is not money and the puzzle is never[5] exactly satisfied; but the bills pass and we will take them as long as[6] other folks do.

[7]*Moon blind horse* Moon eyed[8]. There are some[9] horses who see perfectly well except at a certain change or quartering of the moon.— At that period, no matter when it comes, they are blind.— Horses so affected are liable by any bad management hard work &c to become confirmedly blind

1. Deleted: "Ministers" before "Clergymen?" Entire paragraph cancelled by a slash and a wavy line.
2. Deleted: "as the [*illeg.*] " ; inserted: "by" on a line above [*illeg.*]
3. Inserted on a line above "theory"
4. ".—" and capital "W" inscribed over semicolon and lowercase "w" in "which"
5. Deleted: "clearly" ; inserted above: "exactly"
6. Deleted: "we"
7. Paragraph in pencil.
8. Preceding two words inserted in ink above *"Moon blind"* probably as alternate reading.
9. Inserted on a line above "horses"

In Metaphysical Points.

Manuscript in Duke (26, #33). Inscribed in black pencil and ink on white laid paper, approx. 8¾" x 7¾". Brown rules ⅜" apart. Lower corners trimmed. The second paragraph, added in ink, faintly anticipates "Song of Myself" (1855), sec. 23. The content, the small writing, and the paper indicate this was written before or early in 1855. First printed *N&F,* 120–121 (Pt. II, #130; *CW,* IX, 142–143). Bucke introduces paragraphing not in the MS.

In metaphysical points, here is what I guess about pure and positive truths.[1] I guess that after all reasoning and analogy and their most palpable demonstrations of any *thing,*[2] we have the[3] real satisfaction[4] only when the soul tells and tests by its own arch-chemic power—[5]superior to the learnedest[6] proofs[7], as one glance of[8] living sight, is more than[9] quarto volumes of description[10] and of maps.— There is something in vast[11] erudition melancholy and fruitless as an Arctic sea.— With most men it is a slow[12] dream,[13] dreamed in a moving fog.— So complacent! So much body and muscle; fine legs to walk,— large supple hands—but the eyes are owl's eyes, and the heart is a mackerel's heart.— These words are for the great men, the[14] gigantic few that have[15] plunged themselves[16] deep through density and confusion, and pushed back the jealous coverings of the earth, and[17]

1. Preceding sentence inserted. Deleted: "Pure and Positive Truth about Metaphysical points [*preceding three words inserted on a line above* ".—It seems to me"].—It seems to me"

2. Inserted in ink: "we have" above *"thing,"*

3. Inserted in ink and deleted: "only" following "have" ; following five words inserted in ink on the same line after "only"

4. Deleted: "comes" ; inserted above: "only"

5. Deleted: "something as"

6. Deleted: "and reasoning"

7. Deleted: "and finest reasoning"

8. Deleted: "the" ; inserted in pencil on a line above "sight" : "living"

9. Deleted: "the elaborate" ; inserted above: "quarto volumes of"

10. Deleted: "filling a thousand quarto volumes" ; inserted and deleted: "and" on a line above "ion" in "description" ; inserted: "and of maps.—" following the deleted "and"

11. Deleted: "learning" ; inserted above: "erudition"

12. Deleted: "large"

13. Deleted: "and in a fog too"

14. Deleted: "giants" ; inserted: "gigantic few" on a line above "giants that"

15. Deleted: "reached" ; inserted above: "plunged"

16. Deleted: "out into space" ; inserted above: "deep through density"

17. Deleted: "told us the" ; inserted above: "brought out the" ; "true and" inserted above "great" at the beginning of the next line.

brought out the true and great things, and[18] the sweet things,[19] and hung them like[20] oranges,[21] rounder and riper than[22] all the rest, among our literature and science.— These words are for the[23] five or six grand poets, too; and the masters of artists.[24] I waste no ink, nor my throat, on the[25] ever-deploying armies of professors, authors, lawyers, teachers and what not.[26] Of them we expect[27] that they be very learned, and nothing[28] more.—[29]

What gentlemen! what then? Do you suppose it is for your geology and your chemistry and your mathematics

18. Deleted: "true" ; inserted above: "the sweet"
19. Deleted: "that hang" ; inserted above: "and hung them"
20. Inserted and deleted: "round ripe" on a line above "oranges"
21. Deleted: "on the"
22. Deleted: "ever before, on the limbs of" ; inserted: "all the rest, among our" on a line above "ever . . . limbs"
23. Inserted: "five or six" on a line above "the grand"
24. Deleted: "—" ; inserted: "I waste no ink, nor my throat," on a line above "on the [*del.* huge"
25. Deleted: "huge"
26. Deleted: "let us waste no [*del.*] words ink or [*del.*] breath [*ins. on a line above* "breath" type.—; comma after "not" not deleted, period added; inserted: "Of them" on next line above "we"
27. Deleted: "of them to" ; inserted above: "that they"
28. Deleted: [*illeg.*]
29. Following eighteen words are in ink.

Identical with.

Manuscript in Duke (75). Inscribed in black pencil on verso of "Birth of Hercules." "I Sing the Body Electric" (1855), sec.2, ll. 28–30, 32, depicts a "march of firemen . . . / The slow return from the fire." The date is 1855 or earlier.

identical with the [*MS trimmed*]
years ago—and he was satisfied that they were of that distant date./

Attitudes and expressions of a fire company[1] returning slowly home, with fine flushed faces and loose attire: The[2] bell strikes, a fresh alarm, and on the instant [*MS trimmed*] stop and each has a [*MS trimmed*] and eager, listening look, to[3]

1. Deleted: "of"
2. Deleted: "alarm"
3. Entire entry canceled by vertical stroke.

I Do Not Compose.

Manuscript in Duke (11, #26). Inscribed in black pencil on white laid paper, 4 5/16" x 7 11/16", vertical chain lines, rules spaced 5/16" apart. On verso are lines: "I am your voice . . . / I celebrate myself to celebrate every man and woman." See "Song of Myself" (1855), sec. 1, ll. 1–3. These lines combined with the small neat writing suggest a date before or early in 1855. First printed in *N&F,* 74 (Pt. II, #71; *CW,* IX, 43).

I do not[1] compose[2] a grand opera, with[3] good instrumention and[4] parts[5] which you shall sing as I have[6] written them,[7] and[8] whose performance[9] will give fits to the dilletanti, for its elegance and measure.—[10] To[11] sing well your part of an opera is[12] excellent; but[13] it is not enough.—[14]You[15] should be master of the composers of all[16] operas—[17]and of all tenors—and[18] of all violins and first violins,—for they were all men like yourself, and[19] perhaps less developed than yourself.

1. Deleted: "pretend to"
2. Deleted: "an" ; inserted above: "a grand"
3. Deleted: "choice" ; inserted above: "good"
4. Deleted: "harmonious good"
5. Deleted: "that" ; inserted above: "which"
6. Inserted on a line above "written"
7. Deleted: "and the dilletanti with then [*del.*] have take fits—they will"
8. Deleted: "the" ; inserted above: "whose"
9. Deleted: "shall cannot fail of being so something to" ; inserted: "will" on a line above "cannot"
10. Deleted: "The"
11. Deleted: "compose" ; inserted: "sing well your part of" on a line above "compose an" and into the margin.
12. Deleted: "very well" ; inserted: "excellent" ; inserted and deleted: "enough" ; following "excellent" ; redundant semicolon inserted above, not shown.
13. Deleted: "that" ; inserted above: "it"
14. Deleted: "I would have"
15. Deleted: "shall the" ; inserted above: "should be"
16. Inserted on a line above the wordspace between "of . . . operas"
17. Deleted: "and first tenor of" ; inserted: "and of all" on a line above the deleted "tenor of"
18. Deleted: "first"
19. Deleted: "unless most likely" ; inserted: "perhaps" on a line above "less most"

The Analogy.

Manuscript in LC (#63, sheet #296). Inscribed in faded black ink and some pencil on white laid paper, 3⅜" x 8⅛". Chainlines 1⅛" apart. Rules 5/16" apart. Writing suggests a date of 1855 or earlier. Printed in Furness, 49.

The analogy holds in this way—that the soul[1] of the Universe is the[2] genital master, the[3] impregnating and animating spirit.—[4] Physical matter is[5] Female and Mother,[6] and waits barren and bloomless, the jets of life from the masculine vigor, the undermost first cause of all[7] that is not what Death is.—

1. Deleted: "or[?] Spirit"

2. Deleted: "Father" ; inserted and deleted: "Male and Lord" on a line above "Father, the" ; inserted in pencil: "genital master" ; "genital" inserted before "the" , "master" inserted above.

3. Deleted: "animating[?] and"

4. Deleted: "The Female All [*ins.*] Universal" ; inserted: "Physical" following the deleted "Universal"

5. Deleted: "the"

6. Preceding two words and comma inserted on a line above "and"

7. Deleted: "vigor and motion"

Steamboats and Vaccination.

Manuscript in Duke (16, #39). Inscribed in blue ink on verso of white wove scrap approx. 7⅜"x 5". On recto: "A man of gigantic stature." Numbered at top "4" in WW's hand. The leaf was canceled by a vertical stroke, which usually means that WW used the text elsewhere, but its location has not been found. There is some relationship to his meditations on property and ownership. Cf. "The regular old followers." The date is probably before or early in 1855. First printed in *N&F,* 119–120 (Pt. III, #124; *CW,* IX, 140).

steamboats and vaccination, gunpowder and spinning-jennies; but are our people half as peaceable and happy as were[1] the Peruvians and Mexicans, ere the Spanish navigators introduced[2] to them the blessings of[3] artificial science and of[4] the true faith?—

It is out of this mass of folly, wickedness, and injustice,[5] and its influence,[6] that[7] a man is required to lift himself, as the very first step toward his being[8] perfect.[9]— He must have a very high faculty of independence.— The mere authority of law, custom, or precedent, must be nothing, absolutely nothing, absolutely nothing at all, with him.— High,

1. Inserted on a line above "as . . . the"
2. Deleted: "among" ; inserted above: "to"
3. Deleted: "civilization" ; inserted above: "artificial science"
4. Inserted on a line above "the"
5. Dash deleted.
6. Dash deleted.
7. Deleted: "an individual" ; inserted on a line above "an indi" : "a man"
8. Deleted: "a"
9. Deleted: "man"

A Man of Gigantic Stature.

Manuscript in Duke (16, #39). Inscribed in black pencil on white wove scrap approx. 5″ x 7⅜″. On verso: "steamboats and vaccination." The heroic male is a favorite image in the 1855 poems. The "flowing" as a human quality in the deleted title appears only in "Song of Myself" (1855), sec. 39, l. 976 ("The friendly and flowing savage"). The date is before or early in 1855. First printed in *N&F,* 119 (Pt. III, #123; *CW,* IX, 140).

[1] A man of gigantic, stature, supple, healthy, accomplished, powerful, and[2] resistless[3] is a great man— But when[4] a man with all that is not trapped into any partiality[5]— when he strikes the[6] balance between the eternal average of the developed and the undeveloped—when he goes[7] on the square with those who have not yet[8] climbed as high as he—tender to children and old people and women—indulging most the stupid the sinful and the vulgar—because them the world is most down upon—

1. What appear to be a title and beginning of a paragraph deleted: "Picture of the most flowing grandeur of a man When a man joined to his great power, and wealth and strength, has the knowledge of the [*preceding three words ins. on a line above* "the perfect equanimity"] perfect equanimity and"

2. Inserted on a line above "r" in "resistless"

3. Comma deleted.

4. Deleted: "such an one"

5. Deleted: "or sh"

6. Deleted: "eternal"

7. "goes" written over "is[?]"

8. Inserted on a line above "c" in "climbed"

Tainting the Best.

Manuscript in NYPL (Lion). Inscribed in black pencil on white wove paper hinged at top to similar scrap containing "How mean a person." Total dimensions 7¼" x 7¾". All corners trimmed. Brown rules. On recto: "In vain the Mastodon retreats . . ." ("Song of Myself" (1855), sec. 31, l. 676). The small neat writing, the ideas and the recto indicate a date before or early in 1855. Bucke's text begins with an ellipsis not in MS. First printed *N&F,* 125 (Pt. III, #146; *CW,* IX, 152–153).

tainting the best of the rich orchard of himself. . . . and he who anyway does not respect his own organs and cherish them and strengthen them, and keep himself clean[1] outside and inside—[2] let that man young or old never[3] deceive himself with the folly that the[4] sore stuff[5] is hid by the cloth he wears and[6] makes no avowal.— Though the secret is well hid, though the eye does not see, nor the hand touch, nor the nose smell, the rank odor strikes out

1. Deleted: "not only on his face but"
2. Deleted: "need not"
3. Deleted: "do[?]"
4. Deleted: "bad" ; inserted above: "sore"
5. Deleted: "and the under" ; inserted: "is hid by" on a line above "[*del.*] under"
6. Deleted: "his"

How Mean a Person.

Manuscript in NYPL (Lion). Inscribed in pencil on two pieces of light strong paper, hinged together on long side, all corners trimmed, totalling 7¼" x 7¾". Many pin holes on lower part. Text on [*1*]. On [2] is "tainting the best." "In vain the Mastodon retreats . . ." is on the recto ("Song of Myself" (1855), sec. 31, l. 676). Thus the date of this MS is before or early in 1855. Printed in *N&F,* 124 (Pt. III, #139; *CW,* IX, 149).

How mean a person is sometimes a rich man or a man in a great office—even in the Presidency!

Loveblows, Loveblossoms.

Manuscript not found. Text from *N&F,* 165 (Pt. III, #37; *CW,* X, 10). Bucke calls attention to "Song of Myself" (1855), sec. 2, l. 22. The date is before or early in 1855.

Loveblows. Loveblossoms. Loveapples. Loveleaves. Loveclimbers. Loveverdure. Love Vines. Lovebranches. Loveroot. Climber-blossom. Verdure, branch, fruit and vine. Loveroot. Juice Climber. Silk crotch. Crotch bulb and bine. juicy, climbering mine. Bulb, silkthread crotch and. . . .

It Were Unworthy.

Manuscript in Duke (27, #35). Inscribed in pencil on white laid paper, 2¹¹/₁₆" x 7⅞". Brown rules ¼" apart recto and verso. Corners clipped. Cf. "Song of Myself" (1855), sec. 20, ll. 394–398 and sec. 32, ll. 686–691, which parallels suggest a date before or early in 1855. Bracketed section not in extant MS. The text is from Bucke, *N&F,* 119 (Pt. III, #122; *CW,* IX, 139–140).

[In this . . . Deploying on every side, touch or start from what point you like, are. . .]

It[1] were unworthy a live man to pray or complain, no matter what should[2] happen.— Will he[3] descend among those rhymsters and sexless priests[4] whose virtues are lathered and shaved three times a week,— to whine[5] about sin and hell—to[6] pronounce his race a sham or swindle—to squall out

1. Inserted and deleted: "wh" on a line above wordspace following "It" ; inserted: "were" following and above "unworthy"

2. Inserted: "should" ; on a line above the wordspace between "what . . . happen" ; "s" in "happens" deleted.

3. Deleted: "be a" ; inserted: "descend among those" on a line above "[*del.*] be a" and "rhymeters"

4. Deleted: "and" ; inserted and deleted above: "of" ; deleted: "clean shaved virtue," ; inserted above: "whose [*illeg. del.*] virtues are"

5. Deleted: "hours and weeks"

6. Deleted: "call" ; inserted: "pronounce" on a line above "call [*del.*] his"

After All Is Said and Done.

Manuscript in Duke (4, #3). Inscribed in pencil on white wove ledger paper, approx. 7³/16" x 6", corners clipped. On recto: "It is no miracle", an apparently unrelated continuation of the "touch" passage in "Song of Myself," sec. 28. Cf. "Song of Myself," sec. 4. The date is before or early in 1855. First printed *N&F,* 73 (Pt. II, #69; *CW,* IX, 42).

After[1] all[2] is said and done in the way of argument,[3] the whole[4] raises but bubble of the sea-ooze[5] against that unspeakable Something in my own soul which makes me know without being able to tell[6] how it is.[7] Though the[8] linguists and lore of the whole earth deny what I say, it amounts but to this: So it seems to them.— I simply answer, So it seems to me.— The greatest of thoughts and truths, are[9] never put in[10] print.— They are not susceptible of proof like a sum in simple multiplication

I[11] see myself[12] sweating in the fog with the linguists and learned[13] men.— I look back upon that time in my own days.— I have[14] no mockings or laughter;— I have only to be silent and[15] patiently wait.—

1. Written over [*illeg.*]
2. Deleted: "that can be"
3. Deleted: "the immeasurable it"
4. Deleted: "amount to a" ; inserted and deleted above: "means but a" ; inserted: "is a" ; inserted and deleted: "makes" on a line above "bubble" ; inserted: "raises but" on a line above "[*del.*] makes"
5. Deleted: "in comparison with" ; inserted above: "against that"
6. Deleted: "or prove" ; inserted and deleted: "how that is I know" on a line above "[*del.*] tell or prove" ; inserted before "[*del.*] how . . . know" : "how it is" (*above* "able to tell")
7. Deleted: "If I were opposed by" ; inserted and deleted: "what I felt" above "[*del.*] I were" ; inserted: "Though" above "[*del.*] If" (on the same line before "[*del.*] what I felt")
8. Deleted: "science"
9. Deleted: "not to [*illeg.*] be" ; inserted: "never" on a line above" [*del.*] not"
10. Deleted: "language" ; inserted and deleted above: "writing or" ; inserted on the line following "[*del.*] writing or" : "print." Redundant period not shown.
11. Deleted: "can[?]" . This paragraph is turned into "Song of Myself" (1855), sec. 4, ll. 80–81.
12. Deleted: "struggling" ; inserted above: "sweating"
13. Inserted and deleted: "and" on a line above the wordspace between "learned men.—"
14. Deleted: "gibes nor mocks"
15. Deleted: "to" ; inserted above: "patiently"

The Most Superb Beauties.

Manuscript in Duke (17, #40). Inscribed in black ink on white laid scrap, approx. 2⅜" x 7⅞". Vertical chainlines. Brownish rules ⅜" apart. The thought appears in a modified form in "Song of Myself," sec. 14, l. 259 in which the "beauties" and "blessing" are the wild gander, "Me" and the great catalogues of sec. 15. See also "Truly, what is commonest" and "truly the things commonest." The latter applies the sentiment to language. The date is before or early in 1855. First printed *N&F,* 124 (Pt. III, #143; *CW,* IX, 150) without first sentence.

The most superb beauties[1] are in the cheapest

The[2] divinest[3] blessings are[4] the commonest bestowed every where, and the most[5] superb[6] beauties are the cheapest, the world over.—

1. Deleted: "and"
2. Deleted: "most"
3. Written over [*illeg.*]; "st" added to "divine"
4. Deleted: [*illeg.*]
5. Inserted on a line above "su" in "superb"
6. "est" deleted from "superbest"

Truly, What Is Commonest.

Manuscript in LC (#73, sheet #456R). Inscribed in black ink on two pasted-together scraps of white wove paper. On verso of first scrap fragments of a letter [?] in a "Spencerian" hand. The writing of this MS seems to be early. See "The most superb beauties" for parallel statements. The date is before or early in 1855.

Truly, what is commonest, readiest, cheapest,[1] is often the profoundest, the most curious—has its beginnings the farthest back and is the hardest problem for thought or science[2] from the start[3]

1. Deleted: "of our lives" . Cf. a similar sequence of adjectives in "Song of Myself" (1855), sec. 14, l. 259.
2. Bottom of first scrap; fragments of words visible.
3. Preceding three words on second scrap; fragments of words visible at bottom edge.

The Most Perfect Wonders.

Manuscript in NYPL (Berg). Inscribed in pencil on pinkish-brownish laid? paper approx. 8⅛" x 5⅛". Watermark: a Florentine rose in a double border 4⅝" in diameter. The sentiments and the handwriting are those of 1855 or earlier. Bucke prints the paragraphs in another order in an attempt to follow WW's complicated but unfinished notes for transposition, here recorded in the notes but not followed. (*N&F,* 75 (Pt. III, #2; *CW,* IX, 48). Bucke may have accomplished WW's final intention, but the MS does not quite support him. WW seems to be playing with the idea of identity which he expressed quite differently in "Song of Myself" (1855), sec. 14, ll. 259.

The most perfect wonders of the earth are not[1] rare and distant but present with every person,—you as much as any:—[2]

Man![3] Woman! Youth! wherever you are, in the Northern, Southern, Eastern, or Western States—in Kanada—by the sea-coast, or far inland—[4]

What is more amazing than the[5] sun-rise, the day, the floods of light enveloping[6] fields,[7] waters, grass, trees, persons?— What is more beautiful than the night, the full moon, and the stars?— The prairies, the lakes,[8] rivers, forests,[9] are[10]

Not distant caverns, volcanoes, cataracts, curious islands, birds, foreign cities, architecture, costumes, markets, ceremonies, shows, are any more wonderful than[11] what is common to you, near you now, and continually with you.—

1. Deleted: "an [*illeg.*] letter"

2. The preceding paragraph is in a smaller hand than that of the rest of the MS and was probably inserted.

3. Marked by two lines above and below "Man" and a notation "tr down", which is written on a line above "are" in "you are" . This apparently is Bucke's justification for transposing the paragraphs.

4. Deleted: "the" ; following paragraph begins at the margin with a deleted "Th"

5. Deleted: "day"

6. Deleted: "the"

7. Deleted: "th"

8. Deleted: "t"

9. Deleted: "—all"

10. The preceding eleven words are circled and brought down on an arrow to the final paragraph, meant to follow "any more wonderful than"

11. Circled words brought down to here. Remainder of paragraph inserted on four short lines after "than" and into the margin.

The Test.

Manuscript not found. Text from Furness, 49. It is close in general feeling to "Do you know what," par. 3. The last sentence anticipates "Song of Myself" (1855), sec. 30, l. 653. This was written before or early in 1855.

The test of the goodness or truth of anything is the soul itself—whatever does good to the soul, soothes, refreshes, cheers, inspirits, consoles, &c &c—that is so, easy enough.— But doctrines, sermons, logic??

Human Feet, Awaits Us.

Manuscript in LC (#63, sheet #294R). Inscribed in black ink with black pencil emendations on white laid paper, 12⅞" x 8¼". Faded rules 5/16" apart. The writing and content suggest a date before or early in 1855. See "albot Wilson." First published in Furness, 47.

[*illeg.*][1] human feet, awaits[2] us perhaps at[?] the next corner, or through the range of an ordinary boarding house.

Noble as books and the writers of books are—the leaven of the[3] bread of[4] Life, the[5] stairs of humanity, the cables that hold[6] to[7] us, as to a shore, the freighted[8] supply ship of the past—there is something better than any and all books, and that is the real stuff whereof they are the artificial transcript and portraiture.—[9]

There are plenty who do not own books, but[10] all men[11] and women[12] posess[13] in fee simple the[14] curbless and bottomless mine itself, of[15] whence books are but the dust and scraps.—[16] I[17] have not the great pictures and sculpture of

1. Corner clipped off.
2. Deleted: [*illeg.*]
3. Inserted above.
4. Deleted: "the world" ; inserted above: "life"
5. Deleted: "ladder"
6. Deleted: terminal "s" of "holds"
7. Deleted: "our"
8. Deleted: "cycles[?]" ; inserted: "supply ship" on a line above "cycles"
9. Two preceding words and punctuation inserted above blank space in pencil. Redundant ".—" not printed.
10. Deleted: "where is the man who every" ; inserted above "every" "all"
11. Emended from "man"
12. Emended from "woman"
13. Emended from "possesses" ; deleted: "the"
14. Deleted: "vast[?]" ; inserted above "vast[?]" : "curbless and bottomless"
15. Deleted: "which"; inserted: "whence" ; remainder of the sentence in a smaller hand, probably inserted above following deletion.
16. Deleted paragraph: "I remember [*illeg.*] an evening-party once at an up-town palace, we were with great [*illeg.*] You may not be [*ins.*] on visiting towns[?] [*del.*] terms with the grand family in the up-town palace who perhaps paid a great sum for You"; following fifteen words inserted above "a great sum . . ."
17. Deleted: "You[?]"

the world—the memoirs[?] of art; have not[18] seen the fragment of the true cross[19] in Rome, or[20] the magnolia of art[21] the Last Judgment; but where, under[22] what grade[?] of latitude and longitude, will I[23] on the sea or on the land, be without the autograph of God?— What black and stupid hour is that, while the unspeakable Something[24] in man's eyes any where beams upon[25] me—that[26] I do not feel the hint and the extasy of the presence[27] of God?—[28]

I am[29] not on visiting terms with the rich connoisseur at his palace up town, who shows[30] envying visitors through sumptuous[31] galleries[32] of Rich work[33] from Italy and France, that all are,[34] [*illeg.*] a [*illeg.*] of a million.—*[35]

18. Deleted: [*illeg.*]
19. Inserted: "in Rome" above at end of line.
20. Inserted: "the Last Judgement [*illeg.*]" ; deleted: "Last Judgement" ; deleted above "magnolia" : "that"
21. Deleted and reinserted above line: "the Last Judgement"
22. Deleted: "the sun by day or the stars [*illeg.*] by [*illeg.*] night," ; inserted above deletion: "what grade[?] of latitude and longitude,"
23. Deleted: [*illeg.*]; inserted above deletion: "I on the sea or on the land,"
24. Capitalized over "s"
25. Deleted: "you," ; inserted above: "me"
26. Deleted: "you" ; inserted above: "I"
27. Preceding six words inserted in pencil above "hint of God"
28. Deleted: "himself" ; redundant "?—" not shown.
29. Original beginning deleted: "You [*ins.*] We are" inserted above: "I am"
30. Deleted: "his"
31. Deleted: "his" ; inserted above: "sumptuous"
32. Deleted: ".—" ; inserted and deleted above: "of" ; inserted above: "of"
33. Deleted: "they" ; inserted above: "from Italy and France, that"
34. Deleted: "and I too love to have them with the [*illeg., leaf torn*] many many thousand dollars"
35. No reference point for the asterisk has been found.

Do You Know What Music Does.

Manuscript in Texas (Hanley). Inscribed in black ink and black pencil on white laid paper, 12" x 7⅞". Leaf [3] is 8¼" long. Brown (faded blue?) rules 5/16" apart. A holograph transcript made when the MS was in the Bandler Collection by Emory Holloway and kindly given by him was of assistance in deciphering deleted passages. The transcript is now in the Spencer Research Library of the University of Kansas. Holloway's MS notes call attention to parallels with *LG* 1855. The parallels between paragraph 1 of the MS and "A Song for Occupations" (1855), sec. 4, ll. 95–97 are verbal. That the parallels with "Who Learns My Lesson Complete" (1855) is much more diffuse and less convincing. A further parallel between paragraph 3 and "The test of the goodness or truth" is closer than the latter, but still is only a parallel rather than a source. Page [*1*] in facsimile in William W. Cohen Catalogue, American Art Association, February 5–6, 1929, in Francis and Lozynsky, 171. The date is before or early in 1855.

Do you know[1] what music[*?*][2] does to the soul? Do you suppose that the[3] mere melody of those instruments—. . . — the violencello, sad and sobbing[4] as some human creature—. . . .[5] the cornet, that puts the call of[6] day light[7] and the laugh of hope into voice, and spreads its utterance around like a shower—the organ, president over the rest,[8] representing and embodying them, serious and[9] large, from respect of whom[10] all keep still and know in that presence their best[11] feats would be an impertinence—the brass band whose drums[12] cry All-

1. Deleted: "why"
2. MS torn.
3. Deleted: "melody" ; inserted: "mere melody of those instruments—. . . . ." on a line above "the [*del.*] melody" and "the vio" in "violincello" . WW may have intended to replace the dash before "the violincello" with marks of suspension (written under the dash following "instruments") in the manner of Preface 1855. See *nn*5, 17 below.
4. Deleted: "like" ; inserted above: "as"
5. Marks of suspension over dash. See *n*3 above.
6. Written over "the," which is smeared out.
7. Inserted. Written over [*illeg.*] on a line above the wordspace between "day . . . and"
8. Deleted: "embodying all, with" ; inserted: "representing and embodying them" on a line above "rest [*del.*] embodying all"
9. Deleted: "calm" ; inserted above: "large"
10. Deleted and reinserted above: "all"
11. Deleted: "[*illeg.*] [*illeg.*]" ; inserted: "feats" on a line above second deletion.
12. Inserted and deleted: "shout" on a line above "drums" ; inserted to left of deletion: "cry" ; inserted: "All-alive! and" following the deleted "shout" and above "wake up"

alive! and wake up[13] sleepers[14] from their bedrooms in the brain and put[15] coals of spunk in the[16] flimsiest tinder rags of cowards[17]—. . . . . Do[18] you suppose that in[19] these, touched by the[20] fine players of[21] the world,[22] are the[23] primary of the feelings that move you?— No; there is something else.—[24] This[25] something is[26] in the Soul[27] and eludes description.— No substantive or noun, no[28] figure or phonograph or image, stands for[29] the beatiful mystery.—[30] I can only tell you of it,[31] as one[32] might tell who[33] reaches his neck at night and[34] looks[35] far over sea after the headland of the morning.—

The Soul of Man has within itself the vitality of all that is harmonious or pleasant.[36] Those[37] physical or moral emanations[38] whose attributes we call Beauty and Virtue, and Pride,[39] and such like[40] possess little or nothing inherently;

[2] The reason that any thing pleases the Soul, is that it finds its relations

13. Deleted: "the"
14. Deleted: "in the brain brain of where they"
15. Inserted: "[*del.*] red coals [*two words del.*] the fire"
16. Deleted: "nerves of" ; inserted: "flimsiest tender rags of [*del.*] a" on a line above the deleted "nerves of" and "cowards"
17. Deleted and reinserted: "s" on "cowards" ; inserted: ". . . . ." above dash. See *n*3 above.
18. Written over [*illeg.*], smeared out.
19. Inserted on a line above wordspacing between "that . . . these"
20. Deleted: "greatest" ; inserted above: "fine"
21. Written over "in"
22. Deleted: "give forth" ; inserted above: "are the" . Redundant "the" not shown.
23. Deleted: "sounds" ; inserted above: "primary [*del.*] and" and on the same line "of the feelings" above "of that mo" (in "move").
24. Inserted and deleted with a finer-nibbed pen on a line above ".— [*del.*] ten" : "which music" ; deleted: "ten thousand fathoms"
25. Inserted on a line above "so" in "something" in left margin.
26. Inserted on a line in the wordspace between "something . . . in"
27. Deleted: "which" ; inserted: "and" on a line above and before "eludes"
28. Deleted: "writing" ; inserted: "figure [*del.*] of or phonograph" on a line above the deleted "writing" and "or image"
29. Deleted: "this" ; inserted above: "the"
30. Evidently period inserted before dash; deleted: "which tells far off as the [*illeg.*] stars hint to us from their orbits of millions of leagues afar, tell man that there is a region O Do [*capital over lowercase*] not ask me to" ; inserted: "I can only [*del.*] tell" on a line above "ask me"
31. Deleted: "except"
32. Inserted: "you [*del.*] might [*del.*] ask tell" on a line above "one . . . who"
33. Deleted: "stands" following "who" ; inserted: "reaches his neck" on a line following "tell" and above "stands"
34. Inserted and deleted. [*illeg.*] on a line above "and looks"
35. Deleted: "up at the stars.—; inserted above "looks" : "far over sea after the headland of the morning.—"
36. Deleted: "To that return From it come all and back again address themselves the [*illeg.*] of—every one of" [*preceding eight words ins. on two lines above* "[*del.*] and every"]
37. Capital letter over lowercase. Deleted: "secondary" ; inserted with a finer-nibbed pen on a line above "[*del.*] secondary" and "eman" in "emanations" "physical or moral"
38. Deleted: "that" ; inserted: "whose attributes" on a line above "[*del.*] that" and "we"
39. Preceding two words and comma inserted on a line above "and"
40. Deleted: "as physical life all forms of existence are but unspeakably great as the feet and fingers of the Soul [*last line illeg.—paper crumpled*]" ; inserted above: "possess little or nothing [*del.*] except inherently."

there, and awakes it—and the twain kiss each other.—[41] Yet only the soul burns; the other is impotent. man can[42] suffer or enjoy[43] except in the limits of his individual being; and nothing really enjoys or suffers except the Soul.—[44] The rest are as[45] apples[46] and rice and[47] fish which soothe and gratify the appetite; yet what are they in themselves?

How gladly does the soul welcome all[48] that seeks it.— How it runs to the windows like a beatiful woman whose lover comes to sleep with her that night.— Music, the most spiritual of sensuous[49] enjoyments, gives it some faint[50] sign of[51] the harmony and measure that are[52] of its essence; as a good part of the soul is[53] that which we incompletely describe[54] by[55]

The only test of[56] the virtue[57] or excellence of any thing is that it pleases the Soul.—Whatever thoroughly satisfies the soul is Truth.—

O, theologian, come not to argue with me about God; I can yet[58] comprehend nothing[59] so tremendous as my own soul. I am awed[60] even by its works —by the art and[61] cunning of some fine instrument used in the discoveries of astronomy.— At the huge fact[62] of worlds revolving round their suns—

[3] Cipher it by any rule we will, and then rub all out and work the problem over again, and again, till our eyes blur, we[63] get but one unvarying[64] product,

41. Inserted with finer point: "Yet only [*ins. above* "the"] the soul only [*del.*] burns; the other is impotent.—" on a line above" .— " [*del.*] As As personality" ; deleted: "As As personality"

42. Deleted: "either"

43. Deleted: "any further when"

44. Capital "S" inserted over lowercase.

45. Preceding four words inserted in pencil on a line above ".— apples"

46. Capital "A" in MS on "apples"

47. Deleted in pencil: "honey" ; inserted in pencil: "fish which" on a line above "[*del.*] fish" and "so" of "sooth"

48. Inserted on a line above "welcome . . . that"

49. Deleted: "delights" ; inserted and deleted above: "enjoyments" ; deleted: "touches" following "[*del.*] delights" . Comma not deleted, not printed; inserted above: "enjoyments,"

50. Written over [*illeg.*]

51. Deleted: "its own"

52. Deleted: "part"

53. Deleted: "its craving for"

54. Deleted: "as"

55. Line ends at right margin; three ruled lines left blank.

56. Deleted: "what we call the" ; inserted: on a line above "[*del.*] the" and "virtue"

57. Deleted: "success[?]" ; inserted above: "or excellence"

58. Inserted in pencil and deleted: "just begin to" on a line above "yet com" in "comprehend"

59. Deleted: "more wonderful than" ; inserted above: "tremendous as"

60. Deleted: "at" ; inserted: "even by its works—by" on a line above "[*del.*] at" and "the art"

61. Deleted: "mystery" ; inserted above: "cunning"

62. Deleted: "s" on "fact" ; [*ins. and del.*] "of, and following countless systems of worlds, whose [*ins. and del.*] of suns and their planets"

63. Deleted: "each [?]"

64. Inserted on a line above "one product"

that the Human[65] Soul you yourself[66] by its innate tests,[67] must be the judge and standard of all things, even of the knowledge of God.— Heave[68] for soundings over the whole sea,[69] the lead hits hard bottom here, if no where else.— Whatever the litigation, whatever the cause to be argued, or the knot untied,[70] this is the bar of appeals, the supreme court,[71]

65. Inserted in pencil on a line above the wordspace between "the . . . soul"

66. Preceding two words inserted in pencil on the line following "Human" and above "by its"

67. Deleted: "is the"

68. Deleted: "the lead" ; inserted above: "for soundings"

69. Deleted: "this is the place you touch bottom" ; inserted: "the lead hits hard bottom" on a line above "[*del.*] this . . . you"

70. Deleted: "here" ; inserted above: "this"

71. Deleted: "beyond which stands black Nyx Nyx and labyrinthine chaos.—"

Sweet Flag.

Manuscript in Duke (3, #2). Inscribed on white wove paper approx. 7″ x 6″. Ruled. On verso of "To be at all" (*LG* MS Variorum). Two sets of inscriptions on either side of upper half of leaf; bottom half written across. All entries bear signs of haste. All cancelled by vertical stroke. It is difficult to assign a date. The opening entries suggest "Calamus," the second set suggests "Song of Myself" (1855), sec. 24, l. 537; the two lines of verse at the end, at least "melons with polished rinds," have a verbal suggestion of "Song of Myself," sec. 49, 1. 1296, but the context suggests that he is referring to testicles. The probabilities are that it is earlier than "Song of Myself." First printed in *N&F* and *CW* as noted.

Sweet flag Sweet fern illuminated face clarified unpolluted flour-corn aromatic Calamus sweet-green bulb and melons with bulbs[1] grateful to the hand[2]/

I am a mystic in a trance exaltation[3]

something wild and untamed[4] — half savage/

Coarse[5][*?*] things/

[6]Trickling Sap[7] flows from the end of the manly[8] maple tooth of delight tooth-prong—tine/ spend[9] spend[10]/

bulbous[11]

Living bulbs, melons with polished rinds[12] that smooth to the reached[13] hand

Bulbs of life-lilies, polished melons[14] flavored for the mildest[15] hand that shall reach,[16]

1. Deleted: "sure" ; inserted above: "grateful"
2. End of entry in upper left half. First printed in *N&F,* 165 (Pt. IV, #41; *CW,* X, 11).
3. Set off by a line at left and below.
4. Deleted: [*illeg.*]. Redundant dash not printed.
5. Triggs reads "Common" in *CW,* III, 280.
6. Deleted: "The sweet" ; inserted and deleted: "Trickling"
7. Capital "S" over "s" . Deleted: "trickles" ; inserted above and deleted: "drops" ; inserted above: "flows"
8. Deleted and inserted: "pole" "little"
9. "d" over "t"
10. End of entry in upper right half. First printed in part in *CW,* III, 280.
11. Deleted: "bulbous"
12. Deleted: "the soothing" "the hand to touch" ; inserted above deletions: "that"
13 Written over [*illeg.*].
14. Deleted: [*illeg.*]; inserted above: "flavored"
15. Deleted: "gentlest" ; inserted above: "mildest"
16. Preceding two lines first printed in *CW,* III, 280.

Breathjuice—Airscents.

Manuscript not found. Text from *N&F,* 169 (Pt. IV, #64; *CW,* X, 18). The list suggests "Song of Myself," sec. 2.

Breathjuice—Airscents—Airsmells—Airodor—Loveodor—Airdrifts—Breathsmoke—Airjuice for you—Airsough.

Airscud. Airdrift.

Manuscript not found. Text from *N&F,* 178 (Pt. IV, #124; *CW,* X, 33). Since Bucke frequently conflated distinct MS, there is no reason to assume that the first two entries have any connection with the others, which seem to refer to "Children of Adam," especially sec. 9 (1856) of "I Sing the Body Electric" or possibly "Song of Myself" (1855), sec. 24, l. 530. They may be trial titles, but more probably they are suggestive words and phrases.

Airscud.
Airdrift.
Loveaxles.
Lovepivot.
Sleepripples.
Love-ripples.
Lovejet.
Loveache.
Lovestring.
Glued with Love.
Tiller of Love.

The Mountain-Ash.

Manuscript in LC (Feinberg #18). Inscribed in black pencil on pinkish tan wove paper, probably not *LG* 1855 wrapper, 10³/₁₆″ x 6¼″. Torn off at left from a pad of paper. For similar notes see "Salt works." The connections to "Spontaneous Me" and "Song of the Broad-Axe" indicate a date before 1856. (Gene Edward Veith Jr.)

The mountain-ash, a large shrub, 16 or 20 ft high—northern part of the state of New York—has white blossoms—blooms early in the spring—has then a pleasant perfume—the hill-sides where it grows thickly look *white* from the blossoms.—[1]/

amusements around the fire in the lumbermans hut—the great bright light—the songs and stories—

The lumberman in the woods—goes in in the early winter—makes a hut—perhaps a gang of lumbermen—the pine is the principal timber—the pine grows sometimes thick as a hogshead—100, 150, and even 200 feet high—they cut it in logs of 13 feet.— The maple, the beech, &c are good woods—hemlock, spruce—hardy life, healthy, robust,—food is largely of salt pork, beans, peas,[2] and the like.— The animals likely/[3] to be seen are the wolf, the black bear, and possibly a catamount/ Story of the catamount and the Indian of the Indian of the St. Regis[4]— The Indian lived in his hut in the woods—made sugar-baskets[5] —took a lot into the village—left his little son of five years old to take care of the hut—returned—[6] boy gone—peered around up and down—saw the boy up in a tree in the power of a large catamount who was tossing him up and down—Indian at last fired—the enraged catamount tore

1. For the mountain-ash see "Spontaneous Me" (1856), l. 4. Line nearly across page from left. Following sixteen words crowded in between paragraphs. For the picture of the lumbermen see "Song of the Broad-Axe" (1856), sec. 3, ll. 42–44.

2. Deleted: "&c"

3. Short line seemingly marking a space. Deleted: "Story of" . Following thirteen words indented.

4. The St. Regis Indians were a group of Roman Catholic Iroquois whose reservation was on both sides of the New York–Quebec border.

5. Not listed in *OED, DAE,* or *DA,* but the meaning is probably baskets for carrying or storing maple(?) sugar.

6. The following words are crowded in at the bottom of the leaf.

Poet of Materialism.

Manuscript in Duke (22, #17) . Inscribed in black pencil on the back of an irregular piece of floral wallpaper approx. 7 11/16" x 7⅝". Date, from the small, neat handwriting and the references to Egyptology, is probably before or early 1855. *N&F,* 124–25 (Pt. III, #144; *CW,* IX, 150–51).

[*illeg.*] poet of Materialism—(put this section forward
[*illeg.*] in Reality and demonstration with the opening.) [*illeg.*]—that this earth is under a constant[1] process of amelioration—as it always has been—that it, in some manner not perhaps demonstratable in astronomy, expands outward and outward in a larger and larger orbit—that our immortality is *located* here upon earth,—that we *are immortal*—that the processes of the refinement and perfection[2] of the earth are in steps, the[3] least part of which involves trillions of years—that in due time the earth[4] beautiful as it is now will be as[5] proportionately different from what it is now, as[6] it now is proportionately different from what it was in its earlier gaseous or marine period, uncounted cycles before man and woman grew[7].—That we also[8] shall be here proportionately different from now, and beautiful.[9] That the Egyptian idea of the return of the soul after a certain period of time involved a beautifil [*illeg.*] nature [*illeg.*] mystery [*illeg.*]

1. Deleted: "and"
2. MS torn in two, taped together at this point.
3. Written over [*illeg.*].
4. Deleted: "and" ; inserted: "beautiful as it is now" on a line above "th" (*in* "earth") [*del.*] "and will be as"
5. Deleted: "much beyond" ; inserted above : "proportionately different from"
6. Deleted: "wh"
7. Following twelve words inserted beginning on a line above "n" in "woman" and blank space and ending at foot of the leaf at the right.
8. Inserted on a line above "we . . . shall" in the insert.
9. An [*illeg.*] word at lower right. The last sentence is printed in *N&F,* but is not in the MS, which may have been trimmed by dealers.

Bill Guess, Died.

Manuscript in Duke (4, #5). Inscribed in pencil on white laid paper, 7⁵/₁₆" x 7¼". Vertical blue rules, ¼" apart recto and verso. First published *N&F,* 116 (Pt. III, #110; *CW,* IX, 133–134).

March 20th '54

Bill Guess,[1] died aged 22.

A[2] thoughtless, strong, generous animal nature, fond of direct pleasures, eating, drinking, women, fun &c.— Taken sick with the small-pox, had the bad disorder[3] and was furious with the delirium tremens.— Was with me in the Crystal Palace,—a large broad fellow, weighed over 200.— Was a thoughtless good fellow.—/

Peter——[4]large, strong-boned youn fellow, driver.— Should[5] weighs[6] 180.—[7] Free and candid to me the very first time he saw me.— Man of strong self-will, powerful coarse feelings and appetites—had a quarrel,—borrowed $300—[8] left his father's, somewhere in the interior of the state—fell in with a couple of gamblers—[9] hadn't been home or written there in seven years.— I liked his refreshing wickedness, as it would be called by the orthodox.— He seemed to feel a perfect independence, dashed with a little resentment, toward the world in general.— I never met a man that seemed to me, as far as I could tell in 40

1. This last name does not appear in either the NY City or Brooklyn directories for 1853–1856. There is, however, a "William Guese, laborer" listed in the NY City directory for 1853–1854, and it is possible that either WW or the directory had misspelled the name. The three young men mentioned here were probably itinerant omnibus drivers. Evidence of WW's fondness for men of this sort is especially plentiful in *LG* ("Song of Myself," sec. 47, and "Native Moments" (1860). See also "[*illeg.*] Dick Hunt" and notebooks of the 1860s.

2. Written over "Th"

3. "Bad disorder" is almost illegibly scrawled in contrast to the clerkly hand of the rest of the document. WW was very discreet in his notes. See "[*illeg.*] Dick Hunt."

4. Two short dashes in place of names.

5. Deleted: "guess he"

6. Final "s" written over "d"

7. Written over "200"

8. Preceding five words, initial, and final dashes inserted on a line above "tes" (in "appetites") and "left his father's" . Redundant undeleted dash not shown.

9. Preceding seven words, initial, and final dashes inserted on a line above "the state . . . or" . Redundant undeleted dash not shown.

minutes,[10] more[11] open, coarse, self-willed, strong, and free from the sickly desire to be on society's lines and points.—/

George Fitch.—[12] Yankee boy—Driver.— Fine nature, amiable, of sensitive feelings, a natural gentleman—of quite a reflective turn. Left his home because his father was perpetually "down on him".— When he told me of his mother, his eyes watered.— Good looking, tall, curly haired, black-eyed fellow, age about 23 or 4—slender, face with a smile — trowsers tucked in his boots — cap with the front-piece turned behind.—

10. Preceding thirteen words and comma inserted on a line above "man . . . self-willed"

11. Written over [*illeg.*]

12. In the NY City directory for 1855–1856 are George Fitch, expressman, and George M. Fitch, clerk. Fitch is mentioned again in *"Bloom."*

Bloom.

Manuscript in Duke (16, #39). White laid paper approx. 2½" x 7⅝". Irregularly cut along right edges. Corners clipped. Brownish rules ⅜" apart. Inscribed in pencil. Pasted to a scrap of preliminary notes for "Song of the Broad-axe" (see *"Broadaxe"*), which suggests a date before 1856. It has been suggested that this is Nathaniel Bloom, a member of WW's circle of friends in the early 1860s (*Corr., II,* 80*n*), but it seems more likely that the name refers to either "Gilbert Bloom, carman," or "Gilbert J. Bloom, carman," as listed in the NYC directories for 1854–1855. WW's description here simply does not suggest a literate, prosperous businessman like Nathaniel Bloom. Fitch is mentioned in "Bill Guess, died," which is dated March, 1854, and WW's use of the present tense here suggests that this document is of the same period. First printed *N&F,* 120 (Pt. III, #128; *CW,* IX, 142).

Bloom.—Broad-shouldered, six-footer, with a hare-lip.— Clever fellow, and by no means bad looking.—(George Fitch has roomed[*?*] with him a year, and tells me, there is no more honorable man breathing.)— Direct, plain-spoken, natural-hearted, gentle-tempered, but awful when roused—cartman, with a horse, cart &c, of his own—drives for a store in Maiden lane.—

Not to Dazzle.

Manuscript not found. Text from *N&F,* 71 (Pt. II, 64; *CW,* IX, 37–38). Bucke dates it 1855 or 1856, but the fact that it is in prose relates it not to "Song of Prudence" (1856), ll. 43–45, but to Preface (1855), 716, ll. 264–265. The date is before early 1855.

Not to dazzle with profuse descriptions of character and events and passions. The greatest poet is not content with dazzling his rays over character and events and passions and scenery and does not descend to moralize or make applications of morals. The soul has that measureless pride which consists in never acknowledging any lessions but its own . . . this invariably. But to bring the Spirit of all events and persons and passions to the formation of the one individual that hears or reads . . . of you up there now.

Such Boundless and Affluent Souls.

Manuscript in Duke (5, #7). Inscribed in black ink on irregular white laid paper, approx. 6¼" x 7¾". Rules 5/16" apart recto and verso. The neat handwriting is that of the 1850s, but larger, possibly because it is on larger paper. *N&F,* 121 (Pt. III, #133; *CW,* IX, 144).

Such boundless and affluent souls . . . . bend your head in reverence, my man! they are met through all the strata of life.— Their centrifugal power of love, I think, makes the awfullest forces of nature stand back.— Its perennial blow the frost shall never touch; and what we call death shall go round outside it forever and ever.—

(Every hour of the day and night, and every[1] acre of the earth and shore, and every point[2] or patch of the sea and sky, is full of[3] pictures.— No two of this immortal brood are alike; except that they[4] are all of unspeakable beauty and perfection, and large or[*?*] small[5] alike, descend into that greedy Something[6] in Man whose appetite,[7] is more undying than hope, and more[8] insatiate than the sand[9] with water.—[10])

1. Deleted: [*illeg.*]
2. Deleted: "and" ; inserted above: "or"
3. Deleted: "beautiful"
4. Deleted: "all alike in their" ; inserted above: "are all like [*del.*] of"
5. Inserted: "large or[*?*] small" on a line above "and alike" , "des" (in "descend"). There is also a blurred caret after "alike" , suggesting an alternate position for the insertion.
6. Capital "S" inscribed over lowercase.
7. Inserted: "is more" on a line above "te" (in "appetite") and word space between "appetite . . . underlining"
8. Deleted: "ravenous[*?*]"
9. Deleted: "is [*illeg.*]" ; inserted: "with" on the next line before "water"
10. deleted: "appears at his side at [*del.*] with [*ins.*] his holy baldness flits at his side like a ghost"

Ground Where You May Rest.

Manuscript in Rutgers. Inscribed in black pencil on white laid paper. Faded rules ⅜" apart recto and verso. Numbered 8 (by ?) at top center. On recto: "The money value." The last two sentences anticipate "Song of Myself" (1855), sec. 46, ll. 1226ff. This was written before 1855 or early that year. First printed *N&F,* 126 (Pt. III, #149; *CW,* IX, 154).

[1]ground[2] where you may[3] rest yourself and look[4] quietly[5] upon[6] such, and on the theories of the schools and upon[7] governments and religions.—[8]

All have something noble and true,—,[9] all and every one of them; but[10] not the best that ever was built or ever will be built on earth,[11] can stand as the final[12] destination of man.—[13] Sit awhile, wayfarer.— I give[14] you biscuits to eat and milk to drink; but[15] when afterward you have bathed[16] and renewed[17] yourself in[18] sweet clothes, and staid here a little time, I shall surely kiss[19] you on the cheek, and open the gate for[20] your egress hence.—[21]

1. Deleted: [*illeg. paper trimmed*]; inserted and deleted: "eminent"
2. Deleted: "whence"
3. Deleted: "stand" ; inserted above: "rest yourself"
4. Deleted: "down"
5. Deleted: "as you"
6. Deleted: "those" ; inserted above: "such, and on the"
7. Inserted and deleted: "all the"
8. Deleted: "which" ; inserted above: "All" ; deleted: [*illeg.*]
9. Deleted: "in" ; inserted: "—. all and"
10. Deleted: "are not any the"
11. Deleted: [*illeg.*]
12. Deleted: "resting place" ; inserted above: "destination"
13. Deleted: "O, wayfarer" ; "sit" capitalized.
14. Deleted: "thee apples" ; inserted above and deleted: "berries" ; inserted beside deletions: "biscuits"
15. Deleted: "Thou hast [*illeg.*]" ; inserted: "afterwards you have"
16. Deleted: "thyself"
17. Deleted: "thyself" ; inserted above: "yourself"
18. Deleted: "fresh cl"
19. Deleted: "thee" ; inserted above: "you"
20. Word cut off; inserted above: "your"
21. Deleted: "so speaks the Angel" . Tops of letters from a succeeding paragraph show below.

Poem of "(The Devil.

Manuscript in Duke (14, #36). Inscribed in black pencil on yellow wove scrap approx. 1¾" x 5" (Cf. "Poem of a proud.") Ms II, 63. The text is related to "The Sleepers." (1855), ll. 127–129 (dropped 1876, see *LG CRE,* 627), which is possibly earlier, and certainly anticipates "Chanting the Square Deific" (1865). First printed in Bucke's "Notes on the Text of Leaves of Grass," *Conservator* (February, 1897), 185.

Poem of "(the Devil (counteractive of the common idea of Satan

Left 5 at Jones.

Manuscript in LC (Feinberg). Inscribed in pencil and ink where noted, on the inside front cardboard cover of a book or notebook, 9″ x 7⅞″. Entries separated by lines and in hanging indentation in two columns, the second column beginning with the entry on Henry J. Killmer. On the other side is pasted a picture captioned "Lieutenants E. E. Sill and A. T. Lamson. (From a photograph taken on their arrival at Chattanooga)" torn from an article with the running title "A Hard Road to Travel out of Dixie." Madeleine B. Stern, *Heads & Headlines: The Phrenological Fowlers* (Norman: Univ. of Oklahoma Press, 1971), pp. 99–123, details the relationship between WW and Fowler & Wells, the phrenological firm that distributed *LG* 1855, which they advertised beginning July 6, 1855. Until September, 1855, when a brother left the firm, the company was named Fowlers & Wells, as in this MS. A bill to WW from a bookbinder indicates that a total of 795 copies of the first edition were bound (Feinberg, "Notes on Whitman Collections and Collectors," *LC Cat.,* xii). Details of the transactions recorded appear in the notes. WW made these from July 1855 through January, 1856.

Left 5 at Jones 21[1] Feb. 21—watch March 26th or 7th[2]/ paid $1.20 May 25th[3] Lithe filament / Dr. Ruggles[4] 131 Dean st. /[5] Youmans'[6] 63 State /[7] Henry G. Killmer[8] with Alex Matthew,[9] Liquor dealer 318 Greenwich st. N. Y.[10] / Geo. Flanagan 576 Sixth av. bet. 34 & 35th st. frames /

1. Written over [*illeg.*].
2. Preceding twelve words in ink.
3. "paid . . . 25th" added below, enclosed by curved line.
4. The Whitman family physician. See "Mr. & Mrs. Fitz."
5. Rule above "Dr. Ruggles" and another below with a short wavy mark in ink made below and beyond "st." above.
6. Probably Edward Livingston Youmans (1821–1887), scientific writer and editor. According to Harry Gehman Good in *DAB,* XX, 616, Youmans knew WW as a young man in NY. In the 1850s, Youmans was a popular lecturer on science. See "[*illeg.*] Dick Hunt" and Traubel, I, 101.
7. Following entries in column at right.
8. Carpenter, h. 22 Carlton av., Brooklyn directory 1856–1857. See "Add*resses*."
9. Alexander Mathews, liquors, 318 & 380 Greenwich, h. 108 King, NY City directory, 1854–1855.
10. Preceding entry in ink. Rule under the entry.

Books sent Fowlers & Wells[11]

first———23 copies[11]
second consignment 117
third 100 (40 in paper[12]
taken out of London parcel 4[13]
fourth consignment———12
Fifth Dec. 22 159[14]
Sixth Jan 96 (or 94[15]

256 216[×]60[=]129.60[+]16[=]145.6[+]13[=]158[16]

11. Written slightly above the line, perhaps as a column heading.

12. Feinberg, "Notes on Whitman Collections and Collectors, *LC Cat.*, xi, cites a bookbinder's bill to WW which charged him for 200 copies bound in June 1855. In July, according to the bill, an additional 183 copies were bound, 46 of them in boards. It would seem from this entry that WW kept eighy-three copies, including six of the paperbound copies, and shipped the rest to Fowler & Wells.

13. Fowler & Wells sent copies to its London office, Horsell & Shirrefs. The exact number has not been determined (Allen, 176), but according to Feinberg's bill, 383 copies had been bound by this time. The preceding entries record 240 consigned to Fowler & Wells. WW must have kept 143. The entry implies that WW shipped some of his copies to London, taking four copies out to send to Fowler & Wells. For the fate of this shipment to London see Allen, 176, 382.

14. In December, according to Feinberg's bill, another 169 copies were bound in cloth without the gold leaf of the original binding (*LC Cat.*, xi–xii). WW must have kept ten for himself, sending the rest to his distributors.

15. Feinberg, xii, says 93 copies were bound in January, 1856.

16. The preceding sums written in column. Any connection with WW's bookkeeping in regard to *LG* 1855 is not clear.

Do You Ask Me.

Manuscript not found. Text from Furness, 45. (Gene Edward Veith, Jr.)

Do you ask me what are my own particular dangers and complaints——what is taken that belongs to me——I complain not of myself——What have I to complain of for myself——Everything is mine that I want, and I know of nothing to be had at all which I could not work for and get.

Autobiographical Data.

Original missing. Ten photostats in LC 87 (#'s [*3320–3329*]) show all or part of twenty-one pages, of which at least nineteen are inscribed. *UPP,* II, 86*n* 1, describes the notebook as "a substantial, leatherbacked notebook containing references to the Fugitive Slave Law, which would suggest that it . . . belongs to the period before 1855." *LC Cat.,* 17, gives 15 x 9½ cm. as the dimensions of the original leaves (?). The inscription appears to be in black (?) ink, and there are no signs of printed rules. Portions first printed in *UPP* and Furness, as noted.

Present text is based on photostats with missing passages from *UPP* and Furness. As in many of his notebooks, WW made entries helter-skelter and earlier editors rearranged freely.

The close relationship of certain passages to "Slavery—the Slaveholders—," "As of the orator" (1856) and "The Eighteen Presidency!" suggests that a date before 1855, assigned in *UPP,* might possibly be extended to the winter of 1855–1856. Despite the fact that, whatever the exact date, the notebook comes from WW's great creative period, the entries bear no direct relationship to the poetry of 1855–1856. In fact, some of the contents baffle any theory of WW's development. The jocularly racist reference to "Black Caesar," the comic victim [*3323R*], is in strong contrast to the treatment of blacks in the poetry. Cf. the amusingly self-conscious pose of WW as a liberated man of the world at the sight of blacks in Boston in "English runic." More perplexing are the melancholy wailings of "I am not glad to night" which should date from 1841 or 1842. The notebook probably, however, was written late in the series.

Autobiographical Data[1]

From the middle to the latter part of Oct. 1844 I was in *New Mirror*—[2]

We lived at Vandykes 4th of July 1826

We lived in Adams st in Brooklyn, 1827

I was in Lawyer Clarkes office in 1830—

1. Text from *UPP,* II, 86–87, but surviving photostats show that WW entered autobiographical information intermittently throughout the notebook rather than as one series of entries as in *UPP.* Explanatory footnotes also draw on *UPP.*

2. No known file exists. See William White, *Walt Whitman's Journalism, A Bibliography* (Detroit, 1969), 5.

We moved to Brooklyn in May 1823[3]

Moved to Cranberry st 1824

Moved to Johnson st May 1st 1825

Moved to Tillary st (Martin's) 1st May 1827—moved to own house Nov lived there till Nov 1831

We lived in Henry st the winter before the first cholera summer (1830–1831?)[4]

I was at Clements[5] printing office in the summer of 1831—

I went to Spooner's[6] in the fall of '32.

I was at Worthingtons[7] in the summer of '32

I was at Spooner's when father moved in the country in 33.

We lived at Norwich in 1834.

I went up to Hempstead from New York 1st of May 1836—went to Norwich to teach school in June same year.

I kept the school west of Babylon the winter of 36–7

At Long Swamp the spring of '37

At Smithtown the fall and winter of 37—

Went to Huntington the spring of 38—

We moved to Dix Hills in May 1840

We moved from Hempstead to Babylon in 1836, August

3. Holloway, *UPP,* points out that these dates are not to be taken as conclusive but that "in the main" they are correct. They agree with "Nehemiah Whitman" and are sometimes identical in wording. Possibly WW copied them from that MS.

4. The first cholera summer was 1832. WW's error explains the apparent conflicts with the preceding entry.

5. Samuel E. Clements, owner and editor of the *Long Island Patriot* is described in "Reminiscences of Brooklyn" (1857), *UPP,* II, 3–5; "Printing Office.—Old Brooklyn," *SD, Prose 92,* I, 14.

6. Colonel Alden Spooner, proprietor of the *Long Island Star.* See *UPP,* II, 3; *SD, Prose 92,* I, 15.

7. *UPP,* II, 296*n,* suggests Erastus Worthington Jr., a printer in 1826 Brooklyn directory.

I went from Huntington to Babylon in 1839 (Spring)

Came down to New York (after selling Nina[8]) in the summer of 39

I went to Woodbury to teach school in the summer of 40[9]

Fall and winter of 1842 boarded at Mrs. R. in Spring st.

Spring of 1843 boarded at Mrs. Bonnard's in John st.—

Also at Mrs. Edgarton's in Vesey.

Summer of '43 at Mary's and at Brown's in Duane st.

October 1843 commenced with the Winants'[10]

Edited *Tattler*[11] in summer of '42

Edited *Statesman*[12] in Spring of '43

Edited *Democrat*[13] in Summer of 44

Wrote for *Dem Review, American Review,* and *Columbian Magazines*[14] during 45 and 6—as previously.

About the latter part of February '46, commenced editing the Brooklyn *Eagle*—continued till last of January '48.

Left Brooklyn for New Orleans, Feb. 11th '48[15]

I am not glad to-night. Gloom has gathered round me like a mantle, tightly folded.

8. His horse.

9. See [3326 *L and R*] for continuation of *UPP* text. The localities mentioned are all on Long Island. These autobiographical notes do not seem to agree with rumors that WW taught at Southold, L. I., in 1840 or 1841 or 1842 or 1843 (date varies) as reported in Katharine Molinoff, *Walt Whitman at Southold* (Brookville, N.Y.), 1966.

10. The Edgarton, Brown and Winant establishments are listed in NY City directories, 1841–1844. WW is not listed. He seems to have been very mobile.

11. A New York evening paper. White, *Journalism,* 4, locates three articles.

12. A New York semiweekly. White, *Journalism,* 5, has found no file.

13. A daily. White, *Journalism,* 5, has found no file. *UPP,* II, 88*n* refers to *GF,* II, 6.

14. See *EPF* for WW's contributions.

15. Holloway (*UPP,* II, 88) says this entry is followed by several stubs which do not continue "the form of diary given above."

The oppression of my heart is not fitful and has no pangs; but a torpor like that of some stagnant pool.[16]

2

Yet I know not why I should be sad.

Around me are my brother men, merry and jovial.

The laugh sounds out and the beautiful sound of the human voice a sound I love.

No dear one is in danger, and health shelter and food are vouchsafed me.

3

O, Nature! impartial, and perfect in imperfection!

Every precious gift to man is linked with a curse—and each pollution has some sparkle from heaven.

The mind, raised upward, then holds communion with angels and its reach overtops heaven; yet then it stays in the meshes of the world too and is stung by a hundred serpents every day.

4

Let fools affect humility in the strength of their conceit: this brain (?) feels and claims the divine life which moves restlessly (?)

Shall a clear star deny the brightness wherewith the Hidden has clothed it?

5

Thus it comes that I am not glad to night.—

I feel cramped here in these coarse walls of flesh.

The soul disdains its

O Mystery of Death, I pant for the time when I shall solve you!

[*3320L*][17] *Subjects for articles*

Rapid and temporary manner[*?*] of American changes of popularity[*?*] for eminent statesmen. (in [*illeg.*] of Crawford)[18] (reverse instance, Pi [*illeg.*]/[19]

Answer the objection that democratic forms of gov. not energetic enough in cases of emergency. (Commonwealth of England—directory[*?*] of France.)

16. The text of this and succeeding numbered paragraphs is from *UPP*, II, 88–89. Cf. "Song of Myself" (1855), sec. 29, ll.1299–1308.

17. Part of [*3320 R*] shows in the photostat as well as, possibly, a torn stub. The inscription recto is illegible and is probably a blotting.

18. Possibly Martin Jenkins Crawford (1820–1883), Georgia congressman, who defended Southern views in the debates over Kansas, or the better-known William Harris Crawford (1772–1834), senator from Georgia and secretary of the treasury, who was the favorite for the Democratic Republican nomination in 1816 over Monroe.

19. Short line in center.

[*3321R*][20] Give us turbulence, give us excitement,[21] give us[22] the rage and disputes of hell,—any thing rather than this lethargy of death that spreads like a the[23] vapor of decaying corpses on our land—[24]

Why what was it—that little thing that made the rebellion of '76 —a little question of tea and writing paper only great because involved a great principle[25]

The next worst thing to having such enormous outrages put into laws and acquiesced in by the people without any alarm, is to have them practically carried out. Nations sink by stages, first one, and then[26] another,[27]

I come not here to flatter[28]

[*3322L*] Why[29] confine the matter to that part of[30] it involved in the Scriptures?— /

The influence of the gallows fails[31] /

There is invariably this fact about superior natures; they understand each other, and with similar sight[32] behold the soul, the[33] universe, immortality, and[34] all the aims and arts of men.—[35] /

1*[36] The constitution covenants that the[37] free states shall give up runaway

20. The right-hand edge of [*3321 L*] shows on the photostats and reads as follows: "[*deletion*] persons . . . degrades . . . oral . . . Why . . . meaness[?] . . . a . . . to . . . from an . . . who . . . and . . . soil."

21. Preceding three words inserted above on a line above "ce" (in "turbulence") and "gives us"

22. Deleted: [*illeg.*]

23. "The" inserted above "a . . . vapor" as alternate.

24. Furness, 81, first printed this passage and preceded it with "It is not events of danger and threatening storms that I dread." and followed with "Give us anything rather than this, beat the drums of war." No manuscript source has been located for either. Cf. "As of the orator."

25. Preceding seven words inserted in a balloon above "it—that little thing" . An almost identical sentence is in Furness, 78. Cf. "As of the orator" and "Slavery—the Slaveholders—" [*18*].

26. Deleted: [*illeg.*]

27. Sentence in Furness, 81. See "As of the orator" . Space for several lines of text between this and following entry.

28. Furness, 82. See "As of the orator"

29. Written over [*illeg.*]

30. Deleted: "the"[?]

31. This and the preceding entry were cancelled by two waved vertical strokes; WW seems not to have used them elsewhere. Line across page.

32. Preceding three words inserted on a line above "and . . . behold"

33. Preceding two words inserted on a line above "universe"

34. Deleted: "those [?] fallacies of"

35. Short line from left under "all the aims"

36. No corresponding number or asterisk has been located, but this passage is very close to one in "Slavery–the Slave-holders—" [16] and one in "The Eighteenth Presidency!" First printed in Furness, 79. See "As of the orator" .

37. Deleted: [*illeg.*]

servants—that we all know.— But by[38] the letter and spirit of its most important provisions, we hold the right to decide how to do it, who the runaway servants are, and to[39] perform the whole[40] obligation as we perform any other obligation by due process of law and without any violent[41] intrusion from abroad.—

[*3322R*][42] "O, liberty," said Madame Roland,[43] "what crimes have been committed in thy name!"

"O, Bible!" say I "what nonsense and folly have been supported in *thy* name!"

Calvin burned Servetus at Geneva and found his defence in the Bible. Henry 8th Edward 6th and the bloody Mary offered up scores of victims, at the stake and gallows, for religious opinion, and found their defence in the Bible. The Inquisition also and St. Bartholomew's horrid massacre[44] discover ample authority in the Bible.

[*3323L*][45] I know that[46] America is strong, and supple, and full of growth.— I know we are on good terms with the world, and on extra good terms with ourselves.— Treaties we make with Europe.[47]

Steamships paddle the sea[48] Gold comes from California, and trade is brisk, and the jobbers are busy nailing up goods, and sending them off to customers, and the railroads[49] run loaded, and all goes[50] thriftily.— These things I do not expect to see[51] less of[52] but more,[53] and if any one suppose I am at all alarmed about the prospects of business on this continent[54] he misunderstands me, for I am not—[55] no I see its way clear for a hundred years.— But with all[56] such decking ourselves[57] in the robes of safety and gain, there at the gate[58] sits Mordecai

38. Redundant "by" not printed.
39. Deleted: "settle" ; inserted above: "perform"
40. Deleted: "thing"
41. Deleted: "or unhelpful"
42. The entire page is cancelled by two waved vertical strokes; WW seems not to have used it elsewhere.
43. Marie-Jeanne Philipon, Mme. Roland (1754–1793), a Girondin, at the time of her execution. WW had read a translation of Alphonse de Lamartine's *History of the Girondists* in 1848.
44. Deleted: "all"
45. Cf. "The Eighteenth Presidency!" and "As of the orator" . First printed in Furness, 82.
46. Deleted: "times [*illeg.*]" ; inserted and deleted: [*illeg.*]
47. Sentence inserted.
48. Preceding two words inserted in right margin above and following the preceding MS line.
49. Deleted: [*illeg.*] ; inserted above: "run"
50. Deleted: "gay and"
51. Deleted: "grow"
52. Two illegible words deleted; inserted: "of" on a line above first deleted word.
53. Deleted: "for"
54. Preceding three words inserted on a line above "business . . . he mis"
55. Illegible word deleted.
56. Deleted: "the" ; inserted above: "such"
57. Deleted: [*illeg.*]; inserted above: "in"
58. Preceding three words inserted on a line above "there . . . sits"

the Jew and we know that terrible sign that[59] either[60] we[61] are to have his life, or he is to hang the best part of us on the gallows high.—

What are all[62] these business prospects,[63] these steamships,[64] these fat sub-treasuries and[65] our profitable trade? I do not want these[66] I want brave and large souled men,[67] men[68] not*[69]

[*3323R*] Are these two or three[70] drops[71] any sample[72] of the storm[73] that is cooking for us?—If I thought it was, men of[74] these would be no days of dalliance or of ease[75] or talk.—They would be days[76] for all live all Americans to get on their killing clothes I should advise[77] all live Americans to get on their killing clothes, for there would be a little butchering to be done /

Years[78] ago I formed one[79] of a great crowd[80] that rapidly gathered where a building had fallen in and buried a man alive.— Down somewhere in those ruins the poor fellow lurked,[81] deprived of his liberty,[82] perhaps dead or in danger of

59. Preceding three words inserted on a line above [*illeg.*]

60. Photostat illegible; reading from Furness, 82. See "As of the orator" . Illegible word deleted following "we"

61. Deleted: [*illeg.*]

62. Deleted: "your" ; inserted above: "these"

63. Deleted: "your" ; inserted above: "these"

64. Deleted: "your" ; inserted above: "these"

65. Deleted: "your" ; inserted above: "our"

66. Preceding five words inserted above two illegible deletions.

67. Deleted: "wicked"

68. Deleted: "if"

69. No continuing passage is to be found in the photostats. Furness, 82–83, continues: "without wickedness of some sorts yet looming up into fit proportions to a sublime land and its sublime beginnings." Here he notes that the arrangement of the text in the MS is doubtful and continues: "—Folks talk of some model plantations where collected families of niggers grow sleek and live easy with enough to eat, and no care only to obey a thriving owner, who makes a good thing out of them, and they out of him.—By God I sometimes think this whole land is becoming one vast model plantation thinking itself well off because it has wherewithal to wear and no bother about its pork." See "As of the orator" . The last sentence appears in variant form in "Slavery—the Slaveholders—" [20].

70. Preceding three words inserted on a line above "drops"

71. Deleted: "be"

72. Deleted: "prophecy of If this" following "any" . The preceding seven words inserted at top of page.

73. Inserted below "of the storm" and deleted: "be[?] any prophecy" ; deleted: "of the requirements of the [*illeg.*]" on the next line.

74. Brought up from middle of page on WW's arrow: "these . . . clothes"

75. Deleted: "and"

76. Deleted: "of"

77. Inserted above "all"

78. Original opening deleted: "I was years ago present at"

79. Inserted on a line above "of"

80. Deleted: [*illeg.*]; inserted above: "that rapidly"

81. Deleted: [*illeg.*] ; inserted above: "lurked"

82. Deleted: "and either six[?] in danger"

death.— How every body worked! How the shovels flew! And all for black Caesar—for[83] the buried man wasn't any body else.—[84]

Our country seems to be threatened with a sort of ossification of the spirit. Amid all the advanced grandeurs of these times beyond any other of which we know—amid the never enough praised spread of common education and common newspapers and books—amid the universal accessibility of riches and personal comforts—the wonderful inventions—the cheap swift travel bringing far nations together—amid all the extreme reforms and benevolent societies—the current that bears us is one broadly and deeply materialistic and infidel. It is the very worst kind of infidelity because it suspects not itself but proceeds complacently onward and abounds in churches and all the days of its life solves never the simple riddle why it has not a good time.— For I do not believe the people of these days are happy. The public countenance lacks its bloom of love and its freshness of faith.— For want of these, it is cadaverous as a corpse.[85]

[*3324R*] Going among a large collection of blind persons—who wish that they could see and have all the blessings and knowledge thence—would it make your sight any less valuable to you?/[86]

As to the feeling of a man for a woman and a woman for a man,[87] all the vigor and beauty and muscular yearning—it is well to know that neither the possession of these feelings nor the easy talking and writing about them, and having them powerfully infused in poems is any discredit . . . . but rather a credit.— No woman can bear clean and vigorous children without them.— Most of what is called delicacy is filthy, or sick, and unworthy of a woman of live rosy[88] body and a clean[89] affectionate spirit.— At any rate all these things are necessary to the breeding of robust wholesome offspring.—[90]

[*3325R*][91] In the cheerful performance of the task of presenting some reflections[92] on Temperance,[93] its advantages to all who practice it, /[94]

83. Deleted: "black"

84. First printed *UPP,* II, 89–90.

85. Preceding from *UPP,* II, 90. [*3324L*] appears in part on the photostat but is illegible. A parallel passage appears in "As of the orator" and in "The Eighteenth Presidency!"

86. Line from center to right.

87. Deleted: "and"

88. Inserted on a line above "live . . . body"

89. Deleted: "rosy"

90. First printed *UPP,* II, 90.

91. Part of [*3325L*] appears on the photostat. The entry is apparently only one line long and ends with "Indian."

92. Deleted: "about" ; inserted above: "on"

93. Inserted and deleted: "and" on a line above "its"

94. The entry is deleted by three vertical strokes and line across the leaf below; it seems not to have been used elsewhere.

[3326L] What can be a more admirable aim for the most exalted human ambition, than the wish and resolve to be *perfect?*— Though the carrying out of this resolve requires sound mental purification, the most of it, I think is of a physical nature. How many faults have I!— How many weaknesses!— Ah, if the flesh could but act what my rational mind, in its moments of clear inspiration aspires to, how much better I should be!!— Faint not, heart!— Advance stoutly and perseveringly!

I went to edit the Aurora in April 1842.[95]

In Jamaica,[96] first time in the latter part of the summer of 1839. In the winter, succeeding, I taught school[97] between Jamaica and Flushing—also in February and spring of '40 at Triming Square.—

In summer of 40 I taught at Woodbury.

Was at Jamaica and through Queens co. electioneering in fall of 1840—

[3326R] By the article of Sidney Smith[98] (1826) it appears that at that time certain high orders of criminals had not the privilege of being heard by their counsel in their trials—jury

"I have myself," says Mr Scarlett,[99] the English Barrister *"often* seen persons I thought innocent convicted, and the guilty escape."

Sidney Smith
essays

"Folly, sanctioned by antiquity."
Sidney Smith

(Winter of 1840, went to white stone, and was there till next spring.—

Went to New York in May 1841, and wrote for "Democratic Review,"[1] worked at printing business in New World"[2] office boarded at Mrs. Chipmans—[3]

95. See Joseph Jay Rubin and Charles H. Brown, eds., *Walt Whitman of the New York Aurora* (State College, Penna., 1950). Despite WW's statement, articles attributable to him have been identified from February 23, 1842. See [3326R].

96. The localities are all on Long Island.

97. Deleted: "at"

98. 1771–1845.

99. James Scarlett (1769–1844).

1. See *EPF.*

2. *Franklin Evans; or, The Inebriate* was published in the *New World,* II (No. 10, Extra Series, November [23], 1842) *EPF,* 124–25.

3. Mary Chipman, boardinghouse, 12 Centre St. is listed in NYC directories at least from 1841 to 1844. WW was apparently still there in the spring of 1842, for he refers favorably to Mrs. C------'s" boardinghouse in the *Aurora.* See Rubin and Brown, eds., *Walt Whitman of the New York Aurora,* 22–24, 44–45.

Went in April 1842 to edit the Aurora
Wrote for "sun,[4]" &c[5]
J.W. died at Dix Hills Sept 8th 1845[6]

There is a quality in some persons which ignores and fades away the a-round the hearts of all the people they meet.—To them they respond perhaps for the first time in their lives—now they have ease—now they take holiday—here is some one that they are not afraid of—they do not feel awe or respect or suspicion—they can be themselves—they can expose their secret failings and crimes.—Most people that come to them are formal or good or eminent—are repugnant to them—They close up their leaves then.[7]

[*3327L*][8] The Pretender,"[9] son of James II appeared in Scotland.—This was no avail

1727 George II. (Sir R. Walpole [*illeg.*]) two successive reigns.
1745 Charles Edward, the Young Pretender[10] comes to Scotland, advanced to Edinburgh, was proclaimed king there, Battle of Culloden blasted all his hopes—after which, for six months, he wandered in disguise from cave to cave, and at last escaped to France
Adm. Byng executed.—[11]
1764 George III. (grandson of George II)
1768. Middlesex election. Wilkes' case.[12] Wilkes was three times chosen, and refused by the house.—
1772. dismemberment of Poland between Germany, Prussia, and Russia.
1778. Earl of Chatham[13] died, being seized with illness in the house of lords while speaking.
1789 French Revolution (Bastile taken)
1790 Disruption of Burke, with Fox[14] (Pitt, younger, minister)

[*3327R*]

1791 Another quarrel of Burke with Fox, as he had formerly quarrelled with Sheridan in the House.—

4. The New York *Sun*. White, *Journalism*, 4–5, finds only two articles of 1842 in the *Sun*. Esther Shephard in "Walt Whitman's Whereabouts in the Winter of 1842–1843" *AL*, 29 (November, 1957), 289–96, points out that he worked on *The Plebian* in January and February, 1843, and possibly in October, 1842.

5. Besides the publications mentioned here or elsewhere in this notebook, WW wrote for *Brother Jonathan* in the early 1840s.

6. Jesse Whitman, Jr. See "Nehemiah Whitman"

7. Text from *UPP*, II, 90.

8. Dated entries in column. See also notes on English history

9. The "Old Pretender," James Francis Edward Stuart (1688–1766).

10. Charles Edward Stuart, grandson of James II, attempted to regain the throne in 1745.

11. Admiral John Byng (1704–1757) was executed for neglect of duty.

12. John Wilkes (1727–1797).

13. William Pitt (1708–1778).

14. Two illegible words.

French Revolution. The king by his weakness extortion and tyrany had incensed the people the States' general had assembled—the commons wished one body made of the three orders, and assumed the title of national assembly— Paris was (1789.) environed by a royal army of 50,000. The popular minister, M. Necker, was removed and then the insurrection broke out, the Bastile was destroyed, the king (17th July) visited the hotel de Ville and surrendered himself to the people.— In June, 1791, the king attempted to escape from Paris.— He was caught and brought back National assembly completed a new constitution, which was accepted by the king in Sept. the same year.— The Nat. As. then dissolved, and a new one was chosen, to the exclusion of every member of the former.— (Duke of Brunswick's Proclamation 2nd page.) Sept 21, 1792, new Convention met, and decreed the abolition of royalty, and the formation of a republic.—Since the deposition of the king, the prisons had been filled, with suspected persons; on the 2nd of Sept. they were found open, and a horrid massacre took place.— In Dec. 1792, the Convention tried the king, convicted him and on the 21st of Jan. 1793 he was beheaded.—

[*3328L*][15] Shakspere born in 1564 died in 1615

Sir W. Raleigh born in 1552 was beheaded in 1618, under James 1st

Francis Bacon, Lord Verulam, born in 1561, died in 1626.

Algernon Sidney born in 1617, died in 1683 on the Scaffold.[16] Bold champion of liberty—was beheaded under Charles II.

Dryden, born 1631 died 1701

Tillotson, born 1630 died 1694 Archbishop of Canterbury, writer of sermons.

Sir Wm. Temple born 1629 died 1700

John Locke born 1632, died 1704

George Farquhar, Irish, born 1678, died in 1707. writer of comedies.

Addison, born 1672 died 1719.

Congreve, Irish, born 1672, died 1729. comic writer

[*3328R*] Sir Richard Steele, Irish, born died 1729. commenced "Tatler" in 1709—followed by "Spectator" and "Guardian".—When George I came to the throne, he received the honor of knighthood.

Swift, Irish, born 1667 died 1744 author of "Tale of a Tub," "Gullivers' Travels."

Swift, Rabelais, and Voltaire, have been accounted the three greatest wits of modern times.

Pope, born 1688 died 1744. (Queen Anne)

Sir Robert Walpole, born 1676, died in 1745. (George I)

Isaac Watts, born 1674 died in 1748 (a dissenter)

St. John, Viscount Bolingbroke, born 1672, died 1751.— At George 1st, he

15. In column.

16. Deleted: [*illeg.*]

withdrew to France, joined the "Pretender."— Impeached of high treason, was pardoned, and afterward returned to England. He married a neice of Madame de Maintainon

Camoens, a Portuguese, contemporary of Tasso, Italian. C's poem on the first discovery of East Indies by Vasco da Gama[17]

[*3329L*] Britain

Little known before time of the Romans.— About the beginning of Christian era,[18] had rude forces, infantry and horses—Cesar first visited the island.— Claudius was the emperor, under whom it was subjected. Caractacus sought to free his country, was taken prisoner and carried to Rome.—"Alas! he said how is it possible that people possessed of such magnificence at home should envy me a humble cottage in Britain?"—Boadicia a Briton queen, [*illeg.*] by the Romans, fought her own armies, was routed, committed suicide by poison.— Romans left, after being masters for 400 years.—

After Romans abdicated, the British were so annoyed by the Picts and Scots, that they invited the Saxons, to come over from Germany, and protect them.— They came under Hengist and Horsa, brothers.— Vortigern was their king.— Treachery of the Saxons.—Prince Arthur a native Briton took up arms against them.— Essex Sussex, Wessex[19] &c. Saxon kingdoms.— About 400 years after the arrival of Saxons, they having founded different kingdoms, and, quarrelled—all were united under Egbert of Wessex, who was crowned king of England. At this time St Gregory (Pope) (St George?) sent missionaries to convert them. (Saw some children for sale in the slave market at Rome)

Danes now invaded England, and committed great ravages. "Alfred the Great" fought against them. Edward, Son of Alfred
[*3329R*] Ethelstan, son of Edward.— Edmund, Edward, Edwy.—Edgar.—Edward II.— Etheland II.— Edmund Ironside. (Danes, under Canute [*illeg.*] invaded Eng.) Canute and Edmund, keeping the kingdom in constant war, this nobility obliged them to divide the empire.— Soon after Edmund was murdered, and Canute thereby came into possession of the crown.— Harold, son of Canute.— Hardicanute, another son— Danes deposed, and Edward the Confessor, [*illeg.*][20] king.— Harold, son of a nobleman.— His pretensions were opposed by William, Duke of Normandy.— The crown had been left William by Edward the Confessor.— Pope in favor of William. William entered England, fought Harold, defeated him, and gained the crown. End of Saxon dynasty, after 600 years.

1066. William the Conqueror

1087 William Rufus, son [*William the Conqueror*]

1100 Henry I. (Beauclerk, son of Wm Conqueror

17. Luis de Camoëns (1524–1580), author of the *Lusiads* (1572).

18. Preceding six words inserted on a line below "Little . . . Romans.—"

19. Inserted on a line above "Sussex . . . &c."

20. Inserted on a line above, following "Confessor" and above "King"

1135 Stephen (nephew of Henry)

1154 Henry II. (son of [*illeg.*] quarrels with Thomas a Becket) (Ireland conquered.) Fair Rosamund

1189 Richard I (Coeur de Lion son of Henry II) (Crusades)

1199 John (Magna Charta, at Runnimede)

Understand That You Can Have.

Manuscript in Yale. Inscribed in pencil on three leaves of pink wove paper approx. 9¾" x 5⅝". Bucke's note dates the MS to 1855 or 1856. For other references to "mastering the horse," see "memorials." Printed in *N&F,* 72–73 (Pt. II, #68; *CW,* IX, 39–42).

Understand that you can have in your writing no qualities which you do not honestly entertain in yourself.— Understand that you cannot[1] keep out of your writing the indication of[2] the evil or shallowness you entertain in yourself If you love to have a servant stand behind your chair at dinner, it will appear[3] in your writing,—[4] or if you[5] possess a vile opinion of women,[6] or if you grudge any thing, or[7] doubt immortality—these[8] will appear[9] by what you[10] leave unsaid more than by what you say. There is no trick or cunning, no art or recipe, by which[11] you can have in your writing that which you do not possess in yourself that which is not[12] in you can appear in your writing—no rival of life—[13]no sham for generation—no painting friendship or love by one[14] who is neither friend[15] or lover.— Come, now, I will give[16] the first lesson for a young man, for[17] the newer and greater literati.— Absorb no[18] longer, mon ami, from the[19] text-books.— Go [20]

1. Deleted: "conceal from" ; inserted above: "keep out of"
2. Deleted: "whatever" ; inserted and deleted above: "any" ; inserted: "the" following [*del.*] "any"
3. Inserted: "in your writing" on a line above "ar;—" (in "appear;—") and "[*ins.*] or if"
4. Deleted: "If" ; inserted: "or if"
5. Deleted: "have" ; inserted above: "possess"
6. Deleted: "it will appear" ; inserted: "or if you grudge . . . immortality" on a line above "[*del.*] it will appear" and "—these [*del.*] or"
7. Deleted: "suspect" in the inserted line; inserted above: "doubt"
8. Deleted: "or anything else," ; initial comma not deleted, not shown.
9. Deleted: "more by" ; inserted above: "by"
10. Deleted: "do not say" ; inserted above: "leave unsaid"
11. Inserted: "you can have . . . yourself" on two lines above "which . . . do not"
12. Deleted: "can reserve the result of that which is, [*preceding word and comma not del.*], or that which is" ; inserted: "in you can appear in your writing—" on a line above [*del.*] "can . . . that which"
13. Deleted: "nothing"
14. Deleted: "except he be a" ; inserted: "who is neither" on a line above [*del.*] "except he"
15. Deleted: "and" ; inserted: "or"
16. Deleted: "you"
17. Inserted and deleted: "one of" on a line above "the"
18. Deleted: "more" ; inserted: "longer, mon ami" on a line above [*del.*] "more" and "from" . Comma retained.
19. Deleted: "schools or t" ; inserted: "text-books" on a line above "schools"

not, for some years, to the labors of the recitation room[21] or[22] desk, or on[23] the accepted track of[24] tourists.—[25] Ascend to your own country. Go to the west and south. Go among men, in the spirit of men.— Go to the swimming bath, the gymnasium, the new buildings where the working[26] carpenters and masons are.—[27] Learn of the elements and animals.— Learn to master the horse.— Become familiar with arms.— Become a good fighter, [2] a good rower, a sure marksman, hardy,[28] one that[29] dress and the criticisms of others and the usages of parlors[30] can not master, one who[31] could sleep in a blanket under a tree[32] if need be, one who does not condemn civilization and refinement[33] but[34] grows through them to be superior to them.—[35] What is[36] lacking in literature (can is[37] only be generated from) the seminal freshness and propulsion of new[38] masculine persons.— Books have generated[39] upon[40] books,[41] and religions upon religions, and poems upon poems.— I say a man is to vindicate himself above all things, and a woman above all things.[42] Do not grumble at any[43] fact or condition whatever.— What has been has been well, and what is is well, for nothing but[44] such as they could come out of[45] such as underlay or underlies them.—[46] They also are to underlie what could be built upon nothing better than them.— Sure as the

20. Deleted: "no more" ; inserted above: "not"
21. Comma deleted.
22. Deleted: "the"
23. Inserted on a line above the wordspace between "or . . . the"
24. Deleted: "the"
25. Inserted: "Ascend to your own [*ins. on a line above* "co" *in* "country"] country. [*illeg. del.*] Go [*ins. on a line above the deletion*] to the west and south. All above "ists" (*in* "tourists") ". . . among men, in the"
26. Inserted on a line above the wordspace between "the . . . carpenters"
27. Inserted: "Learn of the elements and animals." on a line above "masons . . . Learn"
28. Inserted on a line above the wordspace between "marksman, . . . one"
29. Deleted: "the dilletante" ; inserted: "dress and the criticisms of others" above [*del.*] "dilletante" and "weighs of"
30. Deleted: "do" ; inserted above: "can"
31. Deleted: "can" ; inserted above: "could"
32. Comma deleted.
33. Comma deleted.
34. Deleted: "learns of" ; inserted above: "grows through"
35. Deleted: "Of all that is" ; inserted: "what is" following the deletion.
36. Deleted: "wanted" ; inserted above: "lacking"
37. "is" inserted over "can"
38. Deleted: "men" ; inserted: "masculine persons." on a line above "new . . . B" (in "Books"). Redundant period not shown.
39. Deleted: "too long"
40. Deleted: "themselves"
41. Dash deleted.
42. Inserted: "I [*del.*] Do not grumble . . . whatever." on a line above ".— . . . well,"
43. Inserted and deleted: "thing now or at any time" on a line under "condition whatever.—"
44. Deleted: "them" ; inserted above: "such as they"
45. Deleted: "what" ; inserted: "such as underlay" or on a line above "[*del.*] what" and "underlies"
46. Inserted: "They also are to underlie . . . than them." on two lines above "underlay . . . sure as"

geological developements follow each other in[47] steady and beautiful order,[48] sure as the saurian ages terminate in more advanced developements—sure as man was prepared for upon the earth—sure as he makes his resistless progress through time, over all impediments, and coming on[49] with renewed vigor from all retrogrades and delays—sure as materialism—sure as the soul—shall arise in this land the[50] literature[51] that shall be eligible to embody not a few phases of life only, but all known and conceivable phases of life, and[52] to identify all men and women and all[53] climates and states New[54] York, Canada, Texas, the Mississippi [3] the planter, the Yankee, the Californian, the native, the immigrant,[55] town government, and the state and federal governments—[56] Literature this[57] of the largest friendship, and the[58] vitalest pride and the truest freedom and practical equality[59] ever known upon the earth;[60] literature[61] the roomiest and least cramped because it shall[62] arise[?] from the[63] broadest geography,—the most diverse because it[64] shall absorb[65] the greatest diversity—[66] the grand organs of whose head[67] shall correspond to the grandeur[68] of its[69] body.[70] Literature not only[71] of the dilletanti and a few pleasant reminiscences,[72] but of all living things and of the past and

47. Deleted: "sure" ; inserted above: "steady" . With this passage, cf. "Song of Myself" (1855), sec. 44, ll. 1165–1167.

48. Deleted: "or as the truth"

49. Inserted on a line above the wordspace between "coming . . . with"

50. Deleted "the" ; reinserted above: "the"

51. Deleted: "which is to typify stan" ; inserted: "that shall be" on a line above "stan"

52. Deleted: "comprehend" ; inserted: "to identify" on a line above "and [*del.*] comprehend"

53. Deleted: "trades and employments landsmen and sailors," ; inserted: "climates and states and the people them" [*preceding four words del.*] on a line below "[*del.*] trades . . . landsmen"

54. Written over [*illeg.*]

55. Deleted: "the federal" ; inserted above: "town"

56. Deleted: "a" ; inserted above and deleted: "The" ; capital "L" inscribed over lowercase in "literature"

57. Inserted on a line above "of"

58. Deleted: "manliest" ; inserted above: "vitalest"

59. Deleted: "yet" ; inserted above: "ever"

60. Deleted: "—A"

61. Deleted: "greatest" ; inserted: "the roomiest and least cramped" on a line above "[*del.*] greatest" and "because it"

62. Deleted: [*illeg.*]; inserted above: "shall"

63. Deleted: "wides"

64. Deleted: "has" ; inserted above: "shall"

65. "ed" deleted from "absorbed"

66. Comma deleted, dash inserted; deleted: "whose immense" ; inserted above: "the grand"

67. Deleted: "are but" ; inserted: "shall" on a line above "[*del.*] but"

68. Inscribed over "greatness"

69. Deleted: "muscular and immense"

70. Deleted: "a" ; capital "L" inscribed over lowercase in "literature"

71. Inserted on a line above the wordspace between "no . . . of"

72. Deleted: "only"

future—[73]Literature for a mighty[74] breed of[75] male and female,[76] represented no longer in their legislatures and executives, but represented better by their[77] successions of poets, orators, debators, readers, musicians, philosophers,[78] equals and mixers with the rest, springing from all trades and employments,[79] and effusing them and from sailors and landsmen, and from the city and the country,[80] making of[81] the vaunted of the past but a support to their feet and so treading it them[82] under their feet.— poets, musicians, philosophers,[83] whom the rest of the world shall not deny, because their greatness shall[84] accept the rest of the world[85] as much as any, also[86] and incorporate it and send back all that it has sent to them[87] with interest more a thousand fold.—

73. Deleted: "a" ; capital "L" inscribed over lowercase in "literature"
74. Deleted: "race" ; inserted above: "breed"
75. Deleted: "man" ; inserted above: "male"
76. Deleted: "woman" ; inserted above: "female"
77. Inserted on a line above the wordspace between "by . . . successions"
78. Inserted: "equals and mixers with the rest," on a line above "ophers" (in "philosophers") and "from all"
79. Inserted: "and effusing them" on a line above "ments" (in "employments") and "and"
80. Deleted: "treading under their feet" ; inserted and deleted: "Literature" on a line above [*del.*] "feet"
81. Inserted on a line above "making . . . the"
82. Written above "it"
83. Deleted: "with"
84. Deleted: "repr" This deletion is followed by a redundant "shall" , not shown. Deleted: "incorporate" ; inserted above: "accept"
85. Inserted: "as much as any" on a line above "world"
86. Inserted: "and incorporate it" on a line above "and send"
87. Deleted: "and interest" ; inserted: "with interest" on a line above.

George Walker.

Manuscript in LC (Feinberg #697). Inscribed in pencil, except where noted, in red leatherette notebook, ca. 5" x 3". Flyleaves, unruled recto and verso, are counted among the pages. Horizontal rules ¼", vertical rules for accounts. The later entries are written upside down on the page. Apparently at some time WW turned the notebook and started making entries from the back to the front (as in "Mr. & Mrs. Fitz"). Although the dates of individual entries are not completely certain, an attempt has been made to reproduce the probable order of inscription. Blodgett dates the notebook between July, 1865, when WW received Emerson's famous letter (see [*34*]), and September 1856, when the new edition of *LG* appeared. Blodgett's assumption was that WW entered the Emerson quotation immediately after receiving the letter, but since it comes at the end of the sequence of upside down entries, it is more likely the last entry in the notebook. WW was probably then engaged in designing the cover for the new edition, which features the quotation, much as WW has it here, on the spine of the book. The dateable entries seem to be from 1856 (but see [*94*] and [*64*]). Printed by Harold Blodgett, *Walt Whitman: An 1855–56 Notebook Toward the Second Edition of Leaves of Grass* (1956; Carbondale: Southern Univ. Press, 1959). Besides the useful notes, Blodgett includes facsimiles of the following pages: [*2*], [*5*] and following fragments, [*10*], [*13*], [*14*], [*17*], [*18*], [*27*], [*33*], [*34*], [*35*], [*37*], [*51*], [*64*], [*85*], [*90*]. (Gene Edward Veith, Jr.)

[*inside front cover*]
George Walker
Edward Smithson[1]
John Swinton (Lewis his bro.[2]
Sam (with black eyes & cap)
Henry Hearne[3]
William Meeker
William Phillips[4]
George P. Morris[5]

1. See "[*illeg.*] Dick Hunt."

2. For John and William Lewis Swinton, see *"Rambles Among Words"* and "[*illeg.*] Dick Hunt."

3. Publisher of the Brooklyn City directory, which lists him at 68 Tillary.

4. A fireman of that name, also in conjunction with the Swintons, is listed in "[*illeg.*] Dick Hunt."

5. Possibly George P. Morris (1802–1864), editor and literary figure. He was owner of the NY *Mirror*, an important literary publication to 1844, and author of the much-memorized poem "Woodman, Spare That Tree." Mentioned in "Starting Newspapers," *SD, Prose 92,* I, 287 and "The Old Bowery," *NB, Prose 92,* II, 595. Listed as editor, 107 Fulton, h. Cold Spring, NYC directory 1855–1856.

Leo
Pete Dempsey[6]
Henry Post (Fulton op. Eagle office[7]
Nick (black eyes 40th st.—small
Joe (Canadian Montreal)
Bill Young (milkman & driver)
George Applegate (tallest)[8]

[*1*][9] Gentlemen, I will be very plain with you.— I see in my country many great qualities.— I see in America not merely the home of Americans, but the home of the needy and down kept races of the whole earth.— I know just as well as you the terrible[10] effects of ages of degradation and caste.— It is a real truth—it is a black and bloody lesson—/

A. Baker, Boots 15 Ann st Stout boots $4 Double water proof $4.50[11]

[*2*][12] It is mentioned that the Irish and German and other foreigners mix in our politics.— Gentlemen with perfect respect I say you you can think what[13] you choose about this;— It is a credit to men and no disgrace to them to take an eager interest in politics.—/

Amherst White, attorney cor Barclay & Broadway/ A. J. Davis[14] 137 Spring

[*5*;[15] *3–4*[16] *stub*][17] The gross and soiled she moved among and was with without repugnance did not make her gross and soiled

[*6*] Not only American literature, but the structures of[18] American social intercourse are[19] household life, are growing up in[20] total severance from the roots and trunks and branches[21]

6. Probably the laborer at 224 E. 17th, NY directory 1855–1856.
7. A Harry Post, mechanic, is listed in "[*illeg.*] Dick Hunt." The office is probably that of the Brooklyn *Eagle*, which WW edited 1846–1848.
8. Mentioned with the same description in "[*illeg.*] Dick Hunt" and "return my book."
9. Notes for a lecture. See "Oratory" section.
10. Deleted: "[*illeg.*] letter."
11. In NYC according to directory. Entry enclosed by horizontal line above and vertical line at left.
12. Deleted: "You" . A continuation of the lecture from [*1*]. In 1855–1856, the nativist Know-Nothing party was at its height.
13. Deleted: "wh"
14. The spiritualist mentioned in "[*illeg.*] Dick Hunt."
15. Bottom two-thirds of leaf clipped out.
16. Traces of writing on [*4*].
17. "Song of the Broadaxe" (1856), sec. 11, l. 241. See [*37*] ff. Cancelled in ink.
18. Preceding three words inserted.
19. Inserted.
20. Deleted: "utter scorn of" ; inserted: "total severance from"
21. Traces of writing visible from clipped out fragment, including an inserted: "growth"

[7][22] for Gymnastic and Athletic/

I heard to-day of a young[23] man who was bequeathed $500,000[24] and wasted it—There are young men who are bequeathed more than that and never put it to good[25]

[8][26] What is there you can conceive more wonderful than what you see around you?
Nothing can be conceived of by the fancy that can be more wonderful than what we see.—

[9][27] Cursed is that age or nation that does not realize itself, and esteem itself,
Wretched is that man who does not esteem himself /

put "Manhattan" for New York all through[28] /

English Johny (49th St Jockey cap) Sam—(49th st round shoulders light clothes[29]

[*10*] (Poem or passage)[30]
the scenes on the river[31] as I cross the Fulton ferry[32]/
Others will see the flow of the river, also,
Others will see on both sides the city of New York and the city of Brooklyn
A hundred years hence others will see them,
Two hundred years—many[33] hundred years hence others will enjoy the flow[34]
of[?] the[?]

22. Bottom half of leaf clipped out. See notes on Health and Hygiene.

23. Deleted: "man"

24. Written over another [*illeg.*] figure.

25. Partially formed beginning of a word, probably meant to be "use"

26. Blodgett notes the similarity to "A Song for Occupations" (1855), sec. 3, l. 61. Cancelled in ink by waved vertical line.

27. Bottom clipped, but loose fragment extant in notebook, as noted below. Verse lines cancelled by waved vertical line.

28. Probably refers, as Blodgett says, to the following draft of "Crossing Brooklyn Ferry."

29. The preceding thirteen words are on a clipped out fragment. It belongs here, as evidenced by the verso: "hundred years hence . . ." [*10*].

30. "Crossing Brooklyn Ferry" (1856). Title partially circled. WW continued writing the poem on the rectos of the succeeding pages and the poem is printed here as it was probably composed. Each page of the poem is cancelled with a vertical stroke. The intervening versos, themselves similarly related to each other, are printed together after the poem. For another passage later used in "Crossing Brooklyn Ferry" see [*88*].

31. Deleted false start of line: "Po[?] O[?]"

32. One of several ferries between NYC and Brooklyn and the one of which WW most often speaks. There was no ferry named "Brooklyn Ferry." For the verse on this page see "Crossing Brooklyn Ferry," sec. 2, ll. 13–19.

33. Clipped. The following is on a loose fragment. On recto is "English Johny . . ." [9].

34. Cut off. Only ascenders of next words visible.

[*13*;11–12 *stub*[35]][36] I too[37] many and many a time have crossed the ferry
I have watched the sea-gulls flapping their wings—[38]
I have seen them[39] floating with motionless wings high in the air at sunset, just oscillating their bodies.
I have seen the[40] glistening
yellow light parts of their bodies and[41] the rest in strong shadow
I have seen them[42] high up slowly wheeling in circles, edging slowly to the south[43]
[*15*[44]] I have looked[45] toward the lower bay to notice the arriving ships.[46]
I have looked on the white sails of the[47] clear[*?*][48]
[*17*] The[49] edged waves, the[50] scooped cups, and the dancing motion,
The yellow masts, the pilots in their pilot-houses, the sailors at work in the rigging,
The swift current, the[51] white[52] frothy wake left by the paddles of the steamboats
The gray walls of granite storehouses near the docks,—the[53] quick tremulous motion of the flukes of the wheels
The flags on the tops of the
[*19*[54]] The continual and hurried[55] crowd of men and women crossing
The reflection of the sky in the water—the[56] blinding dazzle in a track from the most[57] declined[58] sun,

35. Torn out. Writing on stub of [*12*].
36. The verse on the following four pages was worked into "Crossing Brooklyn Ferry," sec. 3, ll. 27ff.
37. Deleted: "have crossed"
38. Deleted: "I have"
39. Inserted above wordspace between "seen . . . floating"
40. Deleted: "bright" ; inserted above: "glistening"
41. Deleted: "leave"
42. Deleted: "thus afa afar off" ; inserted: "high up" above "s" in "thus" and "afa" and "a" in "afar"
43. Final word written below "slowly"
44. Bottom two-thirds of leaf clipped out. For [*14*] see below.
45. Deleted: "ga"
46. Deleted false start of new line: "To"
47. Deleted: "cl"
48. Clipped off. [*illeg.*] ascenders.
49. Deleted: "dancing" ; inserted above: "edged"
50. Deleted: "but"
51. Deleted: "b"
52. Deleted: "brack" ; inserted above: "frothy wake"
53. Deleted: "swift"
54. Bottom third of leaf clipped out.
55. Preceding two words inserted above "ual" in "continual" and "cro" in "crowd"
56. Deleted: "white" ; inserted above: "blinding"
57. Inserted above "e" in "the" and "d" in "declined" . Written over [*illeg.*] initial letter.
58. "ed" written over "ing"

The lighters—the sailors in their picturesque costumes
—the nimbus of light around[59] the shadow of my head in the [*illeg.*][60]

[*21*] (Full poem[61]

I too have— —
    have— have—
I too have— — —[62] felt the curious questioning come upon me.[63]
In the day they came[64]
In the silence of the night came upon me,
What is it now between us?—Is[65] it a score of years? or a hundred years? or five hundred years?
Whatever it is, it avails not . . . . distance avails not and place avails not.
[*23*][66] I[67] too lived,
I too walked upon the solid earth and bathed in the sea
But I, wearied, wavered,
I too[68] was struck from the float eternally[*?*] held in solution.
I too was[69] cohered and received identity[70] through my body,
Of all that I had, I had nothing except through[71] my body
Of all that I have or shall have, it is the same
[*25*]That I am is of my body, and what I am is of my body[72]
What[73] identity I am, I owe to my body . . . . what[74] soul I owe to my body,
What belongs to me . . . . that it does not yet spread in the spread of the universe, I owe to my body[75]
Of all that I have had, I have had nothing except through my body,
Of the make of my body was not my mortal experience only,
My body makes my immortal experience[*?*]

59. Deleted: [*illeg.*] ; "the" written over [*illeg.*]

60. Clipped off.

61. For the following three pages see "Crossing Brooklyn Ferry," sec. 5.

62. For other examples of WW leaving dashes or blanks in structuring his verse see [*41*], "[*illeg.*] Dick Hunt" and "Passage to India".

63. "Crossing Brooklyn Ferry," sec. 5, l. 59.

64. Line crowded in.

65. Originally "Ist" . Final "t" crossed out.

66. Page badly smeared and almost illegible.

67. Deleted: "also" ; inserted above: "too"

68. Deleted: "cohered[*?*]" ; inserted: "was struck" above "too" and the deletion.

69. Inserted in the wordspace between "too . . . cohered"

70. Deleted: "by" ; inserted: "through" above the deletion and "m" in "my"

71. Inserted above.

72. Deleted false start of new line: "That I" . The following line, originally the third line on the page, is brought up by asterisks and WW's notation: "? tr up"

73. Deleted: "soul" ; inserted above: "identity"

74. Deleted beginning of new line: "What"

75. Inscribed as the second line on the page before WW's transposition.

[27] drenched with joy,—had my friends, loved them, was loved by them,—was irritated,—saw hundreds of men and women I loved, yet never told them so,
Had my hopes and dreams,—laughed, slept, had my amours, friendships,
I too—approaching or passing,[76] was called[77] by name by the clear prompt[78] voices of[79] my friends[80] as they saw me[81] passing or approaching[82]
[29][83] You wayward, vain,[84] blabbed, blushed, resented, was shallow,[85] ambitious, curious, fearful, lied, stole, adulterous,[86] a solitary committer, greedy, grudging,[87] —the wolf, the snake, the hog[88] not altogether wanting the covetous wish,—the frivolous word—the cheating look—/[89]
had guile, lust, hot[90] wishes I dared not speak,
Refused my love to those that gave me theirs,/[91]
It is not you alone who[92] know what it is to be these
I too knew what it was to be these—
[*31*]Tighter yet may the bands be drawn,[93]
What thought you have of me, I[94] had as much and more than as much of you,
I have laid up[95] in my stores in advance— for I[96] considered long and[97] friendlily of you before you were born.—/
Who knows but all shall come home to my soul[*?*][98]
Who knows but there are consequences[99] to me seasons and centuries afterward

76. Preceding three words and punctuation marks inserted above "too . . . was called" and "to" in "[*del.*] too"

77. Deleted: "too"

78. Inserted above "voi" in "voices"

79. Deleted: "my" ; inserted and deleted above: "the" ; inserted: "my" above "[*del.*] the"

80. Deleted: "I who" ; inserted and deleted: "as" above "w" "[*del.*] who" ; inserted: "as they" following "[*del.*] "as"

81. Deleted: "as I" ; "ing" written over "passed" and "approached"

82. This line used in "Crossing Brooklyn Ferry," sec. 6, l. 79.

83. "Crossing Brooklyn Ferry," sec. 6. Inserted: "You" ; inserted and deleted above: "that are"

84. Deleted: "that are" following "You" ; deleted: "a blabber," following "vain"

85. Inserted above "ambitious"

86. Deleted: "emerged from"

87. Deleted [*illeg.*] letter.

88. Deleted: "emerging at" ; inserted above: "not altogether wanting"

89. A short line above "had" in the following line.

90. Inserted above "wi" in "wishes"

91. Following two lines crowded in below.

92. Deleted: "are all" ; inserted: "know what it is to be" above the deletion and "these"

93. For the following lines on this page see "Crossing Brooklyn Ferry," sec. 7.

94. Deleted: "have"

95. Deleted: "great" ; inserted: "in my" above "up" and "[*del.*] Great"

96. Deleted: "have thought"

97. Preceding two words inserted in wordspace between "considered" and "Friendlily" and above "Frie" in "Friendlily" . "ily" written over "ly"

98. Line crowded in.

99. Inserted and deleted: "coming" above "ence" in "consequences" ; inserted: "to me" following.

Who knows but I am[1] looking at you now, for all you cannot see me?
[33][2] I believe whatever happens I shall not forget this earth,
I believe I shall walk and walk among men and women.—
Wherever I go I believe I shall often return
There are many words and deeds that will happen that will allure me.
Where[3] any one thinks of me or wishes me[4] that will allure me,
Where the happy young husband and wife are, and the happy old husband and wife are,[5] will allure me.
[35][6] Where[7] the great renunciation is made in secret, that will allure me.
Where personal love reaches toward me, that will allure me . . . . to the prisoner in his cell, or the slave, or the solitary[8] sick person, it will certainly allure me, /
I[9] do not know what is waiting for me[10] to be— [11] But I know[12] that I shall be[13] in great form and nature
I cannot prove it to you or any one . . . . but I know it is so.*
[45][14] What the earth is and where the earth is will allure me
Not more spiritual, not more divine and beautiful than this earth, /

[14][15] *The newer better principle through all my poems.*— (dramas? novels?,[16] compositions of any sort.) /

Present only great characters, good, loving characters.—/[17]

1. Inserted in wordspace between "I . . . looking"

2. It is not clear whether the lines on the following three pages were written as part of the "Crossing Brooklyn Ferry" draft or whether they were conceived separately. The lines do not seem to have been used in *LG* and are not cancelled. A passage used in the conclusion of "Crossing Brooklyn Ferry" is on [88].

3. Inserted over deleted "That"

4. Inserted and deleted: [*illeg.*] above "me" ; inserted: "that" following the deletion.

5. Word incompletely formed.

6. Leaf not cancelled.

7. Deleted: "the" ; inserted above: "the"

8. Inserted above "si" in "sick"

9. Inserted: "do not" above "know"

10. Deleted: ", nor what the being of it shal will exhibit" ; inserted: "to be—" Dash written over ellipses.

11. The following twelve words originally a separate line, brought in by a curved line.

12. Preceding two words inserted above "But . . . that"

13. Deleted: "I know" ; inserted: "in great form and nature" above "now" in [*del.*] "know"] and to the right edge of the leaf.

14. An asterisk is at the bottom of [35], with another asterisk on related lines on [45]. The recurrent "will allure me" indicates that WW intended the lines to go here. The first line and asterisk seem crowded in at the top, suggesting that WW might have adapted the second line to fit into his longer poem ten pages earlier.

15. Just as WW continued his poem on successive rectos, his advice to himself continues on the versos. The advice does not seem to be related to the facing draft of "Crossing Brooklyn Ferry" on [15–35].

16. Question marks above words.

17. Line from left edge and above and below "Present"

Present the best phases of / character, that any one, man or woman is eligible to.

Present noble phases of character for young men /

Combination [18]

I must combine the tenderness and trembling[19] sympathetic manliness of Jean Paul[20] with the strength of Homer,[21] and the perfect *reason* of Shakespeare.[22]

[*16*][23] You may have but a few to (fully,)[24] understand you.—Nevertheless that few rules is to rule[25] the world.—/

[*18*] Convey what I want to convey by models or illustrations of the results I demand.— Convey these by *characters,* selections of *incidents* and *behaviour.*

This indirect mode[26] of attack is better than all direct modes of attack,[27]/

[28]The spirit of the above[29] should pervade ALL[30] my poems. /

[31] Avoid all the "intellectual subtleties," and "withering doubts" and "blasted hopes" and "unrequited loves," and "ennui," and "wretchedness" and the whole of the *lurid*[32] and *artistical* and *melo-dramatic* effects.—Preserve perfect calmness and sanity

[20][33] In the best poems appears the human body,[34] well-formed, natural, accepting itself, unaware[35] of shame, loving that which is necessary to make it complete, proud of its strength, active, receptive, a father, a mother,

18. Originally: "A Combination" ; "A" deleted and both beginning letters overwritten by a large capital "C"

19. "b" written over [*illeg.*].

20. Pen name of Jean Paul Richter (1763–1825). See "Richter born 1763."

21. For WW's knowledge of Homer see "Homer and Shakespeare "

22. For WW's knowledge of Shakespeare see "Shakespeare born "

23. Bottom two-thirds of leaf clipped out.

24. Inserted above "un" in "understand"

25. Preceding three words inserted over "rules" as alternate reading.

26. Initial letter written over "of[?]"

27. Cf. 1855 Preface, l. 110.

28. Fist pointing upwards.

29. Fist above word, pointing upwards.

30. Written in large letters.

31. Pointing fist.

32. "all" written in larger letters.

33. Bottom third of leaf clipped out. Blodgett sees a connection between this passage and the long inventory in "I Sing the Body Electric," sec. 9, which WW added for the 1856 edition.

34. Deleted: "fully-formed" ; inserted above: "well-formed, natural,"

35. Overwritten. Deleted: "that" at the beginning of the next line.

[22][36] They exfoliate pork packing slaughtering[?] pork—the
The[37] hanging[?]carcasses of[38] pork slaughtered—the men in their oil-skin overalls—the[39] scalded— —the packing—
The killing hammer—the hog hook—the gutting[40]

[24] Idea to pervade largely /
Eligibility[41]—I, you, any one eligible to the condition or attributes or advantages of any being, no matter who,—/
3d Feb. Make no puns, funny remarks Double entendres "witty" remarks ironies Sarcasms
—only that which is simply *earnest, meant,* harmless to any one's feelings —unadorned —unvarnished[42] nothing to excite a laugh[43] silence silence silence laconic taciturn

[26] He does not[44]
I do not (wish to) spend my life in a corner
I do not[45] go among conspicuous persons either /

to produce such a public that great performances will not be received with noisy applause but as matters of course.

[28][46] Of me the good comes by wristling[47] for it.[48]
I am not he bringing ointments and soft wool for you,
I am he with whom you must wristle[49] . . . . I am[50]
The good of you is not in me . . . . the good of you is altogether in yourself.
I am the one who indicates, and the one who provokes and tantalizes

36. Badly smeared and almost [*illeg.*]. Cancelled by vertical stroke. See [30] and "A Song of Occupations" (1856), sec. 5, 1. 124.

37. Deleted: "heaps of the" ; inserted: "hanging"

38. Deleted: "pork—the slaughtering" ; inserted above: "pork slaughtered"

39. Deleted: "scalding rooms" ; inserted above: "scalded"

40. Notation "over" with pointing fist, which must refer to [30], on which WW rewrites this material.

41. For what seems to be the earliest use of this term in WW's poetry see "By Blue Ontario's Shore" (1856), sec. 3, l. 3. Entry in hanging indentation.

42. Preceding twenty-two words written in column at left of vertical line. Following ten words written in column at right of line.

43. Small wavy line in the column in the space of a word.

44. Preceding line at top, perhaps inserted as an alternate to "I do not"

45. Deleted: [*illeg.*]

46. Deleted: "I am"

47. Clearly a dotted "i" in MS. See the same spelling below.

48. Preceding four words crammed below line. Evidently the whole verse is a later addition.

49. Cf. "Starting from Paumanok" (1860), sec. 15, l. 235.

50. Deleted false start of new line: "If"

[30][51] The area of pens of live pork—the killing-hammer—the men in their oil-skin overalls—the hog-hook —the scalder's[52] tub—the cutter's cleavers—
the gutting the packer's maul, and the plenteous winter[53] packing

mufti
ulema[54]

[32] I say the land that has a place for slaves and the[55] owners of slaves has no place for freemen.—[56] /

As to her[57]
She is mine—ma femme[58]

[37; 34;[59] 36 *blank*][60] *Full Poem*—indicating, any way, (loosely) the illustrations of the true female character. /

The violent[61] oaths[62] the[63] hiccupping song of the drunkard, the smutty expression, the quarrel,[64]. . . . none of these annoyed[65] her,
She heard them. . . .she heard the taunt, the accusation, the rank word,[66] She

51. Cancelled with vertical stroke. A rewriting of [22]. See "A Song for Occupations," sec. 5, l. 124.

52. "er's" inserted. Deleted: "the gutting, cutting, packing, [*illeg.*]" ; inserted on two lines above and below the deletion: "tub—the cutter's cleavers— the gutting the packer's maul, and"

53. Deleted: "work of pork-" . The deleting stroke extends partially into "packing" and it may be that WW's mark was simply part of his cancellation of the entire passage. "A Song for Occupations," sec. 5, l. 124 reads "the plenteous winterwork of pork-packing"

54. The mufti and the ulama are the arbiters and the interpreters of Islamic law. "Muftis" are mentioned in "Salut au Monde!" (1856), sec. 6, l. 94. Perhaps WW thought of them in connection with the "uncleanness" of pork butchering.

55. Deleted: "me"

56. Entry in hanging indentation. For WW's attitude to slavery see [45], [51], "Slavery—the Slaveholders."

57. Preceding three words inserted above "she is"

58. Written over an [*illeg.*] spelling. WW first used this term in his poetry in "Starting from Paumanok" (1860), sec. 12, l. 157.

59. The famous greeting by Emerson written upside down on [34]: "'I greet you at the beginning of a great career' R. W. Emerson" (see *n*5 at the end of the notes to "George Walker.") Printed as last entry, WW at some time having turned the notebook, making entries from back to front.

60. Cancelled in ink by vertical wavy line. This poem, and a line on [5], were incorporated into "Song of the Broad-Axe" (1856), sec. 11. The 1856 edition does include a "full poem" on the subject, "Poem of Women" ("Unfolded out of the Folds"), but it is unrelated to these lines.

61. Inserted above "oaths"

62. Deleted: "of the drivers,"

63. Deleted: "blackguard" ; inserted above: "hiccupping"

64. Preceding two words inserted above "ssion" in "expression" and the ellipses.

65. Deleted: "Heard"

66. Plural deleted.

knew as she passed[67] the thoughts of the young men[68] . . . . She was not the less considerate or friendly toward them, nothing[68] was concealed from her, ... she was aware . . . . she saw the doers of all
these,
[*39;*[69] *38 blank*] They did not wound her . . . . she was possessed of herself . . . .[70] . . . . she received them as the air received them, or as the laws of nature received them,
She[71] too was a law in nature . . . . she was[72] as great as any . . . . [*illeg.*][73] was maternity, /
[*41; 40 blank*] More than
Her wholesome and
She was silent and at them[74]
Yet she loved them when she saw them or passed among them.—
What made the[75] healthy girl[76]
What made the[77] sensible sweet tempered woman that men so love.
What made[78] the best daughter and the most beloved of her parents,
What made[79] the best wife, the chaste equal of the husband, fully bearing her share,
[*43; 42 blank*] What made[80] home where her presence was
What the performance of all the housekeeping duties,
What made the mother of[81] brave and athletic children,
What made the love that clung to her through through the growth and marriage of her children, and their old age just the same
She was . . .

[*44*] Would you like to know what to produce?
Produce great persons. . .all the rest will surely follow[82] /[83]

67. Preceding three words inserted above "w" in "knew" , "the" , and "t" in "thoughts"
68. The following ten-word clause, originally the final line on the page, brought up by arrow.
69. Bottom half clipped out. Cancelled in ink with vertical wavy line.
70. Preceding five words and both ellipses inserted above ". . . . she received them"
71. Deleted: "too" ; inserted and deleted above: "herself" ; inserted: "too" before the deletion.
72. Deleted: "the greatest law. . . ." ; inserted above: "as great as any. . . ." (WW's ellipses.)
73. Clipped off.
74. For other examples of WW leaving blanks or dashes as he structures his verse see [*21*].
75. Written over "a"
76. Deleted: "and"
77. Preceding two words inserted over a caret above undeleted "a" , which was part of preceding line. Crowding of the subsequent words suggests WW may have been originally filling in one of his blanks, after the "a", then turning the material into a new line by the insertion.
78. Originally "makes" ; "de" written above word. "makes" not deleted, perhaps an alternate reading.
79. Originally "makes" ; "de" written above word. "makes" not deleted, perhaps an alternate reading.
80. Inserted and deleted: "the best" above "de" in "made" and "ho" in "home"
81. Deleted: "the best children, ..." (WW's ellipses.)
82. "By Blue Ontario's Shore" (1856), sec. 3, l. 31.
83. Following entry in a scrawl.

Missing vessels, (ships) at sea—never heard of
—The Schooner of Uncle Dan's[84] sons. / The Pacific

[45][85] say to Slavery
Go, and return no more,[86]/

To Young Men for artists—
(sarcastic)[87]
To Rome!— Go study the human figure—study anatomy—study it along the wharfs and levess, the 'long shoremen,[88] hoisting and lowering cargoes—study the pose of the drivers of horses—[89]

[*51; 46 blank; 47–48 stubs; 49–50*[90] *blank*][91] There is more[92] hullabaloo[93] made for the[94] hourly whims of these 350,000 slaveholders, than,[95] has ever been made, or ever will be made, about the[96] lives on earth, and the eternal lives afterwards of the[97] whole main[98] body of the inhabitants of these states,[99] the good thirty millions of men, women, and children.—

[*61; 52 blank; 53–54 stub; 55–57 blank; 58;*[1] *59 blank; 60*[2]][3] I see[*?*][4]
The Spanish dance with castanets in the chestnut shade to the rebeck and guitar[5]
The courage[6] and nimbleness of the matador[7]

84. Although there were several sailors on WW's mother's side of the family, there is no trace of any "Uncle Dan." WW does not speak of Dan's "sons" as if they were relatives.
85. Asterisk and lines belonging to a previous poem, here printed after [*35*].
86. Preceding entry written in a larger, looser hand. See [*32*].
87. Written above "To Rome!"
88. Deleted: "pulling r[*?*]"
89. For "drivers of horses" see "memorials"
90. Top third clipped out.
91. For the use of the same statistics and the general sentiment see "The Eighteenth Presidency!"
92. Deleted: "ado"
93. Deleted: "raised about" ; inserted above: "made for"
94. Deleted: "unlawful" ; inserted above: "hourly"
95. Deleted: "than would be made about" written on two lines.
96. Deleted: "whole" ; inserted and deleted: "whole"
97. Deleted: "thirty millions of" ; inserted at the beginning of the line: "whole" above "ma" in "main"
98. Deleted: [*illeg.*]
99. Deleted: "the" ; inserted: "the good" above the deletion and "thirty"
1. Drawing of a map showing a "200ft" lot at the corner of McKibben st. (which is in Brooklyn) and a railroad line, just below a "bay" .
2. Rough schematic drawing of a human torso showing lungs, stomach, and heart.
3. Cancelled by vertical stroke.
4. Preceding two words inserted in an almost illegible scrawl.
5. See "Salut au Monde!" (1856), sec. 3, l. 26. The whole passage is a draft for this catalog.
6. Deleted: "of"
7. "t" written over "d"

I hear by the[8] the careless[9] song song of the muleteer loading his panniers with grapes[10]
I see the lithe[11] matador in the arena at Seville[12]
I see the Brazilian vaquero[13] on horseback[14] with his lasso coiled on his arm[15]

[*Inside back cover*[16]]
Joseph Velsor[17] 130 Suffolk 5 x 6 x 12 [*illeg.*]—with moderate arch Mechanics Coffee & Reading Rooms corner 10th st & Avenue D. / (Hewett's pamphlet "on the uses of iron"[18] Miss Libby cor Willoughby & Duffield[19]/ 49 Madison st. / Shirting Mr. Rhodes 244 Bleecker[20] / Map of Mountains & Rivers wholesale 90cts. Wells, 140 Nassau st.[21] / Map of the world wholesale (90cts) / The world's standards & costumes Charts in sheets wholesale colored 38

[94] 70 in paper
5 in cloth & gilt.[22]
Nov. 23[23]

"For Sailors of All Nations" (Inscription on the Mount in Evergreens Cemetery[24]—a simple round column with a square cap supporting a representation of the globe on which the seas and the shores of the continents are outlined/

8. Preceding two words inserted above "hear"
9. Inserted above "song"
10. See "Salut au Monde!" sec. 3, l. 32.
11. Inserted above "ma" in "matador". "t" over "d" in "matador"
12. Preceding three words inserted above "or" in "matador" and "in the" . See "Salut au Monde!" sec. 11, l. 176.
13. Written over illegible misspelling.
14. Preceding two words inserted above "with"
15. See "Salut au Monde!" sec. 7, l. 120.
16. The subsequent entries on both rectos and versos are all written upside down on the page. Apparently at some point WW turned his notebook upside down and began making entries from back to front.
17. Possibly a relative on WW's mother's side. See "return my book" and *n*12.
18. Preceding entry at right of page, enclosed by a curved line. The pamphlet is *On the Statistics and Geography of the Production of Iron* (New York: W. C. Bryant, 1856), the text of a speech made February 21, 1856, by Abram Stevens Hewitt (1822–1903), ironmaster, philanthropist, and later mayor of NY.
19. Preceding word cut off. Brooklyn directory, 1856–1857 lists a James Libbey, customhouse, h. 82 Willoughby, which would be at the corner of Duffield.
20. A NY address. Brooklyn directory 1856–1857 lists a John Rhodes, tailor, h. 56 Adams.
21. Gaylord S. Wells, publisher, 140 Nassau, h. 14 Beekman, NY directory, 1855–1856. He is not listed in John Tebbel, *A History of Book Publishing in the United States* (New York: Bowker, 1972) and there is apparently no connection to the phrenologist S. R. Wells, whose firm of Fowler & Wells published *LG* 1855.
22. Blodgett suggests the reference is to *LG* 1855, which was issued in various bindings.
23. Probably 1855, since *LG* 1856 was published in September, 1856. The meaning of the date is not clear. Illegible marks at upper right.
24. In Brooklyn.

the hills of Abyssinia[25]
The beautiful, strong, black active Abyssinian

[93] "Sight & Hearing" C Scribner[26] / "Stories of the Italian Poets," by Leigh Hunt.[27]

[90; *91–92*[28] *stub*] Full poem /[29]
For the dying treating them and talking to them courageously— /
no whining or praying or tears /

I have all lives, all effects, all hidden invisibly in myself . . . . they proceed from me. /[30]

Gist of my books

To give others, readers, people, the materials to decide for themselves, and *know,* or grow toward *knowing,* with cleanliness and strength.

[*89*][31] Stillman & Durand[32] care of F. W. Christern 763 Broadway
Sunday Courier 15 Spruce
Sunday Mercury 22 Spruce
Sunday Times[33] 162 Nassau
Daily News 129 Nassau st 2d story
Irish American 116 Nassau
Sunday Leader[34] 25 Chambers st
Leslie's Illustrated News 12 Spruce st
Young America 98 Nassau
Citizen; 10 Spruce Police Gazette, 103 Nassau

25. Preceding four words inserted above "beautiful, strong, black" . See "Salut au Monde!" sec. 7, l. 117.

26. James Henry Clark, M.D. (1814–1869), *Sight and Hearing, How Preserved and How Lost: A Popular Handbook* (New York: C. Scribner, 1856).

27. *Stories from Italian Poets* (1846). For Leigh Hunt see "Byron Born at Dover" and Stovall, *Foreground,* p. 241.

28. Traces of writing on [*91*].

29. Deleted at beginning of following line: "add" . See "To One Shortly to Die" (1860).

30. Preceding entry cancelled by vertical stroke. Following entry in ink, cancelled by vertical stroke.

31. Checked off by ticks. List continues on [*88*] and [*87*].

32. William J. Stillman (1828–1901) and John Durand (1822–1908) were editors of *Crayon,* an art journal.

33. WW contributed to the New York *Sunday Times,* 1842–1843 (White, *Walt Whitman's Journalism,* 4). As Blodgett points out, this is not the New York *Times,* to which WW contributed between 1863 and 1865.

34. WW contributed to the New York *Leader* in 1862 (ibid., 63).

Ledger 120 Nassau
Yankee Notions 98 Nassau
Harper's Magazine,[35] Franklin square

[*88*][36] I have seen at night[37]
Where the fires from the foundry chimnys[38] burn high and glaringly into the night[39] and cast strong contrasts of darkness and wild red and yellow light over the tops of the houses, and down into the clefts,[40] the streets.[41]/

Picayune, 114 GNassau
Clipper, 102 Nassau
Observer, 138 Nassau
Churchman
rooms 40 Trinity Building 111 Broadway
American Celt cor Ann & Nassau
Independent
22 Beekman

[*87*][42] O days of the present I will attire you in beauty
I will attire you in as much beauty as the days that are past[43]/
—NY[44] Sun N.Y. Sunday Herald Journal of Commerce Courier & Enquirer

[*86*] *Full poem*[45]
Theme—that which involves gladness, joy,—*all out*—[46]/

Edward H Dixon[47] Editor Scalpel 42Fifth av/[48]
oilworks, —candle making

35. To *Harper's,* WW contributed "Song of the Red-Wood Tree" and "Prayer of Columbus" in 1874, "With Husky-Haughty Lips, O Sea!" in 1884, and "Of That Blithe Throat of Thine" in 1885.

36. Entry cancelled by vertical stroke.

37. Preceding five words crowded in on two lines in a smaller hand at upper left above "Where the" beginning the next line. Possibly meant as an alternate reading for "Where"

38. Preceding four words inserted above "fires . . . burn high"

39. Preceding three words inserted above "ingly" in "glaringly" and "and" and "c" in "cast"

40. Deleted: "of"

41. See "Crossing Brooklyn Ferry" (1856), sec. 9, l. 119. For other lines towards that poem see [*10*]ff.

42. Cancelled with vertical stroke.

43. "By Blue Ontario's Shore" (1856), sec. 8, l. 120.

44. Inserted above "S" in "Sun"

45. Deleted: "There is something" above "involves gladness, joy" ; following three words inserted above "[*del.*] of something" and into right margin.

46. Blodgett suggests "A Song of Joy" (1860).

47. Edward H. Dixon, physician and editor of *Scalpel,* 42 Fifth av., NY directory, 1855–1856.

48. Following entry in ink. "oilworks" is mentioned in "A Song for Occupations" (1856), sec. 5, l. 110.

[85] American society literature[49] is settling itself,[50] in utter defiance of American principles. It is settling itself in accordance with European principles, and on a far larger scale than the European scale—as much larger as the[51] American proportions are larger than the European proportions.— The modes on which it arranges itself involve the idea of caste—involve servants, masters, superiors inferiors.— /

Under the American forms much,[52] something most that is expressed is the European idea of caste, inferiority

[84] *Poem*—comprehending the[53] sentiment of *saluting*[54] Helō!
Halow![55] Hellō!
Halow![56]

[83][57] For[58] broad-ax—See acct of the sack of Rome in 1527 "sweeping on with that horde of Spanish bigots and German unbelievers and Italian brigands to the sack of the old great city[59]/

I see[60] the telegraph lines of the earth /
the crowbar, pickax shovel,[61] spade,[62]
the flail,

[82][63] *axe*—Firemen using the axe to cut in floors or partitions, when the fire is under the floor—or using the axe anyhow. /

[81] Catlin's Indians plates[64] Leggett's[65] 88 Nassau Valentine's NY same place[66]

49. Written above "society" perhaps as alternate.
50. Deleted: "as if for good"
51. Inserted above wordspace between "as . . . American"
52. Deleted: "if not"
53. Deleted: "idea"
54. "Salut au Monde!" (1856), originally titled "Poem of Salutation."
55. "w" written over [*illeg.*] letter and accent mark.
56. Cf. "Poem (subject) ? for recitation"
57. See "Song of the Broad-Axe" (1856), sec. 3, ll. 86–90. See *N&F*, 33–34 (Pt. I, #97; *CW*, III, 160ff.) for other notes toward the poem.
58. Deleted: "battle-a" ; inserted above: "broad-ax"
59. The source of this quotation has not been located.
60. Preceding two words inserted in a scrawl above "the" . Hanging indentation.
61. Preceding two words inserted above "wbar" in "crowbar" and "spade,"
62. Deleted: "shovels"
63. Cancelled in ink by vertical wavy line. See "Song of the Broad-Axe" (1856), sec. 3, l. 71.
64. George Catlin (1796–1872), famous painter and chronicler of the American Indians who knew WW, *Manners, Customs, and Condition of the North American Indians* (1841). This work includes 400 engravings. See Traubel, II, 348–349, 354 and Allen, 521–522.
65. Leggat Brothers, books, 88 Nassau, NYC directory, 1855–1856.
66. Perhaps refers to D. T. Valentine, publisher of *Manual of the City of New York*, the official city handbook issued annually. Entries in hanging indentation.

[78[67]; 80–79[68] *blank*] In conversation, discussion, intercourse, &c.—not to take the position (or drift the talk that way,) of one *wanting compliments*—this must be *real*, because if the *wanting compliments* exist it will show out some how.

[75; 77–76 *blank*] The best Only first rate[69] poems have the quality of arousing in[70] men and women who hear them or read them those thoughts effects[71] that no words can even describe—effects which themselves cannot be described—great effects, proportioned to the ideas,[72] images, and characters of the poem.—

[71[73]; 74 *blank*; 73[74]–72[75]] He[76] so looks at men through the telescope that they are enlarged—while all others reverse the telescope and[77] behold[78] minnikins

[70] axiom for laws, for punishments—/ No punishment shall be provided for the sailor, soldiers, or without its being strictly eligible to be inflicted on the officers, even to the commander in chief.—[79]

[68; 69 *blank*] Poem
holding in terrorem over the heads of men the sure results[80] of all evil /

I see Christ eating his last[81] supper, with the young and old[82] men around him,[83]

[67][84] Where the women enter the public assembly the same as the men
Where[85] women walk in[86] the[87] great processions in the streets[88] the same as the men,

67. Bottom half clipped out. Traces of writing.
68. Top half clipped out.
69. Preceding three words inserted above "The best"
70. Deleted: "those" ; inserted: "men and women" above the deletion and "who hear"
71. Inserted above "thoughts" perhaps as alternate.
72. Deleted: "cha"
73. Upper half torn out.
74. Upper half torn out. Still extant, below tear: "tree) mulberry,' "
75. Cut out at upper corner. Traces of two lines extant: "with [*del.*]" and "sed"
76. Deleted: "sees" ; inserted above: "so"
77. Deleted: "lo"
78. Deleted: "Man"
79. Cf. *DV*, 388–389*n* and "William Grover"
80. "r" over [*illeg.*] letter.
81. "l" written over "s"
82. "old" written over "older[?]"
83. "Salut au Monde!" (1856), sec. 6, l 97.
84. Cancelled by a vertical, horizontal, and short slanted stroke. "Song of the Broad-Axe" (1856), sec. 5, ll. 128–129. See also [37]ff. and [66].
85. Deleted: "they" ; inserted above: "women"
86. Inserted above wordspace between "walk . . . the"
87. Deleted: "streets in" ; inserted: "great" above "[*del.*] in"
88. Preceding three words inserted above "the same"

Where the enter the public assembly and take their places the same as the men, and are appealed to by the orators the same as the men

[66] The water-carriers on a stooping-trot—
The[89] three-year-old child sweeping /

Where[90] women[91] mix in[92] healthy games, the same as men—
Where they run, leap, ride, swim,[93] play at out-door plays, the same as men,[94]

[65][95] I think the genius[96] our continent has complacently gone to sleep, these years, satisfied with having produced the men of the times.

[64] The cities confer with each other from[97] across[98] two thousand miles—the continents[99] talk under the[1] waves of seas[2] /

Lesson for beginners.—[3]

Write every thing—especially poems—*well.*—[4] Mostly because *doing well* passes into a habit—the best habit of art.—

[34][5] [:][6] "I greet you at the beginning of a great career." R.[7]W. Emerson

89. Deleted: [*illeg.*]
90. Inserted above "wom" in "women"
91. Deleted: "mixing" ; inserted above: "mix"
92. Deleted: "all"
93. Deleted: "lead,"
94. See "A Woman Waits for Me" (1856), l. 18.
95. Cancelled by vertical stroke.
96. Preceding two words inserted above "nk" in "think" and "our"
97. Inserted above "acr" in "across"
98. Deleted: "oceans" ; inserted: "two thousand miles" above the deletion and dash following.
99. Deleted: "are"
1. Deleted: "bottoms"
2. The first transatlantic cable, which had been discussed for some time, was attempted in the summer of 1857, but the attempt failed because of breakage August 11.
3. Title inserted.
4. Deleted: "Doing"
5. Upside down on this leaf. Hanging indentation. Whether this was actually the last entry in the notebook is of course not certain. Possibly WW was planning the cover design of the 1856 edition. This quotation appeared on the backstrip.
6. Double brace.
7. Written over original "W."

A Large, Good-Looking Woman.

Manuscript in LC (#79, sheet #764R). Inscribed in black ink on white laid foolscap 12⅞" x 8", torn irregularly at bottom. Blue rules 5/16" apart. Entries separated by a short line in the middle of the sheet. The writing is the small firm hand of the early notebooks. No medical or folkloric source could be found for the story of the unfortunate farmer's wife. No source could be found for the Tom Thumb story. WW had interviewed P. T. Barnum in 1847 (Theodore A. Zunder, "Whitman Interviews Barnum," *MLN*, 48 (January, 1933), 40). Thumb appeared with Barnum's circus in Brooklyn in 1854. There is, however, no record of his meeting WW. Thumb toured the Midwest with Barnum's circus after 1851. Miss Phillipa P. Harrison, to whom I am indebted for diligent but fruitless research, suggests that this sort of story circulates about any popular figure. WW probably wrote this in the 1850s.

A large, good-looking woman, wife of a farmer, has had twelve children; every one of whom died before living a year.— The woman has some serious inward disease, which, the doctor says would have killed her long ago had she not borne children; and that, when she has a child born that lives and grows[1] perfectly well,[2] the woman herself will die.—[3] /

When my little friend[4] Tom Thumb, travelled with the circus he stood behind the stand, in a Missouri settlement, one afternoon, and sold notions.— Amid the crowd, came up the biggest kind of a Western bully, and presently demanded the change[5] due him on the dollar.— . . . . . "O, yes," says Tom, "all but the dollar." ——————————Then crowds the louping[6] giant closer up and cries, "Damn your little heart, didnt I[7] buy three cigars, and give you a dollar bill half an hour ago?". . . . . . Tom was up to Western rigs, and couldn't be persuaded for he had[8] handled nothing but change and a gold quarter-eagle since he open'd trade. On stating this, the baffled ruffian sings out, "Then I lie, do I?—

1. Deleted: "well and"
2. Inserted.
3. Short line between entries midway across leaf.
4. Preceding three words inserted.
5. Deleted: "for"; inserted: "due him on"
6. I.e., "leaping" (OED).
7. Deleted: "just"
8. Deleted: "taken" ; inserted: "handled"

Take that to remember me by[9]!" and reaching over his long arm[10] like a windmill in a gale, hits the poor boy a staggerer that brings the blood from his nose and raises a purple cushion around one eye in short metre.—[11]

The fifteen minutes that passed away before any of the circus people to whom the stand could be decently confided, came within

9. Inserted.
10. Deleted: "like" ; inserted: "like a windmill in a gale,"
11. I.e., "quickly" (*DA*).

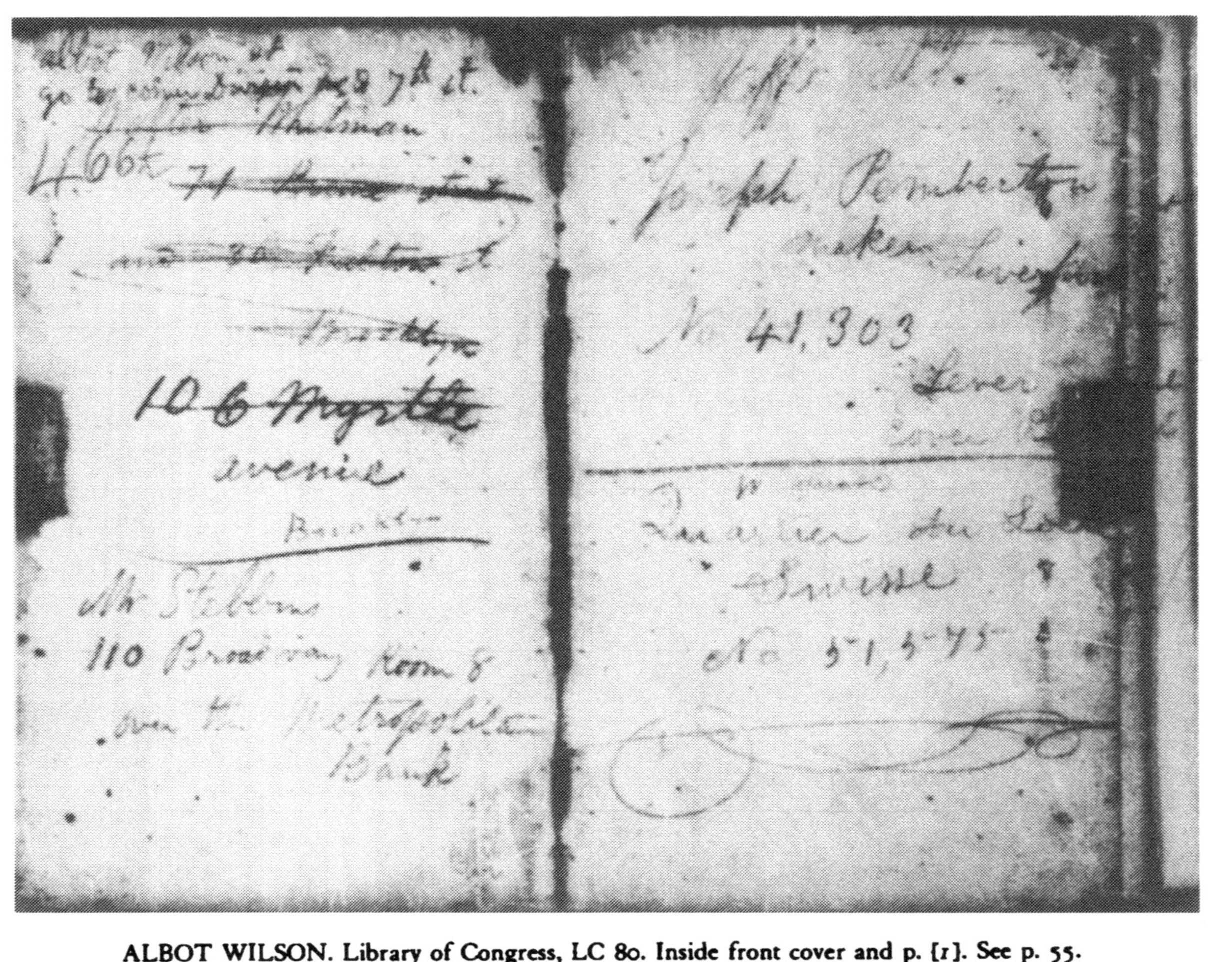

avenue

Brooklyn

Mr Stebbins
110 Broadway Room 8
over the Metropolitan
Bank

Joseph Pemberton
maker Liverpool

No 41,303

ALBOT WILSON. Library of Congress, LC 80. Inside front cover and p. [1]. See p. 55.

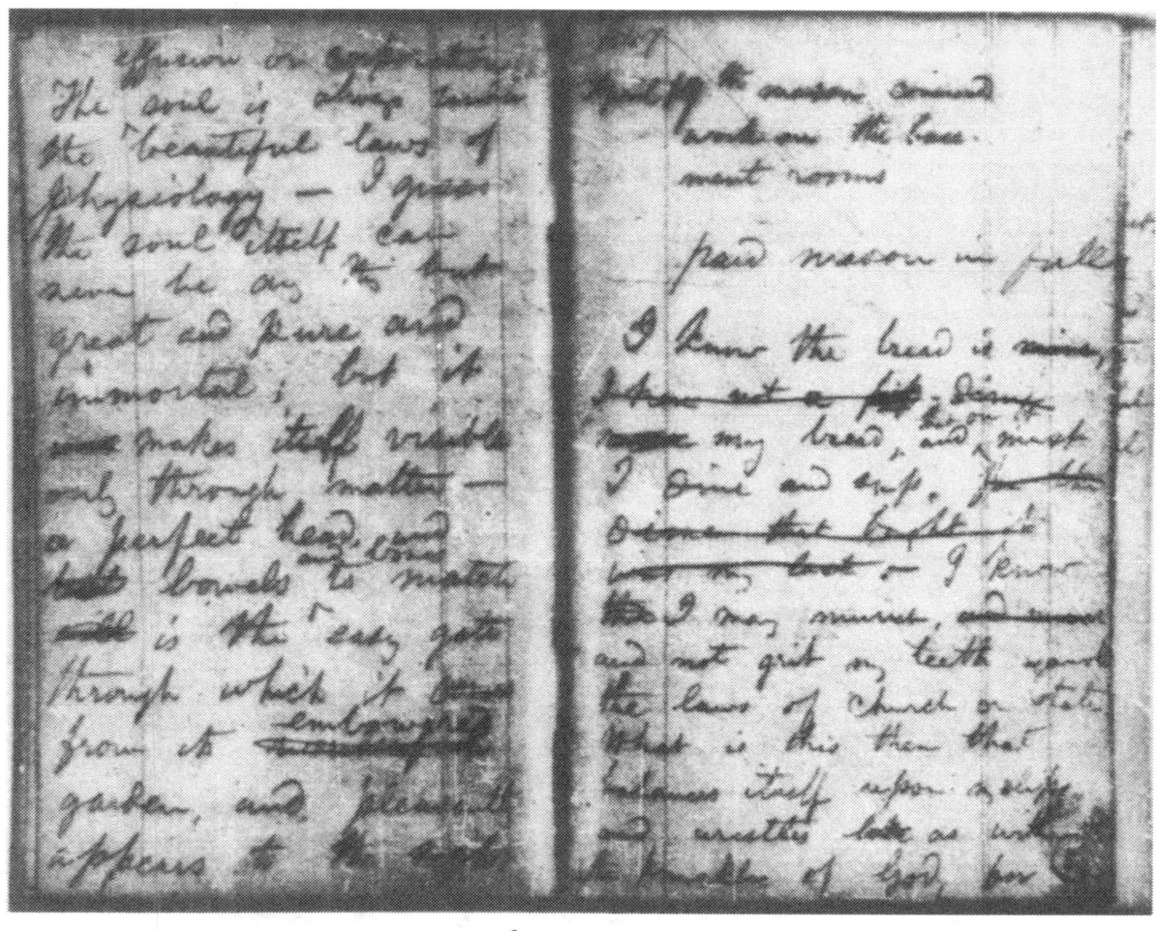
The soul is always [illegible]
the beautiful laws of
physiology — I guess
the soul itself can
never be anything but
great and pure and
immortal; but it
makes itself visible
only through matter —
a perfect head, and
bowels and bones to match
is the easy gate
through which it comes
from its embowered
garden, and pleasantly
appears to the [illegible]

[illegible] mason [illegible]
work on the base.
next rooms

paid mason in full

I know the bread is mine,
[illegible] my bread, and I must
I dine and sup, [illegible]
[illegible] — I know
I may murmur, [illegible]
and not grit my teeth upon
the laws of Church or State
What is this then that
balances itself upon a [illegible]
and [illegible]
[illegible] of God, for

ALBOT WILSON. Library of Congress, LC 80, pp. [16–17]. See pp. 58–59.

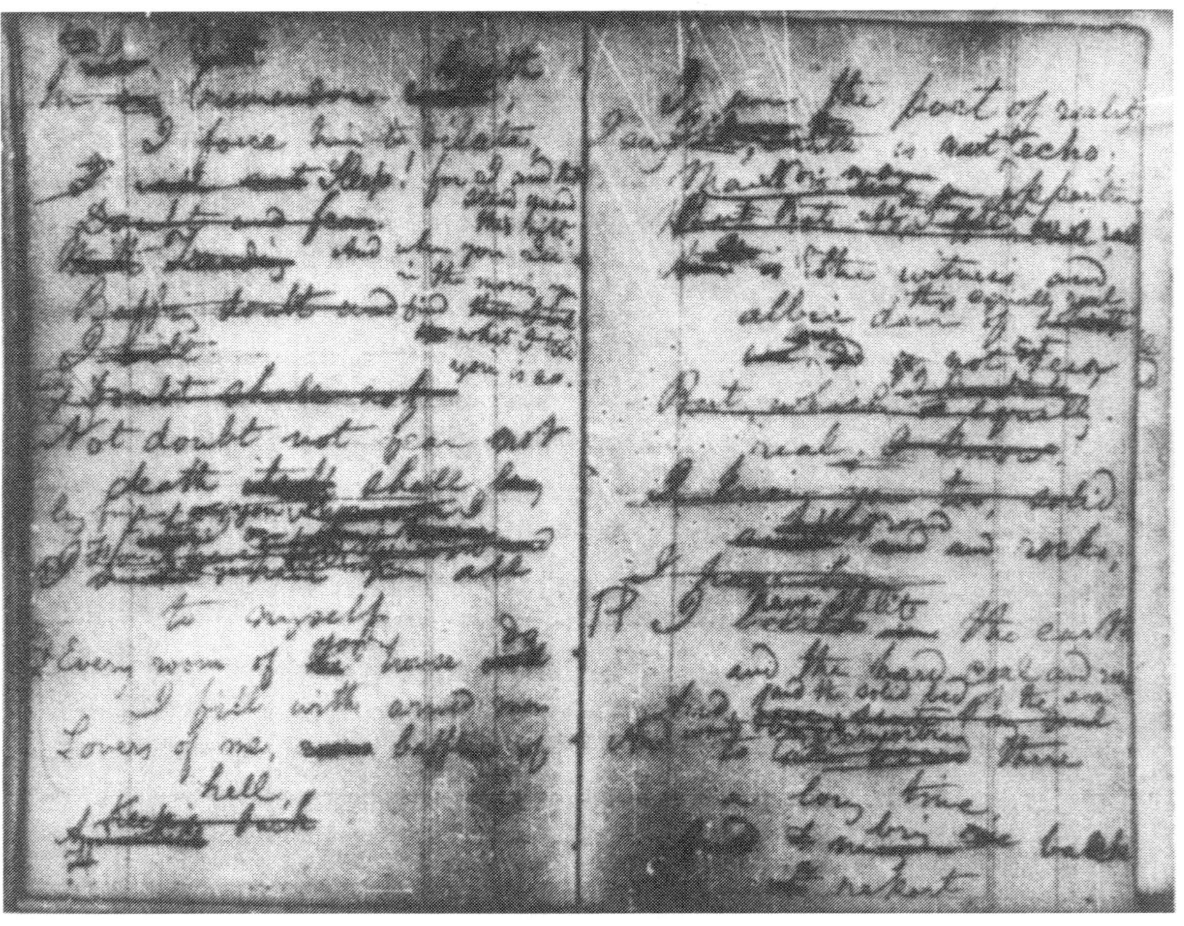

ALBOT WILSON. Library of Congress, LC 80, pp. [56–57]. See pp. 68–69.

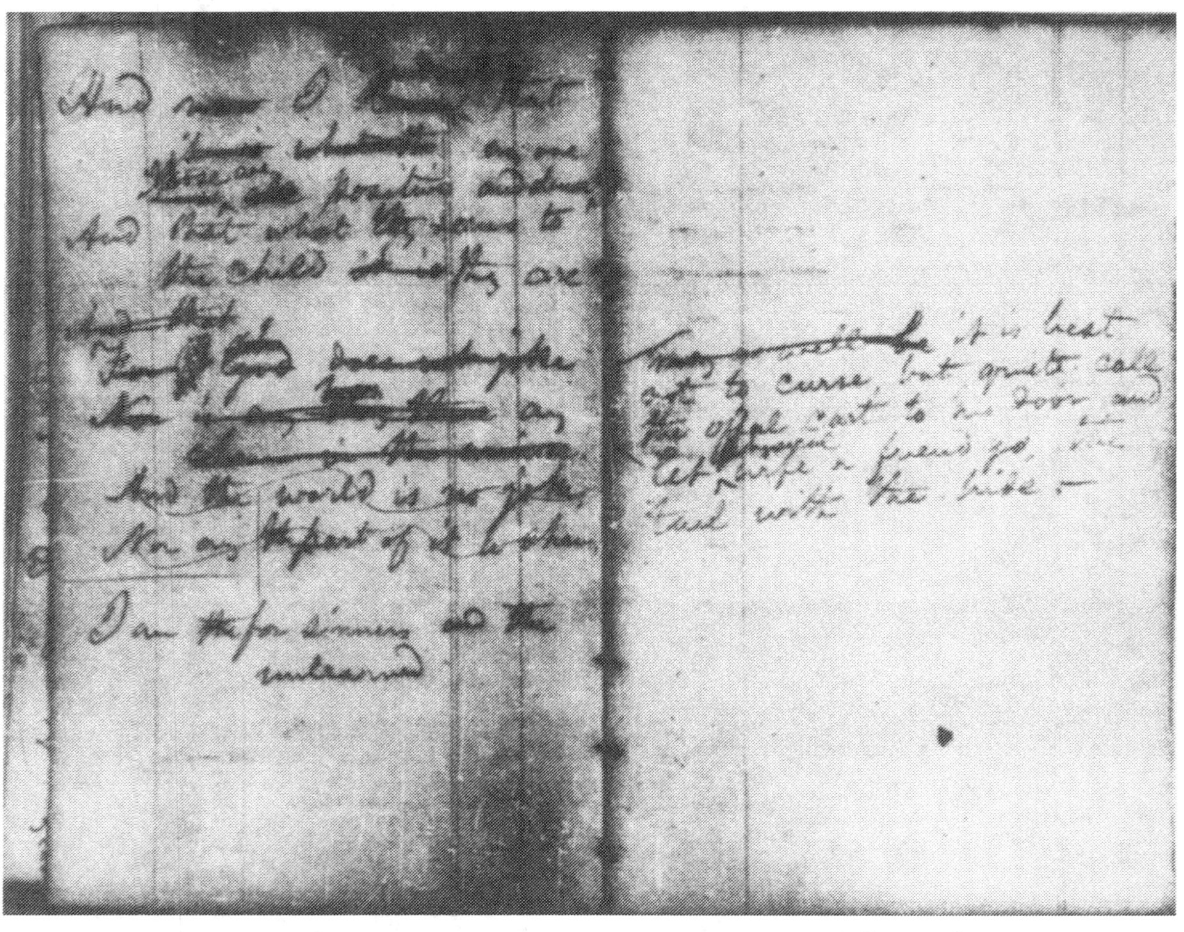

ALBOT WILSON. Library of Congress, LC 80, pp. [58–59]. See pp. 69–70.

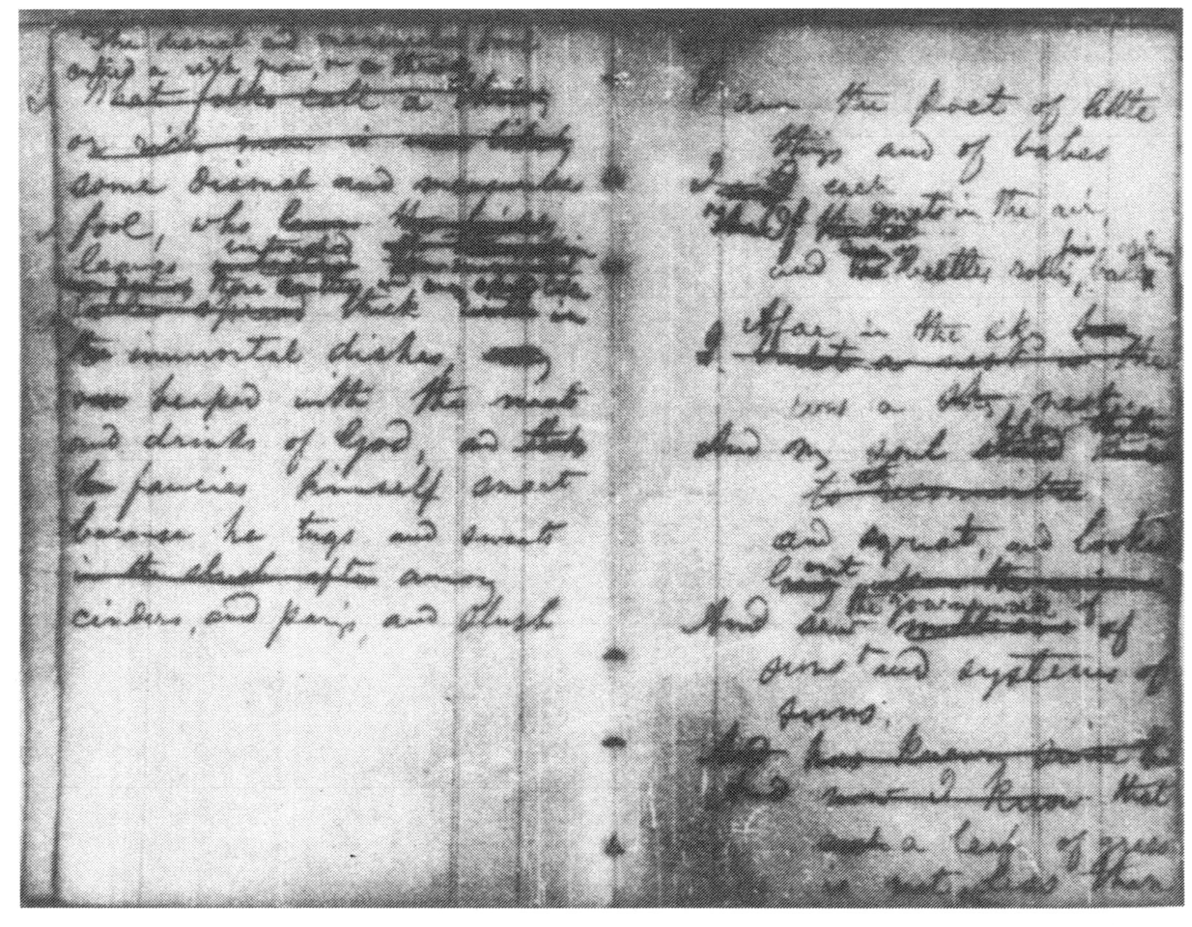

some drunk and vainglorious
fool, who
the immortal dishes
heaped with the meats
and drinks of God, and
he fancies himself a great
because he tips and sweats
cinders, and fancy, and slush

I am the poet of little
things and of babes
Of the gnats in the air,
and the beetles rolling balls
Afar in the sky
was a nest
And my soul staid there
and squat, and looked
out
And saw the journeywork of
suns and systems of
suns,

ALBOT WILSON. Library of Congress, LC 80, pp. [60–61]. See pp. 70–71.

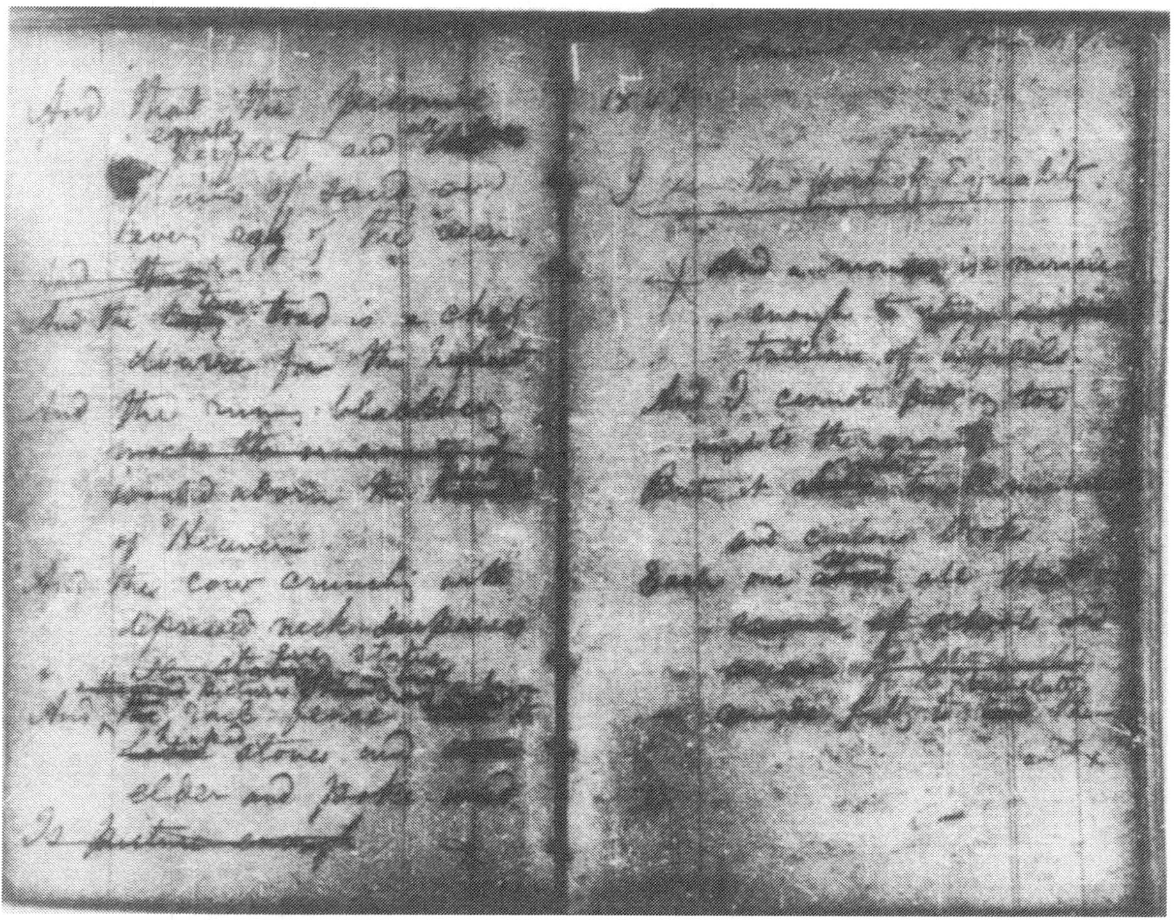

ALBOT WILSON. Library of Congress, LC 80, pp. [62–63]. See pp. 70–72.

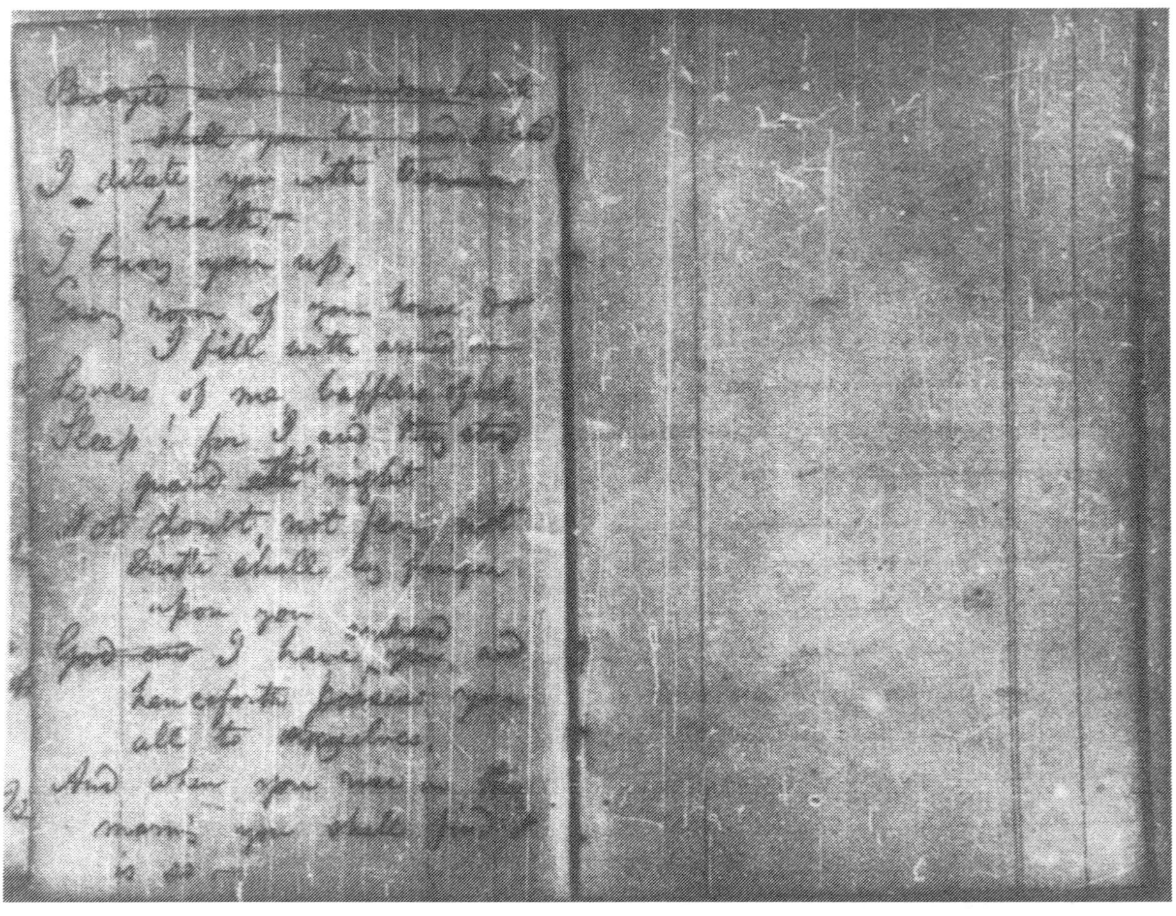

ALBOT WILSON. Library of Congress, LC 80, p. [64]. See p. 72.

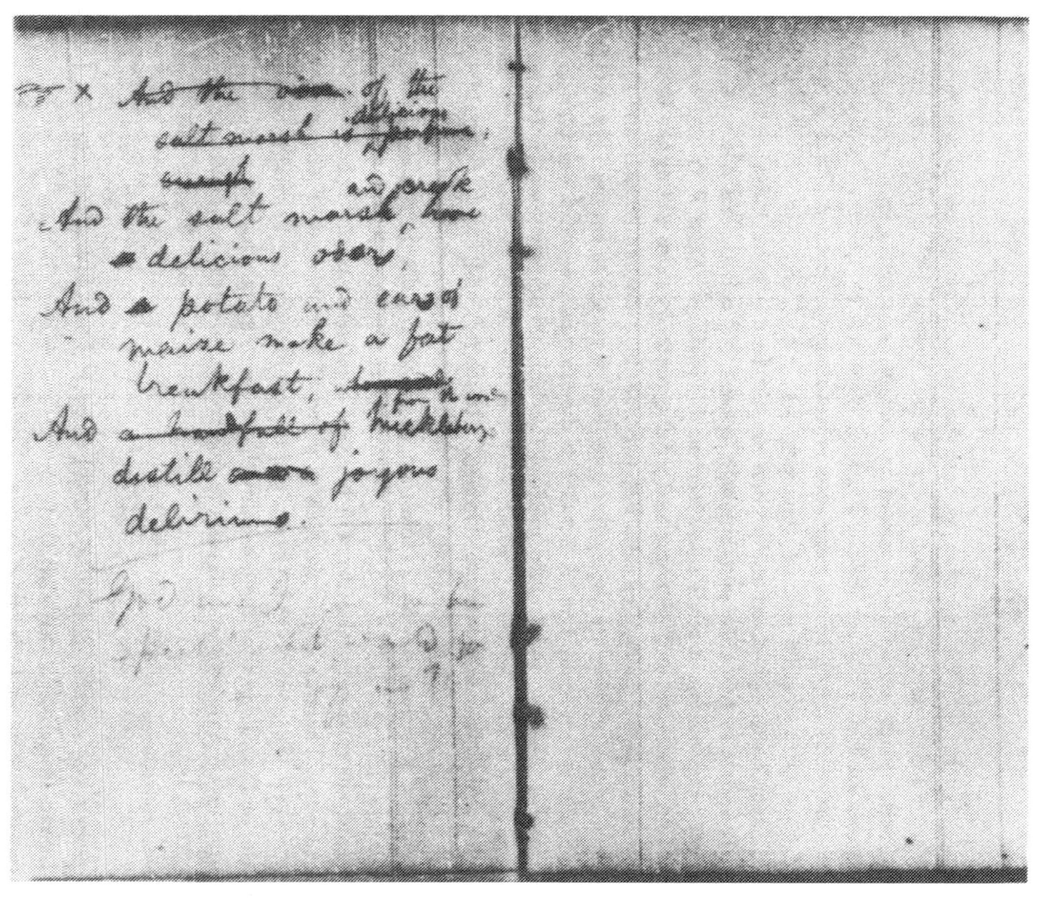

And the salt marsh, and musk
delicious odor,
And potato and ears of
maize make a fat
breakfast,
And huckleberry
distills joyous
delirium.

ALBOT WILSON. Library of Congress, LC 80, p. [66]. See p. 72.

[Illeg.] Dick Hunt.

Manuscript in LC (Feinberg #1514). Inscribed in black pencil, except where noted, on white wove ledger notebook, bound in tan leather, approx. 5¾" x 3¾", rules apart 2" recto and verso. Many entries are separated by straight or irregular lines which may or may not cross the leaf. They are indicated here as elsewhere by a slash. The notebook is no longer completely intact, so the pagination is not altogether certain. Other MSS. may orginally have been clipped out of this notebook, e.g. "Vegetable not wood" and "Poem L'Envoy," although direct comparison has not been possible. Most of the poetry and sketches relate to *LG* 1860 and, although Bowers did not use this notebook in his study of the 1860 edition, it tends to corroborate his findings. While WW was keeping this notebook, he was not only planning and writing poetry but also editing the Brooklyn *Times* (beginning in late January or early February, 1857), educating himself, and making innumerable friends. (These are the earliest long lists of names to survive. The numbers after the names are evidently ages. A number of the same names and descriptions appear also in "George Walker" and "return my book" (which transcribes some of the entries.) The games of "Twenty Questions," which WW had used when he was teaching school (Allen, p. 35), by their references to "drivers," "counters," and "food," were probably played while WW ate with his omnibus driver friends. See C. Carroll Hollis, "Whitman's Word-Game," *WWN* (now *WWR*), 4 (1958), pp. 74–76. WW's dated entries—[*Inside front cover*], [*12*], [*17*], [*18*], [*21*], [*23*], [*32*]—are from December 20, 1856 to May, 1857 and are apparently in chronological order. On [*116*] is a reference to the Police Riot of the summer of 1857. There are a few parallels to poetry WW published in August–September, 1856 ([*55*], [*71*], [*75*], [*77*], [*121*]), but the connections are general, except for a verbal echo on [*75*]. Except for the possibility that these seemingly haphazard entries were made prior to *LG* (1856), the bulk of the notebook can safely be dated 1857. (Gene Edward Veith, Jr.)

[*Inside front cover; outside front cover blank*] [*illeg.*][1] Dick Hunt[2] 68 Stanton /
(The Human Body by Wilkinson)[3]
Mrs. Hicks[4] widow 75 Columbia wooden house with pillars /

1. In upper left corner, set off by curved line. It appears to read "Medium 1/6 size" perhaps a clothing size.

2. Richard Hunt, butcher, employed at Fulton Market, at this address, New York directory, 1857–58. See "return my book"

3. *The Human Body and Its Connexion with Man, Illustrated by the Principal Organs* (London: 1851) by James John Garth Wilkinson (1812–1899), a Swedenborgian and health enthusiast. Emerson praised him in *English Traits* (1857) and one of Henry James' younger brothers was named for him.

4. Not listed at this address, which is in Brooklyn. Possibly Ann Hicks, who kept a boardinghouse, 63 Main, Brooklyn directory, 1857–1858.

Audubon the Naturalist (75cts)
C. S. Francis Diamond Atlas 12mo.— Morse & Gaston pub[5] /
Young's Political History U. S. Derby & Jackson[6] /
Lieut Maury[7] in "Open Arctic Sea" Brooklyn Institute Sat. Dec. 20 /
Mrs. Cornelia[8] Ridgeway—147 South Sixteenth Philadelphia /
Washington Medallion Steel Pen /
Presbyterian Quarterly Review Dec M. W. Dodd[9] /
Is there any English translation of Schlosser's "History of the Ancient World and its cultures." German—1826–34[10]
[*1*] entree stampede, canard[11], (duck) roturier (plebian) /
History of Ancient Art translated from the German of Winckleman[12] 2 vols. 8vo sold by [*illeg.*] & Phinney /
Home Journal —Shaks[?] /
Spirit of German Poetry by Joseph Gostick[13] /
French Literature—Chambers pub Spanish Lit /
Italian Literature.—Chambers pub. / —
Schlegel's History of Literature viz. Lectures on the Literature of All Nations[14] /
Trees of America (serial) by R. W. Piper, M.D. Boston, Munroe & Co.[15] /
System of Physical Geography. By J. M. Warren, 4to 92 pages pub by H Cowperthwaite & Co /
Adventures in the Wilds of the U.S. and British America by Chas. Lanman 2 vols 8vo. Phil. J W Moore[16] /

5. A pocket atlas published in 1857.

6. Andrew White Young, *The American Statesman: A Political History,* first published in 1855, but printed by Derby & Jackson in 1857.

7. Lt. Matthew Fontaine Maury (1806–1873), the great oceanographer, who pioneered the study of ocean currents and who was an early advocate for a transatlantic cable. The lecture referred to was in 1856.

8. Inserted above "Ridgeway"

9. The issue referred to, December 1856, edited by M. W. Dodd, contained an anonymous article on contemporary poetry, reviewing a number of poets including Longfellow, Lowell, and the Brownings (but not WW), and characterizing contemporary poetry as simultaneously "mystic," "practical," and "hopeful."

10. No translation listed in LC *Union List.*

11. Faintly written or erased: "coupee" above "canard"

12. *The History of Ancient Art, tr. from the German of John Winckelmann,* by G. Henry Lodge (Boston: Little, Brown, & Co., 1856). Winckelmann's work was the first great book on classical art.

13. Joseph Gostwick (1814–1887). The book is a series of translations from the German poets with long critical introductions first published in London in 1845 and expanded into *German Literature* (1849; U.S. ed. 1854) from which WW drew heavily for his knowledge of German literature. William Little, "Walt Whitman and the *Nibelungenlied,*" *PMLA,* 80 (1965), 569, doubts that WW knew *Spirit of German Poetry,* though this citation might suggest otherwise. The misspelling occurs on the title page of both books. For Gostwick, see "The celebrated old German poem."

14. Probably *Lectures on the History of Literature, Ancient and Modern* (1812), of which there were various translations from the German. See "Frederick Schlegel 1772–1829."

15. Richard Upton Piper, *The Trees of America* (Boston: W. White). An illustrated series issued in four numbers, 1855–58.

16. This edition published in 1856. Charles Lanman (1819–1895), writer, amateur explorer, and artist. See *Corr.,* III, 327 and Traubel, I, 352.

Capt. Clias Elementary Course of Gymnastics. trans.[17] /
N.E. Historical & Genealogical Register A. R. Phippon 310 Broadway.
[2] Mrs. Rose[18] 72 White st. or 74—husband engraver name on the door /
Look after Arnold Talfourd's[19] "Ancient History" 10 vols. comprising the political, social, literary & Philosophical Histories of Egypt, Assyria, Rome, Greece, &c. (English ed. Dix & Edwards 321 Broadway Look (same place) at Cyclopedia of Geography Chas Knight. 4 vols. quarto /
Frank Bellew,[20] 70 (or 90) West 27th st. /
Youmans,[21] 63 2d av. /
Mrs Price[22] 31 Hicks /
[23]McDonough[24] 16 Hanover place /
Mrs. Chilton,[25] 69 Varick st
[3] Hank Pierce[26] (4th av
Charley (black hair & eyes—round face) 4th av.
Albert, (Mrs. Jones's son.)[27] Jack (—4th av. —now in a N.Y. Express wagon
Frank (Beeswax)[28]
Anson W Turner[29] (oyster Fulton Market)
Charles Brown[30] (Broadway Brownie)

17. Peter Heinrich Clias (1780–1854). A popular manual, frequently translated from the German, of 1816, "intended to develope and improve the physical powers of man." Cf. notes on Health.

18. Ernestine Potowesky Rose (1810–1892), feminist. See "Frances Wright." Her husband, William E. Rose, silversmith, is listed at 72 White st., NY directory.

19. Thomas Arnold (1800–1853), author of classical textbooks, and Sir Thomas Noon Talfourd (1795–1854), lawyer, dramatist, and biographer of Lamb. The two collaborated with others on *The History of Greece* and *The History of the Roman Republic,* as part of the *Encyclopedia Metropolitana* (1848–1858). "Look after" inserted above "Arnold Tal" (in "Talfourd")

20. (1828–1888), caricaturist, newspaper cartoonist, and illustrator. Listed at 70 West 27th, NY directory 1857–58. See "A tip-top caricature" and Notebook 6, *DN,* Pt.III, "Words" [*back flyleaf*], 788.

21. This may be Professor E. L. Youmans (1821–1887), scientific writer and editor, who knew WW. See "Left 5 at Jones." Not listed in NY or Brooklyn directories. A Frederick Youmans, tailor, business address not listed, is in the Brooklyn directory 1857–1858.

22. Mrs. Abby Price, a life-long friend of WW and his family. See "Baily D Damon." Her husband, Edmund, who manufactured pickles, is listed at this address in Brooklyn directory, 1857–1858.

23. Deleted: "R. B. Kimball cor First Place, Clinton st. 7th" Lawyer, 49 Wall st., NY directory 1856–1857. "Clinton st." is in Brooklyn which, together with the notation "7th," probably a date, suggests that the entry refers to an appointment.

24. Eliza McDonough, widow of Peter, listed at this address in Brooklyn directory 1856–1857.

25. Not listed in directories. A NY address.

26. A Henry Pierce, clerk, is listed in NY directory 1857–1858, but the "4th av" suggests a driver on that omnibus line.

27. A laborer and a machinist, both named Albert Jones, are listed in NY directory 1857–1858.

28. For other lists of drivers' nicknames see "memorials."

29. An oyster dealer at Fulton Market, NY directory 1857–1858.

30. A carman, 96 Tenth Ave., NY directory 1857–1858.

Storrs King (or "Fulton" with Jack Garrison[31]
John Schoonmake (Lawyer around City Hall remember Ben Carman
Jakey (James) tall, genteel friend of Brownie)
Jay (5th av.)—19
Bill (Moses) 5th av. 137
Bill—(big, black round eyes, large coarse (formerly Madison Jo—(smallish gallus on Fort Greene[32] (Irish descent playing ball).
Playing [*illeg.*] *ball* [*:*][33] Abe (round red pleasant grayish
keeping tally
John Campbell,[34] round light complex lymphatic, *good-look*
John (light complex—light gray eyes light hair
Tom Gray[35]—smallish (legs)[36] [*illeg.*]
[*4*] Edward Smithson[37] (20) full-eyed genteel boy I meet often at the ferries—Irish or English
Jack Swinton ([*illeg.*] English (23) at Showery's porter ([*illeg.*] Lewis [*Swinton*[38]] (in Bangs & Platts)
William Phillips[39]—(large, light, No 8 engine) (26)
Leo (22) No 8 engine (in Showery's)
Henry Post[40] (stout, mechanic, (26)
George Applegate[41] (tallest)
Bob Fraser[42] (28) policeman (5–6), slow, mild Cor Myrtle &[43] Raymond

31. Perhaps John D. Garrison, a butcher, who might have had ties with Fulton Market. NY directory 1857–1858. The next entry possibly refers to John Schoonmaker, mentioned in "81 Clerman" at "133 Clermont av. Brooklyn." Not listed in directories.

32. In Brooklyn, site of a Revolutionary war fort and later a park. WW agitated for its use as a park while he was editor of the *Eagle*.

33. Brace encloses the names of the four ball players.

34. Perhaps a carman of that name listed in NY directory 1857–1858.

35. Perhaps Thomas F. Gray, driver, NY directory 1857–1858.

36. Inserted above [*illeg.*]

37. Probably also mentioned in "George Walker."

38. Ditto marks in MS. John and William Lewis Swinton. See C. Carroll Hollis, "Whitman and William Swinton: A Co-operative Friendship," *AL*, 30 (1959), 428*n*. For John Swinton see D.W. Wilder" and for William Swinton see "*Rambles among Words*." See also "George Walker" and below, [*22*] and [*34*].

39. A fireman. See "return my book" in which WW recalls, probably transcribing this passage, that they "met in '56 or '7 in ale house" ("Showery's"?) and that Phillips lived in New Jersey. Also possibly mentioned in "George Walker."

40. Mentioned in "George Walker." Not listed in directories.

41. Either a fruitseller at 36 W. Washington, NY directory 1857–1858, or a butcher, Myrtle av., h. 49 Prince, Brooklyn directory 1857–1858. Also mentioned below [*14*], in "George Walker" and in "return my book."

42. Probably Robert Fraser, mason, at 195 Myrtle av. (which was near Raymond), Brooklyn directory 1857–58.

43. Deleted: "Hudson" following "Raymond" ; "Raymond" written in after "Myrtle" and brought up on a line; "cor. Myrtle &" written above "Raymond [*del.*] Hudson"

Tom Haynes (26) driver, Myrtle—mild—
August (Gus) Dutch boy (16) with cake
Bill (23) round faced, blue eyes, light Irish skin (5th av) 7th av
Harry, conductor—Myrtle[44] (Jamaica Academy)
Jim (new policeman) Irish, (round shouldered
Oscar Clark (4th av. liquid eyes now clerk in R.R. Company)
Ed. F. Underhill[45]—Tribune 193–23d st.
Mrs. (lady we hired of in Skillman st[46]
17 Johnson st
4th av. Tracy (26)[47] genteel jovial "Judge"
Tom Harvey[48] (5th av.) smallish, timidish, Irish[49]
"Victory" 13 [:][50]
James Dalton[51] (20) round faced lymphatic lost front teeth
Jack—(20)[52] head more length[53]
[5][54] William Davis,[55] (thin from Portland 23d st[56] /
Bob—(hermaphrodite[?][57]
Long Jack (7th av.)
James Clark (Drunkard cor Raymond)[58]
George Whittock,[59] (Tall carman South ferry
Jake (75 Broadway 49th
William Nash, boy light hair
Jim Cunningham, (boy without thumb)
Johnny Rose[60]

44. Added below "conductor"

45. Edward F. Underhill, reporter for the *Tribune,* 139 E. 23d st., NY directory 1857–1858.

46. Preceding seven words in a smaller hand on three lines and crowded around "17" , suggesting that they were added in a blank space. The word is clearly "hired." Skillman st. is in Brooklyn.

47. Deleted: "rath"

48. A Thomas Harvey, carman, listed at 23 Essex, NY directory 1857–1858.

49. Remaining entry on this page is in black ink. "Victory" is possibly the name of a ferryboat.

50. Brace.

51. Perhaps the sailmaker listed at 2 Oak, NY directory 1856–1857, or the carman of W. 43d, NY directory 1857–1858.

52. Small vertical rectangle divided by horizontal line. Perhaps represents the proportions of the head.

53. Clipping of ferry schedule between NYC and Coney Island.

54. Top of leaf clipped. Present dimensions, 3⅝″ × 3¼″.

55. A Brooklyn address, though Davis is not listed in the directories.

56. "23d st" is written between the lines below "(thin from" and may refer to "Bob".

57. After "herm" letters and word incompletely formed. WW often wrote in this elliptical, stylized way when treating something embarrassing. See below, [*19*], "Bill Guess, died", "81 Clerman." WW possibly meant that Bob was effeminate or homosexual. The latter raises interesting questions of WW's perception of himself.

58. A Brooklyn address. It is not clear which James Clark in the directories WW means.

59. A Mary C. Whittock, widow of George, h. 4 Beach, listed in NY directory 1857–1858.

60. A laborer of that name listed at 204 Fifth, NY directory 1857–1858.

[9;[61] *6 blank; 7–8 cancel*] 4th av.) Brownie, (looks something like handsome Mike hackman
Jack (policeman round, full-sized lymphatic, (eating peanuts night cor Classon & Myrtle[62]
Wm Wilson[63] (Broadway—
Charles Fuller[64]
Johny (round faced—in Dunbar's and engine house—full eyes) and liquid
Pete (smallish—looks a little like 5th av Billy Folk[65]
Wm Vanderbergh,[66] (young fellow, sick, sandy complexion Fulton av. near City Hall
Tom Riley[67] (handsome Irish fighter
John Kiernan[68] (loafer young saucy looking pretty goodlooking
[*11; 10 blank*] Dave. (rich, (white hat.) rides on Broadway
Jack, (big young fellow, sits[69] corner Adams & Myrtle live[70] 4th av.[*:*][71]
Arthur, big round sandy hair coarse, open
Peleg, round head & face young
Wallace,[72] (sailor boy English was in Japan)
John Stoothoof,[73] (police South ferry smallish sized)
Pete Dempster[74] (Cor Kent & Myrtle open faced—gay)
Charles Held[75] (boy son of Mr. Held tuner Mr. Banks, (Lobscouse)[76]
Bill, (engineer Union) 124 4th av 4th
[*:*] Jo (red hair large red face
Teunis[77]—tall—(Yankee)
Pete—not driver
Felix M'Cluskey California

61. A fragment 3⅞" × 3⅝"; top clipped.

62. A Brooklyn address.

63. A tailor, an accountant, a clerk, and a broker of this name, all with addresses on Broadway, are listed in NY directory 1857–1858.

64. Either a Brooklyn printer, 17 York, or a NY dealer in "camphene," an illuminating oil made from turpentine, 289 Greenwich, h. 59 N. Moore. 1857–1858 directories.

65. A William Folk, clerk, chief of police, City Hall, h. Skillman n. Willoughby av., listed in Brooklyn Directory 1857–1858. "5th av." added to left of "Billy Folk."

66. A William H. Vanderburg, lawyer, 82 Broadway, h. Astor, listed in NY directory 1857–1858.

67. Several carmen and laborers of this name, NY directory 1857–1858.

68. Several laborers of this name in NY and Brooklyn directories.

69. Inserted on a line above "corner"

70. "live" written above the ampersand. Perhaps belongs with the entry for "Dave."

71. Brace, enclosing the following two names.

72. A number of Wallaces listed as "seaman" in NY and Brooklyn directories 1857–1858.

73. Listed at 20 Furman n. Joraleman, Brooklyn directory 1857–58.

74. A Brooklyn address. Not listed.

75. Charles Held, possibly "Mr. Held," listed as a pianoforte-maker and piano tuner, 4 Boerum, Brooklyn directory 1857–1858.

76. "Lobscouse" is a sailor's stew made with meat, vegetables, and hardtack.

77. An old Dutch name. See [*14*].

pandon Lennon[78] about 325
John Davenport[79] (Classon tall, genteel)
Charley Smith, 119 or 20, 4th av
Jay 815 (about) or 812
[*12*] Wm Culver[80] (boy in the bath (18) gone to California
James (lame boy in front of Savings bank (13)
Johnny, ([*lame*][81] steel trap)
Jim (boy with Johny Gray[82])
Charley (Mr Rider's boy
Mike Talley (or Dally)[83] the thinnest 25
Pete [*Talley*][84]
Tom Egbert[85] (conductor (sailor open neck (24)
Percival de Clifton
Robert (Dad)
Milton (light complexion, (Ohio) 5th av.
Ben Wallis[86]—(grocery cor Clermont & Myrtle
Northport boys [*:*][87] Edmund Bryant—elder[88]
Melville [*Bryant*][89]
Henry Taylor (Johny Sackback)
Johny Williams[90] (policeman at Fulton ferry N.Y.
Aleck (friend of Andrew.)
Charley Van Dwyne (13) boy on the Nassau sometimes
Mr. Mason[91]—(shoemaker (saw him in Andrew Rome's[92])
Frank (kindling Wood)
Reuben (in the Grand st. frame shop—now driver)

78. A carpenter, h. 108 Carlton av., and a liquor dealer, Fulton av., c. Hanover pl., listed with this name in Brooklyn directory 1857–1858.

79. A real estate dealer, Fulton av., c. Oxford, h. Cumberland n. Greene av., and an auditor, 68 Warren, NY, h. 59 Nassau, listed in Brooklyn directory 1857–1858.

80. Mentioned in "return my book," which transcribes the entry, adding that Culver went to California in " '56" .

81. Ditto marks in MS.

82. A John Gray, carman, h. 465 Greenwich, listed in NY directory 1857–1858.

83. A Michael Dally listed, laborer, 5 Hudson av., Brooklyn directory 1857–1858. No "Talley" or "Tally" is listed. See [*14*], [*17*].

84. Ditto marks in MS.

85. Thomas C., conductor, h. Myrtle av. c. Yates av., Brooklyn directory 1857–1858. See "return my book."

86. An Alfred, grocer, at this address, Brooklyn directory 1857–1858.

87. Brace, enclosing following two names. Northport is on Long Island (written in two lines to the left of the brace).

88. For Edmund and Melville Bryant see "return my book."

89. Ditto mark in MS.

90. 49 Beekman, NY directory 1857–1858.

91. A John Mason of that occupation, 57 Henry, Brooklyn directory 1857–1858.

92. Andrew H. Rome, printer, 98 Cranberry, h. 55 Adams, Brooklyn directory 1857–1858. The Rome brothers printed *LG* 1855 and continued to set up WW's poems for him in proof. See Bowers, xxiii–xxxiii, and "Add*resses*."

Charley Quail[93]—(policeman)
David Stewart—(No. 12)
Peter Ridley (apple pedlr
Abe Debevoise[94] (young boy)
Johny Nevin[95] (22) small quiet, carpenter
Dave Rogers[96]
Jack (5th av.) full brown black beard—(25) brown faced, Feb. 16 '57
Jerry Boerum[97] small, smiling, friend of George,
Phil Stokey (policy player)[98]
Jim Johnson,[99] (saloon & Book)
Woodhull Woolsey[1]
Union Ferry[2] [:]Al (carpenter, Union ferry shop—close by George Wright's[3] bench
Ansel Ketchum[4] (with Tom's bench
Alphonso—new—light haired—Amity st.[5]
[*13*] at Police Station[6] [:] police
Charley—ropemaker
Jerry,—police—looks like Jake Beasly[7] /
Charley—elderly Classon av round[?] white hair
Dave. coachman Halsen[?][8] /
4th av. Mrs. Jones [:][9] Ed, small, black eyes & brows
Bill, big bony Yankee linen coat
Bill big dark complexioned, St. Helena
George, (sulky head sideways
Jim, (looks like Chatman

93. A Charles H. Quail, a clerk, h. 43 Orchard, is listed in NY directory 1857–1858.

94. This family seems to have been active in the drygoods business in New York and Brooklyn. See also "Ike Debevoise" below [*15*]. Both are also mentioned in "return my book"

95. Laborer, 47 Mott, NY directory 1857–1858.

96. The NY directory 1856–1857 lists an artist, r. 73 W. 15th, h. 589 Hudson, and a fish dealer, 10 Fulton market, h. 31 So. 6th, in Brooklyn.

97. A Harman Boerman, grocer, 153 Chrystie, listed in NY directory 1857–1858. "George" may be George Whitman, WW's brother.

98. A "numbers" player.

99. Proprietor of an "eating house, 23 Fulton, h. 8 Hicks," Brooklyn directory 1857–1858.

1. The NY directory, 1857–1858, lists an Ezra W. Woolsey, merchant, 222 Front, who lives on Clinton av. in Brooklyn. The Brooklyn directory 1857–1858 lists an S. W. a carpet dealer, 136 Grand, bds. Wall House.

2. First letters of "Union" and "Ferry" written on two lines before the brace around "Al (carpenter" and "Ansel Ketchum" clipped off.

3. The name is mentioned below [*15*], but it does not seem to be the same individual.

4. Ansel Ketcham, carpenter, Portland av. n. Atlantic av., Brooklyn directory 1857–1858.

5. There is an "Amity St." in both Brooklyn and NY.

6. "at Police Station" written vertically along brace, which encloses the four subsequent entries. "police" is written above "ropemaker" probably as a centered heading.

7. Jacob Beasley, policeman, Myrtle av. n. Graham, Brooklyn directory 1856–1857. Line across the leaf under this entry.

8. There is a Halsey Street in Brooklyn. Line across the leaf under this entry.

9. "4th av. Mrs. Jones" (possibly a boarding house) written vertically along brace, which marks the seven subsequent entries.

Johnny (red faced, small chunky
Mr. Ferris, starter
Johny Mullen red hair. pipe Irish contractor, Jackson [*illeg.*]
Lefferts Laidlaw[10]
4th av. [:][11]
Jack (Davis) light-eyed light haired[12] drunk at Pat Newman's[13]
George, coarse complex low forehead pock mark 4th av.
Al Yankee, thin, medium black moustache now 5th av.
Elisha Jones[14]—foreman
Ab'm Litchalt,[15] small, formerly police now market
Hiram Kellum[16]
Billy Stevens[17]
78? Pat[18] (young, neat jockey cap 8th st.—
Charley—filmy eyes, 4th av.[19]
Jim (Jubal Cain)[20]
Tom Van Brunt[21]
Eugene /
Tom Hyer,[22] Irish 4th av.
[*14*] Joe Downing boy, often at segar store
Oliver (tall, 25,) conductor Myrtle come up in carriage,[23]
Justin (Chousey) boy—(16) blacksmith—come up in the carriaage
George Lavallette (tipsy) son of surgeon in Naval Hospital

10. Book-keeper, White Lead Co., h. 124 Columbia, Brooklyn directory, 1857–1858.

11. A wavy brace marking next four entries.

12. Deleted: [*illeg.*]

13. A NY bar. Patrick Newman, liquors, Lexington av. c. E. 32d, NY directory 1856–1857. See also [*19*].

14. An Elisha C. Jones, agent, 62 E. 33d, listed in NY directory 1856–57. The same name is on [*18*] in conjunction with a sailor. The Brooklyn directory 1857–1858 lists an Elijah Jones, seaman, h. Freeman n. Union av.

15. Abraham Litchult, listed as a policeman in the 1856–1857 Brooklyn directory and as working at Washington market, NY, in the 1857–1858 directory. Address, in both directories, Myrtle av. c. Clermont av.

16. Also mentioned below [*15*].

17. Perhaps William J. Stevens, carman, 375 First av., NY directory 1856–1857.

18. Thin diagonal line through word.

19. Remaining entries on this page written in lower right hand corner, set off by vertical line.

20. Possibly J. H. Cain, grocer, 191 Washington and 238 Fulton, h. S. Second, Brooklyn, listed in NY directory 1857–1858. Following four entries written in right margin and separated by a vertical line from the entries for "Kellum" and "Charley" in double column; rule under "Eugene"

21. Possibly Thomas H. Van Brunt, gold pen manufacturer, 3 & 5 Nassau, Brooklyn directory 1856–1857. He also had a shop in NY, "Vanbrunt & Johnson, pencil cases, 12 Maiden la.," NY directory 1856–57.

22. Listed as a clerk in 1856–1857 NY directory and as a butcher in 1857–1858 directory. Address, in both directories, 201 Hester.

23. Oliver and Justin, in the carriage, are also mentioned below [*15*].

Jim Allen (44) met at Dominick Colgan's[24] told me he was with me in Hablock's school.)
Wm Stewart,[25] police captain tall)
Jack Gill,[26] (elder).
Tom [*Gill*][27]
Bill McCue (Irish—49th st., snub nose
Tom—policeman, cor William & Frankfort sts[28]
Little Dominick (Dominick Colgan's son)[29]
Adolphus Davenport[30] (actor) old boy friend of Ansel Jenning's
Dave Ackerman[31] (bones)
Charles Edwards,[32] foreman in Lockitts Myrtle
Wm Mosscrop[33]—oyster shop Myrtle &[34] [*illeg.*]
Sam Adams—63 Broadway large light com
Frank (30) 4th av. fat round face looks like Louis Cost.
Cornish (tow head) 4th av.
Bill (36) Dunham[35] from Phil. dark face stocky frame
Jim Le---- young fellow light longish hair out by Cannon[36]
Jack (5th av.) with the beautiful beard black
Edward (25) young Brooklyn man printer in N.Y. Times
(ask Tom McEvoy[37] the name of the boy with[*?*] Geo. Leland[38]
Pat—203 (Eighth st) /
Met cor Myrtle & Washington [*illeg.*] [*:*][39] Teunis[40]—round faced brown with moustache

24. Liquors, 238 Fulton, h. 89 Pineapple, Brooklyn directory 1857–1858. See below [*17*], and "return my book."

25. William H. Stewart, this occupation, Kent av. n. Myrtle av., Brooklyn directory 1857–1858.

26. John Gill, driver, 483 7th av., NY directory 1856–1857.

27. Ditto mark. Thomas Gill, driver, 132 W. 36th, NY directory 1856–1857.

28. In NY.

29. See above, *n*24.

30. Scattered references to him in George C. D. Odell, *Annals of the New York Stage,* VI–VII (NY: Columbia Univ. Press, 1927–1949). Apparently a minor but successful actor, he eventually married Lizzie Weston, who seems to have been of greater importance. Not listed in directories.

31. Probably the carman of this name, h. 5 Morton, NY directory 1856–1857. See "return my book"

32. Butcher, h. 46 Carll. Joseph Lockitt & Co., dealers in "provisions," included five stores, one at 177 Myrtle av., listed in Brooklyn directory 1857–1858.

33. Perhaps some connection to Thomas Mosscrop who had a saloon at 166 Myrtle av., Brooklyn directory 1857–1858.

34. Deleted: [*illeg.*]; inserted below: [*illeg.*]

35. Possibly William Dunham, waxmaker, 279 Grand, Brooklyn directory 1857–1858.

36. A street in NY.

37. NY directory 1856–57 lists a dealer in boots, 293 Bowery, and a produce dealer, 49 W. Wash. mkt., h. 289 57th, Jersey City.

38. Possibly the George Leland listed in NY directory 1856–1857 at "hotel, 580 Broadway."

39. Line under "Pat—203 (Eighth st)." Brace enclosing next three entries. "Met . . . [*illeg.*]" written in margin to left of the brace. The address and the names, with the date "March 24" are repeated on [*17*].

40. See above [*11*].

Sam— looks some like Bill 49th india ink on his hand
Mike Dally[41] /
Mike Butler,[42] boy (18) in stone cutters Kent Av.
George Applegate[43] (tallest)
Dan shorter (Myrtle av. market.
[*15*] George Wright[44] 16 (boy 16 in plaster ornament shop, Myrtle n Ryerson
Charley 22 (fireman in the new drab clothes—18 N.Y.
Martin Evans[45] (36)
Ben (19) (tall—bony—big-nosed boy for Hendrickson's express[46]
William (35)—tall dark eyed, moustache ?German formerly Madison av. now Broadway
Martha (15) in Burroughs
George (22) (No[47] 18—tall mild
John Baulsir[48] (28) (pilot Nassau)
John Evans (30) red beard, wrote notice in Woodbury[*?*] Times[49]
Chris Pike (30) in office Fulton av. cars
Thos Shephard[50] (30) pol. 7th st. smallish grey eyes pleasant
Patrick Corr 26 (new Pol Irish boy good looking)
George Moore[51] 21 (tall, thin, works sewing machine
George Matthews[52] 20—(in feed store Graham
Ike Debevoise[53] 20 (black eyes & hair)
Pete Clayton 36 (fat round face cor Myrtle & Fulton Brooklyn police
Charley Held[54] 12—(boy)
Justin 17 (boy, blacksmith from Jersey was in the carriage[*?*][55]

41. See [*12*] and [*17*]. Line across leaf under "Mike Dally"
42. See "return my book." A Brooklyn address.
43. See [*4*].
44. George Wright, plaster, Myrtle av. n. Grand av., h. Steuben n. DeKalb av., Brooklyn directory 1857–1858. Most of the ages, which follow the names, are written above the line on this page.
45. Possibly druggist, Myrtle av. c. Classon av., Brooklyn directory 1857–1858. See "return my book."
46. A company owned by William L. Hendrickson, located on Kent av. near Myrtle, Brooklyn directory 1857–1858.
47. "No." inserted above "18" . Possibly relates to previous entry.
48. For the Baulsir family see "return my book" *n*15. WW nursed John through an attack of typhoid fever. The Brooklyn directory 1857–1858 lists a whole family of pilots, two of them named John, one at 70 Bridge, and the other at 27 Cottage Row, Furman. See "Walt Baulsir" below [*19*].
49. The Long Island Historical Society could not locate the ***Woodbury Times***.
50. Policeman, Kent av. n. Myrtle, Brooklyn directory 1857–58.
51. Tailor, 65 Stanton, NY directory 1856–1857. In 1857–1858 listed as "Shirts, 84 Bleecker."
52. Since Graham Street is in Brooklyn, this is possibly the laborer listed at 248 Gold, Brooklyn directory 1857–1858.
53. Isaac Debevoise, grocer, Flushing av. c. Bushwick av., h. Flushing av. n. Broadway, Brooklyn directory 1857–1858. See "return my book." See also "Abe Debevoise" above [*12*].
54. See "return my book."
55. Cf. [*14*] above, where Justin and Oliver are also mentioned as being in the carriage.

Oliver 21 (tall conductor, slender was in the carriage
Hiram Kellum (25)[56]
[*16*] W. C. Holley[57]
D.C. Holly Real Estate[58] 3 or 5 Nassau on the ground floor /
W Griffith[59]—83 Prospect /
A. J. Davis,[60] 137 Spring st. /
Dr. J. D. Whelpley[61] at Mrs Hildreths cor. Bleeker & Wosster st /
Welsh Church 11th st near 3d av. /
McDonald 335 Broadway room 39 /
Mrs Bloom[62] 57 High /
Geo Wheeler 55[63] 79 Mercer[64]
[*17*] *Soiree dansante* /
Aleck (big, young, (26,) gets out cars at Prince st.
Quaker Ed. (4th av. (33)
Sam[65] (young fellow I met in Dominick Colgan's[66]
John Cunningham—[67]tall thin face No 18
Pete (young married man No 18) bad teeth good eyes

56. Mentioned above [*13*].

57. Entries more widely spaced, in hanging indentation, separated by horizontal lines. William C. Holly, com. mer. and real estate agent, 3 Nassau, h. 31 Hammond, NY directory 1856–1857. "D. C. Holly Real Estate" written on two lines at upper right.

58. Deleted: "5 3" ; "3 or 5" written below; line drawn halfway across the leaf under "3 or 5 . . . floor"

59. A William Griffith, pilot, at this address, Brooklyn directory 1857–1858. Line drawn across under the entry.

60. Probably Andrew Jackson Davis (1826–1910), the noted spiritualist. WW mentions him in a letter dated July 20, 1857. See *Corr.*, I, 43 and III, 441. He is also mentioned in "George Walker," and in 1873–1874 he and his wife are mentioned in "D. W. Wilder." For his possible influence on WW see Stovall, *Foreground,* 154–155, 247, 257 and Howard Kerr, *Mediums, and Spirit-Rappers, and Roaring Radicals: Spiritualism in American Literature, 1850–1900* (Urbana: Univ. of Illinios Press, 1972), pp. 20–21, 199*n*.

61. James Davenport Whelpley, M.D. (1817–1872), editor of the *American Whig Review* 1848–1849. (WW published in that periodical in 1845.) WW clipped and saved two articles of his from the *Review,* before he was editor, one "on style," dated 1845, and the other on phrenology, dated 1846 (see "Bells and Pomgranates"). Whelpley left the *Review* to pursue a financial scheme in Honduras and was impressed into the army of William Walker, the notorious filibuster, for whom he served as surgeon. Whelpley, who survived his adventuring, is listed as "pres., 512 Broadway," NY directory 1856–1857. WW's address is that of Susan S. Hindreth, wid. John, who ran a boarding house at 121 Bleecker. Line across the leaf under "cor. Bleecker and Wooster st" and also under "11th st. near 3d ave." following.

62. A Huldagh Bloom listed at 62 High, Brooklyn directory 1856–1857. Lines across the leaf above and below the entry.

63. Deleted: "79" following "55" ; added, lower left corner: "79" before "55"

64. A NY address. See [*26*].

65. Deleted: [*illeg.*]

66. See [*14*].

67. Two carmen by this name are listed, at 73 Cherry and at 242 Monroe, NY directory 1856–1857.

Tom Lambert[68] (tall young man Mason Myrtle Av
Revand K Field
Valentine Carman[69]
Hank—(in Geo Douglass coffee & cakes)
Bill (tall[70] stout, small mouth fat light blue eyes) (Dunbar's)[71]
George Golder (black eyes & hair deaf one ear 49th st)
Met with Mike Dally[72] March 24 Myrtle n. Washington [:][73]
Teunis—(25) round, brown face, moustache met at Garry Van Dynes[74]
Sam—dark complexion, full eyes, (large figures in india ink on left hand
Mike Dally—
Henry Sinclair (hat shop, Myrtle n Canton
Charley—131(4th av) /
Wm Husted[75] (young man in Myrtle near Clinton)
Sandy (5th av) fancy, "Hallo Walt.)
Tom (foreman (13) "Victory" Wmsburgh
David Barnet[76] (boy) (18) in lawyer's office op. City Hall
Billy (138, 4th av) thin consumptive
[*18*] [:][77] Elisha Jones[78] Bill [*Jones*][79]—the sailor
Dave [*Jones*][80] /
4th av [:][81]
Jack—red faced—marked mouth
Tom (looks something like Frank with Mrs. Hibbard[82]
5th av. Luther Calvin Davis—(coarse red face
Jack MCoon (boy 20 went in Castle Garden[83] with me April 20)

68. Thomas Lambert, no occupation listed, h. Myrtle av., c. Skillman, Brooklyn directory 1856–1857.

69. Butcher and meat inspector, Bedford av., c. Gates av., Brooklyn directory 1856–1857.

70. Word smeared or deleted.

71. Probably a bar. NY directory 1856–1857 lists a Mary Dunbar, wid. James, liquors, 1227 Broadway.

72. See below and [*12*], [*14*].

73. "Met . . . Washington" in the left margin before a brace enclosing "Teunis . . . left hand" . The address and the three names enclosed by the address, Teunis, Sam, and Mike Dally, are repeated from [*14*]. The date perhaps refers to the previous meeting.

74. Garret Van Dyne, ferryman, Myrtle av. n. Oxford, Brooklyn directory 1856–1857.

75. Possibly William A. Husted, carpets, 150 Fulton, Brooklyn directory 1856–1857. NY directory 1856–1857 lists a William F., express, h. 135 S. 3d, Brooklyn. Line drawn above "Wm Husted"

76. See "return my book."

77. Brace marking the three names. The three are also mentioned in "return my book."

78. See [*13*]. Possibly Elijah Jones, seaman, h. Freeman n. Union Av., Brooklyn directory 1857–1858.

79. Ditto. William Jones, seaman, h. 6 Church, Brooklyn directory 1857–1858.

80. Ditto. David E. Jones, seaman, 64 10th, Brooklyn directory 1857–1858.

81. Brace marking the two names; "4th av." written in the margin to the left of the brace.

82. Perhaps Amelia Hibbard, wid. Reuben, h. 13 Forsyth, NY directory 1856–1857.

83. An immigrant station. Previous to 1854, a popular concert hall.

George Rogers 4th av. has been west 3 years
Stephe (boy with Charley Palmer, black moustache)
Henry Hyer[84] (32) Madison av. thin bony bilious—told me of Chinese women[85]
Johny (24) 4th av (white teeth) round clear face, brown eyes
John Van Lear (5th av.) fat, lymphatic, no beard
Bill (4th av.) 27—medium, dark comp & hair—& eyes—? Dutch
Billy (tall young, walked up to Gold[86] st. with, night N. H. firemen's procession
Elias B. Pierson[87] (32) 5th av. been in the rebel army[88] in China
Jo (Lane) starter Madison av. Wall st
Aleck (tall (34)—7th av seen him in Clason av. Sunday.
George (not Jo)[89] ("Brushmaker") 4th av (thin face superb sonorous voice
Wm Craig[90] (young man—Kent av)
[*19*] Saml. D.[91] (or E) Van Etten Milford, on the Delaware river Pennsylvania / Go on the N.Y. & Erie R.R. to *Port Jervis*[92] (fare $2.00 thence by stage to Milford (fare 50 cents) /
son (Charley Etten) /[93]
Charley Hicks (16) boy clear gold complexion & hair—fat—son of Hicks in "Fulton's" engine room
Gus White (25) at Ferry with skeleton boat with Walt Baulsir[94]—(5 ft 9 high—round—well built
Timothy Meighan (30) Irish, oranges, Fulton & Concord[95]
James Dalton (Engine—Williamsburgh)
Charley Fisher (26) 5th av. (hurt, diseased, deprived)
Ike (5th av.) 28—fat, drinks, rode "Fashion" in the great race
Jack (4th av) tall slender, had the French pox[96] (moderate in talk)

84. Perhaps Henry J. Hyer, stonecutter, h. r. 167 E. 24th, NY directory 1857–1858.

85. For WW's knowledge of China see *n*87 below.

86. In downtown NY.

87. Pierson was apparently an important source for WW's knowledge of China. See "June 23d 1857," "British in China," *"Brutish human beings,"* and "return my book." An Elias Pierson is listed as a driver, 32 W. 44th, NY directory 1859–1860.

88. Probably the Taiping Rebellion (1851–1864), which advocated an egalitarian, communal society organized around quasi-Christian beliefs and which attracted some American sympathy.

89. "(not Jo)" inserted above "George"

90. A tinsmith listed at 42 Kent av. Brooklyn directory 1856–1857 also lists a William J. Craig, no occupation given, Kent av. near Myrtle av.

91. Inserted: "(or E)" ; deleted: "Etten"

92. A town in New York at the intersection of the New York, New Jersey, and Pennsylvania borders.

93. Rule across entire page.

94. Walter D. Baulsir, pilot, 106 Prospect, Brooklyn directory 1856–1857. See [*15*].

95. In Brooklyn.

96. The "F" in "French" is marked through by two diagonal slashes. The last two letters of "pox" are obscured, perhaps partially deleted. This is another example of the "Children of Adam" poet's curious reticence and self-consciousness towards sex and the body in his private notebooks. For other examples see [5] and *n*57.

Franklin Sivall[97] (4th av) tallish, gaunt
Mike, (Irish) tallest of the two boys at Newman's[98]
Dan [(*Irish*)][99] least tall
[20] G W Hill[1] cor 18th St & 8th ave. George Waldo Hill /
Talbot[2] 600 Broadway /
Brittan[3] 333 Broadway /
Mr. Ives[4] cor. 4th & South Third over Savings Bank /[5]
Every Monday evening—(soirees.) /
Geo H[6] Riblett 319 2d avenue near 21st
[*21*] Who was the Greek poet Pindar?
Who Merlin? /
Stop at Fowler & Wells and get paper with "Broadway" article
also Prince's catalogue[7]
Engagement at Harrison's[8] Wednesday 3d June /
Moses Stern[9] (tailor) 446 Grand st. N.Y. /
Mr. Goodfellow 65—Tenth st /
R.P. Cooke, M.D.[10] Dentist 3 Great Jones st
[*22*][11] Swinton[12] 51 Macdougal st. /
Dr. Ruggles[13] 24 Warren

97. Perhaps Franklin Sivells, carman, h. 343 Sixth av., NY directory 1856–1857. See "return my book."

98. See [*13*].

99. Ditto.

1. A scrawl. George W. Hill was a builder, h. 459 8th av., NY directory 1856–1857.

2. Jesse Talbot, artist, 600 Broadway, NY directory 1857–1858. See "albot Wilson."

3. Samuel Byron Brittan (d. 1883), spiritualist, listed in NY directory 1857–1858 at this address as publisher and editor of *The Spiritual Age,* a journal "devoted to rational spiritualism and practical reform."

4. Possibly James Merritt Ives (1824–1895) who this year (1857) formed with Nathaniel Currier the famous lithographic firm of Currier & Ives. Listed as publisher, 152 Nassau, h. 164 Bridge, Brooklyn, NY directory 1856–1857. Entry in black ink.

5. A short waved line

6. Inserted.

7. Fowler & Wells was the phrenological firm that distributed *LG* 1855 and that financed *LG* 1856. The article referred to may be WW's "New York Dissected: IV. Broadway," printed in *Life Illustrated,* which was published by Fowler & Wells, August 9, 1856 (*NYD,* 119–124). WW may have needed another copy. "Prince's catalogue" was a popular seed catalogue.

8. Possibly Gabriel Harrison (1818–1902), the versatile Brooklyn artist, actor, writer, and photographer. Harrison took the famous daguerreotype of WW used in *LG* 1855. See *Corr.,* III, 451; Traubel, II, 102, 506, 507. Entry cancelled with short slanted stroke.

9. Listed NY directory 1856–1857. This is given as his home address. Entry written relatively faintly.

10. Richard P. Cooke, M.D., listed with this occupation and this address, NY directory 1856–1857. See "return my book."

11. Not in WW's hand: "E D Carpenter 134½ W. 19th St" . Elliott D. Carpenter, bricklayer, h. 134 W. 19th, NY directory 1856–1857. Also mentioned after Cooke and before Brisbane in "return my book."

12. See [*4*]. William Swinton's address in NYC.

13. Edward Ruggles, physician, 24 E. Warren, Brooklyn directory 1856–1857. He was the family physician. See "Mr. & Mrs. Fitz."

Charley Goen[14] (pier 20)[15]
[23] Chicago Magazine[16] Ross & [*illeg.*] /
Rangers & Regulators of the Tanaha Rob't DeWitt[17] /
Lectures on Human Voice Eveng's of [:][18] Monday 23d March & Thursday 26th [*March*][19] at University Medical College next to Opera House 14th st. /
? Savoir vivre good manners—breeding—gentility—high-style
[24] James Gillan[20] (24) driver Myrtle—large country—open faced
Albany Bill (Madison av.) tall black eyed)
Billy (beautiful—1 Bleecker st[21] 8th av)
Jackson L—(4th av young fellow from Philadelphia
Jack (tallish young Bleecker[22] & 2d st)
?Charley (tallish and goodsized liquid eyed) 4th av—new hand
Charley (East Broadway formerly in Brooklyn
Jack (5th av German birth black eyes & hair 30 now Madison av[23]) /
Jo Baker (23) fine head—4th av
Mike Morrow[24]
Mike—(Bdway) was at Mrs. Hoyts with Dressmaker)
John Brownie—(4th av.) tall, genteel)
?(Jack) Riley
Henry Nelson Hannah[25]
(William (Bdwy) (brother of George, formerly 4th av.)[26]
playing ball [:][27]
Pete (Myrtle & Clermont &c 19 or 20 looks something like George)
Dave—black eyes 25
George Wood (small moustache /
Ike (boy Myrtle) gray eyes) 13

14. Charles Goin, boatman, h. 32 Talman, Brooklyn directory 1857–1858.

15. Not in WW's hand: "A. Brisbane Irvington N.J. Take Newark train at 3 or 5 get out at Market st Depot in Newark, and get into the Irvington omnibus" For Albert Brisbane, the Fourierist, see "return my book."

16. *Chicago Magazine: The West as It Is* ran from March to August 1857.

17. [Alfred W. Arrington], *The Rangers and Regulators of the Tanaha; or, Life Among the Lawless. A Tale of the Republic of Texas* (NY: Robert M. DeWitt, 1856). Much reprinted under various pseudonyms. DeWitt (1827–1877) was a publisher of songbooks and dime novels. A "Regulator" is a vigilante. Entry cancelled by two slanting strokes.

18. Brace, pointing to two dates.

19. Ditto.

20. Possibly Coachman, h. Hunter n. Putnam av., Brooklyn directory 1857–1858.

21. A Brooklyn address. Confusingly, Bleecker St. and 8th St. in NYC also join.

22. A Brooklyn address.

23. Preceding three words, initial parenthesis, and final rule in black ink.

24. Michael Morrow, clerk, 109 Cedar, NY directory 1856–1857.

25. Henry Hannah, mer., 72 Beekman, NY, h. 3d n. 58th, Brooklyn directory 1856–1857.

26. Preceding entry in black ink.

27. Brace, marking subsequent three entries. "playing ball" written to the left of the brace in the margin on two lines aligned on space between entries for Pete and Dave.

[*26; 25 blank*] / Geo. Wheeler[28] 79 Mercer one door above Spring /
Hector Tyndale,[29] 707 Chestnut st. above 7th st. /
Mrs. Sarah Tyndale,[30] corner Main & High st. Germantown: (Germantown Depot corner 9th & Green sts)
[*27*] Clairvoyance (viz *clear seeing* /
E. C. Jones / go over Jersey City ferry take the Morris & Essex RR for Drakesville N.J. Lake Hopatcong 45 miles from N.Y.
Sam Bonnard[31] South 6th st. near Grove Jersey City Inquire for J. B. Forrest engraver
[*28*] Truman & Spafford Cincinnati O. /
Robley[32] cor 18th st & 9th av. Greenwood /
[*29*][33] Meserole st. near Bushwick av.
Schneider's /[34]
Building an iron steamboat foot of North Fifth st.
Wm McConnell[35] sub-contractor five sts. north of Grand

[*31; 30 blank*] (to women—sternly)

Do you suppose you have nothing waiting for yourselves to do, but to embroider, to clean,[36] to be respectable and modest, and not swear or drink?

[*32*] (Spooney)[37] William Place (a public house on the Delaware frequented in the spring by raftsmen)—Go to Port Jervis ($2) thence by stage to William Place's on the route to "Bushville" (Pa)

[*33*] "bold robber"

women rely on men /
the spiritual influence of women, & sex—Mrs. Tyndale's[38] theory /

28. Also mentioned [*16*].
29. WW's longtime friend. A Philadelphia address. See "Feb. 25th 1857."
30. Hector Tyndale's mother, a noted abolitionist. See "Feb. 25th 1857"
31. See "return my book."
32. Possibly Joseph Robley, supt., 18th c. 8th av., h. 18th n. 9th av., Brooklyn directory 1856–1857. Entry in black ink.
33. Top third of leaf clipped out.
34. "Meserole st. . . . av." in black ink. "/ Schneider's /" in brown ink, with an elaborated "S" and the two "e's" and the "s" blotted. The reference is probably to the establishment of John Schneider, brewer, garden and office on Meserole c. Smith, and saloon, 135 Ewen, h. 135 Ewen, Brooklyn directory 1857–1858.
35. Boatbuilder, h. N 2d c. 1st, Brooklyn directory 1857–1858.
36. Deleted: "and"
37. At upper right corner.
38. See [*26*].

That there shall be real and continual comity between The States,[39] the whole of them, or any two of them.[40]
That no State shall be subject to another but each, shall[41] itself have the sole control of its own institutions.

[34] Questions for Swinton[42] To tell me of Etruria

[35] "Hemp, corn, and tobacco, (in Missouri & Kansas /

Hold fast by me![43]

I know very well[44] these may have to be searched[45] many times before they[46] come to you[47] and comply with you.
But what of that? Has not Nature to[48] be searched many times? /
I know they must be persuaded many times a long while[49]

[36] Miss Ellen Grey[50] Bowery Theatre Cor Hicks & Amity before 1st May tall high house free stone. /[51] Wm G. Metzler[52] Tuskilwa Bureau co Illinois

39. Capital "T" and "S" inscribed over lowercase letters in preceding two words.

40. "The States . . . two of them" brought up from bottom of leaf by asterisks and the notation "tr up)" The two lines, in the original order, are in "Starting from Paumanok" (1860), sec. 6, ll. 74–75.

41. Deleted: "be free to [*not del.*] form its own institutions"; inserted: on a line above "free" "itself"; inserted and deleted: "the sole judge of" above "to form its"

42. See [4]. This entry discussed by Hollis, "Whitman and William Swinton," *AL*, 30 (1959), 437.

43. Title inserted with a line above. Entry cancelled by a vertical stroke. Cf. "Starting from Paumanok" (1860), sec. 15, ll. 231–232.

44. Deleted: "that they must be read"; [*ins. and del.*] "sought" on a line above "must be read" ; inserted: "these" above [*del.*] "they:" ; inserted: "may have to be" on a line below "[*del.*] must . . . read"

45. Inserted and brought down by line.

46. Deleted: "will"

47. Deleted: "? —But" ; inserted above: "and comply with you"

48. Inserted above: "be" . Deleted: "read" ; inserted and deleted: "sought" following "be" ; inserted: "searched" below "[*del.*] read" . Short line above "I know"

49. Preceding three words inserted as alternate above "many times" . Line cancelled by short vertical stroke.

50. A NY actress. The date would be 1857, since Ellen Grey did not play at the Bowery in 1858. If the date refers to a performance, and not merely to her address, the reference would probably be to *Fate, or, the Children of Love,* a popular melodrama. See Odell, *Annals of the New York Stage,* VI, 554. A Brooklyn address. Carroll Hollis, "Whitman's 'Ellen Eyre,' " *WWN,* 2 (1956), 24–26, has suggested that she might be the mysterious "Ellen Eyre" with whom WW allegedly had an affair. See "return my book"

51. Ink blotting from following page.

52. Mentioned in "return my book" and "81 Clerman."

[*37*][53] word rifacciamento[54] Bat-ra-chom a om̄ a chy[55]

[*43; 38*[56]*–42 blank*] Oude, (the oldest city in Hindostan) pop. 10,000 /

in Names of Pieces /

some may be called Poem (as Poem of W.W. an American)
some " " Hymn (as Hymn of the Body)
" " " Song as (
" " " simply as (To a Common prostitute[57]
" " " Poemet[58] (as

[*44*] Scoville[59] Maiden lane above William st.[60]

[*45*][61] Noon trains from New York arrive at Rutland[62] at 9 o'clock at night

[*47; 46 blank*] Poem[63]

That is profitable great to you[64] which you carry with you after death
I will carefully earn[65] riches[66] to be carried with me after the death of my body.
I will. . . . .

53. Top third of leaf clipped off.

54. *Rifacimento*—Italian for remaking, recasting, or in a literary sense, a revision. *DN*, Sec. III, "Words," [9], gives "riffacciamento—rumble (sort of mosaic work mixture mess—" . If this is a definition, it could not be identified. Possibly the "mosaic work" refers to the kind of recasting WW had in mind as he was planning his revision of *LG*.

55. *Batrachomyomachia*—"Battle of the Frogs and Mice," the pseudo-Homeric mock epic. In black ink.

56. [*39–40*] is a torn strip with traces of writing, approx. 5¾" x ½". [*41–42*] is a blank leaf, 3½" x 3½" torn out at upper right.

57. "To a Common Prostitute" (1860).

58. See [*159*], [*181*] and Bowers, xxxviii and 260.

59. James M. Scovill of Scovill Manufacturing Company, located at 57 Maiden Lane, NY directory 1856–1857.

60. Calling card of Mr. S. Emlen Randolph. In another hand: "Room 229 St. Nicholas or 123 South 9th Phil[a]"

61. Lower right-hand corner torn out, a piece approx. 2½" x 2¼

62. WW's favorite sister, Hannah, lived in Burlington, Vermont, 45 miles north of Rutland. For Hannah see "D. W. Wilder."

63. "Poem" originally written in the middle of the leaf, above "I will. . . . ." "That is . . . of my body" crammed in above "e will" and has been taken as part of the poem referred to.

64. "great to you" written above "profitable which" as an alternate reading.

65. Deleted: "all the"

66. Deleted: "which I can"

[*49; 48 blank*] All poems, or any other expressions[67] of literature, that do not tally with their writers actual life and knowledge, are lies.

[*51; 50*[68]][69] I will make a song that there is no imperfection in man or woman
And I will make a song that[70] no one thing in the universe is inferior to another, and that all are equally miracles,
And I will make a song that there is nothing more beautiful than death.[71]
And I will make a song that whatever happens to any one may become beautiful
[*53; 52 blank*] And I will make a new song of riches, namely the riches of the body and the spirit, which are before death and after death /[72]

Every Poem of any thing must enclose and express the SPIRITUALITY and JOY of that thing—(of the train of that thing)—(of those things)—not be a mere didactic[73]

[*55;*[74] *54 blank*] Finally after all the physical greatness of the city is attained—after the architecture of the house is finished—then[75] what of the man in the house city[76]? What of the woman?—What is a great[77] city, or a great[78] house, without great men? great Women?[79]

[*57; 56 blank*] Poem of Prophecies— /

—There shall be
(containing prophecies—of all that will probably be in fifty, a hundred, two hundred, &c years hence— /

doctrinaire—theorist/

67. Inserted above "other of"

68. Calling card of James Richardson Jr. In another hand: "256 Asylum Aven Hartford also Southington Highland Plainville Station Conn Hartford Fishkill[?] RR" Holograph calling card of "Edward H. House.) Boston Courier"; in WW's hand: "228 Astor House"

69. Leaf cancelled with vertical line. For this poem see "Starting from Paumanok" (1860), sec. 12, ll. 165–171.

70. Deleted: "there each thing is"

71. This line marked by a curved line at left.

72. Cancelled with two close vertical strokes. Curved line across leaf under "and . . . death"

73. Entry marked with a pointing fist at left.

74. Top third of leaf clipped out. Traces of writing on stub.

75. Inserted: "what of" on a line above "then . . . the"

76. "city" written above "house" as alternate reading. Deleted after question mark: "or" ; inserted: "What of" on a line above [*del.*] "or" and "the"

77. Inserted on a line above "a . . . city"

78. Inserted on a line above "house"

79. See [77] and [*121*]. Cf. "Song of the Broadaxe" (1856), sec. 4, ll. 100–109, and sec. 5.

Strong conviction

Not[80] to volunteer, interfere, or ask questions— / Always *reality—no "funning" no wit*—no[81] ornament

[65; *58 blank; 59–64 clipped*[82]]

Poem of (after Death)[83]

The eliptical style for orations operas
I will be the originator the inventor /

That the extasy of the pythia, the oracles —the divine rage afflatus—that of Christ Hercules &c are just as eligible now[84]

[67; *66 blank*][85]?

Poem of Wise Books

Poem of the Library —(bring in all about the few leading books.

Literature of Egypt,
Assyria
Persia
Hindostan
Palestine[86]
Greece—Pythagoras Plato—Socrates[87]—Homer—Iliad Odyssey
Rome,—Virgil
Germany—Luther

Christ Bible Shakespeare Emerson Rousseau—("Social Contract")[88]

80. Fist pointing to "Not" , which is in a larger hand.
81. Deleted: "iconographies[?] or"
82. Three blank loose fragments: 2" x 3¾", 1¾" x 3¾", 2⅝" x 3¾".
83. Preceding four words cancelled. Next entry marked by pointing fist.
84. Hanging indentation.
85. Entries on this leaf in hanging indentation. Lists of names in columns. Lower third of leaf clipped out. For a continuation of WW's thoughts on a *"Poem of the Library"* see [*71*]. Hollis, "Whitman and William Swinton," *AL*, 30 (1959), p. 444, relates these notes to similar passages in *American Primer* (*DN*, Sec. III, "The Primer of Words," [*58–61*]) and ultimately, and indirectly, to "To Him That Was Crucified" (1860).
86. Added next to column and brought in by curved line.
87. Preceding three names added left of column and aligned before "Greece . . . —Homer" on two lines.
88. See "The Social Contract." Hollis, "Whitman and William Swinton," p. 437, quoting the entire entry, cites WW's spelling of "Rouseaux." Although there is some overwriting at the begin-

[69; 68 *blank*][89] *Motto for all political*[90] *action*

Walt Whitman's terrible Motto.

No nation, once fully[91] enslaved, ever fully recovered its liberty.—

[71; 70 *blank*] (*Poem of the Library*[92]

—first a respectful word to those who in[93] ancient times, and[94] in all times, in unknown nations, have written wise words, or taught them— /

wisdom comes mostly back to the projecter, teller—no matter if no record—[95]/

All my poems do.[96] All I[97] write I write to[98] arouse in you a great personality

[73; 72 *blank*][99] I must not fail to SATURATE my poems with[1] *things, substantial,* American scenes, *climates, names, places, words,*[2] *permanent facts* (*include every important river and mountain animals trees crops, grains, vegetables, flowers*

[75; 74 *blank*][3] Sing celebrate [4]the great[5] ante-conditions of the globe, the gaseous, watery (granitic?[6]) vegetable[7] stages— /

Poem of Precepts /[8] *Poem of Joys and Works*

ning, the ending flourish is not necessarily an "x" . For WW's thoughts on Emerson see "Emerson's Essays—1st series." Written in a column to the left of "Germany" above.

89. A version of "To the States" (1860).

90. Deleted: "philos"

91. Inserted above "enslaved"

92. See [67].

93. Deleted: "all"

94. Inserted above "in"

95. Cf. "A Song of the Rolling Earth" (1856), sec. 2, ll. 82–87.

96. Preceding four words inserted.

97. Deleted: "do" ; inserted above: "write"

98. Deleted: "fo"

99. Hanging indentation. See [99] and Hollis, "Whitman and William Swinton," 444, who relates both entries to "Starting from Paumanok" (1860). Cf. "Feb. 25th 1857."

1. First at left pointing to *"things, substantial"*

2. Deleted: "fo"

3. This line echoes "On the Beach at Night Alone" (1856), l. 9.

4. "Celebrate" written above "Sing the" as an alternate reading.

5. Inserted: "ante" on a line above the word space between "great . . . conditions"

6. "?" written above "granitic"

7. Deleted: "periods" . Three-line space under "stages—" to a rule drawn three-quarters across the leaf above "Poem of Precepts"

8. Pointing fist with a short line written above. "Poem of Joys" is the 1860 title of "A Song of Joys."

[76][9] vegetable in its natural state.[10] not to eat, grows not[11] in U.S., foreign production not a fruit not a wood sea sold at drug stores soft.

[77][12] The greatest thing about a city is—its people [78][13] vegetable[14]

[79] Poem[15]

Poem to one three centuries hence or thirty centuries hence[16]

I, alert,[17] visible, compact, full of life, thirty eight years old,
To you, yet unborn, these.[18]
When you read these, I that was visible am become[19] invisible,
Now[20] it is you[21] compact, full of life, realizing[22] my poems,
If I were[23] with you may be we would love one another
[78][24] Be it[25] as if I were with you—Be not too certain but I am with you

[*83; 80 blank; 81–82 stub*] What would be thought of a surgeon or physician who should be delicate[26] and know only the body as it appears in fashionable

9. Written in column; cancelled with a vertical stroke. See headnote. For other games of twenty questions see [78], [90], [*129*], [*134*], [*136*], [*146*], [*174*], [*178*], [*183*], [*191*], [*192*], "Vegetable not wood," "Hospital Book 12." Hollis, "Whitman's Word-Game," 75, suggests the answer to this riddle is "sponge."

10. Deleted: "to eat"

11. Inserted on a line above "in" "not a fruit . . . soft." in a column following "grows . . . production"

12. See [55].

13. Cancelled with vertical stroke.

14. Possibly the beginning of a game of twenty questions. Cf. [76]. A line of poetry: "Be it as if . . . I am with you" transferred to [79] as last line of poem to which it belongs.

15. See "Full of Life Now" (1860), the last poem in "Calamus." WW was born in 1819; he was thirty-eight on May 31, 1857. It was not part of the original "Live Oak with Moss," later "Calamus Leaves" notebook, of twelve poems numbered in roman which Bowers identified among the Valentine-Barrett MSS. Bowers, p. xl, suggests that this poem may have been written on WW's birthday and that it was to be the final poem in WW's original plan for the third edition of *LG*. See also Bowers, 122, for an intermediate version of the poem. Cancelled with a vertical stroke and a vertical waved line. Title and subtitle in a larger hand.

16. Deleted false start of new line: "To" ; deleted in new line: "To"

17. Inserted and deleted: "formed" above "full of" ; "visible" above "[*del.*] formed" and "[*ins.*] compact,"

18. Deleted beginning of new line: "Now," ; inserted: "As [*del.*] When [*ins.*] you read these,"

19. Inserted on a line above " am . . . invisible"

20. Inserted: "it is" on a line above "you"

21. Deleted: "are"

22. Deleted: "my my" ; inserted and deleted on a line above repeated "my" : "this" ; inserted: "my" on the line before "[*del.*] this"

23. Deleted: "here doubtless it" ; inserted: "with you" on a line below "[*del.*] here do" in "doubtless".

24. Poem continued on facing page. See [78] above.

25. Deleted: "the same"

26. Deleted: "and modest, and treat of costumes and respect the"

costumes?— What is more real than sex? What is there at all the facts of existence but procreation?—[27] These are the very things,—what misses these, misses all. There is just the same reason for my poems, and what they seek to do, to include sex and procreation, as there is for the[28] physician to include them

[*85;*[29] *84 blank*] between 9 & 12 & 1 & 5 (55 Greene[30]/ easy

[*87; 86 blank*] Thomas the Rhymer—Scotch (supposed about 80 years old)[31] died 1299 see p 195–6–7—Scott's Poems[32] /

"the importance of the individual—that is the greatest?[33] saying
the — — — — — — that is the
to — — — — — — — — that is the[34]

[*89; 88 blank*] The idea of *grades* in the mental condition and development of people.— /[35]

The people[36] in strata—remember the vast, largest, most continued popular strata (? strats)—also the various other strata, those of criminals, those of ignorant persons.— Also, in other countries, under other religions and governments.— For instance, the common people, what they are, with their physique, their social customs, amusements, costumes, liberty, slavery, and the rest.— /

This The[37] great fact of grades[38] includes and explains a hundred subordinated facts; without[39] it, the included facts not well understood.—

[90][40] vegetable & mineral
no tool, implement, or instrument. not in the room /
—larger than a foot
on land
is a fixture

27. Deleted: "Yet" ; lowercase changed to capital "T" in "these"
28. Deleted: "surg"
29. Bottom two-thirds of leaf clipped out.
30. At upper right corner, set off by curved line. Rule across leaf above "easy" ; two-line space under "easy" and a rule below two-thirds across the leaf from the left.
31. Preceding five words in a circle to the right under "Scotch"
32. The reference is to *Minstelry of the Scottish Border*. For WW's edition of Scott's poems see Stovall, *Foreground,* 178. Line written under "see . . . Poems"
33. "?" over "greatest"
34. For a similar example of WW leaving dashes or blanks as he structures his verse, see "George Walker" and "Passage to India."
35. Passage crammed in above "The people in strata . . . ."
36. Deleted: "are"
37. Inserted on a line above "g" in "great"
38. Deleted: "comprehends" ; inserted above: "includes"
39. Deleted: "them" ; inserted above: "it"
40. Cancelled with wavy vertical line. See [76].

outdoors /—
public spectacle
figure
chisled—
—on top of a building
not on city building
on Broadway.
no place of amusement
bird
above
is eagle on top
above the St. Germain[41]
on

[*91*][42] Poem of Legacies

—including all that we have received from the past— —tables, languages, figures, measures, literature

[*92*][43]
court plaster
/ all animal / vegetable[44]

[*93*][45] vegetable
not of diet
not wood
in this room
not a cigar
not sold
not about a person
does belong to the premises
not represent any thing
not dry goods
not on a level

41. Hotel, Broadway c. E. 22d, NY directory 1856–1857.

42. Possibly an early proposal for "With Antecedents" (1860).

43. Inscribed on a leaf turned upside down. Cancelled with one horizontal and two vertical strokes. See [*76*].

44. Deleted: "no" ; in another hand: "not in the Room in town and Countery Smaller then your arm not a mecanicks tool not wood not any Diet not any tool Groes in the ground it Groes in the north it Bares flowers it is of a fiber not groe on the vine not in B [*illeg.*]" The misspellings suggest the sort of person with whom WW was playing twenty questions, perhaps his omnibus driver friends.

45. Inscribed on a leaf turned upside down in a column. Cancelled with a vertical stroke. See [*76*]. The answer might be "curtain."

not a cork
above the counter
fast & fixed
touches the wall
No paper

[95[46]; 94 *blank*][47]
Book of Letters ? Poem /

Letter ?Poem[48] to a prostitute
Letter to felon
Letter to one about to die
(end letter to prostitute—
—"I salute you my love, with a kiss on your lips, that you do not forget me—

[97; 96 *blank*] ? whether the right of voting, legal owning, &c. (being "of age") should not be changed from 21 to 18 years—

[99; 98 *blank*][49]? Poem of American Names / the bookbinder's[50] hammer, knife, shears, & folder / the standing press, [*the*][51] embossing press,

[103; 100 *blank*; 101–102 *stub*][52] In Poem of Personality—incorporate all the ideas of the Personal Magnetism articles /[53]

? —*Poem of Large Personality*. (make this poem for women just as much as men)

[105; 104 *blank*][54]/?[55] The Dutch parentage of Manhattan, the English of Massachusetts, the[56] Swedes of New Jersey

46. Most of the top half of leaf clipped out. Cancelled by a slanting stroke.

47. The "Book of Letters" probably refers to the "Messenger Leaves" of *LG* 1860 which includes "To One Shortly to Die" and "To a Common Prostitute." The ending of the latter poem suggested here was incorporated into the MS version. See *LG, CRE,* 386n and *LG MS Variorum*. See also "You Felons on Trial in Courts" (1860), which was part of "Leaves of Grass No. 13" in the 1860 edition.

48. Inserted above "Letter"

49. Hollis, "Whitman and William Swinton," 444, relates this entry to [73] and to "Starting from Paumanok" (1860).

50. Inserted on a line above "hammer"

51. Ditto in MS. Deleted: "stamping" ; inserted above; "embossing"

52. Both entries in hanging indentation.

53. May refer to Bucke clippings #380 ("Personal Magnetism") and #410 ("Human and Animal Magnetism"); *CW*, X, 86, 88.

54. Top clipped out, [*illeg.*] traces of writing visible. Another clipping has been taken from the leaf after the present entry.

55. Entry marked by curved line and "?" Hanging indentation.

56. Deleted: a partially formed "G"

[*107; 106 blank*] personality— [:][57] pride self-esteem self-appreciation egotism elevatedness / the strap and paddle for the punishment of slaves[58] / the young heifer

[*115; 108 blank; 109–114 stubs*]

Make A Poem[59]

(expressed in things[?] and[60] moving acts) involving the idea, that in morals and mental results good, evil, &c, there is the same reciprocal play of effect and causes, as in the physical world. /

When the original men of These States threw off the imperialism of Great Britain, then was dimly roused before the fathers, the vista of a noble government.

[*116*][61] The Mayor this forenoon issued an order to the various Captains, directing them to call in the men at 4 o clock this afternoon and have them deliver up the city property—the Captains to hold on to the Station Houses till the further action of the Common[62] Council

[*117*] Poem of (my brothers and sisters) artists, singers, musicians

[*119; 118 blank*] —1, 2, 3, &c an equal friend of all The States.

[*121; 120 blank*][63] for a Great City

The greatest [*illeg.*] of

—[64]A city may have great temples, avenues, &c but[65] in its common people, their[66] personality, heroism, ruggedness beauty & strength

57. Brace pointing to the next five words written in a column with a line space and a rule from the left margin two-thirds across the leaf

58. Hanging indentation following a line space and a rule above "the young"

59. "A Poem" in a larger hand as a title, followed by a parenthetical insert on four lines at the right of "expressed . . . acts)" aligned on the two lines of "involving . . . morals" . The rest of the text, including the initial "Make," is inserted before the title and the parenthesis. A line is drawn across the leaf under the last line, "physical world"

60. Deleted: "acts"

61. Probably refers to the great Police Riot of the summer of 1857. On June 16 a pitched battle erupted at City Hall between Mayor Fernando Wood's municipal police and the rival police force created by the State Legislature. The riot was put down by the army but the civic unrest and the battle over jurisdiction continued through the summer. See Edward Robb Ellis, *The Epic of New York City* (NY: Coward-McCann, 1966), 276–281. WW wrote several articles for the Brooklyn *Times* on the subject (see White, *Journalism,* 33 and *ISL,* 130–131). Cf. "Memorials." Entry cancelled by a vertical stroke.

62. Scrawled.

63. See [55].

64. Deleted: "The"

65. Deleted: "it [*illeg. letter*]"

66. Deleted: "knowledge"

[*123; 122 blank*] The greater the reform, the greater the personality that is needed./[67]

Poem of Tears[68]

Can I not make a poem in which the tears drop down in great drops?

[*127; 124 blank; 125–126 stub*] animal & mineral
about the person
not in sight
about not Sam
carried in pocket
moves on a joint
Belongs to Cale
this pencil I am writing with[69]
[*129; 128 blank*][70] 1—mineral
2[71] more than a foot
3 not in the room
4 is[72] a conspicuous object in this city
5 is in an[73] elevated position
6 in Broadway
7 private property
8 below Canal
9 in front of a house
10 below the first story
11 no figure of any thing
[*130*] (stone mortar) stone stoop
12 below Worth
13 stone
14 above St. Paul's
15 about the door way
16 at a hotel
17 Astor house stoop

67. Hanging indentation. Three lines space under and a line drawn two-thirds across the leaf above *"Poem of Tears"*

68. Probably "Trickle Drops" (1860). The poem, written in 1857, was one of the early poems included later in "Calamus." It was not one of the "Live Oak with Moss" poems (see [*79n*], above). See Bowers, xlix, lxxii, 94–95. Hanging indentation.

69. The answer, written at bottom of leaf. Questions and answer each cancelled by a vertical stroke.

70. In column. Cancelled by a vertical stroke. See [*76*].

71. Deleted: "l"

72. Deleted: "some"

73. Deleted: "elevated" ; inserted and deleted above: "lofty" ; inserted below: "elevated"

74. "stone mortar" enclosed by a single curved line. Entry cancelled by vertical stroke.

18 not the pillars
19

[*131*][75] Clinic, (or clinique) relating to a bed, bed-ridden—(the lectures, or treatment of a surgeon or phys. given off-hand, as[76] he stands by the patient.[77])

[*134; 132–133 blank*][78] bevel[79] vegetable
not gritty
it is wood
manufactured
it is used as a tool
it is used by any of us in this room)
not used as a support
smaller than my arm
not require the mouth
carried about openly
less than a foot
has a handle
used to strike blows,
used by

[*135*] the Ame

[*136*][80] / mineral
manufactured
instrument
not iron
not a mechanic's tool
not used by us
not for hurt.
sold not at stores
bigger than my fist
not used in medicine or surgery,
not used by any public officer
no precious metal
not in this city

75. Entry in hanging indentation.

76. Inserted: "he stands by the" written on a line above "the patient" ; redundant "the" not printed.

77. Deleted: "is brought to him"

78. Cancelled by vertical stroke. See [*76*].

79. Presumably this is the answer. See [*129*].

80. Deleted at top: "all[?]" . Also at top, nine vertical marks, probably to keep count of questions with a line under across the leaf. Cf. [*inside back cover*]. Following entry and that on the following page cancelled by vertical stroke. In column. See [*76*]. The answer is not given.

is in the U.S.
not in memory of any person
On land /
[*137*] not an edifice
not as a signal

[*138*] Washington Monument at 14th st.[81]

[*145; 139–140 stub; 141–142 blank;*[82] *143–144 stub*] *poem of the*[83] *aborigines*

—introducing every principal aboriginal[84] trait, and name /[85] bring in[86] aboriginal traits in *poem of* (American) *Materials*[87]

[*146*][88] Mineral
not in this room
manufactured
sold at stores
hardware stores (&[89] drug stores
not taken in the stomach
sometimes[90] used in surgery
iron and steel
not an edged tool of any sort
no application to persons
instrument
no handle
mechanic
Carpenters
sometimes more than 9 inches
sometimes less.
smooth[91] points
Joint (square[92]

81. Cancelled by vertical stroke.
82. Nearly half of leaf cut out.
83. Deleted: "Indians" ; inserted above: "aborigines"
84. Written over [*illeg.*].
85. Fist pointing up to preceding entry with a line above the fist and "by in"
86. Deleted: "Indi" ; inserted: "aboriginal"
87. Cf. "Starting from Paumanok" (1860), sec. 16.
88. In column. See [76].
89. "&" inserted.
90. Inserted on a line above "used"
91. Deleted: "one"
92. At upper right, enclosed by curved ine. Entry cancelled by wavy vertical stroke. Presumably the answer, although why a carpenter's square would be used in surgery but not applied to persons remains a puzzle.

[*147*][93]/ Poem of Criminals

Now I[94] betake myself from all others, and go among criminals—

[*155; 148 blank; 149–150 stub; 151–154 blank*[95]] in Poems somewhere put in the Dutch liberty, conscienteousness and good natured tolerance—the settling spirit of Manhattan island—and its prevailing characteristic to this day[96]

[*157; 156 blank*][97] America brings to the[98] test of characters and heroism[99] her own large and new standards

[*159; 158 blank*] ? A poem (or passage in a poem)[1] giving an account of my way of making a poem Poemet[2] Poemot

[*174;*[3] *160–166 blank; 167–168 stub; 169–170 blank; 171–172 stub*] grows both north & south
no shell
generally cooked
eaten at this counter
sometimes sold by the bushel
smaller or larger than Jack's fist
whitish meat
[*175*] eat here every day,
grows in a lump.
([4]may be either mealy or not[5]

[*178; 176–177 blank*][6] Mineral
quite certain not in the room,

93. Top half of leaf clipped off. Line of verse written in hanging indentation.

94. Deleted: "take"

95. Top third of [*153–154*] torn out. Bulk of entry in hanging indentation.

96. Doodling or diagram of small wedge-shaped figures and irregular vertical lines. Perhaps represents twelve ships, some connected by lines, off a coast.

97. Hanging indentation.

98. Deleted: "judgem" ; inserted above: "test"

99. Deleted: "entirely far larger"

1. "(or passage in a poem)" inserted at the top of the leaf above "giving an" . "Poemet" "Poemot" written on two lines following "a poem"

2. See [*43*].

3. Top half of leaf, including some of the questions, clipped out. This missing fragment may possibly be "Poem L'Envoy" on the recto of which is "Vegetable not wood." Entry on this and on the next page cancelled by vertical stroke.

4. Deleted: "no"

5. Answer may be "potato." For what may be the first part of this riddle see "Vegetable not wood," which may be part of this leaf. "Jack" and "eaten at this counter" perhaps suggest that WW played the game while eating with omnibus drivers. For similar games see [*76*].

6. Cancelled by vertical stroke. Hanging indentation. See [*76*].

something made through the use of fire
[7]steel
smaller
carried about one
not a part of another[8] article
not[9] used about the toilet
used by any one
nothing to do with sound

[*181; 179 blank; 180* [10]][11] ? Poem of the past[12]
Poemet[13]

I was looking[14] a long while for the poem of the past and now I have found it
It is the Present—it is the this[15] Earth to-day, and[16] This America, and all languages and inventions
It is the[17] broad show of artificial things, ships,[18] and the interchanges of nations
[*180*][19] It is[20] no more in the rhythmic legends than in all else,[21]
It is not in the[22] old books—it is not in the rhythmic legends,—nor[23] it has not descended[24] in[25] books, any more than all else,

[*183; 182 blank*][26] animal & vegetable in this room not used by drivers worn above the waist not the neck complete in it's [27] a /

7. Deleted: "iron"
8. Deleted: [*illeg.*]
9. Deleted: "a part"
10. WW evidently began the poem on a recto [*181*] and completed it on the facing verso [*180*] which is printed below. See *n*19.
11. An early version of "I Was Looking a Long While" (1860). See Bowers, 168–169.
12. Line deleted: "What of the past"
13. Line deleted: "What is the poem of the Past" . False start of new line deleted: "I was"
14. Inserted: "a long while" on a line above "for the"
15. "this" inserted over "the" as alternate reading.
16. Deleted: "all th Ame"
17. Deleted: "long" ; inserted: "broad" in the word space between "[*del.*] long" and "show"
18. Deleted: "international commer exchanges, books,"
19. Written on MS [*180*]. See above, *n*10.
20. Deleted: "not any more" ; inserted: "no more" on a line above "any more"
21. The following line is written a space below and in a different pencil.
22. Inserted and deleted: on a line above "rythmic" "old books" ; inserted and brought down by curved line: "old books—it is not in" inserted: "the" on a line above the word space between "the . . . rythmic"
23. Deleted: "in [*illeg.*]" ; inserted: "it has not" on a line above "nor" and "[*del.*]" in "[*illeg.*]"
24. Deleted: "to"
25. Deleted: "the"
26. Each entry on this page cancelled by a short vertical stroke. For "Twenty Questions" see [*76*]. Note references to "drivers", perhaps those with whom WW was playing.
27. Word overwritten or deleted.

Poem expressing the sentiment of the joy of old age—of an old person—(? or in the poems of Joys.)[28]

O my old[29] manhood!—my joy!
My children and grandchildren![30] My white hair and beard! My[31] largeness majesty, calmness[32] and[33] majesty from many[34] years![35]
[*185*] O the[36] joy of[37] womanhood!— O ripened[38] happiness at last!
I am more than[39] eighty years of age, in perfect health[40]
My hair[41] too is pure[42] white—[43]I am the most venerable mother[44]—I am complete in myself,
To me[45] all people[46] draw nigh—[47] I[48] attract with[49] more than[50] the attraction of my youth.—

[*184*][51] handsome room, gilt chandeliers /
white-neckcloths— —quaker looking horse-shoe, line of men— /
homily of a reverend gentleman— /
room about one-quarter full /
a regular Yankee Dyspeptic faced speaker, with awkward, see-saw gestures /
very dry speech, the usual platitudes

28. "A Song of Joys" (1860), ll. 86–93. "Poem of Joys" was the 1860 title. For another version of this passage see Bowers, 208. See also "Poem incarnating the mind."

29. Deleted: "age," ; inserted above: "manhood!"

30. Preceding four words inserted on a line above "My . . . and"

31. Deleted: "calmness" ; inserted above: "largeness," ; inserted below: "majesty"

32. Inserted on a line above and preceding "and"

33. Deleted: "peace" ; inserted above: "majesty"

34. Deleted and inserted above.

35. Poem continued on the following recto [*185*]. Upper third of leaf torn out.

36. Deleted: "exquisiteness" ; inserted above: "joy"

37. Deleted: "my"

38. Deleted line: "I am my breast have suckled many so" ; inserted: "happiness at last!" on a line above "[*del.*] my . . . have"

39. Deleted: "seventy" ; inserted above: "eighty"

40. Deleted: "—my" Preceding three words inserted above "[*del.*]—my" .

41. Deleted: "also" ; inserted above: "too"

42. Inserted on a line above "is" and wordspace before "white"

43. Deleted: "I" "My"

44. Deleted: "in perfect health" ; inserted: "—I am complete in myself" on two lines above and to the right of "health"

45. Deleted: "also" ; inserted above: "all"

46. Deleted: "are drawn more than"

47. Deleted: "they"

48. Deleted: "fr[*?*]"

49. Inserted on a line above wordspace between "attract . . . more" and "m" in "more"

50. Deleted: "I am"

51. Notes on a public meeting, led by clergymen, perhaps taken in connection with WW's journalism. For his attitude to the various reform movements see *ISL*, 44–45. Cancelled with several vertical marks.

[*191; 186 blank; 187–190 blank*][52] 12—no legs
13—houses commonly have these things in them
14 mostly[53] in the Kitchen, parlor and bedroom
15 not used about the fire, nor in preparing any thing for the fire.
16 no water
17—no instrument
18 no kind of a box
19 neither a handle nor handles
20 not pliable

[*192*][54] Mineral
manufactured
in sight
used not with food
one complete article
not any vessel
not as large as my hand
no matter about the weather
not about the person
above four feet height
not for sale
not hung up
not handled
not on shelf or counter
driven in horizontally
nail
foil[55]

[*193*][56] Hindostan,[57] from the western sea.—[58]

I look on the[59] Mother, at far removes,[60] of These States,
Mother of[61] languages—mother of the great idea of[62] avatars,[63]

52. See [76]. Entries in column. Cancelled with vertical stroke.
53. Inserted above "in"
54. See [76]. Entries in column. Cancelled with vertical stroke.
55. At upper-right corner of leaf. It is not clear whether "foil" or "nail" is the answer.
56. Eventually to become "Facing West from California's Shores" (1860). See Bowers, 66–67. Cancelled by vertical stroke.
57. Dash deleted.
58. Deleted false start of next line: "Mother"
59. Preceding four words inserted on a line above "Mother,"
60. Deleted: "even"
61. Deleted: "religions,"
62. Deleted: "the"
63. At beginning of next line, deleted: "Like" ; inserted above: "As"

As[64] a child[65] I look afar[66] at the house of maternity, the land of migrations.[67]
I[68] look on the shores of my[69] western sea to behold the old mother of me.[70]
I[71] come westward From[72] the Himmalehs, from the vast plains, from the north,[73] from the flowery islands,[74]
We face home again, as[75] after long travel, growth & sleep
The circle is circled,[76]

[*194*[77]; *inside back cover and outside back cover blank*]

64. Inserted and deleted: "of" above "c" in "child"

65. Deleted: "I turn, seeing his" ; inserted and deleted in balloon: "looking over [*not del.*] [*illeg.*]" on a line above "child" and "[*del.*] I turn" ; inserted: "I look" following.

66. Deleted: "the place" ; inserted: "at the my" and "[*del.*] house" on a line above "afar" and "[*del.*] the place "

67. Deleted new line: "There then is the" ; following twelve words inserted above. "I look . . . sea" enclosed by curved line.

68. Deleted: "stand" ; inserted above: "look"

69. Preceding four words inserted on lines after "look" . Deleted: "the" before "western"

70. Followed by "I" and blank space encircled by a curved line. The continuation is apparently taken up in the revisions on the following line.

71. Inserted and deleted: "We" ; inserted: "I come westward" on a line above "From the"

72. The original beginning of the line, as evidenced by the capitalization, and is inscribed over [*illeg.*].

73. Deleted: "and"

74. Deleted: "how long it is since!—how many generations!" . The following line inscribed last on the leaf, brought up by arrow and WW's notation "tr up"

75. Deleted: "from" ; inserted above: "after"

76. Deleted: "Here" before "the circle" . The placing of this new line beginning is not clear. It may have been inscribed before this final line.

77. Twelve vertical marks at the top left of the inside of [*194*] divided into threes by four smaller marks or commas. Perhaps a record of a score.

Vegetable Not Wood.

Manuscript in Duke (15, #38). Inscribed in black pencil in column on pocket ledger paper, approx. 2⅜" x 3½". Cancelled with vertical stroke. Verso of "Poem L'Envoy." This MS may be a clipping from "[*illeg.*] Dick Hunt," dated 1857, and it is tempting, though not verifiable, to place it at [*174*], which seems to continue this riddle. The answer seems to be "potato." For WW's games of twenty questions see "[*illeg.*] Dick Hunt" [*76*] *n*8. Published in *FC&I,* 17. (Gene Edward Veith, Jr.)

Vegetable not wood
very common
not in the room
used as food
solid
not fruit of any tree
grows in the ground

The Shower of Meteors.

Manuscript in NYPL (Berg). White paper scrap which seems to have been torn from a book or periodical, since fragments of a line of print remain. Inscribed in black pencil. See "and there is the meteor-shower" for a versified version intended as part of "Pictures." See also "other names of Venus." The date is probably between 1856 and 1860. First printed *N&F,* 51–52 (Pt. I, #184).

The shower of meteors—[1]this occurred in the night of 12th 13th Nov. 1833—toward morning——myriads in all directions, some with long shining white trains, some falling over each other like falling water—leaping, silent, white,[2] apparitions around up there in the sky over my head[3]

1. WW's description agrees with that in *Niles' Weekly Register,* 55 (November 16, 1833), 184 and (November 23, 1833), 200–201.

2. Deleted: "the"

3. Preceding three words at upper right on arrow.

The Scope of Government.

Manuscript in LC (Feinberg #926). Inscribed in black pencil on homemade notebook of white laid paper, 6¼" x 7⅜", sewn with white string, no covers. Illegible embossing on [*13–23*]. WW kept this notebook in his usual idiosyncratic fashion. He began with a treatise of the abuses of American government which is strikingly similar to "The Eighteenth Presidency!" of the same year [*3–19*], as usual writing on rectos only. On [*21*] he abruptly began to make notes for a poem "The Insects." Most of [*23*] was torn out, but at the bottom he begins notes for "Assurances" which run through [*29*]. At this point he turned the notebook over, and on the next-to-last recto [*46*] wrote what seems to be a continuation of the political notes. Then, working forward [*45–30, 31*] he wrote sketches for "This Compost." [*37*] is one of his notes to himself about social behavior. Additional sketches for "This Compost" are in Duke (7, #14). See Manuscript Variorum. WW must have kept this notebook in late 1855 or early 1856, probably before the composition of "The Eighteenth Presidency!" if that may be regarded as a finished statement of his disillusion with American politics in 1856.

[*3*][1] The scope of government is always to be kept[2] broad[3]—The question that[4] must premise[5] enactments[6] must be Will this appeal apply[7] to[8] men and women universally?[9] Does it[10] directly or indirectly[11] defend the rights to[12] life, liberty, and property, of each[13] uncriminal man and woman, without any exception whatever?

Whatever is not that broad

1. Feinberg's note accompanying the MS states that pp. [*1–2*] were cut out. Deleted: "That"
2. Inserted and deleted: "very" above the word space between "kept broad"
3. Deleted: "and ample"
4. Deleted: "is to"
5. Deleted: "all"
6. Deleted: "is" "Is" ; inserted above: "must be"
7. Inserted on a line above "eal" in "appeal"
8. Deleted: "universal"
9. Deleted: "Has" ; inserted above: "Does"
10. Deleted: "reference"
11. Deleted: "to preserve" ; inserted: "defend" on a line above "[*del.*] preserve"
12. Preceding two words inserted on a line above "the . . . life"
13. Deleted: "and all men and women" ; inserted: "uncriminal man and woman" on a line across the page and above "[*del.*] men and women"

[5; 4 *blank*] *[14] The government to suit these states is no government of lawyers,—[15] nor a government of dilletanti[16] either.—[17] In[18] politics, in poems, in war, in behavior, one thing tells forever—and that is approp fitness purpose[19] the fit ability ability capability—[20] Not gab, not being genteel, not plenty of money,—none of these[21] save a[22] country.—

The substratum on which the American constitution is based, is, that every uncriminal person is endowed with the right to[23] his or her life, liberty, and the equal pursuit of happiness.—

[7; 6 *blank*] *In what respect does the[24] government of this land represent the strong live——[25] people of this land, this day, or any of these days?—[26] Is there one.—[27] Is this melange A crowd of[28] attorneys, feverish[29] southerners—owners of slaves[30] bleeders of the treasury, bullies without courage, angry[31] dyspeptics from the north, supple human[32] hinges from the same, are they this great America?[33] this this[34] poor scum that has floated somehow into the presidency—these supple [9; 8 *blank*] secretaries—these milliners of[35] diplomats (sent[36] in their[37] poppy-show liveries to[38] dance for us in[39] the cotillions of distant courts)—[40]

—these[41] are they America?— Are they the great nation? of,[42]

14. The significance of this asterisk and that on [7] is not clear.

15. Deleted: "dilletanti [*illeg.*]"

16. In "Words," *DN,* III, 672, WW said he preferred the invented spelling "dilletant."

17. Inserted: "either.—" on a line above ".— " following "dilletanti" . Redundant period-dash not printed.

18. Deleted: "government" ; inserted above: "politics"

19. "approp . . . purpose" written above, on, and below the line following "is"

20. Written above, on, and below the line following "approp . . . purpose"

21. Deleted: "will"

22. Deleted: "man" . Rule across the leaf under "a country.—"

23. Deleted: "liv"

24. Deleted: "A"

25. Two long dashes. Deleted: "American"

26. Deleted: "Not" ; inserted above: "Is there"

27. Deleted: "It is" "Where is" "A" ; inserted: "Is this melange" on a line above "[*del.*] is" and " A crowd of"

28. Deleted: "dyspe"

29. Deleted: "men dyspeptics" ; inserted: "southerners" on a line above "[*del.*] men"

30. Deleted: "seekers of contracts" . This and the two following epithets are in column.

31. Deleted: "speakers" ; inserted: "dyspeptical" corrected to "dyspeptics" above "angry" and "[*del.*] speakers"

32. Inserted on a line above "hinges"

33. The location of this phrase is uncertain. What seems to be a bracket and arrow would place it after "scum" following.

34. Deleted: "Pres" "scum"

35. Preceding two words inserted on a line above "these . . . diplomats"

36. Deleted: "forth"

37. Deleted: "milliner's" ; inserted: "poppy-show" on the next line above "liveries"

38. Deleted: "speak" "show" ; inserted: "dance" above "[*del.*] show"

39. Deleted: "foreign lands"

40. This passage was probably written before the publication of the State Department "Dress Circular" in June, 1856. Cf. "Col Parker's squa mother."

41. Inserted.

42. Deleted: "thirty-two nations"

[*11; 10 blank*] Go back to first principles,—receive[?][43] nothing through parties. I[44] that[?] man a slave who, [*illeg.*][45] to day obeys the[46] authority of any party,[47] no matter how specious their pretensions.— Listen to all, learn from all, consider well what they have to offer, but obey yourself only.—[48] They who[49] fabricate the creeds and commands of these parties, are all infidels—[50] they have no faith in man—they do not dream of any other way to success [*13, 12*[51]][52] except schemings, caucuses,[53] lying, not one lie, but all lies—not one face, but a face for every different section[54] interest.

I tell you[55] *these men are all using you.* /[56]

The[57] performances of government must be reduced to minims. /

Out[58] of[59] thirty[60] enactments passed by the[61] Congress of these States, or by the legislatures, twenty-nine are for petty personal objects, in which the people have no broad interest whatever.—

[*15; 14 blank*] Obey no man

Learn[62] Think upon all subjects for yourselves.—[63] ([64] Learn from all sides but decide for yourselves[65]

43. Rectangular hole in MS.
44. Rectangular hole in MS.
45. Words lost because of hole. Deleted: "[*illeg.*] swallows" "receives" ; inserted above: "to day obeys"
46. Deleted: "commands"
47. Deleted: "whatever"
48. Deleted: "Those"
49. Deleted: "pull the"
50. Deleted: "and scorners of you"
51. Outline sketches of four palmately parted leaves.
52. Embossed at lower right. Deleted: "but" ; inserted above: "except"
53. Deleted: "lies not" ; inserted: "lying" on a line above "[*del.*] lies"
54. "section" written above "interest" as alternate.
55. Inserted above the wordspace between "tell . . . these"
56. Rule across leaf.
57. Deleted: "business" Rule halfway across the leaf under "to minims"
58. Original beginning deleted: "Two"
59. Deleted: "any"
60. Deleted: "laws"
61. Deleted: "state legislature"
62. "Learn" written above "Think" as an alternate reading.
63. Hanging indentation.
64. Loop at left and under first two words.
65. Hanging indentation. This and the preceding sentence inserted in smaller hand at top of leaf.

The remedy is not in authority but in the throwing off of authority.—[66] Then when that which abdicates[67] and was an usurper allowed[68] to do certain work,[69] the true power comes into possession.—[70] It is not this or that party who is going to save America, and make it justify the mighty prophecies and promises which are all that it has hitherto been.— It is in countless breeds of great [*17; 16 blank*][71] individuals, the eternal and only anchor of states.—

I have been informed that it is expected that[72] those who address the people,[73] will flatter them.—[74] I flatter none.— I[75] think I could taunt you rather than to flatter you.—

What have you been about, that you have allowed[76] that scum to be floated into the Presidency? What have you been about[77] that your Congress is filled with little but gab,[78] book-knowledge and[79] tailors clothes,——[80] doughfaces and[81] puttyfaces?

[*19; 18 blank*][82] Do you think[83] liberty[84] and equality have now done with America? That the work is finished, and the dwelling is henceforth[85] secure?—[86] Believe it not? *No* /[87]

66. Deleted: "Then" ; inserted: "Then when [*del.*] false [*del.*] usurper" above "[*del.*] Then" and "that which"

67. Deleted: "is replaced by after his work is done"

68. Inserted on a line above "to do"

69. Deleted: "comes"

70. Inserted and deleted: "I say" on a line above "et"

71. Embossed lower right.

72. Preceding eight words inserted on a line above "Those . . . people" ; "that" inserted before "Those" . Unemended capital on "Those" not printed.

73. Deleted: "are expected to flatter" ; inserted: "will" on a line above "cted" in "expected"

74. Marginal question mark before "that" and curved lines at left of "that those . . . them . . . —" possibly to indicate that WW questioned the passage.

75. Deleted: "come to rebuke" ; inserted: "think I could taunt you" above "[*del.*] come to rebuke" and "taunt"

76. Deleted: "these"

77. Deleted: "What do you send" ; new paragraph: "Can you find nothing but" ; new paragraph: "Do you think nothing" ; inserted: "your Congress is filled with little" above "[*del.*] Do you think nothing" and "but"

78. Deleted: "college-stuffing" ; inserted above: "book-knowledge"

79. Deleted: "tailors" ; inserted above: "tailors"

80. Deleted: "is [*ins. above* "wanted"] ever wanted in your Congress blather"

81. Deleted: "blatherskites?"

82. Embossed at lower right.

83. Deleted: "the experiment of"

84. Deleted: "has" ; inserted: "and equality have" on a line above "erty" in "liberty" and "now"

85. Inserted on a line above "is . . . secure?—"

86. Deleted: "No"

87. Deleted at beginning of next paragraph: "Where are you represented" ; inserted: "What representative have you—what single representative [*del.*] have of you is there"

What representative have you—what single representative of you is there in the Capitol? Where[88]

[*21; 20*[89]][90] The insects.

get from Mr. Arkhurst a list of[91] *American insects*— / ? Just simply enumerate them with their sizes, colors, habits, lives, shortness or length of life—what they feed upon (A little poem of a leaf, or two leaves, only)[92] First enumerate the insects—then end by saying I do not know what these are but I believe that all these are more than they seem

I do not know what they are[93]
I dare not be too assuming over them
I have advised with myself . . .
. . . I dare not consider myself,[94] anymore for my place
then they are for their places

[*23; 22*[95]][96] I
That [*illeg.*][97] know there[98]. . . . which I do not know,[99]
I need no assurances . . . I am he who is pre-occupied

[*25; 24*[1]][2] I do not doubt that From under the very steps,[3] hands, eyes[4] am[5] cognizant of, are[6] looking faces I am not cognizant of—calm and silent faces.[7]

88. Deleted: "in the"

89. See below. [20] is in the back-to-front sequence and is upside down.

90. See also "Whole poem Poem of Insects" for other notes for this poem and Mr. Arkhurst. The layout of this leaf is very idiosyncratic. It appears to end in verse.

91. Deleted: "just" . Wavy line drawn halfway across the leaf from the left under "[*del.*] just" and "Amer" in "American"

92. Sentence taken down on arrow to poetical passage below. Deleted: "end the insects—"

93. Possibly inserted in a lighter hand.

94. Deleted: "in" ; inserted: "any more for" on a line above "[*del.*] in" and "my"

95. See below in back-to-front sequence, p. 291.

96. Top three quarters of leaf torn off. "I" on remaining upper-left corner. Cancelled with a vertical stroke. The lines on [*23–29*] are for "Faith Poem" (1856), now "Assurances."

97. The rest of the sentence is torn off.

98. Deleted: "exists" the leaf is torn off, but the following seems clear.

99. Deleted: "That" ; deleted on new line: "Assurances" "a" "I"

1. See below in back-to-front sequence, p. 291.

2. Page cancelled with a vertical stroke. As far as one can determine from the size and placement of the writing, the whole page originally began: "That besides what I" . Emendatiens in notes 2 and 3 (text to word "cognizant") are at top of leaf. Inserted: "I [*del.*] think" "[*del.*] know do not doubt that" on two lines at the top left of the leaf above "From under"

3. Deleted: "and"

4. Inserted on a line above the wordspace between "[*del.*] besides what"

5. WW did not emend to "are" . (The whole line does not quite make sense.)

6. Deleted: "th calm and looking"

7. Beginning of new line deleted: "That"

I do not doubt but there is far[8] more in myself than I have supposed . . . and more in all men and women . . . and more in my poems than I have supposed

[*27; 26*[9]][10] I do not doubt that there are[11] experiences and growths for me through, time, and through the universes, of which I cannot have the slightest inkling or idea

I do not doubt the universes are limitless . . . in vain I try to fancy how limitless

I do not doubt it is[12] safe for[13] orbs and systems of orbs to[14] play their[15] eternal sports through [*29; 28*[16]] the air—and that I shall one day be eligible to do as much as they, and more then they,

I do not doubt,[17] whatever can possibly happy through any of the worlds is provided for, in the[18] inherences of things,

I do not doubt,[19] whatever can happen in this world, interior or exterior, in America, in the[20] remainder of the[21] earth, among affairs, politics, children, failures,[22] murders, wrecks, degradations death defection[23] is each and all amply provided for

[*31 top half of leaf clipped off, remainder blank; 30*[24]][25]

[*46; 47*[26]; *48; blank*] What is[27] now wanted in these states—and what will[28] be wanted, a hundred years hence,[29] and[30] ever so many hundred years hence—is clear-eyed, well-informed, healthy-brained, bold-mouthed men, —[31] men pos-

8. Deleted: "more in myself more in my poems than"
9. See below in back-to-front sequence.
10. Cancelled with vertical stroke.
11. Deleted: "more"
12. Deleted: "eternally"
13. Deleted: "the mighty"
14. Deleted: "play" before "play"
15. Deleted: "swift plays" ; inserted: "eternal" on a line above "[*del.*] swift"
16. See below in back-to-front sequence.
17. Deleted: "that"
18. Deleted: "natüre" ; inserted above: "inherences"
19. Deleted: [*illeg.*]
20. Deleted: "other"
21. Deleted: "centuries as in pol" ; inserted: "earth" on a line above "[*del.*] centuries"
22. Deleted: "deaths"
23. Inserted on a line above "is"
24. See below in back-to-front sequence, p. 290.
25. Presumably, WW here followed his usual practice of turning the notebook upside down and moving forward on the versos. He appears to pick up the theme of the political notes.
26. Contains line drawings of clover, a leafy twig, some blades of grass and an unidentifiable shape. The leaf is loose and presumably was connected to the missing [*1–2*].
27. Deleted: "wa" ; inserted: "now"
28. Deleted: "always"
29. Preceding two words inserted on a line above "and"
30. Deleted: "every"
31. Deleted: "able"

sessed of such native[32] resolution, that they readily[33] part aside authority, law, custom, officers, popularities,[34] and to[35] walk sternly[36] on with their own divine conviction of what is right.—

[*38; 39–44 stubs*[37]*; 45 blank*] distempered morbid[38]
No, all is fresh,
The[39] berries in the gardens,—how juicy and cool they are!
The fruit of the Apple-orchard[40] and that of the[41] orange orchard—[42] melons, grapes, peaches, pears—I feared they would poison me, but they do not.
As I lay reclining on the grass,[43] how can I not catch some disease? . . .[44] for? probably every spear of grass rises out of what was once some catching disease
[*34; 35–36 stubs; 37*[45]][46] not bring to me[47] a single one of the[48] diseases that have[49] forever laved themselves in it[50]
I[51] cannot believe[52] yet awhile,
I do not see how there can be any thing but disease[53]
[*32; 33*[54]][55] I do not see how[56] nothing but maladies can be[57] resolved back in the earth, and[58] return otherwise

32. Deleted: "firmne"
33. Deleted: "sink all" ; inserted above: "part aside"
34. Deleted: [*illeg.*]
35. Inserted above "and" as alternate.
36. Inserted on a line above "over"
37. Three stubs remain, written on versos only. The inscription appears to be verse. Page cancelled with a vertical line. The following lines are a sketch for "Poem of Wonder at the Resurrection of the Wheat" (1856, now "This Compost").
38. Written one above the other to right of center top.
39. Deleted: "fruits"
40. Original opening deleted: "The" ; inserted: "The fruit of the out of the [*preceding three words del.*]." . "s" cancelled in "Apples"
41. Inserted before "orange"
42. Deleted: "the" There are three dots above the dash.
43. Deleted: "I thought every spear arose out the manure of diseases"
44. Deleted: "for" ; inserted, "for" "? probably" "[*del.*]?perhaps" on a line above " . . . [*del.*] for" and "every" . Question marks above words.
45. See below in back-to-front sequence, p. 291.
46. One stub remains. The inscription is verse. Page [*34*] cancelled with a vertical line.
47. Deleted: "some" ; inserted: "a single one" on a line above "me . . . of"
48. Deleted: "vile"
49. Deleted: "continually each discharge relieve themselves up"
50. Space for one line left vacant. Deleted line follows space: "How can you keep sound you quadrupeds that feed upon crop [*preceding four words del.*] I see you are"
51. Deleted: "will" ; inserted above: "cannot" ; undeleted "not" not printed here.
52. Deleted: "myself"
53. Deleted: "and"
54. See below in back-to-front sequence, p. 292.
55. Top half of leaf clipped off. Leaf cancelled with a vertical stroke. Two lines cancelled separately: "I am in fear" "I do not believe"
56. Deleted: "the earth"
57. Deleted: "buried" ; inserted: "resolved back" on a line above "[*del.*] buried" and "in"
58. Deleted: "I"

[*30; 31*[59]][60]Behold![61]
This is the compost[62] of billions of diseased premature[63] corpses,
Perhaps every[64] mite has once formed part of a sick person
Yet behold![65]
The grass grows upon the prairies!
[*28; 29*[66]][67] Behold the[68] regular[69]
Yet[70]
The bean bursts[71] noiselessly through the ground
Yet the delicate spear of the onion pierces[72] faithfully upward[73]
The[74] apple-blossoms break from their buds[75]
The resurrection of the wheat appears with pale visage[76] out of its graves,
The tinge awakes over[77] willow and the mulberry[78] awake,[79]
[*26; 27*[80]][81] Buds[82] swiftly form upon the vines
The she[83]-birds[84] build[85] nests or brood on[86] them,—the he-birds carol on the trees, mornings and evenings,

59. See above, p. 288.

60. Cancelled with vertical stroke. Two lines separately cancelled: "I do not [*preceding two words del.*] am [*ins. above* [*del.*] "do not"] amazed how the earth can remain so [*three words del.*] vital and calm" "I do not [*del.*] think see how" . Deleted: "Billions of" inserted above: "Behold!"

61. Deleted: "Here is this" ; inserted above: "This is the"

62. Deleted: "are"

63. Inserted on a line above "deceased"

64. Deleted: "grain" ; inserted above: "mite"

65. Deleted: "the shorn earth!" ; deleted at beginning of next line: "Behold how" ; Capital inserted on "the"

66. See above in verse sequence, p. 288.

67. Cancelled with vertical line.

68. Deleted: "fibred trun"

69. "Yet . . . upward" moved down on arrow.

70. Written over [*illeg.*]

71. Deleted: "faithfully" ; inserted above: "noiselessly"

72. Inserted and deleted: "noiselessly" ; inserted above "spears" : "faithfully"

73. Deleted: "to" . Line moved down as noted above. Beginning of new line deleted: "Yet" before "The . . . apple-blossoms . . ."

74. Deleted: "delicate"

75. Line deleted: "appear in May," . Line deleted: "Yet The early wheat puts its re"

76. Deleted: "in its the field"

77. Preceding three words inserted on a line above "willow and the"

78. Deleted: "early"

79. Deleted: "early"

80. See above in verse sequence, p. 288.

81. Leaf cancelled with a vertical stroke. Deleted: "The bot"

82. Deleted: "bud from" following "Buds" ; inserted: "swiftly form upon" on a line above "[*del.*] bud from" . New line cancelled: "The dews rains of April"

83. "She-" inserted on a line above the wordspace between "The . . . birds"

84. Deleted: "of morning and evening, carol"

85. Deleted: "their"

86. Deleted: "their eggs" ; inserted: "them" above "eggs"

The[87] young of[88] poultry break through the hatched eggs,
The[89] new born of animals appear—[90] the calf [*24; 25*[91]][92] is dropt[93] from the cow and the colt from the mare,
[*22; 23*[94]][95] O I am terrified at the earth—it is[96] that calm and patient![97]
It[98] grows[99] such sweet things out of such corruption,
[*20; 21*] It[1] turns so stainless on its axis with[2] all those successions of diseased corpses,
It distills[3] such winds and perfumes out of[4] such infused fætor,
It renews[5] with such unwitting[6] looks its[7] prodigal annual sumptuous[8] crops,
It gives such divine materials to men, and receives such leavings[9] at last!

[*37; 36–35 stubs; 34*[10]][11] An item for conversation everywhere— /

To be simple, nature, as *native as animals are native*—dismissing all the chat, talk of business or money, meaningless talk, criticizing acquaintances and their faults—

To be silent unless something must be said that cannot be left unsaid.

Never to attempt to be witty, or strive after effects——*not one anyhow*

To dismiss the usual amiable aquiescence also—

87. Deleted: "animals young" before "young"

88. Deleted: "fowls a" ; inserted: "poultry" above "fowls"

89. Deleted: "animals" ; inserted: "new born of" on a line above [*del.*] "animals" and "an" in "animals"

90. Deleted: "the" "from" "cow" "the cow"

91. See above in verse sequence.

92. Three quarters of leaf torn out. Cancelled with a vertical stroke. New line deleted: "The" "The" under "mare,"

93. Written over "dropped"

94. See above, p. 287.

95. Page cancelled with a vertical line. Two lines or parts of lines cancelled: "Yet" , "You are very patient"

96. Deleted: "so" ; inserted above: "that"

97. Line deleted: "It [*del.*] does gives such [*del.*] things [*ins.*] ?values to men and receives these what they make themselves [*preceding five words del.*] such leavings bring [*preceding three words ins. above*] at last!"

98. Deleted: "receives those foul corruptions and" ; inserted and deleted: "covers up such" on a line above "[*del.*] receives these"

99. Deleted: "blossoms and grass thence"

1. Deleted: "never tires of" ; inserted: "turns so stainless on its axis with [*del.*] for all" above "[*del.*] never" and "those"

2. Deleted: "for" between "with . . . all"

3. Deleted: "such" "its" ; inserted: "such" on a line above "its"

4. Deleted: "such bequeathed maladies," ; inserted: "such infused" on a line above "such bequeathed"

5. Deleted: "so faithfully"

6. Inserted on a line above "ch" in "such" and "l" in "looks"

7. Deleted: "su"

8. Inserted on a line above "ual" in "annual" and "crops"

9. Deleted: "in return" ; inserted: "at last"

10. See above, p. 289.

11. WW returns to rectos but continues with the notebook upside down.

[*33; 32*[12]][13] O Mother did you think there could ever be a time when I might not—

I walk forth amid the calmness of grass and foliage /

But after a little time I will return among men—

12. See above, p. 289.

13. Lines widely spaced. These lines do not survive in any printed version of "This Compost," but are shown to be part of the original sketches by the sketch in Duke (7, #14). See Manuscript Variorum.

The Old-Fashioned Keel-Boats.

Manuscript in Duke (73). Inscribed in black pencil on white wove scrap, approx. $9^{15}/_{16}$" x $7\frac{1}{2}$", on which are also pasted two unidentifiable newspaper clippings, one dated Wednesday evening, June 19, "Carrying the Mails to California." The other discusses the old-fashioned keel boat of the Mississippi. Of possible years for the clipping, 1857 seems most likely. First printed *N&F,* 79 (Pt. II, #13; *CW,* IX, 57).

The old-fashioned keel-boats and keel-boatmen have, of course, almost disappeared with steamboating.— Still they are occasionally to be seen West, North, on the streams of Kanada, &c

Paul Jones Bore.

Manuscript in Virginia (Barrett). Inscribed in pencil on verso of Williamsburgh tax blank. "Audobon" is WW's spelling. At foot of leaf, upside down, is "Names," probably a heading for other matter. This was written in 1857 or later. First printed in *N&F,* 118 (Pt. III, #'s 115, 116; *CW,* IX, 137–138).

Paul Jones bore for his banner on the Bon Homme Richard, a rattlesnake with 13 rattles—and the motto, "Dont tread on me"—

Audobon proposed the wild turkey as the ensign of America—he says in its native woods, either[1] in flight or perched, it is magnificent bird.

1. Inserted on a line above "in"

A Talent for Conversation.

Manuscript in NYPL (Berg). Inscribed in black ink on white wove scrap 1½" x 7½". Corners trimmed. A note in an unknown hand dates it 1880, but the writing and fine-nibbed pen suggest an earlier date. Further, this sort of moralizing, while very Whitmanesque, belongs to his journalizing of the 1840s through the 1860s. First published *N&F,* 175 (Pt. IV, #106; *CW,* X, 29).

A talent for conversation—Have you it? If you have, you have a facile and dangerous tenant in your soul's palace.—

The Regular Time.

Manuscript not found. Text from *N&F,* 122 (Pt. III, #135; *CW,* IX, 145–146). Bucke prints "The good hostess" and "? seems perpetually goading me" with this MS. Although "The regular time" and "The good hostess" are possibly related, the first exists as a separate manuscript scrap. "? seems perpetually goading" bears no apparent relation to the others. Possibly the two notes on domestic economy bear some relation to a proposed "Poem descriptive of a good housekeeper" ("Rule in all addresses," 1850?) The writing in "The good hostess" is in WW's small, regular early script suggesting a date in the late 1840s or 1850s.

The regular time for baking bread is *one hour.*

The Good Hostess.

Manuscript in NYPL (Berg). Inscribed in black pencil on white laid scrap, 1½" x 4". Blue rules ⅜" apart. For first printing in *N&F,* 122, see "The regular time." The small regular writing suggests a date in the 1840s or 1850s.

The good hostess that could always make fine apple dumplings, except once when she had grand company, and mixed[1] her flour up so rich that[2] it all cooked to tatters in the pot—

1. Deleted: "them" ; inserted: her flour" above "[*del.*] them" and "up"
2. Deleted: "they" ; inserted above: "it"

The World Studies.

Manuscript in LC (63, sheet #297). Inscribed in black ink on white wove paper, 5⅞" x 7¾". Blue rules ½" apart on recto. WW probably wrote this late in the 1850s.

The world studies the portrait, the Book; but here is the living original—Here is

Broadaxe.

Manuscript in Duke (7, #13). Inscribed in black pencil on white paper, approx. 13" x 8". Ruled. Inscribed with opening paragraph followed by three columns separated by vertical lines. Entries separated by rules, here indicated by slashes. Suggestions for "Song of the Broad-axe" (1856). See also *"Bloom."* Date is late 1855 early 1856.

Broadaxe—First as coming in the rough ore out of the earth.— Then as being smelted and made into usable shape for working—then into some of the earlier weapons of the axe kind.— battleaxe—headsman's axe—carpenter's broadaxe—(process of making, tempering and finishing the axe,)—*inquire fully* [1]

Use of the Broadaxe
in cutting away masts when the ship is on her beamends /
in hewing the great timebers for the oldfashioned houses and barns /
passage describing the puttin up of a goodstyled logcabin in the western woods—the whole process—joining the logs—the camping—the fun—the axe /
The silvan woodman or woodboy /
The cutting down of an unusually large and majestic tree—liveoak or other—for some kelson to a frigate or first class steamship— (what wood is the kelson generally?) /
procession of[2] portraits of the different users of the axe—the raftsman, the lumberman, the antique warrior, the headsman, the butcher, the framer of houses, the squatter of the west,—the pioneer /[3]
founding of cities /
Make it the American emblem preferent to the eagle[4]
in ship building /
in cutting a passage through the ice /
the butcher in his slaughterhouse /
full picture the antique warrior always with his great axe—the brawny[5] swing-

1. End of opening paragraph.
2. Preceding two words inserted above "portraits" .
3. No entry between horizontal lines from left.
4. Entry in hanging indentation. End of first column.
5. Inserted above wordspace between "brawny" and "swinging"

ing arm—the clatter and crash on the helmeted head—the death-[6]howl and[7] quick tumbling body and the rush of friend and foe thither—the summons to surrender—the battering of castlegates and city gates— /
building wharves and piers /
full[8] picture of the pioneer /
the Roman lictor preceding the consuls /
the sacrificial priest—[9]Grecian, Roman and Jewish /
What in Scandinavia? [10]
all through the framing of a house—all through—the hewing of timbers—the knocking[11] the beams in their places—laying them regular— /
the framers wielding the axe—their attitudes standing—bending—astride the beams—as the frame is being raised—they on the posts or braces,—holding on—their hands hooked around the plate, the other arm wielding the axe— /

episodic in the cutting down of the tree—about what the wood is for—for a[12] saloon, for a ceiling or floor, for a coffin, for a workbox, a sailor's chest, a musical instrument, for firewood—for rich casings[13] or frames— /
in a terrible fire the use of the axe to cut down[14] connecting woodwork to stop the fire—the excitement—the fireman—the glare—the hoarse shouts, the flames—the red faces [*illeg.*]

6. Inserted above "howl"
7. Deleted: "[*illeg.*] falling raped"
8. Inserted above "of the"
9. Deleted: "both Grecian"
10. End of second column.
11. Written over [*illeg.*]
12. Deleted: "ship"
13. Deleted: "of"
14. Deleted: "the"

A Character.

Manuscript in Duke (74–75). Inscribed in black pencil on faded white wove paper, 9⅜" x 5⅞". Based on a clipping dated "Feb 1856." in WW's hand describing the Rev. Daniel Waldo, a Revolutionary veteran, who had been elected Chaplain of Congress. A number of other clippings on diet, longevity, and phrenology are pasted to it. On the same scrap is "Morality and talent." Written early in 1856. First printed *N&F,* 82 (Pt. III, #18); *CW,* IX, 62).

A Character

94 years old, keeps up with the times, reads the new literature, was a chaplain in the revolutionary army, an intimate acquaintance of Washington, confined in the sugar-house prison in New York City, hale and vigorous and sensible as a man of thirty—Was never sick.

Morality and Talent.

Manuscript in Duke (74–75). Inscribed in black pencil on faded white wove paper, 9⅜" x 5⅞". Pasted to it are a number of clippings on diet, longevity, and phrenology. One is dated "Feb 1856." by WW. O. S. Fowler (1809–1887) and his brother L. N. were eminent phrenologists. WW was attracted by their simplistic psychology and physiology and had his "bumps" read in 1849. Fowler and Wells distributed *LG* 1855 and published *LG* 1856. On same scrap is "A Character." The date is about 1856. *N&F,* 82 (Pt. III, #18); *CW,* IX, 62.

Morality and talent are affected more by food, drink, physical habits, cheerfulness, exercise, regulated or irregulated amativeness than is supposed.—O. S. Fowler.

All Others Have Adhered.

Manuscript in Duke (43, #14). Inscribed in black pencil on tan or faded pink paper, somewhat heavier than pink wrapper paper, 9¹/₆" x 5½". Horizontal lines and vertical cancellation line impressed faintly on verso. Writing is small, neat writing like that of 1850 MSS. Bucke dates it "about 1856." If this is a correct date, this and following MS show WW giving thought to his role as poet just after the publication of *LG* 1855. First printed *N&F,* 70–71 (Pt. II, #61–62; *CW,* IX, 36–37).

All others have adhered to the principle, and shown it, that the poet and savan form classes by themselves, above the people, and more refined than the people; I show that they are just as great when of the people, partaking of the common idioms, manners, the earth, the rude visage of animals and trees, and what is vulgar.— /[1]

The foreign theory is that a man or woman receives rights by grant, demise, or inheritance. The theory of These States is that humanity's rights belong to every man, every woman, in the inherent[2] nature of things, and cannot be alienated, or, if alienated,[3] must be brought back and resumed.—

1. Line full width of leaf.
2. Deleted: "and inalien"
3. Deleted: "may"

A Poem in Which Is Minutely Described.

Manuscript in Duke (17, #40). Inscribed in black ink on pink wove paper (probably wrappers from *LG,* 1855) approx. 10½" x 5¾". See "I Sing the Body Electric," Sec. 9 (1856) and "memorials." The paper and the contents indicate a date of late 1855 or early 1856. First printed *N&F,* 103 (Pt. III, #65), *CW,* VI, 106.

A poem in which is minutely described the whole particulars and ensemble of a *first-rate healthy Human Body*—it looked into and through, as if it were transparent and of pure glass—and now reported in a poem— /
Read the latest and best anatomical works /
talk with physicians /
study the anatomical plates /
also casts of figures in the collections of design /

Iron Works.

Manuscript in NYPL (Berg). Inscribed in black pencil on light tan or faded pink paper, probably *LG* 1855 wrapper stock, 10½" x 5½". First entry in hanging indentation. The source of "A Song for Occupations," sec. 5, ll. 108–109, which were added in 1856. Date late 1855 or early 1856. First printed *N&F,* 117 (Pt. III, #113; *CW,* IX, 135–136).

Iron works

There is a forge in the Adirondack mountains—the "Adirondack forge"— To get to it you land at Crown Point, on Lake Champlain and go back 40 miles /[1]

A forge would be a large rude building with from one to a dozen or more charcoal[2] fires—on which the ore is thrown, and melted—the iron runs down and settles at the bottom, like a bushel-basket-shaped lump—a "loup" or "loop," they call it—

The men are around these fires with huge crowbars—they have to tell the state of the melting by the "feel" of the ore and iron, with these crowbars. /

The forge-fires in the mountains[3] . . . the men around,[4] feeling the melt[5] with huge[6] crowbars,"

The[7] work of[8] colliers[9] and miners,

electro-plating[10]

1. This entry in hanging indentation.
2. Inserted above "fires"
3. Dash deleted; marks of suspension inserted.
4. Deleted: "trying" ; inserted above "[*del.*] trying" : "feeling"
5. Comma deleted; inserted and deleted: "feeling" above word space between "melt" and "with"
6. Inserted above "crowbars"
7. Inserted: "work of" above "colliers"
8. Deleted: "and"
9. Word set off by itself at some distance below and to right of preceding line.
10. Written well below and to right.

In—This Is the Earths.

Manuscript in Duke (8, #16). Inscribed in pencil on white wove scrap, approx. 7" x 6". As Trent *Cat.* suggests, probably the theme of "A Song of the Rolling Earth" (1856). No precise date can be assigned but the probability is late in 1855 or early in 1856. First printed *N&F,* 120 (Pt. II, #125; *CW,* IX, 141).

In[?][1] —This is the Earths word—the pervading sentiment or lesson is to be that the only good of learning the theory[2] of the fluency[3] and generosity and impartiality, largeness and exactitude of the earth is to use all those toward the theory of[4] character—human character

1. Well into left margin.
2. Deleted: "and" ; inserted: "of the" above "[*del.*] and"
3. Inserted as part of above insertion and deleted: "largeness, exa" above "fluency"
4. Preceding three words inserted above "toward character"

Most Poets Finish Single Specimens.

Manuscript in Boston. Inscribed on pink wove paper 10″ x 5½″ damaged slightly at left edge. First entry in black pencil, others in pale black ink. Second entry lettered rather than written. After the second entry WW pasted on a clipping describing the rise of literary nationalism in Hungary and the fund raised for the orphans of Michael Vörösmarty (1800–1855), a national poet. On the backing sheet the clipping is endorsed in black ink "Hungary" and in pencil "orphans of Vörösmarty, the greatest Hungarian poet. June, 1856" (printed separately by Bucke in *N&F,* 159 (Pt. VI, #21; *CW,* IX, 224).

The first entry was first printed *N&F,* 93 (Pt. III, #39; *CW,* IX, 87); the second *N&F,* 93 (Pt. III, #40; *CW,* IX, 87); the third *N&F,* 94 (Pt. III, #41; *CW,* IX, 88). Bucke relates "Most poets" to "Myself and Mine" (1860), ll. 18–19, and "Perfect Sanity" to "Song of the Answerer" (1856), sec. 2, ll. 71–72. WW wrote these between 1855 and 1856.

Most poets finish single specimens of characters.—I will never finish single specimens—; I[1] will shower them by exhaustless laws, as nature does, vindicating not only themselves but[2] successive productions out of themselves, greater and fresher continually /

Perfect Sanity
Divine Instinct
Breadth of Vision
Healthy rudeness of Body
Withdrawnness
Gayety
Sun-tan & Air-sweetness[3]

Heinrich Heine—(just dead) 1856[4] "Pictures of Travel."[5] (1856) portrait—leaning, sleeping head——poems, (as translated) seem to be fanciful and vivacious, rather ironical and melancholy with a dash of the poetical craziness

1. Deleted: "sh"
2. Written over [*illeg.*]
3. Preceding fifteen words printed in large italic letters in column.
4. Preceding three words inserted in pencil above word space between "*Heine*—" and "Pictures"
5. Trans. by Charles G. Leland, 1855.

Produce Great Persons.

Manuscript in Duke (27, #38). Inscribed in black pencil and ink on soft faded pink wove paper approx. 9¾" x 6½". On verso half-erased prose draft for "Song of the Answerer" (1856), sec. 2, ll. 60, 56, 57. (See *FC&I*, 32 and "undeniable might." On left side of leaf over part of inscription left intact is pasted a newspaper clipping summarizing English literary history from the death of Keats and Shelley to the appearance of Dickens in 1835. WW has noted names and dates down the right, erased, side of the leaf. At bottom a clipping annotated *"London Letter* N.Y. Tribune, July 12, '56" mentioning Sidney Dobell, Alexander Smith, and Coventry Patmore. The pink paper is leftover wrapper stock from LG 1855. Identification and first printings are in the notes. The date is 1856, but since *LG* 1856 appeared in September and the drafts of "By Blue Ontario's Shore" and "Song of the Answerer" are still prose, July may be too late. It is probable that having transferred the lines to another paper, WW erased the verso and used it as mounting for clippings he wanted to save. The date is thus early 1856.

Produce great persons and the producers of great persons . . . . all the rest surely follows.— What has[1] been but[2] indicated in other continents[3] in America must receive its[4] definite and numberless growth.[5] the time is arrived and the land got ready, and[6] every present age is to pass the sinewy lesson[7] and[8] add to it.—

Produce great persons . . . . (all) the rest surely follows— [?][9]. The time is arrived and the land got ready, for[?][10] the free growth of that which (the) other continents have[11] which has been indicated[12]

1. Inserted and deleted: "only" above wordspace between "has" and "been"
2. Inserted above "been"
3. Word lost under a blot.
4. Deleted: "natural" ; inserted: "definite" above [*del.*].
5. [*Illeg.*] which may be a deletion.
6. Deleted: "the" "cache [*final* [*del.*] "e" *may be* "each"] century helps"
7. Deleted: ".—"
8. Scrap of clipping (see headnote) covers "a" in "add"
9. Scrap of clipping covers last five letters of "follows"
10. Scrap of clipping covers first two letters of "for"
11. Preceding four words inserted above "has been" perhaps as an alternative reading.
12. These two paragraphs crystallized in the fine line, "Produce great Persons, the rest follows." "By Blue Ontario's Shore" (1856), sec. 3, l. 31. First printed in *N&F*, 97 (Pt. III, #52; *CW*, IX, 95).

Etymology—origin and derivation[13]
—distributes words into parts of speech, tenses, genders, &c /

Syntax—constructing words in a sentence— /

Prosody—accent versification, laws of harmony—[14]

Give[15] me something savage and luxuriant,

Give me[16] large, full-voiced, men[17]

Preterit—past—noting the past tense of a verb, as "I wrote."[18]

13. Following passage written below and in line with "—origin"
14. This and preceding entry first printed in *N&F,* 162 (Pt. IV, #27; *CW,* X, 5).
15. Deleted: "us" ; inserted: "me" above [*del.*]
16. Inserted above wordspace between "Give" and "large"
17. These two lines in black pencil. Extracted by Oscar Lovell Triggs and first printed in *CW,* III, 259.
18. First printed in *N&F,* 162 (Pt. IV, #27; *CW,* X, 5). See also "dithyrambic trochee."

Undeniable Might.

Manuscript in Duke (27, #38V). On recto "Produce great persons." Inscribed in black pencil and black ink as noted on pink wove paper, approx. 9¾" x 6½". The right half of the leaf is almost entirely erased and, moreover, overwritten with "Byron, born at Dover." Nevertheless, the early date and the close connection with "Poem of the Singers and of the Words of Poems" (1856) ("Song of the Answerer," sec. 2) make it worth printing. The material is another draft of the material of "Poet, bard, minstrel." At the bottom of the leaf are two clippings related to "Byron, born at Dover." The date is late 1855 or early 1856. First printed *FC&I,* 32. See illustration of "Byron, born at Dover."

undeniable might—These are some[1] of the varieties of singers:[2]

It is the[3] [*illeg.*][4] glory[5] [*illeg.*] and extract known[*?*] so [*erasure*][6] of things but behind the human race.—[7]

What always indicates?[8] the poet though he may be absorbed even in countries[9] for long portions of[10] time and in the[11] crowd of the pleasant ever[12] rising company of[13] singers.— The singers are[14] the[15] [*illeg.*] hours or minutes of the light or of[16] the[17] darkness but the poet is the[18] perfect light and darkness

1. Preceding four words incompletely erased under in "Byron born at Dover."
2. See "Poet, bard, minstrel" for a list of "varieties of singers."
3. Deleted: "greatest"
4. Deleted: "and"
5. Preceding four words incompletely erased.
6. Erasure. List of names in "Byron born at Dover" begins.
7. *FC&I* reads "but and the human race.—"
8. Question mark above word.
9. Deleted: "and"
10. Preceding two words inserted above "long . . . time"
11. Preceding three words incompletely erased under "Bulwer, Disraeli" in "Byron born at Dover."
12. Inserted above "pleasant"
13. Preceding three words incompletely erased under "Appearance of Carlyle 1827" in "Byron born at Dover."
14. Deleted: [*illeg.*]
15. Preceding two words incompletely erased.
16. Preceding four words incompletely erased.
17. Deleted: "night" ; inserted: "darkness"
18. Preceding three words incompletely erased under "1835 (then 23 years old)" in "Byron born at Dover." Deleted: "complete day and night.—" ; inserted: "perfect light and darkness"

Poet, Bard, Minstrel.

Manuscript in Duke (35, #27). Inscribed in pencil and black ink (as noted) on pink wove paper, 11⅞" x 5¾". Marks of sealing wax on left edge. At left of a line down the middle of the leaf is a column of kinds of singers; at the right of the line "The singers are welcome." Part of the latter is overwritten by "Milton—1608." The latter seems to be a continuation of "The singers are welcome" and the list of singers seems to fit after the first paragraph. However, the inserted "names" in "the singers are welcome" also refers to the list and the reference to singers may be a development of the contrast between poet and singer in "undeniable might." It is probable that each MS is a separate draft of the same essay. These were wittten late in 1855 or early in 1856. First printed *FC&I,* 31.

Poet, bard, minstrel[1]
Songster and Songstress
Rhymester
Versifyer
jongleur
troubadour
Singer[2]
Mystic-singer,
ballad-singer
prose-singer
froth-singer
thrift-singer
moral-singer
song-singer
droll-singer
fable-singer
love-singer
wisdom singer
sea-singer
wit-singer
passion-singer
parlor-singer
echo-singer

1. Written side by side.
2. Preceding entries in ink, succeeding in black pencil.

golden-singer
silver-singer
law-singer
head-singer
heart-singer[3]

The singers are welcome [*illeg.*] most [*illeg.*] poet [*illeg.*][4] The singers do not live long—[5] only the poet lives long.—[6] The singers are [*illeg.*][7] and in most ages plentiful; but vast and rare is the day, and divine is the place, that brings forth a poet.—Not every century nor every five centuries[8] contains such a day, nor does every nation hold such a place. (names)[9] They These[10] may[11] have ostensible names,[12] —but[13] the name of each[14] of them is one of the singers.—The name of poet is reserved till it is taken by

3. A vertical line the length of the leaf separates the two columns.
4. Several lines of erased pencil inscription under "Milton—1608." See headnote.
5. Deleted: "only poet" ; inserted: "—only the poet"
6. Deleted: "It [*illeg.*]"
7. Overwritten.
8. Deleted: "includes" ; inserted: "contains" above "includes"
9. Inserted above. Possibly refers to preceding list.
10. Written above "they" as alternate.
11. Deleted: "taken superior" ; inserted: "have ostensible" above "taken superior"
12. Deleted: "or have them bestowed"
13. Deleted: "their" ; inserted: "the" above "their"
14. Deleted: "that"

And There, Further South.

Manuscript in Duke (15, #36). Inscribed on ledger paper, 4" x 8" in pencil with black ink emendations. First printed in *CW,* III, 284. The writing suggests the 1850s.

And there, further south [1]The[2] early negro at daylight[3] calling his[4] brethren together by[5] the sound of the Carolina yell,[6]

1. Preceding four words inserted in black ink above "the early"
2. Deleted in black ink: "laughing" ; inserted in black ink: "early" above "laughing" . Uppercase "The" not reduced.
3. Preceding two words inserted above "negro calls"
4. Deleted: "—I hear th"
5. Deleted: "to"
6. Deleted in black ink: "to go [*ins. and del.*] ga in a body [*del.*] th gaily[?] to work—"

American American.

Manuscript in LC (Feinberg #618). Inscribed in pencil in two columns on irregular scrap of pink paper, 3¼″ x 4½″. On verso: "been born all" (not printed). The paper suggests a date of 1855 or 1856.

American[1]

American Lectures
New sermons
America-Readings—Voices Walt Whitman's Voices[2]

Narratives tell address elocution primary—primer

1. On following line deleted: "States S"
2. End of left-hand column.

Japanese Women.

Manuscript not found. Text from Traubel, I, 36. Traubel picked up the scrap at the foot of the stove where WW had been burning MS on April 14, 1888. The first sentence is an addition in pencil; the remainder of the text is in ink. "Comparison" and "Self-Esteem" are phrenological terms, which suggests an early date. "From Comparison to Self-Esteem" means "from front to back," such being the locations of the respective "organs." Traubel dated it in the 1850s. First printed Traubel.

Japanese women (mothers) shave their eyebrows

Eighty millions of Tartars may shave the top of the head from Comparison to Self-Esteem, and so on down to the ears; and this may be done for thirty centuries, and be one of the institutions of the Empire. But if a man appears at the end of that time in whose eyes the custom is unnatural and therefore ungraceful, this man will be none the less right because he is denied by a hundred generations, whose coronal fronts were well scraped, and whose pig tails hung down behind.

Man Boy Child.

Manuscript in Duke (7, #14). Inscribed in black pencil in columns on four white wove scraps of varying sizes mounted on two sheets of green paper, probably *LG* 1855 wrapper. On rectos, lines for "This Compost" (1856) beginning "O Mother, did you think." On green paper is "The American people." On versos lists of words used for "I Sing the Body Electric," sec. 9 (1856). First printed *N&F,* 172 (Pt. IV, #84; *CW,* IX, 22–23).

man
boy
child
infant
youth
young man
old man
ami
brother
father /[1]
woman
wife
mother
daughter, sister
amie
aunt,[2]
[2][3]-head
-neck -hair
-ears
iris of the eye[4]
eyes
fringe[5]
nose—nostrils[6]
mouth

1. End of first column. Vertical line the length of the leaf.
2. End of first leaf. At right, parallel with sides of leaf: "1776—to 7" "56—57"
3. Dash or tick.
4. Written opposite "ears"
5. Written opposite "eye"
6. Written opposite "nose"

lips
tongue
teeth[7]
throat
chin
cheeks
temples
eyebrows
eyelashes
forehead
shoulder (shoulder-blade scapula?[8]
elbow
?upper half arm
?lower half arm[9]
wrist
arm-pit[10]
arm-sinews
arm-joints
arm bones
hand
palm
thumb
knuckles
forefinger
finger-points
finger-nails
finger-joints/[11]
breast—breast-bone
breast muscle
ribs[12]
breast-side
back
spine
hips
man-nuts

7. Opposite the succeeding three terms, parallel with sides of leaf: "1856
1776
———
80"
8. Preceding parenthesis and three words written opposite "shoulder"
9. Preceding question mark and three words wirtten opposite "upper half arm"
10. Deleted term: "arm" . Succeeding three terms joined by a brace at left.
11. End of first column. Line the length of the leaf.
12. Written opposite "breast muscle"

thighs
man-balls[13]
man-root
thigh-strength
knee-pan
?upper half leg
?lower half[14] knee
[*illeg.*] leg-finger [?]
leg-fibres
ankle
instep
foot-ball
toes—toe-joints /[15]
skull-frame
brain, (in folds)
spine-hinges and the marrow
hip-muscle
rings of the windpipe
stomach-sac
belly
bowels, sweet and clean
lung-sponges
liver
[3] tympanum of the ear
roof of the mouth
motion of the tongue
voice
articulation of words,
whispering
shouting aloud
tears
weeping,
laughter,
love-looks
love-risings
broad[16] breast-front
ample chest
albumen
arteries
veins

13. Written opposite "thighs"
14. Preceding five words and question marks all on same line.
15. Short line. "toe-joints" written opposite "*toes*"
16. Inserted above "breast"

nerves,
Digestion
pulse
sweat
food
drink
sexuality
health-[17]/
heart
heart-throbs,
blood
veins
list of bones—large and small
skin
freckles
lungs
breathing in and out
ankle-sockets
thigh-sockets
neck-[18]slue
poise of hips
feet
heel
tendon
jaw
jaw-hinges
sleep
running walking
[*4*]sympathies
heart-valves
?palate-valves
nipples
womb
teats

17. Remainder of compound word clipped off. End of first column. Line the length of the leaf.

18. Deleted: [*illeg.*]

Free Cider.

Manuscript in LC (Feinberg #1053). Inscribed in black pencil on recto and verso of white wove slip, approx. 3¼" x 7¾" torn from larger sheet. Brown rules 5/16" apart. The writing suggests this was written in the 1850s.

[*1*] *Free Cider.*—It was customary on Long Island in the country fifty years ago for any one going along with his team, to stop where he knew the place, and without asking any permission to go in and down the cellar, and help himself to cider— Cider was the perpetual drink /

Long Island Character.—Draw the Long Island character different from the New England—the Middle states—or any of the[1] Southern states.— (over)

[2] *Draw a Portrait of an ordinary "great man" and the ambitions of his life* — He is classically education—he is a "perfect gentleman," and associates with "gentlemen".— He goes into "business"—he travels to Europe—is introduced to the courts—he writes a book—perhaps two or three—he is elected to the legislature or Congress—he makes a fortune—he is a well known and highly respected "public character."/

You fired the shot — now I bring them back to you
  Here are the blows you gave me.—

1. Deleted: "old"

Boldness— Nonchalant Ease.

Manuscript in Duke (46, #23). Inscribed in black pencil on slip of white wove paper. The small handwriting is that of the 1840s or 1850s, but it probably was written after 1855. First published *N&F,* 57 (Pt. II, #15; *CW* IX, 7).

Boldness— *Nonchalant ease & indifference* To encourage me or any one continually to strike out alone— So it seems good *to me* —This is my way, *my* pleasure, *my* choice, *my* costume, friendship, amour, or what not.—

Book-Learning Is Good.

Manuscript in Duke (25, #28). Inscribed in ink and pencil on irregular piece of pinkish tan wove paper, approx. 9¾" x 5¾". Cf. "In metaphysical points." For other references to "managing horses" see "memorials." The paper, handwriting, and the parallels to other writings suggest a date of about 1856. Printed in *N&F,* 58 (Pt. II, #20; *CW,* IX, 9–10).

Book-learning is good[1] let none dispense with it—but a man *may* be [?] of great excellence and effect with very little of it.— Washington had but[2] little—Andrew Jackson also—Fulton also.—[3] Frequently it stands in the way of real manliness and power Powerful[4] persons, and the[5] first inventors and poets of the earth,[6] never come from the depths of the schools—never.—[7] There is a man who is no chemist, nor linguist, nor antiquary, nor mathematician—yet he takes very easily the perfection of[8] those sciences, or of the belle lettres, and eats of the fruit of all.—[9] Erudition is[10] large low among the glories of[11] humanity.— I think if those who best embody it were collected together this day in the public assembly,[12] it would be grand.—[13] But the powerful unlearned persons are also grand./

1. Inserted: "let none dispense with it—" on a line above "is . . . may"
2. Deleted: "the ordinary share" ; inserted: "little" above "ordinary"
3. Deleted: "The most" ; inserted: "Frequently . . . and power" on a line above "[*del.*] most" and "Powerful . . . inventors"
4. Capital "P" inscribed over lowercase in "powerful"
5. Deleted: "grand" ; inserted above: "first"
6. Deleted: "have not been" ; inserted above: "never come from the"
7. Deleted: "Books are not to be passed by, read them, but read th[?]"
8. Deleted: "any or all"
9. Inserted and deleted: "Yet" above ".—"
10. Deleted: "not the least of" ; inserted above: "large low among". Neither "large" nor "low" appears to be deleted.
11. Deleted: "the earth" ; inserted above: "humanity.—" . Redundant ".—" after "[*del.*] earth" not shown.
12. Deleted: "rooms,"
13. Inserted on two lines above "be grand.—" to the right edge of leaf : "But the great [*preceding two words del.*] the powerful [*preceding two words ins. above*] unlearned persons are also grand." Cf. the phrase "powerful uneducated persons" in the 1855 Preface, 715, l. 205, and in "By Blue Ontario's Shore" (1856), sec. 14, l. 238.

[14]But all books-knowledge is important as help to [?][15] one's personal qualities, and the use and power of a man.— Let a man learn to run, leap, swim[16] wrestle, fight,[17] to take good aim,[18] to manage horses—to speak readily and clearly and without mannerism—to feel at home among common people, and able to[19] hold his own in[20] terrible positions.— With these

14. Trial start "Book-learning" not deleted, not shown. Inserted: "But all books-knowledge is" on a line above "Book-learning is important" . Redundant "is" not deleted, not shown.

15. Right edge having been trimmed, this word is not in extant MS. Bucke's reading, "helping" , is also possible, though it is evident from Bucke's occasional bracketing, that the MS then was in the same condition.

16. Inserted above "wrestle"

17. Deleted: "—to" ; inserted: "to"

18. Deleted: "—to" ; inserted above: "to"

19. Deleted: "take care of himself" ; inserted: "hold his own" on a line above "care of himself"

20. Deleted: "any" ; inserted above: "terrible"

Sustenance for the Great.

Manuscript in Virginia (Barrett). Inscribed in black ink on pink wove paper, 8⅜" x 5⅛". Bucke's note says that it was written about 1856, which agrees with WW's use of the pink wrappers around this time and the reference to America's now being eighty years old. Printed in *N&F,* 102 (Pt. III, #64; *CW,* IX, 106).

[1] Sustenance for the [2] great geniuses of the world is always plenty, and [3] the main ingredients of it [4] are perhaps always the same.— Yet nothing ever happened to [5] former heroes, sages and poets,[6] so inspiring to them, so fit to shine resplendent light upon them [7] and make them [8] original creators of works of newer and [9] nobler grander, as the events of the last eighty years;— I mean the Advent of America.—

1. Deleted: "The" ; capital "S" inscribed over lowercase in "sustenance"
2. Deleted: "great"
3. Deleted: "some of it"
4. Deleted: "ma"
5. Deleted: "old" ; inserted above: "former"
6. Deleted: "ha"
7. Inserted and deleted: "surpassing all of" on a line above "them as the" ; inserted and enclosed in irregular line: "and make them . . . nobler grander" on a line above to the right edge and down.
8. Deleted: [*illeg.*]
9. Deleted: [*illeg.*]; inserted: "nobler"

Make the Works.

Manuscript in Duke (46, #23). Inscribed in black pencil on scrap of faded white wove paper, approx. 3¼" x 4⅜". A crease, signs of stitching, and a margin at left suggest a notebook. Entries in hanging indentation. For literary comment see Furness, 11, 535. First published *N&F,* 57 (Pt. II, #16); *CW,* IX, 7). Bucke dates it 1856, which is certainly the latest probable date.

Make *the Works*[1]—
Do not go into criticisms or arguments at all
Make full-blooded, rich, flush, natural *Works*[2]—
Insert natural things, indestructibles, idioms, characteristics, rivers, States, persons, &c
Be full of *strong sensual germs*.—

1. *"Works"* printed and larger than written text.
2. *"Works"* printed and larger than written text but not so large as that in first sentence.

Put in a Passage.

Manuscript in Duke (48, #32). Inscribed in black pencil on green wove paper approx. 3″ x 6″. Not a vivid green, faded? to blue on verso. Upper and lower right corners clipped. Hanging indentation. WW insisted on the integrity of his text except under the temptation of Rossetti's refusal in 1868 to edit more than selections. The date of the MS might be any time in the late 1850s. Green paper may be from discarded wrappers from *LG* 1855. First printed *N&F,* 56 (Pt. II, #11; *CW,* IX, 6).

Put in a passage in some poem to the effect of denouncing and threatening whoever translates my poems into any other tongue without translating *every line* and doing it all without increase or diminution

Remember in Scientific.

Manuscript in Duke (17, #40). Inscribed in black pencil on pink wove paper approx. 4½" x 5". Pointing hand opposite each paragraph. First printed *N&F,* 55 (Pt. II, #2; *CW, IX,* 3).

Remember in Scientific and similar allusions—that the theories of[1] Geology, History[2] Language &c. &c. are continually changing—

Be careful to put in only what *must* be appropriate—centuries hence

1. Preceding three words inserted on a line above "Geology"
2. Inserted above "Language"

Cantaloupe. Muskmelon.

Manuscript not found. Text from *N&F,* 179 (Pt. IV, #139; *CW, X,* 36). No Cacique City is listed in modern or nineteenth-century gazetteers. No date can be assigned, but it probably was written before 1860 like the Bucke MS which can be dated.

Cantaloupe. Muskmelon. Cantabile. Cacique City.

Saturday, June 21.

Manuscript not found. Text from *N&F,* 84 (Pt. III, #22; *CW,* IX, 69). Bucke inserted "1856" in brackets after the date and "on" in brackets before "Leaves of Grass." Neither shown here. The date is probably 1856.

Saturday, June 21. It seems to be quite clear and determined that I should concentrate my powers *Leaves of Grass*—not diverting any of my means, strength, interest to the construction of anything else—of any other book.

(In Remarks.

Manuscript in Duke (7, #12V). Inscribed in pencil on white wove ruled paper approx. 4″ x 6″. The verso of a draft of "Great are the Myths" (1855), ll. 16–20. At the beginning of leaf, cancelled with several vertical lines:

> Are the prostitutes nothing? Are the mockers of religion nothing?
> ?(Does the light or heat pick out? Does the attraction of [*ins.*] gravity pick out? /

The date is possibly before 1855, but more probably 1856 or later. Verse section printed in *CW,* III, 272. *N&F,* 104 (Pt. III, #71; *CW,* IX, 109).

(In remarks on myself.
What they say of him
—he was just like other men—he shall not be singled out.
—one of the common

A New Doctrine.

Manuscript in Virginia (Barrett). Inscribed in pencil on pink wove paper, 9½" x 5⅞". Remnants of a clippping on verso. The pink wrapper, perhaps from the paperbound second issue of *LG* 1855, suggests a date between 1855 and 1857. First printed *N&F,* 71–72 (Pt. II, #65, #66; *CW,* IX, 38–39).

a new doctrine—leading feature—

—There is in the soul an instinctive test of the sense and actuality of any thing—of any statement of fact or morals.—*Let this decide.*— Does it not decide?/[1] Thus the soul of each man, woman, nation, age, or what not, realizes only what is proportionate to itself. /

For a new school (or theory) Let the test of any thing proposed in metaphysics be this instinct of the soul—this self-settling power.—

—First however, prepare the *body* it must be healthy, mature, clean, /[2]

Other writers poets[3] look on a laborer as a laborer, a poet as a poet, a President as a President, a merchant as a merchant—and so on.— He looks on the President as a man, on the laborer as a man—on the poet and all the rest, as men.—

1. The remainder of the paragraph is inserted between two horizontal rules the width of the text.

2. Rule across leaf.

3. Written above "writers"

I Do Not Expect.

Manuscript not found. Text from Christopher Morley's introduction to *Manuscripts, Autograph Letters First Editions and Portraits of Walt Whitman Formerly the Property of . . . Richard Maurice Bucke. . .* (NY: American Art Association Anderson Galleries, 1936), n. pag. (Cat. 4251). Morley writes by way of introduction to this quotation: "On the wall of the cabin where I write—it looks out into the woods of Walt's own Paumanok—is a pencil scrawl on a rectangle of green paper. It was written, I think, on a piece scissored from left-over stock of the green wrappers and end-papers of the 1855 Leaves. . . ."

I do not expect to see myself in the present magazines, reviews, schools, pulpits and legislatures—but presently I expect to see myself in magazines, schools, and legislatures—or that my friends after me will see me there.

We Suppose.

Manuscript in Virginia (Barrett). Inscribed in black ink on irregular white wove scrap approx. 8″ x 6¼″. Words trimmed at bottom. The small, smooth handwriting is that of the 1850s.

Like Mark Twain, WW knew the advantages of a striking appearance and the value of publicity, but he was more aggressive. He reviewed both the first and second editions of *LG* anonymously and attempted the same trick several times later in his career. He wrote publicity to be signed by his friends and kept a close eye on what they wrote about him. He lost no opportunity to supply friendly editors with news of his comings and goings. A close reading of the gossip columns of newspapers in New York, Washington, Philadelphia, and Camden, particularly after 1860, would probably turn up a large number of items he planted. A list of self-advertisements in these volumes follows:

Lafayette in Brooklyn, "Biographical Note," *"Walt Whitman,"* "Walt Whitman's second wind," "Memo," "Current Criticism," "WALT WHITMAN," "The Opening of the Piece," "(qu? To make a *Personal,"* "REAL AMERICAN RED MEN," "Whitman democrat" "The newspapers still," "WALT WHITMAN travels north," "WALT WHITMAN who has been," "A tip-top caricature," "IT HAS BEEN GOOD FUN," *"Washington as a central,"* "IS WALT WHITMAN'S POETRY," "Any thing like," "Wealth of Poets," "To getter up," "WHITMAN'S POEMS SUMM'D UP," "July, by the pond," "THE TWO OBJECTIONS See. W Davenport Adam's," "If the following presents," "In fancy picture in Harper's," "Two suggestion points," "for criticism," "How little posterity," *"Walt Whitman's birthday,"* "Jo Swinton," "I suggest inquiringly," *"doubtful* ab't," "pages 26 '7 '8 '9," "—the writers," "for *Motto* page 45," "Seems to me," "—though a big certificate," "A poet's 68th year," "Walt Whitman The generally," "A ¶ of specific," *"Walt Whitman to-day,"* "scraps memos excerpts."

First published *N&F,* 70 (Pt. II, #59; *CW,* IX, 35–36).

We suppose it will excite the mirth of many of our readers to be told that a man has arisen, who has deliberately[1] and insultingly ignored[2] all the other, the cultivated classes as they are called, and set[3] himself to work to write "America's first distinctive Poem," on the platform of[4] these same New York Roughs, firemen, the ouvrier class,[5] masons and carpenters, stage-drivers the Dry Dock boys,

1. Deleted: "rejected" ; inserted above: "and insultingly"
2. Past participle corrected to present and recorrected.
3. Past participle corrected to present and recorrected.
4. Inserted above the wordspace between "platform" and "these"
5. Single parenthesis deleted.

and so forth; and that[6] furthermore he[7] either is not aware of the existence of the[8] polite social[9] models, and the[10] imported literary[11] laws, or else he don't value them two cents for his purposes.

6. Inserted and deleted: "either" on a line above the wordspace between "that" and "he" ; inserted: "furthermore" on a line above "that" and "he" and the deletion.

7. Deleted: "does not seem to be" ; inserted above: "either is not"

8. Deleted: "regular"

9. Inserted on a line above "e" in "polite" and "m" in "models"

10. Deleted: "old" ; inserted above: "imported"

11. Corrected over [*illeg.*], possibly an accidental misspelling.

The Poem.

Manuscript in Trent (8, #17). Inscribed in black ink on green wove paper, 6⅛" x 4⅞". Either because the paper, probably wrapper stock for *LG* 1855, is soft or WW used a broad-nibbed pen, the writing is thicker than usual. The layout on the page is difficult to reproduce. On verso: "recommendation to the young men." As Trent *Cat.* points out, it suggests "Starting from Paumanok," l. 70, and "Mediums," l. 5, both 1860. Bowers however (xl), prints intermediate stages in which the theme has developed into early versions of the two poems. He dates these MS as possibly as early as before July 20, 1857. This MS must then be still earlier.

THE Poem) (? One grand, Eclipsing poem

Poem of Materials /

? several poems[1] Many poems on this model—the bringing together of the materials—*words, figures, suggestions*— —*things*— (words, as solid as timbers stone, iron, brick, glass, planks, &c)—[2]all with reference to main central idea ideas—[3] with powerful indications— / yet loose, fluid-like, leaving each reader eligible to form the resultant-poem for herself or himself.— /

leading *Chicago poem*

1 Written above "Many poems" . Question mark is written before both lines.

2. Initial single parenthesis deleted.

3. Written above "idea" . Rule drawn a quarter of the way across the page above "with" . [*illeg.*] deleted before "with"

On the Other Side.

Manuscript in Duke (47, #29). Inscribed in pencil on scrap of white wove paper with faint rules approx. ¼" apart on recto and verso. First printed in *CW,* IX, 191. The handwriting is that of the 1850s and the reference to the Collins Line places it before 1858, the year the Line ceased operations. The Erie Railroad, founded in 1851, was the longest railroad in the United States.

On the other side is[1] the "barbaric yawp" of a very different[2] poet—as different as a Collins steamship or[3] modern locomotive tearing[4] along the Erie railroad with its train of cars well filled with the men and women of to-day[5] is from the Lord Mayor of London's State barge or his[6] carriage with its[7] adorned slowness and its[8] pageantry and liveries—or as different as the strong and hearty life of the people is from the bookish life of cloisters,[9] and from the etiquet of[10] the English or French[11] courts.—With

1. Deleted: "Walt Whitman with his" ; inserted: "the" above the wordspace between "[*del.*] Walt" and "Whitman"
2. Deleted: "person" ; inserted above: "poet"
3. Preceding three words inserted on a line above "a . . . modern"
4. Deleted: "with its train of cars"
5. Preceding fourteen words inserted above "road [*in* "railroad"] . . . London's"
6. Preceding four words inserted on a line above "carriage with"
7. Deleted: "stately" ; inserted above: "adorned"
8. Deleted: [*illeg.*]
9. Deleted: "or" ; inserted above: "and from"
10. Deleted: "Victor" "St. James" ; inserted above "es" in "James" : "the"
11. Capital "F" inscribed over "fr"

This, or the Equivalent.

Manuscript in LC (# 63, sheet#302). Inscribed in black ink on scrap of blue Williamsburgh tax blank. The subject is probably poetry. The date is 1857.

This[1], or[2] the equivalent to this[3] is[4] already[5] advertised for, and must be supplied.— Let many,[6] no matter how many, try their hands at it—[7]the more the better;—and let[8] the contestants inspire each other, and bequeath themselves to each other, careful[9] less of passing judgments[10] and more of final judgments.

1. Capitalized over lowercase.
2. Deleted: "something"
3. Preceding five words (and the deletion) inserted on three lines above "this . . . is" in upper right corner.
4. Deleted (probably the original beginning): "But[?] work that is"
5. Deleted: "wanted," ; inserted: "advertised for," on a line above "[*del.*] wanted" and "and"
6. Deleted: "persons" ; inserted: ", no matter how many," on a line above "[*del.*] persons" and "their"
7. Inserted: "—the more the better;—" on a line above "it—. . . let" . Redundant dash not printed.
8. Deleted: "him or her who supplies it take the First due [*written above preceding word as alternate reading*] place" . Remainder of the sentence inserted in a smaller hand between deleted lines.
9. Deleted: "not" ; inserted above: "less"
10. Deleted: "but of future"; inserted above: "and more [*illeg. del.*] of final judgments.—" inserted on a line under "[*del.*] but of" . At bottom, clipped off, deleted: "[*illeg.*] These States [*illeg.*]." Deleted: "

A Poem Which More Familiarly Addresses.

Manuscript in Duke (15, #38). Inscribed in black ink on white laid paper, approx. 3 7/16" x 5", horizontal chainlines, conspicuous vertical texturing. Irregularly torn along right edge. Cf. "Poets to Come" and "Recorders Ages Hence" in *LG* 1860. There are no verbal parallels, but the similarities and the neatness of the handwriting would suggest this was written before 1860. Printed in *N&F,* 68 (Pt. II, #51; *CW,* IX, 31).

A poem which more familiarly addresses those who will, in future ages understand me,
(Because I write with reference to being far better understood then than I can possibly be now.)

What Cannot Meet All.

Manuscript in LC (63, sheet #299). Inscribed in pencil on scrap of white laid paper, 3⅞" x 5 13/16". Chain lines perpendicular to writing 1 3/16" apart. Poem on verso. Hanging indentation. Probably written in the 1850s.

What[1] cannot[2] meet[3] all discussions, and[4] open inquiries,[5]— What cannot invite itself[6] to be tried by the ensuing century or ten centuries

1. Deleted: "ever"
2. Deleted: "stand the"
3. Deleted: "any" ; inserted above: "all"
4. Inserted above "o" in "open"
5. Singular changed to plural; deleted: "and connect" ; inserted above: "—What cannot invite" ; "cannot" written above "invite"
6. Deleted: "cheerfully to the calibre of"

(Done Openly) Military Parade.

Manuscript not found. Text from Bucke, "Notes on the Text of 'Leaves of Grass,'" *Conservator* 7 (February, 1897), 186. No date can be assigned. It is placed here because many of Bucke's MS are early.

(Done openly) Military parade. Artllery salute of one war-ship to another. The white smoke from the guns of the fort, firing a salute.

Lect. (To Women.

Manuscript in LC sheet (#275). Inscribed in black ink on white laid paper, Approx. $3^{15}/_{16}'' \times 6^{9}/_{16}''$. Torn cleanly at top from another leaf. The writing suggests WW wrote this in the late 1850s. First printed in Furness, 63–64.

Lect.[1] (To Women[2]
Why should there be these modesties, and prohibitions that keep women from strong actual life—[3] from going about there with men[4]

I desire to say to you, and let you ponder well upon it that the fact that[5] under present arrangements, the love and comradeship[6] of a woman, of his wife, however welcome, however complete,[7] does not and cannot satisfy the[8] grandest[9] requirements of a manly soul for love and comradeship.— The man he loves, he often loves with more passionate attachment than he ever[10] bestows on any woman, even his wife.— Is it that the growth of love needs the free air—the seasons, perhaps more wildness, more rudeness? Why is the love of women so invalid? so transient?

1. At left margin, probably inserted.
2. Curved line at left and under title.
3. Deleted: "going"
4. Sentence inserted on two lines under "To Women"
5. Deleted: "as things are," "no man is" ; inserted: "under present arrangements" on a line above "[*del.*] as . . . m" in "man"
6. Preceding two words inserted on a line above "lov" and "of"
7. Deleted: "does not" ; inserted above and deleted: "never" ; inserted: "does not and cannot" above the deletions.
8. Deleted: "highest and f"
9. Deleted: [*illeg.*]
10. Deleted: [*illeg.*]

Death of an Aged Lover.

Manuscript not found. Text from *N&F,* 175 (Pt. IV, #105; *CW,* X, 29). The painter is unidentifiable. The "our neighbor" suggests a Brooklyn neighbor. No date can be assigned.

Death of an Aged Lover. Our neighbor N. the landscape painter is just dead.

It Was Not the Old Custom.

Manuscript not found. Text from *N&F,* 178 (Pt. IV, #126; *CW,* X, 34). No date can be assigned. The MS is printed in this place because many of Bucke's MS are early.

It was not the old custom (viz.: To abandon the Chief).

Frances Wright.

Manuscript in Duke (31, #10). Inscribed in black pencil on pink wove paper (corners clipped), 9½" x 5¾". No emendations. Frances Wright (1795–1852) was admired by both Walter Whitmans and WW spoke glowingly of her in his last years (Traubel, I, 79, 80; II, 135, 204–206, 445, 499, 500, 517). For her influence on WW see David Goodale, "Some of Walt Whitman's Borrowings," *AL,* X (May 1938) 202–213, and Allen, 138–139. Stovall, *AL,* XXVI, 350–351, suggests that the portrait may be the frontispiece of Amos Gilbert, *A Memoir of Frances Wright* (1855). Mrs. Rose was Ernestine Potowesky Rose (Mrs. William E.) (1810–1892), a feminist who, after marriage to a New York jeweller, lived in the US between 1836 and 1869. WW knew her for several years. See "[*illeg.*] Dick Hunt," "W. Whitman Portland av." "return my book," "Add*resses*." The paper suggests a date perhaps earlier than any of the above. First printed *N&F,* 114 (Pt. III, #107; *CW,* IX, 129–130).

Frances Wright Madame DArusmont
(talk with Mrs. Rose Feb. 9th, '57

Frances Wright was born in Scotland, of gentle lineage—parents died early—educated by uncles,—noblemen; was talented early—of free enquiring disposition—republican—wrote "A few Days in Athens" when 20 years old—Came to America—lectured—had to do with the "Free Enquirer," an atheistical weekly——was a noble, (but much scorned) woman—married D'Arusmont—the great error of her life—he coveted her property—thwarted her—kept exclusive possession of her child, a daughter; Frances had great wealth (Mrs. Rose says $150,000)—D'A. obtained all—even a second bequest left to Frances by a Scotch aunt—Frances had even to sue for a maintenance out of her own property—Judge allowed her $1000 a year—Frances died somewhere about 1853—a heart-broken, harassed woman—all her philanthropic schemes and ideas, coming to nought—(I like much her portrait—engraving—where she is represented seated—)

Municipal Legislation.

Manuscript in Duke (13, #31V). Inscribed in black pencil on white wove paper, 7¾" x 7¾". Blue rules ¾" apart. On recto "I am that angry half-grown boy." See *LG* MS Variorum and "Of a summer evening." The spirit is that of extreme Jacksonian *laissez-faire,* as is the deleted beginning "The best government." It is not the editorial, "Muncipal Legislation," published in the Brooklyn *Daily Times,* Dec. 1, 1858. The writing, however, suggests a date in the 1840s or 1850s.

Municipal legislation, inviting[1] examples[2] in high place, is always inclined to be too meddlesome, and be perpetually multiplying ordinances and restrictions.[*?*][3]

I recommend the[4] abolition of the[5] entire system of licenses or special permits[6] for any business,[7] no matter what.[8] (The control the City Government[9] over the[10] business operations of the citizens must be by general laws, bearing equally upon all, and not by special laws, giving one man or set of men the privilege of engaging in any employment which the rest are prohibited from.)—[11] (Every man and woman[12] has the[13] right free of any special[14] taxes or licences [*?*][15] to engage in

1. Trent *Cat.*, 13, here reads "unitg," which perhaps makes better sense than this reading, but two dots are clearly visible above the "picket-fence" of the first letters.
2. Deleted: "from" ; inserted above: "in"
3. Deleted: "and The best govern" . The last word of the sentence is partly concealed by a dealer's binding.
4. Inserted and deleted: "entire" above "abo" in "abolition"
5. Deleted: "whole" ; inserted above: "entire"
6. Preceding three words inserted above "for any"
7. Deleted: "whatever" . Period and dash not deleted. Inserted above: "no matter what." Comma preceding insertion possibly inserted.
8. The MS here has "tr down" but no point of insertion is indicated. Deleted: "Whatever" ; inserted above: "(The"
9. Deleted: "has"
10. Inserted and deleted: "operations" on a line above "the [*del.*] buying" ; deleted: "buying"
11. The single parenthesis, which is written over the dash, appears to be a later insertion, as does the one before "Every"
12. Inserted and deleted: [*illeg.*] above "man"
13. Deleted: "legal"
14. Inserted: "free of any special [*ins. above* "taxes"] licenses"
15. Preceding seven words inserted. End of last word concealed by a dealer's binding.

any avocation or business whatever,[16] responsible afterward to the authorities for[17] his or her malpractice—the cartman or driver, for instance, when he obstructs the public[18] thoroughfares—the physician for[19] gross injuries to a patient—the tavernkeeper for[20] any habitual nuisance or infringement on the decorum of the neighborhood

16. Deleted: "without" "free of any special license; and"
17. Deleted: "any" ; inserted: "his or her" on a line above "[*del.*] any" and "ma" in "malpractice"
18. Deleted: "street"
19. Deleted: [*illeg.*]. Very heavily crossed out.
20. Deleted: "habitu" "keeping"

Col. Parker's Squa Mother.

Manuscript in LC (#79, sheet #736). Inscribed in black ink on one fold of white laid paper approx. 10¼" x 8". Blue lines ½" apart on verso. Each entry in hanging indentation. The general topic seems to be dress. Possibly WW was contemplating a lecture, for LC 79, sheet #740, is a clipping describing the conflict between Gregory VII and Henry IV and the appearance of the latter barefoot and in his shirt at Canossa. WW endorsed the clipping: "(Lecture episode or *picture* Impressive picture of *moral* power subverting physical power /? remember the incident of Mr Sanford in his plain dress, and plain coach going to the reception at the French Court —? (Tuilleries)— /if used of course should come in very apropos, and be short, specific, [*del.*] plain graphic and plain." Colonel E.S. Parker (1828–1895) was a Seneca Indian and military secretary to Grant. He aided in George Whitman's release (*Corr.*, I, 253*n*23). His mother long refused to wear a hat. Henry S. Sanford (1823–1891) was at the American legation in Paris 1849–1854. When James Buchanan was Minister to London he forced the British court in 1853 to accept him in plain dress. The matter of American diplomatic dress, which roused much controversy here and abroad, was settled by Secretary of State Edward Marcy's "Dress Circular" of 1856.

Col. Parker's squa mother, & the bonnet.[1] Franklin at Versailles in 1777–8— Minister Sanford at the French Court in 1849? 48? 50? 51?/ What are the court costumes of different courts, European, Asiatic, &c? / Mr. Buchanan & Queen Victoria—

1. Each phrase in this MS is in column. Subtopics are separated by a short rule from the left.

Catholics Have Now Such Numbers.

Manuscript not found. Text from Furness, 40–41, which does not identify the source. Furness, 218*n*58, says, "This entry was evidently made for a speech to raise funds for a Protestant hospital or dispensary, as it is followed by memoranda of 'the Disp in 145 Court St.' which was opened 'on the 17th March 1856.' He notes various cases which had been cared for there: 'one of a boy, whose leg was cut off at the heel, case of small-pox 7 times,' etc." The date is in the late 1850s.

Catholics have now such numbers as to place any enterprise within their power. The laity have long desired an opp to aid such a work—the habit of giving only enhances the desire to give. The more we give to the poor of Christ, the more blessed will we be.

No I Do Not Choose.

Manuscript in Duke (47, #27). Inscribed in black ink on verso of blue Williamsburgh tax blank, 8³/16" x 7". The date is late 1857 or later. First printed *N&F*, 59 (Pt. II, #27; *CW*, IX, 11–12).

No I do not choose to write[1] a poem on a lady's sparrow, like Catullus—or on a parrot, like Ovid[2]—nor love-joys[3] like Anacreon—nor even like Homer—nor the Siege of Jerusalem like Tass—nor nor as Shakespeare—[4] (What have these themes to do in America? or what are they to us except as[5] beautiful studies, reminiscencing?)

All those are good—they are what they are—I[6] know they should not have been different—I do not say I will furnish[7] any thing better.—[8] But instead I will aim at high immortal marks—American, the[9] robust[10] large manly character—the perfect woman—the illustriousness of sex, which I will celebrate—

1. Deleted: "of"
2. Capital over lowercase "o"
3. Initial letter written over [*illeg.*]
4. Parenthetical phrase in pencil inserted in small writing in space after "Shakespeare"
5. Inserted.
6. Deleted: "do not say" ; inserted: "know"
7. Initial letter inscribed over [*illeg.*]
8. "Take on up*" before "But" indicates that the preceding twenty-seven words were inserted at the top of the page and preceded by a matching asterisk and should be brought down.
9. Deleted: "perfect"
10. Deleted: "and"

(Do Not This Enough.

Manuscript not found. Text from facsimile in Oscar Lovell Triggs, "The Growth of 'Leaves of Grass,' " *CW,* X, 128. The writing is a scrawl; the left margin is very irregular. Since the thought and tone are in the oracular early manner, it is placed here.

(Do not this enough for a poem[1]
Whoever[2] helps to a good thing for life here,[3] for the life of an individual, or of a city, or of a nation—[4]or helps to a good thing for the continual spiritual[5] life of that[6] individual of all those individuals, for the unknown spheres for myriads of years, perhaps for endless years—

1. Written at upper right with curved line at left and below.
2. Deleted: "does" ; inserted above: "helps to"
3. Deleted: [*illeg.*]
4. Deleted: "he does" ; inserted above: "or helps to"
5. Inserted and deleted below "spiritual" : "over"
6. Deleted and inserted: "that"

Feb. 25th '57.

Manuscript in Trent (45, #18). Black pencil on pink paper now faded to tan approx. 10⅛" x 5½". Actually two scraps, the lower ("Put in my poems") approx. 2¼". On verso are a few fragments of clipping about a Russian poet (?). The quotations on the first scrap are in hanging indentation, with quotation marks (not shown here) at the left of every line. First printed in *N&F,* 126 (Pt. III, #151; *CW,* IX, 154–155).

Feb. 25th '57 Dined with Hector Tyndale[1]

Asked H. T. where he thought I needed particular[2] attention to be directed for my improvement—where I could especially be bettered in my poems—He said— "In *massiveness,* breadth, large, sweeping effects, without regard to details,—as in the "Cathedral at York" (he said) "I came away with great impressions of its largeness, solidity, and spaciousness without troubling myself with its parts"

Asked F. Le B.[3] same question viz: *What I most lacked*[4]—He said—"In *euphony* — your poems seem to me to be full of the raw material of poems, but crude, and wanting finish and rhythms."

Of others the answer has been— "You have too much procreation[5]

Put in my poems

American things, idioms, materials,[6] *persons, groups, minerals, vegetables, animals, &c*

1. Philadelphia importer of china and civic leader (1821–1882), son of Mrs. Sara Tyndale, an abolitionist and reformer. Mrs. Tyndale met WW through Thoreau and Alcott, and Hector met him through Mrs. Abby Price or her family. He was also acquainted with the O'Connors. He served in the war, being brevetted brigadier general for gallantry in 1865. After his resignation, he visited WW at least twice in Washington, in 1866. In 1876, after WW had moved to Camden, he renewed the acquaintance. See "[*illeg.*] Dick Hunt," "D. W. Wilder," *Corr.,* I, 42, 53*n,* 279, III, 25, 26; Allen, 201, 217, 232, 240, 245, 371.

2. Beginning of word written over.

3. Unidentifiable. Fitz James O'Brien, who was called "M. Le Baron" by his friends at Pfaff's, might be the person.

4. Preceding five words inserted on a line above "question— . . . He said—"

5. End of first scrap.

6. Fist pointing up at left of the two lines containing "persons . . . animals, &"

My Poems, When Complete.

Manuscript in Duke (46, #25). Inscribed in black pencil on verso of blue laid Williamsburgh tax blank, 8½" x 4¾". The first paragraph is followed by a clipping, "The Unity of the Bible," which my student, Mrs. Walter Hays, discovered to be from *Ballou's Pictorial Magazine,* 12 (March 28, 1857), 199. The opening sentence: "As in Beethoven's matchless music runs *one idea, worked out through all the changes of measure and of key, now almost hidden, now breaking out in rich natural melody, whispered in the treble, murmured in the base, dimly suggested in the prelude,* but growing clearer and clearer as the work proceeds, winding gradually back until it ends in the key in which it began, and closes in triumphant harmony; so throughout the whole Bible, there runs one great idea—man's ruin by sin, and his redemption by grace; in a word, Jesus Christ, the Saviour." is marked by a waved line and pointing hand in the right margin. Underscores were made by WW. The date is after March 28, 1857.

My Poems, when complete, should be *A Unity,* in the same sense that the earth is, or that the human body, (senses, soul, head, trunk, feet, blood, viscera, man-root,[1] eyes, hair,)[2] or that a perfect musical composition is—[3]

Great Constituent elements of my Poetry [:][4] Two, viz: *Materialism*[5] *Spirituality*[6] The itellect, the esthetic, is what is to be the medium of these and to beautify, govern & make serviceable these

1. See "I Sing the Body Electric" (1856), sec. 9, l. 143.

2. Entire parenthesis is written in a smaller hand and cramped at right side of page opposite the succeeding seven words.

3. Clipping.

4. Brace to right of preceding six words, which are entered on five lines.

5. Written in large letters.

6. Written in large letters. Balance of the text is written to the right of the brace, and "is to . . . there" under the brace.

The Great Construction.

Manuscript in Duke (46, #22). Inscribed in black pencil on white wove paper, 2" x 4". Bowers, xxxv–xxxvi, worries the text, which seems clearly to indicate that in June 1857 WW was formally dedicating his efforts to producing a religious book of 365 poems by (or for?) 1859. The date, which Bowers questions, is in the MS and is June, 1857. Mr. John L. Sharpe III of the Perkins Library at Duke has verified and corrected my reading. First printed *N&F,* 57 (Pt. II, No. 14; *CW,* IX, 6).

The Great Construction of the
New Bible

Not to be diverted from the principal object—the main life work—the Three Hundred & Sixty five—(it ought to be read in 1859.— (June '57)

American Boys.

Manuscript in LC (Feinberg #109). Inscribed in black pencil on white wove scrap, approx. 7½" x 4½". On verso "The th Presidency." Cf. "The Eighteenth Presidency!" The writing is large and sprawling and the lay out approaching that of a title page, as WW's notes often did. The verso and the contents indicate that WW wrote this in the late 1850s when he was explicitly thinking of his role as a lecturer and teacher. Cf. "The great Construction." First printed in *N&F,* 176 (Pt. IV, #109; *CW,* X, 29).

American Boys[1]

A Book

Containing the Main Things—for the formation,[2] reading, reference, & study for An American Young Man /

for Schools—for Study—for individual use— / one for the upper classes of *every school in the* United States.—

1. In upper right corner.
2. Deleted: "an"

Dithyrambic Trochee.

Manuscript in Rutgers. Inscribed in black ink and, where noted, pencil on two leaves of yellow wove paper: [*1*] 6⅝" x 3⅞", torn on all four sides; at the upper right, in another hand, "2" and "9A", circled; [*2*] 6⅜" x 4", cut on right edge, torn on others; at top, in WW's hand, "3", at upper right, probably in another hand, "2." Small, neat handwriting and the subject suggest a date for these notes after 1856 when WW was educating himself. Bracketed section not in extant MS. Text from N&F where short vertical lines have been inserted between metrical feet. Printed in *N&F,* 162–163 (Pt. IV, #28; *CW,* X, 5–7).

dithyrambic trochee iambic anapest,/[1] Hexameter Pentameter dactyl[2] spondee /[3]

pyrrhic, a poetic foot of two short syllables.[4] (an ancient quick military dance) /

Spondee Two long syllables, in poetry. /

Hexameter,—in ancient poetry, a verse of six feet the first four of which may be either dactyls or spondees,—the fifth must regularly be a dactyl—the sixth always a spondee,

So thus hav ing spok en the casque nod ding
Hec tor de part ed.

[2] Iambus[5]

Iambics,

(Anciently—Certain songs, or satires, supposed to have given birth to ancient comedy.)

Iambus—a poetic "foot" consisting of two syllables, the first short, the last long, as in "de-light"

"He scorns—the force—that dares—his fu—ry stay."/

Trochee

(from a Greek word, signifying "to run.")

A poetic foot consisting of two syllables, the first long, the second short.

(I suppose such as this)

Would you—gaze up—on the—wa ters, Of the—lordly—Missis—sippi?/

1. Following four words in pencil. These first eight entries in two columns with a rule across the page under each.
2. Deleted "e" in "dactyle"
3. Following eight words in pencil.
4. Following five words added to the entry and enclosed by curved line.
5. Entries in hanging indentation.

Dactyl

(from the Greek word for "finger," the joint nearest the hand being long, the other two joints short.)

A poetic foot of three syllables, the first long.—the others short (I suppose such as)

"Thun der ing—up ward and—down ward the—sur ges roll'd."[6]

[Hexameters.— Verses whose lines are six poetic feet either dactyls or spondees: e.g.

"Then when An dromache ended said tall bright helmeted Hector."

Dactyl a poetic foot of one long and two short syllables: e.g.

"Oft at the close of the day when the . . ."

Spondee—a poetic foot of two long syllables: e.g.

"Auro ra now fair daugh ter of the dawn."

Pentameter—having five regular feet (as the line immediately above).

Iambus—two short syllables

Trochee—a long and a short syllable.

Pentameter—ancient poetry—a verse of five feet. The two first may be either Dactyls or Spondees—the third is always a Spondee and the two last Anapests. A pentameter verse subjoined to a hexameter constitutes what is called an Elegiac.

Anapest—three syllables, the first two short the last long, the reverse of the Dactyl as

"Can a bo som so gen tle remain unmov'd—when her Co rydon sighs."]

6. End of MS. Remainder from Bucke.

Dithyrambus. Dithyramb.

Manuscript not found. Text from *N&F,* 163 (Pt. IV, #29; *CW,* X, 7–8).

Dithyrambus. Dithyramb. Dithyrambic. From a Greek word a title of Bacchus the signification of which not settled.

In ancient poetry a hymn or song in honor of Bacchus, full of transport and poetical rage. Of this species of writing we have no remains.

A song of Bacchus in which the wildness of intoxication is infused.

Any poem in which ecstasy and wildness are expressed in kind.

Cæsura. Cæsural pause (from Cæsum, the cutting thing). A pause in verse so introduced as to aid the recital and make melody—divides a line into equal or unequal parts.

(?) Other Poets.

Manuscript in Duke (48, #30). Inscribed in black ink on two irregular leaves of pink wove paper, approx. 7⅝" x 5 1/16" and 4¾" x 4 7/16". They may or may not be continuous; Bucke prints them as separate items. The paper and the writing indicate WW wrote this in the late 1850s. First printed *N&F*, 68–69. (Pt. 2, #52–53; *CW*, IX, 31–32).

[*1*](?) Other poets[1] have[2] formed for themselves an ideal, apart from[3] positive life, and disdainful of it—but[4] for me, I[5] ask nothing better or more divine than real life, here, now, yourself, your work,[6] house-building, boating, or in any factory; and I say[7] of every[8] male and every female,[9] he or she can bring out of it all divine? growths? fruits?[10] [*2*] Mine are not the[11] songs of a story teller, or of[12] a voluptuous person, or of an ennuyeed person,— but[13] of an American constructor, looking with[14] friendly eyes upon the earth and men,[15] and[16] beholding the vista of the great mission of The States.—

1. Preceding question mark and two words inserted above deleted "Others"
2. Deleted: "c[?]"
3. Deleted: "a the"
4. Deleted: "as"
5. Deleted: "will offer" ; inserted: "ask" above "otter"
6. Deleted: "the"
7. Deleted: "you" ; inserted above: "of"
8. Deleted: "man" ; inserted above: "male"
9. Deleted: "must make his or her own & you" ; inserted and deleted: "may shape" above "[*del.*] must make"
10. Question marks above words.
11. Deleted: "words of"
12. Deleted: "lo"
13. Deleted: "m"
14. Deleted: "cheerful"
15. Deleted: " . and enjoying" ; inserted: comma under and following deleted period.
16. Deleted: "believing the"

Leading Characteristic.

Manuscript in Duke (46, #22). Inscribed in black pencil on white wove scrap, 2″ x ¾″. The small tight writing is characteristic of the early notebooks and such early MSs as *"The Great Construction."* The date is probably the late 1850s. First printed *N&F,* 56 (Pt. II, #12; *CW,* IX, 6).

Leading Characteristic

To unite all the sects, parties, States, lawyers, disputants, young men, women, (universology) — To be one whom all look toward with attention, respect, love

All Through Writings.

Manuscript in Pennsylvania. Inscribed in black pencil on white laid paper approx. 5¼" x 7⅞", vertical chain lines, faded blue rules recto and verso 5/16" apart. Trimmed with scissors top and bottom. The date, from the small neat handwriting and the subject matter, is probably in the late 1850s. First printed in *N&F,* 56 (Pt. II; #8; *CW,* IX, 5).

All through writings preserve the equilibrium of the truth that the material world, and all its laws, are as grand and superb as the spiritual world and all its laws.— Most writers have disdained the physical world, and[1] they have not over-estimated the other, or soul, but have under-estimated the corporeal—

How shall my eye separate the[2] beauty of the[3] blossoming buckwheat field, from the stalks and heads of tangible matter?— How shall I know what the life is except as I see it in the flesh?— I will not praise one without the other, or[4] any more than the other—the least one of the /

Let the idea of *Equality* stick out—my best— /

Do not argue at all, or compare proofs to demonstrate things—State nothing which it[5] will not[6] do to state as apparent to all eyes.—

1. Deleted: "one" . Dash not deleted, not shown.
2. Deleted: "pleas"
3. Deleted: "flower"
4. Torn, erased spot.
5. Inserted on a line above the wordspace between "which" and "will"
6. Deleted: [*illeg.*]

I Say That Democracy.

Manuscript in LC (#79, sheet #745). Inscribed in black pencil on irregular scrap of white wove paper. The second paragraph is the space of several lines below the end of the first. The small writing suggests a date in the 1850s.

I say that Democracy offers higher and more athletic ideals Persons[1].—[2] They yet sleep.— Who of all these swarms—in the East & West,[3] of writers and speakers courageously steps up to[4] celebrate the savage and free[5] genius of These States?— I know not one.—

Days, years pass, pass away?[6] pass by on

1. Inserted on a line above "als—" in "ideals—"
2. Deleted: "Let all"
3. Preceding five words inserted on a line above "ms" in "swarms" and "of writers"
4. Deleted: "[*illeg.*] the"
5. Preceding five words inserted on a line under "courageously steps up"
6. Preceding two words inserted on a line above "pass by". Question mark above "pass away"

I Know Well Enough.

Manuscript in Duke (26, #32). Two scraps: [*1*] inscribed in pencil in hanging indentations on thin tan, perhaps yellow, wove paper approx. 8^{11}/16" x 5½", torn irregularly along right edge; [2] inscribed in hanging indentations in black ink on white wove paper approx. 3⅝" x 5¾", torn at top, bottom, right. Small, neat handwriting seems to be that of the 1850s. First printed in *N&F,* 123 (Pt. III, #137; *CW,* IX, 148).

I know well enough that man grows up becoming not[1] a physical being merely, but markedly the mental being of the earth,—the esthetic and spiritual being[2]—the benevolent and

But the main thing is, in the same connection, that he is to be the seer of nature—he only can celebrate things,[3] animals, and landscapes— His mentality is a quality to be used toward things, as his vision is used

If he depart from animals and things he is lost.[4]

In other words, man is not only an animal like the others, but he alone has the quality of understanding and telling how divine a thing an animal is—[5] what life, matter, passion, volition are

He alone carries[6] all the substances of the world, by this quality, in himself, and illustrates them.

1. Deleted: "an animal" ; inserted: "a physical" above "[*del.*] animal"
2. Deleted: "of the earth,"
3. Deleted: "and"
4. End of first scrap.
5. Deleted: "See[?]"
6. Deleted: "the" ; inserted: "all the" on a line above "subs" in "substances"

Drops of My Blood.

Manuscript in Trent (14, #36). Inscribed in black pencil more or less in column on scrap of flimsy white wove paper, approx. 3″ x 4¾″. Top and right edges cleanly torn. On verso is "to you an inheritance" (See MS Variorum). Probably notes for "Not Heat Flames Up and Consumes" which as Bowers (lxiv–lxv) points out was written before 1860 or "Trickle Drops" (1860). See also "Breast Sorrel." First printed in Bucke, "Notes on the Text of Leaves of Grass," *Conservator,* 7 (February, 1895), 185.

Drops of my [1] *Blood.*

Native Flames[2] Flames of Confession[3] Moments of Fire.[4] Drops of Evil Flames of Evil *Verses of Evil*[5]

1. Inserted above "of"
2. Written to left and circled by WW.
3. Written to right of "Native Flames" and circled by WW.
4. Written to the left under "Native Flames"
5. Written over [*illeg.*] . Last three entries written in three lines to the right of "Fire"

Breast Sorrel.

Manuscript not found. Text from *N&F,* 164 (Pt. IV, #123; *CW,* X, 33). Probably trial titles for "Calamus," therefore to be dated before 1859. See *"Drops of my Blood."* First printed by Bucke in "Notes on the Text of Leaves of Grass," *Conservator,* 7, (February, 1897), 185, which omitted "Calamus Roots."

Breast Sorrel. Breast Pinks. Breast Currants. Breast Apples. Calamus Roots.

A Main Part of the Greatness.

Manuscript in Duke (27, #28). Inscribed in pencil and some ink on blue Williamsburgh tax form 7½" x 4½". The paper would suggest a date of 1857, which is the date given in Bucke's note, *N&F,* 85 (Pt. III, #26; *CW,* IX, 70). The lines beginning "O I see now" were printed as verse in *N&F,* 14 (Pt. I, #24; *CW,* III, 259) and in "Uncollected Manuscript Fragments," *LG, CRE,* 699.

A main part of[1] the greatness of a humanity is that it[2] never at any time,[3] or under any circumstances, arrives [4] at its finality—never[5] is able to say, Now,[6] as I stand, I am fixed[7] forever.— If any one has the feeling to say, I am fixed—and retains that feeling—then[8] a longer or shorter farewell to the greatness of that humanity.—[9] Every day something more—something[10] unsuspected the previous day.— Always changing, advancing, retreating,[11] enlarging, condensing, widening, being wafted to spirituality.— Always new[12] materialism and things.—

(O I see now that I have the make of materialism and things,
And that intellect is[13] to me but as hands, or eyesight, or as[14] a vessel,[15]

1. Preceding four words inserted in ink. Original beginning of the sentence, capitalized "The" not changed.
2. Deleted: "is at no" ; inserted above: "never at any"
3. Deleted: "nor" ; inserted above: "or"
4. Inserted above "at"
5. Deleted: "so that it can" ; inserted: "is able to" above "it can"
6. Inserted: ", as I stand," on a line above "I am"
7. Deleted: "as I [*del.*] am [*ins.* above "am"] stand"
8. Inserted: "a longer or shorter" on a line above "then . . . farewell"
9. Redundant dash not printed.
10. Deleted: "it unseen" ; inserted: "unsuspected" above "[*del.*] unseen" and "the"
11. Inserted above "enla" in "enlarge"
12. Inserted above wordspace between "Always" and "materialism"
13. Inserted: "to me" above "but"
14. Inserted above "a"
15. Both lines cancelled by diagonal stroke.

The Idea That.

Manuscript in LC (Feinberg, #506). Inscribed in pencil on top half of verso of Williamsburgh tax blank. Traubel says that he found it on the floor of WW's room on September 2, 1888. Although Williamsburgh was incorporated as part of Brooklyn in 1855, all the dateable examples of tax forms are 1857 or later, despite WW's 1888 insertion. First published in Traubel, II, 246.

The idea [1] that in the nature of things, through all affairs and deeds, national or individual, good and bad, each has its inherent law of punishment or reward, which is part of the deed or affair itself, identical with it, and, with its results, goes with that deed, that affair, then and afterwards.—

The idea that the Woman of America is to become the perfect equal of the man.—

The idea of the good old cause, Liberty—that it is to be honored here, whatever day, whatever question, it presents itself in—that the relation of master and slave [this was written in 1855][2] is to go the: same road out of These States, that the relation of kings, lords, and commons, has gone.

1. Deleted: "that of the"
2. WW's brackets and insertion in 1888.

*What We Thought.

Manuscript in NYPL (Berg). Inscribed in black ink with pencil insertions on white wove paper 2" x 6¹³/₁₆", all but lower right corner clipped. An asterisk usually indicates an insertion. Traces of writing are visible at the top of the leaf. The small, neat writing suggests that WW wrote this in the 1850s or 1860s. Printed in *N&F,* 146 (Pt. III, #194; *CW,* IX, 197).

What we thought we knew all about, we know little or nothing about?—[1] and they who presume to teach know least of all about.— It is so[2] unspeakably greater than we thought. There is more miracle in a[3] wave, a rock, a tree than we[4] were attributing to the whole theology?—[5] What children's fables are[6] those you are guaging this mighty thing by?—

1. Inserted in pencil: "?—and they . . . about" ; inserted below the line and deleted: "and they who presume to teach kno"
2. Inserted in pencil above wordspace between "is" and "unspeakably"
3. Deleted: "ro"
4. Deleted: "thought"
5. "?" above word. Deleted after dash: "All our"
6. Deleted: "these we" ; inserted above: "those you"

Salt Works.

Manuscript in NYPL (Berg). Inscribed in pencil on blue Williamsburgh tax form 8⁷/₁₆" x 4⁹/₁₆". Stovall, *AL,* 26 (1954), 340, says WW's source may have been two newspaper clippings, "The Salt Manufacture" (Bucke's No. 124) and "Amount of Salt Made" (Bucke's No. 127). The tax form indicates a date of 1857 or later. First printed in *N&F,* 79 (Pt. III, #12; *CW,* IX, 57). Unlike a similar MS in NYPL (Berg), "Iron works" (see Manuscript Variorum) this was not used for a poem. See also "Maine."

Salt works

At Salina ("Salt Point") now a portion of Syracuse, N.Y. Onondaga Co. (as Williamsburgh is a part of Brooklyn) There are some salt springs,—Also they bore into the neighboring ground—(sometimes 300 ft. deep)—50, 70, 100 ft /

A "block" is erected, in which there are arches, with kettles for boiling the water—these are kept fired under day and night,—till at the end of a week they have to be cleaned of the sediment, coating, &c.—

by the kettles are baskets and ladles to take out and contain the salt—a spout and trough[1] ranging over the kettles lets in the water as it is wanted— /

evaporation supplies the best salt— It is put in bags and large boxes, and sent off on the canals

1. Deleted: "over"

A Simpler System of the Table.

Manuscript in LC (96, sheet #'s 123, 124). Inscribed in black ink on two blue Williamsburgh tax blanks. LC *Cat.* dates it "Before 1860?"

A[1] *simpler system of the Table*

No house, no woman, can be disenthralled[2] until the society arrives at a simpler[3] system of the table.— One dish, cheap,[4] nutritious, plentiful,[5] is enough for a meal.—[6] The complex array of dinner[7], and the labor-costing and money-costing dishes, shall[8] sink away.— A[9] live man must eat;— A[10] great appetite is grand;— Beef[11], rice, fruit potatoes, bread—these in plenty, become a man, twice a day—perhaps even thrice a day;— They are to be plain and rude

[2] It is observed[12] in civilized life in the matter of the table,[13] as in other matters,[14] the trouble and expense are mostly for what is needless, and[15] mars rather than mends—[16] while that really needed is cheap and is soon done.— As to who shall do the work it is just as becoming,[17] when both understand it as, that[18]the man[19] cook for the woman as that the woman[20] cook for the man.—

1. Deleted: "The" ; title then begun with "A"
2. Originally "until it have a" ; "it" deleted; "they" inserted. Entire clause deleted. "until they arrive at a" inserted on caret; "society" inserted after "they" ; "s" added to "arrive"
3. "simple" emended to "simpler" ; deleted: "better"
4. Deleted: "plentiful"
5. Inserted on caret: "very plentiful" above "is" ; "very" deleted.
6. Deleted: "All" ; "The" capitalized.
7. Originally: "of a dinner table,"
8. Inserted: "shall" above wordspace between "dishes," and "sink"
9. Deleted: "man"
10. Capitalized over "a"
11. Capitalized over "b"
12. Inserted: "in civilized life" above "erved" in "observed" and "in the"
13. Deleted: "in civilized life"
14. Deleted: "that"
15. Deleted: "is what"
16. Deleted: "and by [*illeg.*] that what [*illeg.*]" ; inserted: "while that" above "at" of "that" and "what"
17. Inserted: "when both [*del.*] sides understand it as" on a line above "as becoming . . . that"
18. Redundant "that" not printed.
19. Deleted: "should"
20. Deleted: "should"

Content to the Ground.

Manuscript in NYPL (Berg). Inscribed in pencil on white wove scrap approx. 1 7/16" x 3 15/16". Faded rules ¼" apart. The phrase "content to the ground" apparently ties in to a preceding text not found. The other phrases are as notes written at an angle across the page. Small, neat handwriting suggests an early date.

content to the ground the blacksmith shop the brewery[1]

1. Deleted: "saltmaking arsenal nailmaking & themakingofallsortsof edged tools." on five lines under "the brewery" . See "Salt works."

The Greatest Poems May Not Immediately.

Manuscript in Duke (27, #37). Inscribed on wove pocket ledger paper 2⅜″ x 3″, torn from book at right edge, horizontal blue rules ¼″ apart, vertical rules at approx. ¹¹/₁₆″, 2¼″ (double) and 2½″. Small, neat handwriting indicates a date in the 1850s. Printed in *N&F,* 59 (Pt. II, #24; *CW,* IX, 10–11). Bucke concludes, "Let poets. . . ," which is no longer part of this fragment MS, but may have been as suggested by fragments of writing at the bottom edge. On verso: "—seeing this you will no more see [*ins. above*] ridiculous? in the poor man [*del.*] Irishman [*ins.*] shouldering his sheep [*illeg.*]
Then —nor the—
4th av. Charley Smith John, Dutchman elderly—Dan—(linen coat)"

The greatest[1] poems may not immediately[2] be[3] fully understood[4] by outsiders any more than astronomy or engineering may.— The work of the poet is as deep as[5] the astronomer's or engineer's, and his art is also[6] as farfetched.— Science proves itself. . . . .[7]

1. Deleted: "poet" ; inserted above: "poems"
2. Inserted above "be"
3. Deleted: "easily" ; inserted above: "fully"
4. Inserted: "by outsiders" on a line above "stood" in "understood" and into right margin.
5. Deleted: "that of"
6. Inserted: "as farfetched.—" on a line above "also understood" . Redundant ".—" not printed.
7. Suspension marks inserted above deleted ".—"

Every Great Artist.

Manuscript not found. Text from *N&F,* 114 (Pt. III, #105; *CW,* IX, 128). Since so many of Bucke's MS are early, this MS is arbitrarily placed here.

Every great artist, poet, etc., will be found to have some precursors or first beginners of his greatness. Doubtless Homer had though we know them not.

Health Does Not Tell Any More.

Manuscript in Duke (27, #37). Inscribed in pencil on tan wove soft paper, possibly proof paper, 6 11/16" x 5 1/16". The upper right corner is clipped. Probably written before 1860. Printed in *N&F,* 128 (Pt. III, #161; *CW,* IX, 158).

Health does not tell[1] any more in the body, than it tells does[2] in literature.—Which is the poem, or any book, that is not diseased?— (If perfect health appear in a poem, or any book, it[3] propogates itself[4] a great while.) Show[5] health, and native qualities, and[6] you are welcome to all the rest.—

1. Preceding four words written over [*illeg.*] erasures.
2. Written above "tells"
3. Deleted: "surely"
4. Deleted: "while many nations rise"
5. Deleted: "perfect"
6. Deleted: "that which possesses them and"

Tar, Turpentine.

Manuscript in NYPL (Berg). Inscribed in black pencil on scrap of pocket ledger paper. Bucke suggests a relationship with "Our Old Feuillage" (1860), ll. 33 ff. First printed in Bucke, "Notes on the 'Text of Leaves of Grass,'" *Conservator*. 7 (February 1897), 185.

Tar, turpentine, shingles (from North Carolina) / [1]
the lumber-schooner [2]

1. Cancelled entry: "The slaves drive [*preceding three words ins. in a line over*] mules and oxen drawing the rude carts"

2. Cancelled lines suggest "Song of Myself," sec. 33, ll. 835 ff., rather than the jolly local color of "Our Old Fevillage" : "the slave hunt with blood-hounds the pack of negro-dogs chained in couples for the [*ins. above and after* "for"] slave-hunt / the slave hunters [*preceding three words del.*]"

Describing the Death.

Manuscript not found. Text from *N&F,* 118 (Pt. III, #117; *CW,* IX, 138).

Describing the death of seven brothers and their parents—who can say that those were least lucky who died the earliest or under the most appalling circumstances? or that those were luckiest who made the most wealth and lived the longest stretch of mortality?

The Air.

Manuscript in NYPL (Berg). Inscribed in pencil and black ink on blue Williamsburgh tax form, approx. 4⅝" x 6¹³/₁₆". From the use of the tax form, the date is 1857 or later. Printed in *N&F,* 75 (Pt. III, #1; *CW,* IX, 47).

The[1] Air[2] (Space) considered with reference to the earth—as all[3] parts of the universe bear reference to each other, and all other things therefore bear down their influence more or less upon this earth.—[:][4] A Description of those things that may be said to be most closely[5] identified with the air,—(for movement, visibility, occupancy &c) as the orbs, Space, light, heat[6]—(as Silliman[7] says—Cosmical—not Terrestrial) /

The Sea [:][8] All the wonders of the Sea—the Sea covering three-fourths of the land /

The Land [:][9] *Physical* facts of the land—as first its nebulous beginning—then its geology all through to the present—then its *present beauty; reality, & diversity,* as the home of man.—

1. The "A" in "Air" is inscribed over a partially erased capital "S" .
2. The following thirty-three words are in black ink.
3. Inserted: "parts of"
4. Brace.
5. Deleted: "related to" ; inserted: "identified with"
6. Following six words in black ink.
7. (1779–1864), Professor of Chemistry and Natural History at Yale, lectured and published extensively for popular audiences.
8. Brace.
9. Brace. Remainder of MS in black ink.

"The Scout."

Manuscript in Duke (14, #36). Inscribed in black ink on scrap of blue Williamsburgh tax blank, approx. 1⅜" x 4 11/16". "—a *magazine*," "—a *newspaper*" are in column below "poem." See also "Daylight." The date is 1857 to 1860. First printed *N&F*, 178 (Pt. IV, #129; *CW*, X, 34).

"The Scout"

—! a good name for A poem—a *magazine*,—A *newspaper*

That It Perpetually Fibre.

Manuscript not found. Text from *N&F,* 103 (Pt. III, #68; *CW,* IX, 107). According to Bucke's note "The MS of this piece is in a bad state." Because most of Bucke's MS are early this MS is placed here.

. . . that it perpetually fibre and strengthen and vivify all which is good, and erase all which is bad. Compulsion[1] on the other hand, is a temporary support, gained at the price of much bad feeling and reaction. Schools — proud of and valuing it for its good name, works of art, architecture, parks, ornaments, aqueducts, avenues and the perfection of its civilization and conveniences. Every one of these officers should be possessed with the eternal American ideas of liberty, friendliness, amptitude and courage. It is all nonsense to fancy that the sphere of such fine traits can only be on some higher and more diffused and commanding scale, as Governor or Senator or President. The right sort of man will exemplify them just as well here directly at our doors or in our City Hall.

1. *CW,* IX, 107 has a comma.

Employments.

Manuscript in LC (81, sheet # 825). Inscribed in black ink on fragment of blue wove Williamsburgh tax bill. Parenthetical statement in black pencil. The quotation is from Thomas Carlyle's "Dr. Francia" (1844) (*Critical and Miscellaneous Essays,* IV [Centenary Edition, London], 291). José Gaspar Rodrìguez Francia (c. 1766–1840) was elected dictator of Paraguay in 1814. "Quintus Fixlein" is a pseudonym for the German romancer Jean Paul Richter (1768–1825). The Latin source of the idea has not been found. The paper indicates a date after 1857. "Dr. Francia" appeared in American editions of Carlyle's *Critical and Miscellaneous Essays* in 1852, 1855, and 1858.

Employments

Francia, like Quintus Fixlein, had *perennial fire-proof joys, namely Employments*"
XXX (idea from a Latin writer)

No One Will Perfectly Enjoy Me.

Manuscript not found. Text from *N&F,* 68 (Pt. III, #50; *CW,* IX, 31). The tone suggests an early date, in the 1850s.

No one will perfectly enjoy me who has not some of my own rudeness, sensuality and hauteur.

"Animals," Says George Eliot.

Manuscript in Texas (Hanley). Three scraps of paper and two clippings pasted on gray wove leaf smaller than the paste-ons, which looks like a flyleaf of a small book. [*1*] Pencil inscription on fragment of white wove top bound pocket notebook paper, blue rules ¼" apart. [2] Inscribed in black ink on white wove scrap. [*3*] Inscribed in black pencil on white wove side bound small notebook paper, blue rules ¼" apart; upper right corner rounded. The writing in paragraphs [1] and [3] is that of the 1850s or 1860s; that of [2] seems to be the looser, more irregular writing of the 1870s.

"Animals," says George Eliot, "are such agreeable friends — *they ask no questions, & pass no criticisms"*
Mr Gilfil's Love Story[1]

The those[2] stars, which seem so calm & steady,[3] are[4] endless convulsions.

"It is not the handsome people that are the handsomest," says a wise old woman, a friend of mine. Very true; the most beautiful & attractive men & women I have ever known have been technically homely

1. "Mr. Gilfil's Love Story" from *Scenes of Clerical Life* appeared in *Blackwood's Magazine* (March–June, 1857). The collection appeared in Edinburgh and in NY in 1958. WW reviewed *Blackwood's* in the Brooklyn *Daily Times* July 30 and October 7, 1857. Two clippings are pasted below: "Vice stings us even in our pleasures, but virtue consoles us even in our pains." " 'Wit is the god of moments; but genius is the god of ages.' "

2. Inserted above "The"

3. Preceding two words and comma inserted above "calm . . . are"

4. Deleted: "constant"

First to Me Comes the People.

Manuscript not found. Published in *N&F,* 179 (Pt. IV, #136; *CW,* X, 35).

First to me comes the People, and their typical shape and their attitudes—then the divine minor, Literature.

My Two Theses.

Manuscript not found. First published in *N&F,* 167 (Pt. IV, #56), *CW,* X, 15.

My two theses—animal and spiritual—became gradually fused in *Leaves of Grass,*—runs through all the poems and gives color to the whole.

I Say That If Once.

Manuscript not found. First published in *N&F,* 54 (Pt. II, #3), *CW,* IX, 4.

I say that if once the conventional distinctions were dispelled from our eyes we should see just as much.

I do not expect to dispel them by arguing against them, I sweep them away by advancing to a new phase of development where they fail of themselves.

In Future Leaves of Grass.

Manuscript not found. First published in *N&F,* 69 (Pt. II, #55), *CW,* IX, 32–33.

In future *Leaves of Grass. Be more severe* with the final revision of the poem, nothing will do, not one word or sentence, that is not *perfectly clear*—with positive purpose—harmony with the name, nature, drift of the poem. Also *no ornaments,* especially no *ornamental adjectives,* unless they have come molten hot, and imperiously prove themselves. *No ornamental similes at all—not one: perfect transparent clearness* sanity and health are wanted—*that* is the *divine style*—O if it can be attained—

I Want Something to Offset.

Manuscript not found. Published in "Walt Whitman: Unpublished Notes and Letters," *Wake* 7 (Autumn, 1948), 6.

I want something to offset the overlarge element of *muscle* in my poems—it must be counterpoised by something to show I can make perfect poems of the graceful, the sweet, the gentle, the tender—I must show perfect blood, the great heroic gentleman.

Passage in Every "Lecture."

Manuscript in NYPL (Berg). Inscribed in pencil on scrap 2" x 6$^{9}/_{16}$" cut and torn from longer sheet of white cheap wove paper. The subject matter suggests this was written in the 1850s or 1860s. Printed in *N&F,* 170 (Pt. IV, #75; *CW,* X, 20). See also Furness, 208–209, 45*n*.

Passage in every "Lecture"

To those few who understand,
get[1] at the heart
of the theme

1. The correct reading may be "yet"

A Visit to the Opera.

WW's interest in opera during the 1850s produced not only certain elements of *LG,* but an article, "The Opera" (*Life Illustrated* I, N.S. [November 10, 1855], 1, reprinted by Holloway *NYD,* 17–23). This is related to a number of manuscript drafts, the further relationship among which is not entirely clear. It seems preferable to describe the manuscripts and analyze their relationship in one place rather than in individual headnotes.

I. "Steffanone" (LC #47, sheets #125–127). Inscribed in black ink with black pencil emendations on three tattered scraps of white laid paper, 10⅞" x 7¾". LC sheet #126 (here [*1*]) is inscribed "7" in black pencil at top center, apparently in WW's hand. On verso is "here are vast mountains." LC sheet #127([2]) is similarly inscribed "13" On verso is "The New Inland America." LC sheet #125 is placed as [*3*] here, because Steffanone is described as "now in Paris," whereas Alboni, who is described on [*3*], "too is now in Paris." *"Spectacle inside the Opera House."* is similar to "A look around the house," in "A VISIT TO THE OPERA" and the description of Alboni is similar to that in "ITALIAN SINGERS IN AMERICA." Since La Grange sang during WW's residence in NY only in 1855 and 1856 the MS must be not later than that opera season. Alboni sang only in 1852 and 1853.

II. "A VISIT TO THE OPERA." Manuscript in Huntington. (HM 1191). Inscribed in black ink on eight leaves of white, rather porous, wove paper. Leaves [*1–7*], 12½" x 8", leaf 10, 8½" x 8". Numbered 1–10 in WW's hand. Pages 8 and 9 are lacking. (See "The voice is a curious organ.") On the verso of 10 the title is inscribed in black ink lengthwise, on a middle fold, and above it is "(Weekly)" in black pencil also in WW's hand. Published *UPP,* II, 97–101. (Descriptive details are from Mr. Herbert C. Schultz, Curator of Manuscripts, Huntington.)

III. "ITALIAN SINGERS IN AMERICA." Manuscript in Duke (22, #17). Inscribed in black ink on three leaves of white, rather porous wove paper, 7½" x 8", 5⅜" x 7¾", and 5¾" x 7¾". On leaf [*1*] is a curious "tire-tread" watermark which has been found only in "Diary of the War," 22 (Morgan Library), used in *NB,* "Last of the War Cases." The presence of this watermark in "ITALIAN SINGERS IN AMERICA." and "Diary of the War," is fortuitous since the paper is otherwise different. Leaf [*1*] is also of a slightly different color than [2] and [*3*].

The text is discontinuous at the beginning with p. 7 of "A VISIT TO THE OPERA." The top and bottom of leaf [*1*] show signs of trimming and there is no page number. The end of leaf [*3*] is discontinuous with p. 10 of "A VISIT TO THE OPERA." The size of each leaf taken separately and the combined size of leaves [2] and [*3*], which were cut apart at some time, is shorter than the size of the leaves of "A VISIT TO THE OPERA." Since the top of [2] is square, it cannot have been part of [*1*]. These considerations plus the existence of "practice two, three, or four hours" (see below) prohibit identifying "ITALIAN SINGERS IN AMERICA" as the lacking pp 8–9 of "A VISIT TO THE OPERA." It can only be part of a different draft. Since Piccolomini sang in NY only in 1858 and Steffani made his debut that year the date must be 1858 or later. First printed *FC&I,* 18–19. (Mr. John

L. Sharpe, III, Curator of Manuscripts, William R. Perkins Library, Duke University has kindly supplied a number of details.)

IV. "practice two, three, four" Typed transcript by Clifton Joseph Furness on two sheets of his letterhead as Supervisor of Academic Studies, New England Conservatory of Music, no date, of a MS then in the Bucke Collection. According to Furness the MS, presumably one leaf, is marked "page 8" presumably by WW. The beginning is continuous with p. 7 of "A VISIT TO THE OPERA," but not with p. 10. As compared with "ITALIAN SINGERS IN AMERICA," it has additional material at the beginning and end. Otherwise, aside from the absence of the word "now" which is the third word of "ITALIAN SINGERS IN AMERICA" the text is identical. It has 339 words, whereas "A VISIT TO THE OPERA" has 175 to 185 words per page. The original must have been on a larger sheet or have been two pages in length. Furness does not indicate. Therefore it must be part of another draft. The second paragraph is identical with "The voice is a curious organ." (Transcript kindly supplied by Professor Emory Holloway. It is now in the Department of Special Collections, Kenneth L. Spenser Research Library, University of Kansas.)

The relationship of the four separate MSS and "The Opera" in *Life Illustrated* may be as follows. "The Opera" describes the Academy of Music as do "Steffanone" and "A VISIT TO THE OPERA," but tritely emphasizes the cold, heartless, etc., etc., aristocrats in the audience and describes only a performance of Verdi's *Ernani*. The date of "Steffanone" suggests that it was a sketch for "A VISIT TO THE OPERA" which was probably adapted to the prejudices of *Life Illustrated* and its readers. "A VISIT TO THE OPERA," "practice two, three, or four" and "ITALIAN SINGERS IN AMERICA" all seem to be variants of the same essay which, as the references to Piccolomini and Steffani suggest, is 1858 or later. "Steffanone," however, is the earliest draft. Floyd Stovall suggests that WW intended "A VISIT TO THE OPERA" for the Brooklyn *Daily Times,* which he was then editing, but the inscription "Weekly" on "A VISIT TO THE OPERA" suggests a change in his intentions. The three MSS avoid the reverse snobbery of "A VISIT TO THE OPERA" and WW frankly enjoys the spectacle of the wealthy audience. He is also more detailed and enthusiastic about the singers. It seems possible that WW rewrote "A VISIT TO THE OPERA" partly because he was not averse to republishing his own journalism and partly because in it he had not fully expressed his love of *bel canto*. But, despite his genuine enthusiasm for *bel canto* singing, he felt at the same time that Italian opera was too artificial to express American modernity and sketched some ideas for an American opera ("memorials," which dates prior to 1855). The impact of opera and *bel canto* singing has been variously estimated. See Robert D. Faner, *Walt Whitman and Opera* (Philadelphia, 1951) and Floyd Stovall, *The Foreground of "Leaves of Grass"* (Charlottesville, 1973) for full discussion.

Data on the singers and performances are from George C. D. Odell, *Annals of the New York Stage* (NY, 1927–1949) and various musical encyclopedias.

I.

[*1*]7[1]

Steffanone,[2] the true girl of Italy, plump, indolent, dark-skinned, black-haired, rich-voiced, is[3] one of the welcomest vocalists[4] to a New York audience.— Her

1. In black pencil.
2. Balbina Steffanone was popular in NY from 1850 to 1855.
3. Deleted in pencil: "always"
4. Deleted: "before" ; inserted in pencil above "[*del.*] before" : "to"

voice is mezzo-soprano, and her style is easy, rounded, finished, and rather slow, as becomes her.—[5] When warmed up in some scene in Robert Devereux,[6] Lucrezia Borgia,[7] or[8] The Troubadour, Steffanone knows well enough how to be sublime and unsurpassable.— She is now in Paris and very popular there.—[9]

Madame Bertucca-Maretzek[10] has a soprano voice, of considerable power.— She is small, stout, light-haired, blue-eyed, and has a vigorous way[?]of[?]going[?][11] through with her part,[12] an impression.—

[2]13[13]

Spectacle inside the Opera House.—[14]

The appearance of the Opera-house inside, when lit up, and the performance going on, is one of the most splendid that can be imagined.—— Hundreds upon hundreds of gas-lights, softened with globes of ground glass, shed a brilliancy down on the scene.— Seated[15] in the red-velvet arm-chairs of the parquette, and on[16] the rich cushioned sofas of the[17] dress-circle, are[18] groups of the most superbly-dressed women, with[19] the air[?] of politeness and self-possession[20] obtained by mixing[21] with the "best society".— Line after line, party after party, come streaming down the passages[22] the seats they have engaged—[23]under the convoy of the ushers.—

[*illeg.*][24] of man, with perfect-shaped feet[?], arms, and hands.— Her face is regular and pleasant, not beautiful—her forehead low, plentiful black hair, cut short,

5. Deleted: "in"

6. By Gaetano Donizetti, performed in NY in 1849, 1850, 1851, 1864.

7. Also by Donizetti. First performed in NY in 1844 and a popular favorite for years.

8. Deleted: "La Gazza Ladra [by Gioachino Rossini], Steffani" ; inserted above "[*del.*] La Gazza Ladra" : "The Troubadour" [*Il Trovatore* by Giuseppe Verdi].

9. Sentence inserted in pencil in two lines in space to right of end of preceding sentence.

10. Apollonia Bertucca-Maretzek, soprano, sang in NY from 1849 to 1860. She was the wife of Max Maretzek, the impresario.

11. Lower left corner tattered.

12. Lower left corner tattered.

13. Black pencil.

14. Black pencil.

15. Inserted in black pencil above space after sentence. Following "In" not reduced to lowercase in MS.

16. Inserted in black pencil above space between "and" and "the"

17. Deleted: "first"

18. Deleted in black pencil: "swarms" ; inserted: "groups"

19. Deleted: "an" ; inserted: "the"

20. Deleted: "only"

21. Deleted: "much"

22. Lower left corner torn off.

23. Lower left corner torn off.

24. Leaf badly tattered at left. WW is describing Marietta Alboni (1823–1894), a contralto capable of dramatic soprano roles like Norma, who sang in NY in 1852 and 1853. The impact of her singing on WW was very great. With the MS is a clipping from the Poughkeepsie, NY, *Daily News,* in which Frédéric Louis Ritter, Director of the School of Music at Vassar College (see "Kansas & Colorado trip"), reports that in 1879 WW said that more of his poems than he could remember

like a boy's—a slow, graceful[25] style of walk, attitudes [*illeg.*] inimitable beauty, and large black eyes.— We have seen her, [*illeg.*] pathetic scenes, (as in Norma [*illeg.*][26] considering the death of her children) [*illeg.*] real tears like rain[27] coursing each other down[?] her cheeks.— She too[28] is now in[?] Paris, singing at the Grand Opera there.—

La Grange,[29] one of the[30] latest sopranos here[31] [*illeg.*] a most brilliant vocalist, rather French[?] than Italian.—Her voice is[?] capable[?] of producing some effects, [*illeg.*], beyond the power of any [*illeg.*] vocalism[?] in the world; it is [*illeg.*]

II

A VISIT TO THE OPERA,

With some Gossip about the Singers, and Music,
By Mose Velsor,[1] of Brooklyn.

Come reader, would you not like to go with us to the Italian Opera?— We will suppose you are some good fellow of a man—or woman either, it makes no difference—whose days are mostly spent in work; so the Opera will be altogether new to you.

Here we are, up Broadway, turning round the corner to our right hand, down East 14th street—us two[2] part of quite an animated crowd.—

"Book of the Opera?— Book of the Opera? English and Italian," sing out the boys, who run around us as we pass,[3] offering little shilling or two shilling[4] pam-

had been inspired by music and that he thought of Alboni's voice whenever he was writing about a mockingbird or any other bird on a fragrant summer night. The MS description is repeated in "ITALIAN SINGERS IN AMERICA." See also "You know how the one," "Lafayette Aaron Burr," "Restrain Gesture;" "To a Certain Cantatrice" (1860) and "Proud Music of the Storm" (1869), ll. 76–77, 92–94; "Seeing Niagara to Advantage," *SD, Prose 92,* I, 236; "The Old Bowery," *NB,* ibid., II, 592; "Some Laggards Yet, *The Perfect Human Voice,*" GBMF, ibid., II, 674; "Old Actors, Singers, Shows, &c., in New York," ibid., II, 694; "How Leaves of Grass Was Made," ibid., II, 772.

25. Deleted: "&"

26. Leaf torn at left. Vincenzo Bellini, *Norma,* Act II, Sc. 1. WW remembered the experience as late as 1880 ("Seeing Niagara to Advantage," *SD, Prose 92,* I, 236). Deleted: "meditating [?]" ; inserted and deleted above "[*del.*] meditating" : "plotting" ; inserted in pencil above "the" : "con sidering"

27. Preceding two words inserted in pencil above "tears" and "coursing"

28. Inserted in pencil above space between "She" and "is" : "too"

29. Anna La Grange (or de la Grange) (1824–1905), soprano, appeared in NY in 1855 and 1856, but not again until 1868 and 1869. Inserted in pencil above space between "La Grange" and "the" : "one of"

30. Deleted in pencil: "present" ; inserted in pencil above "[*del.*] present" : "latest"

31. Inserted above "soprano"

1. Velsor was WW's mother's maiden name.

2. Two words inserted above "part" ; redundant initial dash not shown.

3. Deleted: "with" ; inserted above "[*del.*] with" : "offering"

4. Preceding three words inserted above "shilling pamphlet"

phlets containing the Italian[5] text of the piece on one page, with the English[6] translation of it on the opposite page.—

What then[7] is the Opera?— The "grand opera," as it is often called?—

For the information of you,[8] our unsophisticated companion, we will[9] say that it is a composition, of the same nature as a play in the theatre, all the dialoge of the characters being sung, or melodiously recited by note, to the [2] accompaniment of a band of instruments, the orchestra.—By acknowledged consent, the music of the Italian composers and singers is at the head of the rest;—Germans, French, English, all bow down to the Italian style.—

In a grand Opera, the story is generally a love-affair—sometimes historical, introducing real personages—all the characters being serious.—Only a class of operas, the "operas buffa," have comic characters. The grand opera, for instance, would be likely to open with a chorus of persons, giving an inkling of the plot, and of what characters are coming on.— There are always, for the principal[10] parts, a soprano, a tenor, and a base; often, in addition, a baritone, contralto, second soprano, second tenor, &c.

THE N. Y. ACADEMY OF MUSIC.[11]

The edifice in 14th st. corner of Lexington avenue,[12] is one of the largest audience buildings in America—and indeed in the world.— It is of elegant architectural appearance outside, especially at night—adorned with its plentiful, round, moon-like lights.—Here we are at the front! What a gay[13] show!— The[14] visiters are now in full tide—the lookers on—The [3] crowds of pedestrians—the numerous private carriages dashing up to the great[15] porch—the splendid and shiny horses—the footmen jumping down and[16] opening the carriage doors—the beautiful and richly drest women alighting, and passing up the steps under the full blaze of the lights—these and their accompaniments, make a sight worth seeing, to a novice—or especially to the country stranger in New York.

The Academy of Music, outside, has, as we said,[17] a large, ornamental stately appearance, with its arch-topped windows and doors, and its brown-colored walls.[18]

5. Deleted: "vers"
6. Deleted: "version"
7. Inserted above "is"
8. Word and comma inserted above "our"
9. Deleted: "tell you" ; inserted above "[*del.*] tell you" : "say"
10. Deleted: "characters" ; inserted above "[*del.*] characters" : "parts"
11. Opened in 1855.
12. Preceding seven words and comma inserted above "edifice . . . largest"
13. Deleted: "sight" ; inserted above "[*del.*] sight" : "show"
14. Capital letter over lowercase.
15. Deleted: "front"
16. Preceding three words inserted above "footmen opening"
17. Preceding three words and comma inserted above "has, a large"
18. Originally a new paragraph began, but WW inserted an arrow and wrote "(run in" in the right margin.

Inside, the house is a perfect success only in the way of sound.—You can hear with ease any where through the building; but in the third and fourth tiers, (including[19] about one third of the auditorium)[20] from nearly half the[21] seats no view of the stage can be obtained at all.— Such is the fault of the construction of the edifice.— The house is probably too narrow for its length; it is shaped like a compressed horse-shoe, but should have been shaped like an expanded one.—

[4] A LOOK AROUND THE HOUSE.

But[22] now from our seat[23] down in the middle of the parquette, let us take a good look around.— The appearance of the Academy, when lit up, and the boxes filled with people, and the performance going on is one of the most[24] remarkable and effective that can be imagined.— Hundreds upon hundreds of gas-lights, softened with globes of ground glass, shed[25] their brilliancy upon the scene.— Seated in the red velvet arm-chairs of the parquette, and on the cushioned sofas of the dress-circle, are groups of gentlemen, and of the most superbly dressed women, some of them with that high bred air, and self-possession, obtained by mixing[26] much with the "best society."

Just before the curtain rises, for fifteen or twenty minutes, line after line, party after party, come streaming down the passages, seeking the seats previously engaged—[27] most of them under the convoy of the ushers.— From every direction opera-glasses are level'd by white-gloved hands.— Those who have been in the habit of going only to the other theaters or places of amusement, will be struck with the [5] quietness and blandness that pervades the whole place, like an atmosphere—no hubbub—no "hi-hi's."

THE ORCHESTRA.—

Now, to the tap-tap of the conductor, the orchestra begins.— What honeyed smoothness! How exact! How true and clear! How inimitable the manner of the conductor, quietly signing with slight waves of his wand, to the right hand or the left! How delicious the proportion between the kinds of instruments—rarely met with in ordinary bands, but here perfect.— The violins, the bugles, the flutes, the drums, the base-fiddles, the violincellos—all, all, so balanced and their results merging into each other.—

19. Deleted: "nearly half" ; inserted above "[*del.*] nearly half" : "about one-third"

20. Deleted: "in" ; inserted above "[*del.*] in" : "from"

21. Deleted: "sle"

22. Inserted "Now" not reduced to lowercase in MS.

23. Deleted: [*illeg.*]

24. Deleted: "splendid" ; inserted above "[*del.*] lendid" and "that can" : "remarkable and effective"

25. Deleted: "a" ; inserted above "[*del.*] a" : "their"

26. Deleted: "only"

27. Deleted: "some" ; inserted above "[*del.*] some" : "most"

Now a rapid passage full of semiquavers given without the least discord by fifteen or twenty violins.— Now the clear warble of the flute—and now a passage in which advances the elephantine tread of the trombones.— Now a solo on the fagotto, relieved by the low, soothing, gulping notes of the base-viols.— And [6] now,[28] a long, tumultuous, crowded grand finale, ending with a grand crash of all the instruments together, every one, (it would seem)[29] making as much noise as it possibly can,—an effect which we perceive you don't like at all, but which we privately confess in your ear, is one of the greatest treats we obtain from a visit to the opera.—

ITALIAN MUSIC AND METHOD.

We have already hinted at the supremacy of Italian music.— The English opera, the tunes of the ballads, &c. sung by the various bands of "minstrels," and indeed all modern[30] musical performances and compositions, are, to all intents and purposes, but driblets from Italian music.— True there are bequeathed to us, from other quarters,[31] some fresh and original tunes, as the native songs of Scotland, Ireland, and one or two other lands; but as to a theory of the lyric art, and its[32] practice too, there is really no other worth the attention of one who wishes to be a good musician[33] only that of Italy.— That is the only large, fresh, free, mag[7]nificent method—and[34] under its auspices alone[35] will there ever be great and perfect American singers, male and female.

Reader, perhaps you have been[36] merely once to the Italian Opera—and didn't like it.— If so, the deficiency was in yourself.— So[37] far-developed, and of course artificial a thing as Italian music cannot be understood or appreciated at once. Then the flurry of a new scene distracts the attention.— If the piece is[38] unknown to you, it were better to procure the English translation of it beforehand and read it over once or twice; for it destroys all the enjoyment of the music to follow it, page by page during the performance.

LONG STUDY AND PRACTICE NEEDED TO MAKE A SINGER.

Few realise the long and arduous study required to make a[39] first-class singer.— Years and years are to be occupied—precept upon precept—and, above

28. Deleted: "at"
29. Parenthetical words inserted above "one" and down right margin.
30. Inserted above "all musical"
31. Preceding three words and comma inserted above "us, some fresh"
32. Inserted above space between "and" and "practice"
33. Deleted: ", but" ; dash inserted and deleted; inserted "only" above "[*del.*], but"
34. Deleted: "only"
35. Inserted above in space between "auspices" and "will"
36. Deleted: "only" ; inserted above "[*del.*] only" : "merely"
37. Deleted: [*illeg.*]
38. Deleted: "new," ; inserted above "is [*del.*] new, it" : "unknown to you,"
39. Deleted: "real" ; inserted above "[*del.*] real" : "first class"

all, practice upon practice.— In Italy there are conservatories of music, where young persons commence in time, under patient and competent teachers— There they[40] [*10*][41] excellent ones—Bettini,[42] Mario,[43] Tiberini,[44] Brignoli[45] and Steffani.—[46] There are no better, probably in Europe or America,[47] than the two last named.—

Many of the[48] opera singers are Jews and Jewesses.—There are some very creditable American singers, of late, making debuts in the[49] Italian Opera. We need a[50] good school, where music can be[51] taught conscientiously and profoundly.—

AU REVOIR.

So,[52] friendly reader, we have filled our column, more or less, with a visit, us two,[53] to the Italian Opera with you, and with[54] random [*illeg.*] ourselves [*illeg.*][55]

40. What was probably part of the content of original MS pages 8–9 can be found in "ITALIAN SINGERS IN AMERICA" as supplemented by the Furness transcript from Bucke's collection.

41. Deleted: "fine" ; inserted above "[*del.*] fine" : "excellent"

42. Alessandro Bettini (1823–1865), tenor, sang occasionally in NY between 1850 and 1852. WW mentions his "pensive and incomparable tenor in Donizetti's *La Favorita*" in "The Old Bowery," *NB, Prose* 92, II, 591, 592; "The Perfect Human Voice," *GBMF,* ibid., II, 674; "Old Actors, Singers, Shows, &c., in New York," ibid., II, 693, and in "Restrain Gesture." The effect of a *bel canto* tenor on WW is attested by "Song of Myself," sec. 26, ll. 601–602. The tenor there referred to may have been almost any one of or all of those he heard, but if he had an individual in mind it was Bettini, whose vocalism he especially praised, Brignoli, or perhaps Mario (see *n*43 below).

43. Giuseppe Mario (1810–1883), generally considered to be the greatest tenor of his period, sang in NY in 1854–1855. WW mentions him less often than Bettini in his published works. See "Plays and Operas Too," *SD, Prose* 92, I, 20, "The Old Bowery," and in *NB,* ibid., II, 592: "he was inimitable — the sweetest of voices, a pure tenor, of considerable compass and respectable power." Manuscript references suggest a deeper response: "memorials" [*33, 48*]. See also "Notes & Memories" and "Specimen Days Grisi and Mario."

44. Mario Tiberini, tenor (1826–1880), made his NY debut in 1855. Less likely his wife, Angelica, since the other names are those of men.

45. Pasquale (or Pasqualino) Brignoli (1824–1884), tenor, made his NY debut in 1854 and remained a popular favorite for twenty years. His death inspired WW's "The Dead Tenor" (1884). WW seems to have been acquainted with him (Traubel, IV, 249, 250).

46. A tenor named Steffani sang in NY in the 1858–1859 season.

47. Preceding four words and comma inserted above "than the two"

48. Deleted: "Italian" ; inserted: "opera"

49. Inserted.

50. Deleted: [*illeg.*]

51. Deleted: "tan"

52. Deleted: "good"; inserted: "friendly"

53. Preceding two words and comma inserted.

54. Deleted: "our"

55. Leaf trimmed; an inserted word "ourselfs[*?*] " and several ascenders visible.

III.

ITALIAN SINGERS IN AMERICA.

This country now has its steady succession of the best Italian singers, male and female.— We do not think much of Piccolomini,[1] the present "rage."— She[2] is not, in reality, as fine a lyric artist as[3] several of those we have heard, in New York,[4] and about whom there has been no furore.—[5]

The best songstress ever in America was Alboni.—[6] Her voice is[7] a contralto of large compass, high and low—and probably sweeter tones never issued from human lips. The mere sound of[8] that voice was pleasure enough.— All persons [2] appreciated Alboni—the common crowd quite as well as the connoisseurs. We used to go in the upper tiers of the theatre, (the Broadway,)[9] on the nights of her performance, and remember seeing that part of the auditorium packed full of New York young men, mechanics, "roughs," &c., entirely oblivious of all except Alboni, from the time the great songstress came on the stage, till she left it again.—[10]

Alboni is a fully developed woman, with perfect-shaped feet, arms, and hands.— [3] Some thought her fat—*we* always thought her beautiful.—Her face is regular and pleasant—her forehead low—plentiful[11] black hair, cut short, like a boy's—a slow and graceful style of walk—attitudes of inimitable beauty, and large black eyes.—We have seen her in pathetic scenes, (as in Norma planning the death of her children,)[12] with real tears, like rain, coursing each other down her cheeks. Alboni is now in Paris, singing at the Grand Opera there.—

La Grange,[13] Steffano,[14] and Bosio[15] are also fine singers—either of them better than the aforesaid lady.[16]

1. WW seems to have first written "Piccolamini." Marietta Piccolomini (1834–1899) made her New York debut in Verdi's *La Traviata,* October 20, 1858, the only season she appeared in this country. The role of Violetta had been created for her, but she did not sing in the disastrous first performance. WW's distaste for her voice perhaps reflects his loyalty to the older tradition of *bel canto,* exemplified by the operas of Donizetti, Rossini and Bellini, which was being replaced by younger composers, especially Verdi, with a dramatic realism. A critic in the New York *Herald* (October 21, 1858), quoted in Odell, VII, 157, points out the shift.
2. Capitalized over lowercase "s"
3. Deleted: "W[*?*]"
4. Preceding three words and comma inserted.
5. WW indicated a new paragraph by a sign.
6. See "Steffanone."
7. Deleted: "what is called"
8. Deleted: "her" ; inserted above "[*del.*] her" : "that"
9. Deleted: "and"
10. WW indicated a new paragraph by a sign.
11. Deleted: "blu[*?*]"
12. See "Steffanone."
13. See "Steffanone."
14. Steffanone?
15. The soprano Angiolina Bosio sang in NY in 1850.
16. Considering WW's high praise of Alboni, it is probable that he meant to refer to Piccolomini.

IV.

Practice two, three or four.

practice two, three, or four hours, every day — perhaps continuing patiently for six or eight years.

The voice is a curious organ, and follows the general health for good or evil.— The body must be vigorous and sound, before the voice can be so. Excess, habitual intoxication, voluptuousness, bad blood, starvation, dyspepsia, a sunken chest, &c, &c, are all obstacles in the way of a fine vocal utterance.

ITALIAN SINGERS IN AMERICA

This country has its steady succession of the best Italian singers, male and female.— We do not think much of Piccolomini, the present "rage".— She is not, in reality, as fine a lyric artist as several of those we have heard in New York, and about whom there has been no furore.

The best songstress ever in America was Alboni. Her voice is a contralto of large compass, high and low—and probably sweeter tones never issued from human lips. The mere sound of that voice was pleasure enough. All persons appreciated Alboni—the common crowd quite as well as the connoisseurs. We used to go in the upper tiers of the theatre, (the Broadway) on the nights of her performance, and remember seeing that part of the auditorium packed full of New York young men, mechanics, "roughs," &c., entirely oblivious to all except Alboni, from the time the great songstress came on the stage, till she left it again.—

Alboni is a fully developed woman, with perfect-shaped feet, arms, and hands.— Some thought her fat—*we* always thought her beautiful. Her face is regular and pleasant, her forehead low—plentiful black hair, cut short, like a boy's—a slow and graceful style of walk—attitudes of inimitable beauty, and large black eyes.— We have seen her in pathetic scenes (as in Norma planning the death of her children) with real tears, like rain, coursing each other down her cheeks. Alboni is now in Paris, singing at the Grand Opera there.—

La Grange, Stefano, and Bosio are also fine singers—either of them better than the aforesaid lady.

The Voice Is a Curious Organ.

Manuscript in Virginia. Inscribed in black ink on white wove scrap 3½" x 8". The writing and the width of the pen point are identical with "A VISIT TO THE OPERA," and this scrap may be part of the missing p. 8, which probably dealt with vocal training. It is identical with the second paragraph of "practice two, three, four hours" . Date, 1858.

The voice is a curious organ, and follows the general health, for good or evil. The body must be vigorous and sound, before the voice can be so. Excess, habitual[1] intoxication, voluptuousness, bad blood, starvation, dyspepsia, a sunken chest, &c. &c., are all obstacles in the way of a fine vocal utterance.

1. Inserted above the space between "excess" and "in" in "intoxication"

The Idea of Reconciliation.

Manuscript in Yale. Inscribed in black ink on thin yellow wove paper, much wrinkled. Approx. 7⅛" x 4¾". The writing is uncharacteristically irregular. Cf. the following LC manuscript with the same title, "The idea of reconciliation," which also seems to have little to do with the stated topic, but is on a Williamsburgh tax form and thus of approximately the same date, 1857 or later.

The idea of reconciliation [1]

The idea of personality,[2] that which belongs to each person[3] as himself, or herself, and[4] that you may so heighten your personality by temperance,[5] by a clean and[6] powerful physique, by chastity,[7] by elevating the mind through[8] lofty discussions, and[9] lofty meditations and themes,[10] and by self-esteem and[11] divine love, that you can hardly go into a room or along the street, but an atmosphere of command[12] and fascination[13] shall exhale out of you upon[14] all you meet—

1. Title in a smaller hand, probably a later insertion.
2. Deleted: "the"
3. Deleted: ", by" ; inserted above: "as"
4. Deleted: "which can be so heightened" ; inserted: "that" above "which" and "you [*del.*] can [*ins.*] may so heighten your personality" above "can . . . heightened"
5. Preceding two words inserted above "by a" and"cl" in "clean"
6. Deleted: "perfect" ; inserted above: "powerful"
7. Deleted: "and" ; inserted and deleted above in left margin: "by"
8. Deleted: "great" ; inserted and deleted above: "high" ; inserted: "lofty" following "[*del.*] high" and above "di" in "discussions"
9. Deleted: "hi[?]"
10. Deleted: "that"
11. Deleted: "lov" ; inserted above: "divine"
12. This word blotted, perhaps deleted, in MS. Deleted: "and"
13. This word blotted, perhaps deleted, in MS.
14. Deleted: "whoever" ; inserted above: "all"

The Idea of Reconciliation.

Manuscript in LC (#70, sheet #375). Inscribed in black ink on verso of Williamsburgh tax form. On recto is blotting from another paper in which can be read the date "Oct 10 '89". The writing and the tax form indicate a date in the late 1850's. Since LC 70 is primarily a collection of notes towards "The Tramp and Strike Questions" (*SDC,* 1882) this MS must have drifted into this group by error. The problem of how it was blotted on the back is insoluble. It may be distantly related to the preceding MS of the same title and of the same period. Date after 1857. First published Furness, 58–59.

The idea of reconciliation—that what has been done, is consumed—Ever, out of its ashes, let new, sweeter, more amicable fruits ripen.—

The idea that no style of behaviour, or dress, or public institutions, or treatment by bosses of employed people, and nothing in the army or navy, nor in the courts, or police, or tuition, or amusements, can[1] permanently elude the jealous and passionate instinct of American standards.—

1. Deleted: "much longer" ; inserted: "permanently" above "[*del.*] much"

A Prostitute.

Manuscript in LC (Feinberg #190). Inscribed in black ink on four leaves of tan wove paper, approx. 12½" x 8". Bottom of [4] torn off. On verso of [1] and [2] is "Important Announcement!" and on [2] and [4] "A live work." The writing is identical. William White, "Whitman as Short Story Writer: Two Unpublished Manuscripts," *Notes and Queries,* 170 (March, 1962), 87–89, also publishes a brief connected beginning of the story, "Bright were the gleams." White dates the drafts in the 1840s, the decade in which WW was contributing short stories to magazines. The writing seems to be larger and looser than that of the 1840s or early 1850s. WW may have turned to fiction writing and to the composition of a book on health and physical training during the financially thin times between 1859 and 1861. The brief draft of the beginning, "Bright were the gleams," set in the salon of a *poule de luxe* (a most unusual locale for WW), suggests the remote possibility that he was inspired by a translation of *La Dame aux Camelias* (novel, 1848; play, 1852) by Dumas *fils,* or especially by Verdi's *La Traviata,* which he almost certainly saw in 1858, or the translation of the play, (1856) or the novel (1857), both under the title *Camille*. For other fiction see "Of a summer evening." For notes on story-writing, see "June 26 '59." First printed by White in *Notes and Queries*.

[*1*][1]A prostitute—large, passionate, unhappy Antoinette—[2]

A young N.Y. Mechanic—the hero—[3] /

A policeman /

Scene in an eating house /

Fulton Ferry— ? rendezvous /

Broadway /

? Open with Broadway in the full tide of a fashionable promenade[4] /

—A street at night—rapid confab /

1. On verso: "Important Announcement!"
2. Hanging indentation.
3. Hanging indentation.
4. Hanging indentation.

Movement—dialogue,—incident—[5] /

Oliver Sanclare, a gambler and lover[6],—absent awhile—on[7] a professional expedition, (or to escape the punishment of some crime committed)—but returns[?][8]—after Antoinette has inviegled[9]

[2][10]An old Quaker lady—good—sensible—(? how to[11] intertwine with Antoinette's affairs—[12] /

A bloody contest— ?[13] dangerously wounded ? by[14] ? Antoinette—interest to hang on the trial[15] /

Proud
Antoinette
A New York Romance of to-day.—

Antoinette's real name Ruth Anderson, a Quaker's daughter /

Josephine an upright noble girl, who loves[16] Hamp Anderson and whom he[17] has been in love with till inviegled by Antoinette.

[3][18]Open[19] with the interview between[20] Lilian and Hamp[21] which there is coolness and[22] breaking up of the engagement—

5. Hand at left and hand at left below point to this entry.
6. Deleted: "gone"
7. Deleted: "an"
8. Bottom of leaf tattered.
9. Bottom of leaf tattered.
10. On verso: *"A live work"*
11. Deleted: "bring"
12. Hanging indentation. The parenthetical statement is in three lines at right.
13. Deleted: "violently"
14. Following words in two lines at right of page. Query to left of both.
15. Hanging indentation. Next entry, evidently a trial title, deleted: "—The Fate of Antoinette"
16. Inserted.
17. Preceding three words inserted above "has"
18. On verso of *"A live work"*
19. Deleted: "the piece"
20. Leaf trimmed on both edges: "w" and "be" trimmed off.
21. Deleted: "Josephine"
22. Word possibly trimmed off at left.

A peaceful cheerful American scene[?][23]— A city home, in a two story house [?],[24] in[25] one of the New York streets[?][26] that terminate at the East River[27]

[4][28]*A few Characters,* rather than many.
Each Character, definitely and strongly drawn.— (not leaving that indistinct impression as in most stories)[29]

The plot with one or two strong leading lines of interest, woven with *decision,* and carried out to the end—*not too complicated*[30]

No sentimental drawling, nor long and sleepy descriptions—[31] /

Dialogue—animation—something stirring—[32] /

23. Word possibly trimmed off at left.
24. Leaf trimmed at left.
25. Leaf trimmed at left. Deleted: "on that"
26. Deleted: "a stree" ; inserted above: "one of the"
27. Leaf trimmed at left and right, torn at bottom. Beginnings of six lines of unidentifiable verse written sidewise on leaf and torn off.
28. On verso: "Birth-influences"
29. Hanging indentation. The parenthetical statement is on two lines at right. Inserted: "as" above wordspace between "impression" and "in"
30. Hanging indentation.
31. Hanging indentation.
32. Hanging indentation.

Bright Were the Gleams.

Manuscript in LC (Feinberg #4). Inscribed in black ink on white wove paper, approx. 11" x 7⅞". Evidently WW had put together in his mind the wild assortment of characters and situations sketched in "A prostitute." First printed by White in *Notes and Queries,* 170 (March 1962).

Bright were the gleams which the mirrors flashed back from the profuse gas-lights of the chandeliers, in the suite of parlors where Antoinette the courtesan received her visitors and friends.— All was in good taste; yet all was rich and elegant.— There were pictures on the walls, and statues in the corners.—

What air was that, from a first-class performer, after a capricious yet harmonious prelude, struck with vigorous fingers,[1] on a fine piano-forte—a noble and pensive song, which the player,[2] repeating on the instrument a few times, followed with his voice—attracting the admiration of the whole company?— It was a quaint old Scotch ballad, a tale of love, jealousy and death.— The laughing and conversation were hushed, as it proceeded, and when it closed, there was quite a silence.—

1. Deleted: "from" ; inserted above: "on"
2. Deleted: "after"

June 26 '59.

Manuscript missing. LC 89 contains photostats of six surviving pages (#3373–#3375). LC *Cat,* 17, gives dimensions of 17 x 10 cm. for the originals. Fortunately, when Emory Holloway examined the original prior to publication of *UPP,* he made two partial transcripts which he has kindly made available. Neither is complete nor are they identical, but they identify material printed elsewhere and suggest an order of entry. The older is in purple typescript and is hereafter referred to as "Holloway's early transcript." The more recent one, in black typescript, may be a recent copy of older notes, and is hereafter referred to as "Holloway's later transcript." (Both transcripts are deposited in the Spencer Research Library of the University of Kansas.) The texts are based on the surviving photostats, Holloway's transcripts, Furness, and *UPP*. Portions, as indicated, were first printed by Jean Catel, "Whitman Conferencier," *L'Ane d'Or,* V (Fevrier-Mars, 1926).

Since a definite order of entry cannot be established, the photostated material is printed first.

Despite the date June 26, 1859 in this manuscript, some of the material relates closely to WW's so-called "Oratory Notebook" (LC 88), which dates as early as 1858. See "Restrain Gesture."

[*3373L*][1] June 26 '59 —It is now time to *Stir*[2] first for *Money*[3] enough *to live and* provide for *M* [4]—*To Stir*[5]— first write Stories,[6] and get out of this Slough

[*3373R*]
The Bell

"Something to make a whole poem of"—[7]
the great bell
Many bells

1. The entry begins halfway down the page. "June 26 '59" written on three lines at right above "time to" . A large pointing hand above at left points toward the entry.
2. Printed in large separated script letters.
3. Preceding two words printed in large script with connected letters.
4. The letter is either very faintly inscribed or partly erased. It is, however, quite clearly *"M"*. Holloway, *UPP,* II, 91*n,* suggests a lover, his mother, or his sister Mary. WW was responsible for the support of his mother and the younger children, but Asselineau, I, 106ff., suggests a male lover.
5. Two words printed in large script with connected letters.
6. As far as is known the latest appearance in print of WW's fiction was the reprint of "The Last of the Sacred Army" (1842) in *Democratic Review,* 29 (November, 1851), (*E P & F,* 336).
7. The various bells are listed in column on the right side of the page.

the Pilot's bell
The fog bell
(the ship's bell that tolls the hour at sea
the muffled bell (funeral)
the cathedral bell (Europe)
The cemetery bell (as at Greenwood)
? The sleigh bells
the Muleteer's bells

[*3374L*][8] *Questions of Life.—*

Alive Beneath the ostensible questions unspoken[9] yet even speaking

[*3374R*] There was a space of 16 ft by 30 through which the body of the animal had left significant traces of its decay.— When the men [10]

Long I was held by the life that exhibits itself,
By what is done in the houses,[11] or the streets, or in company,
The usual pleasures and aims—the intercourse[12] to[13] which all conform, and which[14] the writers[15] celebrate
But[16] I[17] escape and celebrate[18] the untold and[19] carefully concealed life,
I celebrate the need of the love of comrades.[20]

8. The letters on an otherwise illegible leaf projecting from beneath shows that this page was probably written upside-down. With the exception of the last two entries the inscription has been deleted with horizontal lines. It reads as follows:

Have you loved and been beloved?
Have
Are you solitary and without love? Or is your love unrequited?
Do you love to ? And is your love requited?
Unspoken
[*Two uncancelled entries printed in text above*]
Ha

9. Deleted: "they the"

10. Entry cancelled by a vertical slash but not used elsewhere.

11. Deleted: "in the" ; inserted above: "or"

12. Deleted: "of"

13. Deleted: [*illeg.*]

14. Inserted above "the"

15. Deleted: "conform"

16. Deleted: "now"

17. Inserted: "[*del.*] will escape [*del.*] and [*del.*] tr and" above "celebrate the"

18. WW deleted "the" , added "one" , then inserted "the" beginning the next line above and before "untold" . He did not, however, delete "one"

19. Deleted: "and" following "and"

20. An early draft of "In Paths Untrodden" (1860). Bowers, 66, 68, prints a fair MS draft which, since it includes the emendations in this MS, must be later. A variety of MS exist.

I hold it should be the glory and pride of America not to be like other lands, but different, after its own different spirit.[21]

[*3375R, L blank*] quite a first rate ox-tamer (Sam Irwin's description[22]

Directions for Story Writing

Haste along (Don't stop so long to think)—*write quick. Strongly lined and colored.* Only one or two grand culmination-points (perhaps only one is best,) in one story. *Dash off characters at random,* and then fit them in afterward *A strong beginning to arouse curiosity*—and also a well-written ending. *One or two marked characters.* Plenty of incident—Dialogues[23]

One called To Religious Inquirers
To Women[24]

Style[25]

/ Keep steadily understood, with respect to the effects and fascinations of *Elocution* (so broad, spacious, and vital) that although the Lectures may be printed and sold at the end of every performance, nothing can make up for that *irresistible attraction and robust living* treat of the vocalization of the lecture, by me,—which must defy all competition with the printed and read repetition of the Lectures.[26]

Manahatta Lectures "A great city proposed."[27] Do you know whom you celebrate in the name of this haughty and populous city?— You celebrate the meanest and feeblest tyrant that ever press'd the English throne—the Duke of York, duly James the Second—the burner of women and torturer of men, for the least freedom in thought or words. Every time the hitherto name of this city is written with the pen or spoken with the mouth it celebrates that man.— If it remains fastened to

21. Text from Holloway's later transcript.

22. Although "The Ox-Tamer" was not published until 1874, it was apparently composed as early as 1860 (Allen, 267).

23. Text from Furness, 188*n;* inserted here on authority of Holloway's early transcript.

24. Text from Holloway's early transcript.

25. Not in Furness, 33; inserted on authority of Holloway's transcripts.

26. Text from Furness, 33, but inserted here on authority of Holloway's early transcript. According to Holloway's transcripts, here follows a stub about half the width of a leaf on which is pasted by a patch at the top the famous tintype of a woman with hair parted in the middle and falling in curls on either side, about which there has been much speculation. Reproduced *UPP,* II, facing 70. The last word, "world" of "Manahatta Lectures," can be seen on a following leaf in the photograph. First published by Jean Catel, *L' Ane d'Or,* 42.

27. Printed as titles, one above the other, by Furness.

the city, when after times ask what the name perpetuates, they will have to be answered that it perpetuates the memory of that wretch whom his people chased away, but whose memory is preserved here in the grandest freest and most beautiful city of the world!— It celebrates one who attempted the basest violations of his word, of the colonial charter of this very city, and of all human rights! A pretty name, this, to fasten on the proudest and most democratic city in the world![28]

THREE LECTURES ON RELIGION[29]

Finale—state, in a strong manner, (with wierd illustration if necessary), that all I say is but arousing and troubling,—that I can settle nothing—that we are sailing a great sea blown hither and thither and know not our own destination—only this[30] that, whatever it is I, full of confidence, full of joy, know that it is good for me, and that it is divine and great.[31]

Lizzie 89 25th st[32] the true religious genius of our race now seems to say, Beware of churches! Beware of priests![33] above all things the flights and sublime extasies of the soul cannot submit to the exact statements of any church, or any creed.[34]

Enfans d'Adam[35]

There is a lying-in ward—provision is made for women.[36]

O[37] youthful love!
O ? death
O deathly bed!
I sing your[38] gentle song
I sing your[39] love, O faithful love
I sing the with tender tongue[40]

28. Text from Furness, 61; inserted here on authority of Holloway's later transcript.

29. Title as in Furness. See section on Religion.

30. Fist pointing right.

31. Text from Furness, 53; inserted here on authority of Holloway's early transcript. First printed by Jean Catel, *L'Ane d'Or,* 41.

32. Text from Holloway's early transcript.

33. Text from Holloway's early transcript. Also printed in Furness, 41, where the two warnings are printed on separate lines. First printed by Jean Catel, *L'Ane d'Or,* 42.

34. From Furness, 41. Not found in MS sources.

35. Text from Holloway's early transcript. He notes that this entry was on a page by itself.

36. Text from Holloway's early transcript. Holloway notes that it refers to a German hospital on 14th St. Court.

37. Deleted: "joyous"

38. Deleted: "holy"

39. Deleted: "fate"

40. Text from Holloway's early transcript. It is suggestive of "Out of the Cradle Endlessly Rocking," which appeared in the NY *Saturday Press,* December 24, 1859.

Down by the Ottawa
—Down by the Ottawa—lived the young lumberman
—lived with his young wife.[41]

Style

besides direct addressing *to you,* another leading trait of Lectures may well be—strong assertion—("I say")—launched out with fire, or emphasis, or enthusiasm, or anger— (each of the above emotions may come in well in the elocution of lectures)[42]

Style
A main requirement of any Lecture.

(*One leading and simple idea*)[43] Does it embody and express fitted to popular apprehension without too much complication—and the accessories (and other ideas, in themselves, equally great, but, for the present purposes not properly brought too forward) all carefully kept down so that the *strong colors lights and lines* of the lecture mark that *one simple leading*[44] *idea or theory*[45]

The trouble in Lecture style is often the endeavor (from the habit of forming the rhythmic style of *Leaves of Grass*) involuntarily to preserve a sort of rhythm in the Lecture sentences, It seems to me this rhythm, for them, is not only not necessary, but is often dangerous to their character-requirements—which, for speaking purposes, need to be abrupt, sometimes crackling, with strong contrasts.[46]

Do[47] not attempt to put *too much* in one Lecture nor make it too complicated —The elocution should be so broad and spacious as to make a short lecture (in writing) fill up the hour.[48]

41. Text from Holloway's early transcript.

42. Text from Furness, 36; inserted on authority of Holloway's early transcript. First printed by Catel, *L'Ane d'Or,* 42.

43. Not in Furness.

44. In Furness, 36, the three following words are printed on a separate line preceded by a fist pointing obliquely upward.

45. Text from Furness, 36; inserted on authority of Holloway's later transcript. Holloway gives "ONE SIMPLE LEADING IDEA, or THEORY" for the last phrase.

46. Text from Furness, 35; inserted on authority of Holloway's transcripts. First printed by Catel, *L'Ane d'Or,* 42. Holloway transcribes the dividing line.

47. In Furness, 36, paragraph preceded by a fist pointing right.

48. Text from Furness, 36; inserted here on authority of Holloway's transcripts. First printed by Catel, *L'Ane d'Or,* 42.

To The Prevailing Bards[49]

Comrades! I am the bard of Democracy
Others are more correct and elegant than I, and more at home in the parlors and schools than I,[50]
But I alone advance among the people en-masse, coarse and strong
I am he standing first there, solitary chanting the true America,
I alone of all bards, am suffused as with the common people.
I alone receive them with a perfect reception and love—and they shall receive me.
It is I who live in these, and in my poems,— O they are truly me!
But that shadow, my likeness, that goes to and fro seeking a livelihood, chattering, chaffering,
I often find myself standing and looking at it where it flits—
That likeness of me, but never substantially me.

49. Text from *UPP,* II, 91. See "That Shadow My Likeness" (1860). Curiously enough, this poem is not mentioned in Holloway's transcripts, but it clearly is part of the notebook.

50. *UPP,* II, 91*n,* points a parallel in "Not Youth Pertains to Me" (1865), l. 3, but the idea is not unusual in WW.

Signal Bell.

Manuscript not found. Text from *N&F,* 176 (Pt. IV, #114; *CW,* X, 30). Probably in column in MS. Possibly related to notes for "The Bell" in "June 26 '59" Since it is a Bucke MS it probably dates from before 1860. First printed in *N&F.*

Signal bell. Warning bell. Ocean bell. Storm bell. Notes.

A String of Poems.

Manuscript not found. Text from *N&F,* 169 (Pt. IV, 63; *CW,* X, 18). Since this entry and "Theory of a Cluster" have been used to attack the authenticity of "Children of Adam," it should be remembered that explicitly "Adamic" poems antedate explicitly "Calamus" poems, specifically "I Sing the Body Electric" (1855), "A Woman Waits for Me" (1856), "Spontaneous Me" (1856). Since, as Bowers (lxxiii–lxxiv) points out, WW dropped the title "Live Oak Leaves" in late spring, 1859, and adopted calamus as his symbol of manly love, the date must be earlier. First printed *N&F.*

A string of Poems, (short, etc.) embodying the amative love of woman—the same as *Live Oak Leaves* do the passion of friendship for man.

Theory of a Cluster.

Manuscript in Duke (15, #38). Inscribed in black pencil on flimsy white wove paper torn along top and right, approx. 8" x 6⁵/16". Entries in hanging indentation and irregularly placed. The date must be after late spring, 1859 (see "A string of Poems." The use of "cluster" dates from this time also (see "A cluster of Poems"). Facsimile in Trent *Cat.*, facing 28. First printed *N&F*, 124 (Pt. III, #142; *CW*, IX, 150).

Theory of a Cluster of Poems the same *to the Passion of Woman-Love* as the "Calamus-Leaves" are to adhesiveness, manly love. /

Full of animal-fire, tender, burning, —the tremulous ache, delicious, yet such a torment,

The swelling,[1] elate and vehement, that will not be denied, /

Adam, as a central figure and type. /[2]

one piece

Presenting a vivid picture,[3] (in connection with the spirit,) of a fully-complete, well-developed,man[4] eld, bearded, swart, fiery—as a more than rival of the youthful type-hero of novels[5] and love poems[6]

1. Deleted: "and"

2. Preceding seven words inscribed to right of leaf, set off by line curving up at left and across to right, inserted more or less between entries. See facsimile in Trent *Cat.*, 28.

3. Deleted: "of"

4. Deleted: "old" ; inserted above: "man"

5. Deleted: "an"

6. Preceding entry in hanging indentation.

Sea Winrows.

Manuscript in NYPL (Berg). Inscribed in black pencil on white wove scrap approx. 6¼" x 3⅜", left edge torn irregularly. Spaced irregularly down the leaf. On verso: "Sands and Drifts." The relationship between the two is not clear. Bucke identifies this MS as notes for "As I Ebb'd with the Ocean of Life" (*LG* 1860). First published by Bucke, "Notes on the Text of *Leaves of Grass*," *Conservator*, 7 (February 1897), 185.

Sea Winrows
Ocean Winrows
Beach
Beach Winrows
Winrows[1] with sand and sea-hay, — Winrows[2] Sand and scales and beach-hay[3]
    Sands and Drifts
Winrows and Beach-hay Under-foot /[4]
Walking the Beach /
Drift underfoot underfoot Drift /
Wash
Drift at your feet

1. Circled in black pencil.
2. A large ¶.
3. A slant mark below the line in red ink, possibly by Bucke.
4. A red-ink checkmark probably by Bucke.

Sands and Drifts.

Manuscript in NYPL (Berg). Inscribed in black ink on verso of "Sea Winrows." The latter is a note for "As I Ebb'd with the Ocean of Life" (1859) and it is possible that this note refers to a projected collection of sea poems or possibly, as Bucke suggests, "Leaves of Grass. 1," *LG* 1860, 195ff. This 1860 cluster, however, is not unified as a sea-cluster. At any rate neither "As I Ebb'd with the Ocean of Life" nor "Leaves of Grass. 1" were ever placed after "Calamus." Variants of this phrase were apparently used as a trial title between 1870 and 1883, perhaps suggesting "Sea-Drift" (1881). See also "Sands and Drift Mrs Louisa Whitman" and "Drift Sands." First published by Bucke in *N&F,* 170 (Pt. IV, #74; CW, X, 20).

Sands and Drifts / This collection to be transposed so as to come before *Calamus Leaves*

Sands and Drift Mrs Louisa Whitman.

Manuscript in LC (Feinberg #962). Inscribed in pencil on white wove paper, approx. 7" x 6¼". All but first three words cancelled with slanting stroke. On verso is "Short Lectures." Probably an advertisement. The Whitmans moved to the house on Portland Avenue in Brooklyn May 1, 1859 and had a tenant, John Brown, the first of April, 1860 (*Corr.*, I, 51*n*). The date is probably 1859.

Sands and Drift [1]

Mrs. Louisa Whitman, Portland av. first house north of Myrtle av. —[2] a pleasant and[3] healthy location—large new house—has[4] several fine unfurnished[5] rooms,[6] to let with board.

1. At the top of leaf. The following paragraph is considerably below and unrelated to the projected title. See "Sands and Drifts." Small wavy line in the space between entries.
2. Deleted: "has an airy and" . Dash between "has" and "an" not deleted, not printed.
3. Word blotted and smeared.
4. Inserted above "s" on "several"
5. Inserted above "rooms"
6. Preceding two words inserted above "with"

Poem ? Or.

Manuscript not found. Text from Furness, 65–67. It is probable that these entries are quite separate MS. The verbal parallels with "Says" and "By Blue Ontario's Shores," both of 1860, are slight but so striking as to make it necessary to date the entries close to 1860.

Poem ? or [:][1] statement lecture criticism
Suppositious theory as of one who saw where the existing condition of literature was weak, and needed strengthening——What was most needed in America, and through a long range of the future—How the great organizations of machinery, education, refinement, peace, and general social security, make men now (and current literature) deficient in those strong fibres.

Literature to these gentlemen is a parlor in which no person is to be welcomed unless he come attired in dress coat and observing the approved decorums with the fashionable.

He leaps over or dives under for the time, all the reforms and propositions[2] that worry these days, and goes to the making of powerful men and women.——With these, he says, all reforms, all good, will come.——Without these all reforms, all good, all outside effects were useless and helpless.——

He does not lose by comparison with the orange tree or magnolia,[3] with fields that nourish the sugar plant or the cotton plant . . . what strengthens or clothes, adorns or is luscious can be had through subtle counterparts from him——from him magnolia and orange and sugarplant and cottonplant and all fruits and flowers and all the sorts and productions of the earth.

——You must become a force in the state——and a real and great force——just as real and great as the president and congress——greater than they.

1. Brace in Furness's text.
2. Cf. "Says" (1860), sec. 6, l. 18, *LG CRE,* 600.
3. The general thought is close to Preface 1855, ll. 77ff. The magnolia and orange tree appear in "By Blue Ontario's Shore" (1856), sec. 6, l. 79, the magnolia also in "truly the things."

Not (negligible) must be the poets I would have. The poets I would have must be a power in the state, and an engrossing power in the state.

It is not a labor of clothing or putting on or describing——it is a labor of clearing away and reducing——for everything is beautiful in itself and perfect——and the office of the poet is to remove what stands in the way of one perceiving the beauty and perfection.

The very greatest writers can never be understood or appreciated forthwith——any more than the very greatest discoverers. It takes some ages to enfold the scope of the invention of steam-power or printing, or the discovery of America, or the commencement of the greatest breed of poets.

English Runic.

Manuscript in LC (#90, sheets #876–902). Paper-covered notebook, $6^{5}/_{16}''$ x $3^{15}/_{16}''$, blue covers and white wove leaves. Disassembled and mounted. Three blank leaves missing. Inscribed in black pencil, red pencil, blue pencil, black ink as noted. Lines between entries indicated here by slashes.

Although entries are chiefly concerned with WW's trip to Boston between March and May, 1860, to oversee the printing of *LG* 1860, some refer to Brooklyn and New York.

The typographical notes on [*870V–871R*] refer to the printing of *LG* 1860. Unfortunately it was impossible personally to examine the style books cited, so that I have relied on photographic reproductions of the pages cited and on others suggested by staff members of the libraries consulted. Since WW did not use all the types noted, it would seem that the notes are preliminary jottings. The typographical exuberance of *LG* 1860 suggests that it would repay a thorough study by a specialist.

The following type-specimen books were examined. For "Rogers" : *Specimens, Containing a Selection from the Printing Materials Made at This Establishment. Boston Type Foundry.* (Boston, 1857); *Condensed Specimen Book from the Boston Type Foundry* (Boston, 1858); *Condensed Specimen Book from the Boston Type Foundry. John K. Rogers & Co.* (Boston, 1860). All three are unpaged. For "Johnson" : *Specimens of Printing Types, Plain and Ornamental, Borders, Cuts, Rules, Dashes Etc. from the Factory of L. Johnson & Co.* (Philadelphia, 1859).

WW visited Boston at a time of vigorous development. Identifications of sites, buildings and business houses which so impressed him are based on the following sources: Adams, Sampson, and Company, *The Boston Directory . . . for the Year Commencing July 1, 1861* (Boston, 1861); Damrill, and Moores, and G. Coolidge, *Sketches and Business of Boston and Its Vicinity for 1860 and 1861* (Boston, 1860); Henry-Russell Hitchcock, *Boston Architecture, 1637–1954* (New York, 1954); Walter H. Kilham, *Boston After Bulfinch* (Cambridge, 1946); Moses King, *King's Handbook of Boston* (Boston, 1878); Walter Muir Whitehill, *Boston. A Topographical History,* 2d. ed. (Cambridge, 1968). I am indebted to Mr. Whitehill for his patient replies to my inquiries.

A number of entries were published by Clifton Joseph Furness, "Walt Whitman Looks at Boston," *NEQ,* I (July, 1928), 353–370 and Furness, 259–260. For WW's 1881 visit see "on to Boston," etc. For completion of *LG* 1881 see " '81 (Leaves of Grass finished)."

[*870R: Inside front cover*][1] English runic þ

Calamus 2 [*illeg.*] pica rustics[2]

1. In badly smudged black pencil.
2. Pica rustics (Johnson, *Specimens,* 62; Rogers, *Condensed Specimen Book,* n.p.) were not used.

?3 [*illeg.*] pica rustics [?] [:] 60 ¼ line ?

Great primer ornamented[3]

pica rustic P62[4]

2 line pica ornamented No. 7 p. 55 /[5]

"Enfans d'Adam[6]
? (2 line Saxon ornate shade p. 82[7]

2 lines [*illeg.*] in pica modern text p 85[8]

2 lines English scribe text shade p 87 /[9]

Calamus

canon scribe text shade

p. 87 Johnson's book[10]

3 line small[?] pica rustic p 68[11]

[871*R; 870V blank*][12] Boston [*illeg.*][13]

3. A number of Great Primer ornamental characters appear in Johnson, *Specimens,* 69, but were not used. Several Two-Line Pica Ornamented appear on 66, but were not used. The reference to "68" may be to Two-Line Great Primer Condensed Italian (68). The specimen book does not show numbers, but there is a conceivable relationship to the poem numbers in "Calamus," *LG* (1860). Rogers, *Condensed Specimen Book* (1860), n.p., however, shows a Two-Line Brevier Italian with numbers which appear identical.

4. Johnson, *Specimens,* not used.

5. Ibid. None of the seven varieties shown was used. Rule across leaf.

6. Ibid. The three characters shown are Antique Tuscan, which was not used.

7. Ibid. Fortunately WW did not use this extremely ornate character for the title of "Enfans d'Adam," although the Double Paragon Scribe Text Shaded (*Specimens,* 87) which he did use is scarcely more appropriate. The even more ornate title for "Leaves of Grass" (*LG* 1860, 195), an Open Scribe Text, does not seem to come from *Specimens*.

8. Less ornate than Double Paragon Scribe Text Shaded. Not used.

9. Preceded by pointing hand. Johnson, *Specimens*. Another ornate type similar to but smaller than Double Paragon Scribe Text Shaded. Not used. Line three-quarters across leaf from left.

10. Ibid. Similar to but larger than Double Paragon Scribe Text Shaded. Not used.

11. Ibid. Not used. See *n*2, above.

12. In badly smudged black pencil.

13. Probably a reference to the Boston Type Foundry. This establishment, which was at 6 Spring Lane, is listed separately in the Boston directory from the Boston Stereotype Foundry at 4 Spring Lane, which electrotyped *LG* (1860). His printer, George C. Rand and Avery, was at 3 Cornhill.

Chants Democratic 2 line primer or page 32 Johnsons book[14]

2″ Democratic —double Paragon composite p 39 Johnsons book[15]

Calamus 2 line great primer ornamented[?] Rogers book Boston Type Foundry /[16]

canon ornamented p 81 Johnsons book /[17]

Enfans d'Adam 2 line pica ornamented [*illeg.*] Rogers book /[18]

Leaves of Grass double Paragon scribe text shaded p. 87 Johnson's book /[19]

also same page[19a]

six line small pica German text ornamented[20]

See two dashes on p [*illeg.*] Johnsons book[21]

14. There are two two-line Long Primers on the cited page. WW seems to have used "No. 2," which is a slightly heavier type, for the word "Democratic" in the title "Chants Democratic." It appears that he used a variety of the typefaces shown on this page throughout *LG* 1860.

15. Not found. Line across leaf.

16. Widely dissimilar characters of this name are in Rogers, *Specimens* (1857); Rogers, *Specimens* (1858); Rogers, *Condensed Specimens* (1860). None were used.

17. Canon Ornamented No. 2 is a shaded "phantom" type; that is, composed of broken vertical lines. Not used.

18. Examples found in Rogers, *Specimens* (1860) and Rogers, *Condensed Specimen Book* (1858) not used. See *n*7, above.

19. Used for title of "Enfans d'Adam."

19a. Deleted: "four" ; inserted above: "six"

20. It is difficult to see why WW failed to use this extraordinarily ornate and ugly type. Pointed fist before next entry.

21. The dash between the title, "Proto-Leaf," and the first line of the poem in *LG* 1860, 5, is No. 14 in Johnson, *Specimens*, 4½. The others not located. In addition to the information given in footnotes to the text, the following decorative dashes from pages noted in *LG* 1860 have been found in Johnson, *Specimens*, 131: P. 174, half of Border 109; 352, half of Border 32; 358, half of Border 33 plus a central element not located; 359, part of Border 34; 361, part of Border 32 plus a floral center not located; 362, half of Border 33 plus a central element not found; 363, half of Border 32 plus a central element not found; 368 and 372 also use Border 32 but with different central elements. It seems clear that the various ornamental dashes and borders shown in Johnson were not solid pieces of type, but composed of several pieces which could be separated and rearranged. See *LG* 1860, 108 and 166 (not located). The curious curlicue dashes in *LG* 1860, e.g. 105, 127, 159, 174, 176, etc. appear to be combined from various characters from Johnson, *Specimens*, 123. The title "Leaves of Grass," *LG* 1860, 195, appears to be Canon Saxon Open, Rogers, *Specimens*, n.p. Unfortunately the type (if it is that) for the interesting title page could not be found.

[*872-813R*][22] George S. Phillips Chelsea Mass *January Searle*[23] 81 89[24]

[*874R; 872-873V blank*][25] John W A Scott cor of River & Cottage sts Cambridgeport. /

down Lowell st to Forest hill st—turn to the left, 3d house

[*875R; 874V blank*][26] Brookline find Mr Lyman's place Col. Perkins' (dead)[27] Mr Billings 59 Camden

[*876-877R; 875V blank*][28] In the South, (S. C., Georgia &c) "the most beautiful wild flower, in the piney region is the wild pink—the most fragrant the jessamine." blackberries and huckleberries abound—Wilmington, N. C.

[*878R; 877V blank*][29] BLACKS.—You see not near as many black persons in Boston, as you would probably expect; they are not near as plenty as in New York or Philadelphia. Their status here, however, is at once seen to be different. I have seen one working at case in a printing office, (Boston Stereotype Foundry, Spring lane,)—and no dis[*879R*]tinction made between him and the white compositors. Another I noticed, (and I never saw a blacker or woolier African,) an employee in the State House, apparently a clerk or under-official of some such kind. At the eating-houses, a black, when he wants his dinner, comes in and takes [*880R, V blank*] a vacant seat wherever he finds one—and nobody minds it. I notice that the mechanics and young men do not mind all this, either. As for me, I am too much a citizen of the world to have the least compunction about it. Then the blacks here are certainly of a superior [*881* R, V *blank*] order—[30]there is a black lawyer, named Anderson[31] (a resident of Chelsea) practising here in Boston, quite smart and just as big as the best of them. /[32] and in Worcester, they are now put

22. One leaf, numbered thus by LC.

23. Black pencil. George Searle Phillips ("January Searle"), 1815–1889, journalist, editor of the NY *Sun*. He was an enthusiastic admirer of *LG* and wrote in verse "Letter Impromptu," dated from Chelsea, Mass., 1857, which appeared in "Leaves of Grass Imprints" (Boston, 1860), 27–31, and a review of *LG* 1860 in the NY *Illustrated News* 2 (May 26, 1860), 43, which was reprinted in the *Saturday Press* June 30. See Thomas O. Mabbott and Rollo G. Silver, *A Child's Reminiscence by Walt Whitman* (Seattle, 1930), 32–36. Also mentioned in "Add*resses*"

24. Near the foot of the leaf at the right. Black pencil.

25. Blue pencil.

26. When this leaf was mounted, it was reversed, as comparison with [*874–877*] shows, probably because only the verso was inscribed. It should be properly numbered [*875V,*] but LC numbering is followed here.

27. Probably Thomas Handasyd Perkins (1764–1854). His rank was in the state militia and he was a wealthy merchant and public-spirited philanthropist. Rule across leaf under this entry.

28. Blue pencil.

29. [*878R–881R*] in black pencil. Probable order of inscription is followed here.

30. Deleted: "quite as good to have in contact with you as the average of our own color."

31. Preceding two words inserted above "a lawyer . . . re" in "resident"

32. Preceding twenty-seven words in red pencil. Rule across the leaf under "best of them"

on the jury list, two of the names put on being black men, one of them a fugitive slave who has purchased his freedom

[*878V*][33] Converse, Harding & Co. from 3 to 4 million[34] / Beebe & Co 5 million[35] / Jordan, Marsh & Co[36] / prices of real estate in the commercial quarters / in New Devonshire st.[37] on the Blake estate, at auction $10.70 a square foot / on State st. $30 a foot is a not uncom price

[*879V*] C. A. Leonard 21 Stuyvesant st[38]/ routinist[39]/ Mrs. Case 296 Bleecker near Grove / Mrs. Ferris[40]

[*880V*][41] Mr. Shales / among the Algerines / now 84 years of age[42] / 66 years ago—the Eaton affair[43]

[*881V*][44] the Reservoir[45] Beacon Hill the court quarter / walk with Mr. Redpath /[46] the castle—the little courts[47]

Ira Mudgett 85 Dover st corner Washington Boston Mass[48] [*882R*][49] Charles H Horton 52 Tyler st Lowell Mass / C F Hovey sumner st. fine store like Stewarts[50] [*882V*] Federal street the Chaning Building /

33. Blue pencil. Inserted here to follow probable order of inscription.

34. A drygoods store at 75 Franklin St. See [*891V*]. Rule across the leaf under the entry.

35. Dealer in "Yankee notions" at 60–66 Franklin Street. Rule across the leaf under "Beebe . . . mil" in "million"

36. Drygood merchants on New Devonshire Street. Rule drawn under the entry.

37. New Devonshire (or Devonshire) Street crosses Franklin. See [*891V*].

38. Black ink. A New York entry.

39. Blue pencil.

40. Black pencil. NYC directory lists a Leon Case, lawyer, at this NYC address. Mrs. Case is also mentioned at 54 Greenwich St. in "W. Whitman Portland av." and "return my book." A Mrs. Catharine A. Ferris (widow) is listed at the same address in the directory. Nothing further is known of WW's relations with either woman. Possibly WW boarded or roomed at this address. Rule across leaf under the two names.

41. Inserted here to follow probable order of inscription. Black pencil.

42. Boston directory lists an Edward Shales, 210 Tremont.

43. Possibly reference to William Eaton (1764–1811), consul to Tunis 1798, naval agent to the Barbary States. In an attempt to restore the exiled Pasha of Tripoli to the throne he led an astounding march through the Libyan Desert from Egypt to Derne.

44. Inserted here to preserve probable order of inscription.

45. The reservoir on Beacon Hill between Derne, Temple, Hancock and Joy Streets near the State House was something of a tourist sight. It was supported on foundation arches of 14¾′ span and the basin walls were 12′ thick. The Boston Directory for 1861 contains an ad for a winery "under the Beacon Hill Reservoir." See Kilham, pl. xvi.

46. Probably James Redpath (1831–1891), journalist and impresario. He was a journalist in Kansas and author of the first life of John Brown. Engaged in many liberal causes and proprietor of a famous lyceum bureau. He supported WW in his hospital work and was helpful in later years. This note may mark their first meeting. See "MEMORANDA OF A YEAR (1863)," *Corr.*, I, 121–122, 164, 171–172 and Traubel, passim.

47. Preceding entries in blue pencil.

48. Red pencil.

49. Blue pencil.

50. Drygoods store at 33 Summer St. A.T. Stewart's, a famous drygoods store in NY.

[883V; 883R blank][51] *Pavements*

Washington street[52] has all kinds of pavements, Russ. cobble, iron, and a kind they call "kidney stone." The last would make a very good kind of pavement for a street only moderately traveled, but it wears off too quick elsewhere—Some of the "kidney stone," put down last fall, when now taken up *[884R]*[53] Broad st Tilden block & others—granite Wholesale groceries & drugs / in Custom House st the old Custom house[54] / the old buildings on Long wharf[55] storage, & ship Chandelry / also India Wharf[56] */ noblest of all State St. Block*—east of the Custom house rough granite the above probably one of the noblest pieces of com. arch. in the world[57]

[885R; 884V blank][58] In Commercial st.[59] the rush, about 4 o'clock P. M—the carts, drays, trucks, express wagons, crowding—goods, boards,[60] vehicles of all sorts

[886R; 885V blank][61] THE OLD ELM.—[62] This tree has been standing here for an unknown period. It is believed to have existed before the settlement of Boston, being fully grown in 1722, exhibited marks of old age in 1792 and was nearly destroyed by a storm in 1832—Protected by an iron enclosure in 1854 J.V.C. Smith Mayor

[886V][63] Washington st fine trees[*?*] Leopold Furman hot air furnace / Wentworth & Bright Carpets / John Collamore China &c also the adj building on the corner / iron front building of Parker, Towle & Sons *[887R]*[64] Corner[*?*] of Wash[65] also iron front building Am Tract Society toward foot of Washn st /

51. Black pencil, hanging indentation.

52. "I create an immense sensation in Washington street. Everybody here is so like everybody else—and I am Walt Whitman! Yankee curiosity and cuteness, for once, is thoroughly stumped, confounded, petrified, made desperate." *Corr.*, I, 50.

53. Black pencil.

54. Called "new" in 1817. Designed by Uriah Cotting. Whitehill, 85–87.

55. Built in 1710 at the end of State Street.

56. A long five-story building of granite from designs by Charles Bulfinch (1805). Altered 1868, surviving wing demolished 1962.

57. Designed in "Plain American" by G. J. F. Bryant in 1858. Much admired by such later connoisseurs as Kilham. A marginal fist at the left marks the italicized passage, and another the last fourteen words.

58. Black pencil.

59. Then along the waterfront, now considerably back from it. See *[889R]*.

60. Deleted: *[illeg.]*

61. Blue pencil. Hanging indentations.

62. On the Common. Blown down in 1876, but replaced by one of its shoots.

63. Black pencil.

64. Black pencil.

65. Written along left edge beside the following three entries from which it is separated by a vertical line.

Oliver Brewster's cor State st gray granite / Codman Buildings gray granite / Wash st Warren & Co Chickering, pianos very good[66]

[*888R*[67]*; 887V blank*] In Wash st you will not seldom see a spike team of a horse on the lead and two oxen at the wheels,[68] hauling a big strong[*?*][69] box of a wagon /

Franklin (died seventy years ago,) (I suppose Franklin is about the fairest and best Representative man of Massachusetts—remembering also Webster, Emerson and may be one or two others

[*889R;*[70] *888V blank*] Standing on the porch of — Market on Commercial St. the most magnificent blocks of buildings opposite both side of City Wharf st.,[71] of which Quincy Market[72] Buildings are a specimen, noble architecture,[73] fronted with rough gray[74] pieces of stone.[75] and in Clinton st. and down[76] north of it in Commercial st very noble

[*889V*][77] elevation of Washington Park,[78] 110 feet above high water / Reservoir on Prospect Hill—220 feet.[79] / ground at City Hall 70 feet / Highest level in Brooklyn at[80] corner of Hicks and Pierrepont 80 feet / Ridgewood Reservoir, 107 feet /

[*890R*] Geo. S. Phillips, office NY Illustrated News NY City[81] R. M. Hunt architect of south building on south bay—grey stone (carte blanche to finish interior and exterior[82]

66. All of these enterprises were on Washington Street. Preceding two entries in blue pencil with vertical line at left.

67. Leaf reversed in mounting: hinge marks at right; inscription actually on verso but LC numbering followed. Black pencil.

68. Deleted: "dra"

69. Inserted above "big box"

70. Black pencil.

71. Deleted: "espec"

72. Deleted: "block"

73. Deleted: "the"

74. Deleted: "bloc"

75. Three buildings designed by Alexander Parris and built of granite, 1825–1826. At one end is Faneuil Hall, at the other Commercial Street.

76. Deleted: "east" ; inserted above: "north"

77. Black pencil. Deleted: "Highest point on Myr"

78. Deleted: "10"

79. Possibly the park and reservoir were in Roxbury, then a suburb of Boston, King's *Handbook*, 58, 78.

80. Deleted: "B"

81. Blue pencil. See [*872–873R*].

82. Almost certainly an early commercial building of Richard Morris Hunt (1827–1895), most famous for his renaissance mansions. He also designed, however, the Tribune Building (1873) in New York, the first elevator skyscraper. Although Hunt had family connections in Boston, built a

[891V;[83] *890V;*[84] *891R blank] fine buildings*

Franklin street, (all built within the last two years—previously dwellings,)—granite fronts—quite a variety—some quite ornamental—[85] / New Devonshire st.—(we are now in the im. neighborhood of Edward Everitt's residence, and of the late Rufus Choate—Fine[86] brown freestone front block—dry goods[87]

[892R][88]—Yankee manufactures—Lowell & elsewhere /

some of the stores on the same large scale as the best modern[89] wholesale houses in New York, with all the adjuncts of steam-power, great rooms under the walks, lit by Kilby st dry goods[90]

[892V][91] the crowd at Charleston Bridge, when, (at 6) the drawbridge is raised (at sunset)—the[92] sights, Bunker Hill monument—the river, the declining sun—the crowd rushing quick when the bridge is put right

[893R][93] burin—or "graver"[94] i.e. the tool, or "graver" a sort of composite of gouge, chisel, knife, &c used by the engravers—used by wood engravers—also Wm Miller rear of 204 Washington upstairs[95] / Mrs Cheney No 90 Livingston[96]

[893V][97] fine stores on Wash st. (Jones, Ball & Co Rich Ornamental goods & Jewelry (Williams & Everitts, Pictures & Rich engravings)[98] Geo. W Warren & Co dry goods

row of houses on Arlington Street (1859), and is said to have had a Boston office (not in 1861 Directory), he seems to have kept his headquarters in New York (see NY directories). No other reference to this building has been found. Hunt's office records are in the AIA Library in Washington, but are stored. Walter Muir Whitehill suggests that the building was demolished during changes made in the street layout in the twentieth century (personal communication).

83. Blue pencil. Hanging indentation.

84. In black pencil in another hand: "Saml D. Tillman, 7 Spruce st N York

85. The elegant Tontine Crescent (1793) of Charles Bulfinch and other handsome residences on Franklin Street had been demolished in 1857 and 1858.

86. Deleted: *[illeg.]*

87. See *[878V]*. The entire area was shifting from residential to commercial as the land values suggest. Edward Everett (1794–1865), teacher, statesman, orator. Rufus Choate (1799–1859), lawyer, politician, orator.

88. Blue pencil.

89. Deleted: *[illeg.]*

90. Four words on two lines in blue pencil.

91. Black pencil.

92. Written over *[illeg.]*

93. Entry in blue pencil; above, a red pencil line halfway across page from the left. Hanging indentation.

94. Preceding two words inserted on a line above "—i. e. the"

95. Black pencil. This and preceding rule cross the leaf.

96. Black pencil.

97. Black pencil.

98. At 234 Washington Street. According to *Sketches,* 199, the firm had recently opened a picture department.

[*894R*][99] Mechanics Hall—a fine new building, of brown free-stone, in Bedford street, very handsome building[1]

[*894V*][2] Beacon st. / Boylston st / 50[3] acres / 50 / 132 Northampton

[*895R*][4] on Commercial st[5] / opposite and north of the Faneuil Hall Market[6]—several more noble granite blocks

[*895V*][7] the gilt-capped cupola of the State House[8] the old Hancock house[9] with its fan-spreading window trimmings

[*896V; 896R blank*][10] Wash the old Marlboro Hotel & the Adams House / churches[11] the old South / Burnhams window (book store[12] / Mechanics Hall fine new brown free stone Bedford st /

[*897R*][13] the main[14] cattle-yards and slaughter-houses are at Brighton & Cambridge —[15] the beef on the hoof coming thither[16] from all parts of the Northern States, and from Canada—prices, by the quarter,[17] range from 5 to 12 cents a pound. / Mr Snow's story of Wm Evans and his contracts with the city[18]

[*897V*][19] C. L. Heyde,[20] Burlington a real Yankee farm scene, July hay-cutting, the hay-cocks, the loading, one horse grazing, a part of the field not yet mowed, &c / Meadow fine clouds M. J. Heade Providence R. I.[21]

99. Black pencil.
1. Built between 1857 and 1860 from designs by Hammatt Billings.
2. Blue pencil. All rules across leaf.
3. Written above deleted "48" which is written over [*illeg.*]. Below is another "50"
4. Black pencil.
5. Deleted: [*illeg.*]; inserted: "opposite and" on a line above "north of"
6. Designed by G. J. F. Bryant in the 1850s.
7. Black pencil.
8. According to Hitchcock, 7, the dome was copper, and not gilded until 1861.
9. On Beacon Street facing the Common. Built 1737, torn down 1863.
10. Black pencil.
11. Inserted above "the old"
12. On Washington Street opposite the Old South Church, advertised a stock of 200,000 volumes (*Sketches*, 33).
13. Black pencil.
14. Deleted: "markets" ; inserted above: "cattle-yards" above "[*del.*] markets" and "and slaughter-houses" above "are at Brig" in "Brighton"
15. Deleted: "but"
16. Inserted above wordspace between "coming from" and "from"
17. Preceding three words inserted above "range"
18. Entry in blue pencil. This bit of local scandal (?) has not been identified.
19. Blue pencil.
20. Painter and husband of WW's sister Hannah since 1852. They lived in "connubial torment." WW received a letter from Heyde in late March, 1860 (*Corr.*, I, 9, 50). Possibly a description of a painting by Heyde in a Boston gallery. Hanging indentation.
21. Martin Johnson Heade (1819–1904), "Luminist" landscape and marine painter; after a visit to Brazil in 1863 he became famous for his spectacular tropical landscapes. The description of the painting is to the left of the name and separated from it by a waved slant line.

[897*AR*] Silas S Soule, Lawrence, Kansas[22]

[897*AV*] Fine Building /
Washington Building in Washington st. opposite Franklin st material[23] coffee-and-milk color / Seeing the Yankee[24] / (Washington st. seamless goods of felt, from the factory at[25] Matteawan, boots[26] shoes, slippers[27] coats, vests,[28] gaiters gloves, caps,[29]

[898*V*;[30] 898*R blank*] Milk street/
all varieties—great many clothiers / the gt. manf. towns are Lowell & Lawrence / Congress st. Clothing dry goods variety—all kinds / the lobsters the man[?] the stands[31]

[900*R*;[32] 899*R blank*; 899*V*[33]] Summer & Franklin streets indicate the best architecture and for stores, &c[34] /

April 12th Thursday, the grass[35] beginning to look[36] green, on the Common—the buds on the elms are russet,—the young fellows are playing foot ball—Foot

22. Blue pencil. Born in Maine, went to Kansas in 1854. After taking part in the Kansas Free State war, he took part in the daring attempt to rescue John Brown from prison in 1859. In April, 1860, he returned from Boston to his home near Lawrence, Kansas, and wrote back to Thayer and Eldridge, WW's publishers, and Richard J. Hinton, sending a message to WW: "Tell Walt that when he wants to get up another book and thinks he has seen all the world he must take a second class ticket to Kansas and I think it would be very appropriate to name it after a weed called Smart Weed alias Ass Smart." Smart weed is a common roadside weed (one of the polygonums) with an irritating sap. Evidently WW made a mixed, though favorable, impression on Soule. He continues: "Tell Walt that I have a good deal to say about him and when he comes out here the folks will treat him well." At the end of the letter: "Tell Walt to send that book to me." (Typed copy in MS collection, Kansas State Historical Society.) By 1863 he was a lieutenant in the 1st Colored Cavalry Regiment at Ft. Lyon, Colorado. On November 27, 1864, he refused to order his troops to fire at the Cheyennes at the Sand Creek Massacre, but was sustained in the official investigation. He was murdered under mysterious circumstances in Denver in 1865 (Virginia Claire Seay, "Pioneers of Freedom," *Kansas Magazine* (1943), 107–115. See *Corr.*, I, 365, 372, "return my book" and "Walt Whitman Soldier's."

23. Inserted in left margin and above "coffee"

24. Preceding entries in black pencil.

25. Deleted: "Mat"

26. Inserted above "shoes"

27. Inserted on the line following "[*ins.*] shoes" and above "oes" in "shoes" and "co" in "coats"

28. Inserted above "gai" in "gaiters"

29. "(Washington st. . . . caps" in blue pencil.

30. Black pencil.

31. Preceding six words and hand at left in red pencil.

32. This page is actually [900*V*] and was reversed in mounting. The other side, which is blank, bears the LC # [900].

33. In blue pencil, in another hand, on *MS* [899V]: "Simeon Carter Stoneham Mass"

34. Preceding entry in blue pencil. Rule across leaf.

35. Inserted: "beginning to" above "ss" in "grass" and "look"

36. Deleted: "s"

ball! a noble and manly game—there they are—in their shirt [*901R*] sleeves, running crowding[37] tumbling,[38] together quite an inspiriting sight

[*901V*][39] [*illeg.*] shoes [*illeg.*] &c / cor Franklin & Devonshire / Franklin

[*902R*][40] [*illeg.*] whistling and whistling call of the robin, clear and short
as[41] he repeats it over and over—and answered by
As he flits from bough to bough while I walk my walk at early candle light— / with intervals, or quick succession

[*902V*] cor [*illeg.*] & Milk st / fine [*illeg.*] / Pearl st. [*illeg.*] of High street—granite / also the block corner [*illeg.*] Purchase and Pearl st opposite the old store (now Roman Catholic Church)

37. Inserted above "tumbling"
38. Deleted: "crow"
39. Black pencil. Bottom half of [*901R and V*] torn off.
40. Much rubbed black pencil.
41. Paragraph mark at beginning of line.

Leaves of Grass.

Manuscript in Duke (71). Erased pencil passage on leaf [4] of "Bells of Pomegranates." The warning against amativeness seems to indicate a date after the publication of *LG* 1860.

Leaves of Grass—

There is enough amativeness direct— Let [*illeg.*] future be much [*illeg.*] this particular be only as words and passages somewhat modified /

There is enough *prominent self-esteem*—be careful lest this o'er topples, and falls down from too much pride in (see printed page on egotism of poets &c

81 Clerman.

Manuscript in LC (#91). Black leather covered notebook with a fold-over flap fastener. Two scraps inscribed "Physique" in black ink by WW mounted with [903]. Blue wove leaves 6 ⅝" x 4". Blue lines 5/16". Inscribed in black pencil. Entries seem to have been written straight through, in contrast to other notebooks, although versos are occasionally blank. Many blank leaves and stubs are preserved separately. The sketches have been attributed to WW, but there is no evidence that he possessed the technical competence they show. It is more likely that they were drawn by some of the artists among his Pfaffian comrades, possibly Edward F. (or J.) Mullen or John McLenan. (See "William Giggee.") As [907*R*, 922*R*, 925*R* and 928*R*] indicate, the date is 1860–1861. Portions first published in Holloway in *UPP*, II, 91–2, Furness, 84, and Jean Catel, "Tête de Fumeur" and "Tête de Walt whitman par lui-même," *L'Ane d'Or,* V (Fevrier-Mars. 1926 51, 57, as noted. For reproductions of [935*R*, 945*R*, 947*R*, 948*R*] see illustrations.

[903 (*Inside front cover*)] [*illeg.*] 81 Clerman[1] Mr[?] M Leman[2] 81 Claremont Av / Doremus tailor 96 Court st / Charles Hine 174 10th av. between near 21st st & 22d st[3] / Mrs Price 33d st. bet. 7th & 8th av. white marble stoop[4] / Sloan[5] corner—Houston & Thompson basement

[904*R*] Swinton[6] 54th st. Bet. Broadway & 8th av. north side—stone cottage off the st. bet 2 white marble houses. turn [*illeg.*] of When[?] all the[7] future the[8] unknown is waiting for you / Quatuor / Quatruna / Quadriune / Quatruna[9]

1. The address is probably not WW's, as one might expect from its position, for he was living on Portland Avenue. The Brooklyn directory 1859–1860 lists him as "copyist."

2. A Dr. Leman is mentioned as a ward surgeon at Campbell Hospital in "return my book" and *Corr.,* I, 71. The reading is questionable. Possibly John McLenan, The book illustrator. See illustrations.

3. The artist. See "W. Whitman Portland av." Rule across leaf.

4. Mrs. Abby Price (see *Corr.,* passim, and "Baily D Damon") although in March, 1860, WW had addressed her at S.W. corner of Greenwich and Horatio Streets, N.Y. No Price is listed on 33d Street between 1859–1861. Rule across leaf.

5. A Peter G. Sloan is listed as a fitter at 145 Thompson St. in 1859–1860 and as a grocer at 203 W. Houston St. in 1860–1861.

6. Neither William nor John Swinton is listed at this address between 1859 and 1862. See *n* 14 below.

7. Deleted: "unknown" ; inserted above: "future"

8. Deleted: "future" ; inserted above: "unknown"

9. "Quatuor . . . Quatruna" in a column, set off from preceding by rule across leaf; words separated by short dashes. See "Chanting the Square Deific" (1865–66); MSS entry in NYPL copy of *LG* 1860, iii (Arthur Golden, ed., *Walt Whitman's Blue Book* [NY, 1968], I, n. p.); and "Pictures," for the words or WW's reference to a four-person god. "Quatruna," "quadriune" and "quadratura" are not in *OED*.

[904*V*] Ada Clare[10] 86 42d st /

[905*R*] Swinton[11] 54th right hand side going from 7th to 8th av. cottage—next to marble block / Wilkins[12] corner N.E. Amity & Wooster English basement / Ada Clare[13] 86 42d st / Hinton[14] 48 Beekman street

[905*V*] Swinton[15] 739 Sixth av. ring the 3d bell / William Giggee[16] Company E 1st Reg't N.Y. Volunteers[:][17] Col Allen Camp Hamilton Fort Monroe Va.

[906*R*][17a] I stand and look[18] in the dark under a cloud
But I see[19] in the distance where the sun shines,[20] I see the thin haze, on the tall[21] white steeples of the city,[22]
I see the glistening of the waters in the distance. /

Quaterniune /

[907*R; 906V blank*] What is this world literally and diffusely?—
Proletaire

[907*V*] This forthcoming one of Lincoln's is the 19th Presidentiad / Ald. John Leech —old Brooklynite

[909*R; 908R,*[23] *908V blank*] Subject—looking peering in the faces of people, continually passing— /

10. Pseudonym of Jane McElheney (1836–1874), a Pfaffian, called the "Queen of Bohemia," a journalist and actress. WW remembered her tenderly in his old age (Traubel, III, 117). See also *Corr.*, I, 339, II, 285, and "W. Whitman Portland av."

11. See *n*6, above. All rules on this leaf go entirely across.

12. George W. Wilkins, agent, 29 Amity St., NYC. Inserted: "N.E." under wordspace between "corner" and "Amity"

13. See *n* 10, above.

14. Possibly R. J. Hinton, one of John Brown's men, whom WW had met in Boston. See "Add*resses*."

15. William Swinton, editor, in NY Directory 1861–1862.

16. Preceding rule across leaf. See "Wm Giggee" and "return my book."

17. "Col Allen . . ." on brace to right of "Company E . . ."

17a. Deleted: "Where"

18. Deleted: "in" ; inserted above: "in the"

19. Inserted: "in the distance" above "where the"

20. Deleted: "through" ; inserted above: "I see"

21. Inserted above "wh" in "white"

22. Deleted: "in"

23. At top of page a scribble followed by the carefully written name "Arthur Henry" which may or may not be in WW's hand. The rest of the page is filled with variously successful attempts to write "Arthur" and "A." The impression is that WW was attempting to teach one of his "roughs" to write his name. Henry is possibly mentioned in "D. W. Wilder."

(Mullen)[24] [*?*] red olive color woman in Central America /

Paumanok's barefoot sea-boy[25]

[*912R; 909V blank; 910R;*[26] *910V;*[27] *911R;*[28] *911V*[29]] a Poem.
Phantoms—(a dream of the Sea.)
—bring up in a phantasmagoria all the drowned wrecks—the wrecks of the ships—spread the sails—[30]sail them on the sea again—silent, in the mist—the rafts from wrecks—*crowd the sea all over with them thick*—(get a talk with some of the pilots or sailors—

[*913V; 912V blank; 913R blank*][31] name of pieces cluster Kosmic gales Winds of Kosmos Breezes of Kosmos Winds from Kosmos —blow winds of Kosmos (first line of piece)[32]

[*914R*] The omnibus receipts of London are $3,000,000 a year. For the week ending Oct 10. last they were $60,000[33]

Pyle's Dietetic Saleratus 345 Washington st. N. Y. / Kanawha Saltworks Virginia / Wm. H. Jones Dover, New Jersey[34] / Breeze's Express cor Washington & Courtland /

[*915R; 914V blank*] the grappler with his grappling-irons—I see him ahold of the long handles—working them deep in the water, carefully feeling

24. There are various Mullens who were sailors listed in the Brooklyn and NYC directories between 1859 and 1861.

25. The phrase suggests "Out of the Cradle Endlessly Rocking," which had appeared in the *Saturday Press,* December 24, 1859, and in *LG* 1860, which had been printed in May, 1860.

26. In another hand: "A. B. Newcomb 37 Park Row Room 17"

27. Sketch of mustachioed man facing left in tunic and trousers of puffs and slashes style popular in Germany and Low Countries in the early sixteenth century. Lance with pennons or tassels in left hand. I am indebted to Professor Chez J. Haehl, University Theatre, University of Kansas, for identification.

28. Sketch of a woman wearing lowcut dress with short sleeves and skirt flared above the knees and soft cap with tassel. Possibly a ballet girl.

29. Sketch of mustachioed and goateed man facing left holding a glass or beaker. Wears trousers called *pluderhose* and a hip-length sleeved cape called *mandilion,* both popular in the early sixteenth century, and a full peaked cap. I am indebted to Professor Haehl for this information also.

30. Preceding three words inserted above " —sail them"

31. Deleted: "Ben Prince 264 Jay St 9 or 3 o'c" . Rule below drawn across the leaf.

32. Written in column. Parenthetical statement in loop below and to left with pointing hand to "winds" above in last entry.

33. See "return my book." All rules, except as noted, run across the leaf.

34. Short rule from left under entry and rule across leaf under "Breeze's . . . Courtland"

[*917R; 915V*[35]*; 916R*[36] *916V blank*] Nov. 26, '60—Lippard[37] / Gardette[38] account to me, (in Pfaff's) of George Lippards life,—was handsome, Byronic,—commenced[*?*] at 18—wrote sensation novels—drank—drank—drank—died mysteriously either of suicide or mania a potu at 25—or 6—a perfect wreck—was ragged, drunk, beggarly—

[*918R; 917V blank*] *Aholibanah.* (Hebrew.)
"the tabernacle is exalted—" (or raised) /

old specs / Sandy's story of the stage[*?*] driver[39]

[*919R; 918V blank*][40] in adv.

The[41] other poets write with reference to the Costume of the body,—or, at most, with reference to the body, costumed. But I write my poems with reference to the[42] perfect body, divine,[43] irrespective of costumes—in it I have eternal faith beyond all the [*illeg.*] of critics

[*921R; 919V blank; 920R blank; 920V*][44] Arabian (Shanlys book)[45]
I see[46] tombs, built with masonry, with a stone pillar at the head—[47] I see the sex indicated, by the carved turban[48] or by the[49] veil,

35. In another hand: "Henry Beck Jr At Manhattan Gas Works 18th St & 10th ave"

36. In another hand: "M[*?*] Jerry [Jenny*?*] Danforth No 2 Washington place. "Sivori Hotel. Room 11 [*illeg.*]—12—at home *always* till 1 P.M. " Flourished line under "till 1 P.M."

37. George Lippard (1822–1854), popular novelist and lecturer, entered journalism 1841 and published the first of his sensational novels, *The Monks of Monk Hall,* in 1844.

38. On May 14, 1860, Henry Clapp recommended that WW send a review copy of *LG* 1860 to Charles D. Gardette, a Philadelphia writer (Traubel, II, 375). See also William Winter, *Old Friends* (N.Y., 1909), 292, and John Foster Kirk, *A Supplement to Allibone's Critical Dictionary of English Literature,* I (1899), 647–648. As a Philadelphian, Gardette would have known about Lippard's career. He had parodied "With Antecedents" as a promotional device in the *Saturday Press* in 1860 (George Pierce Clark, " 'Saerasmid' an Early Promoter of Walt Whitman," *AL* 27, 258–262).

39. In a sprawling hand. A "Sandy" is mentioned as an old stage driver in 1868 (*Corr.,* II, 54).

40. No printed version has been found. Since it is not cancelled, it is probable that WW never used it. Obviously he was planning publicity for *LG* 1860, published in May. See, for example, *Leaves of Grass Imprints* (Boston, 1860).

41. Inserted above and before "Other" . "Other" capitalized.

42. Deleted: "bod"

43. Deleted: "eternal"

44. Four pencil sketches, three above and one below. The lower one looks like a vertical length of a plant stem. Professor Roland L. McGregor, Department of Botany, University of Kansas, suggests that it looks like a willow branch whistle. Of the three above, the first two are unidentifiable; the third looks like a cross-section of a stem.

45. Stovall, *AL,* 26, 339, suggests Arthur Penrhyn Stanley, *Sinai and Palestine, in Connection with Their History* (London, 1856, N.Y., 1857), but could find no clear source. "Shanlys" (possibly "Stanlys") book written in a loop in the upper right corner of the leaf after "Arabian"

46. Deleted: "the"

47. Preceding seven words inserted above "masonry" and "eye" ("head" on second line of the insert under wordspace between "stone" and "pillar").

48. Deleted: "at the head,"

49. Deleted: "carved"

[922*R*;[50] 921*V*[51]] [[52]To Picture-Makers.[53]

Make a Picture of America as an IMMORTAL MOTHER,[54] surrounded by all her children young and old—no one rejected—all fully accepted—no one preferred to another. Make her seated—she[55] is beautiful beyond the beauty of virginity—she[56] has the inimitable beauty of the mother of many [922*V*] children—she is nether youthful nor aged—around her are none of the emblems of the[57] classic goddess—nor any feudal emblems—she is serene and strong as the[58] heavens.[59]

Make her picture, painters! And you, her statue, sculptors! Try,[60] age after age, till you achieve it! For as to many sons and daughters[61] the perfect mother[62] is the one where all meet, and binds them all together, as long as she lives, so The Mother of These States binds[63] them all together as long as she lives.

[923*R*] Make a "Picture" of the Indian girl looking at the turtle by an aboriginal American creek / Write a cluster of pieces on the sentiment, elevation, acceptation &c of *Old Age*.

[924*R*; 923*V*] Leaf / on a silver ?gold[64] coin /
Through what hands pass'd[65]
a picture—or direction to make[66]

50. At the top of the page is the roughed-in outline of an oval object, perhaps the same as on [921*V*]. Rule across leaf below.

51. MS [921*V*] shows two sketches side by side vertically on the page. The first is a cluster of flowers or fruits growing downwards along a stem below two leaves. The other, perhaps a detail, is of an oval object. Professor McGregor (see *n*44, above) suggests that the cluster "might well be a member of the Figwort family and may be a *Digitalis* or Foxglove."

52. Square bracket in MS. One of the few occasions of its use. Passage first printed in Furness, 60. Paragraph with hanging indentation.

53. See "Pictures," *LG CRE*, 642–649, for discussion of WW's use of the word.

54. The image of the Mother of States was probably suggested by the Civil War and the triumph of the Union. It first appears in *LG* in "By Blue Ontario's Shore" (1867). WW added it possibly before 1865 to *LG* 1860, now in NYPL. See "I say that the spirit"; Golden, ed., *Walt Whitman's Blue Book*, I, 109.

55. Word written over [*illeg.*]

56. Word written over [*illeg.*]. Deleted: "is neither young nor" ; inserted: "has the inimitable beauty" on a line above "young nor"

57. Deleted: "feudal"

58. Inserted and deleted: "beauty of the" above "the heavens"

59. WW here apparently began the "M" of "Make" after "heavens" and deleted it.

60. Deleted: "to achieve it,"

61. Preceding five words inserted on a line above "the . . . mother"

62. Deleted: "of many sons, ——[*illeg.*]"

63. Inserted and deleted: "one" at the end of the line following "so"

64. Written below "silver"

65. The theme is an old one. See, for one version, [Charles Johnstone] *Chrysal; or, the Adventures of a Guinea*, 4 vols. (London, 1760–1765), a scandalous chronicle of the age. E. A. Baker, in his edition (London, n.d.), xii, refers to earlier uses in the eighteenth century. I am indebted to Miss Ann Hyde, Spencer Research Library, for this information. Following this entry is a fragmentary newspaper clipping which seems to tell the same story: "now the purchase price of bread, and now of poison; to-day the comforter of want, to-morrow flung to the street from the jewelled hand of wealth; now the winner at the board, now the last stake of the suicide; in the morning doing duty to buy flowers for the forehead of purity, in the evening the price of infamy and shame."

66. In the left margin a vertical line inside of which is a "p" or "s"

[*925R; 924V blank*][67] Brochure /

Two characters as of a Dialogue between A. L—n and W [*illeg.*] —as in ? a dream /[68] or better ? Lessons for a President elect / Dialogue between WW. and "President elect"

[*926V;*[69] *925V blank; 926R blank*] Two antique[70] records there are—two religions[71] —platforms

On the first[72] one, stands[73] the Greek sage, the classic masterpiece of virtue[74]. . . . —Eternal[75] conscience is there—doubt is there—[76] philosophy, questioning, reasoning, is there.

On the second stands the Jew, the Christ,[77] the Consolator,[78]. . . . There is love, there is drenchèd purity[79] . . . there, subtle, is the unseen Soul,[80] before which all the[81] goods and greatnesses [*927R*] of the world, become insignificant:

But now[82] a[83] third religion I give . . . .[84] I include the antique two[85] . . . I include the divine Jew,[86] and the Greek sage

More still—[87]that which is not conscience, but against it—that which is not the Soul, I include[88]

These, and[89] whatever exists, I include—I surround all, and dare not make a single exclusion.[90]

67. Obviously WW wrote this between November, 1860, and March, 1861. Reproduced in Esther Shephard, *Walt Whitman's Pose,* facing 356. First printed in Glicksberg, 174.

68. Double line from left below "—as in?"

69. This poem written sideways from bottom to top on this and following leaf. First printed *UPP,* II, 91–92.

70. Inserted above "records"

71. Inserted above "platforms"

72. Preceding two words inserted above "one"

73. Inserted above "the"

74. Deleted: "—conscience, justice, reasoning, eternal consc" . The four spaced dots are inserted above "consc" . Inserted and deleted above "consccience" : "philosophy"

75. Capital written over lowercase.

76. Phrase inserted above "philosophy"

77. Preceding four words inserted on a line above "nds" in "stands" and "con" in "consolator"

78. Deleted: "the Jew, the Christ"

79. Preceding four words inserted on a line from the left margin and over ". . . There . . . is"

80. Capital written over lowercase.

81. Deleted: [*illeg.*]

82. Deleted: "I give"

83. Deleted: "modern & second" ; inserted above: "third religion"

84. Deleted: "standing[?]"

85. Two preceding words inserted at right margin with a lighter pencil stroke; "Greek sage" deleted.

86. Following four words inserted with a lighter pencil stroke.

87. Deleted: "More still I include. . . ." ; inserted: "More still—" with lighter pencil stroke on a line above "ude" in "include" and "that"

88. Preceding two words inserted above "Soul" into the right margin.

89. Preceding two words inserted. Uppercase "Whatever" not reduced, not printed.

90. Original reading: "and dare not exclude" : Inserted above "exclude" "make a single" ; "exclude" corrected to "exclusion" by overwriting.

[928V;[91] 927V–928R blank] Why now I shall know whether there is any thing in you, Libertad,
I shall see[92] how much you can stand
perhaps[93] I shall see the crash—is all then lost? /[94]
[929R] What then? Have[95] those thrones there stood so long?
Does the Queen of England represent a thousand years? And the Queen of Spain[96] a thousand years?
And you
[929V] Welcome the storm—welcome the trial—let the waves
Why now I shall see what the old ship is made of
Any body can sail[97] with a fair wind,[98] or a smooth sea

[930V][99] Ship of Libertad

Blow mad winds!
Rage, boil, vex, yawn-wide, yeasty[1] waves
Crash away—
Tug at the planks—make them groan—fall around, black clouds—clouds of death
[930R] Come now we will see what stuff you are made of Ship of Libertad
Let[2] others tremble and turn pale,—let them ?
I want to see what ? before I die,
I welcome this menace—I welcome thee with joy:
[931R][3] Ship of the World—Ship of Humanity—Ship of the ages
? (Ship that circlest the world
Ship of the hope of the world—Ship of Promise

[932R; 931V blank] the vine-hills of Germany (viz: "in Germany the name of the[4] vineyard is *vien-berg* i.e. *vine-hill*") / but in California they plant the vine preferably on flat tracts[5]

91. This and the following page written sideways on the leaf from bottom to top. Entire poem first printed in Furness, 84. WW evidently composed on leaves at random.

92. Deleted: "whether"

93. Inserted above "I" at beginning of line.

94. In column, deleted, below this line: "O! Old England The Queen of [*illeg.*]"

95. Deleted: "you"

96. Isabella II was Queen of Spain in her own right between 1843 and 1868.

97. Deleted successively: "in" "in [*ins.*] before" ; inserted above: "[*del.*] in with"

98. Deleted: "before" ; inserted and deleted above: "[*del.*] before" deleted above: "or"

99. Both [930*R*] and [*V*] are written sideways from top to bottom of the leaf. It seems probable that WW turned his notebook over and began a revision of the preceding lines, thus going from [*V*] to [*R*], especially since the title is on [930*V*]. The leaves have accordingly been reordered here. Poem first printed in Furness, 84. See *n*94 above.

1. Question mark written above "yeasty"

2. Deleted at beginning of line: "W"

3. Written sideways on leaf from bottom to top.

4. Deleted: [*illeg.*]

5. Preceding eleven words with hanging indentation.

[*933R; 932V*][6] Poem on a
Prostitute's Funeral[7] /

adv. or on L of G[8]

The[9] topics of the world,[10]—the world itself with all of[11] its affairs, divide away, and disappear in comparison with those things that come directly home to, or rise up out of[12] your own body and Soul.[13] These are the things made the themes of L of G

[*934R; 933V blank*] Thursday, April 18. 61. / I have this hour, this day r e s o l v ' d[14] to inaugurate for (my se lf) a (p ure) (per fect)[15] sweet, cleanblooded (ro bust) body by ignoring all drinks (but) water and pure milk—and all fat meats late suppers—a great body—a purged, cleansed, spiritualised invigorated body—

[*935V; 934V;*[16] *935R*[17]] (?) Poem
The Hills of Brooklyn,
Here roamed the[18] newly ?[19] landed Hollander
Here stood Washington /
The last war

[*936R*] Poem on the Incompleted /[20]
The Incomplete.
Always unfinished—always incompleted,[21]
The best yet left—the road but fairly started,

6. Pencil sketch facing left of man with moustache and short beard wearing high hat.

7. See "return my book" and "The City Dead-House" (1867). Rule across leaf below.

8. Entry printed in Furness, 65. Furness inserts the word "lecture" in the blank space on the plausible grounds that WW intended to lecture on *LG*.

9. Deleted: "world" "noisy"

10. Deleted: "with all that"

11. Inserted above the wordspace between "all" and "its"

12. Preceding four words inserted above on a line above "your own body" ; "up" deleted and reinserted.

13. Preceding two words appear to have been afterthoughts.

14. The significance of printing or spacing the words below is not clear nor is the use of parentheses. WW was secretive in his notebooks (see "Epictetus"), and it seems clear that this notebook was handled by other people, but the devices conceal nothing. The entry has a certain irony, considering the sketch on [*935R*].

15. Word printed.

16. A pencilled head and shoulders, suggestive of a portrait bust, of a bald, bearded man with a snub nose, vaguely reminiscent of traditional portraits of Socrates.

17. Sketch of profile, facing left, face only. The eyes and heavily shaded tip of the nose suggest a drunken man. There is some resemblance to WW. See [*934R, 945R, 947R, 948R*]. See illustration.

18. Deleted: "H"

19. The question mark is above "newly"

20. First printed in Furness, 48.

21. Original reading: "nev[?] completed" ; deleted: "nev[?]" ; inserted above: "in"

The learning practice so far only practice[22]
The seed but sown—the test the fruit. /

That is best which wears the longest

[*940R; 936V blank; 937V;*[23] *937R blank; 938R blank; 938V;*[24] *939R blank; 939V*[25]] Jos Sprage[26] /

Died Dec 12, 1854 in his 72d year / born in Massachusetts, / Come here before the war of 1812—quite a lad / was in business in New York during the war / was a Jeffersonian Democrat / married at Bedford, L.I. /

[*942R; 940V–941R blank; 941V*[27]] Of My Poem

All the others were singing[28] the distinctions, and what was to be preferred.
Therefore[29] I thought I would sing a[30] song of inherent qualities, in a man,[31] indifferent whether they are right or wrong.

[*943R; 942V blank*] a cluster of poems for children—(fables) / —the earth in space as a story of *the divine ship sailing the divine sea.*

Story of Leonidas /

This,[32] children, is the story of Leonidas, of the race of Hercules,
Twenty-two hundred years before These States.

22. Original reading: "The house" ; "house" deleted; "written" inserted and deleted; "house [*illeg.*]" inserted and deleted; "learning" inserted.

23. Pencil profile sketch of man's head facing left: pronounced aquiline nose and moustache and short beard with two points.

24. Pencil sketch sideways on page from top to bottom. Apparently a proposed new flag for the *Saturday Press.* On a scroll or strip of paper "The Boheamian" in decorative large and small capitals. At left a vertical artist's brush[?] is drawn as if passed through slits in the scroll, at right an unidentifiable object roughly indicated in a similar position. Below the title: "Tate [Late?] Saturdy Press" in large and small capitals.

25. Sketch of male profile (face only) facing right, wearing goatee and smoking pipe.

26. Member of the firm of Reid, Sprague & Co., hardware merchants? No connection with WW is known. Rule across leaf below. All other rules are short lines from left.

27. Full-length sketch facing left of man with long aquiline nose, moustache and pointed beard. Body much smaller than head; right hand holds mallet or gavel.

28. Deleted: "for"

29. Deleted: initial "All" ; inserted above: "Therefore"

30. Deleted: "few" ; final "s" deleted in "songs" following.

31. Preceding three words inserted.

32. Originally lowercase "t"

[*950R; 943V blank; 944R;*[33] *944V blank; 945R;*[34] *945V blank; 946R;*[35] *946V;*[36] *947R;*[37] *947V blank; 948R;*[38] *948V blank; 949R blank; 949V*[39]]

The Cid[40]

Is like the Nibelungen, which in its present form is about the same date)[41] [:] two centuries before Chaucer, primitive, heroic, warlike, stirring full of loyalty & devotion[42]

Consists of 3000 lines.

Could not have been composed later than the year 1200

Subject—the warlike adventures, character, &c. of a Spanish nobleman, Roderigo Diaz (Ruy Diaz) born in the northwestern part of Spain, about 1040. Died in 1099, at valencia, which city he had rescued from the Moors.[43] The title *Cid,* is believed to have come from five Moorish chiefs (or princes,) whom he conquered, acknowledging him as their *Seid* or king—and the additional title, *Campeador,* (Champion), is the popular[44] affix[45] for his efforts in freeing the Country from the Moors—the name comes from a very early date, "El Cid Campeador"—the Lord Champion, or King Champion

[[46]*951R; 950V blank*] —he seems to have passed nearly the whole of his life in warlike efforts, in the service of his Country

33. Pencil sketch of Irish harp with strap at left.

34. Sketch of male bearded head facing left. Almost certainly a sketch of WW. See illustration.

35. Sketch of male head and shoulders facing left. Fat porcine or bulldog features, clean-shaven, large ear, high hat with rounded crown.

36. Sketch of male head and torso facing left. Features indicated by heavy cross-hatching, seems to have heavy moustache and bristling beard. Extraordinarily tall high "silk" hat, which looks somewhat battered.

37. Full length sketch of man seated (?) at table (?) facing left; right arm extended in gesture. Face similar to sketch on [*945R*], but eyes and clear indications of red nose relate it closely to sketches on [*935R*] and [*948R*]. It may well be a caricature of WW in animated conversation at Pfaff's, although most accounts speak of him as an obvserver rather than an active participant. See [*935R, 935R, 945R, 948R*]. See illustration.

38. Pencil sketch of male head facing left; hat with tall rounded crown sketched in lightly. Possibly WW. There is a very strong resemblance to sketch on [*935R*]. See also [*947R*]. See illustration.

39. Grotesque figure sketch facing forward: skull with heart for a body, legs and extended arms sketchily indicated, body pierced by rapier, skull with hair and cap. Figure seems to float against shadowy background, possibly a rising (or setting) sun (or moon) at right. Irregular line surrounds all but lower right quadrant of figure.

40. Based on George Ticknor, *History of Spanish Literature* (NY, 1849), I, 13–14. Written throughout with hanging indentations.

41. Sentence cramped under title at left as if added later, divided from text by irregular line. For *Nibelungenlied* see "Neibelungen-leid Song."

42. Written to right of title. Cf. Ticknor, I, 22, *n*17.

43. Sentence ends in mid-line; new block paragraph begins.

44. Deleted: "expression"

45. Writing is begun at the left in line with "Subject" above.

46. This translation not in passages in Ticknor WW used.

—So the Cid is the great fellow in poetical Spanish history and reminiscence— (as Homer's Achilles, or perhaps as the English Alfred— ? or Roman Æneas.)—

There are numerous "Lives of the Cid," as well as lots of "Ballads," (160 or more,)—besides the old epic itself

He was the great defender of his nation against the Moorish invaders.

The Poem of the Cid is mixt with much fable, very much

[*952R; 951V blank*] It is a contemporary and vivacious song, and chronicle, of[47] those chivalrous,[48] warlike,[49] and romantic times of early Spanish[50] life—full of quaint pictures, hints, opinions, and suggestions

—the very language, just extricating itself from its mother's womb, the Latin— full of the strong,[51] free, individuality of its time—the metre, and rhyme rude and irregular—

—A few pages at the begining are lost

The author of the "Poem of the Cid," is unknown

("Castilian" and "Spanish" seem convertible terms)

[*953R; 952V blank*] The contest between the Christian Spaniards, and the Moors, continued for Seven Centuries—briefly stated the "poem of the Cid," and the other old ballads and poetical Spanish Chronicles, celebrate their countrymens prowess and sufferings, in this war.

(*Castile,*—so called from its many castles) /

It is from this period of tempests and wars, 11–1200[52]—of the Spanish race[53] that we hear the first notes of their wild national poetry, mingled with dauntless war-shouts, and flaunting with banners and curses, and the smiting of steel weapons

47. Deleted: "the" ; inserted above: "those"
48. Deleted: "and"
49. Deleted: "primitive"
50. Deleted: "history"
51. Deleted: [*illeg.*]
52. Dates inserted above "and wars"
53. Preceding four words inserted above "that we hear"

[*954R;*[54] *953V blank*] asonante (a Spanish metrical style, not[55] rhyme, yet giving[56] somewhat the same effect as rhyme, by carefully terminating[57] the lines by with[58] words whose vowels harmonize,—Castilian poetry is alone in this peculiarity—(Longfellow has perhaps[59] imitated it, and come as near to it as possible in English, in his "Hiawatha")[60]

[*955R; 954V blank*][61] "Old Spanish Ballads"
(Ticknor's Hist. Spanish Literature)[62] over 1000, authors unknown—the true antique national poetry—all written previous to the middle of the 16th century

[*956R; 955V blank*] Mr. Rowland, fruit 300 Barclay st / Melissa Rowland 175 Morgan st. Jersey City between Prospect & Grove [*957V; 956V–957R blank*] Oct 14 '60 Thomas P Nichols 69 Carlton avenue[63]

[*958V; 958R blank*][64] I want a Latin motto which conveys the following sense—of the words[65] *Quatuor in Uno* or, better, *Quatuor juncta in Uno / au courant / Quarto / Quatuor /*

[*959–960R*][66] 292 / Quadratura / John Schoonmaker 133 Clermont av Brooklyn/ Wm Metzler Tuskelwa Bureau Co Illinois.

54. Deleted at top of page by a vertical stroke: "Hannah Brush (my grandmother Whitman') and her" . See "Hannah Brush (my grandmother Whitman)." The note is based on Ticknor, I, 112.

55. Deleted: "exactly"

56. Inserted and deleted: "almost" above "the" ; inserted: "somewhat" following "[*del.*] almost " and above "same"

57. WW had originally written: "by a careful termination of"

58. Written above "by" as an alternate.

59. Deleted: "com"

60. Longfellow did not use assonance in *The Song of Hiawatha.* This comment does not seem to be Ticknor's.

61. The top third of the leaf has been torn out.

62. Ticknor, I, 118–119.

63. Listed as a bookkeeper in 1860–1861 Brooklyn directory. Rule across leaf below.

64. See "Chanting the Square Deific," *LG CRE,* 442, and [*904R*] above.

65. Deleted: "Four in One"

66. This leaf seems to have been the flyleaf, and the double numeration is that assigned it by LC. The binding is numbered [*960A*]. All rules run across the leaf. Metzler is mentioned in "[*illeg.*] Dick Hunt" and "return my book."

Mr. & Mrs. Fitz.

Manuscript in LC (#92, sheets #961–992). Despite the LC sheet numbers, WW began keeping the notebook in October, 1860 from what is now the back. He used it briefly in 1862. In 1864 he salvaged it although he was simultaneously keeping "Baily D Damon." The cover label "Hospital note book, No 13" is probably in his handwriting and must date from the later period. The notebook is commercially made and bound in brown leather; the dimensions of the cover are 6¹/₁₆" x 3¾". All leaves are laid paper. [*961, 962 and 992*] are unruled. The LC numbering seems in error, but they are here printed as numbered. Many blank leaves are preserved separately. All other pages have blue lines about a ¼" apart and with a vertical red line on the middle of the page. Inscriptions are in pencil with occasional entries in ink and black ink. The leaves are heavily stained or foxed at the edges. Portions were printed, as noted, by Glicksberg and Furness.

[*991V; 992R,*[1] *V*] Mr. & Mrs. Fitz astronomical instruments 237 (or 438) in 5th st between Av. B and C. (name on the door) / Silver's Jamaica Express 117 or 18 John street / C. H. Haswell 6 Bowling Green[2]

[*991R*][3] *England, in Broadway*
Pass on, fair lord![4]
You

[*990V; 990R blank*] Prince of Wales in New York 1860[5]
The Good[6] Queen's Son[7] Eldest Son
One[8] look[9] I gave and saw

1. Deleted: "[*illeg.*] Whitman Portland av. near Myrtle Brooklyn" . Despite the LC sheet numbers, [*992R–975V*] are the oldest portions of this notebook and are printed first. [*992R*] appears to be the inside front cover. There are rules across the leaf below "(name on the door)" and "Lee Avenue" and "117 or 18 John street"

2. Charles H. Haswell, engineer, house 64 W. 45th, office 6 Bowling Green in 1862–1863 NYC directory. In another hand after "Mr & Mrs. Fitz": "J Talbot Clymer St. 5th house from Lee avenue." Jesse Talbot was an artist. See "albot Wilson."

3. Deleted: "The"

4. Deleted: "of England" ; inserted: exclamation point.

5. The Prince of Wales visited New York City on October 11, 1860. The jottings on this page may have been the basis for the poem "Year of Meteors" (ll. 11–13), first printed in Drum-Taps (1865), in which WW saluted the Prince. Printed *LG CRE,* 700.

6. Inserted in the wordspace between "The" and "Queen's"

7. Inserted above "Eldest"

8. Deleted: "rapid"

9. Deleted: "of"

The[10] Queen's Son
A fair youth
In[11] the barouche[12] drawn by the champing horses.
Pass'd a fair youth with downcast eyes

[*989V; 989R blank*] Mr. Fitz[13]
optical instrument maker 237 Fifth st. between av. C and D. / Henry Reynolds 3d av. right hand side 3d door above 31st street over a coffin store / Mrs. Butt 54 Market street next door to the corner[14] / Powell's Jamaica Express Office 12 Fulton st N.Y. / 2d Brigade Burnside's Coast Division Hatteras Inlet[15]

[*988V; 987 R and V are lacking;*[16] *988R blank*] (Complete Works.) Carl Zimrok's[17] History of the Nibelung Lied Astor Library / "atavism"— ("what the French physiologists call *atavism*"—) Autobiography of a Strength Seeker[18]

[*986V; 986R blank*][19] Feb 1 '62
Sunday, all the mails close at 1.30 P.M.

[*985V; 985R blank*] Capt Geo[20] Folger / 54 Degraw street[21] uncle of Capt Phelon[22] / Dr. John[23] Watson 123 10th st.

[*984V; 984R blank*] Charley Hine[24] No 7 Carroll Place Bleecker st between Thompson & Lawrence /

10. Deleted: "Good"

11. WW originally began "Sent"

12. Deleted: "passing"

13. Deleted: "ast" ; possibly "s" deleted from "Mr." See [*991V*] ante. Rule part way across from left. All other rules on this leaf go fully across.

14. George W. Butt of this address is listed as a stableman in the NY directory for 1862–1863.

15. George Whitman's military address. General Ambrose Burnside had captured Roanoke Island and New Bern, NC, in February and March, 1862.

16. [*986V*] and [*987V*] are missing; on the other side of [*986R*] is [*987R*]. This is probably misnumbering rather than lost material.

17. "Carl" inserted before and above "Z" of "Zimrock" . Karl Josef Simrock (1802–1876), German poet and scholar, translated the *Niebelungenlied* into modern German in 1827. See "Neibelungen-leid Song" for WW's considerable interest in the poem.

18. This title? has not been identified.

19. Three newspaper clippings pasted on: two have to do with postal rates and schedules for the city of Brooklyn, and the other one is an advertisement for a shoe repair shop on Fulton Street in Brooklyn.

20. Inserted above. [*illeg.*] inserted above and deleted.

21. Deleted: [*illeg.*].

22. Possibly the Capt. Henry A. Phelon mentioned in a clipping in "D. W. Wilder" [*1260A*].

23. Inserted above "W" in "Watson"

24. This may be Charles Hine (1827–1871), who painted the portrait which was the basis for the engraved frontispiece of *LG* 1860. The address, however, does not agree with that in the New York City directories, 1860–1862. See "W. Whitman Portland av."

Dr. Ruggles[25] 142 46th st just west of Broadway[26] /

[*983V; 983R blank*] Feb. 20th 1862. 13,000 licensed and unlicensed vehicles in New York City (Stewarts speech at Albany before the Legislative Com. on Broadway railroad application)[27]

[*982V; 982R*[28] *blank*] Delirium tremens patients never attack the doctor

[*981V; 981R blank*] Spofford[29] Assistant Librarian at Washington Congressional Library /

Mrs. Bogle 55 Spring st 2d story front room /

[*980V; 980R blank*] Hospital[30] Charter was got in 1771 foundation laid 27th July '73 / It has never belonged to the city, and the City has never contributed any money to it at any time / the State gives gave donated[31] 12,500 a year for many years this terminated in '59 and now there is no donation

[*979V; 979R blank*] —the Hospital exists now on its own resources—it has no property producing income— / about 38 percent of the patients are gratuitous.— /[32] resources are payments of pay patients—and receipts from the U.S. government, and N.Y. State gov. for soldiers and sailors /

25. Probably Dr. Edward Ruggles (1817–1867), a Brooklyn physician and friend of the Whitman family (*Corr.*, I, 90, 319–320). The address, however, is in Manhattan. No Edward Ruggles is listed in the Brooklyn directories for 1859–1863. There is an Edward Ruggles, physician, listed at 5 St. Timothy place in the 1861–1862 New York directory, but he is not listed between 1863 and 1865. The address given here is also in "William Giggee." See also "Left 5 at Jones" and "[*illeg.*] Dick Hunt."

26. Short lines at left and right.

27. The New York *Times* for February 20, 1862, reports that the State Legislature met at Albany to discuss the pros and cons of installing a railroad on Broadway. A. T. Stewart, a wealthy NYC merchant, represented the Broadway merchants at the meeting and voiced their opposition to the railroad.

28. On [*982R*] is pasted a slip of paper inscribed "1864" in WW's hand. Subsequent entries all are from that year.

29. Ainsworth R. Spofford (1825–1908) became Assistant Librarian of Congress in 1861 and Librarian in 1864.

30. The New York Hospital (or Broadway Hospital), the first hospital of any significance in New York City. The cornerstone was laid on July 27, 1773; the hospital was destroyed by fire when it was near completion, in 1775, and the first patients were not admitted until January 23, 1791. These notes were used by WW in the writing of his four "City Photographs" articles on the Broadway Hospital in the *Leader* in March and April, 1862 (Glicksberg, 18–19, 24–47); "return my book." See also the recollections of Dr. D. B. St. John Roosa written in 1896 concerning WW's visits to the hospital in 1860 ("return my book"). Short line from left.

31. WW allowed all three words to stand. Last two inserted.

32. Rule across leaf.

[*978V; 978R blank*] The U.S. pays 75 cents a day for soldiers / Feb. 24—about 380 patients now in the establishment / pay patients—men are charged $4 a week—and women $3 a week. / [33]patients admitted in '61 3624 /

[*977V; 977R blank*][34] Poem (Religions or in lectures on religion
Put in the idea that we absolutely know *Nothing,* on these mysterious and ever-elusive subject—that they are useful, as suggestive, as soaring up, beyond the demonstrable, the practical, which appeals to mind and sense[35] —That they are precious beyond account as[36] elevating and clarifying, as fine spiritual exercises—but beware! beware!

Know, once for all, they are not true as truths—only as indications or promising spiritual hypotheses[*?*]

[*976V; 976R blank*] The real truth is no doubt infinitely beyond all these little broken and jangled hints

[*975V; 972V, 973 R & V, 974R, 975R blank; 974V*][37] theme for poem
sharpening a knife and fork—crosswise

[*961R*] W Whitman 502 Penn ave 3rd story front room[38] /

[*962R; 961V blank*] father[39] David W Carter Rush Susquehanna co Penn Chas Carter Co D 50th Penn ward A—right leg amp[40]

[*962V*] Reuben Farwell[41] Co H 1st Mich Cavalry 1st brigade 1st division

33. Rule across leaf.

34. [*977V*] and [*976V*] printed by Furness, 47–48. "Religions . . ." set off by waved line at left joined to waved line below. The two paragraphs of the entry are in hanging indentation.

35. WW began the phrase "but about them [*?*]."

36. An incomplete word deleted.

37. Upper half of leaf torn off except for a strip at the left. In another hand: "Mrs Ellen Eyre, station 'D,' New York P. O. Station "D" was at Bible House, 4th Ave. corner of 8th St. Below this entry, in WW's hand: "765 Broadway 3d story front room." "Ellen Eyre" is a woman with whom WW may have had an affair in the spring of 1862. See Allen, 278–280, and "return my book." Ellen Eyre is not listed in the New York directories from 1859 to 1865.

38. WW lived at this Washington address between May 21 and mid-June, 1864. The 1864 directory lists him as a reporter, boarding at 394 L St. North; he is not entered in 1865.

39. Inserted above "David"

40. Preceding five words inserted above "50th"

41. WW and Farwell corresponded with each other frequently during 1864, with Farwell writing the first letter on April 30. WW wrote four letters, Farwell eight; WW's letters are lost (*Corr.,* I, 368, 375, 376). For letters in 1875 and 1878, see *Corr.,* II, 328, 364, 372; III, 431. See [*964V*] below; "Baily D Damon." WW noted his address Aug. 4, 1877, in "Daybook" and at some later date endorsed it "dead" ([74], *DN*). See also "D. W. Wilder," "Typical Soldiers," *SD, Prose 92,* I, 111.

[*963R*][42] orange for Hamblin[43] bed 46—ward C / *bed 34—D*—oranges / Young men in [*illeg.*] U S Insane asylum[44] Sam'l Dixon 1st Penn lt art bat B near Petersburgh[45] Lawrence co Penn / visit to U S Insane Asylum (May '64 /[46] aunty Kitty Henry on N st. about corner 17th house lt brown in front, white on sides—near the corral

[*964V; 963V; 964R blank*] sutler 51st N Y. George's trunk[47] S Kipp cor F & 9th st model house /

Reuben Farwell[48] co H 1st Mich Cav father Leroy Farwell Plymouth Wayne co Mich /

Lieut. A J Liebenan[49] 70th N Y Volunteers 1st Excelsior brigade res N Y 91 west 41st st / Bethuel Smith[50] co F 2d U S cavalry

[*965R*] H P Allen Uniontown Pen /

Aaron Smith co K 51st N Y ward 23 Carver hosp May 15 '64/[51]

42. All rules across leaf.

43. See [*969R*] below.

44. Scribbled at left of Dixon's unit.

45. Grant began an assault on Petersburgh in late May, 1864, but it finally fell only on April 2, 1865.

46. Scribbled after "Petersburgh." At this time, the only hospital for the insane in Washington was St. Elizabeths Hospital, a government-owned institution opened in 1855. Since, in 1863, several rooms were given over to producers of artificial limbs, and amputees were often sent there to be fitted with a limb and rehabilitated, Dixon was probably not a mental patient. See Henry M. Hurd, et al., *The Institutional Care of the Insane in the U.S. and Canada* (1916), II, 146. Rule across leaf.

47. This part of the notebook probably dates from before WW's visit to Brooklyn on June 22 where he stayed until December. On June 18, 1864, George wrote from Petersburg, Va. Letters of October 2 and October 23 report his capture on September 30. Both letters ask his mother to have WW arrange to have his baggage sent home from the regiment. It is possible, however, that since George was in action from mid-May WW had taken some action about his trunk before he went to Brooklyn. He was still in Brooklyn when George was captured and remained there until early December. But see *Corr.*, I, 242*n*. See "Baily D Damon" for an almost identical entry.

48. See [*962V*] above.

49. Liebenan wrote a letter to WW on February 20, 1864 (*Corr.*, I, 375). On [*964V*] below, WW mentions a Leibenan and a Lebenan. These are probably the same person. See also "Baily D Damon" for an almost identical note, and "D. W. Wilder."

50. From Glens Falls, NY. Wounded in 1863 and spent some time in Armory Hospital. The correspondence was reopened in 1874–1875. See "Typical Soldiers," *SD, Prose 92,* I, 111; *Corr.*, I, 149–150, 367, 368, 373, 375, 376, II, 318–319, 364, 372; "a m Dr. LB Russell," "September–October," "Baily D Damon," "some memoranda," "D. W. Wilder"; Traubel, II, 137, 138, 371, 380.

51. On the day before this note was entered, Aaron Smith had written a letter to WW. He wrote again on July 13 (*Corr.*, I, 249, 375, 376). WW mentioned Carver Hospital in an article for the NY *Times,* December 11, 1864, reprinted in "Hospitals Ensemble," *SD, Prose 92,* I, 67.

ward C bed 28 May 16 Michael Gilley age 27 Nativity Germany co G 9th N Y Cav. (died) /—sister Mary Gilley Sheldon wyoming co New York / g s w'd in right hip hit on 7th May / brother John is also wounded (young) ask if he wrote & if so what hosp he is in

[965*V*] [*illeg.*] A Vanaschan co B. 51st NY /

Serg't I K Brown co K 51st N Y [:] Harewood[52] May 28

[966*R*] Judiciary[53] May 15 John Yonkmanard[54] co F 51st N Y vol /

May 19 '64 Jerry Ward[55] ward 13 Lincoln hosp — 4th Ohio friend of Oscar Cunningham[56] /

Jos Ettinger co I 70th N Y Lieut look for the name Liebenan[57] /

Jerry Hartman co B 70th N Y vol Stanton hosp /[58]

Lieut Lebenan[59]

[967*R*; *966V blank*][60] Ward C bed 45 Kenneth Townsend[61] co C 106th N Y w lft lg below knee no bones fract may 24 '64 + book 12[62] /

Ward D bed 9 James M Achor[63] co C 14th Indiana r't elbow bone taken out May 26 '64 + book 12 /

armory ward 2 Darius Lillie[64] co G 44th N Y r't breast, ball passed throg May 64 + book 12 /

52. Harewood Hospital, in Washington. The 51st NY was George Whitman's regiment.

53. The Judiciary Hospital, in Washington, had been hastily erected on the grounds of the old E Street Infirmary, which had been destroyed by fire in the autumn of 1861.

54. Also from George's regiment.

55. See "Hospitals Ensemble," *SD, Prose 92,* I, 67.

56. See "June 20 —'63" for further details on Cunningham. Rule across leaf.

57. See *n*43 above. Rule across leaf.

58. Rule across leaf.

59. Circled in MS.

60. All rules across leaf.

61. See "Hospital book 12."

62. Rule across leaf.

63. See "Hospital book 12."

64. See "Hospital book 12."

Wm H Millis[65] ward B bed 33 co E 8th Penn Cav Bridgeville sussex co Del + book 12 / ward A bed 46 James Hague[66] co H. 1st Del r't lung—Mother has come May '64 *book 12 /

Finley ward 6—bed 59 George L Farnum[67] co C 77th Mass + book 12

[967*V*] Mrs Geo W Briggs[68] Salem Mass /

Justus F Boyd[69] Fleming p o Livingston co Mich/[70]

[968R][71] ward A Jesse Mullery[72] co K 15th New Jersey shot through shoulder or neck ball went downward & is in yet May 64 *see book 12 /

Charley H Harris[73] Co F 4th Vermont gone home furlough *see book 12

ward C bed 30 Cavalier Poland[74] co A 18th Penn Cav r't arm—May '64 *see book 12

bed 30—ward B Geo W Ferguson co D 84th Penn age 19—amp lft. arm above elbow friend Charles Edwards Standing Stone Penn May '64 (died June 64)[75] Lieut Young introduced himself to me)[76]

[968*V*] ward B bed 17 B Benj F Leisenring co C 7th Maryland wants to see Christian Stawm in Av & 7th st market produce & fruit stand large, fresh looking man, red face near centre of market/[77]

65. WW and Millis corresponded with each other on and off until 1880; WW's letters are lost (*Corr.*, I, passim; II, passim; III, 436). WW described Millis' case and recovery in "A Model Hospital," *SD, Prose 92,* I, 86, under date of January 29, 1865. Also mentioned in "Add*resses*" and "Hospital book 12."

66. See "Hospital book 12."

67. See "Hospital book 12."

68. WW received a letter from Mrs. Briggs, probably a contributor, on April 21, 1864 (*Corr.*, I, 375).

69. Boyd, a corporal in the 6th Michigan cavalry, was a patient in Armory Square Hospital in the spring of 1863 ("Walt Whitman Soldier's , " "take (Marg. D Valois)," and "Hospitals/ Culpepper").

70. Rule across leaf.

71. Rule across leaf.

72. In 1864–1865, WW wrote four known letters to Mullery (all of them lost), and Mullery wrote four to WW (*Corr.*, I, 247*n*, 368, 369, 376, 377). See "Add*resses*" and "Hospital book 12."

73. Harris wrote to WW on May 30, 1864, from West Brattleboro, Vermont (*Corr.*, I, 177, 375). See "Hospital book 12."

74. See "Hospital book 12."

75. In large parentheses at left.

76. Scribbled at left and set off by a loop.

77. Rule across leaf.

ward B[78] bed 18 wants pipe—also the man near door in ward C

[969*R*] ward C bed 46 May 64 Wm Hamblin co D 5th Maine wounded 10th lft[79] leg just below knee bone fract came here 26th / wife Louisa M Hamblin Biddeford Maine wrote from Fred'k'g /[80]

ward 23—Carver May '64 Elisha Bailey co B 17th Vermont inf young recruit injured in head by shell—(trouble in bowels

[970*R*;[81] 969*V blank*] Armory building—2d ward bed 34 Frank Magee battery 2 1st Mass heavy artillery —left arm wounded—bone fractured set & healing / sister Miss Mary Susan Magee Marblehead Mass /

ward C bed 8 May '64 Serg't John W Boody battery M 1st Mass hv'y art age 28 father Aaron Boody West Northwood N H / g s w lft thigh (bad) brother E G Boody East Northwood N H (been here) /

Charles[82] Smith ward C bed 7 May '64 co B 91st Penn vol [*illeg.*] right thigh father Leopold Smith 812 Lawrence st above Brown Philadelphia /

bed 39 ward C Pelatiah West[83] W Warner co a 111th N Y. brother Orien Warner Palmyra wayne co N Y g s w r't wrist bad

[971*R*; 970*V blank*] ward E bed 22 / Stephen Lilly co L 1st Maine H art. wounded 19th lost right leg doing very well / father James E Lilly Smyrna mills Aroostook co Maine

[972*R*; 971*V blank*] Lyman T Woods Co I 20th Indiana Wheeler's station Porter co Indiana /[84]

78. Inserted above "18"
79. Deleted: "knee" ; inserted: "leg just" above "[*del.*] knee" and "below"
80. Inserted at left. Fredericksburg[?]. Line across the page under "Maine"
81. All rules across leaf.
82. Inserted above deleted "Leopold"
83. Inserted, above "W" of "West"
84. Rule across leaf.

Did You Ever Think.

Manuscript in Pennsylvania. Inscribed in black pencil with black ink emendation on two pasted scraps: (1) blue Williamsburgh tax bill form, 7⅜" x 4⅛", (2) white wove, 7" x 5½". On verso of white scrap is "Recorders Ages Hence," ll. 9–10 (1860). The date is probably 1859 or 1860. First published *N&F,* 118 (Pt. III, #119; *CW,* IX, 138–139).

Did you ever think, for a moment, how[1] so many[2] young men, full of the stuff to make the noblest heroes of the earth, really live—really pass their lives, year after year, and so till death?— Constant toil—ever[3] alert to keep the wolf back[4] from the door—no developement—no rational pleasure—[5]sleeping in some cramped[6] and dirty place—[7]never knowing once[8] a beautiful happy home—never knowing once in their whole lives,[9] real affection, sweetly returned, the joy, the life of life—always kept down,—[10]unaware of[11] religion—no habitual rendezvous except the bar-room[12]—unaware of any amusements[13] except these preposterous theatres and of a Sunday these[14] those equally preposterous and painful screamings from the pulpits—

1. Deleted: "the"
2. Deleted: "noble-souled"
3. Deleted: "fighting" ; inserted above "[*del.*] fighting" : "alert"
4. Inserted above wordspace between "wolf" and "from"
5. Deleted: "living" ; inserted above "[*del.*] living" : "sleeping"
6. Deleted: "and"
7. End of first scrap.
8. Deleted: "the [*illeg.*]"
9. Deleted: [*illeg.*]
10. Deleted: "aware of"
11. Deleted: "the"
12. Preceding six words inserted above "religion . . . any"
13. Inserted above and deleted: "bar-ro"
14. Two preceding words inserted above "screamings" . Deleted: [*illeg.*] . Inserted: "and harangu [*both del.*] and painful" . Inserted above and to right in black ink: "those equally preposterous"

[Illeg.] of America.

Manuscript in LC (#63, sheet #292V). Inscribed in pencil on irregular white wove scrap. A fragment clipped and torn from a larger text, perhaps a sketch for a poem. On recto a clipping on Paris hospitals, commenting that the nurses are more effective than medicine, with the notation: "Letter from Paris in the N. Y. World," The fairly loose writing suggests a date in the 1860s. The *World* was founded in 1860. There is no real parallel to "A Song for Occupations," sec. 4.

[*illeg.*] of America!
nothing yet done to write about[?] unless[1] what the [*illeg.*] instruments does, etc
perhaps[?] the playing of the [*illeg.*] does to an opera

1. Deleted: "as" ; inserted: "what"

W. Whitman Portland Av.

Manuscript in LC (#93, sheet #s 993–1024). Green paper cover, 6¼" x 3¾" with white label in another hand: "Note Book Walt Whitman." Inscribed in black pencil, ink and blue pencil on white wove paper. One blank leaf is preserved. Portions first printed by Emory Holloway in *UPP,* II, 92–93, and "Walt Whitman in 1862," *AL,* 6 (November, 1934), 266, 268. The notes on the Jamaica Presbyterian bicentennial were used by WW in "Important Ecclesiastical Gathering at Jamaica, L. I.," Brooklyn *City News,* January 9, 1862 (Charles I. Glicksberg, "Walt Whitman, the Journalist," *Americana,* 30, [July, 1936] 481–485). Dates on [993*V*], [997*R*] and the date of the church celebration suggest a date between December 1861 and January 1862. I am indebted to Professor Donald Yeats, Western Australia Institute of Technology, for valuable assistance with the notes.

[993*V* (*inside front cover*); *993R blank*] W. Whitman Portland av. near Myrtle Brooklyn

[994*R*][1] Hines[2] 174 10th av. bet. 21st & 22d Miller[3] 205 8th av. Geo. Potter, 137 West 16th st.[4] Mrs. Rose,[5] 95 Prince / Peale,[6] 15 Hudson [*illeg.*], 2d story, over drug store Billy Anderson, 74 [*illeg.*] st / 86 West 42d st. Ada Clare[7] near 6th av. / John J. Irwin, Grocer, Putnam av. bet. Franklin & Classon / Houghton[8] (Boston) Knickerbocker / George 23d st. large rooms on 6th av.[9] / Bub Cooper 41 Troy[?] st Mrs Bloom 27 Schermerhorn st. Mike Lawn Pete Lawn [:] 23d st No. 7 Aristideo[10] 5th av. / Mrs Case[11] 54 Greenwich av. 3d floor / Al. No. 5 4th av Jan 3d '62 / Jack Abbott [:] 467 Bowery & [*illeg.*] No 7 Butts cor. 12th st & Av. C Gatin[?] saloon

1. Deleted: "Mrs Case 296 Bleecker" . (See *n* 11, below.) All entries are in a single column. Slashes indicate rules between entries.

2. Almost certainly Charles Hine (1827–1871), artist of this address, who painted the picture from which the frontispiece of *LG* 1860 was made. See also *Corr.,* I, 371, II, 130, 131, 366, III, 368, 382–384, 440; Traubel, IV, 378; "81 Clerman," "Mr & Mrs. Fitz," "D.W. Wilder."

3. Franklin Miller, carpets, 205 8th ave.; home, 517 W. 23d.

4. Deleted: "Swinton 154 West 26th st. bet. 7th & 8th av." Probably William Swinton. John is not in NY directories. See *"Rambles Among Words."*

5. Ernestine Potowesky Rose (1810–1892). See "Frances Wright."

6. The next two entries in pencil.

7. See "81 Clerman" . This and the two entries following are in ink.

8. Possibly Henry O. Houghton (1823–1895), the Boston publisher. His firm had NY connections. "Knickerbocker" is possibly the *Knickerbocker Magazine.*

9. This and following entries on page in pencil.

10. Aristideo or Aristides. See "return my book."

11. Wife of Lyman W. Case, lawyer. See *n* 1, above, and "English runic."

[995*R*; 994*V blank*] Mary Hart[12] / 10 Washington street—1st Floor—husband is a pedlar Thomas Dougherty /

[996*R*; 995*V blank*] No 9[13] —5th av. Saturday 21st inst 2d trip down near 9th st in Broadway Henry Taylor

[997*R*; 996*V blank*] James Metcalf, 3^d district Station House, Chambers st.[14] /

Dec 28—Saturday night Mike Ellis—wandering at the cor of Lexington av. & 32d st.—took him home to 150 37th street,—4th story back room—bitter cold night—works in Stevenson's Carriage factory. /

letters for Burnside Ex left at Col. Frank E. Howe's[15] store 203 Broadway

[998*R*; 997*V blank*] The two vaults Subject—Poem[16]

The vault at Pfaffs[17] where the drinkers and laughers meet to eat and drink and carouse,
While on[18] the walk immediatly overhead, pass[19] the myriad feet of Broadway
As the dead in their graves, are underfoot hidden[20]
And the living pass over them, recking not of them,
Laugh on laughters! Drink on drinkers!
Bandy the jests![21] Toss the theme from one to another!
Beam[22] up—Brighten up bright eyes of beautiful young men!
[999*R*; 998*V blank*] Eat what you, haveing ordered,[23] are pleased to see placed before you—after the[24] work of the day, now, with appetite, eat,
Drink wine—drink beer—raise your voice.
Behold![25] your friend, as he arrives[26]—Welcome him, when, from the upper step, he looks down upon you with cheerful look

12. Deleted: "(No)"
13. Probably an omnibus route.
14. I.e. a police station. Entry in black ink.
15. A dealer in scales and safes. George W and the 51st NY Volunteers were with General Ambrose Burnside's expedition against the North Carolina coast.
16. First printed *UPP*, II, 92–93.
17. Pfaff's restaurant was in a basement which extended under the sidewalk at 647 Broadway. The building still stands.
18. Inserted above in the letterspace between "While . . . the"
19. Originally: "passes all"
20. Inserted on a line above "t" in "underfoot"
21. Sentence inserted a line above "Toss the"
22. [*Illeg.*] deleted before "Beam"
23. Deleted: "is"
24. Deleted: [*illeg.*]
25. Deleted: "Welcome" at beginning; inserted: "Behold!"
26. Comma deleted.

[*1000R; 999V blank*][27] Overhead[28] rolls Broadway—the myriad rushing[29] The [*illeg.*][30]
The lamps are lit—the shops blaze in—the fabrics and jewelry[*?*][31] are seen through the plate glass windows[32]
The strong lights from above pour down upon them and[33] are shed outside
The thick crowds, [34] well-dressed—the[35] continual crowds as if they would never end
[*1001R; 1000V blank*] The curious appearance of the faces—the glimpses first caught of the eyes and expressions, as they flit along.
([36]You phantoms![37] oft I[38] pause, yearning, to arrest some one of you!
Oft I doubt your reality[39] you are real[40]—I suspect all is but a pageant.)
The
[*1002R; 1001V blank*] The lights beam in the first vault—but the other is entirely dark /
In the first /

get at Library *Schiller's complete Works* English with new translation by Dr. C.T. Hempel[41]/ New York City during the Revolution, 4to; 195 pages—published for the Mercantile Library Association[42]

[*1003R; 1002V blank*] Anne E. Green in care of Dan'l Hathaway Livery stable keeper Columbus Franklin co. Ohio /
drawers factory Grand street, near Attorney /

[*1004R; 1003V blank*][43] Presbyterian Church of Jamaica—200th anniversary

27. The page is badly rubbed. Since it was apparently no more legible when Holloway transcribed it for *UPP*, the inconsequential differences between our readings are unnoted. Deleted: "Behold the company"

28. Deleted: "passes" ; inserted: "rolls"

29. Deleted: "Broadway"

30. Preceding two words inserted above "[*del.*] Broadway" . *UPP* reads: "rushing Broadway(?)"

31. *UPP* reads: "fabrics vividly(?)"

32. The original reading of this line is difficult to decipher. "fabrics and jewelry[*?*] are seen through" seems to have been inserted between lines on the page. At the same time "the" was inserted to the left of "plate glass" which had been the first word. Before "windows" : "of the" deleted. Twelve words deleted at end of line: "[*illeg.*] the show of the [*illeg.*] and future[*?*] of the [*illeg.*]"

33. Deleted: [*illeg.*]

34. Deleted: [*illeg.*]

35. Deleted [*illeg.*]

36. Deleted: "O" ; inserted: "You" above "ph" in "phantoms"

37. Deleted: "how"

38. Deleted: "stop"

39. Preceding two words inserted on a line above and following "doubt" ; "whether" deleted under the insert.

40. Deleted: "your reality" above "are real" . Deleted: "and must[*?*]" ; inserted: "—I" above and following "[*del.*] and"

41. Two vols., Philadelphia, 1861. This note first printed by Holloway, *AL* (1936), 266.

42. New York, 1861.

43. Each page concerning the anniversary is cancelled with a vertical stroke, which was WW's custom when he used material elsewhere.

Tuesday afternoon 3 oclock[44] 7th & 8th of January / The congregation have just erected two mural tablets—set in the walls of the Church,—on which are inscribed the names of all the deceased ministers—19 ministers altogether—[45] [*1005R; 1004V blank*] Exercises on Tuesday. Prayer by Rev. Nicholas Everett Smith—Scriptures read out of a Bible older than 1776. / Hymn[46] read and from Sternhold & Hopkins, printed in 1714. before Watts was born /[47] Stones inaugurated by Rev. Mr. Oakey[48]—5 or 6 minutes—object of stones, and welcome. [*1006R; 1005V blank*] Rev. James M. McDonald[49] of Princeton, N.J.[50] stationed at Jamaica / Ecclesiastes 1st. 4. "One generation passeth away, and another generation cometh, but the earth abideth forever." / —subject—relation of the permanent to the transient[51] or the gains over the losses in history[52] [*1007R; 1006V blank*] dwelt briefly[53] on the transient nature of earthly thing / Removed as we are from Greece, Egypt, &c we still find engrafted to-day on our own affairs, all that is valuable belonging to them, such for instance as the family institution. / Change the form, but the substance always remain / progress has been made no matter how slow. [*1008R; 1007V blank*] the Church has come over sea to us— / drawing from the very decay of the past, a vigorous life for the future. / Picture[54] a bird's eye of the history of the[55] world at the time of the settlement of this island 200 years ago. England—Russia, Holland, France, &c. Louis 14, Cromwell. [*1009R; 1008V blank*] No English copy of scriptures had yet been—John Eliot's Indian testament had been printed in[56] / The Dutch church in Brooklyn existed. / In 1657 there were but three schoolmasters on Long Island. Rich Jones. / Scho. of Jam was arrested / 1656 Jamaica was settled 1644 Hempstead [*was settled*] [*1010R;*[57] *1009V blank*] Yeniacah[?] Indians—were found here from thence the town was named. / Tribes here were subdued by Capt. Underhill & others / 200 years ago how very humble—thatch & log houses the appearance [?] / in imagination enter one of the houses here—of 200 years ago—food venison &

44. Day and hour at right within a ∧ pointing towards center.

45. Entry first printed by Glicksberg, *Americana* (1936), 478.

46. Inserted: "read and" above and following "Hymn" and over "from"

47. In the *City News* article: "the hymn was recited out of an antique 'Sternhold and Hopkins' printed in 1714 before the lyric Watts was born." (Glicksberg, *Americana,* [1936] 482.) Isaac Watts was born in 1674; his *Hymns* was published in 1707 and *Psalms* in 1719. The first edition of Sternhold's *Psalms* with additions by Hopkins was in 1549.

48. The pastor of the church.

49. Reverend James Madison MacDonald (1812–1876) on the faculty of Princeton Theological Seminary. In 1847, while pastor at Jamaica, he had published *History of the Presbyterian Church of Jamaica, Long Island.*

50. Deleted: "fo" [formerly?].

51. Deleted: "especially"

52. This and preceding entry first published by Glicksberg, *Americana* (1936), 478.

53. Possibly WW meant to delete this word.

54. Deleted: "of"

55. Deleted: "civilized"

56. The *City Press* story reads: "John Eliot's Indian testament had been printed here, but no English copy of the Scriptures had yet been printed." (Glicksberg, *Americana* [1936], 483).

57. Deleted at top of page: "Salut au Monde." WW's mind may have wandered or the entry may have been made earlier. WW adopted this title in *LG* 1860.

fish—bread scarce—dinner indian pudding [*1011R; 1010V blank*] minute description of domestic life here on Long Island at that time / gun killing wolf / Costume—of man & woman of the time / picture of the whole domestic life of people of Jamaica / no of heads in Jamaica in 1683 87 [×] 5 [=] 435[58] whole pop. / Danl Denton's celebrated History of New York 1670, pub in London[59] / Denton was the first[60] town clerk in Jamaica town [*1012R; 1011V blank*] During 7 years preceding 1688. there were 27 marriage 71 baptism 23 burials[61] in a pop of[62] 450 / picture in imagination—entering a home [?] here 200 years ago—conforming to the historical facts as / —conversations some had been in Cromwell's & Charles' battles / some had seen a witch burnt—or told stories of witchcraft. [*1013R; 1012V blank*] —1670—account of a witch at that date here /imagine also the scene presented here on a Sabbath morning—200 years / Abraham Smith beats the drum—to call the people together for the meeting / attendance is compulsory. / men wore three corner'd hats —small clothes, silver buckles—ruffles & wrists—swords—ladies—brocade—[63] hoop'd petticoats [*1014R; 1013V blank*] On the Sabbath, their apparel was simple and appropriate, —neat, but not gaudy./ people enter the Church—a humble edifice built of logs and thatch. / the hourglass stands beside the Bible, to give note of the time. / He then (Rev)[64] glanced at the Causes which led to our forefathers coming here. (skip next page)
[*1015R; 1014V blank*][65] subject for poems

High Tide

every thing culminating—prosperity—all flush—every thing crowded on to the utmost of prosperity—rose-color—wealth—friends—luck— / then Low Tide the reverse[66]

[*1016R; 1015V blank*] May 1672—the town entered into an agreement with Rev. John Pruden, to preach for them, under the Presbyterian system of doctrine. / Jamaica has been Presbyterian from the beginning—and proved her devotion so through a long contest in the early settlement. / This is surely the oldest Presbyterian Church on the American continent—10 years older than the one in Maryland. [*1017R; 1016V blank*][67]—What an advance since that day—there are now 5500 Presbyterian ministers—[68]8000 churches 775,000 communicants—more than double what now exist in Great Britain and provinces

58. Figures written in a column.
59. Daniel Denton (d. 1696), *A Brief Description of New-York* (London, 1670).
60. Inserted: "the first"
61. Written in a column.
62. Deleted: [*illeg.*]
63. Deleted: [*illeg.*]
64. Inserted in wordspace above "then . . . glanced"
65. The preceding entry suggests that this entry antedates the report of the bicentennial. The notes were first printed by Holloway, *AL* (1936), 268.
66. The preceding four words are in a large scrawl quite different from the neat, small hand in which the rest of the notebook is written.
67. The top third of the leaf has been torn off.
68. Deleted: "18"

[*1017V*] coffee & [*illeg.*] / Henry's—next door[69]

[*1018R*] 14[70] millions and a half of Church property / Congregation at[71] present in Jamaica is one of the largest in rural / Whitfield[72] here[73] 1740 & 1764 preached here in Jamaica / last convert made by[74] of Whitfield died in 1840, aged 95 having been a communicant 75 years—here in Jamaica [*1019R; 1018V blank*]—wound up by an appropriate close. / no gulf every really divides one generation from[75] another—[76] / —he took a cheerful view of the present, encouraging all to hope, through the present crisis of our nation. [*1020R; 1019V blank*] Wednesday 8th was a meeting[77] gathering of Clergymen, elders, emigrants &c— / to-day from[78] venerable Dr. Shelton who has been an elder here 40. / Rev. Mr. Crane [*Rev. Mr.*] Everett [*:*] spoke with reminiscences &c / Representation from Philadelphia Rev. Mr. Breed—Rev. Dr. Krebs Rev. Mr. Higbie [*1021R; 1020V blank*] will be published / Rev. Dr. Krebs[79] preached Wednesday night— / Thursday, the Lord's supper will be administered— / —will be the conclusion / Tablets in church from 1666 to 1840 [*1022R; 1021V blank*] Krebs—the Presbytery of New York connection between the church & the family[80] / Rev.[81] Mr. Breed, of Philadelphia / Mr. Reeve of the Presbytery of L. I. / this church has sent out 25 or 30 ministers

[*1023R*] $14 full suit / 3¾

[*1023V*][82] Rosse's "Index of Dates." (in Bohn's Scientific Library.[83] / Hadyn's "Dictionary of Dates."[84] / Stuff for undershirts & drawers 10 (18) 180[85] / neck handkerchief—1 hat 2

[*1024R*] leaves Jamaica 10 mi before 5 and half past 6
[*1024V blank*].

69. Preceding words in blue pencil.
70. WW began to write the figure out.
71. Inserted in wordspace above "Congregation . . . present"
72. Rev. George Whitfield (1714–1770), preacher of the Great Awakening.
73. Inserted in wordspace above "Whitfield . . . 1740"
74. Preceding two words inserted above "rt" in "convert" and "of"
75. Deleted: "one" ; inserted: "another" on a line above following "one"
76. Deleted: "they" and [*illeg.*], beginning of new entry which went no further.
77. Deleted: "of"
78. Deleted: "Rev." inserted: "venerable" on a line above "[*del.*] Rev." and "Dr."
79. Deleted: "deliv" . Possibly John Michel Krebs (1804–1867), from 1842 a Director of Princeton Seminary and, from 1865 to his death, President.
80. Possibly the topic of Krebs' sermon.
81. Deleted: "Reeve" "Dr." ; "Rev." inserted at beginning of entry.
82. Two following entries in ink at top of page.
83. Two vols., London, 1856.
84. A standard work by T. J. Haydn which went through twenty-five editions between 1841 and 1911.
85. This memorandum at the bottom of the page written over some random figures and the multiplication of 18 by 14.

William Giggee.

Manuscript in LC (#95, sheet #s 1026–1045A). Notebook of white wove paper bound in blue paper, 6¾" x 4". Inscribed in black pencil with occasional entries in red pencil, blue pencil and black ink as noted. The paper is soft and the ink penetrates the page. Foliation in this edition follows LC sheet numbers, although an incomplete typed transcript by Joseph Auslander, also in LC, has been followed for its indication of blank leaves preserved separately by LC when the notebook was mounted, as well as for an occasional reading. The notebook seems to date from early 1862 and to have been used not only to note the names of acquaintances and for notes for *LG* but also for journalistic purposes. Aside from the notes for "Brooklyniana" there are also notes for editorials, including the heads. Portions of the notebook have been printed and discussed in Glicksberg, *AL*.

[*1026R*] William Giggee[1] Company E. 1st Regiment New York Volunteers, Camp Butler Newport News Virginia / [*illeg.*] Rankin[*?*] Power[*?*] hotel Park Row opposite[*?*] Astor House /

[*1027R; 1026V blank*][2] The[*?*] Am[*?*] public
the great distinctive purpose aim object drift[3] modern to
The part which It [*illeg.*] plays in /

The distinctive purpose[4] of America[5] is to reduce government to[*?*] its minimum and to make[6] masses of[7] individuals All advantages[*?*] [*illeg.*] collisions [*illeg.*][8] by false[*?*] and[*?*] curious[*?*] ways, with this result—for the current is set and all that seems[9]

[*1028R; 1027V blank*] Individuality[10]

I celebrate the whole man, with his varied parts, animal, mental, and spiritual /

1. See also "81 Clerman" and "return my book."
2. The entire page is badly smeared. An irrelevant sum in red at top of page.
3. The preceding four words are written in a column at the upper right of the page.
4. Deleted: if"
5. Deleted: "is for,"
6. Deleted: "immense Dem[*?*]"
7. Deleted: "superior"
8. Deleted: "by"
9. Auslander's transcript of the following word gives a reading of "seems (terrible striving?) is but [*illeg.*] that [*illeg.*] (but?) in (the result?)" . The MS is now completely illegible.
10. Deleted: above and left: "Through" "America The Modern Spirit . . ." in column.

America The Modern Spirit Democracy Friendship to all nations Spirituality /

[*1029R; 1028V blank*][11] A poem of the deaths of grand and lofty spirited men— / (pick out all the words that embody the ideas of a life of generosity[12] ardor eagerness faith /
and then the words of disappointment dismay ingratitude non-recognition a long list of sorrowful melancholy funereal words[13] see next page

[*1030R; 1029V blank*] Sing the death of[14] Kepler (Columbus, Cervantes, John Brown Burns— Columbus /

pages 207-8-9-10-11 of vol 1 Ticknor[15] /

* * * in 1506 Columbus died at Valladolid, a disappointed, broken-hearted old man—little comprehending what he had done for mankind, and still less the glory & honor that through all future generations awaited his name * * * * * But the mantle of his devout and heroic spirit fell on some of his successors * * *[16]

Columbus was a grander man by far than I thought[*?*]—had [*illeg.*] visions—wrote with unsurpassed vigor[*?*][17] [*illeg.*] command—had the loftiest[*?*] spirit[*?*]

[*1031R; 1030V blank*] the woman who works at making "heart's ease" flowers, and wears out her life—(Mullen's story)[18]/ Miss Kate Barnum Columbus Franklin Co. Ohio

[*1032R; 1031V blank*] poem
wreck of the ship. / the edifice burnt down / the tree decaying / the ? [*:*] but what were these to the man?[19]—the woman—wrecked? Consumed?

11. The entire page is badly smeared. All the "words" in column.
12. Large question mark at left opposite words in column.
13. Pointing hand.
14. Names in column.
15. George Ticknor, *History of Spanish Literature,* 3 vols., New York, 1849. The pages mentioned analyze the character of Columbus with emphasis on his religious aspirations.
16. A quotation from Ticknor, 211.
17. Auslander's transcript reads: "his (spiritual ?) vision wrote with unsurpassed dignity and"
18. Entry in red crayon. Possibly Edward F. (or J.) Mullen, an illustrator for *Vanity Fair* and for books, whom WW knew at Pfaff's. See *Corr.,* I, 85, 127, "Some Old Acquaintances-Memories," *SD, Prose 92,* II, 277, and Groce, George C. and Wallace, David H., *The New-York Historical Society's Dictionary of Artists in America, 1564–1860* (New Haven, 1957). A cartoon by Mullen from *Vanity Fair* depicting Fitz-James O'Brien as a recruiting officer is in Albert Parry, *Garrets and Pretenders* (N. Y., 1933), 54.
19. Question mark above word.

Walking in Broadway—Jan 9 '62, saw the old woman either insane or drunk, wretchedly drest, affectedly promenading the sidewalk

[*1032V*] seething and bubbling year

[*1033R*][20] A few *malignants left* with extract from the "Brooklyn Eagle" /

There[21] is a good feeling opinion prevalent that, now that the Free States are unanimous, there should be a general amnesty, and no casting up of old grudges, and twitting on[22] previous shortcomings. But there are a few malignants yet left at the North. They shelter themselves under the real spirit of toleration which has existed too long here to be rubbed out in a hurry. What [*1034R; 1033V blank*] shall be done with them? /

Canada to the Rescue! /

hold on a little while yet, Canada—but we may want you, if you wish to come[23]/

But while[24] the London Times represents the trade and finance[25] does it not represent the moral,[26] religious, and ? [27] capital of the British Empire. This is the capital that[28] decides ?[29] at last—for it is a perennial force

[*1035R; 1034V blank*] *American Continental Freedom*[30]

the grandeur of the immense masses of material in such a city as New York,[31]

[*1036R; 1035V blank*][32] Make a leaf of grass out of the hemp; the rope-walk, and making rope of hemp[33]—the rope-maker with the hemp bound around his waist— /

[*1036V*] John Crowell 94 Gold st. /

20. Deleted: "The" ; inserted above: "A few"
21. WW had begun the paragraph: "as a general, We cordially join"
22. Deleted: "old"
23. Written in a cramped hand under the heading and above and below a line across the leaf which separates it from what follows.
24. The two preceding words inserted to the left and above. "The" not reduced to lowercase.
25. The preceding five words are inserted on two lines on a caret above "Times . . . does"
26. Deleted: "and"
27. Written above the blank.
28. Deleted: "settles"
29. Written above the blank.
30. Following below is the deleted phrase: *"The blood shed in Baltimore"* This is probably a reference to the attack on Federal troops by the Baltimore mob on April 19, 1861. The entry is separated by a line from what follows.
31. Hanging indentation.
32. Auslander's transcript notes a missing blank leaf here.
33. Deleted: "w"

"Homer & the Homeric Age" by Gladstone the English statesman have it at the Astor Library / English edition $15

[*1037R*] Silver brothers on the blue, your immortal spangles
shine— /[34]

the snow-lake at Nantucket (Mr Clapp's story)[35]

[*1038R; 1037V blank*][36]

An old Brooklyn Landmark going.

a glance at the *Old*[37] *Military Garden*
Before[38] vanishes, to make room for the new Court House.[39]

[*1039R; 1038V blank*] Col Greene—1810–11 / gen'lly[*?*]—1830 / took him at old Eagle Tavern / Masonic lodges / must have been built in 1830[40] [:] Ralph Malbone,[41] over the way Saml Doxsey, kept in 1819 / Washington Garden east side, between Nassau and Concord[42] where the old theatre,[43] kept by Biddy Stevenson / Another garden opposite / Brower[44] Mt Pleasant / Mt Pleasant / another [*1040R; 1039V blank*][45] Black Horse garden junction of De Kalb ave[*?*] / election days—town meeting,[46] / Remsen farm 40 years ago, $40 an acre[47] / gu [*?*]

34. This line does not appear in *LG,* but it suggests a tentative sketch for one of the poems in *Drum-Taps* about the flag.

35. Probably Henry Clapp, editor of the *Saturday Press* and habitué of Pfaff's, who had published "Out of the Cradle Endlessly Rocking." The entry is in red crayon.

36. Auslander's transcript indicates a missing blank verso and recto, but because of the LC mounting it is impossible to confirm that the following should be numbered as a verso. Written lengthwise in ink. Bottom of leaf torn off before writing.

The following entries, [*1038R–1040R*], are notes for *Brooklyniana,* which was published in the Brooklyn *Standard* in twenty-five numbers from June 8, 1861 to November 8, 1862. See *UPP,* II, 222–231.

37. Deleted: "Brook" ; inserted above: "Military"

38. Deleted: "it is torn down and"

39. In "*Brooklyniana*. No. 8" WW describes the Military Gardens. In No. 18 he speaks of the Courthouse as having already been built (ibid., 257, 297–298). This entry is written in black ink on the length of the leaf, the bottom of which had been torn off.

40. Colonel Greene was an eccentric and the builder of Military Gardens. A new building was erected at the Gardens in 1826–1827 of which the upper floor was used for Masonic lodge meetings (ibid., II, 298).

41. WW mentions Malbone as a member of an old Brooklyn family (ibid., II, 296).

42. Preceding six words inserted on two lines above "garden . . . where"

43. The theatre stood from 1828–1848 (ibid., II, 254, 294).

44. WW mentions Brower's Garden as recently having been built over (ibid., II, 298).

45. The page appears to have been clipped off at the top.

46. Ibid., II, 299.

47. Ibid. WW changed the price to $50 per acre.

—Montagu to State—go up to City Hall and go down to the river /[48] Joralemon and Pierrepont property / yellow house used as Hessian hospital[49]

[*1041R; 1039V blank*] *Two words to Maryland*[50]

We have two words to say to Maryland /

$14,000 /

Elevator / —U.S. Warehouse Co —Incorporated Co / have power to issue bonds as certificates /

Contemplating new house at Fulton[51] ferry next spring—

[*1042R; 1041V blank*][52] Geo. W. Carleton 130 Grand st[53]

[*1043R; 1042V blank*][54] I do not chant in my poems the divinity of the brain and spirit of a man[55] only, but the divinity of the animal

[*1044V; R blank*][56] Bowers[*?*] 57 Henry [*?*] / 142 46th bet. 7th & 8th st Dr Ruggles[57] / Mr. Stewart ("Land of Burns") 37 Park Place ? or Park Row /

[*1045 R*][58] [*illeg.*] / 2 [*illeg.*] 3 [*illeg.*] 3 undershirts 2 drawers 2 pr stockings 2 hdkf's / April 18 2 pr [*illeg.*] 5 shirts 2 hdkf 4 undershirts & drawers May 7—12 pieces

[*1045 AR; 1045V blank; 1045AR V blank*] Walt Whitman Portland av. first house north Myrtle, Brooklyn

48. Rule across leaf.

49. Ibid., II, 297. The entry is in black ink. At this point, Auslander's transcript inserts LC [*1042R*] and indicates a blank missing verso and a blank missing recto.

50. See *n*30 above.

51. Deleted in black ink: [*illeg.*].

52. At the top of the page are two names in blue pencil in another hand: "Robertson M. Bryant / Harriet Erwin Malone Franklin Co. N. Y." Each is followed by a rule across the leaf.

53. Also in blue pencil in WW's hand.

54. The top of the leaf has been torn off.

55. The preceding three words inserted on a line above "it" in "spirit" and "only."

56. Auslander's transcript indicates eight blank leaves which are missing here, beginning with a verso. At the bottom of [*1044V*] is written "Dean" in black ink upside down. First two entries followed by rule across leaf.

57. See "Mr & Mrs. Fitz."

58. Auslander's transcript omits [*1045–1045RA*]. Since both of these leaves have glue on the back, [*1045*] may have been a front end-paper and [*1045A*] a back end-paper. Since, however, a fragment of binding, perhaps a hinge, appears at the left in each, this conclusion is not certain. Entries in column.

In the Latter Part.

Manuscript in NYPL (Lion). Inscribed in black ink on three leaves of white wove paper 7¾" x 6⅜". [*1*] and [*2*] are conjugate. On backing sheet with a clipping from a sale catalogue: "476. WHITMAN (WALT.) Auto. MS. . . . ." Possibly this is part of the printer's copy for "Brooklyniana" (*UPP,* II, 222–321) which lacks an account of the outbreak of the Revolution. This was written between 1861 and 1862. The text would seem to belong between "Brooklyniana" No. 4 and No. 5, thus December, 1861. Copious notes for "Brooklyniana" are in LC (Feinberg).

In the latter part of the year 1765[1] while several English men-of-war were lying in the harbor, and after the fort had been put in a complete state of defence by the Royal governor, "the stamps," conveyed in a merchant ship, arrived in the harbor of New-York. The king's stamp officer fearing the temper of the people, notwithstanding the means which had been adopted to overawe them, refused to receive the papers, much less to enter upon their distribution. Upon his refusal, they were transferred, first to a ship of war, and subsequently to the governor's quarters in Fort George. But the people discovered the secret of their landing, and on the instant, hand-bills appeared on every corner, threatening all persons who received or delivered a stamp. On the 31st of October the merchants held a meeting, and resolved not to import goods from England. The next day the people hung the governor in effigy, in what is now the Park. On the same evening they repaired to the fort, and found the soldiers on the rampart ready to receive them. Nothing daunted, they marched to the gate, knocked and demanded admittance. This was of course refused. They then collected in the Bowling Green, and there, within pistol shot of the fort, built a bonfire, upon which they immolated the effigies of the governor along with his chariot, in which they fixed the effigy. In the next newspaper appeared an emphatic semi-official announcement, that the governor "had not issued, and would not suffer to be issued, any of the stamps now in Fort George." The people were not satisfied; they declared that the stamps should be delivered out of the fort or they would take them away by force. Finally, "after much negotiation," they were delivered to the mayor and common council, and deposited in the City Hall.

It seems that this neighborhood of New York, (of which Brooklyn then was, as it now is, a main constituent, if not indeed, as many would claim it to be, the

1. Beginning of unidentifiable pasted-on twenty-three-line clipping, which ends, "and deposited in the City Hall."

better half,) took the lead in political movements, and really gave the cue to the great cause [2] of American freedom and inseperable Union—the same then in the years that preceded[2] 1776, as now in 1861 and 2. The British government understood the importance of[3] our colony perfectly well. There[4] was a military force kept up there. It was the head quarters of His Majesty's American Army. Yet in 1766, it was boldly proclaimed under the very guns of the fort, that the British Parliament possessed not the shadow of a jurisdiction over America. Nor did an apprehension of the men-of-war in the harbor, prevent the New-Yorkers from dragging one distributor of stamps from his hiding-place on the opposite side of the East-River. They even compelled him to sign a resignation of his office before a public magistrate. In the same record are accounts of the dashing movements of "the Liberty Boys," which Marinus Willett, Alexander McDougall,[5] and other patriots subsequently less distinguished than these men of mark, carried through with[6] spirit.

The sending over of these stamps seems to have[7] made the people of Brooklyn and New York[8] frantic to a degree that can hardly now be realized. We have before us as we write a stern old[9] remonstrance against it signed by over one hundred leading merchants of the time—many of them residents, or owners of farms, in Kings County. Among others appear the names of Comfort Sands, and of Messrs. Lott, [3] Duyckman, Bogert, Walton, Lefferts, Kissam, Remsen, and Van Voorhis.[10] Of the leading property owners and merchants of Brooklyn and New York, during the days of the Revolution, it must[11] be remembered, that it was the community which they[12] represented,[13] who were the first to enter into the famous non-importation agreement, which, being followed by the other colonies, did more than any other movement to produce the repeal of the stamp act.[14] That success gave heart to the country for bolder movements.[15]

And while the merchants and property owners fought the attempt to intrude

2. Preceding four words inserted above "then . . . 1776,"

3. Deleted: "the"

4. Beginning of pasted-on ten-line clipping, which ends, "carried through with"

5. Names in small caps, underlined by WW in the clipping. In left margin WW writes "lower case"

6. Final word of the clipping, apparently a hyphenated line ending, blotted; inserted "Spirit" in the right margin

7. Preceding three words inserted above "made"

8. Deleted: "furious" ; inserted: "frantic to a degree . . . realized" on a line above "York . . . before" . Redundant period not shown here.

9. Inserted in the wordspace above "stern . . . remonstrance"

10. The persons named here and above are not in *DAB* or *Appleton's Cyclopedia of American Biography*.

11. Five-line clipping pasted-on, which begins with "be remembered, that" and ends, "for bolder movements."

12. Word deleted from clipping in black ink.

13. Several words deleted from clipping in black ink. Inserted and deleted: "they" in right margin.

14. Word deleted from clipping in black ink. "That" capitalized.

15. ¶ before indentation.

stamps &c upon them by legal[16] documents and remonstrances, the common people[17] in New York and Long Island made direct attacks upon the offending officials. No stamp-distributors'[18] lives were safe here, and they had to flee to the British ships, or to Canada.

16. Deleted: "remon"

17. Deleted: "here" ; following six words inserted on a line above "mon" "in common and "([*del.*] here"

18. WW changed "distributor's" to "distributors' " and corrected the number of "life" and "was."

Occurred on Thursday.

Manuscript not found. Text from Glicksberg, 167–168. The date is 1862.

Occurred on Thursday about sundown April 10th—stage 436—Knickerbocker—policeman 1726, (Macarthy)—outrageous conduct of policeman—pulling the driver down from his stage, tearing the clothes off his back—and then going up to the stables, and taking him off to the station house, and locking him up all night—Brought before Justice Connolly next morning, he was discharged, even on the policeman's own statement.

Most of the Broadway squad of policemen are very well behaved to drivers, (although there are exceptions.) But new police occasionally detailed for some special occasion to Broadway are apt to be very insolent and unreasonable.

Vedder at Brother Jonathan.

Manuscript in Duke (40, #4V). Inscribed and cancelled on white wove scrap, 6¼" x 3¾". On right is leaf 2 of "Nov 23, 62". Elihu Vedder (1836–1923), one of the most prominent American painters of the second half of the century, returned to New York on April 11, 1861 from his first trip to Europe and took up quarters in upper floor back of 48 Beekman Street (Elihu Vedder, *The Digressions of V* [Boston, 1910], 186, 193–194). *Brother Jonathan,* a giant-sized weekly which specialized at first in pirated English literature, was also at this address. WW contributed "Ambition" (1842), "Death of the Nature Lover" (1843), "A Legend of Life and Love" (1842), and "Boz and Democracy" (1842) to it. Vedder knew WW at Pfaff's beer cellar and thought him to be one of the less important people of the circle. Late in life he recalled that "for while Walt Whitman used to sit with his beard and open collar and hairy breast and beam upon the Boys, his beams remained on the outside of you" (Vedder, 218). In 1881 Vedder ordered books from WW (*Corr.,* III, 446). The date is probably 1861 or 1862.

Vedder at Brother Jonathan office Beekman st. —at ½ past 3—in the rear.

To Aid.

Manuscript in LC (#79, item #756). Inscribed in black ink on white wove paper 10¼" x 8³/16". Blue rules approx. ⅜" apart. Set up as title page or poster: rules above and below; first and third lines (in capitals) centered; handwriting very careful. First-line capitols inscribed over script "To Aid." No date can be assigned, but my feeling is that the MS is of his New York years.

TO AID
positively known, extreme cases among
THE POOR
the sick, the aged, respectable women and families destitute, &c. /

*Memorandum.

Manuscript in Pennsylvania. Inscribed in black and red inks with broad nib on white wove scrap, 5⅞″ x 3⅝″. LG 1860 was published May, 1860. This note was possibly written after the failure of Thayer and Eldridge in 1861, when WW was trying to reorder his affairs.

*Memorandum /[1]

The reason is that the copyright 1860, Boston ed'n[2] was entered taken out in the U.S. Dist. Court in Boston, as by law at that time allowed designated[3] —See said Copyright Boston May 1860[4] herewith

1. In red ink. Short line beneath in black ink.
2. Preceding three words inserted above "right" in "copyright"
3. Inserted above "allowed"
4. Deleted: "as" ; preceding three words inserted above "[*del.*] as" and "herewith"

There Is That.

Manuscript in Duke (28, #41). Inscribed in black ink on dark tan wove scrap, approx. 4$^{3}/_{16}$″ x 5$^{15}/_{16}$″. In right margin are two incomplete multiplications: 21 x 13 and 13 x 15. The writing appears to be that of the 1860s, despite the provenance from Bucke. First printed *N&F,* 67 (Pt. II, #45; *CW,* IX, 29).

There[1] is that about these[2] assumptions that only the vastness, multiplicity and vitality of America would seem able to comprehend,[3] to be fit for, and give scope to.

1. Deleted above text: "seem"
2. Deleted: "vast and vital"
3. Deleted: "to be f"

A Fine Warmish Afternoon.

Manuscript at Yale. Inscribed in black ink on two scraps of white wove paper, 12¼" x 7¾" and 3¼" x 7¾", pasted on backing sheets, probably, since pinholes penetrate both leaves, by WW. Binding of MS dates in 1863 without authority, but the NY setting indicates 1862 or earlier. WW continued to promote himself in "human interest" stories. The "Plaza Sketches" have not been located. First printed *NYD,* 227–228*n*.

A fine warmish[1] afternoon—and Broadway,[2] between the two shores of glistening shops, on the east—west sides, in the full[3] flow of its Gulf-stream of fashion,[4] crush handsome women, fops, celebrities, hubbub, countless[5] any well-dressed nobodies, pattering rustle of[6] noisy feet, low hum of[7] human talk, and hoarse and[8] heavy roar of omnibuses.— Omnibuses!— There[9] they go, incessantly—the[10] Broadway line, Fourth Avenue, Yellow Bird, Twenty Third Street,[11] Madison Avenue Bleecker Street—and a score of others.—You see them, dear Sir or Madam doubtless[12] every day, and mark nothing;[13]—yet[14] every thing appertaining to them is a study,—[15] perhaps even a fascination, if you once begin to see it.—One lounging[16] man[17] appears to think so, at any rate.— Do you mind him, as the driver of that handsome Fifth Avenue pulls up, casting at[18] the lounger a friendly

1. Inserted above letterspace between "fine . . . afternoon" and "after" in "afternoon"
2. Inserted: "between . . . shops" ; inserted and deleted: [*illeg.*] ; inserted: "on . . . sides" above "Broadway . . . in"
3. Deleted: "tied," ; inserted above: "flow"
4. Deleted: "silks glistening shops"
5. Deleted: "myriad" ; inserted above: "any"
6. Preceding seven words inserted on two lines above "noisy"
7. Deleted: "voices" ; inserted above: "human talk"
8. Deleted: "rumbling" ; inserted above: "heavy"
9. Capitalized over lowercase.
10. Underscoring deleted.
11. Inserted and deleted: "Eleventh Avenue," ; inserted following deletion: "Madison Avenue"
12. Preceding five words inserted on a line above "m" in "them" and "d" in "day"
13. Colon written over semicolon.
14. Deleted: "all about" ; inserted above: "every thing appertaining to"
15. Inserted: ", —perhaps [*ins.* above "even"] even an pleasure [*del.*] fascination, even [*del.*] if [*ins.*] you once begin to see it."
16. Inserted above wordspace between "one . . . man"
17. Deleted: "seems" ; inserted above: "appears"
18. Deleted: "him a" ; inserted above: "the lounger a"

and inquiring glance, as much as to say, Come take a ride, Walt Whitman? For none other than Walt is it who, in response,[19] turning off from the pave,[20] and seizing the handle[21] swings himself up with[22] spring and elastic motion, and held by lights[23] on the[24] off side top[25] of the stage, with his hip against the rod, as quietly as a hawk swoops to[26] its nest.—

That[27] we find is the subject[28] for the whole of this week's Plaza Sketch—[29] that pet and pride of the Broadway stage-drivers. [2] As onward speeds the stage,[30] mark[31] his nonchalant[32] air,[33] seated aslant and quite at home.—Our[34] million-hued, ever-changing panorama, of Broadway moves steadily[35] down; he, going up,[36] sees it all, as in a kind of half dream.—Mark the salute[37] of four out of[38] each five of the drivers,[39] downward bound; salutes[40] which he silently returns in the same manner—the raised arm, and the[41] upright hand.—

19. Preceding two words slightly above line and in smaller hand at end of line. Probably inserted. Deleted: "steps out" ; inserted above: "turning off"

20. Inserted: "and seizing the stage [*del.*] [*illeg. del.*] handle"

21. Deleted: "steps lightly" ; inserted above: "swings himself up"

22. Deleted: "light" ; inserted above: "springy"

23. Deleted and inserted above.

24. Inserted: "left hand side" above "the . . . top" ; deleted: "left" ; inserted: before "[*del.*] left" : "off"

25. Deleted: "as easy" ; inserted: "of the stage with his hip pressing on rod"; above "[*del.*] as easy" and "as quietly" ; deleted: "pressing on" ; inserted above: "against the"

26. Inserted and deleted: "up" above "ps" in "swoops

27. Two openings deleted: "And this is" ; "That man here we find" above "[*del.*] And" and "subject" ; "That" retained.

28. Deleted: "of" ; inserted: "for the whole of" above "[*del.*] of" and "weeks"

29. Deleted: "here in this" ; inserted above: "that [*illeg.*]" ; deleted: [*illeg.*]

30. Preceding five words inserted above "Mark his" and "non" in "nonchalant"

31. WW did not reduce uppercase "M" in MS.

32. Deleted: "and"

33. Deleted: "as he sits there,—pe" ; inserted above: "seated aslant, and"

34. Deleted: "my" ; inserted above: "million-changing" ; deleted: "changing" ; inserted above: "hued,"

35. Deleted: "by him" ; inserted and deleted: "past" ; inserted "down" above "m" in "[*del.*] him"

36. Preceding two words inserted above "sees"

37. Reduced from plural.

38. Deleted: "every" ; inserted above: "each"

39. Deleted: "that pass him;—a" ; inserted: "downward bound" above "that pass"

40. Made a plural.

41. Deleted: "stra"

Silence.

Manuscript in Yale. Two scraps pasted on tan backing, total dimensions approx. 9⅜" x 7⅞". Pinholes. [*1*] inscribed in ink on white laid paper [*2*] in pencil on browish laid paper. Whole MS backed with tan paper at top and bottom. [*1*] is in the looser hand of the 1860s and is perhaps part of WW's journalism of 1860 and 1862. [*2*] is in the neat, small hand of the 1850s and is related to "Great Are the Myths" (1855), especially ll. 18, 26–28. On verso of [*2*] is "do nothing but lose." The two scraps are unrelated except for the topic. WW apparently pasted them together, perhaps contemplating an essay.

Parsons was a NY street preacher who was arrested December 11, 1853 by order of Mayor Jacob Aaron Westervelt (1800–1879) for his incendiary anti-Catholic, anti-foreign speeches. WW, as political journalist, was interested in the resulting "freedom of speech" controversies. The march referred to took place on December 18. WW's information about Greek statues derives from George Grote's *History of Greece* which he owned and which refers to the Greek hero-worshippers being reduced "to absolute silence" before the statues. (See Floyd Stovall, "Notes on Whitman's Reading," *AL,* 26 [1954], 361.) Miss Marlene Atkinson did helpful research on this MS.

Silence.—Years ago[1] in the Parsons affair, in New York, after[2] Mayor Westervelt had been worsted, a vast mass of[3] some ten to fifteen thousand, after hearing P., on[4] Sunday afternoon, took a freak into their heads to[5] visit in perfect silence the Mayor's house as a rebuke.— They did so; only the trampling of their feet was heard[6] a prodigious army drawing up and standing around[7] his door, and neighborhood, without a word or any insulting gesture or look,[8] for about half an hour, and then dispersed.—[9]

1. Preceding two words inserted in pencil above ".—In the" . Capital "I" in "In" is not reduced in MS.
2. Deleted: "the"
3. Deleted: "ten" ; inserted: "some ten to" above "or" and "fif" in "fifteen"
4. Inserted.
5. Deleted: "adjourn"
6. Preceding eight words inserted in a small hand above "so; a prodigious"
7. Deleted: "there[*?*]"
8. Preceding two words and redundant comma inserted above "re" in "gesture" and "for"
9. End of first scrap.

Silence. (The original god[10] of whom Osiris[11] was one type, in his highest capacity of goodness, was adored by the Egyptian priests in silence,— without words, without movements.—)

The greatest love is that which makes no profession

The greatest anguish is the misery that neither weeps nor complains.—

The greatest contempt utters not a single[12] word.

To the gainer of one or two signal victories the subtle-souled Greeks[13] offered the compliment of a colossal statue, put[14] on a gigantic pedestal, in some public porch.— To the[15] veteran of[16] treble or quadruple of mightiest successes they invariably[17] built a statue strictly of his own size, and[18] planted it on a level with the eye.—

After all there is in eloquence and rage,

I guess[19] there is more still in silence.—

10. Note above preceding three words inserted and deleted: "tr this to last ¶)" apparently referring to section marked by parentheses. Inserted: "of whom" above "god Os" in "Osiris"

11. Inserted: "was one type," above "in his"

12. Inserted above "word"

13. Deleted: "made" ; inserted and deleted above: "frequently" ; inserted: "offered" following the deletion and above "com" in "compliment"

14. Inserted: "on a [*del.*] proportional gigantic pedestal" on a line above "put . . . in a public porch"

15. Deleted: "grand"

16. Deleted: "a dozen" ; inserted and deleted: "twenty" above "[*del.*] of the" ; deleted: "of the" ; inserted above: "treble or quadrupal [*del.*] the of"

17. Inserted above "built"

18. Deleted: "placed" ; inserted above: "planted"

19. Deleted: "that"

Sept '62 Inka.

Manuscript in Huntington. Inscribed in black ink on the front of an unused envelope. Inka is a railway station twenty miles east of Corinth, Miss. Union troops under Rosecrans defeated Confederates under Price there on September 19, 1862. Characteristics of MS have been furnished by Mr. Herbert C. Schultz, Curator of Manuscripts, Huntington.

Sept '62[1] Inka Mississippi / —the dead adjt of the 17th Iowa regiment, with[2] 17 slain men: —in a space 30 or 40 feet square /

1. In a half-loop at right corner.
2. Deleted: [*illeg.*]

www.ingramcontent.com/pod-product-compliance
Lightning Source LLC
Chambersburg PA
CBHW082056090726
47909CB00011B/3061